REXFORD TUGWELL
and the NEW DEAL

BERNARD STERNSHER

REXFORD TUGWELL
and the NEW DEAL

RUTGERS UNIVERSITY PRESS
New Brunswick   *New Jersey*

*Manufactured in the United States of America
by Quinn & Boden Company, Inc., Rahway, New Jersey*

*This book was manufactured with the assistance of a grant
from the Ford Foundation*

To the memory of my shipmates who were lost with the United States Coast Guard Cutter Jackson off Cape Hatteras in the hurricane of September, 1944.

Norman D. Call	Lieutenant (j.g.)	Ohio
William T. Condon	Machinist's Mate 2c	New Jersey
Lawrence F. Cullen	Pharmacist's Mate 2c	Massachusetts
Edwin F. De La Roi	Boatswain's Mate 2c	Nebraska
Joseph S. Flynn	Yeoman 1c	New York
James A. Griffin	Steward 3c	Georgia
Mansel R. Hayden	Seaman 1c	Texas
Thomas S. Hendricks	Sonarman 2c	Tennessee
Hyman A. Karp	Seaman 2c	Connecticut
John H. Kropf	Motor Machinist's Mate 3c	Pennsylvania
Edward J. McCue, Jr.	Fireman 1c	Pennsylvania
Jerome J. Michalski	Seaman 1c	Wisconsin
John Mingione	Radarman 3c	New Jersey
Richard C. Nichols	Seaman 1c	Illinois
James A. Parker	Radio Technician 3c	Texas
Robert Patton	Coxswain	Ohio
William A. Poshinske	Gunner's Mate 3c	Wisconsin
Arthur J. F. Snyder	Radioman 3c	Pennsylvania
Jennings R. Tiller	Seaman 2c	West Virginia
William F. Waters	Machinist	Virginia
Denver C. Welsh	Quartermaster 3c	Missouri
Joseph W. Zimpel	Ensign	Arkansas

To the memory of my shipmates who were lost with the United States Coast Guard Cutter Jackson, Cape Hatteras, in the hurricane of September 1944

Preface

Two or three years ago, at a prep school alumni club meeting, the middle-aged wife of one of the members asked me, "Why are you writing a book about that horrible man?" The question provides its own answer in part. This lady, like literally hundreds of thousands of other Americans of her generation, bases her opinion of Rexford Guy Tugwell on a distorted image which a large sector of the press deliberately created and disseminated in the 1930's. If the lady reads this book, she will no doubt continue to remain outside the circle of Tugwell's admirers. This does not matter because recruitment or conversion is not my purpose. At least she will have encountered an attempt, subject to the various limitations of the writer's capacities, to present an accurate account of Tugwell's role in the New Deal.

There is something to be said for setting the record straight. Indeed, the reader may find in this book what he will consider an overreadiness to grapple with any critic of Tugwell. Before condemning this inclination, the reader should bear in mind just how distorted the popular image of Tugwell really was. In any event, since there are only so many writers who can write only so many books, not every injustice of this kind is rectified. Telling Tugwell's story required additional justification. It appeared to me that his career as a New Dealer merited book-length attention on several grounds: his status as an "insider" from early 1932 until early 1935 provides an important point of entrance to the first Roosevelt Administration; his institutional thought furnishes a criterion against which one can make a meaningful measurement of the New Deal with reference to the question of change in our democratic society; his activities as an administrator are interesting and significant in themselves. When I first wrote to Mr. Tugwell about this study, he replied, "It always strikes me as slightly ridiculous that I should be an object of study; nevertheless, I have to admit that I was around at an interesting time and did have something to do with it all."

There was, of course, the prior question of previous treatments of Tugwell. The most important published studies are "The Experimental Economics of Rexford G. Tugwell," Chapter 6 in Allan G. Gruchy's *Modern Economic Thought: The American Contribution* (1947), and Chapters 7, 8, and 9, dealing with two of the Resettlement Administration's four divisions, in Paul K. Conkin's *Tomorrow a New World: The New Deal Community Program* (1959). "Rexford Guy Tugwell: Institutional Economist" is an unpublished thesis which Maurice Mann submitted to the Boston University Graduate School in 1952 for the degree of Master of Arts in Economics. Tugwell himself has given an account of his experiences as Governor of Puerto Rico in the years 1941-1946 in *The Stricken Land: The Story of Puerto Rico* (1947). His autobiographical *The Light of Other Days* (1962) ends with his entrance into college in 1911. In his voluminous writings about Franklin D. Roosevelt and the New Deal, Tugwell has mentioned himself only incidentally. This book is the first comprehensive investigation, both as to scope and source materials, of his activities in the years 1932-1936. (A chronology of his entire career immediately follows this preface.)

This book is not an authorized study of Mr. Tugwell as a New Dealer. I have submitted only factual questions to him, both in person and in writing, and he has answered all of them briefly and to the point. He has read the first eleven chapters and Chapters 25-27 of this book in manuscript without commenting on the content. On various occasions he has written, "Again I prefer—and presume you prefer me—not to make any suggestions. It does seem in order for me to say, however, that I have no objections to anything." "Reading what you have to say brings up many recollections of old friendships, quarrels, loyalties, and efforts. They do seem long in the past."

This book is not a biography of Tugwell, and it is not a history of the New Deal. It treats the area where the two meet. Its coverage falls into two broad categories: what Tugwell said and what he did—ideology and action. The first category deals with his academic thought and his comments on the New Deal. His academic thought, outlined in Chapters 2 and 9, sometimes serves as the standard by which he evaluates the New Deal. His comments on the New Deal often refer to matters other than the fields of his participation, widening the area of contact just mentioned. In short, Tugwell either had something to do with or has had something to say about nearly every aspect of the New Deal. The second category comprises personal and administrative history. It is hoped that this material, in addition to informing the reader of Tugwell's career in Washington, suggests, even if only indirectly, the experiences and problems of men in the government of this Republic under an unusual President in trying times.

In reading Chapters 2 and 9, which merely are summaries of Tugwell's academic thought, the reader may wonder whether Tugwell's thought came right out of the top of his head. The originality of his ideas is not the point at issue here. The relevant historical fact is that a man who held these ideas was an adviser to the President of the United States. Tugwell was, of course, a product of an aspect of the intellectual climate of his formative period, and his indebtedness to Simon Patten, Thorstein Veblen, Frederick W. Taylor, and John Dewey is acknowledged.

A full account of the context of Tugwell's thought would go back to the early phases of the Industrial Revolution in both Britain and America. Inequities and maladjustments produced protest, and Tugwell derived his ideas from the protesters. During the later stages of the writing of this book, two accounts of the protest in Britain appeared: Herman Ausubel, *In Hard Times: Reformers among the Late Victorians* (1960) and David Roberts, *Victorian Origins of the Welfare State* (1960). Tugwell was influenced by the Victorian thinkers of what Robert L. Heilbroner has called "The Underworld of Economics," especially by John A. Hobson, an underconsumptionist whose works include *The Evolution of Modern Capitalism: A Study of Machine Production* (1894), *The Industrial System: An Inquiry into Earned and Unearned Income* (1910), *Work and Wealth: A Human Valuation* (1921), and *Rationalization and Unemployment: An Economic Dilemma* (1930).

In America Tugwell's heritage in economics went back at least to the founding of the American Economic Association by Patten, Edwin R. A. Seligman, Edmund J. James, John Bates Clark, and Richard T. Ely in 1885. Heirs to this "rebellion," broadly grouped as Institutionalists, included, besides Patten and Veblen, John R. Commons, Wesley C. Mitchell, John M. Clark, Gardiner C. Means, Walton H. Hamilton, and Tugwell himself. Patten was Tugwell's teacher at the University of Pennsylvania, and Mitchell and Means were his colleagues at Columbia University. It is pertinent to note that Ben B. Seligman, in his *Main Currents in Modern Economics: Economic Thought since 1870* (1962) treats Hobson in a section dealing with American Institutionalism, to which, Seligman holds, Hobson was closer in spirit than to the thought of his British contemporaries.

Progressivism, with its optimism, environmentalism, moral fervor, and emphasis on leadership by a benevolent intellectual elite within the framework of a democratic society, was another important source of Tugwell's thinking in political economy. He was particularly influenced by collectivistic Progressives like Charles Van Hise and Herbert Croly. Croly hired Tugwell to comment on the campaign of 1928 for the *New Republic*. Charles Forcey devotes a chapter to Croly in his *The Crossroads of Liberalism* (1961).

Finally, Pragmatism must be mentioned as part of Tugwell's intellectual background. William James, Charles S. Peirce, John Dewey, and George Herbert Mead are names which come to mind immediately in this connection. Tugwell enjoyed exposure at first hand to Dewey's ideas at Columbia. Sidney Ratner's "Pragmatism in America," in *Essays in American Historiography* (1960), is a useful introduction to this subject and places Tugwell among the pragmatists as a disciple of Dewey.

In Chapters 2 and 9 Tugwell's writings from 1922 to 1962 have been treated as a unit. This approach is justified by the consistency over this period of his basic institutional ideas (and inconsistencies are noted at appropriate places in this book). At the same time, this approach does produce some distortion, but only in detail. For example, Tugwell's later statement that it was difficult for an honest businessman to survive in the 1920's, may, when it is related to his thinking of that decade, represent a retroactive attribution to him of over-sharp observation. But his basic diagnosis and prognosis of the New Era are presented accurately in their essentials, and, again, his basic remedial and preventive recommendations have remained fundamentally the same for forty years. Elsewhere in this book Tugwell's statements of opinion are contemporaneous, or their time is indicated by the actual date, the source, or phraseology denoting retrospective comment.

The several books mentioned above, except Hobson's, are of very recent date. This suggests a problem which any historian of the New Deal encounters. The number of works appearing in this field during the course of an investigation is formidable, and there is every indication that this situation will continue indefinitely. Tugwell himself has published seven books in the nine-year period, 1954-1962. (His works are listed in chronological order, within various categories, at the end of this book.)

A note on two mechanical matters will aid the reader: when a cross-reference does *not* include a citation of another chapter, it refers to an occurrence elsewhere in the same chapter; an explanatory list of abbreviations appears in the introduction to the notes.

I wish to thank everyone who has helped or encouraged me in this undertaking. My most obvious debt, as the reader will conclude, is to the many scholars who have worked in the Age of Roosevelt and the New Deal. Several paragraphs in Chapters 10, 11, and 28 have appeared previously in "Tugwell's Appraisal of FDR," *Western Political Quarterly,* March, 1962, and several paragraphs in Chapter 28 have been taken from "Liberalism in the Fifties: The Travail of Redefinition," *Antioch Review,* Fall, 1962; I should like to acknowledge the permission of the editors of these journals to use this material. I am appreciative of the criticism and encouragement offered by Professors Frank Freidel and Arthur M. Schlesinger, Jr., of Harvard University and by Mrs. Lewis Webster Jones. I am especially grateful to Professor Robert E. Moody of Boston University, teacher and friend, whose criticism was particularly valuable because his general views are quite different from my own. I also benefited from the courteous and efficient services of the staffs of the Widener Library of Harvard University, the Chenery Library of Boston University, the Bryn Mawr College Library, the Boston Public Library, the Franklin D. Roosevelt Library, the Oral History Research Office of Columbia University, and the National Archives and Records Service. I am obligated to

Mrs. Peggy Moss, Mrs. Carmel Adams, and Mrs. Anne McCartney for typing the manuscript. I am, of course, alone responsible for the tone and judgments in this book. In this connection I should like to point out that Professor Schlesinger, who read the first twelve chapters of an earlier version of the manuscript, and Professors Freidel and Moody, who read an earlier version in its entirety, have not seen the last chapter which was largely written in the summer and early autumn of 1962. I am also solely responsible for whatever shortcomings this book may have.

I do not think my father, who, as a student at Harvard Law School, actively supported Woodrow Wilson in the election of 1912 and through years of participation in politics until his death in 1940 remained an advocate of the New Freedom, would agree with my final conclusion, but I trust that he would appreciate the effort involved in reaching it. I do not exaggerate when I say that I could not have written this book without the encouragement and support for many years of my mother, Eleanor Bernard Sternsher, who has remained fearless and cheerful through a life that has not been easy. In recent years my wife, Carol Edwards Sternsher, has given me invaluable understanding and assistance.

November, 1962

Tugwell: A Chronology

1891-1904:	Sinclairville, New York
1904-1909:	Wilson, New York
1909-1911:	Student, Masten Park High School, Buffalo, New York
1911-1915:	Undergraduate, University of Pennsylvania
1915-1917:	Graduate student and Instructor of Economics, University of Pennsylvania
1917:	Master's degree received from the University of Pennsylvania
1917-1918:	Assistant Professor of Marketing, University of Washington, Seattle
1918:	Business Manager, American University Union, Paris
1919:	Assistant Manager, Niagara Preserving Corporation
1920-1932:	Department of Economics, Columbia University
1922:	Ph.D. degree received from the University of Pennsylvania
1922:	Promoted to Assistant Professor
1926:	Promoted to Associate Professor
1931:	Promoted to Professor
1932-1933:	Adviser to Franklin D. Roosevelt
1933-1934:	Assistant Secretary of Agriculture
1934-1936:	Undersecretary of Agriculture
1935-1936:	Resettlement Administrator
1936:	Resignation from government effective December 31
1937:	Executive Vice-President, American Molasses Co.
1938-1940:	Chairman, New York City Planning Commission
1941:	Chancellor, University of Puerto Rico
1941-1946:	Governor of Puerto Rico
1946-1957:	Professor of Political Science, University of Chicago
1954-1962:	Published seven books
1959- :	Assistant to the Chancellor, University of Puerto Rico
1962:	Visiting Professor, Summer Session, Columbia University

Contents

Preface vii
Tugwell: A Chronology xii

Part I: Before the New Deal

1. A Biographical Sketch: 1891-1931 3
2. Tugwell's Institutionalism and the Coming of the Depression . 11
3. Mr. Hoover's Economic Policy: 1928-1932 26

Part II: Tugwell the Brain Truster

4. Brain Trust—Campaign—Election: 1932 39
5. Nationalism versus Internationalism 51
6. Roosevelt versus Hoover: The Lame-Duck Interlude . . 59
7. Tugwell versus Hoover: The Twenty-Five-Year Debate . 73
8. Officialdom and the End of the Brain Trust: 1932-1933 . 86

Part III: Tugwell's Thought and the New Deal

9. Tugwell's Institutionalism and Economic Planning . . 91
10. The Ideological Split in the New Deal 109
11. The Two New Deals: 1933-1938 122

Part IV: Professor on the Potomac

12. Intellectual Approaches to Crisis 143
13. The National Industrial Recovery Act and the NRA: 1933-1935 154
14. Proposals for Farm Relief: 1922-1933 170
15. The Agricultural Adjustment Act: 1932-1933 . . . 183
16. Tugwell versus Peek and the Purge in the AAA: 1933-1935 . 194
17. The Department of Agriculture—Conservation: 1933-1936 . 208
18. Tugwell as Whipping Boy: The Attack 223
19. Tugwell as Whipping Boy: The Impact of the Attack . . 238
20. Promotion: 1934 251

21. The Task of the Resettlement Administration 262
22. The Performance of the Resettlement Administration under Tug-
    well: 1935-1936 279
23. Board Member—Errand Boy—Publicist—Idea Man: 1932-1936 . 307
24. Resignation: 1936 321

Part V: An American's Challenge to America

25. Tugwell the "Subversive" 337
26. Tugwell and Communism 357
27. Tugwell and the American Tradition: Evolution—Democracy—
    the Constitution 370
28. Tugwell's Thought and America Today 396

    The Works and Papers of Rexford Guy Tugwell 413
    Notes 425
    Index 499

REXFORD TUGWELL
and the NEW DEAL

Part I
Before the New Deal

———————◆———————

1. A Biographical Sketch: 1891-1931

The predominant popular image of Rexford Guy Tugwell in the 1930's was, among his admirers, that of the urban reformer, or, among his detractors, the city slicker. His actual beginnings were rural. His ancestors came from the southern shires of England. On his mother's side were the Franklins, Rexfords, and Tylers, who moved westward across New York beginning in the eighteenth century. His father's people included the Tugwells, Truslers, and Leaverses. His grandfather Tugwell left Surrey, England, in 1852, landed in New York City, then moved inland to Chautauqua County in the lower part of the western tip of New York State. This grandfather was a cattle dealer known as a good man in a trade.[1]

Tugwell was born in Sinclairville, New York, on July 10, 1891, to Charles Henry and Dessie (Rexford) Tugwell. When he was thirteen years old, his family moved seventy-five miles northward to Wilson, New York, north of Buffalo on the southern shore of Lake Ontario, where his father, who two years before had shifted from the cattle and meat business to canning, purchased a fruit farm. Charles Tugwell soon became a moderately well-to-do orchard farmer and fruit and vegetable canner.

In 1911 Tugwell graduated from Masten Park High School in Buffalo, where he had enrolled for two extra years of secondary education in order to fulfill college-entrance requirements. It appears that his instructors did not see in him the makings of a scholar. The principal wrote his father that the boy was so unappreciative of educational advantages that he might just as well be taken out of school and put to work on the farm.[2] The trouble probably was that Tugwell read so much at home that his classes bored him. As an avid reader he emulated his mother.[3] His father, a journalist later alleged, never understood the

3

"dreaming" lad, raised "carefree and alone." [4] A neighbor refuted this allegation, recalling that the business-minded Charles Tugwell was not disturbed by his son's intellectual inclinations.[5]

It is true that some of Tugwell's boyhood activities were solitary—he raised a prize-winning calf, and in his senior year in high school he covered police courts and city hall for the *Buffalo Courier.* But he also played with the neighbors' boys, joining them in games and the aimless romping of rural youths, and he was very popular with the girls of Wilson.[6] Meanwhile, his intellectual pursuits were neither escapist nor strictly subjective. His high school theme papers evidenced a certain social consciousness.[7]

The boy who enjoyed rural life left Niagara County to make his mark in Philadelphia, New York, and Washington, but he retained a sentimental feeling for the land of his childhood. As a public official in the 1930's he referred in speeches, by way of illustrating agricultural problems, to the erosion of the topsoil in the New York hill country where he had been born,[8] and to overproduction of apples in "my own country" of western New York.[9] In an address which he delivered at Olcott Beach, near Wilson, he expressed a "genuine sense of homecoming," although, he admitted, his loyalties were torn between Chautauqua and Niagara Counties.[10] In 1947 he sent a copy of his book, *The Stricken Land,* to a boyhood playmate with this inscription, "I don't know whether you will like this book, but I should like you to read it anyway for old time's sake." [11] One finds it difficult to dismiss Tugwell's references to his home country as oratorical ornamentation or formality when one reads this passage about his childhood in Sinclairville in *The Stricken Land:*

> To my children the life of my boyhood in that town would seem incredibly simple, no doubt. We went barefoot in summer; the balls we played with were often wound and covered by ourselves; we made our own skis and sleds; and one of my daily duties was to go down to pasture lot and bring home the cow for milking. . . . We had fourteen driving horses in the barn; I had a flock of chickens, a hutch of rabbits, and a maple-sugar house all my own. And dogs—I always had one and sometimes four or five. I could relate the history of every one of them to this day. We spent every summer—or part of it—on Chautauqua Lake, where I could distinguish the steamboats as far away as my boys can now spot a Mariner or a Marauder. And I knew them by their whistles too.[12]

Tugwell left western New York in 1911 to attend the Wharton School of Finance and Commerce of the University of Pennsylvania, expecting to pursue a career in business. During his first two years in college he was immersed in extracurricular activities. He was a member of a social fraternity, Delta Upsilon, and the prom committee. He was toastmaster at the sophomore banquet. He served as managing editor of the college newspaper and as editor of a student literary magazine. Undoubtedly he would not have done well in campus politics. His suavity and literary erudition attracted some students, but few classmates at Pennsylvania knew him well.[13] In his junior year Tugwell abruptly dropped his extracurricular activities and began to study in earnest. Two of his teachers in particular had a lot to do with this change. Simon Nelson Patten told Tugwell he was wasting time on the frivolous side of college life; Scott Nearing advised him that his future lay in economics.[14]

Tugwell believed economics would provide means of rectifying some of society's most serious shortcomings. That he was concerned about social ills was apparent in a poem he wrote in 1915 for *Intercollegiate*—verses which his critics of the New Deal era often cited:

> I am strong,
> I am big and well-made,
> I am muscled and lean and nervous,
> I am frank and sure and incisive.
>
> .   .   .   .   .
>
> I bend the forces untamable;
> I harness the powers irresistible—
> All this I do; but I shall do more.
>
> .   .   .   .
>
> I am sick of a nation's stenches,
> I am sick of propertied czars. . . .
> I have dreamed my great dream of their passing,
> I have gathered my tools and my charts;
> My plans are fashioned and practical;
> I shall roll up my sleeves—make America over! [15]

Tugwell received his B.S. in 1915. He was an instructor in economics at Pennsylvania, 1915-1917. At the same time he studied economics, literature, and constitutional law, earning a master's degree in 1916. He was impressed with Nearing's experimentalism and Patten's institution-alism. In 1917 he served as a special investigator for the Governors' Tri-State (Pennsylvania, Delaware, and Maryland) Milk Commission, of which his dissertation director, Professor Clyde King, was secretary. This work aroused his interest in public regulation. He also served under Gifford Pinchot, then president of the Pennsylvania Rural Progress Association, as a fact-gatherer on the marketing of farm products.

When Nearing was dismissed by the University of Pennsylvania for making allegedly seditious remarks,[16] Tugwell and several others quit

the faculty. Tugwell did not resign because of the attack on Nearing—
he felt Nearing had it coming to him [17]—but because the trustees began
an investigation of the whole department of economics. Nearing, incidentally, once said that of all his students only two—Rex Tugwell and
Bill Tilden, the tennis player—would go far.[18]

In 1917 Tugwell joined the faculty of the University of Washington
as an assistant professor of marketing in the School of Business. Two
of his colleagues at the University of Washington, William F. Ogburn
and Carleton H. Parker, impressed him with their efforts to apply
psychology to the social sciences. In 1919 Ogburn, who developed the
concept of "cultural lag," went to Columbia University, where he served
as a professor of sociology until 1927. Tugwell came to Columbia in
1920. From 1930 until 1939, besides teaching, Ogburn held several positions with government agencies, including one with Tugwell's Resettlement Administration. The two men were together again at the University
of Chicago from 1946, when Tugwell arrived there, until 1951, when
Ogburn retired.

In 1918 Tugwell was business manager of the American University
Union in Paris. In 1919 he returned to his father's farm for a rest. A journalist later noted that Tugwell's experience in Europe unsettled him to
the point of uncertainty as to what to do in life, and that the young
economist had to tramp the old roads near Wilson for more than a year
before steepage in the aesthetic atmosphere of his boyhood cured his
uncertainty and reawakened his interest.[19] Undoubtedly, although Tugwell was behind the lines of battle, he was sufficiently aware of the waste
and cruelty of war to despair at the plight of civilization. But his problem was primarily a physical one—asthma, which was to trouble him the
rest of his life.

His doctors told him to live in the country, to do light work in the
garden, and to write only a little. He built a small house on his father's
farm, staying there while he regained his health. He was able to help out
in his father's business—as he had done during summer vacations from
college—holding the title in 1919 of Assistant Manager, Niagara Preserving Corporation.[20] In 1920 Tugwell was ready to resume his academic
career, and he accepted an instructorship at Columbia, where he was to
help develop the famous Contemporary Civilization course.

Tugwell described his academic contacts at Columbia as a "great influence." Individual faculty members, especially John Dewey and Wesley C. Mitchell, drew his attention. Dewey emphasized the gap between
formal education and social experience. Mitchell was "the bridge between classicism and instrumentalism in economics." Applying their
ideas to the teaching of economics, Tugwell sought to give his students
material relevant to the actual going economy, and he stressed the possi-

bilities of improving economic conditions through "social management." [21]

Tugwell enjoyed what he called "a great intellectual adventure" in "the Columbia experiment"—an instrumentalist attempt to integrate the social sciences and philosophy in dealing with "the insistent problems of industrialism." The faculty labored to reduce the integrated traditional disciplines "to an order which would be understandable to students." The pragmatic orientation of the course, entitled Introduction to Contemporary Civilization, was apparent in one of the objectives of its builders—the assessment of "the contribution to human betterment which each discipline might make"—and in Tugwell's acknowledgment of Dewey's influence. "Many others" also made important contributions, and Tugwell felt a "deep debt" to John J. Coss, Professor of Philosophy, who "made each of us as individuals fertile for the others." Tugwell had "new access to philosophy, history, psychology, and government as well as a change in economic influence in those years which," he maintained, "was formative." [22]

Tugwell was promoted in 1922—the year in which he completed requirements for a Ph.D.—to assistant professor, in 1926 to associate professor, and in 1931 to professor. His rise in rank was rapid as academic careers go. He taught a light schedule, and he was given his head to make studies here and abroad and to work on his books.[23] A critical Washington correspondent later implied that Tugwell was a favored person at Columbia. Nicholas Murray Butler, it was alleged, wholeheartedly approved of Tugwell's theory and method and gave him carte blanche to teach what he would and to devote all the time he wished to writing. Tugwell, it was further alleged, chose to give little attention to teaching because of his customary lack of interest in direct dealing with people.[24]

Too much can be made of Tugwell's light teaching schedule. It was not unusual for a faculty member of an institution which stressed research and publication as well as instruction. He carried a standard load at times—as in 1924, when he gave these courses: Introduction to Contemporary Civilization, Phases of American Economic Life, Proposals for Economic Reorganization, Advanced Economics for Honor Students.[25] He preferred bright students like Jacques Barzun and Joseph Dorfman, his usual policy with them being "not to do more than offer such help as I can give. They do not need encouragement and advice is wasted on them." [26] But this preference is quite common among professors, reflecting a serious interest in subject matter, which, as in Tugwell's case, need not be accompanied by a dislike for contact with people. And the time Tugwell devoted to research and writing during his years at Columbia was not just for his personal edification. He published a number of articles in academic journals and in the *New Republic*, of which he was a contributing editor.

In March, 1928, Herbert Croly, editor of the *New Republic,* arranged for Tugwell to contribute two articles a month, for six months, on "campaign economics." Tugwell's choice of Alfred E. Smith over Herbert Hoover represented a switch from his recent Republican tendencies and a return to his parents' Democracy. His Republican inclinations were based on his desire for an expansion of national power, which the states' rights Democratic party had historically opposed. He concluded that Hoover was committed to Democratic laissez faire, while Smith, in view of his record as governor, was open to education. In the 1920's Tugwell also wrote, edited, or contributed to several volumes. In 1924 he edited *The Trend of Economics,* hoping to stimulate inquiry in all phases of the field.

As for Butler's attitude toward the productive young professor, the president of Columbia undoubtedly approved of Tugwell's educational ideas and scholarly pursuits in a general sense—that is, from the standpoint of viewing academic freedom as the way to truth. This approval did not mean that Butler, whose thought reflected the influence of William Spencer, personally agreed with Tugwell's specific ideas. In fact, in the 1930's the wide disagreement between the two men in the area of political economy became apparent. In a letter of February 13, 1936, to Franklin D. Roosevelt, Butler asked whether Tugwell was to return to Columbia upon the expiration of his leave of absence on June 30. Butler added a protest against the administration's "soak the rich" tax policy.[27] In an article published in 1939 Tugwell condemned the superficial nature of such distinctions as "the one Nicholas Murray Butler is fond of making between 'the sphere of government and the sphere of liberty.'" [28]

As a public official in Washington, 1933-1936, and afterwards, Tugwell was a typical impractical product of an ivory tower in the eyes of many journalists. One referred to him as a "frustrated utopian." [29] *Time* called him "dreamy, reform-minded." [30] A writer in the *Nation* mentioned the young professor who impressed sophomores.[31] This placing of Tugwell among the scholars who fitted into the popular stereotype of the absentminded professor was not justified by the approach to education he adopted at Columbia. In 1927 Tugwell pointed to the "conservatism of education, the inculcation of past standards rather than the freeing and training of intelligence, and the slowness of enlargement of educational programs" as barriers to increased productivity,[32] and he acted on John Dewey's contention that education was becoming divorced from reality—a separation against which Simon Nelson Patten had previously warned him.

In a real sense Tugwell was one of those professors who had a better understanding of the economy than most businessmen of the 1920's. He wrote in retrospect that the generation after World War I, by calling intellectually honest contemporaries—some of whom predicted disaster—"theorists" and "dreamers," hid the true character of its fatal unrealism.[33] Some commentators concluded that Tugwell was "not a typical denizen of an ivory tower," [34] that he was "no stock pedant with ink in his blood and the moldy dust of libraries in his eyes . . . his understanding of practical economics was thoroughly unacademic." [35]

In the summer of 1927 Tugwell spent two months in the Soviet Union. He went there with a group, the first non-Communist delegation of trade unionists to go to Russia. The unionists selected economists and other trained observers to go along with them for both technical assistance and independent observation. The latter group included a lawyer, a labor journalist, Stuart Chase, and nine educators, among whom were Tugwell and Paul Douglas. The Russian economist Kondratieff assisted Tugwell in his study of agricultural conditions. The visitors produced a book, *Soviet Russia in the Second Decade, a Joint Survey by the Technical Staff of the First American Trade Union Delegation* (New York: John Day, 1928). Tugwell, Chase, and Robert Dunn were joint-editors. Tugwell contributed Chapter Three, "Russian Agriculture."

The anti-New Deal press did not let Tugwell forget his tour of the Soviet Union. There were accusations that he desired to Sovietize America because of what he had seen in Russia. Actually, his chapter on Russian agriculture was a scholar's attempt to describe and evaluate what he observed. He did not think the application of Soviet policies to the problems of American agriculture was feasible—the Russians' trouble was underproduction, ours quite the opposite. The magnitude and ambition of the Russians' undertaking did impress him, and he believed that in an academic sense there was much to be learned from observing Soviet development. He departed from Russia unsympathetic with revolutionary tactics and critical of the regimentation of opinion which was an essential part of the Soviet system.

In the 1920's Tugwell mingled freely with the socialists of the League for Industrial Democracy and the Civil Liberties Union. He thought that some of their proposals tended in the right direction, but by no means did he accept all of their theories. A critic later asserted that the platform of the Socialist party accurately expressed Tugwell's beliefs.[36] In fact, Tugwell's economic thought did not include the central tenet of doctrinaire socialism—public ownership of the means of production. He observed in December, 1933, that the government had to spend when the fruitful sources of income shut down in order to reconstruct those sources, not to take them over as the socialists would do.[37]

Tugwell's inquiries ranged over the economy, but he was probably more interested in farmers than he was in urban workers. In the 1920's he made intensive studies of agricultural problems in the United States and Europe, spending his sabbatical year, 1928-1929, studying agricultural policies of European nations. He published several articles on his findings in the *Political Science Quarterly*, the *Annals of the American Academy of Political and Social Science*, and the *Nation*. In 1928, at the invitation of Professor Lindsay Rogers of Columbia, he surveyed the whole agricultural situation for Alfred E. Smith, producing a lengthy memorandum. And he was a lifelong conservationist. Tugwell meanwhile sustained his interest in nonagricultural economic affairs, publishing *Industry's Coming of Age* in 1927 and *The Industrial Discipline and the Governmental Arts* in 1933.

As the depression deepened and governmental policies failed to stop the decline, Tugwell offered both destructive and constructive criticism —in an address to the American Economic Association in December, 1931, and in an article, a booklet, and two addresses in early 1932. These were partly responsible for his recruitment into the inner circle of Roosevelt's advisers in March, 1932, when he and Adolf A. Berle, Jr., at the invitation of their Columbia colleague Raymond Moley and with the Governor's approval, joined the Brain Trust.

2. Tugwell's Institutionalism and the Coming of the Depression

I

In the 1920's the economic aggregates—gross national product, industrial production, and employment—climbed upward, except for mild adjustments in 1923 and 1927, in apparent dynamic harmony. A chorus of Americans sang accompanying refrains: "Permanent Prosperity" and "The New Era." The crescendo of the "Roaring Twenties" drowned out most of the dissonant voices which cited weaknesses and imbalances in the economy. The few unharmonious voices which made themselves heard met with ridicule and rejection. If the dissenter was a professor, the public, particularly its business sector, dismissed his warnings as the wailing of a theorist, an impractical man who had "never met a payroll."

Not many professors gave businessmen occasion to poke fun at theorists who ventured to comment from their ivory towers on the going world beyond the campus. Most educators, Tugwell maintained, were really allies of business, justifying current privileges and orthodoxies. The few who suggested timely adjustments in our society met with the cry, from other educators, of "indoctrination." [1] Tugwell grouped with the press, business sycophants, the orthodox, and the moralists, those teachers who adhered to the "anti-social ideals of 'interested conservatives,'" [2] serving an impossible, imaginary Utopia of reaction. [3] Businessmen, Tugwell observed, did not object to practical-minded professors as such, heaping no scorn upon savants whose public statements agreed with businessmen's views. [4] He might have added that in the 1920's many strong, successful financial and industrial organizations recruited their chief economic advisers from the universities. [5]

Tugwell believed that scholars, especially economists, should get down to the facts—as they, not businessmen, found them—of everyday life and their impact on the whole population. He was dissatisfied with the picture which the facts he gathered about the American economy in the 1920's produced. A brief look at the basic ideas of institutional economists will show that dissatisfaction was then the inevitable attitude of one who belonged to that school of economic thought.

Tugwell, as an institutional economist, believed that man's psychological and mental equipment—"human nature"—had not changed substantially for thousands of generations; at some point in prehistory man set out to go on from where he was by modifying his environment. [6] And, in succeeding centuries, modify it he did, his technological advance

11

proceeding at a giddy pace. With speed went complexity. Man conceived and created new things, devices, and instruments. Each began its own evolution, which simultaneously affected the evolution of the others. Interrelationships produced new totals, which Tugwell called "emergents." Each "emergent" was something more than the sum of its parts. The nature of a city, for example, was distinct from that of any of its parts—streets, sewers, water-pipes, schools, hospitals, and houses.[7] In short, man's environment became incredibly complex, posing ever new problems in social analysis and management.

Man failed to reap the full benefit implicit in his technological ability. He could change his environment, but he could not change his own behavior. Tugwell put it this way: modern processes had been most at home in industry; there had been little progress in thought and morals.[8] In other words, there was a great gap between the physical and social sciences: "The devotion to exactitude, which was a general condition of [technological] invention, has been slow to make any way in social, especially governmental, affairs." [9]

Tugwell, like many other thinkers, referred to the result of the gap between the physical and social sciences as "cultural lag," or, more specifically, "institutional lag." In describing the world in which he lived, man fell behind the rapid changes that technology wrought in an increasingly complex environment. From his descriptions, inadequate to begin with, he derived theories, which became outdated as fast as the descriptions themselves. From his theories he derived social policies. He clung doggedly to old theories, failing to recognize them as theories and citing them to justify antiquated social institutions. Tugwell called the obsolete theories by which man lived "myths." Man had failed to abandon many a false basis for current arrangements because "myths" had become "encysted in a moral and aesthetic system which seems precious, even to those who may have no stake in its favors, because of its familiarity." [10]

Naturally, Tugwell was particularly concerned with "myths" in the area of political economy. Being an inquiring American in the 1920's, he learned that many of the "myths" which most of his fellow citizens followed grew out of the concept of laissez faire. He outlined the origins and history of that doctrine, finding it "useful" in the revolt against mercantilism and divine-right monarchy, but "overworked" by the politically minded leaders of the French Revolution and clothed by its American devotees with a constitutional sanctity for which there was an explanation in terms of practicality, but no constitutional, theoretical, or historical justification.[11]

One of the "myths" of laissez faire was a misconception of the significance of profits—the belief that they were a measure of national welfare.[12] Tugwell pointed out that abusive profits—not moderate rewards to management—resulted in overspeculation and overexpansion, deflecting potential purchasing power into sterile pools and damaging national welfare.[13] The belief in individualism—unrestrained profit-seeking—as accepted, immutable, true, seemed subconscious. Reinforced by orthodoxy and common sense, this belief was relatively immune from outside influences such as the dependence of production on collective organization, more sophisticated modes of thought, and the need, with the intrusion of reality, to form policy and act.[14]

The father of all the "myths" of laissez faire was what we may call the "Smithian total." This concept rested on the assumption that competition would act as an almost God-given automatic balancer, overruling human frailties and enforcing ethical practices. Thus, a society of freely self-seeking individuals, each trying to advance his own welfare, would enjoy the greatest possible total welfare. Tugwell, who saw the whole as more than the sum of its parts, rejected this additive concept of society: "The jig is up. The cat is out of the bag. There is no invisible hand. There never was. . . . Men were taught to believe that they were, paradoxically, advancing co-operation when they were defying it. That was a viciously false paradox." [15]

Tugwell noted that the "myths" of laissez faire won wide acceptance among businessmen—in their thinking if not in their behavior. Considering themselves "practical" rather than "theoretical," they really thought, unknowingly, in terms of a "ready rigamarole which passed for theory." [16] Unaware of their lack of a sound theoretical approach, they also showed a childlike unawareness of their own place, as the end product of technological evolution, in the scheme of things.[17] Obviously, a theoretical approach in itself was not adequate, in Tugwell's view, to meet modern problems. It had to be a "sound" theoretical approach. He was far from amazed to find businessmen clinging to "myths." And he was not surprised to find professors deceiving themselves. He was not surprised— but he was disappointed. He was not surprised because he knew about the sirens who lured the theorist away from reality. It was the line of least resistance to become loyal to a theory which left one living in, and striving to maintain, an unreal, static world.[18] He was disappointed because, as a pupil of Simon Nelson Patten, he expected more from his academic colleagues—especially economists.

Patten, by emphasizing economics as a cultural science, gave his ideas a "realistic twist." Early in the century he adopted the views of the instrumental pragmatists to explain how man adjusted to a new industrial system. It is no wonder that one of his most devoted students came to hold a "functional view of the role of economic science." [19] A further look at the basic ideas of institutional economists will indicate how deep was Tugwell's disappointment at the unrealism in the 1920's of many professors of economics.

The institutionalists believed that "human nature" had changed very little, if at all, for thousands of years. Meanwhile, man had drastically altered his environment. He had created new problems—but he had clung to old approaches (there are, of course, no "solutions"). The gap between the inertia of man's nature and the complexity of his environment left the world running in a monstrously irrational and inequitable manner. The way to narrow the gap was not to change man, but to change his institutions. Institutionalism, nevertheless, was neither amoral nor exculpatory. Institutionalists believed in traditional Western ideals. In fact, a journalist later condemned Tugwell for bringing to Washington an obsession with the immorality of business.[20] Tugwell, it is true, concluded that in the 1920's an honest businessman could not rise.[21] But he also concluded that businessmen would not be different until the system within which they operated changed.[22]

In the early 1930's both President Roosevelt and Professor Adolf A. Berle, Jr., Tugwell's colleague at Columbia, would disagree with Tugwell on the question of ethics. In Roosevelt's view, the depression did not indicate the failure of the Protestant ethic; the collapse came because of men's failure to live up to the code.[23] Similarly, Berle, the son of a Congregational minister, believed the world would be a better place to live in when the men in it were better men.[24] Berle's thesis, which Tugwell did not deny, raised the vital question of timing. Before man reformed in his nature and his ethics, he could, Tugwell pointed out, bring disaster upon himself.[25]

Thus, in the institutionalists' view, placing ethics first would be putting the cart before the horse. Man had to shape institutions and policies so that undesirable impulses would be "taken advantage of or sublimated in a program which is an expression of competing impulses." [26] The institutionalists' ideas about human nature certainly were not original with them. Spinoza, for example, in his seventeenth-century *Political Treatise*, advocated designing laws so that men's undesirable motives would cancel out one another. Adam Smith, too, assumed that through competition the same kind of cancellation would occur—under a negative, "umpire" state in a preindustrial era. But the institutionalists called for a positive control of the framework within which man functioned in an industrial society.

The desire to change institutions rather than men rested partly on the assumption that basic human drives were, as Tugwell asserted, too strong to be channeled by police methods.[27] Thus, his desire to change institutions rather than men was accompanied by a belief in democracy. The converse holds as well. Believing in democracy, he would not have advocated trying to change or regiment men even if he had thought it would be possible to do so. The institutionalists, it is true, thought that men could change to the extent that new institutions would go beyond mutual cancellation of antisocial impulses, encouraging expression of salutary impulses and inducing an improvement in conduct which would become a self-sustaining ethical force.

In the 1930's and 1940's some hostile critics of Tugwell refused to believe that he was a democrat, to whom regimentation, as a means of bringing about change, was unavailable. A magazine article about him, appearing in 1936, was entitled "The Sweetheart of the Regimenters." [28] Some of his opponents charged that he stood for a totalitarian state, basing their accusation on his frequent references to "social discipline" and "democratic discipline." [29] Tugwell's writings and speeches show that he used the word "discipline" in the ecological sense of the discipline of adjustment—men had to think and to conduct themselves in ways which would enable them to make an effective response to the demands of their environment.[30] Imposed uniformity had no place in Tugwell's pragmatic institutional reaction to environmental challenges. In a radio address to the nation in 1934 he stated that "we are living in a democracy," in which Americans had given the administration no mandate to abandon the traditional business system; the people had requested an attempt to readjust, through the method of trial and error, relationships among institutions, and between them and a new economic environment of accelerated technological growth.[31]

We see running through the institutionalists' thought, as in this address, the assumption that change was compulsory. They did not believe in change for its own sake—there was no choice. Society could not go back and literally re-establish a situation from which it had once departed.[32] It could not stand still. The only way to go was forward. And the means of advance was pragmatism. Tugwell came by his pragmatism honestly. His mentor, Simon Nelson Patten, had impressed him with the idea that men could make an efficient adjustment to their environment through planning. His eminent colleague at Columbia, John Dewey, who believed that men could assure progress by designing social mechanisms to meet specific needs, emphasized experimentation as the technique of planning. Pragmatism rejected intellectual regimentation, including the dogmas of Marx and classical liberalism. Tugwell maintained that effective social policy had to be dictated by contemporary resources, techniques, and circumstances; it had to be tuned to the times rather than to an imaginary environment in some Utopia.[33]

Tugwell did not accept it as predetermined that men would choose the reasonable course of going forward with pragmatic adjustment to their environment—even in the face of dire new threats to their existence.[34] They did not have to make this choice—but if they did not, they would be gambling with their very survival. Tugwell's writings abounded in warnings like these: whenever the "oneness of man and nature" was violated, the punishment, often savage, came sooner or later; [35] man had to develop foresight in the use of his inventiveness and accommodate the constantly new environment it produced, "otherwise it can be seen that what he created is likely to destroy him." [36]

The institutionalists' antideterminism suggests a possible dilemma. They contended that men, due to their nature, got and kept themselves in trouble. At the same time, they called upon men to get themselves, without changing their nature, out of trouble. The dilemma dissolves when we note that the institutionalists observed that the intelligence of the race was not equally distributed among all its members. Some men, comparatively few, were more capable than others of understanding and coping with society's problems. Most institutionalists were optimistic about intelligent men's chances of saving civilization. At least they intended to try. Veblen was a pessimist, believing that men could not close the gap between their nature and the machine process. But Patten and Dewey were optimists. They did not despair because the old world of Platonic and Newtonian absolutes was gone. They saw in the new world of science and industry a challenge to man to create, by using his own mind, a new and better life for all.

Tugwell, although he was a keen student of Veblen's works, and despite his occasional melancholy moods, leaned in this respect toward the attitude of Patten and Dewey. In the 1940's Puerto Ricans, who nicknamed their American governors, called him "todo lo huela" (everything smells),[37] but his skepticism regarding contemporary arrangements did not characterize his views on future possibilities. His attitude was that intelligent men should do what they could, working with unflagging energy in the face of known obstacles, to close the physical-social gap. His kind of optimism differed from the commonplace kind which holds, usually without recognizing obstacles, that "everything is going to be all right." Tugwell believed everything could be all right—if men did something about it.

Thus, the institutionalists, while attributing some significance to automatic change in institutions, emphasized the part rational men played in economic affairs. They placed a heavy, crucial burden of responsibility on intelligent men. In this light, Tugwell's condemnation of his myth-making colleagues becomes understandable. Academicians, one would think, had the best chance to make a realistic, disinterested inquiry into economic facts. Unfortunately, Tugwell protested, armchair economists neglected the findings of psychologists, and they allowed the separation of theory from practice to grow wider.[38] Economics failed to consider itself a complete science in the experimental sense, evading its responsibility for policy: "Economics is still social economics and most folk are interested in 'what ought to be done.'"[39] Tugwell considered many professors defenders of the ideals of "interested conservatives," and the conservative habit of mind often failed to recognize the significance of novelty and institutional interrelationships; the consequences of this failure to recognize the process of "emergence" could be devastating.[40] For example, economists failed to understand the significance of scientific management—the "second" Industrial Revolution; they were still "parroting the phrases of Ricardo, Mill, Marshall, and Clark," retreating from "the marketplace and the factory to the library and the classroom."[41] The consequences of their failure turned out to be devastating enough.

Some professors were not among the myth-makers. Like Tugwell, they were enthusiastic about the American experiment but critical of the course of its development.[42] They received no thanks for their warnings. Those who "predicted disaster and preached avoidance" were "theorists" and "academic" and so were not "practical."[43] Often the loudest name-callers were businessmen and politicians, who did their own share of myth-making by "substituting demagogic romancing for future reality."[44] And the censurer of college professors could always count on a hearty second from anti-intellectuals. Indeed, anti-intellectualism was so unyielding that even after crisis called old ideas in question and events proved the joyless professors of the "Jazz Age" right, they were "still accorded the same, or perhaps worse, treatment."[45]

II

Did Tugwell practice what he preached about the obligation of economists to make their studies meaningful in terms of the going economy? We may answer this question by considering what he saw and foresaw as he analyzed economic affairs of the Roaring Twenties. In his doctoral dissertation, published in 1922, Tugwell studied common-law regulation of business in order to determine the claims of government to supervision of economic affairs. He concluded that among the sovereign people's prerogatives, to be exercised through their government, was the right of surveillance of services and prices. According to immemorial usage, he found, services were to be adequate to public needs, and prices were to be reasonable. To assure the fulfillment of these conditions, government had the power to set common limitations and confer common protections.[46]

Tugwell did not advocate government action for its own sake. If business adopted policies of low prices, high wages, and planned use of capacity, foregoing speculative profits and deficits, it would be, happily, "its own government." [47] The economy would then enjoy "continuity"—a term he used often to denote the elimination of violent cyclical fluctuations through the continuous presence of purchasing power to dispose of goods as they came off the production line—and government would not have to exercise its ultimate powers.

In the United States, under laissez faire, business had acquired what Tugwell considered prerogatives of government: "Through the mechanism of incorporation, social functions of the most crucial sorts were appropriated to the uses of money-making. Capital was allocated, production arranged, the places and terms of people's livings fixed—all with a primary view to probable profits—and Government did not interfere." [48] The possession by business of governmental powers did not, in itself, disturb Tugwell. What was more important, assuming the protection of government's right to reclaim the exercising of its powers, was how business managed industry (he used "business" for management and "industry" for production, although not with unvarying consistency).

Tugwell maintained that since business managed industry "all with a primary view to probable profits," it managed it very poorly—that is, without regard for the general interest. His emphasis on the inadequacy of profit-seeking as an overriding impulse suggests Veblen's influence. In his writings Tugwell often referred to Veblen's views on the conflict between businessmen, who sought profits, and engineers, who sought production. He contended that business, in its eager quest for profits, was irresponsible in a social sense. [49]

Tugwell considered the reasons for business' ability to conduct its affairs in a socially irresponsible manner. Above all, business' speculative, exploitative activities enjoyed the approval of laissez faire orthodoxy. That doctrine, which assigned government a negative role, so pervaded Americans' thinking that they—businessmen themselves included—did not know business had received governmental powers. [50] Businessmen who hated dictators acted like them in their own spheres—in the name of democracy. [51] They were able to evade control not only because they operated under the stamp of orthodoxy, but also because most people did not understand the financial structure of the economy. The general public failed to distinguish between the instruments of large-scale production and the speculators who controlled them. [52]

Tugwell cited as evidence of business' possession of governmental powers the chief means by which it promoted its interests to the detriment of the general welfare—"private planning." Businessmen denounced a "planned economy," but they planned their own particular economies whenever they could. The antitrust laws seldom stopped them; their planning took place out of the public's sight, without concern for public advantage—and, equally significant, without concern for mutual advantage. Each group of planners aimed to profit by sacrificing other groups, although such offerings would be, as Tugwell observed, "eventually, though they may not realize it, at a sacrifice to themselves." [53]

Thus, the inner contradiction of laissez faire—the use of freedom to suppress freedom—produced an inequitable economy. In the absence of centralized responsibility to the public interest, the most efficient or the most ruthless developed private centers of control. The efficient did not necessarily have to conspire to monopolize. They bested their competitors and grew large. Since bigness was a "self-enlarging advantage," monopoly "could result from natural growth" which the antitrust laws had been unable to hinder.[54] As for the ruthless, who preached individualism, they did not intend to conquer nature but to exploit their fellows; opposing any limitations which protected the plundered, they had no complaints so long as all got an equal start—except, of course, their own children.[55]

There were at least two obvious possible results of a situation in which business, brandishing governmental powers, boomed while government was prostrate: (1) economic autocracy could develop as private planners supplanted government (actually, business in the 1920's was in many respects already more powerful than government in economic matters—in fact if not in theory); (2) economic ruin could come about if the private planners, "wholly out of social control, . . . unbalanced the system in their own favor to the extent of destroying their own markets." [56]

Tugwell's analysis of the economy in the 1920's did not end with the general judgment that business possessed and abused governmental powers. He described in some detail the abuses and the consequent maladjustments which threatened collapse. But first let us consider his analysis in brief outline. A technological revolution had begun in the early part of the century and was still going on. Productivity per man-hour went up; production costs went down. Here was a gain in technological efficiency which should have benefited society. It was reasonable to expect that industry would turn out more and better goods, cheaper and faster, for more people. This expectation even survived the collapse of the new economy. As late as October, 1930, President Hoover told an American Federation of Labor convention that both labor and management agreed "the savings from these reduced [production] costs shall be shared between labor, employer, and consumer." [57] What actually happened was that business did not pass on its savings to workers in the form of higher wages or to consumers in the form of lower prices. Nor did farmers, partly due to public policies which business dictated, receive a fair share of national income. Accordingly, business' profits piled up. Business kept some of these profits for protective reserves. It expended some of them in various ways which did not add to general purchasing power. Most significantly, it often put them into plant expansion without adequate deliberation. This thoughtless action was deceptive in its impact on the economy because it increased employment and acted as a stimulant—for a while.

Tugwell warned against the inevitable results of practices and policies which enlarged productive capacity without increasing and spreading purchasing power. Sooner or later factories would produce more goods than people could buy—overproduction. Or, looking at the other side of a two-headed economic coin, one could predict that people would not have enough purchasing power to buy all the goods factories produced —underconsumption. The basic maladjustment, described either way, would, if it went uncorrected, wreak economic havoc. Unfortunately, stock-market speculation put a false front on the economy, concealing its essential lack of balance and preventing timely remedial action.

The people who made crucial economic decisions in the 1920's paid little heed to Tugwell's forebodings. Finally, in 1932 he reached important listeners. The main features of his analysis of the collapse of "permanent prosperity" appeared in Franklin D. Roosevelt's speech in acceptance of the Democratic presidential nomination in Chicago on July 2, 1932. Roosevelt presented views he held before he met the Columbia economist.[58] But the section of his speech dealing with the *causes* of the depression sounded like straight Tugwell to anyone familiar with the latter's writings of the 1920's.

By the 1950's economists were in general agreement on an analysis of the origins of the depression fundamentally like Tugwell's. *Fortune,* a magazine widely respected in business circles, published an article which included graphs that strikingly showed discrepancies in the period 1920-1929 between rapidly rising factory productivity (55%) on the one hand and slightly increasing wages (2%), slightly decreasing consumer prices (3%), and drastically declining farm prices on the other; between rising capital investment and falling sales of durable consumer goods after 1926; and between the amounts of income received by various fractions of the total population.[59]

Tugwell's specific comments on aspects of his economic analysis—technological advance, wages, prices, farm income, and profits—deserve attention. He called the "nationalizing of business" and Taylorism, the techniques and processes of scientific management, the two transforming economic forces of the last half century. They included the breadth and depth of business penetration.[60] He attempted in *Industry's Coming of Age,* published in 1927, to describe and evaluate Taylorism. He saw in Taylorized industry a productive potential that staggered the imagination. He envisioned a time when technology would free man from the compulsions laid on him by nature, making physical work obsolete.[61]

The road to leisure and plenty, however, would not be an easy one. It would require repaving through changes in attitudes, policies, and institutions. In order to carry on in peacetime the kinds of institutional experiments which would give us the amount of production we had shown we could turn out in time of war, we would have to develop what William James called a "moral equivalent of war." [62] In order to accept reductions in the need for human effort as the machine process mastered industry, we would have to change our thinking, separating work from income and giving up our attachment of moral importance to the connection between them.[63] We could conceivably create a "Third Economy" of basic public works, neither socialistic nor in competition with private enterprise, which would absorb that part of the labor force not required to meet the ordinary economic needs of society.[64]

We did not, of course, have to look to the future for problems created by high productivity. Some of them were already with us. Tugwell was concerned with technological unemployment as it affected both the individual worker and the whole economy. He deplored the inadequacy of attention and funds devoted to the retraining of displaced workers.[65] He questioned the classical assumption that business, in increasing its labor force as the returns from sales of an enlarged product came in, passed enough of its returns on to new employees to enable them to absorb additional production. When machines replaced men, business' income increased by the amount of that saving, and total buyers' income decreased. It is true that business, if it sold its increased product to buyers other than displaced workers, then employed more labor, as well as machines, but since part of its incremental income was "sterile"—it did not go into wages and thus purchasing power—new hiring did not stimulate the economy enough to offset the loss of wages by displaced workers.[66]

Technological unemployment naturally entered into Tugwell's discussions of wages. After all, wage statistics, which showed that real wages in the United States were the highest in the world, referred only to workers who had jobs. From the standpoint of economic stability, the relationship between labor's total purchasing power and total production of salable goods was what counted. Figures supported Tugwell's contention that technological unemployment cancelled out additions to purchasing power through new hirings and wage increases. In the 1920's, he noted, employment in manufacturing industries declined slightly, and total factory payroll barely held its own.[67] Meanwhile, factory production increased. Tugwell insisted that despite high real wages it would be best for the nation if labor tried as hard as it could to raise its share of technological gains in order to assure a market for industrial products.[68]

Price reductions, as well as wage increases, would help keep consumption in line with production. As a graduate student Tugwell was concerned with protection of the consumer's interest—a concern he later brought to the New Deal. And the principal protection—or abuse—of the consumer's interest involved prices. Laissez faire had not, as it was supposed to have done through competition between producers, provided adequate price protection for consumers. Nor had technological advances, as they were supposed to have done through cutting costs of production.

Tugwell studied the comments of the technologists themselves on price policies for Taylorized industry. At first they had shown little concern with the social implications of their work, only dimly recognizing "the risk involved in putting it to the sole service of business." Later, after 1910, the engineers began to think about the meaning of their work and its social aspects. As early as 1912 some prominent Taylorites concluded that "small profits make good business, . . . that large profits always tend to diminish business" and would prevent the reductions in costs of production which Taylorism had achieved from benefiting the economy. The engineers, Tugwell noted, were beginning to see that prices did not simply happen but were decided upon. Tugwell himself concluded that when the organizers of the trusts added scientific management to the weapons in their economic arsenal, the situation called for public price controls.[69]

Price behavior in the 1920's justified the engineers' earlier misgivings. It failed to fit into the classical sequence—lower costs, lower prices, greater demand, more employment, more production—because competition did not operate in the classical manner. The most efficient were supposed to win the market, but market-capturing, Tugwell noted, was a very complex process which seldom followed classical lines. Market-capturing required several years for raising capital, expanding plant, and increasing efficiency—years in which prices were retained at the old rate. Often the next step was a merger, which kept prices up for another indefinite period. As plant expansion outran increases in sales, unused plant added to overhead, which business sought to carry by charging abnormal prices (not based on costs). These discouraged buyers.[70]

In short, prices did not come down fast enough to enable demand to absorb the greater supply resulting from improved technique and enlarged capital commitments. In the end, business sacrificed low-price, full-capacity profits for high-price, restricted-operation profits. There was, for a time, a race between rising production and falling prices. Unfortunately, Tugwell observed in 1928—the year after Edward Chamberlin submitted his doctoral dissertation to Harvard University, beginning deep theoretical inquiry into the "stickiness" of prices set by monopolies and oligopolies—not enough businessmen had been converted to a low-profit, large-volume policy.[71] The classical sequence depended on progressive price reductions, and they proved to be the fly in the ointment.

In the 1920's the farm population received a disproportionately low portion of national income. Along with workers who did not receive significantly higher wages, and consumers who did not benefit from continually declining prices, farmers could not purchase their share of industrial products. Tugwell was an earnest student of the plight of agriculture from the early 1920's on—even more so toward the end of the decade, when he became involved in the thinking which eventually found legislative expression in the Agricultural Adjustment Act of 1933. For the present, it is pertinent to note that insufficient purchasing power on the part of rural producers injured urban producers. The farmers' predicament was a basic aspect of the lack of balance in the economy of the New Era.

While business, as figures for farm income, prices, and wages indicate, did not pass enough of its savings from technological advance on to the general population, profits grew. To put it another way, a good part of these savings which became profits should have gone into purchasing power if prosperity were to be sustained. Classical economists assumed that buying power was adequate because they believed the very act of production automatically provided enough funds to assure purchase of the product (Say's Law). We know now that this did not happen, that the growth of profits in the 1920's was a short-run affair. Where, specifically, did profits actually go?

Tugwell, who believed that the processes which classical economists described took place nowhere but in their imagination, sought an answer to this question. He traced out corporate directors' allocations of funds received from the disposal of goods, listing these kinds of disbursements: (1) retention of a protective cash balance or surplus reserve; (2) investment in the securities of other corporations; (3) permission of the use of funds in the open money market on call; (4) expenditure for plant expansion; (5) expenditure for distribution costs and "business luxuries" such as advertising; (6) lending to stock-exchange speculators; (7) lending abroad. None of these, except plant expansion, enlarged domestic purchasing power; and plant expansion, while it increased employment and wage payments for a time, enlarged product even more.[72]

Investment of corporate surpluses in plant capacity for the production of goods in excess of purchasing power would result eventually in the piling up of goods in warehouses, which would set in motion a vicious circle of collapse: shutdowns, unemployment, further reduction of purchasing power, more shutdowns. Yet, corporate surpluses were very difficult to reach in the interest of the public welfare. Certainly the banking and credit system did not introduce into business' capital commitments a scrutinizing factor with sufficiently sobering effects. In fact, the banking and credit system, Tugwell asserted, was just as much to blame as business for faulty anticipations and overextension.[73]

Two features in particular of Tugwell's analysis gave rise to a response. Some defenders of the status quo saw in his objections to the "misuse" of profits a desire to put an end to the profit system—something it was impossible to do, he stated, "if by profit we mean the reward a man receives for his services and for his investment of time, effort and foresight." He preferred low, continuous profits based on new efficiencies to high, cyclical profits based on "the practice of that economic cannibalism which regards man as the proper prey of man and one individual's destruction as an advantage to another." [74] Abusing the profit system was the best way to ruin it.

Tugwell's comments on advertising also earned him a scolding. He advocated, the rebuke read, abolition of the advertising industry as a social and economic waste. Tugwell became "a name always enough to send shivers down the spine of any advertising man." [75] Actually, Tugwell credited advertising with serving a legitimate marketing function in helping consumers to make intelligent choices between different products.[76] He saw waste in efforts to turn trade from one firm to another when their products were identical.[77] Some of the funds spent in these efforts would have benefited the economy more if they had gone into purchasing power. To economists who argued that advertising created purchasing power, Tugwell would have replied that the desire to buy and the ability to buy were two different things—not even motivational researchers, who caused housewives to buy as much as a third more than they intended to when they went into supermarkets, could prevent recessions in the 1950's.

As a New Dealer Tugwell waged a fierce fight against false advertising. At no time, however, did he recommend abolishing the advertising industry. And he never suggested, as he was accused of doing, interference with freedom of the press, for which he had deep respect. (In 1934 Mussolini told Tugwell Roosevelt's program would fail.[78] When Tugwell asked why, Mussolini replied, "You have to shut down the press." Tugwell recalled with glee the Italian dictator's failure to appreciate the American heritage.[79])

It is pertinent to point out that Tugwell's analysis was similar to J. M. Keynes's contention that withholding of wages in order to invest in capital plant was permissible in the nineteenth century but not in the 1920's when investment opportunities were dwindling—the "maturity" or "stagnation" concept. Tugwell also shared Keynes's view that government spending was the way to end inertia. We should also note that Tugwell's ideas differed from Keynes's in several important respects. In Tugwell's view, the creation of opportunities for investment through the restoration of effective demand would unleash the forces of technology. Keynes, on the other hand, was not concerned with the productivity-increasing aspects of investment. Nor did Keynes devote particular attention to industrial organization, a matter which Tugwell's emphasis on Taylorism caused him to consider. This consideration resulted in a certain ambiguity in Tugwell's approach to the "maturity" thesis and led to his proposing detailed plans for industrial co-ordination, including centralized allocation of resources and price controls in accordance with the institutional concept of "concentration and control" or collectivism as opposed to trust-busting or atomism. Finally, Tugwell advocated utilization of contra-cyclical fiscal policy only as second best to co-ordination, and he only belatedly grasped the various ramifications of Keynesian deficit spending.

How serious were the maladjustments Tugwell's analysis revealed? His expectation was that "we were headed for a good deal of trouble . . . and the time would come when our much-praised system would break down because of overinvestment and underconsumption." [80] There was no basis in fact for one author's observation that Tugwell's complaint about "draining the last cent of profit" was heard only in bad times.[81] Tugwell's articles in the *New Republic* in 1926 and on the presidential campaign of 1928 described deficiencies in the economy and warned of collapse if remedies were too long delayed. He listed critical problems which would confront the next President: power, farm relief, unemployment, and the assurance of continued prosperity—for although industrial affairs appeared to be running smoothly, the smoothness was not real but only apparent. Chronic difficulties plagued farming, bituminous mining, and textile and shoe manufacturing. A few bad spots like these would inevitably spread throughout the entire economy.[82]

It is appropriate to note, in conclusion, Tugwell's emphasis on purchasing power as "the only thing which can keep industry alive. Destroy . . . or weaken it . . . and you injure every part of industry." [83] He was not worried about our ability to produce—our technology would take care of that. But when consumption and production got abidingly out of balance, he predicted disaster. When catastrophe came, it took him—after two and one-half years of depression—off the campus and into the world.

3. Mr. Hoover's Economic Policy: 1928-1932

Tugwell's published comments on Hoover's policies began with his series of articles in the *New Republic* on the campaign of 1928. In these articles Tugwell questioned Hoover's reputation as a practical man. The GOP candidate, he conceded, was a superb administrator as far as he went, but his schooling in the orthodox lessons of nineteenth-century laissez faire doctrines did not allow him to go far enough. According to Hoover's ideas in political economy, government was only to assist but in no way control business.[1] Concerned about industrial weak spots and low farm income, Tugwell asserted that Hoover's views prevented him from detecting symptoms of sickness. Tugwell wondered whether Alfred E. Smith would sponsor "effective industrial control which might effect a cure, or will he offer the cheaper and easier way of meeting problems only in crisis and refusing to see them until the crisis arrives— as Mr. Hoover [does]?"[2]

As election day neared in 1928, Tugwell's comments became harsher. In September he wrote, "One is forced to the conclusion that Mr. Hoover is either a very bad economist or that he is intellectually dishonest"—a difficult choice for intelligent people who had conceived Hoover as the engineer in politics. Tugwell thought it strange that Hoover's followers were disposed toward apology. They maintained, he noted, that it was not the real Hoover who, for example, advocated enlarged foreign commerce while outdoing Calvin Coolidge in supporting protective tariffs. Tugwell concluded, "If he believes the stuff he talks, there is nothing to be gained in electing him. If he does not believe it, when can we trust him?"[3]

In the early part of 1932 Tugwell reviewed the first three years of Hoover's administration in two addresses, an article, and a booklet:

"Responsibility and Economic Distress," National Advisory Council on Education, Economic Series, Lecture No. 14, National Broadcasting Co., January 30, 1932; Chicago: University of Chicago Press, 1932.

"Discourse in Depression," address, Columbia Teachers College, *Tugwell Papers.*

with A. T. Cutler and G. S. Mitchell, "Flaws in the Hoover Economic Plan," *Current History,* January, 1932.

Mr. Hoover's Economic Policy, New York: John Day, 1932.

Tugwell recalled that he wrote the comprehensive booklet after it had become apparent that Hoover did not intend to sponsor any sufficient remedies and "my indignation got the better of me." Based on a classification and analysis of the thoughts in all of Hoover's published writings and addresses, the booklet had a large sale.[4] Governor Roosevelt read it, and it had some influence on his decision to take Tugwell into the Brain Trust.[5]

Tugwell found that Hoover was practically the opposite of the engineer in government that many Americans thought he was. He did not act on facts but evaluated them according to how they fitted, or did not fit, into an economic faith. One foundation of this faith was his inheritance of a nineteenth-century set of ideas in political economy. These ideas, emerging in a period of economic expansion unaccompanied by governmental controls, attributed prosperity to the absence of controls. Tugwell, on the other hand, believed that after the Civil War our economy, as he later put it, "just grew" as abundant resources provided a "margin of tolerance." [6]

Hoover's ideas on prosperity took the specific form of the "business confidence" thesis, which, as Tugwell summarized it in 1957 in *The Democratic Roosevelt*, held that "only when business venturers felt the future to be secure would they initiate and carry on those enterprises which, totaled together, made up the capitalist 'system.'" [7] What gave business venturers a sense of security was a "hands off" attitude on the part of government. Government, of course, could aid business, but, Tugwell protested in 1928, it could not regulate closely.[8] Business would thus be confident that there were no strings attached to government assistance.

Hoover, Tugwell also noted in 1928, acted on the confidence thesis, keeping government on the sidelines except to support business' own program as it evolved from profit-seeking motives.[9] If the government's remaining on the sidelines, except to help businessmen play the game according to their own rules, created confidence, obviously government's intervening in economic affairs in any important way or changing the rules would damage confidence. In particular, Tugwell remarked in *The Democratic Roosevelt*, government spending "would cause inflation; inflation would cause a loss of confidence; and that loss of confidence would stifle enterprise and decrease employment." [10]

In sticking to the confidence thesis, Hoover could cite a theoretical rationale which Tugwell traced back to Lord Brougham's observation that nothing could be done for workers directly because frightened capital would stop hiring labor. Tugwell suspected that the "whole wages-fund doctrine of the classical economists was shaped to this policy of 'avoidance.'" Andrew Mellon restated the doctrine as the "trickle-down" theory—shift taxes to the poor, and the wealth of the relieved rich would find its way downward—and Eugene Meyer echoed Mellon in advocating the creation of the Reconstruction Finance Corporation. The "trickle-down" idea, Tugwell commented in 1953, "would crop up a little later as 'business confidence' and be presented all over again as though it had not been refuted a hundred times in theory and practice." [11]

A second foundation of Hoover's economic faith was his own fabulous economic success. That his personal experience reinforced his belief in the prevailing theories of his time requires no elaboration. A third foundation of Hoover's economic faith lay in his personality. Louis B. Wehle, who served under Hoover in the Department of Commerce, doubted "whether the world ever understood the depth of Hoover's shyness that then amounted to an intensely morbid fear of adverse criticism." This fear prevented Hoover from putting his "unique combination of mental, spiritual, and humane qualities, his technological masteries, and his knowledge of the world's life to effective use for the lasting benefit of the nation." "An obscure defect in personality, not in character," Wehle concluded, "proved a major national misfortune." [12] Morris L. Cooke, a Philadelphia engineer and later head of the Rural Electrification Administration, recalled that Hoover was moody and extremely cautious. When a drive for funds for his relief work was not going well, he was "in the depths of despair"; a few weeks later he was "as excited as a boy." He once told Cooke he would not take the Belgian relief job unless the books were kept by the Bank of England—"he would not take chances." [13]

Tugwell, too, in 1932, detected—from a study of the President's statements and policies rather than from personal contact—Hoover's personality defect. In time, Tugwell commented, Hoover became so sensitive in his fear that legislation might imply a reversal of his doctrines that this phobia went a long way toward preventing action of any sort. The struggle between Hoover's ideas and reality had damaging psychological effects. Becoming less and less able to face reality, he gradually succumbed to the prestige of his office, tending to believe that what he said was true because he said it. He systematically whittled down damaging reality, deliberately twisting evidence which reflected on the basis of his policies. In the end, Tugwell concluded, Hoover clung to his business-confidence thesis by "ballyhooing for better business and hurling invective at 'pessimists.'" [14]

The comments of Wehle, Cooke, and Tugwell suggest a psychological sequence which is both interesting and of importance in American history: (1) Hoover had a morbid fear of adverse criticism; (2) one way of avoiding criticism, he thought, was to take only limited action; (3) the justification for taking only limited action was that everything was going to be all right; (4) everything was going to be all right—and Hoover kept saying so—because: (a) his policies would create business confidence—the key to recovery and prosperity; (b) people who predicted otherwise had bad motives and/or were mentally unbalanced; (c) facts which indicated otherwise were erroneous. Thus, Hoover's ideas and personality traits were mutually reinforcing in support of his policy of limited action.

Regarding item (b), in 1932 Tugwell noted Hoover's tendency to accuse his critics of exploiting human suffering for political gain, and he called the President's aptness to assert that his critics were unbalanced the "last refuge of the mentally troubled." [15] Regarding item (c), Tugwell discussed at some length Hoover's handling of facts. The President, Tugwell wrote in *Mr. Hoover's Economic Policy,* believed that he proceeded from particulars to generals, that he was an engineer and pragmatist par excellence. Actually, Hoover clung to "fixed ideas inherited from a vanished past." He had a mania for facts and an obsession for acting on them—"if they will only behave." He maintained that progress in the past proved the "fundamental correctness of our system." The halt in progress after October, 1929, did not move him to consider whether there were basic defects in our economy. "We judge by fruits," Tugwell stated, "so long as their production requires no change in our customary attitudes." Tugwell granted that it would be justifiable for Hoover to point to progress as proof of soundness if he would show the relation between cause and effect.[16]

Tugwell concluded that in causal analysis Hoover had a "curious twist of mind, seeking to establish itself on fact, yet resting solidly on received ideas." In fact, in Hoover's statements there was no causal analysis, only citations of simple concurrence. For example, in a message to Congress in 1929, referring to the tariff of 1922, Hoover associated the retention of that tariff with economic well-being. He overlooked "one thousand other reasons for prosperity," describing several years of history in terms of a single reference. Tugwell protested that if tariffs caused prosperity, they must also cause depressions, for there had been a tariff increase at the start of the last slump. Hoover's reasoning regarding antitrust laws was similarly perverse.[17]

Hoover's reactions to data on unemployment were a significant case in point. In 1928 Tugwell complained that Hoover, despite his sponsorship, as Secretary of Commerce, of valuable research on unemployment, failed to recommend action to help jobless workers.[18] In 1932 Tugwell stated, regarding unemployment, that Hoover had "denied or shaded" facts which did not fit into his dogmatic, theological-like concepts in political economy, had "evaded administrative responsibility," and had made only "false gestures" toward relief.[19] In 1957 Tugwell recalled how

Hoover was "repeatedly guilty of minimizing the number of unemployed" —a juggling act which Frances Perkins exposed.[20]

Thus Hoover held to his faith. He did so despite his superior mental powers and his knowledge that the world had changed. In 1928, in his *American Individualism,* he showed familiarity with technological advance and called antitrust legislation, a reaction to that advance, "itself proof that we have gone a long way toward the abandonment of the 'capitalism' of Adam Smith." [21] "He had been aware," Tugwell noted in *The Democratic Roosevelt,* "of most knowledge in the economic field." [22] He held to his faith despite the facts available to him about the suffering recent changes had visited on many people, even though he possessed strong humanitarian qualities. Human suffering, Tugwell recalled, had an intense meaning for Hoover.[23] Finally, Hoover held to his faith despite the failure of businessmen to behave in the public-spirited manner he expected of them, and, above all, despite the continuous decline of the economy.

Hoover's expectation that businessmen's conduct under a government favorably disposed toward them would be public-spirited was a key corollary of his business-confidence thesis. It accounted for his belief that mere requests of business for co-operation would be effective. Business' response to Hoover's requests did not justify his assumption. Business disregarded its pledge of early 1930 to maintain wages and employment, desperately trying to cut them faster than prices fell. The President's appeal to Wall Street and the commodity exchanges to stop short selling which depressed prices to unnaturally low levels appeared, in Basil Rauch's opinion, "timid to the point of absurdity" when the president of the New York Stock Exchange told a House committee that stock exchanges depended on short selling for their very existence.[24] Business' behavior, Tugwell later declared, showed that the "business classes have always wanted government to 'inspire confidence' by being supine." [25]

Tugwell's opinion of businessmen's conduct during the depression, as he stated it in 1954, was that "they were just poor sports." [26] In 1932 and again in 1935 he asserted that businessmen had deliberately risked dire consequences to the system, not for social but for private reasons, while expressing horror of governmental interference. When the gambling mechanism betrayed the manipulators, they expected the government to rescue them. They were "always ready to shift the burdens which they create onto the shoulders of those least able to bear them, always unwilling to pay the social costs of the policies which they have fastened on our people. . . ." "A lamentable lack of sportsmanship," Tugwell continued, "has characterized the reactionaries throughout the crisis—a kind of sportsmanship which would rule them out of their favorite sports by common consent." Their unsporting refusal to share the burdens of the times with the rest of the American people, "regardless of ability to help and regardless of favors of the past," was reflected in the government's emergency policies and was the "ugliest feature of our system." [27] As a New Dealer Tugwell offered some specific examples of poor sportsmanship. In 1933 he called the gold standard a "convenient retreat for the monied," who could convert their holdings into gold, immunizing themselves from social change.[28] In 1935 he observed that business was able to co-operate, without governmental sponsorship, to control its production, but objected when farmers tried to do the same thing—allegedly because farmers would co-operate under governmental aegis.[29]

In 1928 Tugwell had pointed out a lack of sportsmanship among bankers. The Federal Reserve Act, which they originally denounced, had only theoretically placed the banking system above politics. The system actually "reflected the current administration's notion of the government's relation to business," and within the new structure the banks, especially the big ones, were able to carry on in their "usual selfish fashion." [30] They contributed to economic collapse, Tugwell averred in 1933, by feeding the speculative boom of 1929, which was "largely financed through a system loosely conceived." Banks discovered the elaborate fiction of setting up affiliates for speculation with depositors' funds, weaving complex nets of finance through the old laws and creating and manipulating securities to the profit of "speculators who pretended to be bankers." [31] Yet, when the crash came, Hoover proposed establishing the National Credit Corporation in the hope that the strong banks would voluntarily form a credit pool to help the weak ones. The big banks, Tugwell maintained in *Mr. Hoover's Economic Policy*, rebelled at the responsibility of supporting the small ones.[32] The NCC collapsed, leaving the whole burden of saving the banking system to the government.

Historically, Tugwell contended in "Discourse in Depression," businessmen had been able to "manipulate legislation in such ways as to escape most of the penalties involved in a system which is maintained to support their functions and to protect their privileges." [33] In the 1930's they would again be saved by government, but this time their rescuer would not be the kind of a government they liked. Under Hoover, whom they considered their friend, the decline went on. Hoover had time to test his policies, and their ineffectiveness was evident in economic statistics. In early 1930 he obtained promises that wages and production would be maintained. In May, 1930, the stock market crashed again, and a two-year decline in prices and production began. There was a vast increase in unemployment and a systematic reduction in wages. For over a year he accepted the collapse as an inevitable liquidation of inflated values that should be permitted to run its course. As a matter of fact, while wage losses for 1930-1931 were from 12 to 15 billions, dividend payments increased by 200 to 300 millions. These payments, Tugwell recalled, showed that business was gambling on a sudden end to the depression.[34] In other words, business had confidence. Yet, the liquidation went on longer than Hoover thought it would. Still, he clung to his confidence thesis.

In his first attempt to meet the depression, in early 1930, Hoover urged that confidence was the key to the situation. During the remainder of 1930 he described the decline as a dislocation, an adjustment. In 1931 he stressed the European origins of the depression, although he admitted that at home there had been wild speculation and loose methods with harmful effects. These abuses did not shake his faith. In the same speech in which he cited them, he voiced what Tugwell, in 1932, called a "lyric encomium" of businessmen.[35] Hoover's efforts to restore confidence by making optimistic statements became, in the public mind, what Basil Rauch called "comic diversions from the realities of life." [36]

In October, 1931, under the sheer weight of disaster, Hoover, Tugwell commented in 1932, "finally and perhaps reluctantly took steps." [37] If the confidence thesis delayed his taking action, it also determined the nature of the action he eventually took. And his program of late 1931 did not bring back confidence. In the spring of 1932 he blamed proposed measures providing for expansion of the currency and direct federal unemployment relief, bills which passed the House but not the Senate, for business' failure to regain confidence.[38] In the fall of 1932, after he suffered defeat at the polls, he urged his confidence thesis upon the President-elect.

In 1932 a bitter Tugwell declared that a pep talk to business leaders was Hoover's "single contribution to the whole problem of depression and unemployment in the first two years." [39] If this was an unfair remark, it was even less fair, Tugwell recalled, to charge, after Hoover had initiated his program of October, 1931, that he had done "nothing" about the depression—a charge Roosevelt made during the campaign.[40] Hoover, it is true, was inflexible, and "inflexibility is a quality no person in political life can well afford." [41] His ideas and his personality limited his action, which rested on what Tugwell referred to in 1957 as the cyclical theory that "what went down would come up whether anything was done or not." [42] He felt that "a time of crisis was not one for reform. Confidence was the first need," *but,* Tugwell insisted, "he did, in fact, exhaust every resource he could allow himself to meet the situation." [43]

Certainly the presence of Hoover in the White House should have given business confidence. He carried on, Tugwell stated in 1932, the Harding and Coolidge tradition of a weak government in Washington with an almost "Quixotic intrepidity," even being unafraid "to present the spectacle of a chief executive who passionately desires a limitation of the functions of his office," and leaving "dangerously little . . . of governmental power. . . ." [44] Even if Hoover had given business confidence, "business recovery," Tugwell declared in 1934, would not have been enough. Tugwell saw scant recognition of the basic consequences of technology among those who were obsessed with this "speciously simple 'recovery' formula—attractive because it appears to avoid the necessity for both thought and reform." [45]

II

When Hoover's relative inaction failed to sustain business confidence, he at last determined on action to achieve that end. In 1932 Tugwell studied the economic beliefs behind Hoover's program of October, 1931, and the program itself, stating what he thought was wrong with it. "Flaws in the Hoover Economic Plan" held that as profits increased in the 1920's, values of goods, real estate, and securities became inflated. There was no equivalent growth in purchasing power. Values represented capitalization of prospective earnings from industrial and land holdings, and earnings depended on prices. With the deflation which followed the crash of 1929, prices and values dropped despite the "step by step" fight of financial and business interests to hold them up. Hoover believed that the decline in prices was exaggerated, warranting no such drop in security values as had taken place. Fear threatened the American banking structure by driving down the values of the stocks, bonds, and mortgages which banks held. In short, Hoover saw the deflationary process as largely psychological. Running through the measures he took was "the theme of 'restoring confidence.' All are intended to support values which have presumably declined too far." [46]

Tugwell listed Hoover's measures, which were "premised on optimism and a dogged faith in the institutions of Coolidge prosperity." [47] After the banking situation had become extremely precarious during September, 1931, Hoover announced his six-point plan for financial relief. Two points referred to the Federal Reserve System, one to the Land Banks, and three called for new financial mechanisms: a revived War Finance Corporation, a National Credit Corporation, and a new bank pool. Hoover also had in mind two other major credit plans: one, for the rescue of railroad bonds, had not been announced by the time Tugwell's article was submitted for publication; the other, announced on November 14, was to benefit building-and-loan and real-estate operators by the establishment of twelve home-loan banks. "The whole policy," Tugwell concluded, "is calculated to save the banks—agricultural, commercial, and investment—which are holding paper valuations representing capitalized incomes far above those obtainable at present price levels." [48]

Obviously, Tugwell did not agree with Hoover that the decline in values had been unwarranted. In both his article and his booklet of early 1932 he insisted that lower prices were needed to match diminished purchasing power, and "an accompanying decline of capital values would seem to be required." [49] He stated that to support frozen assets was to wager that they would soon be salable at higher prices, but prudent forecast, he asserted, would look toward revaluation on a lower level rather than toward a rise in prices supporting values at any former level.[50] He held that the confidence thesis failed to answer a crucial question: if the government's credit policy fostered confidence which resulted in a resumption of production, who was going to buy the new product if it were to sell at prices protecting capital at present valuations? [51]

Tugwell reasoned that no successful recovery policy could disregard the restoration of purchasing power. Hoover's remedies applied to the top of the economy—financial institutions and productive enterprises. Tugwell did not object to aid at the top, but, because he did not accept the confidence thesis, he insisted on aid at the bottom too. He deplored Hoover's failure to bolster the economy at both ends. In *Mr. Hoover's Economic Policy* Tugwell quoted this statement by Hoover on relief: "I am opposed to any direct or indirect dole. The breakdown and increased unemployment in Europe is due in part to such practices." This remark moved Tugwell to offer a "tempting syllogism":

> Our troubles originated in Europe.
> Europe's troubles are due in part to the dole.
> Therefore, our troubles originate in the European dole!

Hoover believed that direct federal aid would destroy Americans' character and liberty. He also opposed indirect aid—he vetoed Senator Robert Wagner's bill for employment exchanges. He accused Senators who differed with him on the question of government contributions to Red Cross aid to drought sufferers of "playing politics with misery." Senator Robert La Follette recalled Hoover's urging Congress to provide relief for German children in 1924. The President replied that that was "different"—ravages of war made self-help impossible.[52]

Tugwell believed that relief was necessary on both humanitarian and economic grounds. It was "obviously right," he remarked in 1935, "for the community to see that the unemployed and helpless are fed, clothed, and preserved in decency and self-respect . . . even the logic of reactionaries shrinks from the conclusion that it could ever be good business to permit potential producers and consumers of goods and services to perish. . . ." [53] This was in line with what he had said about relief in 1932. Not only did Tugwell want to keep potential customers for business alive, but he also wanted to make them actual customers again as soon as possible. Hoover's program of local and private relief had disbursed $800,000,000, which could not compensate for the 12 billion dollars in wages that 10 to 12 million unemployed had lost.[54] Besides, Tugwell protested, the funds which the President's Emergency Unemployment Relief Committee provided came partly from wage earners—from municipal governments which raised funds by taxing the rank and file of citizens.[55]

Tugwell could not see economic logic in drawing relief funds from that portion of the population with low purchasing power. In "Discourse in Depression" he recommended shifting purchasing power to those who lacked it through increased, progressive income and inheritance taxes, and public works and federal unemployment relief—for we needed the "repairing of a nationally damaged purchasing power, *not confidence, but actual power to buy.*" [56] (In advocating efforts to raise the income of that portion of the population with a high consuming "propensity," Tugwell was coincidentally using a Keynesian term.[57])

Hoover, Tugwell recalled, was "so afraid that people's characters would be undermined by doles that he seemed immune to their suffering. Humanitarian that he was, he was an even more stubborn moralist." [58] He considered it wicked to receive income as a gift from government. Such a gift undermined character because it "destroyed incentive to work; it taught people that they might get something for nothing. It tended to reward laziness, shirking, and shiftlessness." [59] Hoover could see unemployment increase, Hoovervilles proliferate, and human suffering beyond estimate grow, "and still not be shaken in what he knew to be right"—not that he was an indifferent or an insensitive man, but "it was simply that there were resorts which were not available." [60]

In "Flaws in the Hoover Economic Plan" Tugwell saw the President in a dilemma. The policy of extended credits could leave the government with a "deed of trust on an overvalued economic system," but if Hoover reversed himself, the banks would fail. Hoover believed that strengthening the credit behind industry, agriculture, railroads, and banks would relieve uncertainty, halt the decline in price levels, and restore opportunities for profitable business. This was wishful thinking, Tugwell believed, so long as there was inadequate aid at the bottom. Hoover's program anticipated a reversal of the downward trend of commodity and security prices, but it was of "no assistance at all in increasing the incomes of employed and unemployed consumers." Without the stimulus of purchases, business activity would decrease, and prices and market

quotations would decline still further. Without a comprehensive recovery program, the government's banking activities would leave it
"holding the bag—empty." [61] "Flaws in the Hoover Economic Plan" ended
on a depressing note. The conclusion was that lower prices and security
values, accompanied by wider distribution of purchasing power, "cannot
be fitted into the credit policy of the administration." [62] The last sentence bemoaned the fact that Hoover's policies offered no "guarantee
in any event that prices, security values, and consumer purchasing
power will be brought into a balanced relationship." [63] The prospect
was one of continued unbalance and decline.

In 1932 many people overlooked Hoover's humanitarianism, his moral
beliefs, the economic assumptions behind his confidence thesis, and his
constitutional scruples—the federal government must do everything to
help people help themselves but nothing to help them directly. In "Discourse in Depression" Tugwell charged that Hoover's whole emergency
program had been "framed with reference to the protection of privilege rather than any calculated analysis of cause and cure." [64] By
the spring of 1932 many ordinary citizens—farmers, workers, unemployed
—joined Democrats and Progressives in Congress in making the simple
accusation that the President showed class favoritism in failing to meet
the needs of any group except big business, and in the fall of 1932
the charge that Hoover was only interested in protecting business was,
Basil Rauch has observed, a potent argument in bringing about his
defeat at the polls. [65]

Efforts to make Hoover appear dour, taciturn, and callous to the people's plight amounted to a "smear campaign," but, as Dixon Wecter has
noted, he lent himself to the role of scapegoat because he had neither
the communicable personal warmth of his opponent nor a comprehensive
program. [66] Certainly his program appeared top-heavy to most people.
For the relief of farmers suffering from drought in 1931 he recommended
loans, when secured by property, to be used only for supporting property
values. Western Senators complained that farmers would be unable to
feed their cattle unless they fed themselves first, and the growing
ranks of the unemployed, who saw local and private relief shrinking,
now knew, Rauch has remarked, what to expect from Washington. [67]
To many people the RFC was proof of Hoover's alleged class favoritism.
The same people who clamored for an RFC, Marriner S. Eccles has
pointed out, opposed the use of government credit for the relief of the
distressed and unemployed. [68] Later, Hoover vetoed the Wagner-Garner
relief bill to extend RFC loans to small businesses and individuals.
The Home Loan Banks were another example of top-heavy aid. They
helped to keep mortgage-lending instruments afloat, Wecter has written,

but their "effect in removing the incubus of worry and loss from the backs of individual homeowners proved disappointingly small." [69]

Hoover continued to reaffirm his faith in business and himself, even asserting that "from this one [depression] we shall gain stiffening and economic discipline." [70] Tugwell did not agree that the system produced depressions for our own good, or that suffering was a necessary part of capitalism. In "Discourse in Depression" he thought the "regime of laissez faire, with modifications, might be made to work far more justly than it does at present." During periodic stagnations, if we had to have them, there was no reason for allowing the incidence of distress to fall so heavily on workers and farmers. [71]

If people misjudged the motives behind Hoover's program, they were hardly pleased with its effects. They lost confidence in the confidence thesis, which had had two and a half years to work its recuperative ways, and a doctrine of individualism which did not permit their government to aid them directly in their distress. The conclusion was only too logical, Tugwell later commented, that "if prosperity belonged to the Republicans, the depression did too. . . ." [72] People wanted new doctrines that would explain the causes of the depression better than Hoover had done and indicate a less painful cure. Academic economists, on the whole, had little to offer, while radical doctrines—running from orthodox Marxism through native panaceas such as the single-tax, share-the-wealth, and funny money—did not appeal to most Americans' basic conservatism. The people had no definite policies to rally around, but they were through with Hoover's program. In Rauch's opinion, by the fall of 1932 the majority of Americans, including businessmen, were ready for unconventional experiments. [73] If Hoover's allegations that those who disagreed with him were knaves or fools were true, by 1932 there were a lot of wicked, wild-eyed people in the United States.

Twenty-five years later, commenting on the recession of 1957-1958, Tugwell stuck to his emphasis on aid at the bottom and purchasing power. He did not "think this slump is going any further. We've got the base to lick it. People have money. They're not broke as they were in the '30's." [74] Regarding the confidence thesis, he declared in *The Democratic Roosevelt:*

> As could be seen clearly enough later, no more hollow and naive theory ever established itself as an orthodoxy; it would amaze historians to see how anxiously, and at what pains, the theory was propagated.

> That goods and services could not be bought by an impoverished people would seem so simple a fact as to be incontrovertible; but

there were few—and those mostly intellectuals—who recognized it in the early years of the great depression. Everything, therefore, was done but the necessary thing.[75]

Thus, the Democratic presidential nomination in 1932 would be a ticket to Washington, and the nominee's advisers could count on a move to the capital if they wanted it.

Part II
Tugwell the Brain Truster

———◆———

4. Brain Trust—Campaign—Election: 1932

I

Raymond Moley and Samuel Rosenman have told the story of the formation of the Brain Trust.[1] Each has claimed that he conceived the idea of going to universities to get men who would give Roosevelt the expert, professional advice on national issues which he needed as a prospective presidential candidate. Such conflicts of claims for responsibility were, Tugwell believed, unavoidable in participants' accounts of the New Deal. "Insiders," often lacking full knowledge of others' contributions, naturally tended to place themselves at the center of developments in which they played a part.[2]

Two men have received credit for coining the name, "Brains Trust" (the later form, without the first "s," will be used here except in quotations). The biographer of Louis Howe, Roosevelt's personal secretary and political adviser, attributed the appellation to her subject.[3] Tugwell followed the prevailing version in referring to James M. Kieran, Albany correspondent of the *New York Times*—and somewhat of an "insider" in 1932—as the inventor of the label for Roosevelt's professorial advisers.[4]

Moley and Rosenman concentrated on Columbia University for practical reasons which Moley has explained. Working with Basil ("Doc") O'Connor, Roosevelt's law partner, they listed possible campaign topics. Moley then listed experts on each subject. They decided to bring these men to Roosevelt one by one. Because Roosevelt wanted to emphasize the plight of the farm population, Tugwell was the first choice. Moley and Tugwell were colleagues at Columbia and neighbors, but they were not close personal friends. Moley knew about Tugwell's studies of agriculture, and he was particularly impressed by the address, "Discourse in Depression," which Tugwell made at Teachers College, Columbia, in early 1932.[5] After Moley read a mimeographed copy, he discussed the speech with Tugwell.[6] This discussion led to additional meetings in which Moley "was persuaded at least that my views were sharp, specific and practical—that, in fact, they offered a tenable alternative to the policies of the Hoover administration."[7] Moley concluded that Tugwell would get along very well with Roosevelt:

> He was ignorant of politics. But he was a first-rate economist who had pushed beyond the frontiers of stiff classicism, and his original and speculative turn of mind made him an exhilarating companion. Rex was like a cocktail: his conversation picked you up and made your brain race along. At the same time there was a rich vein of melancholy in his temperament—frequently finding expression in the doubt that any politician could or would take steps to relieve the paralysis creeping over our system. And that gave his presentation of ideas a certain moving quality.

Moley brought Tugwell to Rosenman's apartment, where, Rosenman recalled, the eager professor of economics spoke at length on the farm problem and the action it required. According to Moley, O'Connor remarked with something of awe, "He's a pretty profound fellow, isn't he?" Rosenman, too, thought Tugwell would do. The next interview would take place in Albany. In *The Democratic Roosevelt* Tugwell described his and Roosevelt's reactions on meeting one another.[8] He was keyed up before the encounter. "I was taken out of myself," he noted, because after indulging "to the point of immoderacy" in public criticism of Hoover and the business leaders who "presided so pretentiously and so blindly" over the spreading depression, "now I could turn to a more constructive kind of activity." Given this opportunity, "I should have been a strange young man had I not been instantly fascinated."

Tugwell was more than "fascinated." The Roosevelt personality disarmed him, to say the least: "Meeting him was like coming into contact with destiny itself. It was a tremendous, an unnerving experience, only to be realized and assimilated over a long time." But Tugwell was still able to make his points: "Either the impact of this meeting did not prevent me from expressing myself or Franklin was extraordinarily patient about extracting from me what I so badly wanted to say." Tugwell wanted Roosevelt to understand "the futility of the old approaches." The economic collapse of 1929 was "not contemplated in any of the received explanations." Therefore, "none of the approaches to remedial action was of any use." In retrospect Tugwell thought that by 1932 Roosevelt "had come," even if in a mostly unconscious way, "to some such conclusion himself." In any case, the Governor's reaction was favorable: "He was certainly receptive. And he found in what I had to say, I believe, an adequacy of explanation he had not heretofore been able to find . . . he felt then that what was needed was opening out to him and he explored it eagerly."

As the first choice of the board of selection, Tugwell "broke the ice." Roosevelt's ability to communicate with him made it easier for others who followed. The chief beneficiary was Adolf Berle, "the only other, besides Ray and myself, who was regularly present at those unique meetings in the red plush surroundings of the Executive Mansion that spring." Thus, Tugwell met the requirements for admission to the Roosevelt circle. He passed the tests which, Moley noted, others failed because they were overspecialized intellectually or were unable to simplify and generalize their ideas for campaign purposes. As just noted, Adolf A. Berle, Jr., Professor of Law at Columbia and an authority on corporate organization, also survived the screening process. The three professors— Moley, Tugwell, and Berle—and the two lawyers—Rosenman and O'Connor—composed the original Brain Trust. As the group began its work in the middle of March, it had no time to lose. Roosevelt's campaign had gotten under way with the primary in North Dakota on January 22.

The Brain Trust held a few preliminary meetings in New York. Then the professors moved on to Albany. They would take a train in the afternoon, later roaming over the field of economics with the Governor until past midnight. Just before Roosevelt left to attend a Governors' Conference in Richmond on April 25 and to vacation in Warm Springs for a month, he formally acknowledged his staff of five. He told Moley and Rosenman that he hoped the group would continue to prepare material and possibly send a memorandum to Warm Springs. Moley asked, "Who, specifically, are 'you fellows'?" Roosevelt named Sam, Doc, Rex, Berle, and Moley, instructing the last named, "You put in whatever you want to and pull the whole thing together so it makes sense politically, which makes you chairman, I guess."

The Brain Trust worked at a feverish pace for the next several weeks on various memoranda. Tugwell studied the tariff structure and analyzed the farm remedies proposed in the 1920's. With Henry Morgenthau, Jr., then chairman of Roosevelt's agricultural advisory commission, he prepared elaborate notes on a farm program. Moley and Rosenman edited the memoranda, while Moley worked out a broad philosophic statement as a preface. On May 19 Rosenman left for Warm Springs with a heavy brief case. When Roosevelt returned in early June, the Albany meetings resumed. The Brain Trust was more now than a research group. Ernest K. Lindley, the knowledgeable journalist, called it a board of economic strategy for the campaign.[9] The professors worked up memoranda, and they examined proposals from all quarters—"one of the most onerous tasks of Moley and myself," Tugwell recalled, "had been to scrutinize the more serious suggestions for governmental action in the crisis." [10] But what subjected their efforts to the requirements of strategy was speech-writing.

The famous "Forgotten Man" speech of April 7 was Moley's. The "Concert of Interests" speech in St. Paul on April 18 was Tugwell's. In this speech, Tugwell judged, "a major stroke was in fact delivered. But I admit . . . that I may be prejudiced. In all honesty, also, I must admit to no more real authorship than any but a very few of the numerous speeches of that year allowed anyone to claim. Franklin was almost always the real author. I wrote, but he rewrote, in the manner Sam Rosenman has so elaborately and faithfully described." [11] Roosevelt's speech on May 22 at Oglethorpe University was his boldest expression of the Brain Trust's experimental and holistic views. Oddly enough, no one in the academic sector of the Brain Trust had anything directly to do with that address. Ernest K. Lindley, then Albany correspondent for the *Herald Tribune,* wrote it, and James Kieran of the *Times* made some critical comment. Both of these journalists were intimately familiar with the Brain Trusters' ideas. Senators La Follette and Wagner refused to believe that Tugwell had not had a hand in this speech.[12]

In the latter part of June, Tugwell attended a meeting of agricultural economists in Chicago. There he learned of the latest proposals for a farm program. At the end of June he watched another meeting, much larger and livelier, in Chicago—the Democratic convention. Jesse Straus of Macy's store provided a room for Tugwell and Moley in the Drake. They spent most of their time in Louis Howe's suite in the Congress. They were merely spectators, having nothing to do with the political maneuvering. On the morning of July 1, when—after an all-night session of the convention—Roosevelt's prospects seemed dim, Tugwell and Moley found the Congress full of "hell and desperation." They went to the Stadium with Harry Hopkins, Chairman of the New York State Temporary Emergency Relief Committee, to witness their chief's eleventh-hour triumph.[13] Tugwell and Moley then joined the victory celebration at the Congress. A later arrival was Bernard M. Baruch, suspected of having supported Smith for the nomination. His greeting, "Well, boys, we won," astounded Tugwell,[14] who, with Moley, distrusted the newcomer. In retrospect, Moley saw Baruch's appearance as "a gesture of loyalty to the party ticket . . . the act of a good sport." [15] According to Tugwell, Moley continued to distrust Baruch after the convention, but "he was not in-clined to recall it very vividly when he was writing *After Seven Years.*" [16]

Roosevelt's acceptance speech on July 2 was disappointing to Tugwell. He had submitted passages for consideration, and he had especially urged a bold, specific proposal of the domestic-allotment plan for farm recovery. The passage on agriculture partially satisfied Tugwell's demand—which, he recalled, "may or may not be taken to represent something of an achievement for my efforts." And he found Roosevelt's presentation of the causes of economic collapse even more satisfactory.[17] It was Roosevelt's failure to outline a recovery program that disgruntled Tugwell. "Unfortunately the excellent analysis of depression was not followed by the statement of a remedial program that was at all adequate." Tugwell's drafts had discussed economic planning, price controls, social management of investments, and emergency public works and relief. "All that was, to my great disappointment, left out." There was a "digression into simple reformism . . . that . . . had nothing to do with recovery."[18] Despite the dashing of his hopes, Tugwell did not undervalue the over-all effect of the acceptance address: "But of course its status as a state paper is one thing, and the air of hearty elation and high optimism with which it was delivered is another . . . since victory was in the air, words already mattered less than the appearance of competence and stability."[19]

While the Brain Trust carried on its intellectual activities, Howe and James A. Farley pursued their objectives—the nomination, then election. There were rumors of friction between the professors and the political managers. Howe, in particular, was supposed to have held the Brain Trusters in something close to contempt.[20] There is no evidence to support these rumors. Moley had enjoyed close, cordial relations with Howe since 1928. During 1932 they conferred frequently. Howe, Moley recalled, became reasonably familiar with the ideas expressed in the acceptance speech, and "contrary to the impression of political wiseacres, he had no objection to them."[21] On July 3 Roosevelt told Moley that policy, with Moley in charge, and the political side, which Howe was to head up, were to be separate. A few days later Moley confirmed the division with Farley, and Howe agreed to send all policy ideas along to the Brain Trust. The two groups agreed to keep out of each other's affairs, and, Moley noted, they kept the agreement.[22]

Howe's biographer wrote that he watched the Brain Trust only for its loyalty to Roosevelt. He was not capable of jealousy in this matter because he was a part of F.D.R.[23] Mrs. Howe could recall no indication that her husband disapproved of the Brain Trust.[24] Howe and Moley continued to work together right up to March 4.[25] Tugwell, for his part, indicated his attitude toward the political managers in his description of the victory celebration at the Biltmore after the election, where Roosevelt appeared on a balcony between Howe and Farley, "as was fitting enough."[26] Later, when Howe's function diminished due to the sweep of events and his last illness, Tugwell and others went out of their way to channel papers through him for the benefit of the dying man's morale.[27]

The political contributors, as well as the political managers, were, Moley noted, either in general sympathy with the Brain Trust or disinterested.[28] Nor was there discord between political officeholders and the professors. By October Senators Key Pittman and James F. Byrnes were actively working with the Brain Trust. As the campaign progressed, Senators, Congressmen, state bosses, and local politicians sat in with Roosevelt and Moley on the drafting of speeches (only Rosenman, O'Connor, and Moley of the Brain Trust actually went on campaign trips).[29]

In *The Democratic Roosevelt* Tugwell described relations between the professors and the politicians during the campaign as generally friendly. He gave two reasons why the politicians accepted the academicians more readily than many observers thought. "The sensitivity of politicians to the probable sources of influence," he noted, "is extreme." They felt that "anyone close to a candidate must have the one kind of influence they understood." (In this instance the politicians, "as they watched us at work and wondered what we were up to," grossly misestimated the Brain Trust's influence on Roosevelt. "We were embarrassed; we knew how little we counted." [30])

Another reason for the politicians' attitude, Tugwell remarked, had to do with speeches. "One thing the politicians could understand: speeches had to be written. They were part of the ritual of campaigning . . . and they had to be done with care." On the negative side, a mistake in a speech was "too horrible to contemplate." On the positive side, a speech "represented the outward face of . . . grand strategy." In 1932 "the politicians felt particularly inferior in these matters." The Democrats' old cliches and shibboleths were, even the politicians perceived, obsolete. Something new was needed. Although the electorate would probably vote against something, "its opposite had to be formulated. If the Brains Trust could do that, its members had at least to be tolerated. The best the politicians knew how to do for us was to treat us as a respected member of their own trade union. We came to appreciate the compliment." [31]

As for the professors, they had no intention of encroaching on the politicians' functions. They were aware, Tugwell commented, that the operations of the political committee had "a natural priority. But we were not overconscious, in our sector, of this urgency." The Brain Trusters dealt with subject matter—social forces and their impact on each other—that was "not timeless, but it was general." They were interested in politics "only as it had to do with grasping and keeping power." It was "no more than one of the recalcitrant variables with which an analyst must deal." [32]

Inevitably, Tugwell explained, the Brain Trust "had to come down to earth" as Roosevelt "made contact with one or another issue that forced, or threatened to force, his hand." There was an almost unconscious adaptation. "We began to approach the general problem through specific issues," learning to discuss agriculture, banking, railroads, foreign trade, and other sectors of the economy which were in distress in terms that a politician—a candidate and a president—could use.[33] Even the politically oriented efforts of the Brain Trusters did not interfere with the politicians' work. On the contrary, what the professors looked upon as a program of public policy and remedial action was to the politicians material for a successful campaign.

Thus, it appears that many commentators confused the situation in 1932 with developments after Tugwell became Assistant Secretary of Agriculture and Moley Assistant Secretary of State. It is true that soon after March 4, 1933, there were intimations on Capitol Hill of hostility toward the "classroom cabinet." Politicians reportedly resented appointments of non-heelers and were annoyed at the professors' methods. Moreover, Tugwell—although he was friendly with several "Progressives" in both the House and Senate—often failed to go out of his way to improve his personal relations with the politicians. He made no pretense of being a practical politician—Lindley sensed that he would prefer never to be known as one.[34] And he met hostility with a certain disdain.

Perhaps, with the election out of the way, friction between the politically sensitive, elected members of the administration and the academic, nonpolitical members was inevitable. Be that as it may, let us return to the more harmonious situation of 1932. Back in New York after the convention, the Brain Trust found itself still without a home. Finally, in late July, the Brain Trust set up headquarters in the Roosevelt Hotel, separate from the offices of the Democratic National Committee across the street in the Biltmore.

The original group sought the advice of various people from time to time. The most active addition was General Hugh Johnson, Baruch's disciple. He met Moley and Tugwell at Baruch's home, contributing data which had been gathered for Alfred E. Smith in 1928.[35] Tugwell's and Berle's views on a fundamental approach to the economic crisis differed from Johnson's. Johnson, Tugwell remembered, believed that government's basic function was to give reassurance to business; government also had to end the crisis. Reductions in public expenditures and taxes, Johnson reasoned, would fulfill both functions. Tugwell considered "seductive" a doctrine which held that "with one motion government could reduce its importance and discharge its most pressing responsibility."[36]

II

In August Tugwell began to suffer from hay fever. In September, because victory appeared certain and the need for the kind of material which the Brain Trust provided had diminished, he went to Mexico for two weeks of respite from a high pollen count.[37] The basic work on Roosevelt's two major speeches in September was done. The preparation of the farm-policy address, given at Topeka on September 14, had begun in late June when Tugwell attended a meeting of agricultural economists in Chicago. Roosevelt was familiar with the equalization-fee and export-debenture schemes which farm interests had proposed in the 1920's. In the spring of 1932 Tugwell told him that a group of agricultural economists, financed by the Laura Spelman Rockefeller Fund, was working on "something better than the old schemes." The Governor sent Tugwell to the Chicago meeting, sponsored by the Giannini Foundation for Agricultural Economics, to study the new plan and find out whether it met with general approval. Tugwell spent an hour on the telephone explaining the plan to Roosevelt, who then called back a few minutes later, saying, "I don't get it yet. Put it in a telegram." [38]

At the meeting in Chicago, Tugwell "discovered" Professor M. L. Wilson of Montana State College, one of the principal authors and promoters of the Voluntary Domestic Allotment Plan. Tugwell made arrangements for Wilson to visit Hyde Park in August. In that month Wilson went to New York, where he spent a whole day with Tugwell and Moley. He explained the VDAP, estimated the extent of its support among farm-organization leaders, and evaluated its economic and political possibilities.[39] When the Brain Trusters took Wilson to see the Governor, he found that Tugwell had already done a good job of selling the idea. Wilson had no doubt about Roosevelt's position.[40]

Moley has told about the drafting of the Topeka address.[41] He asked Wilson to prepare a memorandum as a basis for a speech and to go over it with Henry A. Wallace, the Iowa publisher of a farm journal. Moley received Wilson's draft on August 23. He correlated it with the work done by Hugh Johnson, Morgenthau and his assistant Herbert E. Gaston, and others. In turn, Tugwell, Berle, Johnson, Morgenthau, and Gaston scrutinized Moley's draft. Wilson then made some final suggestions. Moley called the speech first-rate "substantively and strategically." Roosevelt spoke in general terms, but there was no doubt that he referred to the domestic-allotment plan. Wilson and Tugwell were overjoyed; they congratulated one another on what they had accomplished for the farmer.[42]

The other important speech in September was the "economic maturity" address at the Commonwealth Club in San Francisco on the

23rd. In *The Democratic Roosevelt* Tugwell made a surprising disclosure about this speech, suggesting that historians had misinterpreted it. Proceeding from the thesis of "maturity," the address called for policies of "consolidation, conservation, sharing of product, and the like." It seemed a reversion to the collectivism of the Oglethorpe speech. "The trouble was that . . . he [Roosevelt] was actually, no matter what that speech said, in retreat from this position." Besides, Roosevelt "was much more an optimist than he appeared in that speech." [43]

Tugwell told why historians erred in attaching great significance— as they were inclined to do—to the themes of maturity, collectivism, and pessimism as expressed in the San Francisco speech. "For once" Roosevelt "was caught without even a moment for revision. He never saw that speech until he opened it on the lectern." Berle wrote it, with some assistance from Tugwell which was "not altogether congenial." Tugwell felt that "we were on the verge of a vast expansion if we recognized our collective nature and socialized our product." He shared Roosevelt's optimism, but there was a "deep difference" between their concepts of collectivism.[44]

Tugwell believed that collectivism and abundance could develop together. But, it should be pointed out, his recollection in 1957 of his ideas as of September, 1932, on economic expansion did not square with statements he made on several occasions in 1933. In an address to the Annual Meeting of the Federation of Bar Associations of Western New York on June 24, 1933, for example, he said, "Our economic course has carried us from the era of economic *development* to an era which confronts us with the necessity for economic *maintenance*." [45] This may have been an instance in which Tugwell's immediate concerns differed from his long-run expectations. In any event, it was one of the few cases in which there was a divergence of his earlier from his later comments.

In the latter part of September Tugwell was back in New York. He, Berle, Johnson, Pittman, Byrnes, and Moley reviewed Roosevelt's speeches to date. They decided their candidate had yet to take a stand on three major issues: fiscal policy; industry, labor, and relief; and foreign policy.[46] None of the speeches in the last month of the campaign was a major effort comparable to the Topeka address. In fact, Roosevelt, for reasons Professor Frank Freidel has indicated, did not make a foreign-policy speech.[47] Hugh Johnson wrote the fiscal-policy speech, and Moley revised it.[48] Roosevelt delivered it at Pittsburgh on October 19. He made a promise which was to haunt him in the future—a 25 per cent reduction in government expenditures. He was, Moley asserted, wholly sincere—"none of us, then, was a member of the 'borrow and spend' school." [49]

The Boston speech of October 31 on industry, labor, and relief occasioned the only major quarrel within the Brain Trust. The members agreed on coverage; they disagreed vehemently as to phrasing. Tugwell and Berle favored a detailed statement of the program for industry and labor. They advocated a sharp attack on those men in government and industry who had countenanced existing abuses. The others, especially Moley, recommended a general outline of the program in a moderate tone. They reasoned that since the public was weary of the campaign and Roosevelt was a sure winner, it was time for dignity and conciliation. Roosevelt followed Moley's tack.[50]

In *The Democratic Roosevelt* Tugwell assessed the work of the Brain Trust from March, 1932, to the election in terms of Roosevelt's reactions to the group. The professors found Roosevelt's positive response—his eagerness, the quality of his thinking processes, and his progress from well-informed amateurishness to "all-round competence" in his understanding of complex economic matters—"remarkable." And they were amazed at his performing this intellectual feat while he was Governor of New York and an active contender for the presidential nomination. "As academic observers," Tugwell noted, "we could be excused if we were amazed and even, perhaps, if we found ourselves, quite without wishing it, enlisted in a cause." [51] Tugwell's enlistment in the Roosevelt cause was an expression of his personal loyalty. This fidelity would outlive Roosevelt. But devoted service did not mean uncritical acceptance. Nor did it rest on Roosevelt's adoption of the policies the professors advocated—which suggests the limitations of Roosevelt's reactions to the Brain Trust.

Roosevelt seemed to accept Tugwell's and Berle's explanation of the depression. Yet, there were intellectual and political obstacles to his acceptance of the remedial program which that explanation called for. His instinct made it difficult for him "to get outside the logic of laissez faire or to think in any reforming terms except those of the progressives in which he had been schooled." The Democratic politicians, of course, did not want a sure winner to rock the campaign boat unnecessarily with the presentation of anything novel, disturbing, or controversial. Later, Roosevelt would find that "even in crisis the terms of a revised theory were politically unacceptable." [52]

Tugwell discussed at length how these intellectual and political considerations determined the conduct of the campaign. They resulted in Roosevelt's adopting the "principle of secret amputation" rather than the "rule of the mandate." "Secret amputation" was a term Tugwell coined for his own amusement as a label for the political strategy of Cordell Hull, who told him and other younger members of the administration in 1933, "You don't tell a man about it when you are about to cut off his leg. If you do you scare him half to death before his real trouble comes upon him." In other words, Tugwell commented, "if you have to do some social reorganizing, you do it as quietly as possible. You play down its implications . . . give no advance notice . . . pretend that nothing unusual is happening." The "rule of the mandate" referred to Robert La Follette's contention that "nothing of importance could be done without support, and support could be had only by painstaking education of potential supporters." [53]

Some of the Brain Trusters urged that 1932 was "a time when radicalism would be politically desirable." But the politicians' "deluge of opposite advice was overwhelming." Roosevelt decided for expediency. In retrospect, Tugwell did not think that Roosevelt's decision was as basic as it seemed at the time. The candidate had not been won back to atomism or trustbusting. He had concluded that it was "so traditional, so accepted, so widely believed to be the economic reform most needed" that he could not possibly get a mandate for the collectivist policies he had been discussing with the Brain Trust.[54]

Thus the campaign was a "safe" one. There was a shift from the holistic "Forgotten Man" and "Concert of Interests" speeches of April and the "experimental planning" speech at Oglethorpe University in May to atomistic Progressive reform in the Columbus, Ohio, speech of August 20, with only occasional bows thereafter—at Topeka and San Francisco—to the philosophy of social management.[55] Tugwell remembered the Oglethorpe speech as the "high tide of collectivism." [56] The trend of these speeches, moreover, supported Tugwell's assertion that Roosevelt used the Brain Trust for his own purposes. The professors were aware from the start that Roosevelt intended to make the final decisions. Tugwell recalled, "The truth was . . . —and we never for a moment forgot it—that we, like the others [the politicians], were being used by the principal in this grand political venture." [57] "Our memoranda were merely the instruments he . . . used on which to play a tune . . . of his own composing." [58]

Another "safety" device was Roosevelt's expression, in effect, of a desire to be President of all the people. He persistently made a distinction between Republican voters and Republican leaders. He welcomed support from solid industrialists and businessmen—"strange political friends," Tugwell observed, "for a suspected leftist." [59] As a result of his cautious tactics, Roosevelt lost a minimum of potential votes. "Very few voters," in Tugwell's opinion, "reversed their intention of casting their ballots against Hoover." [60] On the other hand, Roosevelt did not win a mandate for a specific program. The program, bold and coherent, was there in his speeches, but the people did not see it beneath the generalities. (It should be noted that Hoover and Ogden Mills saw it clearly.) The people, Tugwell noted, voted against a regime that had let them down and for the "big, easy, smiling man" who offered "vitality, charm, a sense of confidence in the midst of spreading fear . . . it was certainly as vague as that, but it was pervasive and strong. It was the way of democracy." [61]

Tugwell considered Roosevelt's appeal personal—"everywhere he went the people . . . responded more to his personality than to his intellectual appeal." [62] And his triumph was personal—except in the South and New England he outran Democratic Congressional candidates. In view of Roosevelt's personal majority, "it seemed too bad," Tugwell felt, "that he had not appealed for a mandate instead of retreating to a safe, general, and discursive strategy." [63]

Tugwell did not overestimate his contribution to the victory. "I will not say that the work our group did was wasted," he wrote, "but certainly it played little part in the success of his campaign." [64] In fact, all the time and effort Roosevelt devoted to "this rigorous Brains Trust course in socio-economics," in view of its obvious irrelevancy to politics, were "a measure of his amazing confidence in the future." [65] But Tugwell was satisfied that he had done his best. He left the victory celebration at the Biltmore and "went early home to bed with a sense of a job completed—and if not well done, then done as well as posterity had a right to expect of a fairly badly trained, even if earnest, student of contemporary affairs." [66] But the completion of one job meant the beginning of another.

5. Nationalism versus Internationalism

During the period of Hoover's lame-duck presidency—from the election of November 8, 1932, until the inauguration of March 4, 1933—he offered several policy proposals to the President-elect. Then and later Hoover condemned Roosevelt's reaction to his suggestions, maintaining that the President-elect's attitude torpedoed a recovery that had begun in July, 1932. Ernest K. Lindley, Moley, and Tugwell, among others, have defended Roosevelt's conduct in the lame-duck interregnum. This controversy, the subject of the next chapter, requires a preliminary discussion of trade, intergovernmental debts, and currency in the context of the differences between the President-elect and the Brain Trusters on the one hand and Hoover on the other with respect to their ideas on international economics. The conflict between these two positions became strikingly apparent during the lame-duck interval.

I

Roosevelt accepted the explanation of the depression in terms of domestic maladjustments which Berle, Moley, and Tugwell—whom we may call the "nationalists"—presented to him. Moley listed the three distinctive features of the nationalists' thought: (1) they assumed that the causes of our economic illness were internal, and internal remedies were called for; (2) they believed that government, in addition to extending its regulatory power to prevent abuses, also had to develop controls for stimulating and stabilizing economic activity; (3) they rejected the atomistic, trustbusting Wilson-Brandeis philosophy, believing in "concentration and control"; they agreed on the preservation of equality of opportunity, but recognized that competition, as such, was not inherently virtuous.[1]

A letter of 1934 to Tugwell from Gardiner C. Means, a Columbia colleague whose research Tugwell encouraged and whose views he respected, indicated the importance which the two economists placed on restoring and increasing domestic purchasing power as the way to recovery. Means suggested the possibility of a study by the Bureau of Home Economics, USDA, of consumer demand for nonagricultural products—assuming that average family income could be raised, for example, to $3,000. "If such a study were made," Means wrote, "I believe that much of the talk of the importance of foreign markets for manufactured goods would disappear." [2]

A number of Roosevelt's subordinates were not nationalists. They maintained that increased international trade was vital to recovery. Secretary of State Cordell Hull was the leader of the free-trade advocates. In early February, 1933, before Hull was appointed, Moley told Roosevelt that Hull personified the philosophical opposition to New Deal nationalistic policies.[3] Hull did not object very vehemently to the nationalists' policies on intergovernmental debts and currency stabilization, but he stood for international laissez faire.[4] On the question of free trade he was an unyielding doctrinaire.

Moley and Tugwell looked at free trade in terms of practical possibilities rather than from a theoretical standpoint. They both considered free trade a long-run desideratum. In the short run, Tugwell asserted in early 1933, the administration had to consider the effects of any move in the direction of free trade on the standard of living of the American worker.[5] Moley, conceding that the theoretical argument for free trade was convincing, would agree to its immediate implementation only if one hundred years of history could be wiped out.[6]

Free trade was a policy Hull could not go back on, Tugwell recalled, "even if hardly anyone wanted to see it implemented."[7] Tugwell thought the administration might work out some sort of compromise like a reciprocal trade program. Roosevelt mentioned reciprocal tariffs in his Seattle campaign speech, "using a formula the Brains Trust was rather proud to have worked out."[8] Reciprocity, of course, involved a number of possibilities. Hull called for multilateral reductions of tariffs; among Roosevelt's advisers, Berle, Moley and Tugwell—but not Charles Taussig, President of the American Molasses Company and an adviser on Caribbean affairs—favored reciprocal trade agreements on the British model.[9] The difference was essentially between an unconditional and a conditional most-favored-nation clause.

(Under an unconditional clause the United States grants the reductions it gives to one nation on certain imports to all nations which give the United States most-favored-nation treatment. Under a conditional clause the United States grants the reductions it gives to one nation on certain imports to a second nation, if the second nation matches the concessions which the first nation grants to the United States. The unconditional clause is intended to reduce tariffs all over the world. The conditional clause requires negotiations with one nation at a time, promoting a selective rather than a general reduction of American tariffs.)

By mid-1933, when the nationalists considered international trade agreements, they kept in mind the aims of the Agricultural Adjustment Act and the National Industrial Recovery Act, which were intended to raise prices in the American market. These Acts provided for tariff increases in the event that American prices rose faster than world prices, inviting an avalanche of imports—provisions that were inconsistent, Tugwell later remarked, "with all the talk about reduced barriers and more trade." [10] Devaluation of the dollar partially offset the discouragement of foreign purchases of American goods involved in protecting the domestic price level. This offsetting effect would, in turn, be offset if stabilization of currencies occurred at levels unfair to the United States.

In a real sense, the difference between Hull and the nationalists was one of timing. The New Deal, Moley insisted, could not start a crusade for free trade and at the same time attain its essential objectives—agricultural-industrial balance, stability and security of livelihood, and adequate domestic purchasing power. Roosevelt resorted to modified protectionism to enable experiments in raising wages and prices to get under way. "It was not," Moley observed, "that tariff reduction was per se incompatible with the economics of the New Deal . . . but there was a crucial question of timing and method" which the Hull school ignored.[11]

"Timing and method" hinged on the policies of foreign nations. If they had been quickly co-operative in international economic relations, the United States could have responded in a like manner. They were not, and the nationalists concluded, Tugwell recalled in 1940, that "international sentiments were unrealistic and clouded every issue; we could not count on that sort of relief." [12] To a realistic administration, adoption of a nationalistic policy was not a matter of choice, and it was not based on strict adherence to a doctrine. In 1933 Tugwell maintained that it was "nonsense to say that because we were forced to follow that course for the time being we . . . had become determined nationalists." [13]

Reference to the differences between the nationalists and internationalists may convey the impression that the nationalists dismissed international aspects of the depression out of hand. Tugwell's comments show that this would be a false impression. In 1933 he pointed out that the United States emerged from World War I as a creditor-exporter. Europe would not accept the situation, closing her markets with tariffs and quotas and impounding funds for exchange.[14] On the other hand, as he wrote in retrospect, restating his views of the 1920's, "the sins of Europe were at least shared by the United States." We made no efforts toward tariff reduction, and the Republican policy of disposing of surpluses by creating purchasing power abroad through loans was "distinguishably among the causes of the trouble." [15]

In 1933 Tugwell referred to the dire consequences of "the sentiment of nationalism carried into inappropriate economic fields." The United States, he noted, could not go it alone in adopting an internationalist policy. We too were "caught in the universal movement toward isolation" —a trend which "may be reversed by slow, hard stages, but that reversal has not yet begun." [16] On another occasion in 1933 he declared that recovery would be harder without international co-operation, and that the Western world would not be set right until the trend toward national-ism was reversed.[17]

In time, the New Dealers did adopt an internationalist economic policy, demonstrating that they were not doctrinaire nationalists. The stabiliza-tion of the dollar in January, 1934, the creation of two Export-Import Banks in February and March, and the Reciprocity Trade Agreements Act of June marked the end of economic nationalism in foreign policy. Thus, looking back, Tugwell could write that "one could make more of this struggle with the internationalists than is warranted by the is-sues." Roosevelt often humiliated the nationalists and "nervewrackingly" delayed adopting decisive policies. But he did free the nation from international exchange speculators. He resisted currency stabilization on European terms. And in 1934 he launched the reciprocal-trade treaties, which were internationalist but less so than free trade. The international-ists, on the other hand, also had victories. They preserved the "most favored nation" policy, and for all practical purposes the United States forgave the intergovernmental debts.[18]

Thus, we can now see that what the nationalists won was time—the crucial factor which, according to Moley, the Hull school ignored. Tugwell, acting as Moley's lieutenant, made his contribution to the fight for time by getting the date of the London Economic Conference post-poned from April until June.[19] How decisive this victory was is hard to say. It does not appear that the New Deal would have got off the ground or that the nation would have gained much in 1933 by following an internationalist policy on European terms. In any event, it is ironic that Tugwell, who staunchly supported Roosevelt's nationalist, Amer-ica-first policy, became "un-American" in the opposition press when he called for new food and drug legislation.

II

In describing Moley's and Tugwell's nationalist position by contrasting it with Hull's internationalist views, we have got ahead of our story. Somewhat earlier the nationalists clashed with another internationalist, President Hoover. Unlike Hull, Hoover was not a free-trader. Rather, he stressed rationalizing intergovernmental debts and stabilizing currencies.

Turning to Hoover's ideas on the causes of the depression, we find that historians often refer to them quite briefly, mentioning his tendency to stress events in Europe and his inconsistency. Hoover's reasoning in this regard is not easy to follow. In their detailed study of Hoover's policies during two years of depression, Tugwell and two of his colleagues concluded that Hoover had not developed a "formal and coherent theory" but only "some hypothesis, however vague" concerning the causes of the depression. They did venture to say that the "administration's theory of our economic difficulties probably runs more in terms of European disturbances than American shortcomings." [20]

Hoover was quite familiar with Europe's financial affairs. During the depression European politicians declared that World War I debts were responsible for unbalanced budgets, inflation, high taxes, and lagging industrial recovery. They called for cancellation. Unlike Coolidge, Tugwell noted in *The Democratic Roosevelt*, Hoover understood the dangers involved. He knew that the settlements, "apparently so generous, . . . probably would not be carried out." He also "must have known but did not admit . . . that the best reason they were unlikely to be carried out was an unwise action in which he had concurred"—the Smoot-Hawley Tariff. But this was not Hoover's story in the campaign of 1932.[21] His story, as later summarized by Tugwell, was that ". . . the depression was an after-effect of dislocations remaining from war in Europe; that it had begun there and spread to America; that it was not a particularly serious matter because foreigners bought only a small percentage of American production in any case; that it would soon be over; and that minor precautions would be needed. . . ." [22]

Hoover, in maintaining that events in Europe caused the depression, assumed that the American economy was basically sound. If the American economy were basically sound, "natural" remedies should have been sufficient to cure an illness that was "not a particularly serious matter." On April 24, 1930, Julius H. Barnes, Chairman of the National Business Survey Conference, declared, "American business . . . is achieving a restored stability by a philosophy peculiarly its own, and through methods probably effective in no other country and in no other era." [23] Barnes undoubtedly had in mind Hoover's persistent calls for business confidence. In any event, "natural" remedies, together with "minor precautions," did not make our troubles limited and temporary. Europe suffered a financial collapse in 1931—beginning with the failure of Vienna's great Kreditanstalt in March and reaching a climax with Great Britain's departure from the gold standard in September—and the United States experienced another wave of business liquidations and bank failures.

Hoover reacted to these events with his statesmanlike proposal in June of a one-year moratorium on debts and reparations. At home, in October, he persuaded the stronger banks to set up a National Credit Corporation. In January, 1932, Congress, at Hoover's request, chartered the Reconstruction Finance Corporation. Hoover's measures, international and domestic, were in line with his assertion in October, 1931, that "the world is suffering more from frozen confidence than from frozen securities." [24] The moratorium eliminated, at least for the time being, what he considered significant sources of international uncertainty. His domestic program of support for financial institutions and productive enterprises rested on the belief that the way to recovery was through restoring confidence at the top of a basically sound economy.

The story of the European collapse and its impact on the United States has often been told—especially by Hoover. He repeatedly maintained, Tugwell pointed out in 1932, how uncertainty spread over Europe, ruining our foreign trade and debt collection.[25] He and his supporters were inclined to de-emphasize or ignore other aspects of European-American economic relations. The signer of the Smoot-Hawley Tariff Bill was in a vulnerable position on the question of trade. And evidence of withdrawals of currency for hoarding and increased gold exports—which paved the way for a banking collapse—was available long before Hoover showed a willingness to act to control them.

The things Hoover left out of his account of Europe's impact on America suggest a line of inquiry. When the depression did not turn out to be limited and temporary—as it should have been according to the explanation of its origins which emphasized events in Europe—why did Hoover not re-examine his premise that the domestic economy was basically sound? He did not do this. Then why did he not, when he concluded that European developments—which, in the context of his thought, could not undermine the basic structure of the American economy—were at least capable of depressing domestic economic activity, take steps to counteract this impeding impact?

Hoover could not bring himself to invoke the Trading with the Enemy Act of 1917 to control movements of gold but intended to bring order out of chaos in international financial relations by trading concessions on debts for concessions from European nations on currency stabilization and other economic questions. He first presented his scheme to the President-elect at a White House meeting on November 22, 1932, in connection with the forthcoming Economic Conference (later he presented it on December 17 and 20, 1932, and January 20, 1933). He had been unable to get negotiations under way, he explained, because his hands were tied by Congress. Moley replied that under the Constitution Hoover did not have to ask Congress for permission to negotiate with foreign powers on debts.[26]

Hoover, in insisting that settlement of these international matters was essential to a restoration of confidence, which was in turn necessary to recovery, deviated from his original opinion that European developments could not seriously affect America's economic well-being. But he did not contradict his axiom about the basic soundness of the American economy. He clung to that proposition to the end. On February 17, 1933, he wrote to Roosevelt, emphasizing the gravity of the domestic financial crisis—perhaps an implicit recognition of defects in the domestic economy and a partial divergence from his European thesis—but he still stressed the need to restore confidence.

It is pertinent to note that in this letter Hoover requested of Roosevelt a public pledge that there would be no modification of the gold standard. Since other nations had gained an advantage over the United States in world markets by devaluing their currencies, Hoover assumed, in making his request, that foreign nations would be quite cooperative and make important concessions at the Economic Conference.[27] Their attitudes and conduct would prove this assumption wrong (Hoover had been similarly mistaken in his assumption that through the National Credit Corporation the strong banks would help the weak ones). Roosevelt acted on the opposite assumption. Determined, with the support of Moley and Tugwell, to protect his domestic price-raising program, he would make no agreements on currency stabilization and trade which put the United States at a disadvantage relative to those nations which had previously departed from the gold standard. Thus, he rejected Hoover's proposal of November 22, 1932, that the United States trade, in advance, concessions on debts for European concessions on other economic matters.

Intergovernmental debts, it should be emphasized, posed a delicate, difficult problem at best. In *The Democratic Roosevelt* Tugwell observed that "politicians on both sides had made capital of the situation—especially the Europeans," who found it popular to promise they would obtain forgiveness or refuse to pay. Roosevelt would find forgiveness politically difficult because "American annoyance with European war debtors was widespread." He had to be very cautious about the debts, a "highly sensitized subject" on both sides of the ocean. It was at his insistence that debts were left off the Conference agenda—an omission which angered the debtors.[28]

There was more than politics behind Roosevelt's position on the debts. His nationalist advisers called forgiveness "largely a banker's idea." Bankers maintained that with governmental debts out of the way Europeans would have enough dollars to pay private debts. The nationalists, Tugwell recalled, were inclined to argue the reverse. "It was not true, as it had been put out by propagandists, that payment was impossible. It was just inconvenient for the bankers." And Hoover's position was the bankers' position.[29] "We believed, all of us," that the British and the French, who were determined not to pay, "not only should but could." [30]

Moley, too, wrote, "We were profoundly certain that protestations of inability to pay were in large part untrue." "Trading" concessions on debts for concessions on other economic matters "looked to us like asking a man to pay admission to a gambling casino." It was necessary to show

the Europeans "we knew what was up and refused to be outtraded."
Moley hailed Roosevelt's rejection of Hoover's proposal, at the White
House meeting of November 22, of a revival of the Debt Commission
as the President-elect's first step to "differentiate his foreign policy from
that of the internationalists." [31]

Instances in which Hoover assumed that the co-operation necessary
to the implementation of his plans would be forthcoming have psychological implications. In fact, the same can be said about his dogged
adherence to his theory of European origins of the depression—the
historian William Miller remarked that the shrinkage of American export
markets was "pounced upon by Hoover as an appropriate 'foreign'
scapegoat for the American catastrophe." [32] European politicians similarly pounced on America's insistence on debt collection. In 1931 a
German author went further, in effect reversing Hoover's thesis by attributing Germany's economic ills to emulation of the United States. [33]

In late 1932 Hoover finally hinted that there was something fundamentally wrong with the domestic economy. He referred to abusive
financial practices, revealed by Congressional investigations, as "wicked
manipulations." Likewise, the nationalists recognized the importance of
international economics. Yet, if the difference between Hoover and
the nationalists was in emphasis, it was not a slight one. The European-
origins theory was superficial; it overlooked too much.

Did Hoover delay and limit his action on domestic matters because
he believed in the European thesis, or did he come to believe in the
European thesis, which neglected so many facts, because he could
not act with the speed and range which recognition of certain facts
about the home economy might have suggested to him as appropriate?
There was a definite connection, Tugwell recalled, between Hoover's
emphasizing European origins and the fact that he "pooh-poohed the
statistics of decline" while insisting that prosperity was "just around the
corner." [34] It was from this internationalist position that Hoover presented his proposals to the President-elect and condemned Roosevelt's
reactions to them.

6. Roosevelt versus Hoover:
The Lame-Duck Interlude

Economic deterioration went on relentlessly during the year between Tugwell's presentation of his probing of Hoover's program and Roosevelt's inauguration. The new administration faced a situation which Moley called "superdeflationary." Accordingly, by early 1933 Tugwell's views had changed somewhat from those he held in early 1932. Previously he had called for a lowering of prices and positive measures to restore purchasing power as policies which would provide a basis for putting the economy back on a rising course. Hoover's failure to adopt these policies had resulted, as Tugwell anticipated, in further decline. If a timely lowering of prices at first would have helped prevent continuous decline, it was now too late for price decreases to do much good.

Tugwell still stood for a balanced relationship between production, costs, prices, and purchasing power, but by late 1932, he remembered, there was "another range of fact to be considered . . . which loomed larger as the campaign progressed. And it was more important [than direct changing of prices] in shaping the New Deal program. . . ." Tugwell referred to the dislocation of established relationships caused by prolonged deflation. Such dislocation was not only a matter of debts but also of exchangeability. Panic had taken hold when "evidence of ownership had moved toward worthlessness." [1]

A person repaying, in 1932, a debt contracted in 1928 found that 1932 dollars were worth more than 1928 dollars, and they were harder to come by. With a reduction in the value of dollars to the level at which debts had been contracted, debtors would be able to get enough dollars to satisfy their creditors. "The incurring and discharging of debt— one of the central mechanisms of capitalism—could," Tugwell recalled, "then go on freely." [2] This kind of inflation, which the increase in the value of the dollar in a deflationary period subsequent to the contraction of debt made necessary if debtor-creditor relationships were to be going ones, was called "reflation."

Reflation, which contemplated the raising of commodity prices, was a middle course according to Ernest K. Lindley, whose two volumes on the early New Deal are indispensable. Rigid deflationists wanted to bring the overhead weight of debt and taxation, built up at a higher price level, down to the lower price level. They assumed that the price

level would not drop as the overhead was cut down. Extreme inflationists wanted to raise the price level enough to support the highest levels
of the old debt structure. They ignored the fact that the top level was
"no longer a plateau but a series of peaks with deep valleys in between."
Outright inflation would cause further dislocation in those sectors of
the economy which had already adjusted to lower levels.[3]

Hoover had preserved some of the peaks in the debt structure by
using federal credit, but he had done nothing effective to raise commodity prices. The new administration, Lindley explained, proposed a corrective compromise: "An orderly reduction of the peaks of debt and
taxation and the raising of commodity prices until debts and prices were
again in a workable relationship to each other."[4] Tugwell supported
the middle course. In February, 1933, he advocated selective price
adjustments—"Some prices ought to go down; some ought to go up"—and
he opposed inflation beyond reflation: "General inflation will not procure
the results we want . . . it would be favorable to those groups which
never adjusted themselves to the new price level; it would injure those
who had done so. . . ."[5] As a public official he deplored the failure of
the NRA to use a selective price-fixing program.[6] He backed the efforts
of voluntary debt-adjustment committees. And he worked to raise the
prices of farm commodities.

Inflationists, especially those in the Committee for the Nation, blasted
Tugwell. Deflationists considered him "wild" on the monetary issue.
Among academic economists he "lost face all around."[7] Extreme leftists
felt that he contradicted himself in favoring aid at the top. The inflationists were, from their point of view, justifiably belligerent—Tugwell
was against them. The deflationists might have seen, with calm analysis,
that monetary and price policies designed to revive the discharging of
debts would give creditors about as good a return as they could expect
after more than three years of deflation. The leftists failed to understand
that Tugwell had never opposed aid at the top, and that reflation and
price-raising did not comprise the whole program—there was to be a
concerted attempt to build up purchasing power at the bottom.

It is to be recalled that Tugwell criticized Hoover not for aiding the
top but for not aiding both top and bottom with what he later called a
"Diversified Attack."[8] The new administration had no intention of standing by while credit institutions collapsed. On May 22, 1932, Roosevelt
referred to the possible need for a reflationary policy in a way which
showed concern for the creditor interest.[9] From early 1932 on the
Roosevelt inner circle was deeply concerned, Tugwell recalled, that
the "banks by then were in an alarming condition and the decline
in values had jeopardized all sorts of credit institutions. . . . It began
to seem like a choice between very general bankruptcy and such a

complete reconstruction of values as could be accomplished by government action." [10]

Perhaps militant leftists judged reflation in terms of its supporters, among whom were a great many businessmen. It is hard to say what would have happened if the new administration let deflation run its course to the bitter end, but by 1933 most businessmen were afraid to find out.[11] A number of "sound money" Eastern Democrats with the creditors' point of view did not oppose the fall of the dollar to its "natural" level from March to August, 1933. They—Dean Acheson, Bernard Baruch, Professor Frederic Mills, Ralph Robey (a financial writer), Alfred E. Smith, O. M. W. Sprague, and James P. Warburg, among others—did oppose the "artificial" measures for further devaluation which began in October.[12] So did Tugwell. He and Moley both told the President that the theory of Professor George F. Warren of Cornell University that changes in the price of gold would cause commodity prices to vary proportionately was nonsense.[13]

Thus, Tugwell was, if the distinction will be allowed, a reflationist but not an inflationist. And, in terms of his institutional economics, reflation was only an emergency adjustment, a patching-up policy. In a note of the early 1930's and an article of 1948 he held that in the short run monetary measures could raise prices, halt deflation, and save middle-class investments—insurance policies, homes, and farms—but they could not "achieve a situation in which everyone could buy everyone else's products because his own sold at 'parity.'"[14] Continuous economic balance required more fundamental institutional reforms of a sort which the American people had been unwilling to accept. Instead, Tugwell later concluded from a study of the role of the cheap-money doctrine of prosperity in American history, they had resorted to inflation as a kind of abrupt general bankruptcy, in crises of mounting debt after periods of unsound expansion, when ordinary processes of bankruptcy were too slow—as in 1837, 1873, and 1929. Even though any suggestion of inflation infuriated the creditor classes, "inflation was one of those facilitating devices which had always maintained the business system."[15]

Nor was Roosevelt an inflationist. According to Moley, the President was not determined on inflation on March 4, 1933. He was consciously waiting after March 13, when the banks reopened, to see whether the preservation of the monetary standard would not entail "greater sacrifices in terms of shrinking money incomes than the American people would bear." He was also aware, especially after a count of noses in the Capitol on April 18, of the possibility that the political forces demanding uncontrolled inflation might overwhelm any effort to preserve the gold standard. The President, Moley concluded, abandoned the gold standard not to implement any monetary theory but to prevent further deflation. He accepted the Thomas amendment to the farm bill, which vested control over inflation in the President, to circumvent uncontrolled inflation by Congress.[16]

Tugwell had no part after March 4 in the decision-making on measures affecting currency.[17] (These included the President's proclamation of March 6, the Emergency Banking Act of March 9, the official departure from the gold standard on April 20, when Secretary William Woodin stopped the export of gold, the Warren gold-buying experiment in October, and devaluation by an act of Congress in January, 1934.) His opinion, however, expressed before inauguration, that the administration possibly, even probably, would have to go off the gold standard and resort to reflation was in line with the position Roosevelt took in refusing to follow Hoover's recommendations on currency policy during the lame-duck period.

Reflation, the attempt to bolster financial institutions by deliberate measures to raise prices through gold and currency management, could not be divorced from international finance. "Nothing could be done here," Tugwell wrote in retrospect, "without either foreign consent or without deliberately establishing a policy of isolation." [18] On the international, as well as the domestic, aspects of gold and currency policy, Hoover and Roosevelt disagreed. On November 22, 1932, Hoover and Ogden Mills, Secretary of the Treasury, met in Washington with Roosevelt and Moley. In the only published account of this meeting by a participant, Moley related Hoover's emphasis on the foreign causes of the depression.[19] International instability, Hoover said, was the only threat to recovery. Hoover's remedy for international ills, which Tugwell had summarized in early 1932, was: (1) calm the debtors with a moratorium; (2) scale down reparations and public debts; (3) work for currency stability by collaborating with France, the leading European gold nation.[20]

At the meeting of November 22, Hoover proposed that a single body of delegates represent the United States in debt negotiations, the Disarmament Conference, and the London Economic Conference. He wanted to facilitate "trading"—scaling down debts in exchange for concessions on tariffs, monetary stabilization, and disarmament.[21] Roosevelt rejected this proposal, declined to participate in the appointment of a Debt Commission, and suggested that debt negotiations be carried on through regular diplomatic channels.[22]

Roosevelt objected to "trading" because he assumed that his all-important domestic program would probably hinge on price-raising, and he wished to assure protection of this program from foreign interference. The protection of increased domestic prices against foreign dumping in the American market would require dollar devaluation and the maintenance of tariffs. International currency stabilization before devaluation, Moley noted, would be unfavorable to the United States.[23] Similarly, tariff reductions required international co-operation.

Debt payments were due in December, 1932. If Roosevelt made concessions on them then, how could he be sure that the debtor nations would reciprocate at the Economic Conference to be held in the spring of 1933? He was unwilling to make concessions before the Conference, at which he would be able to see how much foreign nations would concede. And they would have to be willing to make concessions if international monetary stabilization were to be fair to the United States. When, at the Conference, the Europeans showed no disposition to make concessions to the legitimate interests of the United States, Roosevelt stuck to his nationalist position, although he reached his end in what Tugwell afterward called a "most embarrassing and awkward way." [24]

In his famous letter of February 17, 1933, Hoover again expressed his ideas on recovery to the President-elect. Now, with the banking system in convulsion, Hoover stressed domestic developments. Agitation for money tinkering, publication of RFC loans, and fear of Roosevelt's unannounced policies had damaged confidence, he maintained, bringing on a banking collapse which was now out of hand. He urged Roosevelt to issue a statement that (1) there would be no currency tampering—preservation of the gold standard; (2) the budget would be balanced; (3) government credit would not be exhausted by the issuance of securities.[25] Roosevelt did not comply with Hoover's request.

Hoover was justifiably concerned with the domestic situation, which now was superdeflationary. Yet, aside from aid at the top, he had relied on "natural" cures for domestic ills. "Natural" cures should have been effective if there were validity to Hoover's European interpretation of the depression, which assumed that the domestic economy was basically sound—providing Hoover, failing to get foreign co-operation, had taken action to protect the economy at home from foreign influences.

These included the threat of a flooding of the American market by goods from foreign nations with depreciated currencies. There was also the danger, Tugwell pointed out in *The Democratic Roosevelt*, of leaving the United States at the mercy of international financiers, who "wanted to manage prices and exchanges; they did not want it done by governments. What they intended was that all the nations should be tied to a gold standard which, in fact, was no standard at all, since under it the purchasing power of currencies would fluctuate as widely as the price of gold itself. Speculation in gold was a specialty with several European groups." [26] Meanwhile, both the hoarding and export of gold, with their disastrous impact on the banking system, continued apace.

Having failed to get the international co-operation on currency essential to price relations which would be fair to the United States, Hoover took no alternative action. His administration was resourceful to its end in finding reasons not to act. Theodore Joslin, Hoover's secretary, stated that the Governor of Michigan "lost his head" when he closed the banks in his state on February 11, 1933; and the guaranteeing of deposits, it was reasoned, would not stop withdrawals, "considering the attitude of the people." [27] These judgments overlooked certain pertinent facts. The Detroit Clearing House and the Michigan State Bankers Association made a joint request to the Governor to declare a bank holiday; postal-savings deposits increased from 150 million to 1 billion dollars between June 30, 1928, and June 30, 1933, which refuted the assumption that guaranteeing deposits would not affect the people's attitude.[28]

Hoover did make some eleventh-hour concessions to Roosevelt's position, but with reservations that prevented action. After requesting Roosevelt's co-operation as late as February 28, in early March he offered full co-operation "in any line of sensible action." On the evening of March 2 the outgoing administration made proposals which, according to Woodin, for the first time were worth serious consideration. Representatives of the Federal Reserve Board and the Treasury suggested a proclamation closing the banks. That evening, and on the afternoon of March 3, Hoover asked Roosevelt to promise that the Democrats in the new Congress would not repudiate a proclamation, under the Trading with the Enemy Act of 1917, controlling foreign exchange and withdrawals of currency and gold. Hoover stated his belief that such a proclamation would make it unnecessary to close the banks. Roosevelt said he could give no assurances on Congressional reaction. Hoover did not issue a proclamation.[29]

Resort to a World War I statute raised a constitutional question. Hoover's Attorney-General was inclined to think that the Act was no longer valid. Roosevelt's Attorney-General-designate, Senator Thomas Walsh of Montana, stated that in an emergency he would deem the needed powers legally available. Walsh died just before the inauguration. On March 3 Roosevelt had not heard the opinion of Homer Cummings, Walsh's replacement. On the basis of legal advice, Hoover had less reason to feel free to use the Trading with the Enemy Act than Roosevelt, but he was willing to do so if he could get from Roosevelt "an assurance and a commitment in terms of absolutes" on the attitude of the next Congress.[30] Apparently Hoover's failure to act was determined less by constitutional scruples than by fear of disavowal.

Earlier in 1933, unencumbered in this instance by his relations with Roosevelt, Hoover had issued a call for action. His annual message to Congress centered on the "urgent necessity of immediately passing banking reform acts, in view of the scandals which had developed and the weakness which had been proved in the whole banking system." [31] Why had he failed to call for action, in view of dramatic forewarnings of weakness in the banking structure, in 1930, 1931, or 1932? Some of his supporters later claimed that he had carried on a vigorous campaign for bank reform for three years. Moley refuted this claim, quoting John T. Flynn, who quoted Professor H. Parker Willis of Columbia. Willis, technical adviser to the Banking Committee in the preparation of the Glass bill, said "what everyone at the time knew to be true, that not only did Hoover do nothing to support the Glass bill but actually 'retarded and prevented its passage.'" [32]

The attribution to Hoover, in retrospect, of timely, vigorous action suggests the intellectual and psychological limitations on his action operative throughout his administration. Tugwell noted that Hoover himself, in his *Memoirs*, "may possibly have exaggerated to some degree the promptness and energy with which the crisis was met." Hoover certainly worked hard. That he did everything he listed, in a summary of his policies under nine headings, when it should have been done could be questioned. In Tugwell's judgment the last five items on the list were qualifications which severely restricted action on the first four.[33]

Hoover's intellectual limitations were ones of inflexibility in application, not ones of inadequate understanding. He had a penetrating grasp, for example, of the international gold situation. He was aware that hoarding threatened to paralyze the banking system. He knew that countries with depreciated currencies were flooding our markets, causing unemployment and hurting American farmers. In his address to the National Republican Club in New York on February 13, 1933, he comprehensively surveyed possible courses of action: (1) international stabilization of currencies—Hoover believed that if anyone could announce at once that such action would be taken, price levels would rise immediately; he stated, as he had to Roosevelt on November 22, that debtor nations would concede on this point in return for debt concessions; (2) nationalism, with increased tariffs, curtailment of agricultural production, and a long road of adjustments into unknown and uncertain fields; (3) departure from the gold standard and currency tinkering —this would lead to a world-wide economic war with certain destruction at home and abroad.[34]

II

Hoover has always maintained that recovery was under way in July, 1932, but Roosevelt's conduct in the lame-duck period frightened business and reversed the tide. Specifically, Roosevelt failed to dispel fears

of his obvious tendency toward inflation by joining Hoover in reas-
suring business on this point. In general, Roosevelt refused to co-operate
with Hoover on a program which would sustain the recovery that had
begun in July. The result of Roosevelt's attitude, Hoover's argument
went on to say, was renewed decline, culminating in the banking
crisis of February, 1933.

In his book, published in 1934, Theodore Joslin listed the Democrats'
misdeeds of the lame-duck period in detail. Roosevelt showed no intention of reciprocating Hoover's willingness to go more than halfway
in co-operation. He stated that he would handle international debt and
currency negotiations after March 4 rather than co-operate with Hoover.
He refused to give Senator Carter Glass, a hard-money man, assurances
which would make Glass willing to become Secretary of the Treasury.
John N. Garner forced the publication of RFC loans. The Democrats
restated their intentions of making huge public-works expenditures and
reducing tariffs. Congress refused to co-operate on the budget and on a
bankruptcy act.[35]

These misdeeds, combined with Roosevelt's silence on many aspects
of his intended program, according to Hoover's secretary, damaged confidence and, consequently, destroyed recovery. Because of the announcement of RFC loans, depositors feared that the banking system would collapse. Because it was "obvious to every thinking person that the forces
of experimentation, inflation, and tinkering with the currency had been
elected," and because enormous expenditures and deficits were "fore-
gone conclusions," people feared that the government's credit would not
stand up.[36]

These fears, Joslin asserted, brought recovery to a halt. Amid general
uncertainty about events after March 4, employers marked time, and the
whole country hesitated. The election was followed by a collapse which
saw the economy resume a downward course with increasing speed.
Bank withdrawals increased as people demanded gold; national firms
transferred their funds from interior banks to larger banks; and over a
thousand banks failed. With the depreciation of foreign currencies, foreign goods poured over tariff walls, and the dollar fled the country.
Orders for several hundred millions, placed by business in September
and October, were cancelled.[37] Two supporters of Hoover, in a book
published in 1936, seconded his secretary.[38] Neither account exaggerated the collapse (from December, 1932, to March, 1933, the index of
production fell from 64 to 56—an all-time low [39]). Both assumed that
with Roosevelt's co-operation the President and the President-elect could
have prevented economic collapse and the banking crisis of February,
1933.

At one point in his *Memoirs* Hoover placed the initial impact of Roosevelt's attitudes in the pre-lame-duck period. Politically, only a quick up-turn in the economy could have saved Hoover—as he knew. He thought the July recovery was his salvation, but to his regret it was halted, he said, by the elections in Maine at the end of September. It now looked as if Roosevelt would be the next President. "The fears of the business world at Roosevelt's announced policies [later it would be Roosevelt's un-announced policies] started a downward movement for the next six weeks which greatly nullified our hopes of mitigating the political in-fluence of the depression." [40]

How significant was the July upswing in the economy which Roosevelt, according to Hoover, frustrated? Did it represent what would have been —with Roosevelt's co-operation—a prolonged, decisive rise; or was it a limited deviation from a continuing trend of low-level economic ac-tivity? In Hoover's view business confidence produced recovery, or, conversely, recovery meant that business had confidence. There was striking evidence, however, that business lost confidence some time be-fore 1932 and had not regained it as near to July as the spring of 1932. There was also evidence that business did not regain confidence with the upturn in July.

The pre-July evidence consisted in drastic forewarnings of a banking collapse—almost as drastic as the 1933 collapse itself. The Comptroller-General's Annual Report to Congress for the fiscal year 1931-1932 noted the importance of hoarding in bank failures, stating that in the autumn of 1930 there began a recognizable trend toward demanding currency for hoarding purposes.[41] Hoover was aware of this development. In late January, 1933, he requested a report on hoarding. He learned that the average daily withdrawal of currency from circulation was from 10 to 15 millions—amounts "sufficiently large to cause concern," Joslin commented, "although they were not as heavy as during the crisis the year before." Confidential daily Treasury reports on hoarding contained figures which "compared with only a few millions one way or the other for months previously." [42]

Exports of gold increased in February, 1933, although they were far less than in the first six months of 1932.[43] Hoover knew this. On February 13 he told the National Republican Club in New York: "We ourselves a year ago suffered from the effects of such a movement." [44] In his letter to Roosevelt of February 17 he wrote: "We are confronted with precisely the same phenomena we experienced in late 1931 and again in the spring of 1932." [45] Additional evidence of a loss of confidence by business was the continued failure of banks—although at a reduced rate—after the creation of the RFC, which provided aid at the top in accordance with the confidence thesis. The RFC helped, but it was not enough. Thus, severe blows struck the banking system well before the depositors' panic of early 1933. In his later comments, however, Hoover did not treat the collapse of 1933 as the final phase in a sequence of recurring crises. Nor did others who attributed the collapse to Roosevelt's pre-presidential conduct.[46]

There was also evidence that a significant portion of the business community did not regain confidence with the upturn in July. The United States Chamber of Commerce, which took the lead in business' demand for some sort of a scheme of industrial co-ordination, continued to show an unabated interest along this line. Apparently, the mild rise of July, which Hoover hailed, did not convince a number of businessmen that he had achieved a fundamental cure of economic ills. Nor was the average citizen impressed by the rise in July. "Looking at his meager pay envelope, the soup kitchens and bread lines, [he] felt hardly better and yearned for a change." [47]

From the standpoint of economics, it is to be noted that the slight relative rise in July took place far down on an absolute scale of activity. Obviously, given a depressed economy, a rise had to start at a low level. But that low level had been reached during the Hoover administration. If that administration took credit for the upturn in July, it also had to accept responsibility for the previous decline. It may be said in Hoover's defense that it takes time to halt an economic decline and then reverse the trend, but there had been a continuous decline for nearly three years before July, 1932. Had the policies which permitted that decline finally taken effect, getting at the root causes of the depression? Many Americans thought not.

Basil Rauch attributed greatest importance among the factors contributing to the final crisis to those which had a long background. He granted that business was concerned during the lame-duck period about the Democrats' general inflationary tendencies and rumors of their specific inflationary intentions. Business confidence also suffered damage for other reasons. Senate investigations revealed unsound practices by managers of great banks. Moreover, even the most conservative banks, after three years of falling values, bankruptcies, and foreclosures, were in a weakened condition—the most important reason, in Rauch's opinion, for the loss of confidence. The fact that only one-sixth of domestic withdrawals in February, 1933, were in gold and gold certificates indicated that fear of inflation was less important in causing runs on banks, hoarding, and the flight of the dollar abroad than fear that the banks were unsound.[48]

The banks' lack of soundness was, in turn, even when one takes into account banking abuses in the 1920's, essentially a result before it could be a cause of general economic weakness. The economy of the 1920's was characterized by maldistribution of income and deficiencies in purchasing power. Concentrated income went into stock-market and real-estate speculation in unduly large amounts, leaving about a third of bank assets tied in with these uncertain markets.

According to classical economics the maladjustments of the 1920's would eventually correct themselves. Thus, classical theory did not demonstrate that the July upturn was fundamental because it did not allow for a "great depression" in the first place. Classical economics assumed, in a slump, a reduction but not a collapse of purchasing power. Business' orders of several hundred millions, which Joslin mentioned, were small compared to the billions labor had lost in wages. Joslin did not show where the purchasing power to absorb the new product—if business had not cancelled its orders—was coming from. And business would have needed confidence that there would be customers for its goods—not confidence in Hoover's beneficence—if it were to continue placing orders.

The results of the Maine elections, which, Hoover said, halted the July recovery, suggest flaws in the confidence thesis. If the voters had no confidence in Roosevelt, they could have rejected him at the polls, especially in the traditionally Republican state of Maine, by supporting a President in whom they did have confidence. It could be argued in Hoover's defense that businessmen, who feared Roosevelt and whose confidence Hoover considered the source of prosperity, cast only a small percentage of the total vote. But many businessmen themselves had given up on Hoover's confidence thesis. Besides, if the confidence policy had been effective in the previous three years, a Roosevelt victory would not have appeared probable, and businessmen would not have been concerned with his intended policies. People did not want Roosevelt in so much as they wanted Hoover out. Roosevelt's election was a result before it could be a cause of lack of confidence.

Having raised questions about Hoover's "July recovery" thesis without defending Roosevelt's conduct, let us consider the case for the President-elect's position. Ernest K. Lindley, in *The Roosevelt Revolution: First Phase*, defended Roosevelt's stand.[49] Lindley noted that Hoover could not recommend to Congress most of the important measures in Roosevelt's program "without repudiating his political principles and swallowing some of his most earnest campaign utterances." Even if Roosevelt and Hoover had agreed on policy, there was no precedent, and no provision in the Constitution, Lindley observed, for participation in executive functions by a President-elect. Lindley's reference to Hoover's inability to accept Roosevelt's program indicated what Hoover meant by "co-operation." In November, December, and January, Hoover tried to obtain a commitment to his foreign policy from Roosevelt; on February 17, 21, and 28 he requested acceptance of his domestic policies by Roosevelt.[50] Lindley commented: "It developed that Mr. Hoover's desire was less to co-operate in putting Mr. Roosevelt's policies into effect than to persuade Mr. Roosevelt to support Mr. Hoover's policies."

On the currency question, Lindley held, silence was Roosevelt's best alternative. If he even hinted that "sound money" might require devaluation, he might precipitate an immediate panic and speculation in gold. If he pledged no currency tinkering, future developments might force him to go back on his word—"Mr. Hoover had helped undermine his prestige by making optimistic statements which everybody knew were not supported by fact." As to probable future developments, Lindley commented that the gold standard meant something to financiers and corporations who were making large conversions into gold—in contrast to the average citizen who, caring nothing about the gold standard, went to the bank to get currency—"but most of them were intelligent enough to see that the suspension of specie payments probably would come soon no matter what anybody might say."

If Roosevelt committed himself to Hoover's policies, some of the outgoing administration's unpopularity might rub off on the incoming one. If he had to reverse his policies of November in March, his prestige would suffer. If, lacking the power of an actual President, he tried to manage the lame-duck Congress and failed, he would lose good will in Congress—where he would need help later when he could more effectively demand it—and prestige with the public. "Most important," Lindley wrote, "he could not afford to risk impairment of his prestige in the eyes of the American people." Thus, the "chances were overwhelming that the effect of a statement from Mr. Roosevelt would have been not to stop the demand for currency and gold, but to injure public confidence in him and destroy his chances of dealing effectively with the situation after March 4."

Moley minced no words in commenting on Hoover's letter of February 17. He noted that during the campaign Roosevelt had "torn to shreds" the analysis of the origins of the depression which Hoover presented in this letter—and Hoover knew it. The letter requested a "promise that could not honestly be made, for things had already gone so far that temporary suspension of specie payments seemed inevitable." It "assumed that Roosevelt would succeed—where Hoover had repeatedly failed—in hornswoggling the country with optimistic statements which everyone knew weren't justified." People put their money back into banks on March 12, when Roosevelt asked them to, "not because he promised the things Hoover asked him to promise," but because he had given them assurances of the reopened banks' safety. "This completely refutes Hoover's theory that Roosevelt could have stemmed the bank panic by the making of a statement about the currency." Regarding Hoover's emphasis on stabilization and the maintenance of the gold standard, Moley commented: "The argument that we could have persuaded Great Britain to return to the gold standard in the winter of 1932-33 or even to stabilize at that time if we made concessions on debts was obviously illusory." [51]

Tugwell, too, thought it was too late for words to be of any help. He recalled that drastic reduction of gold reserves through speculation on foreign exchanges and withdrawal and hoarding at home, together with depositors' withdrawals, had "impaired the position of the banks . . . [and] made the doing of business all but impossible." [52] Of Hoover's remark on February 13 that the United States' holding to the gold standard was "one Gibraltar of stability in the world," Tugwell wrote that this was a "curious view in February of that year. There was no Gibraltar of stability" for the unemployed, dispossessed farm and home owners, insurance policyholders whose companies were insolvent, industrialists whose factories were closed, or even the banks which held gold—"within a month they would all be refusing payments to depositors." [53]

Supporting Moley's nationalist position, Tugwell, in 1933, pointed out in syndicated columns and unpublished statements that gold was important only internationally. Domestically, people cared only about the relationship of money to goods as reflected in prices. [54] On June 30, 1933, the United States possessed 4 billions in gold. Currency and public and private obligations in gold totaled over 70 billions. It was possible to maintain a gold standard only so long as people did not ask for gold. [55] With deflation and the accompanying liquidation movement, Roosevelt had to stop payments in gold, call in recent withdrawals, and make all American coins and currency legal tender for all debts simply because gold was no longer obtainable. [56] It was also necessary to put the value of the dollar beyond the influence of foreign manipulations in order to protect a domestic rise in the commodity price level. [57]

Roosevelt's proclamation of 1:00 a.m. on Monday, March 6, placing an embargo on gold exports and declaring a bank holiday, amounted to a recognition of the facts of life—on March 4 New York had brought the number of states that had declared bank holidays to thirty-five. On Tuesday, March 7, via Moley, Roosevelt approved Woodin's suggestions for a banking act in twenty minutes. On Thursday, March 9, he sent his message to Congress at 3:00 p.m. and signed the Emergency Banking Act at 9:00 p.m. Basil Rauch stated, "The confidence for which Hoover had pleaded for three years had been restored within two weeks by Roosevelt." [58] Moley declared, "Capitalism was saved in eight days." [59] "When the banks began to open," Tugwell recalled, "redepositing, to the bankers' amazement, began almost as if nothing had happened; and presently business was going on at the old stands." [60]

If Hoover did not deny that capitalism had been saved, he maintained that the cost of the rescue was both exorbitant and unnecessary. His critics might say that his confidence thesis not only delayed his acting to meet the depression and determined the nature of the limited action he finally took, but was also the basis for his judgment of his successor's policies. Be that as it may, Hoover blamed Roosevelt for the reversal of the recovery that began in July, 1932, and he attributed the slowness of recovery through the 1930's to Roosevelt's program after March 4, 1933. If the troubles of 1929-1933 were the "Hoover depression," the difficulties of 1933-1941 were the "Roosevelt depression."

7. Tugwell versus Hoover: The Twenty-Five-Year Debate

Roosevelt did not live to enjoy a retirement in which he might have answered Hoover's criticism, but others defended his actions. Tugwell not only replied to Hoover's condemnation of Roosevelt's conduct in the lame-duck interlude, but he also rebutted Hoover's charge that the New Deal delayed recovery. Tugwell, it is true, shared Hoover's desire for quicker recovery. He believed that the policies which he personally preferred would have produced a faster upturn, but he vehemently rejected Hoover's implication that a continuation of the policies of the years 1929-1933 would have revived the economy more effectively than the New Deal.

In late February, 1933, Hoover, in a letter confirming a telephone conversation, specifically blamed Tugwell for contributing to the banking crisis of that month—a crisis that Hoover considered the last phase of a decline which Roosevelt's unco-operativeness had set in motion. A reference to this letter was first published in 1934, Hoover alluded to it in 1952 in his *Memoirs,* and Tugwell commented on it in 1954. In his *Memoirs* Hoover also pronounced judgment on the New Deal. Tugwell criticized this assessment in several articles in the late 1940's and early 1950's—particularly in an article of 1953, "The Protagonists: Roosevelt and Hoover"—and in *The Democratic Roosevelt* in 1957.

I

On February 25, 1933, Tugwell had lunch with James H. Rand, Jr., Chairman of the Board, Remington Rand, Incorporated. Rand telephoned to the White House a summary of their conversation. Hoover repeated Rand's message in a confirming letter. References to this letter appeared in books by Hoover's secretary (1934), Lawrence Sullivan (1936), William I. Myers and Walter H. Newton (1936), John T. Flynn (1948), and Hoover himself (1952). Myers and Newton gave the complete text:

> I beg to acknowledge your telephone message received through Mr. Joslin, as follows: "Professor Tugwell, adviser to Franklin D. Roosevelt, had lunch with me. He said they were fully aware of the bank situation and that it would undoubtedly collapse in a few days, which would place the responsibility in the lap of President Hoover. He said, 'We should worry about anything except rehabilitating the country after March 4th. Then there would be several moves; first, an embargo on exportation of yellow chips; second, suspension of specie

73

payments; third, reflation if necessary, after one and two, and after that arrangements would be made for the so-called business man's committee of 60 prominent manufacturers who have been invited to spend half a day with Mr. Woodin on Tuesday [March 7] in an attempt to gain support of the business interests for a program.'" I also have your suggestion that in consequence of this attitude I should at once demand of Congress a general guarantee of bank deposits. When I consider this statement of Professor Tugwell's in connection with the recommendations we have made to the incoming administration, I can say emphatically that he breathes with infamous politics devoid of every atom of patriotism. Mr. Tugwell would project millions of people into hideous losses for a Roman holiday.[1]

Tugwell's remarks, in John T. Flynn's opinion, confirmed Hoover's impression that Roosevelt did not want to save the banks and people's savings but "was thinking of the political advantage of a complete banking disaster under Hoover."[2] Sullivan stressed the impact of Tugwell's statements on New York financiers, who received word of the conversation on the afternoon of the 25th. It was, Sullivan asserted, this authoritative "inside information" which controlled events during the final week of the Hoover administration as the financial community "began to brace itself for the final shock."[3]

Hoover was undoubtedly highly suspicious that Roosevelt might place politics above patriotism. In a memorandum to Senator David A. Reed (Rep., Pa.) he wrote, "If it is precipitated, the responsibility lies squarely with them for they have had ample warning—unless, of course, such a debacle is part of the 'New Deal.'"[4] It did not occur to Hoover that his suspicion could in a sense be reversed. Unable to admit that his policies were ineffective, he came to identify them with the national welfare, mistakenly believing that history would vindicate him. Accordingly, he would place his own inability to admit error above the national welfare, jeopardizing the banking system rather than changing the policies to which he had held for three years. His was not conscious rationalization since he believed his policies would save the nation, and his patriotism was beyond reproach. Because he could not believe that policies other than his own were feasible or acceptable in the American system, bad motives were a likely explanation of Roosevelt's refusal to follow his lead.

As for Sullivan's view, chronology tends to undermine it. Weaknesses in the banking system were plainly evident long before February 25, 1933. The final panic itself was under way by the middle of February. Sullivan noted that the banking community was informed, for the first of several times, in November that Roosevelt contemplated some form of currency manipulation; and that by January the bankers were convinced of Roosevelt's intention of going in for inflation.[5] Thus, it does not appear that Tugwell's remarks in late February could have shocked the financial district.

Hoover's letter to Rand obviously did not tell Tugwell's side of the story. Tugwell's flippant "we should worry" did not indicate his real feelings at the time. Marriner Eccles, an Ogden, Utah, banker, after testifying before a Congressional committee, went to New York in late February to see Tugwell. Eccles found the professor far from flippant as they lunched in a drugstore booth. Tugwell was despairing because it "was clear that nothing could be or would be done to stop the final collapse." Eccles, who knew the details of the banking situation—moratoriums, failures, withdrawals—felt that events justified Tugwell's gloom.[6] Hoover's letter of February 17 to Roosevelt, Tugwell recalled in *The Democratic Roosevelt*, "was not a warning that was needed. What was happening was apparent to everyone." [7] Tugwell's attitude was roughly analogous to that of the Republican farmers of the Midwest who crossed party lines in 1932 because they believed nothing would be accomplished until a new president took office.

Although Tugwell was gloomy, this mood did not account for his saying "we should worry." In 1954 he commented on his remark to Rand:

> I knew members of the Rand family from my home territory in upstate New York. James Rand knew of me for years. He paid little attention to me until it became known that I was to have something to do with policy. When Rand invited me to lunch, he called me "Rex." He was snooping around for information for his own speculative purposes. I certainly did say, "We should worry. . . ." I said it by way of evasion. I wanted to lend a light, airy tone to my conversation so that Rand wouldn't know how to take it. In other words, I wasn't going to tell him a damn thing. Hoover, who was understandably in bad shape in the lame-duck period, took it seriously.[8]

Tugwell made a serious tactical error. It would have been difficult to put off Rand with a simple "we should worry," but Tugwell should have stuck to his intention of not telling a "damn thing." He had no business mentioning, even with studied offhandedness, a specific three-point program. He should have been aware, especially after his "off-the-record" interview with a journalist made front pages earlier in February, how quickly private statements got around. Certainly, besides personal feelings, he had no respect for Rand's motives. His talkativeness was attributable to a lapse in self-control or a miscalculation at the moment, carelessness, or extreme naïveté, or all of these.

Tugwell soon learned that he was right about Rand's "speculative purposes." On March 14, 1933, Rand wrote to "Dear Rex," enclosing a confidential analysis of the banking situation and remarking, "I have nothing but praise for the leadership of the President." He suggested a deposit-insurance plan and favored raising the price of gold to 36 from 20.67 to help farmers, debtors, and creditors. On November 15, 1933, Rand sent Tugwell a summary of the "vicious propaganda emanating from the vicinity of Broad and Wall"—certain financiers intended, he warned, to break government bond prices and bring the administration to its knees.[9]

Apparently, Rand sought to cultivate the friendship of those men who happened to be in office—which suggested, in a general way, some ulterior motive. Specifically, his recommendation of an increase in the price of gold betrayed a speculator's interest. He became a leader of the Committee for the Nation, which lobbied for outright inflation. In 1934 it was William Wirt of this group who, in a letter released by Rand, charged that Roosevelt was only the Kerensky of the New Deal, and Tugwell (an anti-inflationist) would eventually take over. Hoover, who called Rand a "responsible industrialist," [10] and his supporters did not know that there was more to Tugwell's "we should worry" than met the eye.

II

In his *Memoirs* Hoover made these judgments of Roosevelt's policies: (1) the depression extended from 1929 to 1941; (2) recovery was rapid in other nations with free economies, but New Deal devices prevented peacetime recovery; (3) the New Deal attempt to collectivize the American system of life was the chief preventive of recovery; (4) the depression was "ultimately in name ended only by war." [11] Hoover supported his judgments with figures which, Tugwell noted, had been "collated patiently over the years with engineering neatness." They proved what he had always insisted was fact about the depression—"the Republicans had had it licked but the Democrats had interfered and prevented recovery until war had intervened and saved them. It was quite safe to go back to the Republicanism of the 1920's." [12]

Tugwell agreed with points (1) and (4). During "strictly New Deal times . . . unemployment would never be nearly cured, nor would industrial activity nearly reach the levels of capacity. But all during this period there would be unbalanced budgets and a more or less uncontrolled inflation." [13] Roosevelt "had to go on and on . . . subsidizing the most demanding elements of the economy . . . until W.P.A. merged into war production." [14] Point (2) overlooked a number of obvious facts. For example, the Scandinavian nations, which suffered least from the depression, had producer and consumer co-operatives and extensive social legislation. Great Britain, in order to achieve a balanced budget, which Hoover would have approved, cut unemployment benefits and made poor relief harder to get. But she did not attain a modicum of recovery until 1931, when she recovered part of her export markets by devaluation of the pound, which Hoover would not have approved.

Point (3) was the one to which Tugwell objected. Hoover maintained, in effect, that the New Deal slowed recovery by attempting too much. Tugwell contended that the New Deal delayed recovery by attempting too little—from the standpoint of either an institutional or a Keynesian economist. New Deal economic policy never had "the straightforwardness and simplicity it should have had." [15] The "alternative to Hoover's 'proof' was the horrid suggestion that recovery had not occurred because actually there never had been any New Deal as Hoover defined it. That is to say, prices and investment had not been controlled and the resort to spending had never been sufficient." [16]

As an institutional economist, Tugwell regretted the neglect of basic reforms. Inflation concealed the failure to achieve recovery and prevented a direct encounter with the problem of creating co-ordinating institutions.[17] Nevertheless, spending, which was not the ideal stabilizing device, was the best tool available under the circumstances. The more the administration spent sooner, the less it would have to spend later. The 1933 appropriation of 3.3 billions for relief and public works was an astronomical figure to conservatives. Senators La Follette and Wagner knew that 12 billions would have been a more realistic sum. In Tugwell's opinion, the two Progressive Senators were "quite right, if what was wanted was what was professed to be wanted—the relief of unemployment," but "the reason there was always wavering and insufficiency was that President Roosevelt felt just as much convicted of sin when the budget was unbalanced as Hoover had been." [18] Thus, in retrospect Tugwell asserted that halfway Keynesianism was not enough, but that is what we can call his recommendation in 1933 of an expenditure of 5.5 billions.

The recession of 1937-1938 seemed to support Tugwell's views on spending. He noted that an "attempt had been made in 1936 to withdraw subsidies and relief spending. The recession of 1937 showed that it could not be done in an inarticulated economy." [19] The authors of an article in *Fortune*, March, 1955, entitled "Why the Depression Lasted So Long," attributed the recession to Roosevelt's inconsistent fiscal policy, specifically his budget which reduced the government's contribution to buying power by about 3 billions.[20] The recession was overcome when Roosevelt resumed spending at the behest of Marriner S. Eccles and against the urgings of Henry Morgenthau, Jacob Viner, and the "Byrd-Hull-Harrison-Garner axis." The reason there was opposition, Tugwell recalled, was that as recovery progressed in the early 1930's, "the number multiplied of those who, in spite of the plain lesson being unfolded before their eyes, refused to believe that it had been induced by governmental measures. Indeed, they claimed the contrary with more and more effect." [21]

Thus, there was little comfort for Hoover and his supporters in Tugwell's judgment that the New Deal failed to achieve quick, full recovery. A point Hoover overlooked is that the reason it took the patient—the economy—so long to recover is that he was so sick. Our economy had fallen drastically from a situation in which, as Walt W. Rostow put it, "full employment is needed, in a sense, to sustain full employment. . . ." [22] It was a long, hard climb back to healthy mass consumption. On second thought, Hoover did not overlook this point—he denied it. He thought the patient was basically of sound health. We cannot say for certain what would have been the result of a continuation of his mild medicines. Economic experience before and after 1932 does not appear to support Hoover's assumption that his treatment would have been a cure. It is certain that by 1932 a majority of Americans wanted a new doctor.

But Hoover stuck to his thesis. He had to, Tugwell remarked, because "if Roosevelt had been right in 1932, business had brought on its own debacle and complete freedom of enterprise was no longer a tenable policy for the nation." And stick he did. "When candidates wavered, and seemed to accept the New Deal, when even the platforms became equivocal on some doctrinal issues," Hoover was "always standing somewhere in the shadows to remind newcomers where their faith had to center." He always maintained a lofty moral position—"an impatient democracy had preferred to follow a siren voice." He found it difficult to accept rejection by the people because he "felt so virtuous about the whole thing." He would not, he said, resort to panaceas and shortcuts, even if they promised success at the moment, if they would ultimately harm the American way of life which rested on 150 years of experience and effort. Intellectually, Hoover remained consistent. "Few men in all history," Tugwell asserted, "can have played a Premier role in comparable circumstances and have kept their ideas so inviolate." Tugwell attributed this obtuseness to "immersion in an ideology immune to events." [23]

Hoover's letter of February 17, 1933, to Roosevelt was, Tugwell observed, "about as far as a human being ever went in sticking to his guns while the ship went down. There was the clear implication that the Republican party was to be absolved of all blame for the depression," which began as the aftermath of war, continued due to "shocks from abroad," and was about to be overcome by efforts which irresponsible Democrats frustrated. [24] Twenty-five years later, on February 27, 1958, in an address to the New York Chamber of Commerce, Hoover spoke in terms of economic fatalism. [25] On August 9, 1959, on a television program, "Meet the Press," Hoover, now mellow and more philosophical and less self-regardful than when he was President, seemed to give away his case. He asserted that the basic heritage and vigor of the American people had survived war, depression, and bad administrations so that we were in a position to meet new problems. He did not give away his case, of course, because he would have classified the Roosevelt administration as one of the bad ones, never conceding that it contributed to survival.

Tugwell judged that Hoover carried on the debate with Roosevelt into a third decade with significant success. "In the midst of the rising panic the Republican rationalization was almost lost; only Hoover and a few others kept it alive. As soon as recovery began to be apparent, it would grow, along with the expanding economy, until a decade later, or even before, it would come to full bloom." [26] In 1952, when Hoover restated his thesis in his *Memoirs*, he had final proof in the defeat at the polls of Roosevelt and everything he stood for.[27] While he once seemed to stand almost alone, Hoover now found his thesis accepted "in perhaps the dominant intellectual majority"—pundits, teachers in schools of business, radio commentators, and financial writers repeated it quite casually —and "this *would* be conclusive." [28]

The press teemed with statements of Hoover's thesis. Tugwell cited an article entitled "New Dealers Still Blame Hoover," which appeared on the financial page of the *Chicago Daily News*, February 9, 1953. This article maintained that the deflation Roosevelt caused by his unwillingness to co-operate and by declaring a bank holiday was "many times more severe than anything that happened under Hoover. . . . Billions were unnecessarily sacrificed in bank assets in order that FDR could have his fun. But the man in the street never got that picture. The present generation of New Deal writers probably never heard of it." [29] In 1958 a column by David Lawrence carried the head, "1933 Bank Holiday Was Unnecessary." [30] In another column, a month earlier, Lawrence wrote, "Mr. Roosevelt absolutely refused to co-operate . . . and the result was a 'bank holiday' which was so severe that it brought on the 'Roosevelt depression.' This lasted far longer than the 'Hoover depression.'" [31]

Businessmen, too, considered the Republican victory of 1952 as their own.[32] Tugwell traced the evolution of their attitudes from 1929 to 1952 in some detail in his series of articles in the *Western Political Quarterly*, 1948-1953. He compared the businessmen of the New Era unfavorably with the nineteenth-century moguls. Overrated in the 1920's, businessmen were bewildered in 1929 and completely lost face. They turned for aid to an instrument they had done so much to weaken—"the despised, the bought and sold, the debauched—the government!" [33] Some observers saw them as repentant. Tugwell saw "only a lot of badly scared men who will return to their old habits as soon as they dare." [34] By 1934, as in an article by one of Tugwell's critics, they were calling for a return to laissez faire.[35] Roosevelt, Tugwell recalled, was now "a crazy fool of a reformer for continuing to insist, in the better times of partial recovery, that what had been weepingly promised in the fake-repentance of a stormy day should now be carried out." [36]

In 1937 businessmen suggested measures for recovery which were the same, Tugwell wrote, as the ones which "had proved inadequate before, but they were just as determined to try them again as if they were not of record." In his message to Congress of November 15, 1937, Roosevelt talked about the "restoration of confidence." Although he had said many times that he stood for capitalism, not socialism, he yielded to Morgenthau's urgings that he "reiterate the futile formula." [37] Endless charges in the newspapers that Roosevelt deliberately tried to destroy confidence referred, Tugwell noted, to the confidence of business that it would be treated as it had been up to 1929. Roosevelt was not willing to pay that high a price for confidence. When business found that its return to its position of the 1920's was not to be tolerated, "it judged that it was to be treated with uniform intolerance." [38]

But, in the election of 1952, businessmen concluded, the confidence thesis and Hoover were vindicated. Tugwell disagreed. He thought that there were no great differences on foreign policy, that there was about 90 per cent agreement on domestic policy, that the voters chose the candidate they thought could best handle the outstanding issue—the cold war. They voted neither for nor against any theory of prosperity. The Republican party, moreover, made concessions to which Hoover was never reconciled, absorbing social security and other "social minima." The difference between the two parties in 1952, Tugwell maintained, was between 86 and 96 per cent free-enterprise theories of prosperity. Hoover went on asserting that Roosevelt's position never shifted. Democrats attributed to Republicans a complete lack of sympathy with labor, consumers, and common people. "The truth is both have given way by some four per cent. To that extent the debate [Hoover vs. Roosevelt] has become unrealistic, beside the point." [39]

Indeed, looked at in perspective, Hoover and Roosevelt showed significant similarities. Roosevelt, Tugwell commented, operated within "somewhat the same limitations as did Hoover," believing in the same private and public virtues. Both had a concern for national character. Both thought liberty precious. Both had a strong attachment for private enterprise. Both favored a balanced budget. The long debate between them "is misconceived if it is thought to proceed from morals or orthodoxy on the one side against immorality or unorthodoxy on the other." Roosevelt unbalanced the budget, devalued the dollar, and involved the government in the direction of enterprise "because these expedients were forced on him by depression and war. In resorting to them he was, in his own mind, doing wrong. And so he was sensitive to attack." [40]

Yet, differences, "if less than is usually thought," were, in Tugwell's opinion, "still significant." Although they were "a matter of degree rather than of kind," they were there.[41] Hoover was willing to make unprecedented departures from laissez faire, but there simply were some "resorts that were not available." If Hoover followed his principles too far, "they were not different from the Roosevelt principles which on occasion were modified or attenuated." Both considered themselves liberal capitalists. Thus, the two Presidents differed on "a question of instrumentalism— what was end and what was means and what could therefore be properly manipulated and what had to be regarded as untouchable." Roosevelt's concern for human welfare "overrode any principle of government or any conception of business. . . . Institutions were instrumental." [42] As a democrat and a capitalist, he was more flexible than Hoover just enough to have, in addition to an RFC, a Relief Administration. Hoover "sent a rowboat out to save the Bigs . . . the future President heard Littles as well as Bigs." [43]

In a real sense, Roosevelt was more of a democrat than Hoover, who, in the words of Professor William E. Leuchtenburg, "possessed almost no political gifts. He had an aversion to the tortuous practices of democracy. Lacking skill at political maneuver, he met every situation with the directness of a rhinoceros." [44] Roosevelt's concern with democratic processes suggests that what Hoover called a conflict between two philosophies of government was really a clash between two theories of prosperity. In any event, it is easier to compare their policies by dropping the use of the word "philosophy" and the problem of determining at what level it applies. It is clear, for example, that both men were democrats and capitalists rather than totalitarians and socialists. Since both sponsored government action to aid the economy, the difference between them is not necessarily clarified by speaking in terms of "positive" and "negative" government. Since Hoover's trade-association movement anticipated Roosevelt's NRA, to talk of "individualism" and "collectivism" does not tell us enough. The difference seems, again, to turn on a question of implementation.

It was a question of less flexibility and more flexibility. Both were essentially nineteenth-century men. They faced problems arising from twentieth-century technology. Both left the previous century reluctantly, and—perhaps the difference lies here—Hoover more reluctantly than Roosevelt. Possibly the world Hoover recalled, say 1885 to 1914, was a better or happier world for Americans. Who can say? The question is academic. In 1929 that world was gone. Roosevelt had an inkling of the world to come. He "reluctantly came to see (even if the conviction was implemented so poorly)," Tugwell concluded, "that an intelligent and

democratic collectivisim is the *sine qua non* of individualism and liberty
. . . because . . . there is no return to the good old days without abolishing technology, and that failure to develop the instruments of collectivity
will result in dreadful penalties as they did in 1929." [45]

Tugwell judged that Roosevelt's action, starting at a point a little left
of center, saved the domestic economy. At the moment of crisis, he devoted a "bare minimum" of several billion dollars, spread among consumers, to tempt goods out of warehouses. "Wails and groans and . . .
the most violent opposition of press and pundits" accompanied this
"temporary salvation" of the economy.[46] If the New Deal barely saved
the system and strengthened it with some "built-in stabilizers," a quarter
of a century later the nation had not yet met the problems of the twentieth century head-on. But we must not get ahead of our story. As Professor
Mario Enaudi has stated, "No man can be held responsible for the ultimate unfolding of all the consequences that may flow from the decisions
in which he played a vital initial role. . . . No historical appraisal of
Roosevelt can go much beyond the frame of reference imposed by the
events and conditions that belonged to his times." [47]

Tugwell judged the supporters of Hoover's thesis harshly, observing
that with recovery there had been a "wide conspiracy to pretend that
the whole cataclysm had been caused by the measures taken for recovery." He continued: "When it was said that the minimum measures of
the New Deal *were responsible,* the ultimate hypocrisy had been
reached; for those who said it knew that it was false. They said it risking
the further disaster of such counsel, in complete cynicism, because they
themselves would gain, they thought, from the country's loss." [48] Tugwell did not judge Hoover himself so harshly. Hoover was sincere. His
thesis "had to be believed, a psychiatrist might have said, because a return to the Republicanism of the 1920's would otherwise cause a new
depression. Democratic responsibility not only had to be accepted, it was
true." [49]

This comment of Tugwell's suggests once again that psychology, as
well as politics and economics, sheds light on Hoover's judgments. There
is no reason to conclude that his actions during the lame-duck period were
not subject to the same limitations which restricted his reactions to
economic deterioration in the previous three years. While Roosevelt's
explanation of the depression was mechanistic, Tugwell noted, Hoover's
was psychological.[50] And he did not believe that there was any explanation other than his own.[51] Thus, he clung to his confidence thesis, but
it cannot be said that he did not identify it with the national interest as
well as his own.

Hoover's emphasizing the July upturn and the lame-duck interval—
a period when someone else was available with whom to try to share
responsibility—fitted into the reaction pattern of a man who could not

abandon certain ideas, and who had a morbid fear of adverse criticism of the results of determining public policies on the basis of those ideas. In a larger sense, of course, Hoover did not really have responsibility to share or transfer. He was not personally responsible for the depression, as his opponents often said he was. His reactions to it, however, warrant close scrutiny by historians.

His reactions to the gold problem showed that his action was as restricted in 1933 as it had been in 1930, 1931, and 1932. A close comparison of Moley's comments on possible courses of action with Hoover's comments on them reveals that what Hoover considered the desirable course—currency stabilization at a level fair to the United States—was unattainable, and that the attainable courses—nationalism and departure from the gold standard—were, in Hoover's estimate, undesirable. Accordingly, he did not act. His last hope was for a change of psychology between Roosevelt's inauguration on Saturday and the next business day on Monday.

Hoover suffered terribly in 1932 and 1933. He distrusted Roosevelt, Tugwell wrote, "as profoundly as it is possible for one man to distrust another." Moley thought Hoover had the "look of being alone, but still of going on and on, driven by some damned duty." That duty, Tugwell observed, was to minimize the disaster which Hoover believed was involved in Roosevelt's accession. Hoover suffered, moreover, because for the first time in his life something he touched did not turn into a success. "He could not believe that it was true, and he would not believe it until the day of his death." He would spend much of the rest of his life in "tortuous ratiocination intended to show—and to convince others—that the obvious was not fact." [52] Comments on Hoover's *Memoirs* support Tugwell's conclusion. Arthur S. Link said that in them Hoover "claims much and concedes nothing," and John D. Hicks remarked on "the unwillingness of the author to concede that he could ever have been wrong on anything." [53] There were harsher comments: "It may be preferable (as the recent memoirs of Herbert Hoover suggest) that embittered men whose lives have come to be identified with great national catastrophe should follow a policy of taciturnity if the only alternative is published recrimination." [54]

III

Hoover's "1941" thesis produced several corollary theses. One was that Roosevelt took us to war to divert the country's attention from unsolved domestic problems. John T. Flynn wrote: "Saved now by the war from the disaster . . . in 1938 . . . he could now rise out of the ashes of a mere New Dealer to become a modern St. Michael brandishing his sword against Hitler and all the forces of evil throughout the world." [55] Moley flatly rejected such an implication. Those who made it "do not know their man. Roosevelt was no cold-blooded opportunist. In fact, he felt so intensely the need to do right that he was incapable of sustaining a planned duplicity." He could shift to foreign affairs more easily because internationalists had for so long been describing them in moral terms.[56] In *The Art of Politics* Tugwell rejected the charge that Roosevelt deliberately brought on World War II and called the claim that the President conspired to precipitate Pearl Harbor "nonsense," giving his reasons for this conclusion.[57]

Another corollary thesis, advanced by Eliot Janeway in *Life*, April 30, 1945, and cited by Tugwell, was that Roosevelt "did not want to resolve the crisis but only to keep it going so that he could ride it perpetually as a ship rides a storm, knowing that what was most fundamental was for him to stay ascendant, thus providing for American continuance, however divided." Tugwell stated that this thesis simply was not true. "On the contrary, he wanted above all things to solve the domestic crisis: he considered that his place in history would be determined by this test."[58] Tugwell later remarked that "politically it was better *to be recovering* than *to have recovered* and to have reached stability," but he attributed partial recovery to confusion in policy rather than to political calculation.[59]

A third corollary thesis, closely related to the first two, was that Roosevelt had no alternative policies to those which failed to bring about recovery by 1938.[60] Tugwell, in the year after his resignation of December 31, 1936, talked to the President on several occasions.[61] He concluded that by early 1938 Roosevelt for the first time showed that he understood the leverage which Keynesian fiscal policy could exert. He also judged that by February, 1938, Roosevelt gave "undisputable signs of recovery from Progressive orthodoxy." He "at least understood the need for social management rather than economic reform. It would take the sharp and costly recession of 1937 to drive the lesson home." The President, of course, did not achieve the grand objective of national balance by the creation of co-ordinating institutions. "The war would intervene, for one thing."[62] By 1938 Roosevelt had to sacrifice domestic reform in order to obtain adequate support in Congress for meeting the Axis threat— "to him so overwhelmingly the most important contemporary objective that compromise of almost any sort, if it was really required, was worth the price."[63] Thus, the President was pulled away, he did not flee, from domestic difficulties.

A fourth corollary thesis was the "capital strike" idea, an old concept which appears among the erroneous Federalist predictions of probable developments in the event of a victory for Jefferson in 1800. James M. Burns, referring to the slowness of recovery, stated that "investors were still immobilized by their fears of government."[64] Dexter Perkins, noting the failure of business to regain confidence, cited annual-average figures for capital investment: 1925-1929, 9.5 billions; 1933-1939, 1.0 billion.[65] In 1958 Arthur Krock of the *New York Times* pointed to the persistence of unemployment and low profits, 1933-1939, despite all sorts of expensive make-work schemes, as proof that "free enterprise and not government is the true source of jobs," supporting, by implication, the "capital strike" thesis.[66]

It is true, as Robert L. Heilbroner has stated, that while government investment in the 1930's was meant as an aid to business, "it was *interpreted* by business as a threatening gesture." [67] It is also true, as two other writers on economics asserted, that the novelty of legislation and business' situation resulted in a lag in investment. On the other hand, as these two writers pointed out, "what really shapes business decisions to buy capital goods is not a vague sense of confidence or doubt, not necessarily even an inflationary or deflationary government policy, but the outlook for sales and profits." [68] As for Perkins' figures, the 9.5 billion annual average for 1925-1929 represented overinvestment. Business was not going to expand its capital plant when it was not using the capacity it already had—at least not in the wake of a collapse.

A fifth corollary thesis was the translation of the partial failure of the New Deal with respect to unemployment into total failure. The facts of recovery were that there were still about 7 million unemployed in 1937, even though the gross national product was 5 per cent above the mid-1929 level—the previous high—by the beginning of the third quarter of 1937. Full employment would have required a 25 per cent increase in gross national product because labor's productivity had increased 15 per cent and the working force 10 per cent. It is interesting to note that in 1961 Democratic Senator William Proxmire called New Deal fiscal policy a failure as a cure for unemployment. The Senator made this judgment at a time when increasing productivity and an increasing labor force contributed to significant unemployment even in prosperous times. Perhaps this will cause historians to give the New Deal a higher mark when they consider what Professor Alvin H. Hansen, replying to Proxmire, called the "bottomless pit" from which recovery in the 1930's started.[69]

Despite Hoover's "1941" thesis and its corollaries, a perverse minority of intellectuals adhered to Roosevelt's explanation of the depression. This bothered Hoover, Tugwell noted. He could excuse others—they had suffered too much, they had chosen the "easy and wicked way out," rejecting the "honest but trying" struggle he had outlined. As for politicians, their persistence was understandable. But the failure of intellectuals to be set right was "downright dangerous—heresy might spread." [70] Perhaps historians were the most perverse intellectuals. Basil Rauch remarked, "It is an inescapable fact that no one, except Hoover in his memoirs, has used this thesis—that Hoover saved the country and Roosevelt ruined it—to write the history of the period." [71]

8. Officialdom and the End of the
Brain Trust: 1932-1933

As inauguration day approached in 1933, Tugwell had to decide whether to return to Columbia or go to Washington in an administrative post. If some of his critics were correct, the decision was an easy one. Tugwell, they claimed, after years of writing, now saw his chance for action and seized it eagerly. The manner of Tugwell's appointment as Assistant Secretary of Agriculture and his attitude in early 1933 toward government service—that is, toward his own entrance into officialdom—refuted his critics' claim.

The typical story in the press of Tugwell's appointment was that he persuaded Roosevelt to appoint Henry Wallace Secretary, and Wallace reciprocated by naming him Assistant Secretary.[1] George N. Peek, first head of the Agricultural Adjustment Administration and a foe of Tugwell, flatly alleged that Tugwell secured the appointment of Wallace for his own purposes.[2] It is true that Tugwell urged the appointment of Wallace, and that Wallace urged the appointment of Tugwell. But there was no "corrupt bargain" involved. Moley recalled that "it was largely Rex Tugwell who persuaded Roosevelt to appoint Wallace."[3] By the end of the summer of 1932 Tugwell "sold" Wallace to Moley, who joined him in urging the appointment. In Moley's opinion, Roosevelt would have chosen Wallace anyway. Roosevelt liked Wallace, who was a distinguished man in the Corn Belt, a Republican for Roosevelt, and a champion of New Deal farm policies.[4]

Moley identified one active candidate for the Agriculture post—Henry Morgenthau, Jr.[5] He had the support of an important collector of party funds—Henry Morgenthau, Sr. Morgenthau studied farm management at Cornell under Professor George F. Warren, he owned an orchard and dairy farm near Hyde Park, and he was the proprietor of *The American Agriculturalist,* a Poughkeepsie farm journal. He served under Governor Roosevelt as chairman of an Agricultural Advisory Commission and, in Roosevelt's second term, became Commissioner of Conservation. Tugwell recalled that Roosevelt never seriously considered Morgenthau for the Agriculture position in the Cabinet.[6] A Washington correspondent reported that Roosevelt rejected Morgenthau as "too Eastern and too Judaic."[7] Morgenthau's political claim to the office was certainly less than that of Wallace, who represented the Republican farmers who had crossed party lines to vote for Roosevelt. Besides, Roosevelt probably resented Morgenthau's campaign for the position. In any event,

Roosevelt and Howe, Moley noted, soon made it clear that the appointment of Morgenthau was "out of the question." [8]

Tugwell had dealings with both Wallace and Morgenthau from the middle of 1932 on in connection with work on the farm problem. He got along very easily with Wallace, but it appears that he and Morgenthau did not hit it off too well. Before the election Tugwell was involved in the formulation of a crop-reduction plan, while Morgenthau was busy lining up the support of farm leaders. The two men came into closer contact when Roosevelt sent them to lobby for a farm bill during the lame-duck session of Congress. Apparently Morgenthau preferred independent activity—even when Roosevelt assigned him to work with a group. Harold Ickes, in his diary, referred to Morgenthau's unco-operative conduct—not his independence but his obstructionism. At Warm Springs in December, 1934, Roosevelt, Ickes, Tugwell, and Harry Hopkins were discussing the public-works program for the following year. Morgenthau, Ickes recorded, was "always raising some childish objections . . . I find it difficult to hold my temper." Ickes complained to Tugwell that it was hard to get anywhere with Morgenthau sitting in. Tugwell replied, "That's Henry." [9]

Undoubtedly there were differences between Morgenthau and Tugwell besides those which became apparent as they worked on the farm program. Morgenthau followed the economics of Professor George F. Warren, his Cornell mentor. Tugwell did not think much of the monetary theories of Warren, "who, curiously enough, became a President's adviser, not on his professional subject but on his avocation of currency reform." [10] Morgenthau also supported the "business confidence" thesis which Tugwell rejected. At any rate, when Peek was informed in February, 1933, that Morgenthau and Tugwell did not "jibe at all," [11] he received information which was essentially correct.

If Morgenthau was out (in May, 1933, he would become head of the Farm Credit Administration, which combined nine credit agencies and administered a 2.3 billion farm mortgage relief program), who was in? Prognosticators kept guessing wide of the mark, naming Morgenthau, Tugwell, and Professor M. L. Wilson of domestic-allotment plan fame as possibilities. In February *Kiplinger's Farm Letter* named Cully Cobb of Georgia as the next Secretary of Agriculture. No one thought Wallace would be Secretary.[12] The appointment was really decided upon in December, 1932. Before Roosevelt went to Warm Springs for a rest, Moley noted, he wrote to Wallace in Des Moines. Moley kept in touch with Wallace by telephone until he and Howe were able to wire Roosevelt, "Corn Belt in the bag." [13] Later in December, Wallace and Tugwell visited Roosevelt in Georgia. Russell Lord, biographer of Wallace, stated that no direct offer was made at Warm Springs, but it was pretty well understood that Wallace would be the choice. On February 12, 1933, Wallace received a written request that he accept the office of Secretary.[14]

Frank Kent, widely read *Baltimore Sun* political commentator, averred in his column of February 9, 1935, that Roosevelt forced Wallace to take Tugwell into Agriculture.[15] Journalist Blair Bolles asserted during the campaign of 1936 that Wallace had virtually refused to become Secretary unless Tugwell served with him.[16] Bolles was nearer the truth. Wallace did express a strong desire that Tugwell be made Assistant Secretary. He said he was reluctant to make the suggestion, "For, Rex, I really ought to be working under you." [17] It was only two weeks before inauguration when Tugwell agreed to go to Washington. On February 22, 1933, Wallace wrote to Roosevelt that he was "pleased to have the loan of Rex for Assistant Secretary of Agriculture." [18] Tugwell was not the first professor to serve in the USDA, but his appointment was unique in that it broke the tradition of choosing professors from state agricultural institutions.[19]

Wallace did not have an easy time of it in persuading Tugwell to take the post of Assistant Secretary. Tugwell was aware that government service was quite different from academic life. He knew very little about politics. What contact he had had with politicians—when he lobbied for an agricultural bill during the lame-duck Congress—he found distasteful. He freely remarked that the legislative performance he witnessed made the thought of his going to Washington repulsive.[20] On the other hand, it seemed logical that if Tugwell went to Washington at all, he should go into Agriculture (he undoubtedly could have had for the asking any one of several other positions—possibly with the Tariff Commission or the Federal Trade Commission). He had been a serious student of the farm problem for about a decade. As an institutional economist, he naturally would be interested in a social device like the AAA. And, as an amateur conservationist, he recalled, he weighed the possibility of working with the Forest Service against the reasons for remaining at Columbia.[21] Moley indicated the tentative nature of Tugwell's response to Wallace's request:

Rex had entertained doubts similar to mine on the subject of public office. Wallace's confidence in him, his own liking for Wallace, the big chance of helping set up the new farm program, and his concern about the international aspects of the program won from him a qualified decision. He decided to take the post for three months and then go to Europe on a tour of study and observation. Destiny filled different orders, however; the three months lengthened to more than three-and-one-half years. . . .[22]

Tugwell's entrance into the government was part of the dissolution of the Brain Trust. The writings of most journalists who covered the capital or commented on government did not indicate that the President's advisory group had broken up. Newspapermen could not agree on what the qualifications for membership in the Brain Trust were and how many men met them, but they continued to use the term as they had in the past. David Lawrence made some apparently contradictory remarks about the Brain Trust. In 1934 he charged that the Brain Trusters, "innovators without standards and principles," controlled the making of laws.[23] In 1935 he observed that journalists made a mistake when they referred to the academicians in government as the Brain Trust because there really was no such cohesive corps of presidential advisers.[24] Lawrence did not really contradict himself because, in his view, the professors in Washington did not have to meet in order to work out a legislative program—they were attuned to revolutionary doctrines of worship of the state, and "their hearts beat as one." [25]

Lawrence was correct when he wrote that the Brain Trust did not continue as a cohesive group in Washington. A long-time capital correspondent stated that the Brain Trust was a newspaperman's fabrication.[26] Ernest K. Lindley noted that individual members of the Brain Trust, including a few of the later recruits, had access to the President, but that after March 4, 1933, there was no longer a definite body which could be called the Brain Trust. There were, Lindley remarked, various subsidiary Brain Trusts and scattered individuals working at their own particular tasks.[27]

Lawrence was incorrect when he said of Roosevelt's advisers that "their hearts beat as one." The so-called Brain Trusters disagreed among themselves on many fundamental points. According to Max Lerner, they represented at least nine different schools of economic thought, and they did not agree on either means or ends.[28] George Soule commented that the differences among the professors in government reflected the disagreement among academicians throughout the nation. In Soule's opinion, the popular belief that most professors supported Roosevelt was not true, and there were sharp divisions among those who did.[29] It would require a great deal of space to list these divisions. Tugwell's and Warren's disagreement on monetary matters has been mentioned. Perhaps another example will illustrate Soule's point. Roosevelt's gold-buying experiment of October, 1933, was generally attributed to Warren and James H. Rogers of Yale University, yet these two professors were far from being in complete agreement on monetary policy.

Under such circumstances, Soule concluded, a well-knit plot to control the government was not possible.[30]

Comments by the original Brain Trusters themselves supported Lindley's observation that "by the time the brains trust received wide publicity, it had ceased to exist as an institution." [31] Roosevelt considered the Brain Trust's services valuable—he wrote to Sam Rosenman on March 9, 1933, "Your contribution of Ray and Rex was probably the best that anyone made during the whole campaign." But the President rejected Rosenman's suggestion that he retain the Brain Trust as it was—"as a staff to gather materials for study and for speeches, as a group with whom the President could, as formerly, 'bat around' ideas." Rosenman argued that the Brain Trusters, if given administrative jobs, would have neither the time nor the ability to see beyond the trees, due to personal or departmental interests, "when their job should be to help the President in his concern about the forest." Rosenman noted simply that the President did not agree.[32]

Moley's view was the opposite of Rosenman's. The Brain Trust was "simply a group of informed people doing, jointly, what a group of informed people ought to do under the circumstances." With Roosevelt's election, its job was done. Moley asserted that there was "no place in a free government" for an integrated group of men who had power without responsibility. The Brain Trusters could, if they chose, be brought into the government as presidential advisers with appropriate official status.[33] These remarks of Rosenman and Moley show how absurd were the references to a conspiratorial Brain Trust. Tugwell, too, recalled that the Brain Trust "dispersed into officialdom" after March 4.[34] Moley placed the date of dissolution earlier: "As I determined it should be on election eve, the 'brains trust' ceased to exist on November 8." It never met as a group from that day on. Former members met individually, Moley explained, "but their contributions no longer became part of a unified product—a draft speech or a recommendation on policy offered as a group suggestion." [35] Members of the original group continued to help on speeches, but, Rosenman pointed out, not as a team.[36]

Thus, references after March 4, 1933, to the Brain Trust were necessarily loose and inaccurate. The press conferred membership on anyone not in the government upon whom Roosevelt called for advice, as well as on officials who were frequent visitors at the White House. Tugwell merely insisted on the deletion of a misleading term when he wired Donald Geddes of Columbia University Press on June 19, 1933, regarding a book about seventeen American educators: STRONGLY DISAPPROVE USE OF THE REAL BRAIN TRUST.[37]

Part III
Tugwell's Thought and the New Deal

———————◆————————

9. Tugwell's Institutionalism and Economic Planning

Tugwell's institutional thought led him to deplore our failure to face the realities of modern economic life. This lapse, he maintained, resulted in business' acquiring and misusing governmental powers. The eventual outcome of this situation, he warned, would be self-destruction. Now we shall consider the long-run remedial and preventive prescription which grew out of Tugwell's institutional thought.

Tugwell did not emphasize his institutional design in connection with his criticism in early 1932 of Hoover's policies. He concentrated in his constructive comments on proposals to bolster purchasing power through immediate action in the fields of taxation, relief, and public works. By early 1933, he was concerned, in addition, with reflation—price-raising—in both its domestic and international aspects.

When Tugwell went to Washington as an appointee of the new President, however, he hoped for a favorable response to his long-run reconstructive plans—as distinguished from short-run recovery measures in the emergency. Of course, he devoted most of his energy to his assignments in the Department of Agriculture and the Resettlement Administration, but an understanding of his role in and attitude toward the New Deal requires some knowledge of his institutional schemes (Chapter 9) and Roosevelt's reactions to them (Chapters 10 and 11).

I

What did Tugwell offer as a way of correcting economic maladjustments—summed up under the headings "overproduction" and "underconsumption"—and preventing their recurrence? The main elements of his program of "planned capitalism," which was to assure "continuity," were few: centralized allocation of resources (centralized control of capital investment), price controls, and a federal incorporation law. Why did Tugwell believe there was a crying need for these devices? Obviously, because, in his opinion, present economic practices, from the standpoint of long-run general welfare, did not work. They did not work because private interests acquired and abused, or misused, public powers. *Why did they abuse or misuse these powers?* Tugwell claimed that many of them would have done so even if they had wished otherwise. His claim suggests that we have come to a question to which the answer is neither obvious nor simple. His own answer determined the nature of his recommendations for economic planning.

We may outline Tugwell's answer at the outset, before considering it more closely: (1) in the unplanned sector of the economy special interests, being unco-ordinated, worked at cross-purposes, causing instability; (2) the advanced state of technology meant that there was going to be some planning one way or another in some sectors of the economy, and private planning—which followed from government's loss or neglect of its powers and was done by groups co-ordinated within but not between themselves—also caused instability. It is easy to see how he could proceed readily from this answer to these propositions: (1) planning must provide for co-ordination affecting the whole economy; (2) this co-ordination must serve the general interest.

In the unplanned sector of the economy many businessmen were efficient in their own operations, without being able, in most cases, to see the whole scheme within which they conducted their businesses. They did not understand their relationships to other businessmen, and they were unaware of their social function. Specifically, in economic terms, they did not have knowledge of the whole capital-investment and market situations in their particular industries, and they did not see that grievous social consequences—like unemployment—sprang from their miscalculations.

Businessmen in a given line, lacking inclusive information about their industry, were inclined to think of the same thing at the same time. In prosperous times, Tugwell pointed out, they tended to assume an unlimited market, each optimistically making capital commitments—plant, machinery, materials—out of surplus. With resulting overexpansion went the expense of unused facilities, which caused increased selling prices and thereby made marketing more and more difficult.[1] Thus, the overexpansion which businessmen brought about, going their separate ways in making capital investments, ended in painful contraction.

Was it possible for businessmen in a given industry to co-ordinate their capital investments? Tugwell thought so, holding that such co-ordination on a large scale was not only possible but inevitable. Would this much co-ordination—within industries—give the economy stability? Tugwell thought not, for reasons we shall take up after examining his assertion that technological progress was conducive to economic collectivism.

Tugwell maintained that maximum efficiency in applying principles of scientific management to the use of expensive equipment which represented the latest technological development called for bigger productive units.[2] As firms in a particular industry became larger and fewer, they could more easily co-ordinate activities, and they did—despite antitrust laws. Those laws, Tugwell declared, left the government "pitting itself against inevitable, unconquerable industrial forces."[3] Their advocates were "atomists."

We may, to characterize one phase of Tugwell's economic thought, call him an "anti-trustbuster." Many of his writings justify the coining of this term. He laid the antitrust movement to society's failure to recognize the inevitable technique for governing industry. Antitrust laws compelled business confusion, thwarting co-operative impulses which current economic trends demanded. Because "what was sound and economically necessary was branded as wrong legally," the urge to co-operate, Tugwell concluded, had to express itself "indirectly and unhealthily." The new industrial structure had to lead a subterranean existence, but, even though it was an illegitimate outcast, it grew like a well-nourished child, preying on its oppressors.[4]

Politicians pretended that antitrust laws were effective, that illegal business combinations did not exist. They preached littleness as a simple vote-getting reaction—successfully. Really big business had few votes, even losing, as time passed, the political loyalty of its employees. "Money alone did not make the political mare go," Tugwell asserted, and politicians won elections partly by taking advantage of a sentiment which, while it did not produce effective antitrust laws, was strong enough to prevent the positive development of an effective alternative policy.[5] Politicians carried the pretenses of their campaigns into office. They got themselves tangled in contradictory statements of public policy. They urged promotion of free competitive enterprise along with what Tugwell described as a set of wholly opposing aims such as utilization and co-ordination of the "plans, functions, and resources" of industry, labor, agriculture, and government.[6]

In *Mr. Hoover's Economic Policy* Tugwell carefully analyzed President Hoover's statements on the revision of antitrust laws and found them utterly confusing. Hoover recommended cautious revision to encourage development of co-ordination through the trade-association movement. The President, according to Tugwell, was concerned that acts of combination would provoke government interference which would stifle the will to enterprise.[7] Apparently the individualism which Hoover often referred to did not call for any particular kind of behavior on the part of individuals, such as steering clear of co-operative business management. Hoover's "individualism" seemed to mean a "hands off" policy on the part of government. Like Hoover, Tugwell favored government sanction of combination, but, unlike the President, he insisted that public supervision accompany public permission.

In his message of December 3, 1930, Hoover considered the prevention of monopolies of vital public importance. He also stated that competition was not desirable in "those enterprises closely related to natural resources." He deplored wasteful and destructive competition due to "prohibitive interpretation" of a law intended to enforce competition. He wished to "determine if these evils can be eliminated without sacrifice of the fundamental purpose of these laws." This wish, Tugwell commented, was "a desire to have his cake and eat it too." Hoover, Tugwell added, faced squarely with fact and theory in his professional field, left himself on a rack of indecision: "Those instances in which it [competition] is not good are those in which it is enforced. Where it is not enforced combinations exist." The President's trouble, Tugwell concluded, was his failure to see wasteful and destructive competition as the "natural characteristics of a certain stage of the private exploitation of natural resources." [8]

Obviously, Tugwell did not infer that inevitable combination necessarily gave the economy stability. The combinations of the 1920's did not promote continuity because (1) businessmen co-operating within a given industry still lacked knowledge of where they fitted into a larger scheme—that is, they lacked information about the relative position of their industry in the schedule of capital investments for all industries; and (2) private planners did not act in the public interest. Continuous stability, Tugwell maintained, required, besides *intra*industry co-ordination, over-all or *inter*industry co-ordination. Without over-all co-ordination there would be overinvestment in some industries and underinvestment in others. The economy, considered on a national, total basis, would suffer serious inefficiencies.

In addition to creating means of achieving over-all co-ordination, society would have to assure that such co-ordination promoted the general welfare. Certainly the *intra*industry planners of the 1920's worked against the public interest, making speculative capital investments and manipulating prices for maximum short-run profits. Possibly *inter*industry co-ordination could provide the protection of the general interest which was missing in the 1920's, with little more government participation in, and supervision of, economic affairs than marked the prosperity decade.

Even under such permissive circumstances an all-embracing system could bring disciplinary pressure to bear on supposed co-ordinators who tried to take advantage of other businessmen and, therefore, of people at large. An all-inclusive system, unlike the classical-model economy of laissez faire (many, small, equal competing enterprises) or the partial, private planning of the 1920's, would automatically and immediately identify would-be speculative, exploitative groups for all to see, presumably moving a united opposition to take corrective action against them. In any event, government would need powers with which it could, if necessary, act to protect the public interest.

The phrase "concentration and control," which Charles R. Van Hise of the University of Wisconsin used before World War I, summarized Tugwell's ideas on society's accommodation of technology. "Concentration" denoted unhampered development of huge productive units for technological efficiency. "Control" meant guarantees that the new industrial structure would benefit society as a whole. The two had to go together. In a modern industrial system there would always be co-ordinators, and they would hold the keys to power. The choice, Tugwell declared, was between a "supertrust outside our political forms (which may swamp the state in the backwash of its progress) and an assimilation to the state of the going system." [9] Either the government would supervise the planners, or the planners would supervise the government. It was difficult to overemphasize the importance of protecting the public. In 1926 Tugwell expressed doubt "whether the technical forces suitable for attacking nature will not break up our society unless they are strictly regulated in the general interest." [10]

Tugwell had some harsh things to say about businessmen who abused the public interest, but he did not invariably condemn them in personal or ethical terms. He once called them "a set of irresponsible and certainly self-interested people who half-manage and half-neglect affairs of whose consequences they have no adequate conception." [11] Yet he did not blame them personally for their antisocial attitudes because it was unrealistic to expect "conformity to a design which does not exist, nor to a sequential program which is not laid out." [12] Tugwell by no means approved of unethical business practices. He believed their elimination lay not in a transformation of human nature but in institutional reforms. The trouble was not with men but with the system. He prescribed an institutional framework for business so arranged that, without any detailed check being made on businessmen's conduct, individual enterprises, no matter who owned or managed them, would necessarily operate in the general interest.

The institutionalists did expect to "change" human nature, in time, to the extent that institutional changes would bring out men's better side. In fact, this "change" would be essential to the continued success of any scheme for social management of economic affairs. "Yet," as the Bard wrote in *The Winter's Tale,* "nature is made better by no mean but nature makes that mean." The problem was where to begin. Tugwell presented as a point of entrance to the problem of bringing about a more ethical, equitable economy a program for industrial co-ordination. He did not set it down in great detail. Some commentators scoffed at his brevity as a resort to the license granted dreaming academicians who were not responsible for framing and executing public policy. Others attributed his unwillingness to "blueprint" a finished system to his pragmatic outlook, his recognition that rigid theoretical commitment would not allow the flexibility which a complex, dynamic, and un-predictable economy would require.[13]

In the 1920's Tugwell referred in his writings to the inherent weakness of an unmanaged economy which lacked direction of investment and price controls.[14] In *The Industrial Discipline and the Governmental Arts,* published by Columbia University Press in 1933, he outlined his ideas on the means of management in a short (thirty-three pages) chapter, "Government and Industry." *Intra*industry associations would create planning boards for each industry. The effectiveness of these boards would rest on the voluntary co-operation of the businesses within an industry. Employers, employees, and consumers would work out plans for production, prices, division of markets, and working condi-tions. When matters became *inter*industrial in scope, they would pass over to the jurisdiction of a central planning board. This central board would represent the various industries and the government. It would be a "mediating and integrating body," co-ordinating *intra*industrial plans into a national planning program. It would also be a research organization, gathering the data needed for such a program. The central board would retain two crucial functions for itself: final supervision of capital investment and control of prices.

Tugwell wished to prevent a recurrence of the disastrous results of uncontrolled capital investment in the 1920's. He suggested two ways of channeling capital investment into the right places, in the right amounts. A tax on undistributed profits would force surplus funds into distribution, compelling businesses to go to the regular investment mar-kets to get funds for expansion. These markets, which had a wider point of view than individual businesses, would carefully examine in-vestment proposals for soundness in terms of the economy in general. Tugwell also recommended a federal incorporation law which would provide for some control over new capital issues. The history of incor-poration laws, he pointed out, had seen competition between states to attract industry. Out of this competition came confusion and mighty corporations which abused their excessive powers.[15] As early as the first decade of the century President Taft sought to correct this unhealthy situation, proposing a federal incorporation law in 1909 and again in 1911. Tugwell thought such a law would be an important part of a larger plan to co-ordinate capital plant with Americans' economic needs.

Price controls, in Tugwell's view, were essential to the maintenance of balance between production and consumption. Price policies which failed to pass on technological gains to consumers eventually resulted in a recession. Rigid price policies in a recession made the decline worse. Price controls fitted precisely into "concentration and control." Tugwell held that any attempt at positive control of prices without invalidation of the ideology of antitrust laws would be futile.[16]

Finally, in *The Industrial Discipline*, Tugwell stated that an effective national planning program would have to assure protection of certain vital interests such as essential weaker businesses, technicians, workers, consumers, and farmers. He wrote elsewhere about wages, his comments on this subject reflecting the lagging of wages behind rising productivity per man-hour in the 1920's. In the 1950's, when the reverse was sometimes true, he did not insist that labor should seek higher wages at all times. It was his view that labor, in seeking to maximize its income, often displayed a much too narrow interest.[17]

Price controls would, of course, afford basic protection for consumers. Tugwell also wanted specific representation in a national planning program of the consumer interest. As for farmers, *The Industrial Discipline* naturally was not directly concerned with them, but the maintenance of a balanced relationship between industry and agriculture would be a necessary function of any mechanism for economic stabilization. In other writings Tugwell had a lot to say about agriculture. As a New Dealer he did his best to promote protection of the interests of both consumers and farmers. Of the two groups, the farmers were better organized and more vocal. More was done for them.

Tugwell laid down some general guide lines for the operation of his co-ordinating scheme. *Intra*industry boards would work from the bottom up. A central planning board would oversee *inter*industry affairs from the top down. How far down would the direct jurisdiction of the central board reach? Tugwell answered this question in explaining the concepts of "conjuncture" and "direction." The idea of "conjuncture" grew out of his holistic thought. Parts were not significant when taken alone. They had a contributory significance in relation to the whole, which had a behavior pattern distinct from that of its parts. Where a part came into direct relationship with the whole lay the area or level of "conjuncture." [18] "Direction" included ends and means. It meant the definition of objectives *and* their achievement through planning—

giving as well as pointing out direction.[19] The central board would furnish "direction" at the level of "conjuncture."

In practical economic terms, the central board would not, for example, take cognizance of the details of factory operations such as workers' dress. It would start with, and be limited to, "direction" at the other end of the economy, concerning itself with matters of broad social significance. For instance, an industry's plans for capital investment involved the general public interest since they would, if miscalculated, cause maladjustments affecting the whole economy. And well-founded calculations had to be based on *inter*industrial information. Thus, the central board would adopt a synthesizing rather than an analytical approach to the economy. It would attempt to grasp the whole before considering parts. The whole, Tugwell explained, would not be a lifeless mechanical additive, but a unique "emergent" to which each part was necessary in suitable proportion.[20] He illustrated his concept of the "emergent," conjunctural whole with references to biology, which had been one of his favorite subjects in high school. He drew a parallel between the evolution of societies and that of multicellular organisms. The lives of both complex wholes conditioned those of all their members. Both developed loci of leadership. The higher forms of both were democratic, all parts interacting with the seat of direction when decisions affecting all parts were made.[21]

II

Tugwell's mentioning physiological and political democracy suggests the main line of attack against his planning proposals. Objectors avowed that his scheme could not work in a democracy. It was, they alleged, socialistic, Marxist, Sovietist, totalitarian. Tugwell was aware of these charges and their sources. He answered the accusations, and he insisted that planning could be consistent with democracy. In identifying the opponents of his program, Tugwell remarked that some serious students of public affairs, in an age devoted to analytical methods, considered his synthetic ideas too unorthodox.[22] The loudest cries of "unorthodox" came from businessmen who hid behind orthodoxies to veil their speculative activities. They did not want the future laid out in clear, objective, even if tentative, terms because they thrived on uncertainty and could not survive exactitude.[23] They were interested in gambling, in keeping society insecure in order to create conditions which provided gamblers' risks.[24]

Politicians, too, Tugwell observed, turned away from a planned future. They attributed all appropriate attractions to an uncertain future—campaign promises were notorious—while exploiting the popular impulse toward an uncomplicated and undisciplined past.[25] Businessmen joined in the appeal to the past, attributing the vast gains in economic well-being of the previous two centuries to uncontrolled initiative. Tugwell disagreed with them: "This period [of great gains] was indeed also the one of least control. But the demand for business freedom followed rather than preceded technical change. The desire was to take advantage of cumulative possibilities rather than to further them or to make certain of their benignity." [26] There is no real conflict between this view and that of Edward C. Kirkland and Allan Nevins, who have stressed the heroic qualities of America's industrial pioneers. To imply that there might have been other ways of building our capital plant is not to deny that they built it and that they were heroic. In this statement Tugwell did not judge them as men. He referred to them as logical products of a certain stage of America's economic development. In this context he considered them significant individuals.

Tugwell's opponents were a formidable force, and their charges were barbed. Many of his critics called his ideas socialistic, especially after he made this statement in December, 1931: "Business will logically be required to disappear. This . . . is literally meant. The essence of business is its free venture for profits in an unregulated economy." [27] They cited his call for the disappearance of business without referring to his definition of business. In context, the end of business meant the end of laissez faire. In 1932 important businessmen such as Henry I. Harriman, President of the Boston, and later of the United States, Chamber of Commerce, were insisting that the preservation of capitalism required the abandonment of laissez faire.[28] Senator Hugo Black, later a Supreme Court Justice, asserted in 1934 that there was nothing in Tugwell's works about doing away with private ownership.[29] Black thereby refuted the claims that Tugwell was a socialist.

Tugwell did not look upon business and government as opposite interests, one of which had to push the other out. In the depths of the depression he wrote that government had certain tasks to perform, but government was not business. The more industry did, the less government would have to do.[30] He also remarked that while public ownership applied to some utilities, "in others we shall equally certainly have to rely on individual initiative. . . ." [31] In fact, the early New Deal planned its relief program to avoid interference with private enterprise —thus being compelled to resort to inferior projects—and to provide customers for business, but business, Tugwell commented, was "cruelly satirical about a program shaped to its own criteria." [32]

As for planning, Tugwell considered the issue between private and public ownership beside the point. He had "no feeling [about it] one way or the other." [33] For "what is important beyond all else is the achieving of publicly oriented direction whether of publicly or privately owned or operated agencies."[34] Planning, far from being socialistic, would save capitalism. The capitalists themselves practiced planning through the trade-association movement. In order to avoid canceling out each other's efficiency, they needed an institutional framework for over-all co-ordination.

Tugwell not only rejected the central tenet of doctrinaire socialism—public ownership of the means of production—but he also repudiated Marxism in general—as theory and as Russian practice. He found himself unable to discover the inevitable superiority of a doctrinaire system. It seemed to operate well so long as doctrine fitted facts, but a system constructed without deference to preconception would have greater survival value in the long run. Certainly, Tugwell maintained, Marxism did not fit the facts of industry after the advent of Taylorism.[35]

What did Tugwell think about Marxism in Russia? This question is suggested by allegations that his ideas resembled Soviet theory.[36] In his opinion it was both gain and loss for others that "objectives should suddenly have become dominant in Russia; gain, because administrative feasibilities may be tested; loss, because so many Russian character-istics infuse them."[37] The Russians had an opportunity to show what planning could accomplish—in a dictatorship, not in a democracy. It was logical for the Russians, as followers of a deterministic philosophy which assumed certain inevitable results, to give first place to objectives. It was logical for them, as Russians, to use harsh means to attain their objectives. And it was logical for Tugwell, as an anti-determinist, to deny that ends justified means. As to means, he wrote that simple conformity to process would produce an insane world; as to ends, dominance of objectives, without consideration of administrative possibilities, would result in endless disputes.[38] In Tugwell's experimentalist view both ends and means would have to be flexible and interacting, and projections into the future tentative.

Tugwell's attitudes toward socialism, Marxism, and Sovietism made two points which his critics missed: (1) setting up a planning mecha-nism did not require making a choice between oversimplified alterna-tives—the isms; (2) planning in democracies did not mean they had to abandon their heritage. One of Tugwell's foes said "planned capitalism" was not "social control," "democratic process," "planned economy," or "experimentation"—it was "bureaucratic dictatorship."[39] Tugwell con-tended in 1926 that America's democratic spirit generated an "invincible objection" to Communism and Fascism with their suppression of dissent. The United States' democracy could manage economic affairs as efficiently as dictatorships. Planning in a democracy depended on vol-untarism and the aid of functioning managers of the economy. It began where class warfare and hatred ended.[40]

In answering the charge of "regimentation," Tugwell admitted that there would be some under planning—just as there always had been. In an unco-ordinated economy, he noted, business had adopted predatory policies involving a kind of regimentation which "usually did not go by that name"—the herding of workers into factories for eight, nine, or ten hours a day and the payment of inadequate wages.[41] Under planning it would still be necessary for men to submit to the discipline of machines. This submission would be a desirable kind of regimentation, setting men free to develop the most important aspects of individualism.

Tugwell held that "there must always be a certain amount of regimentation," but co-ordination would end human exploitation and the predatory practices of big business, "which already have gone far toward the regimentation of workers, of producers, and of consumers." The use by class-party dictatorships in certain foreign nations of repressive police measures leading to "intolerable regimentation of what we regard as fundamental human rights and liberties" should not, he declared, blind us to the fact that there were desirable as well as undesirable kinds of regimentation, and that we had some of the latter in our own society.[42]

Besides insisting that planning could fit into a democracy, Tugwell suggested ways of achieving this union. He approached the problem on two levels. Culturally, it was a question of reconciling the esoteric and the exoteric—expertness and public opinion. Institutionally, it was a matter of creating an agency which could plan effectively outside of the realm of politics while remaining subject to public control. Since his graduate-school days, Tugwell thought such a planning device was legal in a democratic setting. Consumers' rights, as established in common law, to adequate goods and services at reasonable prices were the basis of the public interest in economic affairs.

In the nineteenth century antitrustism was conceived as a policy to protect the public interest, but trustbusting was out of tune with technological developments in the twentieth century. Big business had been unable to put up a strong defense against antitrustism, on the basis of technological superiority, because shortsighted wage and price policies left few contented consumers. Business wanted an end to antitrustism but a continuance of private economic privileges. "Only at last gasp," Tugwell stated, "would any business man admit that public rights were involved in his enterprise." [43] However, if the public decided to support a policy of anti-trustbusting as a way of promoting the general welfare, it had a legal right to create means of implementing that policy and to invest them with power to protect the public interest.

One of Tugwell's phrases, "The Superpolitical," [44] indicated the kind of problems a planning agency would handle and the necessity of keeping politics out of its work. The problems of planning were for disinterested experts to tackle. As civilization advanced, its problems became more complex and difficult, and not many people were able to understand them. The number of people who could think for themselves had always been very small. Tugwell thought the intelligence of the race ran constant, every generation having "some one-half-of-one per cent of gifted individuals whose cerebrations suggest change." [45] Serious students of government such as Henry Adams in *The Degradation of the Democratic Dogma* and Walter Lippmann in *The Public Philosophy* inevitably came up against the problem of reconciling expertness with democracy.

Tugwell cited the well-made budget—he learned something about budget-making from his experience in the late 1930's as Chairman of the New York City Planning Commission—as a creation of experts which benefited all other institutions. The formulation of a budget was not democratic if "democracy means that with reference to technical matters all judgments are to be considered equal." But a budget was a democratic instrument, in a higher sense, because it helped "make the participation of each after his fashion effective in government." [46]

Another phrase used by Tugwell, "The Fourth Power," [47] denoted his recommendation of the establishment of a planning agency outside the three traditional branches of government. He explained why he believed that officials of the existing political system, with their comparatively short-run and necessarily political interests, could not effectively discharge the responsibility of planning (that is, exercise the "directive power") in the public interest. He analyzed the "leadership system" which American political organizations used, concluding that the ability to get ahead in politics and the ability to rise to statesmanship in public service seldom went together. In fact, political success hampered even the official who possessed the qualities of statesmanship and who also hired experts. He, like other political leaders, usually compromised between giving away whatever was necessary to hold his party organization together—payments of various sorts at the general expense (privileges)—and acting in the general interest.[48]

If planning called for experts, and experts could not operate effectively within one of the three existing branches of government, placing them in a new fourth branch was a way of employing their services for public purposes. Putting the experts beyond the reach of political pressures would refute the prediction that planning would simply be a substitution of politics for business—and that politicians would be worse looters than businessmen.[49] On the other hand, putting the experts completely beyond the jurisdiction of representatives of the public could leave the general interest at the mercy of undemocratic impulses. How, specifically, did Tugwell propose to implement planning in a democracy?

The "Fourth Power" would be exercised by experts meeting highly selective qualifications. Their terms of appointment would be relatively long—longer than any others in government except those in the judiciary. The planning body would function under a "rigorously fixed procedure of expert preparation, public hearings, agreed findings, and careful translation into law—which are in turn subject to legislative ratification." [50] The public would have something to say at the beginning of the process and a final say at the end. The experts would not determine social aims. They would devise ways of managing the economy to achieve the general aims which the public indicated it wanted to realize.[51]

Tugwell believed the federal government could create the kind of a planning body he had in mind without gathering in from the states any more powers than had already been delegated or appropriated with judicial consent, and without exercising more controls over private business than those already in use.[52] He preferred business self-government to direct governmental planning.[53] Democratic voluntarism, through a co-ordinating mechanism, could make it unnecessary for a planning agency to exercise by fiat its reserved powers to control capital investment and prices.

Tugwell asserted time and again that planning could be democratic. He stressed the sequence of technical proposal, public discussion, and considered adoption. Of course, according to his proposal, once a plan had received legislative approval, it would not be subject to discard at anyone's whim, but it would still be flexible—that is, changeable by constitutional procedure.[54] He considered the very creation of a planning mechanism in itself a democratic action. Planning—the exercise of governmental powers—was going to take place anyway. Believers in democratic procedures would prefer that "representative public power rather than self-interested private groups" function at the level of "conjuncture." [55] Planning, being "based on substantial agreement," would be more democratic than most governmental processes; it would regularize and make effective "what is otherwise done but is not done as well as is required in society." [56]

Tugwell readily admitted that planning, a politically neutral technique, could be used by dictatorships. In totalitarian states planning was dictatorial and militaristic. In a free society planning could foster democracy, which denoted the beliefs that government sought to institutionalize, as churches sought to institutionalize theologies. Some people called economic planning undemocratic, Tugwell said, because they incorrectly identified democracy with laissez faire capitalism. To the average citizen democracy was not a system but a "latent, ever-ready revolt" against oppression lying deep in men's natures.[57]

Tugwell's proposals may, in view of America's historic hesitancy to go in for economic planning, sound unrealistic, if not fantastic. Nevertheless, he thought the need for institutional reform was so pressing that what he suggested was little enough. And he did not expect early enactment of his recommendations. He was aware that the chief obstacle to his program would lie in stubborn public opinion. A firm believer in democratic evolution, he saw no way of applying his ideas effectively without public support.

Tugwell felt he could hardly exaggerate the urgency of the need for co-ordinated management of the economy. In his view, the environmental compulsion to adjust—to accommodate larger combinations which were often intent on destroying one another—involved the question of racial survival.[58] Democratization of "direction" was essential, he insisted, "if technique is to be allowed to have its way in the world without at the same time destroying it." [59] In this light, Tugwell maintained, the steps he wanted society to take to achieve a minimum of order—"as much consistency as is required" for practical purposes of assuring economic stability—were "relatively few but . . . momentous." [60]

It was possible to indicate the general nature of the "few but momentous" steps very concisely. Society simply needed to apply the principles of scientific management at the higher level of social management. All of this suggests the cliché, "more easily said than done." Certainly a planning agency, in applying the principles of scientific management on a general scale, would encounter many difficult problems. But, such problems aside, what about opposition—briefly mentioned above—to the establishment of a planning agency in the first place?

From his study of biology Tugwell concluded that the nature of men made it difficult for them to participate in co-ordinating, integrating schemes. Among ants and bees, whose societies behaved like single organisms, co-operation had its final triumph. For a human society to acquire a "brain" was an entirely different matter. Individual humans, unlike single ants and bees, had highly developed brains, which they used in specialized activities. Although these activities had become functionally interdependent, co-operation among intellectually individualistic humans had been slight. Yet, the new world of contracting time and space required that men reconcile specialization and integration.[61]

Business, as well as biology, militated against planning. Co-ordination could not be effective unless businessmen adopted new attitudes in place of the ones they had acquired in an unco-ordinated economy. The passion of their outbursts against planning showed that it would not be easy for them to change their ways. They rejected the idea of "planned capitalism" out of hand—if there were any planning, there would be no capitalism. Tugwell summarized their protest: planning would regiment every detail of the economy, jamming "arbitrary production schedules down the throats of a liberty-loving people" and even interfering with freedom of consumption.[62]

Business spokesmen also took another tack, drawing lessons, they claimed, from European history. Herbert Hoover denounced planning as the first stage of the step-by-step development of dictatorships. Raoul Desvernine, Chairman of the National Lawyers Committee of the American Liberty League, in his book, *Democratic Despotism*, warned that the United States, in undertaking planning, would lose the kind of democracy which promised to last in Great Britain and the Scandinavian nations. Ernest K. Lindley pointed out flaws in Hoover's historical analysis and Desvernine's deductions from current history. He noted that what Desvernine denounced as "democratic despotism" in the United States amounted to far less governmental management of the economy than the "economic liberalism" of Great Britain and the Scandinavian nations, which Desvernine approved. "Such antagonists of the 'totalitarian' states as Messrs. Hoover and Desvernine," Lindley commented, "apparently do not think that managed economies are inconsistent with democracy anywhere except in the United States"—the only important nation which considered waiting for "natural" forces to bring recovery a fit, or even defensible, policy.[63]

Business had plenty of company in its opposition to planning. Old Progressives, Tugwell observed, suggested weakening industry to match a weak government, looking upon any positive change in government as socialistic and immoral.[64] Militant leftists condemned Tugwell's program for its gradualism and flexibility.[65] They held that if there were any capitalism, there would be no planning. Tugwell, in reply, called Marxists old-fashioned. They stuck to "a philosophy which antedated the modern phases of industrialism." [66] He dismissed advocates of laissez faire and antitrustism, as well as Marxists, as doctrinaires. None of them, he said, related policy to actual conditions, and any of them, as policy makers, would be equally destructive.[67]

The public responded favorably to antiplanning arguments because of the elementary state of information about planning. Schools did not teach, and organs of opinion did not insist, Tugwell wrote, that we had to achieve organic relations among economic elements and prevent any part of the whole from exploiting the others. The events of the 1920's and 1930's taught that "exploitation returns to torment even its authors," but there was "a kind of determined refusal to draw the lesson." This refusal was due, again, to people's lack of knowledge about planning.

They did not understand that the machinery of planning would be strictly impersonal and that they would have a part in creating the development plan in democratic fashion.[68]

Despite his awareness of the obstacles to creating co-ordinating institutions, Tugwell believed Americans could and would do it. He was certain that man had in his rich nature the contriving ability to foresee, control, and agree, through "social mechanisms capable of containing and mastering the forces and materials to be understood, controlled, and socially accepted."[69] He saw in American civilization a generalized but deep "cultural faith" that our nation could achieve a better life for all. Yearning for fulfillment of this faith, Americans had moved beyond unquestioning acceptance of old institutions to the extent that their inclinations were divided between the old and the new.

Tugwell saw "a democratic republic torn by internal struggles yet hoping to find a competence" which could survive twentieth-century challenges.[70] Americans knew their history and were tired of insecurity.[71] Some day they would demand co-ordinating devices which would give them economic plenty and spiritual freedom.[72] "Some day" meant they still had time—but they did not have forever. Writing in retrospect about the economy of the late 1930's, Tugwell remarked, "Monopolies were growing, but they were private. Matters were getting out of hand."[73]

Thus, the penalty for institutional lag could be disaster, the reward for institutional reform an "economy of abundance"—a concept Tugwell borrowed from Simon N. Patten to indicate a situation in which co-ordination released the total potential of America's productive energy and provided for a full flow of goods to all the people. During the New Deal one of Tugwell's critics, Frank Kent, ridiculed the "economy of abundance" as a dream comprising "most farsighted schemes for the happiness of us all."[74] Others deplored the failure of the government to achieve it.[75]

III

Tugwell the New Dealer, in contrast to Tugwell the professor, was primarily concerned, of course, with emergency and recovery measures rather than long-range planning. It is necessary to take into account the time-range context in which he expressed himself in order to gain a clear understanding of his ideas on a given issue. He supported a number of policies on a short-run, stop-gap basis that did not harmonize with his long-run institutional ideas. He recalled that it was necessary to consider semi-permanent plans which would be effective after temporary devices had been discarded and forgotten,[76] but the first job in the early 1930's was to get the nation back on its feet.

Tugwell's views on agriculture, trade, and fiscal policy, among others, exemplified the differences between his short- and long-run preferences. In 1934 he called AAA devices expedients, some of them drastic, for adjusting supply to the market of the moment.[77] He foresaw the inevitable reaction against the original crop-reduction program, advising departure from emergency methods as soon as possible.[78] He believed that seekers of a permanent solution to the farm problem would have to concentrate on land use, especially the retirement of submarginal lands.

Tugwell opposed immediate adoption of a doctrinaire, unqualified free-trade policy. The nature of trade was such that the United States could not go it alone. Until other nations co-operated, he contended, it was best to make limited, specific agreements one at a time. He gave his long-run ideas on trade in an address to a meeting of the International Institute of Agriculture in Rome on October 24, 1934. He called for international planning through such devices as import and export boards and conferences for co-ordination of trade in certain commodities. He wanted it to be known that he was speaking as an individual and not as a public official. The President did not think such a distinction was possible, and he was unenthusiastic about Tugwell's making the speech at all.[79] Roosevelt was right. The press assumed that the White House stood behind the speech.[80] Tugwell often ran into such difficulties when, as a government executive, he expressed his academic opinions.

Tugwell's long-run views on fiscal policy refuted charges, provoked by some statements he made in the heat of political turmoil, that he was a fomenter of class warfare. He did favor, as a short-run policy, redistribution of income through graduated income taxes and government spending. This policy was constitutional, and he considered it necessary for building up and spreading purchasing power in order to get the economy going again. Tugwell, it is true, occasionally made belligerent remarks in the 1930's like this one taken from a speech he made to California Democrats in 1935: "We have no right to expect that the disestablishment of our plutocracy will be pleasant. These historic changes never are. We have, however, the duty of avoiding violence." [81] This particular sentence moved critics to call him a preacher of class hate.[82] It is ironic that even the belligerent Harold Ickes, writing in his diary about the speech which included this remark, commented: "I agree pretty generally with Tugwell in his social outlook, but I do think he might guard himself more carefully in what he says and writes." [83]

Tugwell's long-run views on fiscal policy revealed a quite different attitude toward class relationships. He looked upon taxation and spending for redistribution of income as an emergency policy which business brought on by abusing its powers in the past. In 1934 he voiced his preference for a "socially wise policy to socialistic taxation" as a means of distributing technological benefits.[84] In the long run, he later warned, fiscal policies that put an intolerable burden on upper- and middle-class incomes would have dire consequences. The decreasing number of unsubsidized citizens would "revolt at some point short of losing all their privileges to others whom they regarded as inferior to themselves"— as they had done in Nazi Germany and Fascist Italy.[85]

Thus, Tugwell concluded that government spending was a crude device for correcting permanent unbalance. The recession of 1937, which followed the withdrawal of subsidies and relief expenditures in 1936, showed that such a withdrawal was disastrous in an unco-ordinated economy. A co-ordinated economy, he declared, would yield "such an increase in benefits and such a diffusion of them as will satisfy those who are presently below standard without reducing everyone to misery." [86] Then class relationships could be characterized by a phrase that Tugwell coined in 1933, and which he and the President used often —"a concert of interests."

10. The Ideological Split in the New Deal

I

There were two main schools of economic thought in the New Deal. Tugwell was a follower of the collectivistic philosophy of "concentration and control." This philosophy, resting on the gospel of efficiency, contemplated the emergence of large productive units as the logical result of invincible technological advance. Tugwell called for protection of the public interest amid the industrial giants through "social management." His aim was protection of the public interest in the broadest sense—fair shares for all in an expanding, stable economy.

The Progressive atomists, or trustbusters, also saw hugeness resulting from technological advance, but they had a different way of protecting the public interest. They demanded the breaking up of the industrial Goliaths and the restoration of the classical competitive model of many, small, equal enterprises. They did not wish to change the institutional arrangements of the capitalist system. Their objective was to make the capitalists behave—through reforms in the fields of banking and securities as well as through trustbusting.

In addition, the Progressives' program for recovery emphasized the restoration of business confidence, which required orthodoxy in the handling of the banking system and in fiscal management. Thus, Progressivism permitted increased spending—including expenditures for relief, welfare, and public works—while also providing for progressive taxation as the source of funds. And the Progressives accepted social security, which, Tugwell later remarked, by assuring everyone a minimum, served as the "necessary floor" for laissez faire.[1] In other words, Progressivism did not basically change the game. It enacted some new rules and, by means of minimal guarantees, sought to give everyone a chance to play.

Embodying these two schools of thought, the New Deal exhibited a split personality. Tugwell attributed this dichotomy to Roosevelt's refusal to choose between "concentration and control" and enforced atomization. The San Francisco Commonwealth Club campaign speech of 1932 outlined both policies. Similarly, in the last years of the prewar period, after 1935, Roosevelt sought to discover a positive control of prices without violating the trustbusting ideology. But he did not dare to let go of either. This desire to reconcile opposites, Tugwell recalled, was an impossible challenge and the source of costly confusion.[2]

Placing the President in the center of affairs in this manner may convey the false impression that one can explain the history of the period in terms of the impact of this single personality. There was, as there always is, an interacting relationship between the man, especially since he was a politician in a democracy, and his times (a subject which Dexter Perkins has handled skillfully and judiciously [3]). Leon H. Keyserling, the New Dealer, insisted that a courageous, forward-looking Roosevelt made a difference.[4] Tugwell would agree with Keyserling, but, looking back, he also pointed out the President's typicalness, stating that Roosevelt's hesitation to make a choice was characteristic of Progressives in general. They were torn between attachment to their traditional attitudes and the demands of a new technological era.[5]

Indeed, the American people on the whole wanted assistance in a palatable form—assurance of security in a new age without abandonment of familiar ways. They looked upon the depression and the reactions to it in the way of public policy as temporary deviations, a detour off the broad highway we had traveled in the 1920's. A great deal of time and energy was wasted, Tugwell recalled, in the search for that highway.[6] Yet, the American people, unwilling to go forward, sensed that it was not possible to go back to the good old days. And so, Tugwell concluded, like their President, who, as he edged away from difficult reality, was more typical of the American mind than the Brain Trusters appreciated at the time, they lingered between two worlds.[7]

In retrospect, Tugwell noted that Roosevelt, born in a mansion rather than a log cabin, and educated at Groton, Harvard, and Columbia, "could be as blind to reality as were farmers and workers because his own education had been quite as defective." [8] He was understandable, Tugwell wrote, "as symbol, agent, and vessel of our contradictions, our hopes, our external cynicism and our internal reaching for fellowship. . . . He was like the rest of us and was not to be understood in any other way. His New Deal would not have turned out to be like us or in tune with the times if he had been different." It was generous while catering to greed, orthodox in economics while showing some slight understanding of economic evolution, niggardly while spendthrift. It was confused "because that is what we were like, and what the man was like whom we had chosen to lead us." [9]

Whether Roosevelt himself was a decisive force or whether he was typical, or whether, as was undoubtedly the real case, he was both, it is a useful analytical device to place him at the center of affairs. But before we consider the anti-Progressive and pro-Progressive forces acting upon him, we shall find it helpful to identify a trait of the President which accounted for his ability simultaneously to entertain both collectivistic and Progressive ideas. This trait was what Tugwell later labeled Roosevelt's "fly-paper" mind—"quick, retentive, and full of useful information, but marked by a genuine indifference to *systems* of all sorts." [10] His schooling had taught him mostly things that were not so, and he instinctively wanted a new interpretation, but his fly-paper mind kept him from committing himself to a systematic application of either collectivistic or atomistic policies. James M. Burns, who deplored Roosevelt's failure to adopt the Keynesian system, referred to the President's "staccato" intellectual habits.[11]

In his thoughtful moments Roosevelt understood the momentum of collectivism, but he could not visualize its practical embodiment in acceptable institutions. That is, the institutions of collectivism were unacceptable to Americans, Tugwell held, because they would require the sacrifice of private privilege and speculative hope. Thus, the President, while partly rejecting the old and partly accepting the new, tended to follow his basic inclination toward nineteenth-century Progressivism, which, from Tugwell's standpoint, involved antique reforms of antique abuses. This fitted in with Roosevelt's intellectual aversion to systems since Progressivism was an enforced no-system.

Roosevelt's aversion to systems also related to a factor which Tugwell stressed as an anti-Progressive force working on the President—*crisis.* If Roosevelt came into the crisis uncommitted to any new systematic solutions, he also was uncommitted to—in fact had rejected—classical economics, and so was better off than Hoover and most politicians and economists. One could say that he came into the crisis with a philosophy but without a program. His philosophy was one of positive government, the use of the power of government to restore balance to the economy by subordinating private to collective interests, by replacing selfish individualism with co-operation, and by aiding the underdog. He believed that political democracy could not exist side by side with economic plutocracy. This was a "state of mind and heart thoroughly familiar in the United States," Moley asserted, but it was not a program adequate for a President.[12] Tugwell, too, maintained that Roosevelt did not know on March 4, 1933, exactly what he was going to do.

But he had to do something. And the crisis, Tugwell recalled, was not only the reason for action, it was also the opportunity for action. He emphasized this opportunity, attributing the AAA and the NRA to a few months of acquiescence in executive leadership: "Only by the accident of vast patronage in emergency agencies would President Roosevelt have, for a few months, the lever to move things off center and to come into some control of business." [13] In 1935 Justice Benjamin Cardozo underlined what had happened in 1933 by stating the position of "old-fashioned liberalism which rested on legislative superiority" and issuing a reprimand for "delegation run riot." [14]

Tugwell issued his own reprimand for another reason. Given the demands and the opportunity of the crisis, Roosevelt gave some vent to his penchants for *statism* (most of which was of the welfare variety), *experimentalism,* and even a *tentative collectivism.* However, Tugwell judged, the President remained predominantly a Progressive, and he took far from full advantage of the opportunity which the crisis provided. All the emergency produced, Tugwell noted in 1939, was the "dusting off of some atomic reforms that had been lying around for fifty years—unused or safely mismanaged by hostile administrations." [15] Thus, 1933 had been a "lost year of opportunities passed over." The President had fallen back on the re-establishment of confidence and the restoration of trust in old institutions. That Roosevelt's policies had a "success d'estime for the moment was seized on for too much justification. It is still true that Americans would have followed him anywhere on that day, and that he had no place to take them." [16]

Tugwell's views were in accord with Dixon Wecter's observation that the New Deal was not "an explicit program drafted under Roosevelt's direction in 1932, but a general attitude toward government for the people later shaped by the urgency of circumstance." [17] In Roosevelt's reaction to the circumstances of 1933 the anti-Progressive elements— crisis, welfare statism beyond classical "umpire" statism, experimentalism, and a tentative collectivism—were offset by Progressive elements. Foremost among these was what we have called the basic inclination of the President himself. This was his Progressive orthodoxy, the origins and content of which Tugwell discussed at great length in his later writings.

Evading the question of environment versus heredity, we can see, in any event, that Tugwell traced the origins of the President's Progressive orthodoxy back to an early time. They accounted for his failure to show, like others of his background, surprise and resentment at the questioning of old arrangements as the dignity and mutuality of human relations in America broke down. He could be expected to have been removed from this questioning and this deterioration, and certainly he could be expected to treat his family prosperity, which antedated the English invasion of New York, as a matter of established right. But there was in him an antique sense of responsibility. It was not, however, directly connected with the changed nature of relationships. It rested, rather, on what Tugwell described as a "certain mild indignation at the antics of the newer rich, a Dutch sense of need for the restoration of order, and an English feeling for fair play—what his distant cousin, an earlier President, had called 'the Square Deal.' " [18]

Tugwell pointed out, in effect, that the derivation from these origins of Roosevelt's reactions to changes in American life ruled out anything "radical" in the usual sense of the word. If Roosevelt's amazement at the crash of 1929 was less than might have been thought possible, "he too had not been immune to our national myths" [19] and he too had a "weakness for what was familiar and trusted." [20] In other words, the collapse of 1929 was not, in his mind, the result of a failure to adjust to fundamental and invincible evolutionary changes in American life. Rather, it was the result of behavioral changes which represented a departure from tried and true conduct.

The phrase "the antics of the newer rich" suggests the core of Roosevelt's Progressive orthodoxy. If these antics offended his Dutch sense of order and his English feeling for fair play, they also were incompatible with his belief in the capitalistic business system and in the Protestant ethic. In economic terms he discussed these antics as mismanagement of corporate surplus. In ethical-religious terms they were simply bad behavior, and, Tugwell commented, his "underlying faith in business would really be measured by the capacity he would retain for outrage at each instance of bad behavior." [21] Thus, "disaster would be laid to departures from the old paths of rectitude," and "the New Deal was to be an attempt to re-establish the old virtues." [22] Business must be Christian rather than rapacious, economical rather than spendthrift, small-scale rather than large-scale in the size of its units, competitive rather than monopolistic, and democratic rather than absolute.

Concern with the "antics of the newer rich" revealed, in addition, the influence on Roosevelt's attitudes of Uncle Ted, who wanted men of means to behave in such a manner as to "prevent any just discontent becoming a factor in the socialistic movement." [23] Tugwell referred continually to Roosevelt's sense of continuity from the Progressive T. R., maintaining that the "parallels in the two Roosevelt careers are too close to be accidental." [24] He believed Roosevelt was worried about the comparisons which posterity would make between himself and T.R., and he was certain F.D.R. studied T.R. "if for no other reason than to make a better record." [25] The Hyde Park Roosevelt paralleled the Oyster Bay Roosevelt in the nationalism of the early New Deal, in the Pure Food and Drug Bill, in conservation measures, and in Progressive reforms such as the creation of the Securities and Exchange Commission and the Holding Company Act. Each "thought of himself as saving the capitalist system by making the capitalists behave. . . ." [26] There were differences too. Franklin was the natural, out-and-out Progressive. Theodore might have become so after 1912, but he lost the election. It remained for Wilson to exploit his knowledge that the long ground swell was toward Progressivism and to create a setting for Franklin in the Democratic party.

If Roosevelt's Progressivism had unique origins, it was not unique in its content. It was, Tugwell concluded, the Progressivism of Alfred

E. Smith, of Tom Johnson of Cleveland, of Brand Whitlock of Toledo, of Henry Hunt of Cincinnati, of La Follette and other Westerners, of the muckrakers, of a stronger labor movement—all promoters of education in public grievance. It went no further than would make the system operate tolerably. The government could "only regulate; it could not initiate. It had no part, actually, in the running of the business system. It could prevent abuses and check unwise policies, but it could only indirectly stimulate activity or ensure expansion. It could affect credit policies and the price level, but it could not direct investment or substitute its judgment for that of the bankers who were in contact with borrowers." [27] Thus, Roosevelt spent "a lot of time . . . planting protective shrubbery on the slopes of a volcano." [28]

II

If Roosevelt's basic inclination was toward Progressive orthodoxy, there were men in his entourage to reinforce it. They were Felix Frankfurter, agent for Justice Louis Brandeis, and Hugh Johnson, agent for Bernard Baruch. Later, beginning after Moley's departure, Benjamin Cohen and Thomas Corcoran, apostles of Progressivism, gained direct access to the President. This inclination and this reinforcement proved a formidable combination. That is why Tugwell did not judge his own failure as an educator harshly. His admission that he and Berle may sometimes have been at fault in method and motive as they presented their ideas to the President was "tempered by the certainty that not much more could have been done anyway. Mr. Roosevelt was getting what he thought he wanted." [29]

Journalists often lumped the Progressives and the collectivists together as "radicals" among Roosevelt's advisers. The *Washington Herald,* for example, in May, 1934, noting that the American people were "sick of the Brain Trust," associated Tugwell with Frankfurter, Corcoran, and Cohen.[30] In fact, Moley remarked, Frankfurter "thoroughly disapproved of the NRA. . . . He disliked Rex Tugwell. . . . For the whole philosophy of planning Frankfurter maintained intense opposition." [31] On the surface Frankfurter practiced the usual amenities, writing to Tugwell in December, 1933, "Aren't you having a swell time? Even from this end that's clear." [32] But Frankfurter made his basic position clear in another note, which came to Tugwell by way of the White House in May, 1934. He recommended that defenders of reform legislation collect utterances which had been used against T.R., Charles E. Hughes, and Wilson.[33]

Frankfurter has been introduced here as an agent of Brandeis, and it was about the Justice that Tugwell, in retrospect, wrote frequently, referring to him as the Progressives' prophet. Brandeis' prescription for the economy comprised regulation, antitrustism, taxation, and spending of tax receipts for welfare purposes. Taxation, of course, was related to antitrustism or atomism since the power to tax was the power to make small. This prescription, Brandeis believed, was all that was needed. In Tugwell's opinion it was a vast oversimplification. It showed, like Brandeis' *Other People's Money*, that money, credit, capital, and currency were always administrative matters on which liberals were not quite clear. Consequently, the first Progressive administration to come along dealt roughly with the financiers, but, Tugwell recalled, "no systematic change was in the cards." [34]

Tugwell called Brandeis "one of the New Deal's astonishing paradoxes." As one of the earlier discoverers of Frederick W. Taylor, Brandeis had "suggested that Taylorism might save the railroads. But as an interesting illustration of the impregnability of orthodoxy, he had seen no connection between this and the inevitability of large-scale operations. He had gone right on using all his influence for atomization." [35] Brandeis was "a wolf in sheep's clothing—more accurately, a doctrinaire parading as an instrumentalist. Brandeis very early drew certain conclusions from his experience which hardened into prejudice. These in time came to seem to him axiomatic. And he applied them without scruple." [36] According to Brandeis' "simple" Progressive orthodoxy, big business and big finance had caused the depression. Their admission to governmental partnership in the NRA had set up a "kind of unnatural union," and the partnership theory was unacceptable to the many representatives around the President of Brandeis, than whom, Tugwell asserted, "no figure loomed larger" in Roosevelt's Valhalla. [37]

As a Supreme Court Justice, Brandeis, Tugwell explained, had to exercise his influence discreetly, but he had "two means of enforcing his dogmas, and both were used on Roosevelt with devastating effect." Brandeis had his disciples, and he had the threat of unconstitutionality. Frankfurter was the first disciple, and through him, "mostly the staffing of New Deal agencies was controlled and dissenters were got rid of. And because Brandeis was, after Holmes's death, the most influential member of the Court among intellectuals and liberals—and with Roosevelt—a word from him was very nearly a command." This was more true after the adverse decisions on the NRA and the AAA, in which Brandeis joined with reactionaries like James C. McReynolds and Willis Van Devanter. Like them, he wanted to destroy the New Deal, "if for quite other reasons. He had, in fact, given warning and he was merely making good." [38]

Tugwell recollected how business, after it recovered from its fright of the emergency, poured its renewed strength into "its lobbies, its control of mass communication media, and its resistance to change of any sort." [39] Even earlier, in the crisis, business had an important voice in the shaping of the New Deal through its spokesmen in the Roosevelt circle, influencing the President toward fiscal orthodoxy. Later it was able to pervert the NRA. Thus, it was a "curious coalition of speculators and old-fashioned progressives" which overcame the forces of modernism. [40]

The most important figure among the speculators was Hugh Johnson's principal, Bernard Baruch, whose influence for a "business confidence" cure for the depression Tugwell recalled at some length. Roosevelt was wary of Baruch, suspecting him of having supported Smith for the nomination in 1932. But, Tugwell concluded, Baruch was willing to switch his allegiance to the winner in order to gain power, and Roosevelt placated him because of his influence in the Democratic party, especially with many Southerners in Congress. [41] The highest tribute to Baruch's influence on the New Deal was paid by Thomas Corcoran, [42] which, perhaps, illuminates the "curious coalition" of businessmen and Progressives that Tugwell mentioned. On the question of collectivism, however, this coalition did not hold together. Tugwell indicated this when he noted that the Brandeis influence prevailed after the departure of Peek and Johnson, the "Baruch twins." [43] This comment did not mean that Tugwell approved of Peek's brand of collectivism in the AAA and Johnson's in the NRA. He certainly did not.

The whole matter of Baruch's position on collectivism is a confusing one. Margaret Coit noted that his greatest service during Hoover's term was in "heading off several somewhat hysterical measures, including a proposed peacetime War Industries Board." [44] On the other hand, in the spring of 1930 Baruch proposed to the Boston Chamber of Commerce the formation of a Supreme Court of Industry. [45] This proposal, like the War Industries Board and the NRA, leaned heavily on Baruch's philosophy of industrial self-government. But he believed, Miss Coit elucidated, that while these organizations should protect capital and labor, they must never allow them to forget the general public. [46] Tugwell felt that Baruch's kind of collectivism did not provide for adequate protection of the public interest. Perhaps Baruch's concept of industrial self-government under governmental sponsorship was a compromise between two positions which Miss Coit attributed to him: his conviction that with the rise of consolidated corporate power "only big government could see and plan for all" and his mistrust, "natural to one who had lived under Reconstruction," of concentrated governmental power. [47]

One other comment on Baruch's position seems justified. He was opposed to a peacetime War Industries Board. The NRA, of course, was that, although it was created, it is true, at a very critical juncture in peacetime—which only supports the judgment that his views gave intimations of a panic philosophy. He seemed to favor pulling out all the stops in a crisis and then, when the crisis had passed, returning to the good old days of business as usual.

In addition to Roosevelt's basic inclination and its reinforcement by Brandeis, Frankfurter, and Baruch, political considerations made for orthodoxy in policy. This does not mean that the President's politics was simply a matter of doing whatever would win him the most votes. His problem was to determine, as a politician, just how much change, which he deemed desirable as a statesman, society would accept. Returning to teaching in 1946 as a Professor of Political Science at the University of Chicago, Tugwell emphasized in his writings the limitations which politics placed on executive action.

Tugwell pointed out that in our democratic society, with its separation-of-powers or checks-and-balances system of government, the President had to weigh the criteria of efficiency against probable Supreme Court opinion in choosing instruments.[48] He also had to appease Congress, which, Tugwell held, was a natural opponent of the executive and, except in extreme crisis, represented minority feelings in the country.[49] The necessity of entrusting administration of policies to subordinates resulted in further compromise with Congress. Administrators, receiving instructions only as to ends, were prone to make deals with key legislators, accepting "practical" or "orthodox" solutions as to means and postponing the quest for long-range goals.[50] The American people themselves, whose feelings Congress did not usually represent, were not doctrinaire, and they would support only so much reform in a generation—largely in crises and only so much even then.[51] The "people," of course, fell into a number of categories. In the center the middle-income group, widening with recovery, took on a conservative color.[52] To right and left were political forces which significantly affected Roosevelt's policy calculations.

Basil Rauch contended that "thunder on the right" pushed the President away from collectivism and toward Progressive orthodoxy. He blamed Roosevelt's opponents of the Liberty League type for introducing class antagonisms into public affairs and for refusing to compromise or co-operate with the administration. They forced the President to appeal to farmers and labor in order to make up for the loss of conservative support.[53] James M. Burns also stressed the "cumulative impact of attacks from the right." [54] Rauch's and Burns's statements imply resentment, even revenge, in Roosevelt's motivation.

Tugwell, too, noted that the President was responsive to the barrage of adverse criticism which the right laid down in 1934 on administrators to the left: Ickes, Perkins, Hopkins, and Tugwell himself. But Tugwell maintained that in a real sense Roosevelt's reaction was one of acquiescence rather than revenge. The President occasionally showed his irritation at criticism from the right, but, "more important, he can be seen in retrospect to have allowed his policy to be shaped by a desire first to escape from the continual manifestations of ill will, and second to find among the multiplying signs of opposition some real haven of political friendship." [55] In other words, Roosevelt, seeking to preserve the capitalist system, was very sensitive to "traitor to his class" accusations, and avoiding them was one of the reasons he reverted to orthodox Progressivism. This return, however, did not bring him big business' political support. For a political base he had to look elsewhere.

Tugwell and Roosevelt discussed the forces on the extreme right as a latent threat to democracy. This threat, rooted in the assumption that people would willingly give up liberty in return for security and "disguised as super-patriotism of various sorts," awaited an appropriate opportunity to come out into the open under a leader with the requisite "charm, tradition, and appearance." [56] It was Roosevelt's duty to keep an appropriate opportunity from arising. Meanwhile, if "thunder on the right" was a latent threat as a revolutionary alternative to democracy, "thunder on the left" was, in Tugwell's opinion, a "clearer present danger." In *The Democratic Roosevelt* he made some lengthy remarks on the colorful figures on the left, listing among the demagogues, left and right, Father Charles Coughlin, Milo Reno, Dr. Francis Townsend, Gerald L. K. Smith, William Lemke, and Huey Long. Next to Huey Long, whom Tugwell, for a time, was supposed to pacify, the others were "after all pygmies." They were not new in American history. They were "another 'know-nothing' movement, anti-intellectual and completely irresponsible. And, as usual, there soon developed a following of the ignorant and malicious, always latent in any population." [57]

The demagogues, Tugwell observed, "never had an intelligible program. They seemed to agree only on a nonsensical enlargement of inflation that was already one of the most criticized phases of the New Deal." They had "no place in a peaceable movement. They lived on trouble," and an improvement in conditions would return them to obscurity. Their "one chance was to propagate impossible goals and to condemn Franklin not for having done nothing but for not having done enough." [58] With the passage of welfare legislation, the demagogues were "forced to become more and more extreme. This allowed Franklin, as a national figure, to occupy more and more of the area left of center." Huey Long, for example, helped in the passage of the Social Security Act, the Revenue Act of 1935, and relief and public works appropriations. "He inveighed against all of these," Tugwell recalled, "but that he denounced them as insufficient, along with his fellow demagogues, certainly contributed to their passage." [59]

"If 1934 was the year when the reactionaries made the most noise," Tugwell wrote, "1935 was dominated . . . by thunder on the left. . . ." [60] Thus, if Roosevelt responded in 1934 to thunder on the right by deciding to turn toward Progressive orthodoxy, the thunder on the left of 1935 facilitated and accelerated the implementation of a policy previously decided upon. In this sense, Tugwell's analysis was in accord with that of Rauch and Burns, who stressed thunder on the right. We shall never know, of course, how Roosevelt worked out his political calculations. As Tugwell explained, "This was not the kind of difficulty Franklin ever asked for advice about. He did on occasion, as he was considering a problem, talk with those around him rather as though he were thinking out loud. But he came to his conclusions and made his dispositions without saying what it was he was trying to do. Anyone was free to draw his own inferences; but as for himself, he would not admit that any change had taken place." [61]

Tugwell drew his own inferences about "a number of combined estimates" on Roosevelt's part. The President, he deduced, determined that the "weight of the movement still lay with the older orthodox progressives." If their policies were "developed in all their ramifications, the likely defection of reactionaries in the South . . . would be offset by strength among urban workers and city machines. . . ." Moreover, simplicity lent orthodox Progressivism great attractiveness. [62] This allurement was a formidable political factor. Or, to state the converse, neither politicians nor the people were ready to accept the complexity of collectivism. Indeed, regardless of his secret thoughts, this was Roosevelt's basic calculation. He decided, Tugwell noted, that "not only Brandeis but the country as a whole was still at the trust-busting mental age. The time to collectivize had not come. It was obviously his judgment, furthermore, that the exercise of his leadership, the use of his talents for persuasion, and all his political contrivance would be unequal to the task of collectivization." [63] But Roosevelt's backing off collectivism did not mean that he had abandoned it. Nor had he given up his "grand conception of a new political alignment," [64] the one about which he communicated with Wendell Willkie in 1944. At some later date the time would come for collectivism under a genuine Progressive party.

Tugwell went so far as to claim that Roosevelt, beneath his heritage and orthodox inclinations, was a "wholeness man who, out of discretion, gave ground to atomism," although his "commitment was never clear or complete." [65] Similarly, Roosevelt, beneath the appearance that he was a party man, was a Progressive Democrat who, out of discretion, postponed the formation of a new party. He could make no advance without winning elections. [66] He "ought to be allowed some leeway by his supporters. But he must keep them. And this he thought he could do by being progressively orthodox." [67] He resolved to "put himself in the main stream of progressivism before trying to harness and transform it. He had not been able to redefine and reorient the movement. He must swallow its orthodox tenets even if he choked a little. The retrogression went all the way back to atomism, hanging on to the holistic conception only in a few accepted fields, such as natural-resource development, conservation, and the provision of social minima." [68]

Thus, if economics required collectivism, "politics required that collectivism be camouflaged as competition . . . congenial collectivism." [69] Meanwhile, "to make use of hostility to bigness was one way, Franklin conceived, of approaching, by indirection, the planning necessary to a high-energy economy." Progressivism "might eventually evolve, or be made to evolve, into an adequate social philosophy." [70] Thus, Roosevelt's basic calculation that collectivism was politically unacceptable reflected the American people's willingness to support only so much reform in a generation. Looking at American history in terms of a pendulum's swing —and there are poorer analytical devices—one could not expect the American people to experience a disastrous depression without insisting on some reforms. But they did not base their demands on doctrine, and by 1936 the reforming impulse was fading fast.

Samuel Lubell, the noted political analyst, called 1935 "The Year of Decision": "To go back to the old order [of unchallenged business dominance] or to move forward to something different? That was the question. . . ." The spate of social legislation in 1935 was the politicians' answer, and the election of 1936 was the people's stamp of approval.[71] In speaking of the situation after 1935, however, one would have to change Lubell's use of prepositions. Now the people wanted to go on "with" something different rather than "to" something different. America in 1936, of course, was different from America in 1929, and in time would become more so as the result of legislation already passed. This much the people approved. That they did not want further reform was indicated by public-opinion polls. By cross-tabulating two polls, Elmo Roper showed that only 5 per cent of Roosevelt's most enthusiastic supporters in October, 1936, thought he would, if elected, become more "radical," and 59 per cent thought his policies would remain about the same.[72]

This reference to public opinion suggests a problem which political scientists raise when they consider the leadership qualities of a President —the question whether he leads or follows public attitudes. James M. Burns concluded that Roosevelt was not a creative political leader because he refused to "risk endangering the integration of his followers in trying to improve their position" (four years later, in 1960, Burns took a different view of political limitations on executive leadership, confining presidential exercise of significant power to "moments of sharp crisis . . .").[73]

Tugwell's position as of 1936 was in line with Burns's. In that year he felt that Roosevelt should ask the American people for a mandate for collectivism.

In retrospect, Tugwell was more of a political scientist than an economist and more philosophic in his judgment. He stressed limitations and obstacles, expressing disagreement with some of his modernist friends who were impatient with the political needs of the head of government.[74] He noted that in a democratic government the experts' decisions were modified by the political compromises between the concessions necessary to hold the organization together and acting in the public interest.[75] He disagreed with Burns on Roosevelt's creativity as a political leader, pointing out that the President exhibited the "ambivalence of a political reformer seeking to bring about changes while maintaining his own sources of strength." [76]

Tugwell also objected to Professor Richard Hofstadter's essay which described Roosevelt as an "opportunist." [77] The President, Tugwell asserted, had a "bulldog determination concerning objectives and a completely contrasting flexibility concerning means." Hofstadter "failed to rate highly enough Roosevelt's persistence and determination in pursuit of his real objectives." [78] Commenting in 1960 on his essay of 1948, Hofstadter stated, "My opinion of F.D.R. has gone up as my understanding of what can and cannot be done in the political process has increased. I have more respect now for the 'broker function' of the politician that F.D.R. represents so well." [79]

If in the end Roosevelt did not achieve all that he wanted, Tugwell concluded, "it was because the situations he had to deal with were impossibly difficult. An analysis of any one effort in detail almost always shows endless resources and determination. Failures from poor technique are few." [80] Thus, the "question whether in these compromises Franklin allowed expediency to overcome his duty to press for the policy the nation should have been persuaded to adopt is one it is not possible to answer." No one could so closely analyze the imponderables of political support. Roosevelt had to make a judgment and he made it.[81] In any event, to sum up, a clash between antiorthodox factors—crisis, Roosevelt's experimentalism, statism, and tentative collectivism—and pro-orthodox factors—Roosevelt's heritage, its reinforcement by Progressives like Brandeis and businessmen like Baruch, and the limitations imposed by politics —produced a Progressive New Deal.

11. The Two New Deals: 1933-1938

I

Historians customarily relate the collectivism-Progressivism conflict to the concept of two New Deals, which Basil Rauch first popularized. They have called the transition from the First New Deal of 1933-1934 to the Second New Deal of 1935-1938 a shift from the New Nationalism to the New Freedom, from a planned economy to a compensated economy, from a managed economy to a mixed economy. We should note, however, that in detail this division of the New Deal was not so clear-cut. Historians, especially those concerned with the history of ideas, run the risk of imposing on events a neat pattern that was not necessarily there at the time. James M. Burns pointed out the fluidity of the transition from the First to the Second New Deal. He indicated the inadequacy of ideological explanations of the shift, he denied that there was a "consciously planned, grandly executed deployment to the left," and he remarked that "events have ways of committing leaders to new positions."[1]

Certainly the two New Deals overlapped. Professor Eugene O. Golub listed objectives common to both: economic security, a higher standard of living, aid to underprivileged groups, and orthodox Progressive reforms to make the capitalists play fairly.[2] Professor Eric F. Goldman identified security as a theme common to both.[3] Professor Daniel R. Fusfeld described the philosophy running through the two New Deals as economic interventionism (governmental responsibility for prosperity) based on a new view of the place of the individual in society (security) and a new position on the social responsibilities of the businessman (the belief that individual gain was not always synonymous with the social good).[4]

Thus, we find Tugwell supporting part of the Second New Deal during the First as he called for action to assure economic security and a higher standard of living for the underprivileged non-staple farmers. He finally obtained the establishment of the Resettlement Administration in 1935. When the Second New Deal got under way, he recalled, he urged that the Food and Drug Bill, which he had also supported during the First New Deal, was "strictly in the line of the new philosophy—to regulate industry, but not to require of it planning or performance. If manufacturers were to be required to conform to wages-and-hours requirements and to treat each other fairly, they ought also to be asked to treat their consumers fairly."[5]

That Second New Deal policies appeared in the First New Deal, and vice versa, indicates that confusion and inconsistency characterized both. Tugwell underlined this situation when he listed in *The Art of Politics* the several theories of recovery, all of which had staunch supporters among thoughtful men, from which Roosevelt made his choices. These theories were "roughly recognizable" as (1) the business solution—deflation, easing up on business regulation, restoration of confidence; (2) monetary—infusing currency into the system to restore price levels and start things going and, because gold was the standard of value, affecting prices by manipulating the price of gold; (3) consumers' purchasing power—making purchasing power available to consumers to start factories going, thus reducing unemployment; (4) fiscal—manipulating interest rates (making money "easy") and increasing or decreasing federal spending; (5) balance—the equalizing of income among mutually supporting groups.[6] (Tugwell's basic commitment was, of course, to balance.)

From Roosevelt's simultaneous sponsorship of policies coming under opposing theories it followed, Tugwell remarked afterward, that his administration was inconsistent if reference is made solely to economic theory.[7] This inconsistency has led to the textbook axiom, expressed even by students who credit Roosevelt with having saved the capitalist system, that he "played it by ear" and that the impact of the haphazard, unco-ordinated, and wasteful New Deal was more or less accidental—due less to intelligence and planning than to luck. The other extreme in interpretation, Alfred Kazin has noted, portrays Roosevelt as "more calculating than he really was" and the New Deal as "planned, theoretical, coherent."[8]

Tugwell's comments on the confusion of the New Deal, in both its First and Second phases, suggest that the truth encompasses both of the interpretations we have mentioned. In *The Democratic Roosevelt* he rejected the contention of Roosevelt's critics that reversals and inconsistencies were proof that "most of the time he knew neither what he was doing nor why he was doing it."[9] If Tugwell considered Roosevelt an opportunist concerning means, he stressed an antithetical determination concerning objectives.[10] The President's objectives were the themes, described by Professors Golub, Goldman, and Fusfeld, which were common to both New Deals. In Tugwell's opinion, "a bright thread of intention ran through the confusions and contradictions."[11] Thus, consistency at least applied to the "why" of Roosevelt's action. As for the "what," Tugwell recalled that Roosevelt "had to deal *de novo* with more and more complicated situations," making decisions which seemed unwise to some people. But "for none of them is it true that there was no reason or that there was no authority to lean on."[12]

Tugwell did not doubt that the New Deal could have been more consistent and more effective economically.[13] In any event, at least Roosevelt was an experimentalist, and experimentation meant that some advantage could be taken of various theories. Granville Hicks, the ex-Marxist, asserted that the New Deal proved American experimentalism more efficacious than the Marxist-Leninist system and demonstrated the resourcefulness of the American people.[14] In addition Roosevelt was a humanitarian. Expressing themselves through his experimentalism and humanitarianism, feelings, philosophy, and intentions were as important as economic theories in giving the New Deal thrust in a general direction and in producing remedial action. Perhaps it is reasonable to conclude that the New Deal was partly accidental in detail but not accidental in general.

Having pointed out an overlapping of the two New Deals in connection with Tugwell's participation in the Roosevelt administration (the RA and the Food and Drug Bill), we also see the same phenomenon in his later analysis of the President's policies. Tugwell identified several Second New Deal elements which appeared during the period of the First New Deal—and even earlier. There was Roosevelt's speech in the "safe" campaign of 1932 at Columbus, Ohio, on August 20. This address, which reversed the call for social planning and experimentation of the Oglethorpe University speech of May 22, was in the Brandeis tradition. The suppression of Berle and Tugwell as administration associates in March, 1933, accorded with immediate Presidential action—especially the Emergency Banking Act of March 9 and the Economy Act of March 20, which were more consistent with the views expressed in the Columbus speech than with the Brain Trusters' ideas. They were also in line with the orthodox views of the business half of the "curious coalition" of Baruch and Brandeis.

Tugwell asserted in 1928 that the Federal Reserve System was not discharging its responsibilities in the general interest,[15] and in early 1932 he suggested that the government might be a more efficient banker than private groups.[16] In 1933 he welcomed the Glass-Steagall Banking Act of June 16 as a "great step forward," but it did not "go all the way in creating a consolidated, national banking system." [17] He noted in his diary, "We should have set up a national bank in the crisis; now it's settled." [18] In an article of 1948 he wrote that Roosevelt's handling of the banking crisis "fitted in with Mr. Baruch's constant leaning toward retrenchment and the restoration of business confidence," for it was the conservative representatives of finance and industry whose technique was used.[19] In 1953 Tugwell rejected the interpretation that Roosevelt could not "have done other than he did. . . . It seems that those who argue against the existence of alternatives minimize the . . . readiness of a paralyzed people to accept drastic solutions offered by a trusted leader." [20]

In 1957 Tugwell backed off this position somewhat, emphasizing Roosevelt's concern with the lack of personnel to run a new kind of system and the pressing need for "simple restoration of a system people understood under conditions that would assure them of future safety." [21] But this later remark did not necessarily represent a complete retraction. Tugwell had conceded earlier that he "may have been wrong," that this could have been another instance of Roosevelt's "superior instinct for social action, that the middle class might somehow have revolted and torn up the streets or invaded stores." Nevertheless, Tugwell still felt that in the crisis Roosevelt confused "the welfare of a few with the welfare of all." [22]

To sum up, in Tugwell's view there were two general means of attacking the financial crisis of 1933: nationalizing of the banking system and the use of national credit as a balancing mechanism (although he may have exaggerated in retrospect his awareness as of 1933 of the possibilities of compensatory fiscal policy). He argued for these alternatives, "although I was excluded from actual decision-making in financial matters, as policy [the Emergency Banking Act and the Economy Act] was adopted in early New Deal days." [23]

Tugwell held that even the AAA and the NRA, the obvious expressions of the collectivism which historians consider characteristic of the Brain Trust's ideas and the First New Deal, did not reflect the demise of the Progressives' influence. He commented in retrospect that the publicity which these two Acts and the Brain Trust received gave the public a distorted view of the relative positions of the collectivists and the Progressives in the Roosevelt circle. [24] Despite the creation of the AAA and the NRA in the crisis of 1933, Roosevelt clung to his Progressive heritage. [25] He turned away from the Brain Trust and to the alternative which was "available and ardently argued for by those he admired"— especially Mr. Frankfurter, deputy for Justice Brandeis. [26] We should also note in this connection Tugwell's contention that the beneficiaries of the AAA and the NRA set out, and were allowed, to upset the balancing and co-ordinating intent of those agencies. [27]

In late 1933 the original Brain Trusters, Tugwell recalled, suffered a defeat in the matter of monetary policy. Roosevelt's confidence in "practical" advice wavered when recovery faltered, but he again took it, this time from Professor George F. Warren and Henry Morgenthau, adopting the futile gold-buying scheme. Eventually, Tugwell wrote, "the practical course . . . gradually and embarrassingly . . . had to be abandoned." [28] (In this connection, Tugwell's use of the word "practical" is not entirely clear. In terms of his general approach, the gold-buying scheme was practical because its advocates considered it an alternative to the expansive fiscal policy which business deplored. Presumably Morgenthau rather than the theorist Warren represented the business point of view in this instance. At the same time, a number of important businessmen shared Tugwell's opinion on the gold-buying gambit.)

So far we have said that historians commonly refer to two New Deals, but that in order to avoid oversimplification we must bear in mind that the two New Deals overlapped. We have remarked that this overlapping is evident in the limitations to which the original Brain Trusters' influence was subject as early as 1932. Expressions of their collectivism did not put the atomistic Progressives to flight, and their ideas in the field of finance—that is, strictly speaking, Tugwell's, not Moley's, ideas—received slight consideration as Roosevelt followed the advice in this area of orthodox, "practical" businessmen (Tugwell and Moley agreed in their opposition to the gold-buying scheme but disagreed on spending and the handling of the banking system). The Progressives, unlike the businessmen, opposed NRA and favored an expansive fiscal policy. Thus, while the Progressives contained the original Brain Trusters' collectivism, the businessmen, who favored their own version of the "partnership" brand of collectivism, set aside Tugwell's preferences in financial and fiscal policy.

Now we come to a third step in our approach to the two New Deals. Having first pointed out their separation, then their blending, we return to their separation by noting that Tugwell accepted the two-New-Deals analysis as generally valid. In *The Democratic Roosevelt* he called Rauch's conclusion a "just comment. Franklin was in process of making a complete turn-around. It is no exaggeration to speak of the situation after 1934 as a Second New Deal." [29] Tugwell's account in the middle third of *The Democratic Roosevelt* (pages 210-454) of the atomists' victory over the collectivists and Professor A. M. Schlesinger's narration in *The Politics of Upheaval,* Boston: Houghton Mifflin, 1960 (pages 211-443), are the most detailed treatments of the shift from the First to the Second New Deal. These two descriptions are in accord on the basic nature of the transition but differ on the matter of the timing of Roosevelt's re-formulation of his views. In Tugwell's version, Roosevelt decided on a new departure in policy in late 1934 and launched his new program in early 1935. Schlesinger, too, attributes to the President the decision in late 1934 that a new approach was needed, but he depicts Roosevelt as not synthesizing the new measures in his mind until mid-1935. Tugwell's analysis is searching but difficult to follow because it lacks chronological order. It is worth our while here to provide the chronological sequence that we do not find in his report.

In *The Democratic Roosevelt* Tugwell mentioned some of the developments of 1934 which represented a reversal in the direction of orthodox Progressivism. The Gold Reserve Act of January 31, in fixing the value of the dollar at 59.06 per cent of its former gold value, prepared the way for the stabilization Roosevelt had "so emphatically rejected just a year before." The Reciprocal Trade Agreements Act of June was "another and even more startling about-face"; it was the same Act Roosevelt had refused to submit to Congress in 1933. It was, however, "far from being the free trade of the theorists. . . . It was thus not so considerable a departure from the nationalism of the early New Deal as was sometimes represented." Another reversal of mid-1934, after the Clarence Darrow report, was the change in Roosevelt's pro-big business NRA policy.[30]

The Securities Exchange Act and the Communications Act of June, while they were not contrary to previous policies, were also part of an orthodox Progressive drift. This trend was not without exceptions. Roosevelt treated the Labor Disputes Act in an equivocal manner which offended the Progressives and in October seemed to reverse his field again in NRA policy, to the dismay of both orthodox Progressives and collectivists (orthodox Progressives were doctrinally opposed to big business and the NRA to begin with, but, short of abolishing the NRA, they agreed with the collectivists that government rather than business should dominate the agency). Yet, despite the President's twistings and turnings in the election year of 1934, the Progressive tendency prevailed. In fact, Roosevelt's October speech to the American Bankers Association, the one which the Progressives deplored for its apparent retreat on the NRA issue, was, in Tugwell's judgment, a phase of a groping back toward orthodox Progressivism.[31]

The bankers were not too enthusiastic about the comparatively conciliatory speech, and they were not too happy after the elections when the President once more changed his NRA tune to the Progressives' delight. But this last switch, too, proved temporary—from the standpoint of the collectivists. The trend of a longer, although not in Roosevelt's mind a permanent, run was developing out of his search for a new policy. This search, going on beneath the friction between the President and the bankers, foreshadowed and characterized the Second New Deal. The new policy, Tugwell remarked, "had to be acceptable in a majority sense; it had to be capable of managing indirectly to maintain a stabilized and expanding economy; and it had to seem—although this was perhaps part of the first requirement—a development, not a replacement, of the business system." [32]

In other words, Roosevelt was giving up on the direct controls of collectivism, returning to the indirect controls of regulatory Progressivism. Yet, he expected business, which under collectivism had enjoyed its partnership with government in the NRA only so long as it was the senior partner, to depict regulatory Progressivism as radical and anti-capitalistic. It was not intended to be that—"a replacement of the business system"— but neither was it to be "a development of the business system." It was only to seem so. Regulatory power lay outside of the business system. It resided with government, which, Roosevelt told the bankers, "by the necessity of things must be the leader, must be the judge of the conflicting interests of all groups in the community, including bankers." Here the President was voicing the earlier Roosevelt's view that the various sectors of society, equal to each other, are not equal to government. Unfortunately, "this preachment," Tugwell observed, "was lost on Franklin's hearers." [33]

Thus, according to Tugwell's account, by the end of 1934 orthodox Progressivism held sway at the White House. Roosevelt had returned to the position he had assumed during the campaign of 1932 under the pressure of politics. The departure of old hands and the arrival of new personnel accompanied the shift in policy and objectives. The only new official at the cabinet level was Morgenthau at the Treasury, but the top level of secondary assistants was "almost wholly replaced with Frankfurter nominees. This was achieved through two of his energetic lieutenants—Corcoran and Cohen—who personify this Second New Deal as the Brains Trust personifies the First." With a great deal of embarrassment Roosevelt had ousted Peek and Johnson, "the Baruch twins," and the influence of Brandeis now dominated. "From this time on, collectivism and planning would have no place in Franklin's policy. Whatever he secretly believed, he had now publicly placed himself in the older progressive tradition, and there he would stay." [34] (Tugwell, too, favored the ouster of Peek and Johnson, whom he here placed with the collectivists; their version of publicly sponsored collectivism, however, relegated government to the role of junior partner.)

The implementation of the new policy decided upon in 1934 began with a bang in 1935. The President's State of the Union message of January 4, 1935, assumed recovery and stressed the themes of reform and social justice. [35] It outlined a program of three types of security: (1) the rescue of stranded populations through efficient use of natural resources and intelligent distribution of the means of livelihood; (2) security against the major hazards of life—unemployment, old age, illness, and physical handicaps; (3) housing. [36]

The year 1935 saw changes in relief policies. Local agencies, receiving federal assistance, took over the care of 1.5 million unemployables on relief rolls. The Works Progress Administration, under Harry Hopkins, superseded the FERA and all but a few normal public building operations of the PWA. The function of the WPA was to create a work program for the 3.5 million employables and to integrate it with the planned development of natural resources.[37] Executive orders under the act appropriating $4,000,000,000 for relief also established, in addition to the WPA, the National Youth Administration and the Resettlement Administration. The Rural Electrification Administration was another agency organized in 1935.

Major legislation in that year of intense activity included: the Social Security Act, the National Labor Relations (Wagner-Connery) Act, the Public Utility Holding Company ("death sentence") Act, the Motor Carrier Act, the Air Mail Act, the Banking Act of 1935, the Gold Clause Act, the act amending the TVA, and the Revenue ("share the wealth") Act of 1935. This listing, Tugwell contended, does not "convey the sense of energy radiating from the White House, but by inference the inquirer will know that leadership was largely responsible." [38]

Tugwell had got an inkling in early 1934 of the social philosophy which underlay these specific measures, and to which Roosevelt was yielding, when the President accepted unemployment insurance "at a time when both Hopkins and I were inclined to argue for the more flexible method of a permanent relief and public works system" ("A Third Economy," as Tugwell later called it in a speech in April, 1935). Roosevelt thought of social security as the "necessary floor" for the laissez faire to which he was reverting, and "he wanted it to be comprehensive. He wanted to assure everyone of a minimum; above this, the system could operate without more regulation than would assure fairness in competition. He still thought that a good deal of planning and even of directing would be possible, but it would not be formidable. It would consist of strategic pressures used at focal points where there was leverage. But this concept was still hazy in his mind." The first confirmation of this earlier clue came in June, 1934, when the President discussed the transition from the First to the Second New Deal with J. M. Keynes, the eminent British economist.[39]

Tugwell referred to the policies of the Second New Deal as "the kind of thing the old gentleman on the Supreme Court approved." The government could give relief, expand welfare measures, and undertake public works, but the President "must abandon his leaning toward collectivism. He must support free enterprise and keep the government out of it." The Court would approve any kind of spending, but "he would not be allowed to plan or to make any arrangements for social management." Despite his veneration of Brandeis, Roosevelt's first impulse, "so far as this was a warning from the Court," was to resist the judges, "adherents of an obsolete social philosophy." Unfortunately, Tugwell concluded, Roosevelt's Congressional allies were "even more convinced that the old ways were best. He gave in." [40]

Tugwell commented on several instances in which the President himself indicated the social philosophy of the Second New Deal. There was, of course, the message of January, 1935, on the State of the Union. It followed the decisive victory at the polls in 1934, despite which Roosevelt "had some worrying critical appraisals from those whose respect he valued," and "the first policies had not succeeded too well." He had done a great deal of thinking about all the major issues he would probably face. This reflection, together with the nature of the State of the Union message, led to the conclusion that the President had quite consciously rejected the First New Deal.[41]

Tugwell considered Roosevelt's famous "breathing spell" statement of September, 1935, a significant indication of acceptance of orthodox Progressivism. This statement was a response to a letter from Roy Howard, head of the Scripps-Howard newspapers. After the Revenue Act of 1935 became law on August 30, Howard wrote the President that business considered it a punitive rather than a revenue measure, that business badly needed a "breathing spell" during which "experimentation" would come to a halt. Roosevelt replied that the administration had substantially carried out its program, and that "the breathing spell of which you speak is here—very decidedly so." The President's letter included an explanation of the theory behind the tax bill which was, Tugwell noted, "an effective statement of the progressive attitude." [42]

Roosevelt said, in effect, that the Revenue Act, the Social Security Act, and the reforms of banking and utilities, taken together, "constituted a whole governmental economic policy. And it did. Bob La Follette, for instance, began to see now that it was emerging as an alternative to the collectivism in which he believed. I recall his talking to me about it in a disappointed way. He thought the new policy hopelessly insufficient. Insufficient or not, it was obviously what Franklin had determined on. And he felt, moreover, that he had now reached a safe position." Thus, Roosevelt "had fallen back on . . . what Justice Brandeis had said he could have." Collectivism, with the government as senior partner, was out. Reliance must be on "regulation to establish fairness among competing enterprises. Competing was a policy in itself. On the other hand, there was no limit to the regulating, provided that it was necessary to fairness, . . . there was no limit to the taxing power, and there could be no interference with spending for welfare purposes the funds raised by taxation." [43] (Nevertheless, Roosevelt would try to balance the budget for 1936-1937.)

Tugwell maintained that the President, in conforming to a three-pronged national economic policy—regulation, taxation, and spending—"was telling the unperceptive businessmen that their own theory had prevailed. They could have no objection, in principle, to what was now being done. It was all in conformity with the laissez faire they so strongly professed." There would be taxation of incomes to support purchasing power and welfare, and there would be regulation to assure effective competition. "But this was nothing to get excited about; it was not revolutionary. It was, indeed, in the most realistic sense, reactionary. It went back." Businessmen, Tugwell asserted, should have supported "the necessary corollary to their own theory." The reason that they did not accept the "breathing spell" as it was meant was because it was one-sided. Roosevelt had meant what he said in his speech to the bankers in October, 1934—"How could the representative of the state negotiate with business as an equal?" [44]

Finally, Roosevelt's "Rendezvous with Destiny" acceptance address at Philadelphia on June 27, 1936, showed that "he had indeed come all the way back to the orthodox progressive line. It was a speech Bryan might have made, or La Follette, or Uncle Ted in 1912. . . . But something was added now—an appeal to city folk in all the fast-growing industrial centers." The First New Deal was abandoned. Its triad of farmers, workers, and businessmen, working with the government so that each group might acquire strength, claim a fair share of national income, and obtain "a method and devices to make good its claims," now lost a member. Big businessmen replaced the financiers as public enemies, and, in a "most remarkable phase of the campaign," the New Deal embraced the hitherto neglected small enterpriser. This embrace logically resulted in Thurman Arnold's antitrust drive, which eventually faded out quietly in the face of industrial expansion for war purposes. [45]

In 1936 Roosevelt, feeling that the crisis had passed, determined on a balanced budget. The disastrous result of this fiscal orthodoxy was the recession of 1937-1938. In the campaign of 1936 the President once again failed to ask for a mandate, playing it safe despite the high probability of his victory. Nor did he interpret his plurality of 11,000,000 votes as a mandate for further pursuit of a New Deal for the American people. In 1937 Congress rejected Roosevelt's Supreme Court reform and his proposal to reorganize the executive department, but it did pass some important legislation, establishing the Farm Security Administration and the United States Housing Authority. In early 1938 Congress enacted the second Agricultural Adjustment Act.

Tugwell accepted the common judgment that the passage of the Fair Labor Standards Act or wages-and-hours law in May, 1938, marked the end of the New Deal, so far as legislation was concerned (the impact of previously enacted measures was, of course, continuing). Indeed, 1938 emerges from Tugwell's analysis as an interesting year. Besides (1) the end of the New Deal, other developments of 1938 included: (2) Roosevelt's clear comprehension by the end of the recession of the potentialities of Keynesian policies; [46] (3) Roosevelt's understanding, which had come to him gradually and through painful experience, of the need for social management rather than economic reform;[47] (4) Thurman Arnold's trustbusting; and (5) Roosevelt's decision that stopping Axis aggression had first priority, which meant that it was too late for him to apply his new knowledge. No longer possessing sufficient political capital to use in bargaining with the reactionary Southerners, who were so powerful in Congress and had never reconciled themselves to Roosevelt and the Hamiltonian New Deal, the President halted the New Deal as the price of adequate preparation for the coming world conflict. He traded domestic reform for national security.[48]

Even without additional New Deal legislation after 1938, there were previous gains which could still be lost. Thus, in *The Stricken Land* (1947) we find Tugwell deploring Congress' conduct during the war, when it killed off New Deal agencies one by one by perverting the legislative process into a struggle among private interests for advantage. Congress, incapable of truly "public" action, prevented executive action.[49] By 1942, Tugwell concluded, the reactionaries were dominant, and there was very little left of the New Deal.[50] The President provided the epitaph in 1944 when he stated his preference for the title of "Dr. Win-the-War" over that of "Dr. New Deal." Yet, while Tugwell often raised the question whether Roosevelt compromised too much by giving away more than he got in return, his over-all judgment of the President's response to the foreign threat was favorable. He judged that Roosevelt, in prodding a complacent, pacifistic people, represented by a recalcitrant Congress, into preparations for meeting the challenge they would soon face, exhibited his greatest statesmanship as he had never done in domestic management.[51]

In summarizing Tugwell's account of the two New Deals, we have had occasion to mention developments in almost every year from 1932 to 1944. To select one year as the key year in the transition is to oversimplify the process whereby the orthodox Progressives' persuading prevailed. This process, Tugwell noted, is unlikely ever to be revealed in any detail, although the results are plain enough.[52] Nevertheless, we may venture the opinion that in terms of Tugwell's institutional thought the indicatory year was 1935, when Roosevelt acquiesced in the Supreme Court's decision and never again espoused the concept of governmental responsibility for conjuncture. Roosevelt might have turned to collectivism in 1938 if the war had not intervened, or, as Tugwell thought, after the war if he had lived. We shall never really know. As it was, after 1935 the President did not attempt to make any basic changes in our social and economic institutions. Predictions, such as Frank Kent's, that Roosevelt's re-election, accompanied by an unco-operative attitude on the part of business, would bring about a drastic swing to the left and the end of the Constitution, courts, and individual liberty proved puerile.[53]

II

Although Tugwell commented at length on the shift from the First to the Second New Deal, he played a purely passive role in this transition. He stated in 1934 that he was "glad to sink my personal preferences in [Roosevelt's] program and to do all that I could to help in carrying it out." [54] Accordingly, he publicly accepted the Second New Deal, as in his political speech at Los Angeles in October, 1935. Privately, he told Harold Ickes in February, 1935, that the administration had done "all that it can be expected to do in the way of social advance . . . and the big interests have him [Roosevelt] stopped." [55] Tugwell, nevertheless, made an indirect but significant contribution to the Second New Deal. He was largely responsible for the appointment as Special Assistant to the Secretary of the Treasury in December, 1933, of Marriner S. Eccles, whom he had met in February, through Stuart Chase, and again in November, when he had invited Eccles to Washington to discuss means of combating renewed deflation.[56] Tugwell later referred to Eccles as the "unconscious Keynesian of the administration." [57] He always wrote with a note of pride about Eccles' accomplishments in banking and fiscal policy.

With the Banking Act of 1935 Eccles became Chairman of the Board of Governors of the Federal Reserve System. Tugwell gave this Act his enthusiastic approval, recalling that "Mr. Eccles, whose counsel this writer had strongly recommended to the President, was largely responsible for its shape. . . ." [58] Fiscal policy, Tugwell recollected, did not become "really effective for public purposes" until after Eccles became Chairman of the Federal Reserve Board. Tugwell regretted that the administration had not followed Eccles' advice in 1933 that it take immediate, sweeping measures for rebuilding purchasing power and for reorganizing the credit system. Instead, it followed the advice of "practical" business leaders. The result was confusion, delay in recovery, and additional years of suffering for the unemployed and their families. Eccles' remedy, Tugwell wrote, "had in the end to be accepted, even if in modified form, and with an admixture of noxious inflation." [59] Tugwell also lauded Eccles' stand against Morgenthau during the recession of 1937-1938. Eccles, from his "very powerful position . . . used all his influence to sustain the recovery he felt was now gaining momentum." [60]

In Tugwell's opinion it was Eccles who, with Harry Hopkins' assistance, finally brought about Roosevelt's conversion to Keynesianism. We say "finally" because Roosevelt's fiscal orthodoxy was formidable and yielded only very slowly to pressures which called for unorthodox policies. "Those who worked with him," Tugwell remembered, "were always aware of his longing for economy, a balanced budget, and a sound dollar. . . ." [61] Unbalanced budgets he "tended always to consider . . . evidences of incapacity. . . ." [62] Roosevelt did surrender to necessity, and "orthodox handling of the government's credit did finally, even if reluctantly, give way." [63] Harry Hopkins, Harold Ickes, and numerous other New Deal administrators, Tugwell commented, "could testify with what reluctance President Roosevelt was forced into deficit spending and how he resisted it at every step." [64] Thus, while Roosevelt "made many moves that only a believer in a compensated budget would make, . . . he had a secret longing to balance the national accounts." [65]

Tugwell recalled how "estimates of need were always pared down; this project or that was taken off the list; for a long time every project was regularly cut from 10 to 25 per cent." [66] Tugwell was familiar at first hand with the paring process. In June, 1935, at the suggestion of Acting Budget Director D. W. Bell, Roosevelt allotted the RA $7,000,000 rather than the $9,000,000 requested.[67] In a memorandum of July 15, 1935, Tugwell requested funds for the land program (USDA, USDI, RA) during the current fiscal year. Opposite each item appeared the President's penciled notations, calling for reductions of 1 to 5 million dollars.[68]

Tugwell listed several developments which reflected Roosevelt's fiscal orthodoxy. There was the famous Pittsburgh speech of October, 1932, in which the candidate promised to reduce the current cost of government operations by 25 per cent. He also promised recovery through the restoration of purchasing power, which meant spending. Looking back, Tugwell held that this inconsistency made the speech "irresponsible." [69] The appointment of Lewis Douglas as Director of the Budget was another conclusive indication of Roosevelt's fiscal views. Tugwell later attributed this choice to Douglas' "fervor for economy matched by only two other contemporary statesmen—Senator Byrd and Representative Taber." [70] Douglas helped draft the message calling for the Economy Act, which became law on March 20, 1933, and in enforcing this Act he demanded cuts which Tugwell considered unrealistic.[71] In early July Tugwell, accepting Eccles' analysis, objected to Douglas' contention that recovery to date justified holding back some of the public works appropriation.[72] Indeed, Tugwell and Douglas clashed bitterly as members of Ickes' Special Board for Public Works.

Roosevelt's request in 1933 for a public works appropriation of 3.3 billions (appropriated under the NIR Act) was slim in the opinion of Tugwell and Senators La Follette and Wagner.[73] According to Moley, Tugwell recommended an appropriation of 5 billions.[74] In March, 1934, Roosevelt, finding himself caught in what Tugwell afterward referred to as "this contradiction of his own making: . . . trying to reduce and expand simultaneously," adopted a novel budgetary concept in his message to Congress. He mentioned "ordinary" and "emergency" categories. This device neither pleased the spenders nor fooled the savers, but the President was resorting to camouflage, Tugwell recalled, in order to relieve himself of "the guilt he felt . . . over the budgetary deficit." [75]

In 1936 Roosevelt was determined to get the government out of the relief business, which he thought he could do without hurting recovery, and balance the budget. He had always undertaken relief measures, Tugwell noted in retrospect, "haltingly and not with claims of discovery and shouts of virtue." [76] He was "from the first prejudiced against relief as such . . . he was just as much convinced as Hoover had been that unearned income eroded character." [77] His real intention in 1936, Tugwell believed, was "to balance the budget even, if necessary, by liquidating WPA. He had hoped so much that he had refused to recognize signs of trouble and had waited too long when he did." [78]

The "trouble" was the recession of 1937-1938. The first signs of the slump were unmistakable in the summer of 1937, but Roosevelt hesitated to take the advice of La Follette, Wagner, Ickes, Wallace, Hopkins, and Eccles rather than that of Morgenthau and Jacob Viner. Eccles recalled, "As I came to know him . . . Roosevelt was at heart far more the budget-balancer . . . than some of his sharpest critics." [79] Finally, Hopkins and Eccles prevailed. On April 14, 1938, Roosevelt asked Congress to resume large-scale spending. "This was the first time—after four years—" Tugwell wrote in *The Democratic Roosevelt*, "that he appears to have accepted, not only theoretically, but as a matter of positive governmental virtue, the management of income and outgo as a regulator of the economy." In bringing about this conversion, Hopkins harped on soup lines, apple peddling, and despair, while Eccles argued in economic terms. Confirmation came in 1939, when the President telephoned Eccles to commend him on his performance in a radio debate with Byrd: "You made the problem so simple that even I was able to understand it." This remark, Tugwell noted, "was intended as persiflage. As the old saying goes, however, there may have been more truth in it than poetry." [80]

Tugwell's account in *The Democratic Roosevelt* of the President's conversion to fiscal unorthodoxy denies the assertion of some students that the conscious application of Keynes's ideas by the New Dealers began soon after his visit to the United States in June, 1934. Tugwell, who was host to Keynes in Washington, did not attribute any significance to this visit: "Someone remarked after he left that for the first time, after long talks with Keynes, the President knew what he was doing. But I was present at some of these interchanges, and Keynes' attitude was more that of an admiring observer than that of an instructor." [81] Tugwell laid the "Keynesian myth" to Roosevelt's behaving "in what later came to be called the Keynesian manner—that is to say, he kept feeling for a 'balanced economy rather than a balanced budget. . . .' " But the "explanation of what seems to students a causal relationship between Keynes' theories and Franklin's policies," Tugwell concluded, "is that Franklin lived in an intellectual climate created not by Keynes alone but by many others as well who were considering the same problems." Orthodoxy in economics and political science were gradually yielding to new findings. Although Roosevelt did not read the original literature, he was "sensitive to such changes . . . and his sensitivity had been increased by his explorations of the depression with the Brains Trust." [82]

Like Eccles and the President, Tugwell himself was an "unconscious Keynesian." Like Eccles, Tugwell approached the concept of compensatory fiscal policy in a positive way before the President did. In this matter Tugwell was two steps ahead of Hoover, a step ahead of Roosevelt, and a step behind Eccles. In 1932 Tugwell criticized Hoover for permitting the federal deficit to increase, but he did not oppose unbalancing the budget as such. He was more concerned that the measures which Hoover undertook through deficit financing would not produce the recovery and balanced budget which Hoover expected within two years. He maintained that Hoover's mistaken expectation of quick recovery resulted in grossly inadequate relief.[83] Tugwell also called for public works and unemployment compensation to revive purchasing power.[84] But in 1932 none of the Brain Trusters thought systematically of planned deficits as an instrument of recovery.

They warned Roosevelt that he was overestimating possible economies and underestimating the funds that would be needed for relief and public works, but, Tugwell recalled, "even to those who were more realistic . . . fiscal conservatism did not seem an impossible policy. To me, for instance, it seemed in order to pay for these expanded programs from increased taxation. I was against inflation." Inflation was, of course, in prospect, but that was something which "none of us was aware of at the time." By late January, 1933, however, "these were . . . very nearly moot questions." [85]

In the extreme crisis which faced the new administration in 1933 Tugwell began to move toward Keynesianism without being a Keynesian. When Eccles spoke to him in New York in February, 1933, he found Tugwell only generally versed in the ways government could use money, credit, and fiscal policy to promote economic revival.[86] Entries in Tugwell's diary in April, 1933, confirm Eccles' impression. Tugwell noted La Follette's fear that an expansionist program would not come soon enough after the conservatory measures involving banks, railroads, and corporations. "The answer," Tugwell added, "is government expenditures." He stated that "huge issues will be necessary; but something must be done about unemployment, and neither taxpayers nor creditors, if there is inflation, will like it." His general view was that "what this administration must concentrate on is a grand effort for the resumption of production in normal ways . . . along with the expansive fiscal policy which needs to accompany it." [87]

By the time the legislation of the Hundred Days had been enacted, Tugwell had decided that the fiscal year was not sacred, and that the fiscal period should be long enough to be typical over a cycle.[88] Believing that the administration's spending and taxing policies were constitutional,[89] he insisted in 1933 that Ickes' PWA was not spending money fast enough. He favored projects which would put many people to work quickly, expressing, in an argument with Frances Perkins which Ickes reported, a wide view of what constituted creating wealth.[90] He also advocated public works as a stimulant to heavy industry.

As for relief, in 1934 Tugwell called the FERA the "foremost of all the recovery agencies." [91] In 1935 he spoke of the FERA as significant because it "began at least a partial restoration of buying power." [92] He had in mind not only the direct recipients of relief funds but also the enterprisers whose customers they would be. Sixty to 70 per cent of work-relief funds, he later pointed out, went directly for wages.[93] (Another fundamental aspect of the administration's attitude toward private enterprise, Tugwell recollected, was its decision that relief would involve a lot of leaf-raking since the government was not going to take over production.[94] There was always, of course, the humanitarian reason for relief which appealed to the Progressives' concept of governmental responsibility. In 1935 Tugwell declared that the government had been niggardly rather than wasteful in denying the "ruthless doctrine of survival" and in protecting 10 million families from the poverty which "industrial ruthlessness" inflicted on guilty and innocent alike.[95])

Tugwell claimed subsequently that he suggested Roosevelt's division of expenditures into "ordinary" and "emergency" categories in March, 1934.[96] This was another indication of Tugwell's abandonment of the arbitrary fiscal year as the period of time within which the budget must be balanced. But the emergency did not make of Tugwell a reckless spender, as Frank Kent said he was.[97] He was aware, he recalled, that too many conventional public works could create a heavy burden of maintenance expenses, driving up tax rates and reducing communities' available income. A depression was a good time to build a lot of desirable public works, but "they should be the apex of a pyramid whose lower courses are supporting public enterprises." [98] This remark of 1947 was in line with Tugwell's attitude in 1935, when he stated that public works would have to be paid for and listed the returns accruing to the RFC, HOLC, FCA, RA, and PWA from the capital assets they had financed.[99]

Tugwell's original expectation that increased taxes would pay for increased emergency expenditures, currently, proved unrealistic. He gave it up, turning to the Keynesian-like scheme of achieving balance over a period longer than a fiscal year, but he did not think it through at first. In time, he commented in *The Democratic Roosevelt*, he learned that what goes up does not easily come down.[100] In this connection it should be recalled (see Chapter 9) that Tugwell advocated increased public expenditures merely as preferable among short-run alternatives for stimulating recovery. The "practical" course, he later wrote, led to stagnation, and "inflation was doubtless better than stagnation. If we could not have planned rebalancing, inflation was a possible recourse, although it was a dangerous national habit to acquire." [101] In this context he was quite certain about what he would recommend when the recession began in 1937. By that time he was no longer in Washington. He did have access to the White House, visiting the President in late December, 1937, and again in the middle of January, 1938.[102] But Tugwell did not "sell" Roosevelt his "golden theories" of deficit financing —as John T. Flynn said he did.[103] It was, however, his nominee Eccles whose advice the President finally took.

III

The First New Deal is often described as "pro-business." In this light Tugwell, at the height of his influence in 1933 and 1934, becomes "pro-business"—which, in terms of his institutional thought as he expressed it relevant to the NRA, he was. As Basil Rauch and William Miller have held, he was "pro-business" in the sense that he, Moley, and Berle looked upon business as the instrument of recovery.[104] But he did not contemplate a return to the business dominance of the 1920's, and he opposed certain policies—in banking, fiscal, and monetary matters—which "practical" businessmen urged on the President during the First New Deal.

This characterization of the Brain Trust and the NRA of the First New Deal as pro-business requires further qualification. While Moley, Berle, and Tugwell were all holists, emphasizing economic co-ordination rather than conflict, they had different concepts of the relationship between government and business. Professor A. M. Schlesinger, Jr., skillfully summarized these variations on a theme: "Moley thus thought essentially of a business-managed economy, with government serving as a clearinghouse of information and as a means of facilitating business co-ordination. Berle thought more of a government-business partnership, with government promulgating new social ideals and inspiring businessmen to a sense of ethical responsibility. Tugwell thought of a government-managed economy, with government making the key decisions and reorganizing economic institutions so as to produce a more fool-proof business order." [105]

These variations left plenty of room within a collectivistic framework for different approaches to the NRA. Tugwell recalled that to him the NRA represented "a holism congenial, fundamentally, only to big business." He also maintained that the titans of the industrial and financial world did not appreciate the fundamental nature of the NRA—or, to put it another way, they "hoped for more . . . they had no moderation. They proceeded to abuse their privileges and to subvert the intention of the organization. Self-interest became unintelligent and destructive. They were not only defeated at the polls, they were struck a heavy blow by the Supreme Court. That many of them were jubilant about the Court's decision does not affect this generalization. Many of them did not recognize NRA as their own because it was linked with the hated New Deal." [106]

The orthodox Progressivism of the Second New Deal was anti-business at one level—the stricter the regulations the less business liked it. In terms of Tugwell's collectivism, orthodox Progressivism was anti-business in its neglect of efficiency but pro-business since it was fundamentally an expression of laissez faire. In retrospect Tugwell wrote that the Second New Deal, "apparently so characteristically a season of battles with the financiers, was actually an attempt to find a rapprochement with business, but not one stultifying to government." [107] If the Second New Deal was inadequate as a total policy, it was acceptable to Tugwell as far as it went. The food and drug bill was a classic example of the attempt to make businessmen behave. Moreover, the spending policy of the Second New Deal was, in Tugwell's view, pro-business in that it provided loans to enterprises and purchasing power for their customers.

The decline of Tugwell's influence, such as it was, during the so-called anti-business Second New Deal would appear to reinforce the obvious inference, just mentioned, about the pro-business First New Deal, but, again, qualification is called for. During the high-spending Second New Deal we find Tugwell eventually arriving at a roughly Keynesian position, but *only after he had given up hope of seeing implementation of collectivism*. He had, of course, advocated huge expenditures for relief and public works as early as 1932. This was partly based on pragmatism, partly on humanitarianism. It also reflected the influence on Tugwell of the underconsumptionist views of John A. Hobson rather than Keynes.[108] Later, Tugwell came to a fuller recognition of the possibilities in fiscal policy for compensatory action, and he recommended Marriner S. Eccles to the President. But even then Tugwell, as an institutionalist, disapproved of deficit financing as a permanent policy of stabilization. Besides, Eccles was the kind of a man the President was looking for during the evolvement of a trend rooted in pragmatic political and economic developments—not in Tugwell's policy preferences.

If the use of the "pro-business" and "anti-business" labels produces confusion, this complexity suggests, in turn, a simple conclusion about Tugwell. While he occasionally referred to businessmen as "Tories" and "poor sports," his emphasis on aid at the top as well as the bottom of the economy indicates that as a holistic thinker he took an impersonal view of business and its place in the scheme of things. Perhaps we can clarify a good deal of the confusion among American liberals by deriving from Tugwell's account of the two New Deals this summary of the attitudes of the opposing groups:

Big Business

favored bigness but opposed the NRA when business was not the senior partner.

opposed regulatory Progressivism when regulations were too strict.

The collectivistic Progressives

favored bigness, preaching the gospel of efficiency, but they opposed the NRA when business was the senior partner.

opposed regulatory Progressivism as a total policy.

The atomistic Progressives

opposed bigness and the NRA.

favored regulatory Progressivism but opposed business as the maker of the rules.

Doctrinally, the atomistic Progressives called for the eradication of bigness, and big business had more in common with the collectivistic Progressives. Practically, the antitrust laws never really threatened bigness, and big business was both more familiar and more comfortable with its fight with the atomistic regulators than with its conflict with the collectivists over seniority in a partnership. Thus, Tugwell could say that with the Second New Deal business' "own theory had prevailed."

This was not easy to see amid the controversy of the Second New Deal, especially since economic arguments in America, as Professor J. K. Galbraith has shown, are characterized by sound and fury in excess of substance.[109] And every historian who deals with conflicts in American history may obscure the assumed rules of the joust and the point, made by a British observer, that in the face of conflict the "harmonies, the continuities, or the sheer weight of popular indifference may be equally important."[110] In this context, conflict, as Tugwell maintained, can be a good thing. Its absence "inevitably means that progress is made more difficult; and overlong resting in the status quo may result in an accumulation of maladjustments and wrongs whose correction may sometime be forced in a near-revolutionary overturn. Such an overturn occurred in 1932, for instance, after three reactionary Republican administrations." [111] Even opponents of the New Deal—First and/or Second—will concede that amid the heat of controversy in the 1930's some light was shed on our economic problems in a democratic debate.

Part IV
Professor on the Potomac

———◆◆———

12. Intellectual Approaches to Crisis

We have reached that point in Tugwell's career at which he was about to move from campus to capital as an appointee of the administration which Americans had elected to govern them in crisis. We have also noted that his general ideology eventually succumbed to a rival doctrine. Thus, his participation in the New Deal from March 4, 1933, through December 31, 1936, was subject to this limitation, and he suppressed his personal policy preferences to contribute what he could in the emergency. As a preface to the consideration of his contribution, this chapter summarizes some of the ideas—which, with the exception of the "concert of interests" concept, were somewhat more specific than his general holistic ideology but less precise than an administrator's reasoning—that he brought to bear on the bleak conditions of the early 1930's.

I

In early 1932 Tugwell remarked that since the autumn of 1931 there had been a taint of panic in the air as more and more people concluded that the capitalistic structure was collapsing.[1] He himself was exasperated at the time he made this remark. He described the capitalistic world as a prostrate one in which the United States commanded no confidence.[2] He noted in retrospect that if his criticism of the Hoover administration "now seems a little bitter, a little overurgent, it is to be remembered how far our economy had then sunk and how weak and ineffective were the measures with which Mr. Hoover hoped to defeat depression."[3]

Tugwell was in a bitter frame of mind when he was taken into the Brain Trust in March, 1932. Looking back, he thought it "accidental that the furious resentment which was eating me in that third depression spring should, for an instant, have appealed to the dramatist in Ray Moley . . . that it should have survived the scrutiny of Messrs. Rosenman and O'Connor . . . that the Governor should have found the energies useful which that resentment generated." As the Brain Trust began its work, pressures from unemployment and deflation mounted visibly from week to week. Hoover's policies were discredited, while the economy made protesting noises because there was sand in its gear box. "But high above these sounds there had begun to rise frightened wails from the self-appointed chiefs of finance and industry." [4]

By the fall of 1932 panic was sweeping across the land. After the election Congress was in chaos. The nation was confused and despairing. Normally self-reliant people were desperate. "It is part of the kindness of mere time," Tugwell later commented, "that we are unable to remember the worst of our besetting terrors. There was a kind of crowding hysteria in the air . . . no one could escape . . . its awful prevalence." [5] By March, 1933, the American people were ready and eager for new departures in governmental action. In the 1920's, Tugwell recalled, publicity, ceremony, preaching, ballyhoo in the press, descriptions in textbooks, and wishful thinking had concealed the realities of the economic system. "Americans had lived too long in a dream world. Even those who had created it had forgot that it was all a fairy story." As Roosevelt took office, the people "could not comprehend . . . a strange, a crazy, a frightening world which had been exposed by the economic earthquake of 1929 . . . nothing was as it seemed to be." [6]

Bewildered as they were, Americans awoke from their dream with a vengeance. Our institutions, Tugwell stated in 1935, had affronted human dignity, provoking an invincible determination—undeterred by reverence for vested property rights or concern about consistency in policy —to get things straightened out.[7] Americans, he later wrote, usually allowed their representatives to make policy without a mandate or to have no policy—"unless that neglect suddenly caused us inconvenience or sacrifice, when we instantly rose against it, no matter what the consequences. . . ." [8] But as soon as the crisis was over, Tugwell remembered, there was a tendency on the part of both Democrats and Republicans to "minimize the discredit into which the system had then fallen. . . ." [9] By 1934 Tugwell's critics were condemning him for some of the statements he had made in 1931. In the Capitol Senator Burton K. Wheeler came to his defense, declaring that in 1931 "many in this room" wondered whether our government would survive.[10]

One of the themes in Tugwell's writings which indicates how critical he considered the situation in the early 1930's is the *prevention of revolution*. In 1947 he noted that "Roosevelt had inherited what was nearly a Civil War too from the intransigent Mr. Hoover; radicals and reactionaries were eager to be at each other's throats," and he hailed the PWA, FERA, and WPA as "noble institutions—at least one half of a program which saved the nation from revolution." [11] His contemporary remarks were just as urgent.

In early 1932 Tugwell warned that Hoover's policy of aid at the top was "more than poor sportsmanship; it is shortsighted. Such ruthless exploitation, such ungenerous grasping, may finally engender revolutionary attitudes." [12] About a year later, in the concluding passages of *The Industrial Discipline,* he insisted that we had been "unconsciously creating a situation in which the revolutionary tactic might be resorted to successfully." So long as we did not devise ways of freeing the potentialities of our techniques, the "contrast between what we are and what we might be will lodge itself firmly in every worker's mind," suggesting that control be taken away from people who could not produce a better society from the excellent materials at their disposal. There was no use in pointing out difficulties because "there are always those who have alternative suggestions for meeting those difficulties." It was both possible and necessary to experiment at once "before it is too late. Otherwise, we are surely committed to revolution." [13]

During his stay in Washington, Tugwell continually referred to the averting of revolution in 1933 and the necessity of preventing a recurrence of such an emergency. In April, 1934, he commented that the New Deal was inevitable since people would not starve in the presence of abundance; the only choice before Americans was whether the revolution was to be violent or orderly and legal.[14] In May, 1934, he stated that we continuously faced the challenge of enlarging the capacity of our social and economic system to absorb young people "without political violence, social demoralization, or economic chaos." [15] In June, 1934, in a statement which he prepared for the Senate Agriculture Committee's hearings on his promotion to Undersecretary, he called the Old Guard, "in their opposition to achievable reform while it is possible, . . . the real friends of violent revolution." [16]

In a speech in April, 1935, Tugwell remarked on the explosive implications of unemployment for both domestic and foreign affairs. Unemployment sardonically represented human resources which, if unused, "will demand expression and that expression will invariably take the form which history shows is characteristic of societies which lack the intelligence to anticipate revolution by reform and imperialism by recovery." [17] In October, 1935, Tugwell, speaking frankly as a political partisan before the Democratic State Central Committee in Los Angeles, declared, "Another Harding, another Coolidge, another Hoover entrusted with leadership now, would set us back as many decades as we were set back before—and at the end of it there might not be another genius to avert a revolution." [18]

II

Nations have, of course, lived through revolutions. In Tugwell's opinion there was the deeper problem of *survival* itself. He was not really worried about a revolution after Roosevelt's first term got under way, although after the hectic first "Hundred Days" there was still a lot to do. He was concerned that the need to formulate remedial measures in the emergency might result in a neglect of thinking in long-run terms about the prevention of crises in the future.

Tugwell himself continued, in the midst of his administrative activities, to think in a long-run context. In the USDA he stressed the need for a permanent land-use program as an effective way of attacking the farm problem. He also emphasized the implications of destructive use of the land for survival. After he left Washington, he dwelt in several articles on the subject of survival at some length and with a certain urgency. He wondered whether the institutional changes he considered necessary "may be brought about within the time still allowable." He wondered because the democratic process depended on education, meaning persuasion, which in turn depended "to an extent which is appalling on the engaging of an interest which has been able to accumulate wealth and so carry on an expensive propaganda." [19]

In his post-government days Tugwell supplemented his consideration of institutional change in political economy by studying ecology. This was a natural outgrowth of his interest in agriculture, which so vividly demonstrated the "oneness of man and nature." He presented ecological problems in terms of a drama still in progress—the conflict between man's creative and destructive abilities. Man's freedom, his power to make his own decisions, was "identified with his far destiny." But it had limitations. "The power to choose is not given with the provision that choosing wrong may be done without penalty." Tugwell averred that "these issues led to other than individual questions too." If survival were to be assured, "its conditions have got to be set in terms which do not refer to individual ambitions. . . ." If man were to avoid destruction, he had to keep in mind that the "oneness of man and nature" was everlasting. Defiance or neglect of this fact inevitably brought penalty. "Often these costs were hidden or deferred but never forgiven or mitigated." Man could not now make survival certain by going back, but "only by going forward, solving one technological problem after another. . . ." [20]

III

Economic fatalism was repugnant to Tugwell, whose training stressed experimentation in institutional adjustment. His views were irreconcilable with the Marxist assumption that men could not correct the defects of capitalism and the laissez faire postulate that these flaws were self-correcting. He insisted that between these extremes, and within their traditional democratic system, Americans could consciously create an institutional foundation supporting an economy of stability and plenty. In 1928 Tugwell asserted that Americans habitually courted disaster by letting things drift until it was too late. They refused to follow a constructive course, neglecting to control events of the greatest public significance in order to prevent eventual collapse.[21] As a New Dealer he continued to express his *anti-deterministic views*, partly because he believed that Americans were prone to take an interest in institutional change only in times of distress.

In April, 1934, Tugwell published an article with the anti-deterministic title "America Takes Hold of Its Destiny." In the same month he told students at Dartmouth College that Americans did not take tragedy lying down, which was "right—our purpose is . . . set toward its circumvention."[22] In May, 1934, he rejected the contention that periodic depressions were outbreaks of bad luck.[23] In August, 1934, in an address at Clemson College, he declared that the South, using democratic processes and federal agencies, had shown that we could "make our economic kings our servants, whether these kings be called King Cotton, the Gold Standard, Rugged Individualism, or a Protective Tariff."[24] In June, 1935, Tugwell assured the graduating class at the University of New Mexico that they could enjoy modern, flexible, efficient institutions, "turned to the uses of liberty, democracy, and good living," but "you cannot have these things by default. You will have to create them . . . to protect and nurse them and perhaps to recreate them as conditions change again and again."[25]

Tugwell's anti-deterministic statements after he left Washington were somewhat more general and philosophic. He observed that only "once in a while is something really determinative injected into human affairs—although perhaps not often."[26] Nevertheless, it was perhaps illogical to suppose that a man-made world could be managed by men with tolerable efficiency. But the need to do so was overriding. It was vital that "the logic of creation and management should run within the same limits." If one set of men continually created problems, and another set had to face their consequences, "the situation may well get out of hand."[27] In the end, difficulties did not discourage Tugwell. As an institutionalist he assumed that social arrangements, being works of man, could "be made, within the resources at disposal, in conformance with an objective." [28]

IV

Among those who believed that men could act to determine their fate there were significant differences. Some expected to reform and rebuild society more thoroughly and more quickly than others. They were young, eager, idealistic, and doctrinaire. Many of them found jobs in the New Deal in 1933. When the press made a distinction between practical and idealistic reformers, it placed Tugwell among the latter despite his *aversion to crack-pot do-goodism.*

It is true that Tugwell was young (forty-two on July 10, 1933), but he was neither as young as he looked nor as young as many people thought he was. Nor is there necessarily a correlation between age and ability to deal with social problems. Moreover, while most New Deal reformers came from urban backgrounds and the long fight against municipal corruption—Moley, Ickes, Hopkins, Frances Perkins, Jerome Frank, Frederick Delano, Charles Merriam, Louis Brownlow, Leonard White, Frederick Howe, Morris Cooke, and Henry Hunt, to name a few —agricultural relief required the services of Wallace, Morgenthau, George N. Peek, Chester Davis, Mordecai Ezekiel, Louis Bean, William Myers, and Tugwell.[29] It was inaccurate to classify Tugwell with the urbanites—young militants or long-time Progressives. Moley, who noted that there were New Dealers "who represent the two great truths . . . an ideal Truth and a practical Truth, Truth like a wild swan and Truth like a faithful dog," did not do so. He attributed to Tugwell three and a half years in the capital of "courageous and intelligent thinking." [30]

In 1926 Tugwell censured "all or nothing" idealists.[31] During the campaign of 1932 he noted that into Roosevelt's headquarters poured hundreds of suggestions from well-meaning people—little formulae which their authors thought would "solve the world's difficulties." [32] In 1934 he admonished, "Workers for the New Deal are too often obsessed with some thirty-day panacea for solving everything without the necessity of thought." [33] In 1935 he cautioned against "casual proposals to fix things up during the next convenient weekend." [34] In *The Democratic Roosevelt* he recalled that Mrs. Roosevelt evidenced a power of growth when she "came to understand finally how little good it was possible to do individually and directly, and how necessary it was to sublimate the philanthropic impulses into social programs and permanent systems." [35] Thus, while he deprecated doctrinaire idealists, Tugwell did not exclude emotion from the motivation of policy makers whose aim was to promote the general welfare. He simply pointed out that emotion would be self-defeating if it resulted in neglect of hard thinking. He protested in his memoir that in attributing to him an affinity for crack-pot do-goodism, the press linked him with something that was foreign to his nature.

V

While Tugwell rejected thirty-day panaceas, he conceded that relief measures would be inefficient. They were, he maintained, made necessary by an institutional structure that was inefficient to begin with. It produced crises which called for immediate action, leaving little time for careful, long-range planning. In fact, as in agriculture, an emergency program was one thing, reconstructive planning something else. Tugwell underlined this difference, stressing *the stop-gap nature of relief.*

Tugwell asserted in his later writings that "the adequacy of institutions ought not to be judged by the way crises are met, but rather by the number there are," [36] and he held that "sound industrial and commercial life is better than . . . efficient and adequate relief." [37] As a New Dealer he had asserted that relief was neither efficient nor adquate because it was difficult to meet crises after they had arisen. In an emergency it was necessary to administer relief under the "strain of attempting to do in a hurry what should have been done forty years ago"—establish security against the various risks of society such as unemployment, illness, and old age.[38]

Certainly, Tugwell observed in a speech in 1934, relief was necessary —"we have had . . . to accept conditions as they were and do first things first"—but it hardly touched on the real problem. Unfortunately, the community was inclined to minister to charity rather than to replace it with rehabilitation. Public opinion had not encouraged going very far beyond relief in dealing with the "fundamental economic and sociological problems set us by the breakdown of the Old Order." Relief without reconstruction was not only an inadequate policy with respect to those whom it affected directly, but it was also a poor policy from the standpoint of society as a whole. Tugwell declared that we could not "forever go on providing subsistence to the idle at government expense. This will never be more than subsistence and it will kill the thing . . . we are trying to foster"—self-development of citizens, each of whom would play his proportionate economic role.[39]

Tugwell's view on relief was, in short, that an ounce of prevention was worth a pound of cure. It was our responsibility to solve problems by planning not to have them. We had to break what he considered a vicious circle. The unco-ordinated enterprises that brought on crises also determined the way in which crises were met, preventing institutional changes for the promotion of the general welfare. We had a choice, he concluded in his 1934 address, between giving people pittances as charity and giving them access to income they have earned as a right.[40]

VI

Thus, Tugwell blamed a faulty institutional structure for crises. He also had some caustic words for the businessmen who engaged in the harmful practices which prevailed within the loose structure. He escaped from this seeming contradiction when he attributed immorality ultimately to institutions, not individuals. As a social scientist he had an *impersonal attitude toward business*. In an article of 1941 he chided historians for their "condemnation of nineteenth-century industrialists . . . on humanitarian rather than economic grounds." [41]

Tugwell asserted that business' expropriation of governmental powers and its speculative, predatory practices were inevitable in an uncoordinated economy. Individual enterprisers were not concerned with the general interest, he commented in 1939, because "laissez faire is so disconnected, and causes and effects . . . are so apparently unrelated that management of affairs without reference to the 'state of the industrial arts' is possible. Of course it is not"; sooner or later penalties had to be paid, although often not by the people who brought them on.[42] It was the "nature of contemporary institutions," he wrote in 1953, which "forced on the sycophants and apologists they supported so generously . . . the praise of piracy, of miserliness, and of cunning." [43]

These later comments were in accord with Tugwell's remark in 1934 that "for all this I would not have you think that I impute blame to anyone." [44] In fact, he blamed everyone. Elaborating on this question of general guilt in a later article in which he reviewed American economic development during the century ending in 1929, he noted that very few Americans thought that high living standards "had been won in spite of, rather than because of, the system of laissez faire." They howled down the few doubters and, in a "new era," accepted "things incredibly against common sense"—wild speculation and ravaging of natural resources. Not everyone participated, but "certainly the orgy had at least been condoned." Similarly, business' encroachment on government was done more or less with general consent. Future generations could not complain against any special group. What had happened to the government and the land at the hands of exploiters had been the responsibility of all.[45]

In absolving individuals of responsibility for economic collapse and in recommending institutional changes, Tugwell knowingly tied the Gordian knot which institutionalists must untie. He stated in 1935 that our enemies were not individuals so much as they are institutions,[46] but it was individuals, after all, who supported institutions. Changes in institutions would have to stem from changes in individuals' attitudes and conduct. That the latter would not change easily Tugwell was well aware. He assumed that those who had thrived under old institutions would, in normal human fashion, accept some nonfundamental reforms and expect a quick revival of the good old days. They were, he wrote in 1934, "the sincere group of willful beneficiaries of the Old Order, who—in the words of a gifted Englishman—sat 'waiting for the twentieth century to blow over.'"[47]

But, Tugwell believed, education and crisis would eventually enable bold, intelligent leadership to gain majority consent to needed institutional changes. And, like Simon Nelson Patten, he presupposed that the changes themselves would at first sublimate, then eradicate, the customary exploitative activities and attitudes of the recalcitrant minority. If, as he said in 1934, it was "the system which makes us behave in these ways,"[48] it would be a new system which would make us behave in new ways. Changes in behavior would result partly from compulsion—the elimination of opportunities for profits for the unscrupulous—and partly from habituation in a new ethical atmosphere. Then, as he had declared in 1933, "from the point of view of the public the old sentiment of fear of big business will become unnecessary."[49]

VII

Tugwell's attitude toward business fitted in with his concept of the economy as a "concert of interests." Roosevelt used this phrase in a campaign speech at St. Paul on April 18, 1932, and he used it many times after that. Tugwell had invented it to represent his and Berle's collectivism as opposed to the atomism of the Brandeis school. He recalled his intention to "convey the necessity for encompassing in a system, subject to control, all the forces and functions of our society, each contributing its due part."[50] A "concert of interests" excluded class warfare, rejected Adam Smith's idea that the greatest total good derived from nonco-operating individuals, and connoted the opposite of the one-thing-at-a-time reasoning of classical economics. Tugwell, of course, stressed the concept of a "concert of interests" before he hit upon its identifying label. In the 1920's he wrote about the interdependence of economic activities, indicating the danger which weak spots held for other sectors. In early 1932 he criticized Hoover for failing to work for balanced relationships between prices, consumer purchasing power, and security values.

Tugwell recalled that when he first met Roosevelt in early 1932, he found the Governor "a man of much information . . . but he was weak on relations, on the conjunctural, on the joining together of forces and processes, especially in the national economy." Such knowledge, which could suggest national solutions to national problems, was not used by governors. Roosevelt acquired it during the campaign. By March 4, 1933, he was definitely not "one of those who regard the fortunes of the nation as the simple sum of the fortunes of its groups." He had learned the lesson that was the "first door which opens outward toward genuine national policy." [51]

In Washington, Tugwell disagreed with the parochially minded bureaucrats of the USDA. In his view agriculture was linked up to the whole economic system. Thus, when Tugwell referred to balance in agriculture —between producer, processor, distributor, and consumer—he inevitably applied this concept to the relationship between agriculture and industry as well. And he naturally advocated balance within industry, stating in 1933 that no one of the three parties in industry—the consumer, labor, and the management-owner group—should be in a position to dominate another.[52] In short, he emphasized the interrelatedness of all parts of our complex economy. Any upset of the delicate balance of price and income relationships would bring hardship to rural and urban populations alike.

Americans had to recognize that balance was necessary before they would support attempts to achieve it. Tugwell tried to promote such recognition, affirming in 1935 that the broad principle upon which we could find our common ground was the growing consciousness of joint interest. Injury to one in the form of poverty or unemployment was the concern of all. The incidence of these misfortunes did not depend on the faults or merits of individuals. No one was immune from spreading unemployment and economic paralysis.[53] Balance, he had asserted in 1933, would provide full employment and economic expansion, for it was not to be "attained in a static sense, with an absence of progress." It would be necessary continuously to improve methods and quality of production in order constantly to raise the standard of living and give Americans greater leisure.[54]

In retrospect Tugwell concluded that New Deal measures had done no more than imply the concept of a balanced whole. Roosevelt, as a politician, had to convey to many groups the "feeling of solicitude and even favoritism," but he also had to struggle against the pressures from each which might upset the necessary balance among them all. His greatest efforts were not directed toward relief for groups or classes; they "centered rather in one policy which would be national." NRA, AAA, money and budget management, relief, and taxation were intended to be contributory to this policy. Roosevelt was not highly sophisticated in these matters, and he had to deal with a nation which was even less so. In struggling for a policy which would "include and subdue" the various interests, he found that each group and region expected favors, being unwilling to moderate its demands even for the sake of achieving balance.[55]

In an article published in 1949, Tugwell scolded the farmers as an interest group.[56] He explained that for emergency purposes the authors of AAA had thought of the economy as a dichotomy, dividing income into agricultural and industrial and attempting to reduce farm production so as to bring its prices into parity with industrial prices ("parity" meant a ratio of exchangeability between the two kinds of goods comparable to that which had held in the period 1909-1914). The authors of AAA hoped that the economy, when rearticulated, would go forward as a whole. There was general improvement, but it was not due to balance. "The carefully conceived program, as is so often true, fell into bargaining among economic groups." Congress, lacking conviction and criteria in this matter, "responded to the strongest and most immediate pressure" regardless of long-range effects. Business' objections to AAA were especially ironic—farmers, after all, had learned from industry the technique of price maintenance through cutting production. The result was "something far from well calculated to achieve the effect. But it was something." AAA, together with currency devaluation, farmers' and consumers' subsidies, work relief, and a two-price system (with some dumping abroad), achieved a tolerable situation.

Although the farmers' condition had improved, especially with the war, Tugwell saw no reason to give up the quest for balance. He pointed out that the wartime market depended significantly upon inflation. It was still necessary to assure the fundamental soundness of agriculture so that it would not again be a critical weak spot. But, if farmers had suffered disadvantages in the past, they were at fault when they wanted everything else regulated in their interest. "Parity implied a condition of well being for others than farmers." They, too, for their own interest, had to develop a concept of the general interest and play their role in "perfecting machinery for maintaining the integrity of all the parts of a balanced whole." If the farmers of the 1940's did not appreciate this lecture, they had to concede that it came from one of their staunchest supporters of the 1920's and 1930's. Perhaps they had forgotten, or had never learned, that Tugwell advocated the general interest above all.

13. The National Industrial Recovery Act and the NRA: 1933-1935

The National Industrial Recovery Act has been the subject of a vast amount of study and comment. Its novelty, scope, and complexity make this attention understandable. Putting Tugwell in the center of a discussion of this legislation involves unavoidable distortion, but what he had to do with it and what he had to say about it merit consideration.

I

The novelty of the National Recovery Administration, created under Title I of the NIR Act (Title II authorized public works), was in its enactment. There was nothing new about the ideas behind it. For years business had desired to eliminate destructive competition through self-government under a relaxation of the antitrust laws. Labor had wanted higher wages, shorter hours, and, to achieve them, guaranteed rights of organization and collective bargaining. Others, like Tugwell and Moley, had a more general view, following Van Hise's concept of "concentration and control"—legalization of the invincible combination movement and the establishment of social controls to protect the general interest. Tugwell wrote in greater detail about implementation and advocated more government intervention than Moley did.

Reviewing the background of the NRA in *The Democratic Roosevelt*, Tugwell classified business' aspirations as negative and positive. On the negative side was the withdrawal of competitive influence from areas where competition was unprofitable and gave an advantage to unscrupulous exploiters of labor and consumers—the elimination of "unfair practices." On the positive side were additional advantages in forming trade associations: "exchanging information concerning standards, methods for attaining efficiency, the general conditions governing manufacture and sale, statistics covering the industry, and so on." Tugwell noted that the NRA, looked at as a way of giving industry responsibility for establishing standards of decent social behavior and for eliminating the "nonconforming few who persisted in 'unfairness,'" was a logical extension of the trade-association development which Secretary of Commerce Hoover had sponsored.[1]

Regarding the trade associations' positive advantages in exchanging information, Tugwell remarked that they did not violate the antitrust acts, but "they did easily merge into prohibited practices, such as division of markets and agreements about prices."[2] His institutional

154

thought contemplated the legalization of some of these prohibited practices—provided the public interest were represented and protected. In
1933, in *The Industrial Discipline,* Tugwell described a tentative, experimental mechanism for industrial co-ordination. It would comprise
an Integration Association for each industry and a central Industrial
Integration Board. The central Board would co-ordinate the various
industries' plans and reconcile them with a general plan submitted by
the government's representatives (from the controlling public agency)
on the central Board. Thus, plans respecting production, prices, division
of markets, working conditions, wages, allocation of capital, security
issues, and the like would evolve from bottom-up and top-down recommendations. Possibly the associations themselves could largely manage
these matters, but there would definitely need to be a public advocate
in two areas: allocation of capital and regulation of prices. In instances
of recalcitrance the controlling agency would be able to invoke appropriate sanctions—publicity, fines, and expulsion.[3]

Tugwell recalled the New Dealers' thought that the NRA "at best . . .
might lead to industry planning—that is, the estimation of needs and
the adjustment to them of investment; this in turn would provide a
basis for national planning, thus reducing waste, raising standards, and
increasing real incomes."[4] Business leaders, too, such as Henry I. Harriman and Gerard Swope, advocated industrial co-ordination and the
adjustment of production goals to estimated needs. This, they assumed, would bring forth the necessary investment. "They did not,"
Tugwell noted, "stress the reverse, that other investments ought to be
prohibited, but that was inherent in their argument."[5] This comment
indicates that Tugwell's holistic views were broader in scope than the
ideas of the business community.

The NIR Act, as it turned out, dealt largely with the elimination of
"unfair practices." What was done in the NRA in the area of positive
advantages which "easily merge into prohibited practices" was done
privately, for the benefit of private interests. Private price-fixing, in
particular, became a target for critics of the NRA. The NIR Act did not
provide for outright price-fixing, but it allowed minimum price determinations, cost protection, loss leader control, emergency price-fixing, and
the provision of waiting periods in open-price systems. Minimum price
determinations probably had the most far-reaching effect—not because
of the number of cases in which they were applied, but because of the
pressure brought to bear in that direction.[6]

In *The Democratic Roosevelt* Tugwell commented on labor's interest
in the NIR Act as well as on the attitudes of business and the former
Brain Trusters. He referred to the labor people as "hovering about and
confusing the issues . . . interested only in establishing once and for

all" collective bargaining, minimum wages, and maximum hours. In retrospect he thought it might have been better to pass separate labor legislation and to "keep the Recovery Act to a narrower scope. But that may have been politically impossible. Franklin thought so at the time." [7] (After the Supreme Court invalidated the NIR Act on May 27, 1935, the famous Section 7A, guaranteeing the right of collective bargaining, was restated in the National Labor Relations Act of July 5, 1935; and the wages and hours provisions of the NRA fair-practices codes for the various industries were embodied in the Fair Labor Standards Act of June 25, 1938.)

The different points of view were apparent in the formulation of the NIR Act. This task, Tugwell recalled, required the reconciliation of the ideas of those who were interested in labor's demands, those business-men who "wanted mostly to escape the restrictions of the antitrust acts," and those who were "concerned to see a new start made in the relations of government and industry, substituting partnership for trust-busting." [8] The latter group included—besides Moley, Berle, Tugwell, and others—Hugh Johnson, who was a latecomer to the Brain Trust in 1932. Johnson's experience in the War Industries Board of World War I under his idol Bernard Baruch proved pertinent to the NRA.

Before we turn to the formulation of the NIR Act, let us consider Tugwell's explanation in *The Democratic Roosevelt* of the views of the President who supervised this activity. An argument over ways of eliminating unfair practices in business had been going on, Tugwell observed, for more than half a century. Roosevelt had acquired definite ideas on the subject. He tended to think in terms of government in-terference "only in the area beyond the reach of voluntary action"—wage minima, child labor, labeling of goods. Voluntary organizations would eliminate other unfair practices. The government, besides setting stand-ards for wages and so on, could legitimize these voluntary organizations. Progressives "of the old sort" objected, maintaining that trade associations so legitimized would engage in monopolistic practices with regard to markets, production, and prices. The Progressives would give the Federal Trade Commission wider powers to establish standards, "but otherwise vigorously enforce free competition in the interest of fair trading." [9]

But "legitimize" came to mean more to Roosevelt than sponsorship. To go back some years, in a "cloudy" speech in Troy, New York, in 1912 he referred to co-operation in industry rather than competition as the means of promoting the "liberty of the community." Thus, at this early stage of his public career, he expressed, however vaguely, disillu-sionment about competition as an organizing principle. In 1912 he was still "searching for a way to state a more positive policy" than trust-busting.[10] In the years 1922-1928 Roosevelt was head of the Construc-

tion Council, one of the trade associations which "belonged to an attitude or approach that stood in complete contrast to trustbusting." Tugwell called this experience one of Roosevelt's significant contacts with
the economic system. It "taught him that purely voluntary self-regulation
did not work," and it clearly foreshadowed the policy embodied in the
NRA—"partnership with industry." This phrase was "obviously intended
to soften the fact of government intervention." [11]

In early 1932 the Brain Trust brought to Roosevelt the concept of a
"concert of interests"—"one idea . . . which he could never quite let
go." It was translated into legal language as "parity," "adjustment," and
"codes of fair practice." [12] In September, 1932, in his famous San Francisco speech, he stated that "business men everywhere are asking for
a form of organization which will bring the scheme of things into balance. . . ." [13] Thus, on the verge of the presidency, Roosevelt was
ready to entertain suggestions for industrial co-ordination.

The formulation of the NIR Act was a kind of organized confusion.
Legislators, economists, businessmen, and labor people—through their
organizations and individually—worked on schemes for industrial co-ordination and recovery. In early 1933 literally dozens of plans were
available. In Washington there were two important study groups at first.
Senator Wagner was the central figure in one, Assistant Secretary of
Commerce John Dickinson in the other. Tugwell had contacts with
both groups. Jerome Frank brought Tugwell's ideas to Dickinson.[14] Leon
Keyserling, a Harvard Law School graduate whom Tugwell brought to
Washington in March, became Wagner's legislative assistant.[15] This kind
of overlapping was common in the capital, and the Wagner and Dickinson
groups inevitably merged.

As late as April 4, 1933, Roosevelt and Moley agreed that government
and business thinking had not yet sufficiently crystallized to justify any
further moves at that time. The passage by the Senate on April 6 of
Senator Hugo Black's AF of L 30-hour bill stirred the executive branch
to action. Roosevelt asked Miss Perkins to prepare an alternative bill.
Both she and the President were aghast at the opposition of business
leaders to her proposals, and on April 11 Roosevelt told Moley to get
in touch with the various groups in Washington known to be working
on plans for government-business co-operation. Moley, swamped with
other work, soon found that he could not "get on top of the job." On April
25 he met Hugh Johnson in a hotel lobby and persuaded him to work
on the problem.[16] Johnson went at his task with characteristic impetu-
osity. He locked himself in his hotel room, went through all the principal
plans in twenty-four straight hours of work, and came out with a two-
page draft of a bill.[17] He then called on Tugwell and Donald Richberg
for help.[18] Richberg's experience as counsel for the Railroad Labor

Executive Association was valuable to Johnson, who was weak on labor questions.

Finally Roosevelt ended the confusion which, by authorizing a number of people to do the same job, he had helped create. He told the various assignees to get together and come up with a bill. Miss Perkins claimed a key role in bringing about this unity of effort. In *The Roosevelt I Knew* she recalled that when she learned of the work Wagner, Johnson, and Tugwell were doing, she complained to the President that "no cabinet member is in on it." Roosevelt asked Tugwell to let the Secretary of Labor know what was going on. In the Treasury Department building she found Tugwell and Johnson, who had been "working for weeks under a mutual pledge of secrecy." They were stingy with information, giving her only the "barest outline" of their plan. She found it much like the Wagner scheme and reported this duplication to the President. Roosevelt then asked her and Henry Wallace to arrange a meeting of the two groups.[19]

Moley noted that the President called the "usual compromise session at the White House" and ordered those present to agree on a bill.[20] In any event, Wagner, Dickinson, Johnson, Perkins, Richberg, and Tugwell met in the office of Budget Director Lewis Douglas. The chief difference between the Wagner-Dickinson and Johnson bills involved disciplinary powers. Johnson supported codes with a vigorous licensing power for the swift punishment of recalcitrant minorities. Tugwell backed Johnson's insistence on stiff penalties. The conferees rejected Tugwell's disciplinary device—a reserve fund, acquired through a processing tax, for distribution among compliers.[21] Ironically, Johnson, for reasons Professor Schlesinger has explained, turned wholly to voluntarism in implementing the NIR Act.[22]

According to Johnson the two bills were reconciled in a few days with no more than "slight misunderstandings at the outset, which were resolved by Rex Tugwell. . . ."[23] After his initial contribution to compromise, Tugwell dropped out of the discussions due to his administrative duties; Wagner, Johnson, Richberg, and Douglas did the main job of writing.[24] Tugwell's participation did not justify assertions in the press that, as columnist Frank Kent avowed, while a group wrote the bill, "it had to be in the head of one man"—Tugwell, who "sold" the NRA to the President.[25] Another hostile journalist, implying that Tugwell had a final say, stated that the NIR Act "was not sent to Congress until Rexford Guy Tugwell had made his critical emendations of the text."[26] In a real sense the men who wrote the bill merely put pen to paper as a final, formal act. If the former Brain Trusters had something to do with the NIR Act, it was because their ideas coincided with the demands, voiced most forcefully by the Chamber of Commerce, of the business community.

The NIR Act was presented to Congress on May 13 and signed by the President on June 16. It did not pass, Tugwell later observed, "as easily as it seemed in retrospect. There was a kind of ganging up of those who did not see at once how they could use it to advantage. . . ." [27] The Act authorized committees representing management, labor (protected by Section 7A), and the public (or consumers) to draw up codes of industrial practices. "Practices" covered a lot of ground. The actual content of the various codes depended on the implementation of the Act by the National Recovery Administration, set up under Hugh Johnson.

As the NIR Act became law, the attitudes of various groups toward it indicated that it would have a stormy career. Tugwell recalled these attitudes, noting differences among businessmen. Some of them objected to the Act because "they did not like the power government seemed to have." They were the ones "who benefited under the going rules because they knew how to escape their application." Other businessmen saw in the NRA "an opportunity for aggrandizement." And they did not conceal their intentions—testimony before Congressional committees showed that they contemplated price-fixing. Labor, too, was out for what it could get under 7A. If labor leaders had to concede to business in the way of price-fixing to achieve the goals of many years, "they were prepared not to worry overmuch about that." [28]

The Progressives in Congress objected, Tugwell noted, because of their heavy investment in the antitrust acts. Many legislators with atomistic tendencies were worried from the first not about the very wide delegation of authority to the President which the Supreme Court later rejected, but about "the implication of an unacceptable collectivism." They asked whether the bill was not "drawn largely from the philosophy of Mussolini or the old German cartel system." Senator Wagner replied that it was not.[29]

The original Brain Trusters, Tugwell remembered, had mixed feelings about the NRA. They believed, Moley excepted, that a national collectivism would require that government rather than business "make final determinations and ultimately . . . regulate the process of conjuncture in the public interest." As they learned that businesses still hoped to determine production and price policies in their own interest, they began to wonder whether they had created a Frankenstein. Would big business and big labor play their old game, "conspiring to further a mutual interest which would be far from coincidental with the public good?" At the same time, the Brain Trusters viewed the possibilities of the NRA with some optimism, which led Tugwell to remark in retrospect that they had no right to expect that the "conjunctural function could be more strictly administered . . . knowing businesses and politicians as they did—not to mention the offended progressives." [30]

The consumer interest was low man on the administrative totem pole. Consumerists had great hopes for the NRA, and technically they were to participate on an equal basis with industry and labor in code-making. Tugwell considered consumer representation vital. A full explanation of the ineffectiveness of that representation would be a lengthy one. Briefly, the consumer division of each industrial committee was weak because of the lack of an organized, vocal constituency, the unavailability of an adequate number of sufficiently experienced personnel, and the consequent delay in getting started. The Consumers' Advisory Board fought a hard fight, but the other interests determined the basic policies of the NRA.

II

Up to this point nothing has been said about recovery, which, after all, was the raison d'être of the NRA. In fact, in 1933 nothing very definite was said about a theory of recovery in connection with the NRA. There was some emphasis on increasing purchasing power by raising wages. This would be done directly through code agreements and indirectly through placing a floor under prices, thereby eliminating cutthroat competition with its accompanying wage reductions. There was an expression—in the maximum-hours provisions—of the "spread the work" idea of the Black 30-hour Bill. And it was also conceived, Tugwell recalled, that the codes would tend to "increase efficiency, reduce costs of production, make marketing more orderly, and, by granting businessmen privileges they had long sought, encourage expansion." [31]

In any event, it was the urgency of the recovery problem, Tugwell later wrote, that determined the early history of the NRA. There was an increase in industrial activity beginning in March, but it was partly speculative. Goods went to inventory as producers acted to avoid the higher wages, yet sell at the higher prices, expected under the NRA. By mid-July this early rise was tailing off. At the same time, only one major code—cotton textiles—had been written. Some special, dramatic steps seemed appropriate. Roosevelt concluded, Tugwell noted, that reflation—to promote debt adjustment and the issuance of credit—and the direct inducement of industrial activity through relief and public works were not enough. Besides, relief was "bad for people" and public works were "so slow as to be ineffective as an immediate stimulant." [32] The President found what he wanted in the re-employment agreement which Hugh Johnson suggested.

The President's Re-employment Agreement—which we may call the

Blue Eagle, its famous symbol—was a blanket code designed to hasten the code-making process and provide an opportunity for the NRA formula to show what it could achieve in the way of recovery. It set minimum wages and maximum hours, and it prohibited child labor. Signers agreed not to raise prices beyond resulting payroll increases and not to buy from nonsigners. In a short time 2,300,000 employers in businesses hiring 16 of a potential 25 million workers signed up.[33] A flood of specific codes poured in for NRA approval, and the agency's work load increased enormously. Tugwell had nothing good to say for the Blue Eagle either at the time or in retrospect. In July, 1933, just before Johnson launched the Blue Eagle on the 21st, Tugwell told the Special Industrial Recovery Board, "I am just scared to death. I am afraid of the commitment and of getting the President into this. If we strike what a number of us anticipate, which is a flattening out of markets and a precipitous drop right in the midst of a ballyhoo campaign, we will look like ten cents." [34]

In *The Democratic Roosevelt* Tugwell referred disapprovingly to the Blue Eagle theory. If all employers simultaneously expanded their labor forces while maintaining wage rates and keeping prices stable, the resulting wage payments would buy the enlarged product. A self-supporting recovery "spiral" would get started. This theory, he noted, "appealed to naïve hopes for painless restoration of accustomed conditions." It was unfortunate that the Blue Eagle "necessarily got itself inextricably mixed up with code-making." And, "most fatal of all," it neglected to set up an enforcement organization. "It even omitted the irreducibly necessary governmental representation on the code authorities to see to it that industry behaved in the civilized manner envisioned in the self-government theory." Under these circumstances the Blue Eagle was "most agreeable to those who still hoped to escape from depression without changing the institutions to which they were accustomed." Many businessmen calculated that they could "take advantage of the compliance of all the rest." From the start the Blue Eagle was "sabotaged by . . . its most enthusiastic supporters." [35]

Thus, under Johnson, who was fanatically determined to get codes written, the NRA neither provided for co-ordination—especially from the point of view of a planner like Tugwell—nor satisfactorily settled the question of government-business relations. To get his codes Johnson made fundamental concessions on price-fixing and production controls.[36] In effect, business became the senior partner. And big business manipulated the codes to the disadvantage of small business. Later, after the failure of the Blue Eagle and the biased but devastating Darrow report of March, 1934, Johnson began to crack down on business. By this time the colorful, volatile, domineering Johnson and his agency were in a situation perilous to the potential benefits involved in the concept of business self-government under public sponsorship. Professor Schlesinger has described the NRA's dilemma. Business domination of the NRA looked like "the halfway house to the corporate state"; but if NRA decisions went against business, a political storm would "either overthrow NRA or cause the government itself in self-defense to march much faster on the road to statism." [37]

Moley maintained that the basic difficulty in the NRA was the attempt to combine emergency with long-run policies—recovery with industrial reorganization.[38] The basic difficulty in the recovery program was what Professor Schlesinger has called "the conundrum of prices"—the problem of devising "techniques which would raise prices enough to maintain decent wages and hours without raising them so much as to dry up purchasing power, restrict production, or introduce new rigidities into the economy." [39] Tugwell, especially concerned with the restoration of purchasing power, condemned the NRA's price policies—as determined by big business—as restrictive of recovery and expansion.

Perhaps the basic difficulty which the hard-headed Moley pointed out made an unsatisfactory solution of the price conundrum inevitable. The NRA seems to have taken on more than it could handle. It had to draw the line between undefined fair practices and practices in restraint of trade. It had to codify the practices of a massive, complex economy, eventually approving 557 basic codes, 189 supplementary codes, and the labor provisions of 19 joint NRA-AAA codes.[40] In order to put together a staff which understood business practices, it had to recruit personnel from the industries whose practices were being codified. Six hundred code secretaries were also the chief executives of the related trade associations—yet these policy makers were supposed to be impartial.[41] Their presence in the NRA, Tugwell recalled, made this version of government-business partnership an "unnatural union." [42]

Inevitable or not, the policies of the NRA were unacceptable to Tugwell. In *The Democratic Roosevelt* he referred to the "selfishness and indiscipline which was to break down NRA almost before it got well underway." The evidence which "at once became noticed" indicated that business was going to free itself of government domination and exploit the NRA codes, adopting restrictive price policies. In a short time bigger businesses were "cynically exploiting the code-making process" to the disadvantage of their smaller competitors and labor (they used the NRA to "prevent strikes but not to raise wages"). In 1934 there was nearly a Congressional investigation of the NRA by disaffected Progressives, to whom Johnson was a "kind of bête noire." It would have disclosed "favoritism to big business, tolerance of restrictive practices, including price controls, and a favoring of employers as against employees. . . ." Tugwell blamed Johnson for creating a chaotic situation by failing to infuse the code-making process with any general principle and by granting businessmen "many freedoms they could not safely be allowed." [43]

The record shows that Tugwell protested in 1933 and 1934 against the policies which he deplored in retrospect. Sitting in for Wallace on the Special Industrial Recovery Board, he insisted that the NRA's price policies—as they appeared in the first extensive codes—would decrease purchasing power and restrict economic activity.[44] He harped on the price problem so persistently that he apologized to Johnson.[45] But he kept on stressing the adverse effects of too-high prices on purchasing power and expansion. As time went on, Tugwell became disenchanted with the Administrator. At first he had had high hopes for Johnson, crediting the General with character, brains, honesty, and progressiveness— along with poor personal relations—and noting in his diary his "doubt if anyone is a much better planner for believing in it as a principle." [46] By the summer of 1933 he was fighting a losing fight against Johnson's policies as the President rendered the Special Industrial Recovery Board ineffective at Johnson's request.[47] In the fall of 1934 Tugwell was among those urging Roosevelt to replace Johnson,[48] even though Johnson had reversed his field after the Blue Eagle fell to earth in late 1933. The Administrator resigned in late September, 1934.

Tugwell's connection with two additional aspects of the NRA should be mentioned. There was some disagreement over the relationship between increases in agricultural prices and industrial prices. At the outset of the New Deal farm prices rose quickly. Then industrial prices began to catch up, and personnel of the USDA and the AAA protested. Johnson absolved the AAA Administrator George Peek (another Baruch disciple and an old friend), Wallace, and Tugwell of any responsibility for propaganda alleging that the NRA program was prejudicial to agriculture. But he insisted on a stepping-up in the rate of increase of industrial prices so that they might catch up with farm prices. Peek and Tugwell, who disagreed sharply on many policy matters, would not give away agriculture's original gains. They contended that the historically disadvantageous position of farm prices justified their initial spurt. But, declining to go along with AAA partisans, they conceded in late 1933 that equal rates of increase would now be fair—that is, economically sound.[49]

Tugwell was only indirectly involved in another aspect of the NRA— potential co-ordination of NRA operations with the public-works program authorized by Title II of the NIR Act. Like the Progressives in Congress, Tugwell advocated a huge public-works program.[50] And his institutional ideas on the centralized allocation of resources fitted in with Johnson's desire to revive capital-goods industries with specific applications of public-works funds. In early 1933, however, Tugwell was not thinking in terms of the particular kind of co-ordination Johnson had in mind. In fact, Miss Perkins found only a "meager" public-works program in the original Tugwell-Johnson plan for industrial co-ordina-tion.[51] Title II was, moreover, a last-minute addition to the NIR Act, made out of political rather than functional considerations.

In March, 1933, Moley suggested to Senator La Follette, Senator Ed-ward Costigan, and Tugwell, over the dinner table, that if the recovery and public-works bill were tied together they would tend to carry each other through the White House and Congress.[52] Moley's strategy was adopted, and it worked. Title II appropriated 3.3 billions for public works. This figure, Moley noted, was a compromise between the 900 millions which Hoover could find in useful projects and the 5.5 billions which Tugwell and others suggested.[53] When Roosevelt designated Johnson to administer Title I and Ickes to administer Title II, the General seriously considered resigning. Roosevelt thought the two men would work things out, but Moley's prediction that they would not proved accurate. Johnson's cherished scheme for specific co-ordination was con-fined to the general level of comparative pace. "What happened," Moley commented, "is that Johnson moved ahead altogether too fast and Ickes moved at a snail's pace." [54]

Either Johnson was quick to forgive and forget, or the disagreements to which he was a party were discussed on a high level. In any case, in his book published in 1935 he remarked that although he was alleged to have had fights with a number of men—Homer Cummings, Mor-genthau, Daniel Roper, Lewis Douglas, Wallace, and Tugwell—"up to the very end no unkind word was ever passed." As for Wallace and Tug-well, although they "probably did not agree with me on some questions of policy, it was never the subject of quarrel or controversy." Ironically, Johnson's most heated arguments were with his old friend Peek.[55]

III

Tugwell's public statements on the NRA were naturally more general and calm than his private remarks. His lengthiest published comment on the NRA while it was still alive came after Johnson had taken steps in early 1934 to put reins on big business. In an article written in April, 1934, Tugwell called the NRA "a charter for experiment and research, for invention and learning." He warned that speculative producers would attempt to write codes in support of restrictive practices, and he asserted emphatically that co-ordination did not mean limitation. There was no need for "hoarding our gains against a poverty-stricken future. We must devote ourselves to organizing and expanding resources and capacities.

Abundance compels changes in ideas and institutions." The key to abundance was "the management of purchasing power, provision of which can release the potentialities of vast producing equipment." The key to the management of purchasing power was protection of the consumer through rigorously lowered prices. The alternative to low-price, high-volume sales was taxation to return part of the profits to consumers. Tugwell preferred a "socially wise policy to socialistic taxation." [56]

Comments on Tugwell's remarks on the NRA indicate that there would have been no shortage of critics of his views no matter what he said. One reformer considered Tugwell's statements "perhaps a little too favorable." [57] A vehement critic accused him of insincerity, of disguising his dictatorial preferences with the use of the terms "co-ordination" and "partnership." [58] A favorable commentator noted that when Tugwell protested against inadequate consumer protection in the NRA, producer interests howled that he wanted business run without profits.[59] On the other hand, a former Communist, Louis C. Fraina (Lewis Corey), charged that Tugwell was an apologist for the NRA who emphasized consumption because he was really concerned with "markets to absorb the output of industry and insure capitalist profits." [60]

After Johnson resigned, the NRA began to contract and simplify its activities. On May 25, 1935, less than a month before its date of renewal (or expiration), it was declared unconstitutional. Tugwell continued to comment on the NRA and the Court's decision in the years which followed. In late 1935 he spoke about the perversion of the NRA. As soon as our industrial leaders regained "something of their lost morale," he noted, they sabotaged the NRA, adopting the restrictive practices and seeking the selfish gains they had adopted and sought in the unorganized competitive system.[61] This perversion, he commented in 1947, involved "competitive advantages measured perhaps in the billions as compared to millions in any other period." In comparison the "exploitative excursions" of the nineteenth century, which, as a college student, he had considered "aggression to end all aggressions" and unmatchable in their "imaginative immorality," were child's play.[62]

Tugwell wrote about the Court's decision several times in the years 1939-1952. It was acceptable to him insofar as it condemned administrative abuses leading to scarcity. The Justices, he remarked, no matter what they said, were probably "actuated by the same revulsion felt by the whole public—a withdrawal from the depravities of artificial scarcity into which the agency had fallen." [63] But, on a more fundamental level, he found the Court's decision inadequate. The Justices were "governed by ideas which went even beyond the beginning of industrialism," and the industrialists who applauded the decision did not understand that they, themselves, were "the end-product of technological evolution." [64] In short, the Court punished government for recognizing any need for the conciliation of group conflicts, thereby disallowing "the thesis that society had passed out of the individual and entered the group stage of functioning, when the truth was that even that stage had been left behind." [65] Thus, the administration was rebuked for treating the bigness of business as a "technical rather than a moral problem." Roosevelt received a sharp reminder of his apostasy in departing from the textbooks, and, with the punishment of unorthodoxy, "another tilt at windmills would have to be undertaken for the sake of progressive pride." Out of their pigeonholes came the antitrust laws for another battle against "simple wickedness." [66]

And so the NRA, in Tugwell's view, never came to grips with the basic problem it might have tried to solve. He noted that the trust movement had continued apace in the 1920's under Secretary of Commerce and President Hoover—"a poor record for the outstanding champion of competitive individualism. . . ." [67] This development squared with Tugwell's views because the "ideological concomitant of the machine process was operational wholeness. That was the original meaning of NRA. Other measures [antitrust laws] were purely repressive." [68] The NRA, recognizing the failure of enforced competition, made an attempt at a "sort of recapture of the government's pricing power, even if by indirect approach. . . ." [69] This attempt failed with the initial perversion of the NRA and—after the agency showed vague signs of getting on the right track—its death in court. Its destruction was understandable since judges and economists, confusing business with society, had always shied off from the implications of recognition of a public interest in prices; they avoided looking straight at the consequences of private price-fixing.[70] They put the NRA out of business, but the basic problems remained.

The role of the President himself in the career of the NRA was the subject of lengthy comment by Tugwell in *The Democratic Roosevelt.*[71] Briefly, the President's strategy, as Tugwell described it, was to make a "kind of bargain." He would overlook aggressions if business would carry out the re-employment agreement and acquiesce in the agreements which labor wanted so much. In other words, "the unwise codes were a bribe." When Tugwell warned the President, vigorously and in detail, that the NRA's policies would result in restriction, higher prices, and more unemployment—rather than their opposites—Roosevelt revealed the second phase of his strategy. He replied that "once he had substantially all industries under the blanket the job of revising would begin." He believed that, given enough powers, he could see to it that the NRA resulted in expansive co-ordination and not restriction. Tugwell was "not at all satisfied with his explanation, or optimistic about the reform he suggested."

With the failure of the Blue Eagle, Roosevelt did shift in late 1933 into the second phase of his strategy. Meanwhile, the Warren gold-buying scheme diverted public attention from this change. The shift became more definite in 1934. An Executive Order of January disallowed monopolistic and discriminatory practices under the NRA codes—"the policy he had disbanded the Recovery Board for insisting on." In March, when the Darrow review staff was set up, the President called for "balanced recovery," with lower prices, higher wages, and moderate profits. He reverted to the antitrust approach, which was to be modified for welfare purposes—the elimination of child labor, sweat shops, and starvation wages. "Gone were industrial planning and partnership with industry." Roosevelt explained the new policies in a fireside chat, presenting to the electorate "nothing but the most orthodox of institutions." And the people were reassured.

What Roosevelt wanted to bring about and what happened were two different things. In fact, his handling of the NRA, Tugwell judged, was one of his poorest performances. The agency, which had not fallen into "irrecoverable ways," certainly needed a sharp change in policy under new management, Tugwell agreed, but the concessions which Roosevelt made in phase one prevented the realization of the reforms contemplated in phase two. The President "alienated practically every interest that might have given him support. This had been unnecessary." In the face of ample warnings he was stubborn. He perversely delivered himself to his worst enemies. He had "no adequate answer for any of the critics," and he "would go on toward defeat ungracefully and without alternatives."

Specifically, Roosevelt alienated the Progressives and businessmen. In trying at the outset to please the latter, he displeased the former. Thus, he "never again had united progressive support and never again could expect the Congress to pass any measure that did not have conservative approval." Meanwhile, business, which, in perverting the NRA, had not fulfilled its part of the bargain, may not have been justified in its reaction to Roosevelt's shift in policy. But it had made cautious concessions on child labor, wages, and hours, and nothing had been said against its assumption of senior status in the NRA partnership. Now that it was going to get nothing in return for its concessions, it felt betrayed.

When the end of the NRA came, Roosevelt was relieved—although he "covered his relief with a careful camouflage of indignation" and, ironically, used "so fortunate a reverse as a club with which to beat the reactionary justices." His feeling of relief, Tugwell concluded, was in terms of the current situation. The abandonment of the NRA and the reversion to regulation was an "expedient action, not one he believed could be permanent for modern industry." Modification of his public statements did not mean that he had lost the "conviction that bigness had come to stay and that control was its concomitant."

This reference to the expediency of abandonment implied that the NRA idea deserved another trial at some future date. Did it? Tugwell thought so, on the grounds that it had not had a fair trial in the first instance. In the end the agency had become, he wrote in 1940, an "interesting mechanism—a representative board—capable in itself of adaption and evolution, and possessing the possibility of enormously reducing the frictions of industry, but which never got a chance to operate and to prove itself in action." [72] But, as it was until shortly before its fall, the NRA did not get at the basic question of "concentration and control," and it deserved to fail. [73] Tugwell, of course, judged the NRA in terms of his long-run institutional views, which assumed a continuing need for such a social device in a highly technological economy. In stressing long-run considerations, he may have exaggerated the abuses of the NRA and underestimated its immediate contributions.

Professor Schlesinger, in one of the most forthright defenses of the NRA, has maintained that price policies and monopolistic practices under the NRA did not hurt small businesses so much as the wages and hours provisions of the various codes. And if the NRA was not successful as a recovery measure, it did keep the bottom from falling out of the economy in a deflationary disaster. On the positive side, the NRA gave an important boost to morale, providing a symbol and a program and defeating economic fatalism. In the social field it established the principles of minimum wages, maximum hours, elimination of child labor, and collective bargaining. It gave the consumer status and in general stressed decency in economic behavior. It served an educative purpose, gathering valuable information on industry, leading people to think in terms of national policy, and—as we know with hindsight—training personnel for a future crisis (Pearl Harbor was not far off). [74]

Schlesinger specifically noted Tugwell's preoccupation with price policy in terms of the classical model of the competitive market—despite the iconoclasm of his other economic views. "The hard fact was," Schlesinger wrote, "that the causes of price rigidity went a great deal deeper than anything written by trade associations into NRA codes, and that its cure was beyond the power of NRA to achieve." [75] It should be said in Tugwell's defense that he was familiar with Gardiner Means's studies of the relative inflexibility of industrial prices, but Schlesinger's implication that Tugwell overestimated the potential of the NRA may be justified. In September, 1934, in a lengthy memorandum to the President, Tugwell referred to "lowness" and "flexibility" as if he assumed that an effective NRA could control prices as desired.[76] On the other hand, in the context of Tugwell's institutional thought, an *effective* NRA would be only a part of a comprehensive scheme calculated to achieve "balance." This would answer Schlesinger's protest that the "problem here was not the level of price but the gross failure of demand, and this was something that NRA by itself could not reverse." [77]

Whatever disagreement there is between Schlesinger and Tugwell involves emphasis in details. Their basic conclusions coincide. Schlesinger observed that the unfortunate aspect of the NRA was not the conflict between big and small business, but the clash between special and public interests.[78] Tugwell remarked in *The Democratic Roosevelt* that the NRA might have emerged as an "adequate social philosophy" if the "pattern of partnership had been carefully established and if it had not been used by faithless businessmen to gain advantages they might have known they would not be allowed to maintain." [79] Both men, in effect, pointed out a principle that suggested a limitation of "self-government" and indicated the requirements of a successful social agency. No single segment of the economy has a wide enough viewpoint to deal effectively with national problems; and, as Professor Schlesinger stated in an earlier work, the result of mistaking class interest for the national interest is national disaster.[80]

Finally, we should consider a dilemma which arises from Tugwell's thought. He maintained that only crisis called into question accepted institutions, giving progressive leadership a chance to operate. On the other hand, he had stated in 1921 that expanding economic situations should be the basis for business regulation, that business regulation should be planned and experimental rather than the product of emergencies.[81] In other words, when social agencies will work well we cannot have them; and when we can have them they will not work well.

It may be that public opinion will always lag behind institutional needs in a crisis—as it did in 1933, when, Tugwell recalled, Americans were not receptive to the idea that they "must live together as co-operators and not as competitors. . . ." [82] Nevertheless, perhaps a meliorative conclusion regarding the domestic economy can be derived from this discouraging dilemma after all. If a new kind of agency suffers in a crisis the inevitable defects of a first try under emergency conditions, it does set a precedent and provide experience which can prove valuable in a subsequent crisis—even though new crises present new problems. And we do not look for another crisis as severe as that of 1929. At least we have some reason to believe that we have learned a lot about avoiding severe depressions.

14. Proposals for Farm Relief: 1922-1933

Farm prices dropped precipitously in the recession of 1921 and stayed down. The agricultural depression was under way long before the general collapse which started in 1929. In 1922 there began a decade of study, discussion, publication, and legislative proposals to promote "farm relief." During most of this decade professors, farm-organization leaders, and Congressmen were "in advance" of both the executive branch of government and the people at large—including farmers. Finally, in 1933 the farm interest won expression in the form of national law. The present chapter provides background for the enactment of this legislation, summarizing and comparing the McNary-Haugen scheme, the domestic-allotment plan, and Tugwell's remedial device of 1928.

I

In *The Democratic Roosevelt* Tugwell listed five causes of the farmers' troubles in the 1920's: (1) the sudden uselessness of the new land called into production by the demands of war; (2) the changes in diet from starch to protein; (3) the development of synthetic fibers; (4) over-capitalization of farm lands in prosperous years; (5) inability of farm owners to discharge their debts with the income from cheapened crops.[1] Crops, moreover, cheapened for historic reasons as well as those especially characteristic of the 1920's. Farmers received low prices for what they sold and paid high prices for what they bought—that is, they sold their products at prices determined in a world market and bought manufactured goods whose prices were set in a tariff-protected market. Because of their lack of co-ordination as producers and sellers, the necessity of allowing a margin for the whims of nature, and the interval between production commitment and marketing, farmers were unable to adjust supply to demand with anything like the speed and efficiency with which industrialists made this adjustment. These disadvantages meant that farm prices rose more slowly than industrial prices in good times and fell more rapidly in bad times. They combined with current handicaps to deprive farmers of a proportionate share in the prosperity of the New Era.

Looking ahead for a moment to the end of the Prosperity Decade, we find Tugwell noting in 1928 that our integrated economy was vulnerable to a weakness in any of its parts and citing low farm income as a danger point.[2] By 1932 the position of the farmers had collapsed. The force with which the depression struck them down is indicated by a few figures:

Farm Prices	1909-14: 100	1925: 156	1932: 65
Cash Income	1929: $7 billion		1932: $2 billion
Share of National Income	1929: 12%		1932: 5%[3]

In 1934 Tugwell, in typical holistic fashion, offered figures which related farm prices to other prices:

Exchange Value of Farm Products   1909-14: 100
1929: 91   Feb., 1932: 50[4]

In the 1920's the land agencies of the Departments of Agriculture and the Interior, Tugwell remarked in an address of 1933, "largely followed the direction given them by their initial creation," failing to adjust to new conditions after wartime prosperity faded. The Division of Land Economics of the USDA was an exception. It studied the basic economic problems concerned with land and developed broad information on the subject.[5] (In an article of 1949 Tugwell also lauded the Office of Farm Management, later the Bureau of Agricultural Economics, which, under W. J. Spillman, compiled valuable cost-of-production figures.[6]) But "there was no single Federal agency to guide settlement and create policies."[7]

Nor did the people of the farm belt understand the situation which later produced disaster. The West, Tugwell recalled in 1952, was full of hopeful small capitalists whose chances of realizing their hopes were disappearing by 1929. They faced an invasion by merchandise chains and manufacturers, through dealer contracts, of trades and occupations involving clothing, groceries, tires, shoes, and farm machinery. Western farmers became tenants or found their properties so heavily mortgaged that it amounted to the same thing. But these individualists were "no more distinguished than the rest of the people for their recognition of facts." While the "reality of independence escaped them . . . they clung to its appearance," preserving, "out of all reason, a heartbreaking confidence in their ability to rise again by getting the best of one another." By 1932 the gap between the farmers and the professors, organization leaders, and members of Congress was closing. Farmers were at last aware that machinery "started a revolution in agriculture which changed it from a 'way of life' to an industry much like any other."[8] They showed at the polls that they wanted national action on what they considered a national problem. It is to the proposals for action that we must now turn.

The 1920's saw the development of two basic approaches to the farm problem. One stressed marketing, the other production. Both sought the same end—an equitable relationship between agriculture and the rest of the economy, a fair share of national income for farmers. The difference between them was over means. The marketing approach took the form of the McNary-Haugen scheme—named for its sponsors in Senate and House. Representatives of the farm bloc, a product of agricultural distress, kept McNary-Haugen bills, Tugwell later noted, "in and about the Congress for years." The farmers of the whole nation centered their hopes in these proposals. Legislators, professors, farm-organization leaders, and other individuals contributed to their formulation. "But," Tugwell commented, "if there was one individual more than another who could claim authorship—or perhaps original sponsorship—it was . . . George N. Peek." [9]

Peek, who had served under Bernard M. Baruch on the War Industries Board, was a manufacturer of farm implements. In 1922 he and Hugh Johnson, a War Industries Board colleague, wrote a pamphlet, *Equality for Agriculture*. They publicized the concept of parity, translating it into a statistical index and bringing about agreement on it between the USDA and farm-organization leaders.[10] In *The Democratic Roosevelt* Tugwell judged that Peek's "was far from an original mind, and the ideas were more those of various agricultural economists than his own." [11] In any event, Peek did his best during the 1920's to indoctrinate farmers with the ideas of group action and compulsory co-operation, weakening their traditonal reliance on individualism.[12] In 1928 Peek went to the Democratic convention in Houston and sold his program to Alfred E. Smith. It appeared in the platform. Smith, Tugwell recalled, "hedged his acceptance . . . with a commitment to set up, and to accept the findings of, an agricultural commission—after he became President." [13]

McNary-Haugenism or, more specifically, Peekism centered on the equalization-fee scheme and marketing agreements. The equalization-fee scheme provided tariff protection for a fair (parity) domestic price for farm products. A government corporation would purchase at the domestic price that part of the crop which exceeded domestic needs and sell it on the world market for whatever price it would bring. Losses on exports would be made up out of a fund to which farmers would contribute a fee for each unit of product they sold. Marketing agreements involved a number of possibilities. The enabling provision in the AA Act was brief and general. A specific marketing agreement could include provisions pertaining to any number of the following: (1) prices which the processor paid to the producer; (2) marketing practices; (3) labels and standards; (4) prices which the consumer paid at retail. Peek, who was primarily interested in (1), had high hopes for marketing agreements as a means to agricultural recovery.

While McNary-Haugenism got the headlines in the 1920's, another school of thought on the farm problem was developing. Finally, as the farm-relief movement neared the goal line in the early 1930's, the advocates of the domestic-allotment plan stole the ball from the McNary-Haugenites.

The domestic-allotment plan called for a direct effort to hold supply down to demand. It would rest on voluntarism, but it would offer tangible inducements to farmers in order to win their co-operation. Briefly, the plan included these steps: (1) calculate the total prospective sale of export crops in the domestic market (the domestic allotment) and, using historical amounts of production as base figures, allot a specific amount of production to each farmer; (2) provide for payments which, when added to the selling price, would give the farmer a parity return on the domestically consumed portion of his product. On production in excess of the domestic allotment farmers would receive only the prevailing world prices. The proponents of the domestic-allotment plan argued that their scheme, in making it clear to farmers that production above domestic demand would lower the average price, would effectively discourage excess production. They pointed out that under the equalization-fee scheme each producer would sell whatever he decided to offer—all of it on the same basis.[14] They maintained that a viable, effective program had to begin at the production end of the farm problem.

It is interesting to note that an affinity for ideas pointing toward production controls (but stopping short of the final step until late 1932) developed within the administrations of Presidents who did not favor a major farm-relief program. The National Agricultural Conference, called by Harding in 1922, counseled farm organizations to look to world supply-and-demand factors so that they could advise their members and "propose measures for proper limitation of acreage in particular crops."[15] In 1930 Secretary of Agriculture Arthur M. Hyde declared: "I want to emphasize the need for equitable, intelligent, systematic, and collective action to bring supply into better relationship with demand. . . ."[16] In a Special Report of December 7, 1932, the Federal Farm Board, after its disastrous experience with requests for voluntary reduction of acreage, finally and reluctantly recommended a version of the domestic-allotment plan.[17] The lame-duck Congress took no action on this recommendation.

It was Mordecai Ezekiel, a USDA economist assigned to the Federal Farm Board, who proposed the domestic-allotment plan to that body. Ezekiel was in contact with the allotment advocates, who, by the latter half of 1932, had become an influential force in the Roosevelt camp. From small, quiet beginnings they had come a long way. The pioneers in the formulation of the domestic-allotment plan were W. J. Spillman of the USDA, John D. Black of Harvard, and Beardsley Ruml of the Rockefeller Foundation. Spillman published *Balancing the Farm Output* in 1927 (New York: Orange Judd Publishing Company). His name, Tugwell wrote in 1949, "will forever be associated with the growth of rural social action." [18] In 1929 Black published *Agricultural Reform in the United States*. He coined the phrase "domestic allotment" and, at Ruml's suggestion, explained it in his book—in Chapter Ten, reprints of which were widely circulated in the farm belt.[19]

The man who "really led the fight" for the domestic-allotment principle was Milburn Lincoln Wilson of Montana State College. Originally a McNary-Haugenite, he informed Black in 1930 that he was switching to the superior allotment idea. Through correspondence and propagandizing he recruited to his cause Henry Wallace, Senator Peter Norbeck (Rep., S. D.), and Henry I. Harriman, President of the Boston Chamber of Commerce and holder of large agricultural interests in Montana.[20] Wallace, too, was originally an equalization-fee man. He remarked in 1929 that the McNary-Haugen plan would result in very little increase in acreage.[21] In the next year or two he decided that some kind of check on production was necessary.

II

Tugwell came into direct contact with the allotment group in 1932. Meanwhile, during the 1920's, he had carried on his own studies of the farm problem. These investigations led him to conclusions which made him receptive to the domestic-allotment scheme. Tugwell's rural background and the emphasis he placed in his economics on purchasing power naturally aroused his concern for the farmers' plight. It was an exaggeration, if a lack of interest in other aspects of the economy was implied, to say that he "made the economics of agriculture a life study." [22] But his investigations certainly belied the widely held opinion, as expressed, for example, by Ambassador William E. Dodd, that he "knows little of agriculture." [23]

Tugwell attended the National Agricultural Conference in 1922. Between 1924 and 1930 he published several articles on the farm problem in academic journals and the *Nation* and wrote an analysis of Russian agriculture in connection with his trip to the Soviet Union. He also made his knowledge available to two would-be Presidents. During the late 1920's and until 1931 he corresponded with Governor Frank Lowden of Illinois.[24] For Alfred E. Smith's use in the campaign of 1928 he prepared a lengthy memorandum.[25] Tugwell did not meet Smith in 1928.[26] The McNary-Haugenites had the New York Governor's ear.

Two of Tugwell's studies in the 1920's deserve special attention. An article, "Farm Relief and a Permanent Agriculture," appeared in *The Annals of the American Academy of Political and Social Science*, March, 1929, 271-82. This article represented a long-run approach to the farm problem, centering on conservation. Soil erosion, Tugwell declared, was the "greatest single danger to the United States in its ultimate consequences." Outlining the stages of the evolution of agriculture in America, he called for public policies which would encourage practices "suited to our soils, climate, and the needs of our people." He opposed indiscriminate assistance intended to make agriculture "profitable as it is." He rejected the McNary-Haugen plan as uncritical aid which embodied "no attempt to gauge the future or to penalize inefficiency or antisocial techniques." A backward agriculture, acting as a "drag on the whole economic system," required relief, but why "should we support by federal aid a kind of agriculture which will ruin the last good land we have?" The nation had a right to insist on assurances of sound conservation practices in return for assistance rendered. Tugwell concluded with a pragmatic plea that we examine government intervention "dispassionately and without preconception to see whether the necessary things can actually be accomplished through it."

The memorandum for Smith, which Tugwell began preparing in 1927, treated the causes of the farmers' plight; then it dwelt on immediate policy. Tugwell surveyed the various proposals for farm relief, adding his own to the list. He had undertaken this study with a certain zeal when Belle Moscowitz and Judge Joseph M. Proskauer asked him to submit a report to the Governor. As it turned out, Smith did not examine Tugwell's memorandum with any care. Tugwell was certain, he recalled, that "after the export-subsidy boys got hold of Smith at Houston," the Governor did not read his report, and he told Mrs. Moscowitz and Judge Proskauer that it was pointless for him to stay around.[27] But if Tugwell did not gain a hearing from this Democratic presidential candidate, he did from the next one. And the ideas he expressed in his memorandum of 1928 presaged his responsiveness to the domestic-allotment plan in 1932.

In an unsigned article, "A Plank for Agriculture," *New Republic,* July 4, 1928, Tugwell summarized some of the findings on surplus disposal which he presented in the Smith memorandum. An outline will indicate the extensive and intensive coverage of the memorandum itself:

I. Continuing and Strengthening the Work of the USDA
II. The Farm Bloc
III. The Disadvantages of Agriculture
    Tariffs
    Credit Facilities
    Taxation
    Transportation Rates
    Techniques

The Differential between Crop and Animal Care
Land-Use in One-Crop Areas
Bargaining Power as a Seller
Overhead Costs
Slowness of Turnover
Short-Run Inflexibility of Supply
Inelasticity of Demand for Staples
Marginal Lands
The Chronic Surplus
IV. A Summary of Proposals for Agricultural Relief
Laissez faire
A Government Marketing Agency
Outright Bounties: Export Debentures
Aid to Self-Help: Statistical and Technical Information
Assistance to Co-operatives
McNary-Haugenism
V. The Elements of a Program
Elements Subject to Legislative Regulation
Tariffs
Credit Facilities
Taxation
Transportation Rates
Encouragement of Large-Scale Operations
Encouragement of Co-operatives
Improvement of Techniques
More Orderly Marketing
Checking Supply
VI. The Advance Ratio Price Plan

Tugwell's references to techniques, large-scale operations, and marginal lands suggest the kinds of long-run considerations he treated in his article in *The Annals*. But the burden of this memorandum was recommendations for immediate action. He found some proposals—aid to self-help and assistance to co-operatives—inadequate, and the others—among which he paid the most attention to McNary-Haugenism—unsound. He believed that any attempt to control the surplus and affect prices without getting directly at supply would be locking the barn after the horse had been stolen. He offered his own program, the Advance Ratio Price Plan. In examining it, we can see why he was responsive to the domestic-allotment idea four years later.

Tugwell first identified and defined the main source of agriculture's troubles: "The surplus presents itself as the heart of the difficulty. The surplus is excess production . . . over what would be taken by consumers at a normal price, which is a price meeting costs of production and allowing a customary margin." The harmful effects of the surplus determined the objective of his plan, which was "to maintain a ratio of some constancy between the index of agricultural prices and that of other prices. . . . The annual output of agricultural commodities ought to exchange for the annual output of industrial commodities in a constant ratio." Tugwell noted that in times of falling prices agriculture characteristically fell below industry. When this happened, it meant that "the farm output is undervalued in terms of the industrial output." Even if the total money relationship remained constant, it could "still conceal an undervaluation of agricultural goods . . . because of a larger surplus problem" in agriculture than in industry. In the emergency there was only one way to attack the problem: "Controlling the planting of crops so as to meet the normal demand eliminates the surplus and stabilizes prices without price-fixing."

Except for a concluding comment on constitutional questions, a description of "Mechanisms of the Advance Ratio Price Plan" comprised the rest of the memorandum. A government board, or an agency approved by the government, would be the marketing agent for farmers. It would establish a ratio price, based on a statistical survey of costs, a year in advance. It would buy at the ratio price only the product of a certain acreage—estimated to meet normal (domestic plus foreign) needs. It would contract for this acreage, rationing it out on the basis of averages for the previous five years. The agency would create a fund to bear losses. Some profits would go into this fund, while excess profits would go on a pro-rated basis to the participating producers. Efficiency would gain greatly from the calculation of the advance-ratio price on the basis of production costs, since this would encourage larger operations on the part of the best growers.

Although the fund for insuring against losses was akin to McNary-Haugenism, the heart of Tugwell's scheme resembled the domestic-allotment plan. Unlike the McNary-Haugenites, Tugwell would attack the surplus problem directly. And his scheme would include all agricultural products—"except those whose ratio-price history was higher than the general index"—while the McNary-Haugen plan "increases prices to domestic consumers for the benefit of only certain classes of farmers." Those "certain classes" were the big staple growers.

Other mechanisms related to sales in local and auction markets and the alleviation of the farmers' historic disadvantages with reference to railroad rates, storage costs, credit facilities, and legislative regulation in general. An additional mechanism merits attention. Tugwell stated that tariffs could be used or not used, depending on whether it was thought desirable to sell surpluses abroad at less than domestic prices. McNary-

Haugenism depended on this kind of dumping, something which, Tugwell maintained, "would seldom be advisable on account of the legitimate objections that would come from domestic consumers." He suggested that the farmers' agency prevent all importations except those consigned to it by contract, "leaving the tariff issue out." Running through Tugwell's proposals, as the potential source of the farmers' ability to overcome their old disadvantages, was the theme of the benefits of centralization. A single agency, acting for the farmers, would possess statistical data which it could use to advantage through its naturally formidable bargaining power.

Tugwell believed that under his scheme the surplus would be "cut down to manageable size," but it would still be a problem. Even though the agency would consider carry-over in allotting acreage for a new season, natural causes could result in a variation of up to 25 per cent. Allowance for this factor, together with variations upward, would make removal of surplus virtually impossible. There would still be a need for surplus disposal through storage or exports. Tugwell also believed that his scheme would be difficult to administer, "but less so than the other proposals." He foresaw possible constitutional difficulties with respect to abridgment of the right of contract and the Fifth Amendment. He was not certain "but that Attorney-General John G. Sargent was correct in forecasting the probable attitude of the present Supreme Court towards the McNary-Haugen proposals." If they were unconstitutional, so was his scheme—and vice versa. He asked rhetorically whether, if his scheme were rejected by the Court, it would receive enough support to work on a voluntary basis. His answer was that even if the Court accepted it, ease of enforcement would still depend on popular support. His "own preferences would be for a more direct attack," but if Sargent were correct, "this difficulty may as well be avoided in future proposals and price relief sought by a means to which all assent. . . ."

III

Since Tugwell's scheme would pay the advance-ratio price for the normal export product, he had not quite arrived at the domestic-allotment idea by 1928. But he was moving in that direction. He had moved far enough so that the basic differences between his ideas and those of a McNary-Haugenite like George Peek were visible. Before looking at differences, however, we may briefly consider *similarities*. Both the McNary-Haugen and the domestic-allotment camps had the same objective—assuring a fair share of national income for farmers. Both, and the McNary-Haugenites first, stressed group action and quasi-voluntary co-operation. In fact, Peek inadvertently stimulated thought favored by the allotment advocates and opposed to his own. He said so much about the effect of the surplus on farm prices that he helped to stimulate consideration of production controls as policy.[28]

We may now consider the important *differences* between the McNary-Haugenites and the allotment proponents, or, let us say, Peek and Tugwell. Tugwell's article in *The Annals* indicates his concern with *conservation* as a long-run factor and accounts for his criticism of Peek for his lack of such concern. Other differences derived from the difference over *production controls*. It may be said that those who opposed such controls were compelled to emphasize marketing and trade devices as means of disposing of surplus. On the other hand, those who favored such controls naturally gave a lower priority to matters of marketing and trade. From 1922 until he resigned as AA Administrator on December 15, 1933, and after, Peek was against production controls. The failure of the marketing schemes of the Federal Farm Board did not change his ideas. During its sway he called talk about controlling production "extremely dangerous." [29] During the campaign of 1932, during the lame-duck period, and into the new administration, Peek called for a sweeping program for farm recovery—without decisive measures for crop reduction.

During the hectic winter of 1932-1933 Peek conferred daily with interested parties on a farm bill. He was dismayed at the emphasis Wallace, Wilson, Ezekiel, and others placed on production controls, complaining that the farm leaders were being dominated by economists.[30] In February and March, 1933, he testified at hearings held by the Senate Committees on Finance and Agriculture that marketing agreements would be the most important part of a farm bill. He stated that he would agree to direct interference with supply only as a last resort in a great emergency (February), or if a slight proportion of the maturing crop threatened to destroy the whole industry (March), adding the puzzling remark, "That is what happens with unregulated, uncontrolled supply. . . ." [31]

Gilbert Fite, Peek's objective biographer, pointed out an inconsistency in Peek's thought. Peek had talked for ten years about giving farmers the kind of influence on prices which business and labor had achieved, but "he was unwilling to follow the policies of business and restrict output." It was his "deep-seated antagonism to a program of economic scarcity for agriculture which would not permit him to take this last logical step." Production controls, he believed, would weaken the backbone of the nation and the capitalistic system—the independent landowning farmer. It was "this belief which . . . forced him to oppose any program of restricted production." [32]

After 1927, when he began to prepare his memorandum for Smith, Tugwell was as consistent in his support of production controls as Peek was in his opposition to them. In his article in *The Annals* in 1929 he declared that "unless surpluses were controlled, they might grow so large as to swamp any thinkable administrative scheme." He contended that the McNary-Haugenites contradicted themselves in objecting to crop controls as a departure from laissez faire. Their plan called for a very active government, but they would not move to the heart of the problem. Tugwell protested that "literal interpretations of doctrine, and hysterical fears of allowing the camel's nose to get under the tent, have served to bring doctrine into dispute. Free enterprise as a useful system will be more questioned than it might be if it were interpreted more flexibly. . . ." [33] Three years later he got his chance to promote effectively the production controls which, he recalled, "every realist knew to be necessary." [34]

For the *marketing agreements* which Peek considered the most important part of a farm bill Tugwell had some very harsh criticism. In *The Democratic Roosevelt* he attributed them to clever and powerful processors, middlemen, and financial houses, who were "determined that there should be no reduction in the volume of goods passing through their hands." To them the domestic-allotment plan was anathema. They favored marketing agreements and dumping because they hoped that the agreements would give them—in return for higher prices to farmers—exemption from the antitrust laws. Then they would pass their higher costs, and maybe more, on to consumers. Tugwell concluded that "the processors were more influential in shaping policy than the farmers," and the man "who most prominently represented this point of view" was George Peek. [35]

The conflicting views of Peek and Tugwell on *foreign markets* related to their ideas on production controls. Peek believed that there really was no such thing as overproduction. The government's task was to maintain parity prices at home and find markets abroad for the surplus. He testified before the Senate Finance Committee in February, 1933, that the "vacuum created in the world's agricultural markets by our withdrawal is being filled by other exporting countries. . . ." He told the Senators production controls were not necessary. What was needed was the reopening of normal export markets through international trade agreements, reciprocal tariffs, application of foreign debt to payment for our exports, and stabilization of international currencies. [36] On other occasions Peek expressed a curious idea about export markets. He urged farmers to refuse to reduce production of exportable crops unless the government compelled industry to reduce its overseas sales. Gilbert Fite commented that industry and agriculture did not compete for foreign markets to the extent that Peek assumed they did. In fact, reducing industrial exports would result in a decrease in total sales of farm products because of a shrinkage in domestic demand. Peek's scheme, Fite concluded, had "no particular merit." [37]

Tugwell's rejection of Peek's ideas on foreign markets resulted not only from a primary concern with production controls. It was also based on a different estimate of foreign markets. American farmers, Tugwell pointed out, had not withdrawn from export markets—they had lost them in the nonmilitary conflict after World War I between national self-sufficiency programs. Thus, Tugwell later wrote, Peekism was a "stubborn refusal to recognize reality" which did not make sense in the circumstances.[38] Tugwell by no means favored withdrawal from export markets. He observed in 1933 that agricultural adjustment would be "much easier if our goods could move to foreign markets." [39] Nor did the domestic-allotment plan call for withdrawal, as Peek—with what Fite called "a degree of uncertainty and confusion"—implied that it did.[40] The allotment plan allowed for the production, in addition to domestic needs, of whatever product could be profitably exported. The alternative to production controls, Tugwell recalled, was the sale abroad of "something like twice the volume of farm products sold in recent years. That this was a hopeless dream was all too apparent." [41] Even Peek conceded, in a letter to William Randolph Hearst in the summer of 1932, that foreign markets were not what they used to be.[42] But he did not relent in his opposition to production controls.

Peek and Tugwell differed sharply in their concepts of the place of *tariffs* in a farm program. This difference, again, arose from their disagreement on production controls. Peek and the McNary-Haugenites emphasized "tariff effectiveness" for farm prices. But historically tariff-protected industry had geared its production primarily to the home market—something which Peek was not willing to do. The McNary-Haugenites, Tugwell remarked in his memorandum to Alfred E. Smith, wanted preservation of the domestic market for American farmers without upsetting the organization of agriculture on an export basis. The logical outcome of protection of the home market, Tugwell insisted, was organization along domestic lines. A student of farm policies has held that the "chief fallacy" of the McNary-Haugen plan lay in its tariff provisions. He quoted Peek's friend, Chester C. Davis, who pointed out that a nation cannot sell exports if it does not allow imports.[43] Davis' comment also applied to Tugwell's Advance Ratio Price Plan, which provided for imports only through specific arrangements in specific instances. But Tugwell and the allotment advocates did not want to have their cake and eat it too. The McNary-Haugenites, on the other hand, after providing tariff protection, still had to dispose of surplus through export. In all probability this would require dumping with all its bad effects.

The tariff also pertained to the *calculation of fair farm prices*. Beginning in 1922 Peek encouraged the compilation of figures which showed a ratio of farm prices to industrial prices that was disadvantageous to the farmer. He proposed to overcome this disadvantage by making the "tariff effective." Later he used the term "parity," but he did not mean by this a ratio price calculated on the exchangeability of agricultural for industrial goods in a historical base period. Peek stuck to the "tariff effective" idea down into the 1930's. On April 30, 1932, in a letter to Roosevelt, he urged the Governor to come out in favor of some mechanism which would make the "tariff effective" on the domestically consumed portion of export staples. Peek was enthusiastic over Roosevelt's major farm speech at Topeka in September, 1932. He congratulated the Democratic candidate and added that the "principle of making the tariff effective for agriculture should be stressed." [44]

The allotment supporters, too, began by referring, as Professor Black did, to a "free trade price plus the tariff" for the domestic crop.[45] In time, they shifted to the use of the term "parity" in the specific sense of an index price related to some historical base period (they eventually settled on 1909-1914 as an era of fair exchangeability of agricultural for industrial products). This shift enabled them to avoid the complicated and sometimes contradictory tariff policies which the McNary-Haugenites formulated, for, it should be noted, calculations of a "tariff effective" price and a "parity" price were different and would not necessarily yield the same figures. M. L. Wilson was convinced by 1932 that the tariff was not a valid basis for determining a fair price. He suggested sticking to it for the time being because people had been so educated to "this tariff effective business." [46] He would find Tugwell responsive to his views. In his report to Smith, Tugwell had asserted that the tariff did not account for all of industry's advantage over agriculture, and the very name of his scheme—the Advance Ratio Price Plan—indicated his opinion in this matter.

By early 1933, "parity," for which Peek, to his lasting credit, had fought for more than a decade, was widely accepted in its "ratio price" rather than its "tariff effective" version. But there was no love lost between the two main schools of thought on the attainment of fair farm prices, however they were calculated, as the opportunity neared for translating "parity" into law.

15. The Agricultural Adjustment Act: 1932-1933

The promotional activities in the early 1930's of the advocates of the domestic-allotment plan took on added significance after the Democrats nominated a presidential candidate who, if elected, would sign a farm-relief bill. In August, 1931, a Conference on Economic Policy for American Agriculture met at the University of Chicago. M. L. Wilson summarized the Conference in a pamphlet, *Land Utilization*. Tugwell wrote Wilson that he liked his line of reasoning.[1] Within a year the two professors would meet. That was after Tugwell had become a Brain Truster and, with Henry Morgenthau, Jr., had taken charge of the Brain Trust's agricultural division. Tugwell learned about the latest version of the domestic-allotment plan in the spring of 1932 from Beardsley Ruml and spoke to Roosevelt about it, although not in detail.[2] Meanwhile, in April, a group of allotment supporters met in Chicago, creating a promotion committee of five men, including Wallace and Wilson.[3] Wilson then went to Washington to publicize the plan in the last full session of a Hoover Congress. It was at this juncture that Ruml introduced Wilson to Tugwell. According to Russell Lord, the two professors "took to each other at once." [4]

They met again at a meeting of agricultural economists which opened in Chicago on June 23. After the general session Tugwell and Wilson had a private discussion, during which Tugwell had to struggle to keep Wilson on the narrow subject in which Roosevelt was interested.[5] Tugwell also conferred with Wallace, Ezekiel, and several others. "And," he recalled, "to show how close a margin we worked on," what he learned from them "went to Albany by wire; and it came back to Chicago by plane—incorporated in Mr. Roosevelt's acceptance speech." [6]

In the acceptance address of July 2 Roosevelt spoke in general terms, referring to "reasonable" tariff protection for export staples, in return for which the farmers would "agree ultimately to such planning of their production as would reduce the surpluses. . . ." Tugwell was disappointed. He had urged a statement of Wilson's plan in specific terms, and he continued to insist that Roosevelt should give the farmers a program rather than vice versa.[7] But, Tugwell later explained, Roosevelt, the politician, wanted assurances of practicability and wide consent.[8] The farm leaders had been arguing for years over the relative merits of various plans. This was no time to push on them a new plan which he himself did not fully grasp. In July, 1932, Tugwell later noted in his diary, Roosevelt had yet to comprehend the shift from "tariff effective" to "ratio price" parity.[9]

On July 25, 1932, Wilson wrote to Tugwell, informing him of fund-raising activities for a campaign to publicize the allotment plan. Businesses which sold to farmers were the chief contributors. Wilson also filled Tugwell in on the background of Henry I. Harriman, whom he quoted as saying that the Hoover administration was "growing worse from day to day. . . ." Wilson was happy to learn that Tugwell and some of the friends of the Governor were going to meet Harriman.[10] On August 7 Wilson wrote to Tugwell, stating that he was going to Washington, as the representative of the Governor of Montana, to seek help from the RFC for drought-stricken farmers.[11] Wilson then went to New York, where he spent a day with Tugwell and Moley, and to Hyde Park, where he concluded that, due to Tugwell's efforts, Roosevelt's position on the allotment plan was sound. Back in New York, Tugwell and Wilson met Wallace, who was on his way to see Roosevelt.[12]

Now, in the middle of August, the agricultural Brain Trust concentrated on preparations for Roosevelt's major speech on farm policy, to be made at Topeka on September 14. On September 28 Wilson wrote to Tugwell, "I have just . . . offered a thanksgiving to the Gods for you in recognition of what you have done through the FDR camp to put the . . . Allotment Plan on the map. It is all due to you . . . we are deeply appreciative and want you to accept us as fellows in the pragmatic economic fellowship."[13] Tugwell's reaction to Wilson's accolade was both modest and accurate. According to Gilbert Fite, he "gave credit where credit was due—to M. L. Wilson."[14]

In a letter to Tugwell of October 8 Wilson expressed his misgivings about farm politicians' opposition to the allotment plan. Peek, he noted, was not a politician, and he was "a good fellow on general principle . . . open and frank, very friendly to the allotment plan as far as he understands it." Wilson suggested that Roosevelt should say little about the tariff "but press hard on the constructive side of the program." The farmers were going to vote Democratic not because of Roosevelt's different tariff ideas, "but because they think he will give them a new deal." Wilson warned that the "farm fellows are going to keep pressing for inflation and the cheaper dollar."[15]

Wilson's letter of October 24 summarized the situation in the West. Farmers, lacking education in production control, thought prices could be raised "by magic without any effort by them." Many farm leaders did not understand the allotment plan because they were "wedded to the equalization fee and don't want to know." They thought "FDR's not going to be firm and will take any plan they propose." John Simpson of the Farmers Union was "going around saying that Roosevelt told him there would be five billion dollars in printed money." Wilson also pointed out that the resolution of a meeting of the three big farm organizations in Chicago on October 11 did not mention production controls. The organizations stressed suspension of foreclosures, amendment of the Farm Marketing Act, and enforcement of laws on trading in commodity futures. Wilson declared, "If FDR will stand firm, he can get what he wants; if not, there will be no production control—the heart of the problem to you and me." (This did not mean that Wilson and Tugwell were not interested in other devices. For example, in this letter Wilson proposed the creation of debt-adjustment committees, instead of Simpson's "funny money," for cutting farmers' debts.) Wilson concluded his letter of October 24 with a tribute to Harriman, calling him a "Greek hero" who had stayed with the allotment plan despite a "panning" from General Mills and the Chicago Grain Exchange. He enclosed, as he had with his letter of October 8, a legal opinion on the constitutionality of his scheme.[16]

Tugwell echoed Wilson's warning in a letter of November 3, stating that the farmers, who had granted few concessions to Roosevelt during the campaign, "will try to get what they want out of the allotment plan without giving anything in return in the way of restricted production." Wilson replied on November 28 that he was "convinced that the allotment plan without production control will simply stimulate production."[17]

After the election the agricultural Brain Trusters tried to get a bill through the lame-duck session of Congress. They hoped to get price-raising legislation in operation before the spring planting season in order to prevent a collapse of the whole farm credit structure. Tugwell and Morgenthau went to Washington. On December 12 Tugwell addressed a meeting of about forty representatives of farm organizations. He emphasized "parity" over "tariff effectiveness."[18] By mid-December agents of the major farm organizations were actively collaborating with Tugwell, Wilson, Ezekiel, and Frederick P. Lee, a Washington attorney experienced in drafting farm bills since McNary-Haugen days.[19]

At Roosevelt's suggestion, Tugwell returned to Washington in early January. On the 6th he and Wallace heard the House debate on the Jones Bill (Marvin Jones, Dem., Texas). Then they went to a meeting of House Progressives. Tugwell concluded that a processing tax would have to be used to avoid the constitutional ban on price-fixing. He was uncertain about the incidence of both burdens and benefits under the allotment plan, noting in his diary, "We will have to try it."[20] The next day Tugwell again met with Fiorello La Guardia and other Progressives. He approved such meetings because he thought the "bill should win by education, not force." He felt that even if the bill were to fail in the Senate, or Hoover were to exercise his veto, discussion would improve the proposal. A few days after the Jones Bill passed the House on January 12, Roosevelt told Tugwell, "Get it through the Senate, and maybe Hoover will sign it." [21]

During January Tugwell conferred with a number of interested persons, including the farm-organization leaders Edward O'Neal and Earl Smith, Senator James F. Byrnes, Henry I. Harriman, Beardsley Ruml, and Roosevelt. Ruml reported that the millers had pledged their cooperation; he was now going to try his hand with the packers. Tugwell told Roosevelt that the bill should include dairy products. He agreed, at Roosevelt's request, to seek Huey Long's support. He recorded in his diary his misgivings about the initial cost of farm legislation. He hoped it would pay for itself in the emergency.[22]

After passing the House in mutilated form, the Jones Bill failed to get through the Senate. Ernest K. Lindley observed that the lame-duck session fiasco gave Tugwell a distaste for politics and service in Washington which Roosevelt and Wallace could not overcome until just before inauguration.[23] Tugwell recalled how the New Dealers' efforts in the short session were "frustrated by jealous or bargaining legislators." One might have expected passage after all the argument and agreement, but the agreements were illusory, and the processors prevailed with Congress. The debate found proponents of agricultural relief "much deeper in old quarrels." And the final check was furnished by Ellison "Cotton Ed" Smith of South Carolina, Chairman of the Senate Committee on Agriculture.[24] In late February Edward O'Neal told Tugwell that the Smith cotton bill would probably pass the Senate. Tugwell then got Marvin Jones to put the quietus on it in the House. Tugwell told Jones that although Roosevelt would not make any public statement on the subject, the Smith bill would split the West and South when for the first time in years there was a chance for national agricultural legislation. Tugwell concluded, "It is up to you whether you play ball with us." [25]

The January entries in Tugwell's diary describe difficult relations with Morgenthau, a disciple of George F. Warren and William I. Myers of Cornell. The Cornell group stressed tax relief, credit reform, reduction of distribution costs, and monetary measures as the means to farm recovery. Tugwell shared Morgenthau's interest in credit reform, and after the election he asked Ezekiel and D. L. Wickens, also of the Farm Board, to undertake a study. He later brought the two groups together in Albany, where they agreed to a joint study. But Morgenthau went his own way. There were at least two possible reasons for his conduct. He opposed the parity principle, as Tugwell learned at the meetings of farm leaders in Washington on December 12 and 13, and he was trying "to stay in the center of the picture" because he "wants to be Secretary of Agriculture." Tugwell noted that Morgenthau "does not trust my adherents, which is foolish." Finally, after Morgenthau had a quarrel with Moley, he came to Tugwell in a conciliatory mood. He said he wanted to avoid a row. Tugwell replied, "Consult us and keep the lines of authority straight." Morgenthau now seemed convinced that Tugwell was a "workhorse and not a rival." [26]

Looking back, Tugwell attributed the lack of co-ordination in the agricultural Brain Trust to Roosevelt's carelessness in making commitments and assignments and his failure to see the issues involved. Roosevelt's speeches of 1928 and 1930 revealed views on agricultural policy which were a "mixture of back-to-the-landism together with . . . Peekism." [27] It was not until the latter part of January, 1933, Tugwell remarked in his diary, that Roosevelt showed "for the first time that he has thought about the depths of the bill." [28] His conversion from "tariff effectiveness" to "parity," however, did not eliminate disunity. Tugwell promised himself that he would not "fight Morgenthau until the last minute," but he would then "if necessary." [29] As it turned out, Morgenthau went along with Roosevelt's decision. The fight would be with Peek.

With Roosevelt's inauguration there was certain to be, at last, some action for farm relief. On Sunday, March 5, 1933, a White House conference rejected the idea of acting on the agricultural situation through a proclamation—consent was necessary.[30] On Wednesday, March 8, Wallace and Tugwell urged the President to hold the special session of Congress, which was to open the next day, until it passed a farm bill.[31] On the evening of the 8th Wallace wired farm leaders across the nation to come to Washington. Tugwell presided at a preliminary conference on March 10.[32] The main meeting took place in Wallace's office on Sunday, March 12. A committee of farm leaders then went to the White House with their proposals, received a Presidential go-ahead, and Frederick Lee began drafting a bill, a penciled copy of which Roosevelt sent to Tugwell.[33] On March 16 the President sent the bill to Congress.

Tugwell recorded in his diary that there was strong opposition immediately from packers, millers, and spinners, who enjoyed adequate representation in Congress. But the bill got through the House in four days. Its supporters were "busy day and night trying to save it in the Senate." Fortunately, from Tugwell's standpoint, the opposition was split between those who thought the benefits more than offset subjection to controls and those who made the opposite calculation. At the same time, there was "no real push" behind the bill in Congress. It was not enough for radicals like Wheeler, and it was too much for conservatives and

Jeffersonians. Thus, the bitter fighting was between determined minorities. Tugwell concluded that in any event "there will be a law because something is needed." [34] The AA Act became law on May 12.

II

The reader may have concluded that the allotment advocates succeeded by May, 1933, in putting Peekism out of the picture. In fact, Peek, too, was active from 1931 on. In 1933 he was a power to be reckoned with, and the AA Act included his ideas as well as those of the allotment group. Peek's biographer and Peek himself give us an account of this period.[35]

During most of what Fite called "The Farm Board Interlude" Peek remained silent out of sympathy for the administrators of what he considered a futile law. Finally, on November 11, 1931, he publicly urged the addition to the Agricultural Marketing Act of the equalization fee. He did not expect the Hoover administration to act on his proposal. In 1930 he had decided to work for Hoover's defeat, and earlier in 1931 he had indicated privately that his first choice for president was Roosevelt. In the summer of 1932 Peek, like Wilson, took his case to Congress. His proposals called for payments for domestically consumed crops, aggressive marketing abroad, and no production controls—even though he conceded in a letter to Hearst at about this time that in a changed world more drastic remedies than the McNary-Haugen scheme might be in order.

The domestic-allotment group considered Peek's support vital. They valued his political influence more than his ideas on farm relief. Perhaps, Fite suggested, they thought they could convert him to acreage restriction. "If so, they did not know George Peek." In August, 1932, Roosevelt requested Peek's suggestions for the Topeka farm-policy speech. Peek suggested declaring for higher domestic prices and avoiding commitment to any specific plan. During the campaign Peek did everything he could to win the Midwest for Roosevelt, and he considered the latter's triumph his own. From December, 1932, until February, 1933, Peek was in Washington, where he conferred daily with farm leaders and others on legislation in the lame-duck Congress. He did not join Tugwell, Morgenthau, Wilson, and Ezekiel in their meetings with farm leaders on December 12 and 13, but he kept in touch with the conferees from his hotel room. He began to feel that the allotment advocates had the inside track. On the 16th he told Earl Smith that he thought Tugwell represented Roosevelt. In retrospect he remarked, "I cannot say that he represented himself as speaking for Governor Roosevelt. I can say that he did nothing to dispel the impression that he was." Regarding the mid-December meetings, he recalled, "The farm leaders

. . . turned over the whole job . . . to Messrs. Wallace and Tugwell. These gentlemen accepted the responsibility with alacrity. Tugwell knew what he wanted."

Peek stayed in Washington for a time after the failure of the Jones Bill. After he testified before the Senate Finance Committee on February 14, emphasizing marketing agreements, he returned to Moline. He was in the capital once again to attend the meeting of farm leaders which Wallace called for March 12. On the 15th he told Wallace and Tugwell that he had warned the processors that they were through "ganging" the farmer. Tugwell told him to present this kind of talk to the President. On the 18th Peek and Tugwell found themselves getting along less harmoniously—to put it mildly.

They and Wallace and Earl Smith met to discuss Roosevelt's request that Wallace submit a memorandum on his plans for administering a farm law by the 20th. Tugwell said they would have to get busy. Peek interposed, "I can tell you in fifty words how to proceed." He outlined a plan under which advisory councils and representatives of both producers and processors would work out procedure for each commodity. Tugwell objected, "We must write the regulations." Peek replied, "You know nothing of the intricacies of the business of different industries."

On March 24 Peek testified before the Senate Committee on Agriculture. He suggested that the farm bill be flexible but emphasize marketing agreements. The very next day Wallace told the Senators to stress production controls. On April 1, Peek recalled, he told Wallace, "the same men who had messed up legislation last December were doing the same thing again with this new bill." On April 2 Peek, Wallace, Tugwell, Jerome Frank, and Frederick Lee held a meeting during which Peek vowed to oppose restriction of production with all his might. On April 6 some tobacco men told Peek they were fearful of the young men in the USDA, especially Tugwell and Ezekiel. Chester C. Davis also said he was afraid of the "theoretical" Tugwell.

The basic division continued right down to, and beyond, the signing of the AA Act into law. On April 22 Wallace stated in a memorandum to the President that, although any possible inflation might help the farmer meet fixed charges, inflation would not obviate the need for production controls.[36] Peek, for his part, understood his opponents' position: "Neither Mr. Wallace nor Mr. Tugwell knew much about the bill, but there is no doubt that they had in their minds the restriction of production." Peek must have thought he could handle them because on May 3 he agreed to become AA Administrator. It should be pointed out that Peek took some time to make up his mind—Wallace offered him the post on March 12. Peek's first reaction was to suggest Baruch, to whom

Wallace offered the job on March 18. Tugwell, Peek noted, "obviously was not pleased at the trend of affairs." On March 25 Peek remarked to Alf Stone, a farm partisan, "No man with any sense would take the administrative job and have such men as Tugwell and Ezekiel in a position to run rings around him."

Peek finally accepted at a White House meeting on the evening of May 3. Wallace, Roper, Miss Perkins, Woodin, and Cummings of the Cabinet were there. James A. Farley, Lewis Douglas, Morgenthau, Moley, Tugwell, and others were also present. After the meeting Roosevelt combined Peek's and Wallace's organizational charts to Peek's satisfaction. On May 12 Peek wrote Wallace, indicating his understanding that the Administrator would act for the Secretary, differences being settled by the President. "It is perhaps impossible at the present juncture," Peek concluded, "to state even broadly the policies that should prevail. . . ." He mentioned among the possibilities "reduction of acreage or reduction of production as the case may be." (It should be kept in mind that Peek looked upon production controls as a last resort.)

Peek's note to Wallace indicated the *omnibus nature of the AA Act.* "In it," Tugwell later observed, "the Congress simply delegated to the President and the Secretary the power to choose whatever scheme seemed best and put it into action." [37] In other words, there was something in the Act for everyone. For the allotment group there were benefit payments on the domestically consumed portion of the crop. For the McNary-Haugenites there were marketing agreements, quotas, and (Section 12B) the use of processing taxes to pay for losses on exports. There were also several other devices. Senator Smith's cotton-option plan gave the farmer an option on cotton held by the old Farm Board in return for acreage reduction. Another provision enabled the government to lease land from individual farmers in order to take it out of production. The government could maintain prices through loans on storable crops or through direct purchase. One subsection gave the Secretary licensing powers pertaining to the authorization and enforcement of codes of fair practices among marketers. "Probably never in American history," Professor Schlesinger has commented, "had so much social and legal inventiveness gone into a single legislative measure." [38]

The administration of this ingenious measure—with Wallace as Secretary, Tugwell as Assistant Secretary, Peek as AA Administrator, and a variety of policies authorized—led to a bitter clash. We may ask, perhaps in omniscient retrospect, how such a freakish situation developed. Ernest K. Lindley noted that the administration wanted a new law quickly—before spring planting if possible—and did not know which device would be best for which crops. [39] As the proponents of various policies argued, Wallace "had not much hope," Tugwell recalled, "that these quarrels could be resolved in the Congress," and he recommended an omnibus bill to the President. Roosevelt responded favorably. He never liked to put all of his eggs in one basket. His usual practice was to demand preliminary agreement among all concerned. During the campaign he had refused to abandon this practice when Tugwell urged the allotment plan on him. Tugwell was for "establishing commitments which then turned into mandates. But I never won my point, in agriculture or anything else. Franklin took the advice which, as a politician, I suppose his instinct also approved. He left everything fluid, general, and discursive." In the case of the AA Act, when time did not permit general agreement beforehand, Roosevelt, in characteristic fashion, "left to the ministrations of time and his own mediating talents the issues thus remaining unresolved." [40]

It is quite possible that there would have been no battle such as occurred in the AAA in 1933 if a McNary-Haugenite did not hold the post of Administrator. Why was Peek chosen? There can be little doubt that his appointment facilitated passage of the farm bill in the Senate. [41] He was a Baruch disciple, he had had administrative experience in business and government, and he enjoyed prestige with farmers. It was better to entrust this novel legislation, the Senators thought, to the mature Peek than the upstart Brain Trusters. It looks as if the administration, in accepting Peek's services and rejecting his policies, deceived him for political purposes. But a political explanation is not necessarily a complete one. The allotment advocates seem sincerely to have believed, as in Wilson's letters to Tugwell, that Peek would accept their ideas if they seemed reasonably appropriate to a particular situation. Peek's reference in his note to Wallace on May 12 to "reduction of acreage or reduction of production" may have stimulated this belief. Was Peek himself engaging in a bit of deception? Apparently not. He was a lion rather than a fox. There appears to have been some wishful thinking on both sides about converting the opposition. Out of such miscalculations comes trouble.

Peek thought his opponents were foxes. His own explanation of how the unhappy situation in the AAA came about dwelt on conspiracy. In *Why Quit Our Own*, published in 1936, he bitterly charged that the AA Act, in giving production controls equal status with his marketing agreements, was the product of an eleventh-hour conspiracy on the part of a handful of economists and professors, led by Tugwell, against the farmers and the American people. He alleged that the "bill was the composite of a variety of ideas contributed by Tugwell, Morgenthau, Ezekiel, M. L. Wilson, some other professors and economists and perhaps Henry Wallace. It was not the farmers' measure." [42] The farm organizations were "willing to buy anything" in an emergency. By the middle of March, Peek observed, "Tugwell appeared satisfied that he was getting whatever he was after." [43] A number of commentators supported Peek's implication that Tugwell was primarily responsible for the provisions of the AA Act. For example, in a 1936 campaign piece Richard Barry asserted that the farm leaders did not see the bill or any part of it before Congress received it; the printer's copy exhibited copious marks in red pencil, "and it is known that Professor Tugwell is addicted to a red pencil." [44]

In leveling accusations of conspiracy at Tugwell in his election-year book, Peek overlooked a number of things. He neglected a decade of agitation by farm interests. From this agitation had emerged a number of proposals. Coolidge and Hoover had rejected them. Rejection led to frustration, and frustration led to new proposals, which moved toward control of production. As for the processing tax, Fite pointed out that it was only a short step from the equalization fee.[45] By 1928, Fite asserted, "the idea of compulsory cooperation, the parity concept, and the principle of acreage restriction had all entered the thinking of agricultural policy makers." [46] By 1930, Fite added, the Farm Board's experience had shown that curtailment of production was essential to an effective price-support program.[47] Peek implied that these developing ideas were kept a secret. If that were true, it was despite his own efforts and those of Wilson, Tugwell, and Wallace, all of whom, according to two historians, "helped to provide three years of the most intensive economic education the American people ever received. . . ." [48]

Coming down to the three months before the farm bill went to Congress in the middle of March, we find that Peek was in touch with the December meeting of farm leaders by telephone, and that he attended the March meeting in Wallace's office. Wallace listed as the authors of the bill himself, Lee, Frank, Ezekiel, Tugwell, Peek, Charles Davis, and Charles Brand.[49] Davis and Brand favored Peek's approach. It is interesting to note that in 1936 Peek named only Lee and Ezekiel as authors.[50] In any event, the opportunities the farm leaders had, either directly or through Peek, their self-appointed agent, to learn about the bill were enough to undermine Peek's conspiracy thesis. Incidentally, the objections which Peek voiced in 1936 to the authority, established by conspiracy, of the Secretary—the "czar" of agriculture [51]—did not square with his testimony before the Senate Committee on Agriculture in 1933. Then he had advised that the legislation must be flexible, giving broad administrative powers to the Secretary.[52] This is what the farm organizations, after the lame-duck farce in Congress, desired.[53] And Congress itself, Tugwell wrote in retrospect, was ready to delegate its powers. This was "not attributable to the influence of any one person. It was the result of panic." [54]

When the legislative struggle began on March 16, Ernest K. Lindley noted, the farm bill enjoyed the support of seven leading farm organizations.[55] Basil Rauch averred that, in view of the farmers' support of the domestic-allotment plan, Peek's charge that the farm organizations had little to do with the AA Act had to be taken "in the narrow sense of actual participation in its writing. . . ." [56] Henry Wallace maintained that "the bill carried out the wishes of the farm leaders' conference" in early March and was in many respects the "logical crystallization of the long struggle for adequate farm legislation." [57] Stuart Chase declared: "If any American believes that the New Deal agricultural legislation was the product of dreamers, long-haired professors, and agents from Moscow, he is a pretty good dreamer himself. It was the product primarily of local farmers crying to be delivered from their competition." [58] Fite concluded: "It can be hardly overemphasized . . . that the New Deal program was not the work of wild-eyed radicals, eastern college professors, or impractical idealists. It resulted from the work of hard-bitten practitioners, many of whom leaned toward political conservatism." [59]

Finally, we may point out a few more facts relevant to Peek's conspiracy charge. Roosevelt told him in early March that the bill must contain both approaches—Peek's and Wallace's.[60] Thus, despite the eclipse of the marketing-agreement idea after 1929,[61] the bill did include Peek's pet schemes, and in 1933 he had a full opportunity to try out his ideas in the dairy industry. Lastly, under all the circumstances he described, Peek took the job of Administrator. Uncertainty and confusion, yes. Conspiracy, no. As the result of the omnibus nature of the Act, Tugwell noted in *The Democratic Roosevelt*, "the differences were merely transferred to the administrators who continued to differ." [62] And what a battle they had!

16. Tugwell versus Peek and the Purge in the AAA: 1933-1935

Now we can see that a battle in the AAA was virtually inevitable. In early 1933 Tugwell did not see this clearly. An April entry in his diary indicates that he favored Peek for the post of AA Administrator. He preferred a "hard-boiled Progressive," but Peek would bring the Baruch faction's support and the processors' co-operation. Thus progress would be slower, but surer. Peek's other assets were his grasp of the possibilities in the marketing-agreement section of the AA Act, his administrative ability, badly needed for an untried program, and, above all, his loyalty to the cause of agriculture.[1]

On the other hand, Tugwell had some misgivings about Peek, a conservative in philosophy who "may oppose production controls and urge too much on marketing agreements and dumping abroad." Older and wealthier than Wallace and Tugwell, Peek had powerful friends. There was the possibility that he "may run off with the show." Still, despite his doubts, Tugwell was somewhat naïve. Twenty years later he added to his diary the comment that he "should have been certain Peek's appointment would not work." In the struggle for power in Washington, "ruthless to a degree unbelievable to the outsider," Tugwell was "not yet tough enough." He believed the best in people, ignoring jealousies and intrigues. But, he noted, "I learned." [2]

There were two main differences between Peek's and Tugwell's ideas on a farm program. Peek wanted to concentrate on marketing agreements as the means to the recovery of agriculture; Tugwell stressed control of production—as an emergency measure (he remarked in his diary that crop restriction was negative and temporary compared to land utilization, necessarily the core of a long-range plan [3]). Each saw usefulness under certain circumstances in the other's preferred device. The dispute between them was over relative emphasis.

So long as the AAA used both devices, in whatever ratio, marketing agreements themselves were a second source of differences. In Peek's view, the purpose of marketing agreements was domestic disposal of farm products at higher prices for farmers. In Tugwell's view, higher prices would not necessarily be parity prices. Relying on acreage restriction to assure disposal, he contemplated a broader function for marketing agreements. He maintained that they should take into account retail prices as well as the prices farmers received.

Peek's view of agricultural recovery was essentially a narrow one. His policy, he indicated in a frequently quoted remark, was going to be "to try like hell to raise farm prices." His experience in the 1920's with the defunct Moline Plow Company helped to explain his intention. He saw farmers primarily as a market for goods. He was, Tugwell later commented, a brother to those who sold things—seedsmen, fertilizer manufacturers, and others—and wanted farmers to be able to pay for them. "That was a simple impulse and Mr. Peek was an altogether simple man." [4]

Peek ignored the problem of what happened to farmers after increased prices brought them the cost of production and a margin. As one observer put it, he "suddenly went native" when it came to dealing with the processing system which had kept the ratio of retail to farm prices high; he left it to Tugwell and others to devise ways of bringing farm prices into line with farm costs, then cursed them out as socialists for refusing to "fall for the old bunk" that higher farm prices, and not the cost of living, were the test of an effective farm program. [5] In *The Stricken Land* Tugwell noted that Peek was interested in specifics. He did not worry about "the country" or "the economy." [6] Meanwhile, Tugwell wrote in *The Democratic Roosevelt*, Peek anticipated the failure of the domestic-allotment plan and a return to "his own preference for giving responsibility to the processors." [7]

Tugwell's view of agricultural recovery was a holistic one. He was concerned with the relationship between agriculture and the rest of the economy. In his diary he denied the concept that the governmental departments represented "interests." [8] He insisted that undue increases in retail prices, accompanying increases in farm prices, would be translated into higher wages and higher prices for industrial products. Then the farmer, whose purchasing power was an important element in the health of industry, would be back where he started. Thus, as Tugwell stated in a speech in 1934, farmers, industrialists, workers, and consumers had common interests in an intricate, delicate balance of price and income relationships. [9]

The keynote of the holistic thinkers was "reduce the spread." In 1933 Tugwell described the "spread" as "that vast, uncharted region between the six cents a pound the farmer gets for beef cattle, and the fifteen to seventy cents a pound the consumer pays for it." [10] This emphasis on the "spread" explains his assertion in 1934 that the "mandate of consumer protection contained in the Act is second only to that of raising the incomes of farmers"; and in connection with consumer protection through price policies there arose the "intimately correlated question of . . . standards." [11] Tugwell pointed out that selling inferior products to the consumer was the same as overcharging him in its harmful effect on his purchasing power.

The broad view related to the anti-trustbusting ideology. Tugwell held that packers and canners, in return for exemptions from the anti-trust laws, should open their books to the government in order to assure protection of the public interest.[12] The issue was between controlled and uncontrolled monopoly. The processors maintained that the "young liberals" in the AAA sought access to company books as a means of promoting socialistic control of business.[13] The matter of access to books had been a bone of contention at least since the Federal Trade Commission had investigated meat packers two decades previously. Professor Edwin G. Nourse concluded that the question of access to books was, "more than any other," the one on which the marketing agreements went aground.[14]

The broad view met with opposition in the form of the more specialized "farm leader" view—well represented both inside and outside the USDA. When the agricultural forces "accepted the preferred program," Tugwell recalled, "they were no more actuated by concern for the whole than any big businessman who exploits the whole by monopolizing a part."[15] At the same time, Tugwell protested in 1934, the processors and distributors bitterly resisted the AAA Consumers' Counsel's attempts to write into marketing agreements provisions for standards of quality, identity, labeling, and package fill.[16] When the big staple farmers and the processors joined hands, the opposition to the broad view took on added strength.

Peek, in concentrating on the single objective of raising the prices which farmers received, did not practice what he had preached in the 1920's. On May 15, 1933, he declared that the AAA's activities would involve "as little interference with established institutions and methods . . . as is consistent with the fixed purpose of the law; namely, to raise farm prices."[17] In a press release of September 1, 1933, it is true, he deplored waste in distribution at the consumer's expense,[18] seeming to show concern with increasing the percentage of the consumer's dollar which the farmer received. But the first of these two statements characterized his policy. His biographer concluded that "when it came to implementing his program, Peek was surprisingly charitable with the processors and handlers of food products."[19]

Tugwell's attitude toward the processors, compared to Peek's, suggests that Professor Nourse put it mildly when he wrote that marketing agreements went into effect with "rather different views as to their meanings."[20] Tugwell recalled that the processors opposed production controls because they did not want the farmers' bargaining position to improve; they were willing, however, to pay farmers more—provided marketing agreements exempted them from the antitrust laws.[21] They thought, Tugwell recorded privately in 1933, that the AAA would help them increase the "spread." [22] Publicly, he had some harsh words for them, as in a talk which he gave in 1933 to the Food Industries Advisory Board.[23]

Tugwell may have been unnecessarily tactless and unduly severe in his comments to and about the processors. Peek thought he was.[24] After all, the Food Industries Advisory Board expressed the desire of the processors it represented to eliminate unfair trade practices, pay parity prices, and reduce the "spread." [25] But in action the processors were a tough-minded, self-interested group, and they often enjoyed the support of the major farm leaders. The big producers, Russell Lord observed, were willing to "go easy" on big operators in the matter of final prices if the farmer got a "thicker cut." Lord found this difficult to understand "when old-line agrarians had for years been creating a 'personal devil' of the middle man." [26] Describing the alliance of big farmers and processors, Wesley McCune noted that Charles Holman, Secretary since 1921 of the National Co-operative Milk Producers' Federation, defended the distributors. Henry Wallace called Holman's group "distributors masquerading in overalls." [27]

Undoubtedly the processors and distributors had honest differences of opinion with the General Counsel and the Consumers' Counsel. At the same time, their viewpoint was essentially narrow. Recounting the quarrels of the early 1930's before a subcommittee of the Senate Committee on Agriculture in 1937, Holman said, "We resented the establishment of a Consumers' Counsel in a farmers' agency." [28] The processors, Tugwell recalled, continued, after the resignation of Peek, their friend (wittingly or unwittingly), to do all they could to disrupt administration.[29] In March, 1935, as Tugwell was preparing to take charge of the Resettlement Administration, he received a memorandum which summarized the results of a legislative investigation in California of the influence which processors exerted on farm leaders and agricultural agencies of the state government.[30] Perhaps the best indication of the processors' aims and strength was the AAA's failure, noted by Professor Nourse, to achieve significant reforms in marketing.[31]

The formulation of a marketing agreement was a tedious, complex process. It involved public notice, informal discussions, formal hearings, review by the appropriate commodity section of the AAA and the Consumers' Counsel, a conference with processors and handlers, a formal hearing on the revised draft, final agreement, and, again, public notice.[32] Disagreements among and between growers, processors, and distributors—and between them and the AAA—delayed the process as the positions we have just reviewed met in a head-on collision at the administrative level.

II

During Peek's term as Administrator, from the middle of May to the middle of December, 1933, the first basic difference—production controls versus marketing agreements—overshadowed the second—narrow versus broad functions of marketing agreements. The leaders of the opposing factions were Peek and Tugwell. Among Peek's supporters in the AAA were Chester Davis, Chief of Production, and Charles Brand, Co-Administrator. Brand held to Peek's line more closely than Davis. Peek's supporters outside of the AAA included Baruch and Edward O'Neal. Baruch's involvement was general and indirect. His biographer thought that his objections to the AAA were illogical since it was trying to do what the McNary-Haugen bills had attempted.[33] O'Neal, representing the Farm Bureau Federation, found people inside the AAA who were responsive to his views.

Tugwell, holding no official post in the AAA, led from a position behind the front. General Counsel Jerome Frank and Consumers' Counsel Frederic C. Howe, especially Frank, bore the tactical burden. They enjoyed the support of their respective divisions, which included some militant young radicals and some Communists who concealed their Red affiliations. They also received help from USDA personnel besides Tugwell: Paul Appleby, Wallace's assistant; C. B. Baldwin, Appleby's assistant; Mordecai Ezekiel, now Wallace's economic adviser; and Louis Bean, a statistician.[34] Wallace himself, reluctant to quarrel, gave only occasional aid before he finally took a decisive stand.

Tugwell and Frank worked in close association. Professor Felix Frankfurter of Harvard Law School was Frank's original sponsor. The successful young corporation lawyer had been slated for the job of USDA solicitor, but Roosevelt stopped the appointment at James Farley's request. It turned out to be a case of mistaken identity, and Tugwell, whom Frank had been advising on the NRA part of the NIR Act, was embarrassed. He recommended Frank for the General Counselship in the AAA.[35] For a while in 1933 Tugwell, Frank, and Wallace had adjoining rooms at the Cosmos Club. Later, after Wallace brought his family to Washington, Frank and Tugwell shared an apartment.[36]

There were, at first, friendships and ties of mutual respect which crossed the lines of differences, but when bottlenecks in the whole process of orderly administration developed, personal antagonisms became intense.[37] Peek recalled that "the General Counsel's office appeared to be the neck of the bottle, and it was quickly reported to me that . . . Frank was dealing directly with Messrs. Wallace and Tug-well. . . ." [38] While Peek insisted that the young liberals were trying to use the marketing agreements to promote socialism, they maintained that he was the bottleneck: he opposed production controls, after supporting them in a public statement, even though he was Wallace's subordinate in the decision-making hierarchy; he brought in his own men, duplicating the AAA's staff at many points; and he ignored Frank, retaining Frederick Lee as his personal counsel at his own expense. One knowledgeable observer commented that the stubborn, self-willed Peek "tried to run the whole show and apparently believed up to the bitter end that he was Roosevelt's favorite." [39]

Russell Lord, an eyewitness, reported that the fight soon became a dirty one, marked by shabby techniques: planting questions in press conferences, slipping out trial balloons to certain correspondents, cultivating columnists with anonymous tips, and—the lowest trick of the zealots in any organization—holding up papers or decisions by burying them in detail or "tricking them out" with legal or bureaucratic harness. "Both sides had learned to do good, as each saw it, on the sly." [40]

The clash between Peek and Wallace over administrative authority began as soon as, even before, the President signed the AA Act on May 12. When Tugwell noted in his diary on April 13 that Congress "will have to concede executive powers in agriculture in this emergency," [41] he did not foresee how much trouble the delegation of those powers would cause. But Peek must have foreseen it—despite his assertion after he left the administration that Wallace's emphasis on acreage controls took him completely by surprise. Peek was familiar with Wallace's policy preferences, and his requiring direct access to the President as a condition of his accepting the position of Administrator indicated that he expected to have fundamental differences with the Secretary.[42]

Wallace, for his part, wrote to the President on May 15, objecting to "Mr. Peek's insistence on using you as an umpire between him and myself. . . ." This tactic, Wallace continued, "will involve you unnecessarily in administrative detail and will prove to be a fundamental handicap to unified administration. . . ." Wallace respected Peek's ability and sympathized with his desire to raise farm prices, but, as a matter of administrative necessity, he was asking Roosevelt to renew formally a previous verbal assurance that the Secretary was Peek's superior.[43]

Peek conceded on the question of production controls for the 1933 planting season. The prospect, on the basis of crops already planted, was one of staggering surpluses in cotton, wheat, corn, and hogs. Referring to the cotton-reduction program in a radio talk on July 14, Peek declared, "what has transpired . . . marks an epoch in American history." [44] He did not recall this enthusiasm in 1936 when he wrote, "I had no part in shaping the program . . . there seemed nothing to do but go along with it in view of the existing emergency." [45]

In September serious differences developed over the formulation of two marketing agreements—one for sugar, the other for tobacco. Wallace followed the Legal Division's advice and rejected an agreement which the sugar industry had written because it increased the "spread" without helping the growers.[46] Peek objected to the sweeping specifications on access to company books which the Legal Division wrote into the flue-cured tobacco agreement. In early October he took the dispute to Roosevelt and received Presidential backing.[47] Perhaps this incident led him to overestimate his credit rating at the White House political bank.

By November, when plans for acreage controls for the 1934 crop were being developed, Peek was fighting mad. On November 15 he sent a memorandum to Wallace, stating that Frank had become impossible and requesting his removal. When Wallace failed to reply, Peek repeated his request in a memorandum of November 25.[48] Frank had been ready to resign a number of times before this, but Wallace and Tugwell had held him in line.[49] Wallace's silence in the face of this showdown amounted to a choice of Frank over Peek. More important than friendship was the basic agreement of Wallace, Tugwell, and Frank on policy. Besides, Wallace was getting fed up with Peek's taking problems directly to the President.

An incident occurred in late November and early December which appears to have been the last straw for Peek. He had arranged for the subsidized export to Europe of a large quantity of butter, and he requested an advance of $500,000 out of processing-tax revenue to make up the difference between foreign and domestic prices. Wallace was in Warm Springs, and Tugwell, as Acting Secretary, turned down Peek's request. Tugwell explained his action in a memorandum to Wallace and Peek on December 2. The memorandum, an essay on the evils of dumping, satisfied Wallace. Since April Peek had been accusing Wallace and Tugwell of destroying foreign markets. Now he accused them of shelving the farm policy which Roosevelt had promised the American people. He directed his charges at both men because he believed, as he recalled in 1936, that Tugwell "was not acting on his own." He asserted that no dumping was involved because the importing nations made no objections.[50] He did not mention the reactions of butter-producing nations or American housewives.

Peek's assumption that Tugwell "was not acting on his own" was correct. Gilbert Fite reported a telephone conversation between Tugwell and Wallace on the evening of November 27.[51] Tugwell himself later offered a brief but adequate explanation of his and Wallace's co-operation. He recalled, "Henry went out of town for that one." [52] If Wallace did not choose to come directly to grips with Peek over the butter matter, he soon had no choice about facing his adversary. Peek did not take the butter decision lying down. He told Wallace that according to his (Peek's) original stipulation with the President, he "should have to discover from the President in person exactly how he wanted the Act administered." If the President wanted the Wallace way, Peek would leave. If he preferred Peek's way, Wallace's course was to co-operate. The showdown on interpretation never came, Peek wrote, because the President sent for him and offered him a new job. [53]

Peek failed to explain that the President offered him a new job precisely because a showdown had come. Peek had challenged Wallace's authority in such a way that Roosevelt had to make a choice. Tugwell had helped to bring about this situation. His issuance of the decision on Peek's butter-export scheme not only moved the Administrator to challenge Wallace, but it also caused the President to summon Tugwell to the White House. If Roosevelt was displeased, Tugwell, according to his memoir, was angry too. He told the President that Peek's opponents were fighting the President's battle. They discussed the possibility of another job for Peek, and Tugwell suggested something connected with developing foreign markets. [54]

The end of Peek's tenure as Administrator now came quickly. On December 6 he received a "slap" from Wallace which *Time* credited to Tugwell. [55] In a press conference in Wallace's office, which no one who attended "will ever forget," the Secretary, with Peek at his side, "calmly said that Peek's milk agreements were a failure and proceeded to write Peek's work off as a total loss. Yet it was done too impersonally and too adroitly for Peek to take offense." [56] It is true that the first and most important marketing agreements, covering the handling of milk in the Chicago area, were on the verge of collapse. In October Chester Davis had recommended production controls for the entire dairy industry, and Professor Nourse later cited the milk agreements as a demonstration of how little it was possible to accomplish through regulation of marketing. [57]

On the evening of the 6th Peek, Wallace, and Hugh Johnson met with the President. [58] On the 7th Wallace and Tugwell visited the White House in the morning, and Peek saw the President twice during the day; on Peek's second visit Roosevelt asked him to resign. [59] On the 11th Peek and a number of his supporters (Brand had resigned at the end of September) submitted their resignations. [60] On December 15 Peek agreed to become the President's Special Adviser on Foreign Trade, in which position he was to co-operate with the State Department. Roosevelt was relieved. There was now no need to be concerned that Peek would be outside the administration, attacking the farm program.

One version of Peek's departure from the AAA had Tugwell suggesting that the President make Peek Minister to Czechoslovakia, with a roving European assignment as a salesman for American farm products.[61] Tugwell's memoir gives the impression that it was Roosevelt who mentioned the post in Prague as a possibility. Tugwell recalled that he, himself, "did not act positively for Peek's ouster; his resignation amounted to a choice on the part of the President." He also remembered that he was fond at first of the "bluff, shrewd, persistent" Peek and tried to be conciliatory for a while. Later he made no effort to pacify Peek, finding him "essentially stupid." Thus, it appears that despite Tugwell's disclaimer of any positive action on his part for Peek's removal, there was a great deal of substance in Gilbert Fite's conclusion that Tugwell, "more than anyone else," wanted to get rid of Peek and maneuvered to force him into resigning.[62]

Tugwell naturally approved the President's decision, but he thought it had been delayed too long. He later referred to Roosevelt's political-administrative technique of letting fights go on a long time before choosing sides.[63] This technique may have been effective politically. Administratively, it was bad for policy and morale—at least in the case of the AAA.[64] Other commentators asserted that Roosevelt decided for radicalism. Mark Sullivan called the fight in the AAA a "struggle between contrasting ideals of government." [65] *Time* described Peek's opponents as "Socialists" or "near-Socialists," led by Rex Tugwell.[66] Peek himself, the *Des Moines Register* remarked, tended to call "everyone . . . in Washington who disagreed with him either a fool or a knave." [67]

It is true, as Gilbert Fite remarked, that a number of lawyers on the AAA staff, many of them bright young urban liberals, were less interested in raising farm prices than they were in controlling business in some authoritarian way outside of the American tradition.[68] But the fight in the AAA could be accounted for without reference to their activities or influence. And Tugwell, Frank, and Howe were no Reds. In his book, *Save America First*, Frank condemned Marxism.[69] As for Howe, the old-time Progressive, in Moley's opinion he "innocently scared the daylights out of business men with talk natural to him after many years of gentle agitation." [70]

Some commentators disagreed with Hugh Johnson, who thought his friend Peek had been "kicked in the slats." [71] J. F. Carter stated that Peek clung to his "vest-pocket" remedy, the equalization fee, long after European countries' trade policies had made it unrealistic. Carter saw in Peek's new assignment "poetic justice with a dash of irony . . . Peek thought the farm surplus ought to be exported. Let him try to export it!" [72] Fite made some harsh comments on Peek's farm program, concluding that it was oversimplified in separating agriculture from the rest of the economy, and inadequate to handle ever-increasing surpluses. He criticized Peek for seeing only "black and white on the farm question—never gray." [73]

III

The year 1933 was one of frustration for those who wished to use marketing agreements to peg retail prices in their own interest, those who expected agreements to bring substantial gains in farm prices, and those who hoped to reform marketing practices. [74] The second battle in the AAA, in 1934, centered not so much on differences in basic views as on the administration, in detail, of marketing agreements.

Before Peek left the AAA, he told his successor Chester Davis to "get rid of Frank and that crowd." [75] Davis thought he could handle them, and there was some basis for his confidence. His educational background, his knowledge of economics, and his elasticity of mind were superior to Peek's. Russell Lord described Davis as "kind and intelligent, humorously self-deprecatory, cordially open-minded, and capable of continued learning." Lord listed Davis' assets: agrarian sympathies unconfined by formulated landlord agrarianism, years of experience in dealing with businessmen, an aptitude for presiding without bias over negotiations at long conferences in the AAA, an ability to ease personal tensions and keep disagreements above a personal level, and a talent in skilled, patient administration. [76]

Tugwell did not oppose Davis as he had opposed Peek. By 1934 he had little to do with the AAA. He did make Davis angry on one occasion, in June, 1934, when he publicly criticized large packers, with whom Davis was then negotiating, for refusing to open their books. [77] But he played a part in the 1934 battle only indirectly—the "young liberals" still considered him their moral leader. The differences between Davis and the "young liberals" involved administrative technique rather than broad policy. A McNary-Haugenite who had shifted to the allotment plan, Davis also believed that gains were to be made in the reform of marketing. But he did not want agreements which would be beneficial to the farmer to fail because of doctrinaire insistence on some ideal requirement. He accepted what he could get if it seemed reasonable, Nourse commented, "biding his time for the accomplishing of results not obtainable at the moment." [78]

For all his moderating qualities of intellect and personality, within a year Davis had taken from the "young liberals" about all that he could stand. Two incidents at the turn of the year (1934-1935) exhausted his patience. One was a clash with the Consumers' Counsel over the standards clause in a marketing agreement for asparagus. The other, more important and not just a matter of administrative technique, was an attempt by the "young liberals" to tie in social reform with benefit payments to cotton farmers. The Cotton Section, the Consumers' Counsel, and the Legal Division of the AAA had agreed on a workable compromise under which landlords who signed acreage-adjustment contracts would agree not to reduce the number of their tenants during the first year of operation. While Davis was away on a trip, the Legal Division reinterpreted the AA Act and ordered state administrators in the South to enforce in the second year of operation a ruling which virtually compelled landlords to keep the same tenants on the same land and in the same houses. An uproar in the South reached Davis, who flew into Washington "with his jaw shut tight." Wallace, who, like Davis, was aware of the serious problem of farm tenancy in the South, agreed with the Administrator that the "young liberals" had gone beyond the purposes of the AA Act in a wholly impractical way. He gave Davis, who was "tired of sharp tricks," permission to handle the situation as he saw fit.[79]

On Monday, February 4, Davis issued a mimeographed sheet announcing a reorganization of the AAA. He fired Frank and four members of the Legal Division: Lee Pressman, Victor Rotnem, Francis Shea, and Alger Hiss. He demoted Howe and dismissed Gardiner Jackson of Howe's staff, elevating Calvin B. Hoover to the post of Consumers' Counsel. The next day, before the start of a meeting of the Emergency Council at the White House, Wallace told the President about Davis' action. When the press got wind of the story, Wallace and Davis scheduled a press conference, which proved an exceedingly trying occasion for Wallace. The Secretary told the hostile reporters that Frank was removed for the sake of harmony, not because of his social or economic views. Davis, too, stressed administrative considerations: "It was just a mounting difficulty in getting things done, and, after all, our job is to get things done."[80]

Wallace's only reference to Tugwell was, "Mr. Tugwell is out of town and you will have to ask him what he thinks of this change." (Raymond Gram Swing called Tugwell's absence "a godsend if there was to be a purge."[81]) The reporters did not have to wait long. Tugwell, recuperating in Florida from an attack of influenza, flew back to Washington to save Frank and company. He was too late. The President had already told the press that he did not intend to intervene in this internal matter in the AAA.[82] Tugwell went to the White House and resigned to the President. He expressed his willingness to go to Interior, assuring the President that he preferred to work with the reputedly difficult Ickes than to stay with Wallace, who was preparing to "take a broad jump from a bowl of jelly." Roosevelt, aware that Interior wanted Tugwell for conservation activities, told him to stay in the USDA for the time being and talk it over with Wallace. Wallace wanted Tugwell to stay in Agriculture, with the understanding that he would have nothing to do with the AAA. Tugwell replied that he was Davis' superior officer and would not stay on such terms. On February 9 Ickes telephoned Tugwell, telling him to sit tight until he (Ickes) got back from a trip. On February 20 Tugwell told Ickes he would go back to Columbia except for his loyalty to the President. Ickes said that he hoped to get an Undersecretaryship for conservation and would be happy to have Tugwell take the job.[83]

Ickes did not get his Undersecretaryship at this time, and Tugwell, receiving reassurance from Roosevelt, remained in the USDA. Reassurance took the form of appointment to a new "operating council" of the AAA and the promise that Tugwell would have a responsible part in the expenditure of work-relief funds. In addition, Frank and his followers were to get new government jobs.[84] There was also some consolation for Tugwell in the probability that Hoover, the new Consumers' Counsel, would advocate policies similar to Howe's.[85] But Tugwell was bitter about the firings, telling Ickes they were a "sell-out."[86] Despite Roosevelt's reassurance, he considered himself "squeezed out" of the AAA, and he turned his interest to the Resettlement Administration.[87] In *The Stricken Land* he noted that, having been impressed at first with the AAA's democratic procedures, he soon saw the agency as the big farmers' captive. He had concluded that only the processors, equipment manufacturers, and 20 per cent of the farmers would come off well under the AAA; sharecroppers, tenants, and farm laborers were "having a hard time" sharing in its benefits.[88] The RA would help them. Meanwhile, Tugwell's relations with Wallace were deteriorating.[89]

Again, press reactions were varied. *Time* reported that "the biggest single bevy of Brain Trusters in the Administration had been quietly but firmly turned out as trouble-makers."[90] On the other hand, Raymond Gram Swing, writing in the *Nation*, declared that the dismissals were not a purge of radicals but an expression of the political power of processors, distributors, and big producers to prevent a shift of economic power from themselves to the public in the interest of the consumer and the small producer. It was, Swing concluded, the "end of an era . . . the defeat of the social outlook in agricultural policy."[91]

Again, differences in the AAA could be explained without reference to the radicals' activities or influence. Professor Schlesinger has pointed out that the Communists in the AAA could hardly affect policy. They had to govern their words and deeds so as to hide their identity from Wallace, Frank, and Tugwell, and "the nature of the farm problem was such that it did not lend itself . . . to Communist purposes." [92] Another student of the radicals in the AAA concluded that "the team did not accomplish very much" before Davis broke it up.[93] Among loyal Americans, Tugwell and Frank wanted to reduce the "spread." They were also interested in the small farmer—that is, they were concerned about the distribution of increased farm income. Davis understood this broad view, but he faced the reality, as Swing conceded, of dealing across the table with producers, processors, and distributors who could exert formidable political pressure.[94] Wallace, finding himself in the middle, had remarked before the firings that "in Rex and Chester I've got two ill-matched horses in harness together." [95] At the time of the dismissal he commented that "people with the highest ideals don't have the same conceptions. . . ." [96]

The inevitability of a clash was probably inherent in the situation —the attempt, as in the case of the NRA, to reconcile short-run and long-run objectives, recovery and reform. Davis had to put recovery first, and the AAA, partly due to the nature of its origins, did become the big farmers' agency. One would not have to accept all of the implications of Peek's well-known declaration that the Department of Agriculture was not the "Department of Everything" to concede that the potentialities of the AAA were limited. Perhaps special agencies could more effectively represent the consumer and the small farmer. In any event, while little was done for the consumer, small farmers benefited from the creation in the spring of 1935 of the Resettlement Administration. From that time on Tugwell had very little to do with the AAA and spent only about an hour a day on departmental affairs.[97] Running the RA was a full-time job.

In later years Tugwell's relations with Wallace regained their original warmth. He placed a high valuation on the Iowan's "genuine worth," [98] and he defended Wallace against attacks by militant reformers.[99] He reversed his harsh judgment of 1935, noting that as a fight developed quickly "right under his nose," Wallace compromised for a time in the hope of pleasing all. When the Secretary could no longer postpone a choice of sides, he felt unable to oppose the lobbyists he had nursed back to health. Tugwell did not condemn him for having this feeling— he "conceived he had to be a statesman." Where Wallace made his mistake, Tugwell concluded, was at the start in depending on the professionals: farm leaders, lobbyists, graduates of land-grant colleges. "I took the other line." [100]

Nor did Davis bear any grudge against Frank, who, before his death in 1957, served as special counsel to the RFC, Chairman of the SEC, judge of the United States Court of Appeals for the Second Circuit, and lecturer at Yale Law School. When Frank became a judge in 1941, Davis, borrowing from Kipling, sent him this telegram:

And only the Master shall praise us, and only the Master shall blame;
And no one shall work for money, and no one shall work for fame;
But each for the joy of the working, and each in his separate star,
Shall draw the thing as he sees It, for the God of Things as They Are! [101]

If Frank's sponsor, Tugwell, had been Davis' adversary at the tactical level, he might have received the same telegram in the same year when he became Governor of Puerto Rico. In any case, Davis recognized that there could be honest differences between men who, each in his own way, sought to build a better America.

17. The Department of Agriculture—
Conservation: 1933-1936

Until he became Resettlement Administrator in the spring of 1935, Tugwell worked hard as Assistant Secretary and, after his promotion in June, 1934, as Undersecretary of Agriculture. His efforts may be summarized under three headings: reorganization, special assignments, and conservation.

I

At first Tugwell, in performing his duties, enjoyed excellent relations with Wallace. There was disagreement among commentators as to the influence of each complex man on the other. John T. Flynn suggested that Tugwell, with his superior mind, dominated the relationship.[1] Moley, on the other hand, wrote that Wallace captivated Tugwell with his modesty, charm, and intellectual radicalism.[2] John Chamberlain emphasized differences between the Assistant Secretary and his chief— Tugwell was "too much of a total planner to get along with the more pluralistic Henry Wallace."[3] Russell Lord, who observed both men in action, remarked that Tugwell neither enchanted nor bewitched the argumentative Wallace. They were contrasting personalities—the cool, debonair, skeptical, occasionally curt, and cagily fighting Tugwell, and the rumpled, ardent, shy, folksy, religious, frontally attacking Wallace. But, Lord concluded, they had two important things in common: "respect for the scientific attitude and contempt for the lower levels of political ingratiation and behavior." And beneath their contrasting personalities they had a warm regard for each other.[4]

About the middle of 1934 the relationship began to cool. This was largely a result of the conflict over AAA policy. That clash would not have affected relations between Tugwell and Wallace if there had been no crossing of the lines of jurisdiction which Wallace originally laid down. Tugwell was to be responsible for the old-line bureaus, while Wallace himself was to concentrate on the AAA. In practice this allocation of work did not stand up. For one thing, administrative boundaries could not confine intellectual interests. Wallace, an agricultural scientist and a student of statistical methods, was keenly interested in departmental work.[5] Tugwell, a student for the past decade of proposals for farm legislation, had a heavy investment of time, energy, and thought in the AAA. He also had an informal link to that agency and the Surplus Relief Corporation in the person of Jerome Frank.

Administrative necessities, moreover, required a formal crossing of lines. When Wallace was absent, Tugwell represented the Secretary in the AAA, serving, in effect, as a consultant on major economic policies.[6] Tugwell also sat in for Wallace at Cabinet meetings while the Secretary was out of town seeking farmers' co-operation.[7] At these White House gatherings Tugwell, of course, represented the USDA as a whole. In addition, it appears that Wallace had shortcomings as an administrator. Tugwell recalled that the Secretary's in-between position in the AAA fight hurt his general administrative effectiveness.[8] Tugwell complained to Ickes, who noted in his diary in December, 1934, that "I have had a feeling for some time that Agriculture is badly administered. . . . Henry Wallace is not a good administrator. . . . The other Assistant Secretary, Dr. M. L. Wilson, is as bad as, or worse than, Henry Wallace when it comes to executive work." This situation, Ickes concluded, left Tugwell with "a lot of responsibility without the necessary power," especially since Wallace "insists on keeping men in important posts in Agriculture whom Tugwell regards as untrustworthy and lacking in ability." [9]

Earlier in 1934, in September, Harry Hopkins told Ickes that there had been a falling out between Wallace and Tugwell. Hopkins was of the opinion that Wallace was becoming more conservative.[10] Such a break was understandable to Russell Lord, who commented that the hazy division of labor produced an "anomalous situation, certain to crack wide open; it was simply a matter of time." [11] The low point in the Tugwell-Wallace relationship came with the explosion in the AAA of February, 1935.

Despite differences over policy and difficulties in administration, Tugwell was able to do a lot of solid work in reorganizing the USDA's old-line bureaus. He had, Professor Schlesinger has noted, "a profound belief in an expert civil service," and he considered it his "obligation to give the Department's scientists and technicians the wholehearted official support which previous administrations had denied them." [12] Tugwell had shown his interest in an efficient, effective USDA in 1928 in his report to Alfred E. Smith, in the section "Continuing and Strengthening the Work of the Department of Agriculture." In 1933 he showed how deep this interest was by agreeing, in undertaking the task of reorganization, to take the "heat" off Wallace. The Secretary would tell the bureau chiefs and other bureaucrats, when they objected to changes, that Tugwell was close to Roosevelt and he, Wallace, was helpless.[13]

Reorganization does not make a lively story, but it had a basic, permanent effect on departmental operations. The project was under way as early as January, 1933, when Roosevelt, anticipating a broad program for agriculture, asked Wallace, Tugwell, and M. L. Wilson to draw up working plans for reorganizing the USDA as an instrument of national planning.[14] By March Tugwell, busy with the AA Act among other things, was attacking the problem of reorganization directly. He received valuable aid from Lee Strong, later Chief of the Bureau of Entomology and Plant Quarantine, who headed the Departmental Reorganization Committee; William Jump, Budget Officer of the USDA; and F. B. Bartlett, his administrative assistant.[15]

Reorganization, in Tugwell's estimate "an immense and thankless task," was inextricably connected with budgetary matters. Budget Director Lewis Douglas laid down an ultimatum to the USDA calling for a 60 per cent cut in funds for research, which was tied in with forty regulatory acts and occasional additional statutes. Tugwell hoped through reorganization to save the best activities, and he fought Douglas face to face on the Special Board for Public Works, proposing selective reductions instead of the Budget Director's meat-axe approach. Tugwell also tried to wean the President away from Douglas' antiresearch views. He considered research a long-time need, and he insisted that it took a long time to bring research to a productive state. Halting it was like cutting down a forest.[16]

Tugwell claimed personal responsibility for the establishment of one research facility, the National Agricultural Research Center at Beltsville, Maryland. Several Bureau Chiefs suggested its creation, and he was able to fulfill their request only because emergency funds were available.[17] He encouraged research in another way not directly related to reorganization by arranging for the renewal of American membership in the International Institute of Agriculture. During the lameduck period he talked to Simon J. Lubin, son of the Institute's founder, David L. Lubin, and he won the President's and Senator James F. Byrnes's support for renewal.[18] In the fall of 1934 Tugwell represented the United States at the Institute's annual meeting in Rome. Desk work did not satisfy Tugwell's urge to learn as much as he could about the USDA. On a field trip from August 17 to September 20, 1933, he visited ten western states, meeting personnel of the Bureau of Public Roads, the Forest Service, and various irrigation and conservation activities. This tour, he recalled, convinced the department that he was a "serious collaborator"; and, he concluded, "thirty days in the field was worth five years in an office." [19]

Among Tugwell's special assignments, his appointment to the Surplus Relief Corporation, which reinforced his informal connection with the Corporation through Jerome Frank, deserves mention. This agency used emergency funds to purchase surplus commodities for free distribution to various relief organizations. It functioned, Tugwell later wrote, "for many years and handled millions of tons of produce. But it might as well have not existed so far as the New Deal critics were concerned;

they preferred to pretend that the paradox of hungry people and crop controls remained unresolved." [20]

Another special assignment involved Tugwell in the allocation of sugar-production quotas among the United States, its insular possessions, and Cuba. He received this assignment in early 1934 after negotiations through the summer of 1933 had failed to reach a satisfactory conclusion. In the summer of 1934 Hawaiian planters and Frank Kent, among others, charged that Tugwell was partial and arbitrary in setting quotas.[21] It appears that there would have been complaints no matter how the quotas were set. Reconciling the interests of domestic, Puerto Rican, Hawaiian, Philippine, and Cuban growers was, Tugwell remarked in *The Stricken Land,* a "wholly impossible" task which had to be undertaken and brought to some result. Congress favored the Louisiana and western beet growers. The State Department, for reasons of foreign relations, favored Cuba. Every group had its extremely single-minded lobbyists. In fact, it was the failure of private negotiations in 1933 which had resulted in a request for government intervention. After many conferences in which the interested parties jockeyed for position, a system of import and production quotas was eventually written into law. But no group admitted fair treatment, each harboring grudges against the others and the government. The whole story, Tugwell concluded, "would make a book in itself." [22]

Tugwell's belief in the economic principle of efficiency determined his judgments, if not his current policy recommendations, in the sugar situation. He told a Congressional committee that sugar was a "parasite industry" in the United States. "God knows," Ickes concurred, "that this is true." [23] The President, too, thought the beet-sugar situation was "scandalous." [24] Tugwell afterward remarked that the tariff exemption on Puerto Rican sugar artificially created and maintained an economy of contradictions and paradoxes which supported the inefficient.[25] He went to Puerto Rico in March, 1934, to learn more about the island's economy.[26] He studied needs in rural rehabilitation, soil conservation, and redistribution of land-holding, and he suggested a plan for a soil survey, which the USDA ordered and Governor Blanton Winship approved.[27] On his return to Washington, Tugwell recalled, he discussed with the President his conclusion that some drastic changes, with less emphasis on sugar, were needed in the Puerto Rican economy. Roosevelt displayed an extensive knowledge of the Caribbean, referring to dietary deficiencies and unexploited resources. Tugwell decided that he needed time to think out Puerto Rico's problems in relation to our whole colonial policy.[28] He would be well prepared when Ickes sent him to Puerto Rico in the early forties as a fact-finder and then as Governor.

II

Tugwell's work on reorganization and his special assignments both related, at least in part, to conservation, a subject which brings us to the heart of his concern for agriculture, rural America, and their significance for national welfare. Beginning in 1921, he wrote a number of articles on conservation. In 1933 the desire to fulfill the aspirations he had harbored for years as "an earnest, if relatively amateur, conservationist" was, he remembered, a decisive factor in his decision to go to Washington.[29] There his major efforts involved the conservation of the nation's natural, or physical, and human resources.

Conservationists recognized Tugwell as one of their own. Upon his appointment as Assistant Secretary he received a congratulatory letter from Ovid Butler, Executive Secretary of the American Forestry Association, who remarked that "conservationists in general are gratified." [30] Now, as a public official, Tugwell had to make his views on conservation known to a wider audience. He did this in the years 1933-1936 in a number of articles and speeches. The basic theme Tugwell stressed was that nature imposed rules on men, and violation of these rules brought, slowly but surely, severe punishment. In May, 1935, he cited the experience of China, pointing out how the abuse of the soil in the four hundred years after 1500 reduced Chinese agriculture to a pitiable plight. This had serious implications for Americans, for we, too, had subjected our land to an orgy of exploitation in the nineteenth and twentieth centuries.[31] A kind of Gresham's law, Tugwell remarked a month later, seemed to apply; "the worst practices triumph over the best if they are brought into competition." [32] Retribution was delayed but inexorable, and nature, Tugwell stated in April, 1935, "is just now presenting the bill." [33] In 1934 he had referred to the bill as 30,000,000 acres of land utterly ruined and many farmers in abject poverty.[34]

If abuse had been the keynote of the past, action was the demand of the present. Everyone could support conservation measures, Tugwell asserted in 1934, because they were literally conservative and above politics.[35] Conservationists, however, could not assume public support, which, he wrote in April, 1935, required specific attractions and practical results. Scientific conservationists who criticized the wastefulness of easy land policies of the past "may fail to give sufficient weight to the fact that the earlier policy of conservation did not make sense in terms of what people wanted, and that it did not work. . . ." [36] A practical program, Tugwell declared (also in April, 1935), would be national, for "drought, flood, and disaster know no local divisions." [37] The following month he insisted that an effective policy would combine conservation of natural and human resources.[38]

Tugwell considered himself fortunate to be working under a President who was a staunch conservationist. In *The Democratic Roosevelt* he traced his subject's lifelong preoccupation with conservation back to the lessons he learned as a boy from his father at Hyde Park. James taught Franklin that "trees and grass, well-tended crops, contented animals— these belong to the round and rhythm of nature." The young Roosevelt did not forget. "The earth and its inhabitants—plant and animal—he always treated as something especially precious. There was no outrage he would so indignantly prevent, or punish when he could, as the maltreatment of farms or forests, either as the result of carelessness or rapacity." After James's death another Roosevelt, President of the United States, set an example for the young Franklin in promoting conservation. Tugwell made much of Franklin's emulation of Theodore, noting with reference to conservation that "here again he was cultivating an interest of Uncle Ted's." [39]

As a young man Roosevelt bought additional land at Hyde Park for experimentation, especially in the planting of many trees.[40] As a young state legislator in 1910 he received the chairmanship of the Committee on Forests, Fish and Game. In this heretofore comparatively innocuous post his efforts, described by Tugwell in an address in 1935, were energetic and effective.[41] As Governor of New York he sponsored a program which, as Tugwell summarized it in another address in 1935, included land retirement, reforestation, the rationalization of social services such as roads and schools with regard to taxable values, and, above all, steps which eventuated in the development of Tompkins County as a demonstration area for planning "based on local initiative and local enterprise, but carried out co-operatively and with help from the state and the federal government." [42] Meanwhile, Roosevelt's concern for conservation expanded, Tugwell later concluded, into a regard for the welfare of others.[43]

When the subject of conservation came up, Tugwell recalled, Roosevelt talked in a way which revealed "a pattern within which his mind and spirit felt at home with ambition. I followed it up rather shamelessly. True, this was congenial to all I believed and hoped. But its usefulness was in the entrée it furnished. Again and again we explored the delights of country life, detailed the possibilities of improvement. . . ." [44] The heavy exchange between Roosevelt and Tugwell of reports, memoranda, letters, and notes also showed their ardent mutual interest in conservation. When Tugwell spent two days at Warm Springs in November, 1934, the President took him to an erosion-control project on his 1,700-acre farm at near-by Pine Mountain.[45] In January, 1935, Tugwell sent material to the President for use in a speech or letter in acceptance of the Sir William Schlick Memorial Medal from the Society of American Foresters.[46] In May, 1935, when Tugwell spoke in Albany before a meeting commemorating the fiftieth anniversary of the founding of New York's Forest Preserve, he sent a copy of the address to the President, adding, "I thought you might like to see how I hold the story of your early connection with the conservation movement at the Albany meeting you asked me to attend." [47]

The President put his ideas on conservation into practice most directly in the Civilian Conservation Corps. A Washington correspondent stated that Tugwell suggested the creation of this agency.[48] Actually, it had been one of Roosevelt's pet ideas since his Governorship, and he had discussed it with Louis Howe.[49] He shared it with Tugwell, the latter remembered, after the election of 1932. One evening when he and his Brain Truster were alone, "we began to talk about forests, wild life, and their conservation, and he sketched the outlines of what afterwards became the Civilian Conservation Corps." [50] This was "not an overnight thought. . . . He had a kind of vision, born, no doubt, of his long love for the forests as well as his concern for people. . . ." [51]

The CCC was not a division of the USDA, but Tugwell played a part in shaping it into a going agency. In December, 1932, he exchanged views on such an agency with Major Robert Y. Stuart, Chief Forester.[52] He worked with the Secretary of Labor, since Frances Perkins' Department was to handle recruitment. There was also the problem of organized labor's misgivings about the CCC: the fear that it would threaten wage standards and the insistence that union labor build the camps.[53] Assurance that union labor would provide housing and appointment of Robert Fechner, vice-president of the Machinists, as Administrator of the CCC conciliated labor.

Other problems were the planning and execution of conservation projects and morale—health and recreation. The USDA and the USDI were to be responsible for works, and Army reserve officers would take charge of the management of the camps and all other activities.[54] Tugwell explained the structure and purposes of the CCC in an address, "Jobs in the Woods," over the Columbia Broadcasting System on March 18, 1933. The President, he said, was about to suggest to Congress that there existed an opportunity to "offer a job of the sort most men like to do. In the great woods there is health; men can recover the manhood which has been sapped by years of uncertainty and drift." [55]

Privately, Tugwell was certain that "unemployment will assure passage." [56] Other conservationists also saw in unemployment a chance to promote their cause. Ovid Butler, in a letter mentioned above, wrote Tugwell, "We trust that your ideas regarding employment relief can be extended to state forests. . . ." They would provide "opportunities for constructive, character-building employment. . . ." [57] P. A. Herbert,

Professor of Forestry at Michigan State College, sent Tugwell a memorandum, "Conservation Work Projects as a Means of Alleviating Unemployment," outlining a scheme for employing 2,000,000 men at a cost of $2,000,000,000.[58] Congress, too, was responsive to proposals for putting men to work. On March 29 the President's vision became a fact.

The CCC was the most popular of all the New Deal agencies, but there were some whispers among diehard opponents about preparation for war. Tugwell recalled that calling on the Army was a last-minute idea of Louis Howe's. It was simply that the Army had equipment for work in the woods. Roosevelt, it is true, did think it would be good experience for reserve officers to have to exercise leadership without benefit of military regulations, but this was an afterthought. The main concern of the administration was for millions of boys who were neither attending school nor working. They were loitering in city streets, a potential or actual source of harm to themselves and society. In the forests they could do themselves and the nation a lot of good.[59]

Statistics support Tugwell's recollection. In 1934 he pointed out that the labor force had increased by 5 millions since 1928. The tendency to re-employ men who had lost their jobs in 1929 left unemployment concentrated in the 18-29 age group. This was the group (18-25) the CCC was designed to help.[60] Lewis Meriam concluded that the CCC did an excellent job,[61] and Tugwell in 1957 felt "especially proud to have been his [Roosevelt's] agent in some of this work. . . ."[62] He also observed in the 1950's that when "the nation returned to its care for the land and other natural resources, and tired of temporizing with juvenile delinquency, the Civilian Conservation Corps might be reconstituted."[63]

The President did not originate but gave effective sponsorship to another conservation agency outside of the USDA—the Tennessee Valley Authority, which undertook conservation in all of its aspects. Tugwell had only one important contact with the TVA, which he described in 1950, and its significance was academic. In the fall of 1933 Arthur E. Morgan, Harcourt A. Morgan, and David Lilienthal, the TVA's executive board, visited him in Washington. They asked "whether, in the opinion of one who might possibly know the President's views, they were supposed to be a government, a planning and co-ordinating agency, or a public corporation devoted to certain specific tasks."[64]

Neither Tugwell nor anyone else knew the answer because Roosevelt had not given it. The visitors "did not get what they came for but they did get the ventured suggestion that the Authority might well approximate a new kind of government." Tugwell deduced his opinion from his limited knowledge of the President's thinking on TVA. In any event, his "ventured suggestion" went unheeded. Tugwell's retrospective opinion was that the President had mistakenly concluded that it was possible to enhance both state and federal power at the same time, and Lilienthal had promoted a kind of "grass roots democracy" which shaped the TVA "toward an accommodation of the forces and interests already present in the situation in such a way as gradually to render it harmless to them." [65]

III

In the USDA itself Tugwell strove to protect and expand the old-line bureaus' activities and authority in conservation. We find him, for instance, warning Roosevelt against sportsmen's attempts, through legislation, to weaken the Secretary's authority to issue regulations under the Migratory Bird Treaty Act, and suggesting to the President the strengthening of the Bureau of Biological Survey.[66] Or, on another occasion we find him protesting to the White House that the "total funds now proposed for wild life restoration is about the same as that spent on mosquitoes this year." [67]

Tugwell made a major attempt to strengthen the USDA Food and Drug Administration's conservation of human resources. As a result of this effort his career suffered significant adverse consequences (see Chapters 18 and 19). In the present context we should mention his supervision of the most important old-line bureau concerned with the conservation of natural resources—the Forest Service.

His tour of USDA installations in the West in 1933 convinced Tugwell that a revamping of the administration of the Forest Service was necessary. Each Forestry division seemed to him a principality in its own right, running things to suit itself.[68] When Major Stuart committed suicide in October, 1933, Tugwell practically begged Ferdinand Silcox to become Chief Forester. Silcox, a long-time conservationist now working in labor relations, had been out of the Forest Service for sixteen years. He accepted the post and held it until his death in 1939. Silcox brought vigor and imagination to his task, expanding the Service's conservation programs and encouraging research. He was happy in his work, Tugwell later noted, because "forestry was a field in which public investment could be considerable in a truly productive sense without meeting the implacable resistance met almost everywhere else." [69] In his eulogy of 1940 Tugwell called his selection of Silcox in itself a significant contribution to the cause of conservation.[70]

One particularly difficult task the Forest Service tackled under Silcox was the execution of the President's "shelterbelt" idea of defeating dust storms by planting millions of trees in a 100-mile strip along the 100th meridian from Canada to Texas. In September, 1934, Tugwell reported to the President on this work, requesting 15 millions of drought-relief funds for acquisition of land, planting of trees and grass, and resettlement of people on better land.[71] Silcox continued and improved the Service's research. He benefited from the previous survey of European forest programs conducted by Arthur C. Ringland, whose report had impressed Tugwell.[72] He produced studies, which Tugwell forwarded to the President, of the forest situation in the United States, including case histories of communities ruined by "cut-and-get-out" lumbering methods.[73]

Tugwell and Silcox paid close attention to the formulation of the NRA's Lumber Industry Code. The President requested their opinions in this matter, and they offered them—partly in vain—on several occasions in 1933 and 1934. The Forest Service insisted on strengthening the protection of the public interest in Article Ten. In November, 1933, Tugwell wrote to the President that under Article Ten the industry got what it wanted "without giving in to the public interest—especially in the matter of enforcement." In May, 1934, Tugwell expressed to the President his approval of a report by Silcox which called for committing the industry to co-operation in public action. In June, Tugwell asked the President to make a public statement on the conservation provisions of the forestry industry codes.[74]

Tugwell made an important contribution to a new agency which was to become, in 1935, a part of the USDA—the Soil Conservation Service. Again, his selection of an administrator was significant. His choice was Hugh H. Bennett, who had come from the University of North Carolina to the USDA in 1903 as a laboratory assistant in the Bureau of Soils. Since 1929 he had been in charge of moisture-conservation activities in the Bureau of Chemistry and Soils. In that year, after years of pleading, he had also obtained funds to study the effects of erosion.[75]

In the summer of 1933, $5,000,000 of Public Works Administration funds was allocated to erosion control. Bennett, now director of the erosion experiment stations in the Bureau of Chemistry and Soils, heard that the Department of the Interior was going to use the money for a terracing program and call it a soil-conservation program. He went to see Tugwell to argue that terracing alone would fail. Supporting practices of strip cropping, contour plowing, crop rotation, and grassed waterways were essential, he declared, for erosion control and conservation of rainfall. Tugwell responded warmly to the angry man, whom he called the "father of soil conservation." He agreed with Bennett, telling him, "I'll see what I can do to direct the use of the money. . . . You're going to have a leading part in whatever program is agreed upon." [76] Tugwell wanted Ickes to set up a special bureau for Bennett in the PWA. Ickes followed part of this recommendation, making Bennett Director of the Soil Erosion Service but taking it into the USDI. Bennett, on loan from the USDA, assumed his duties on September 19, 1933. He had a big job to do.

In 1934 the SES surveyed the nation, exclusive of urban and water areas, finding that only 578 million of nearly 2 billion acres had suffered little or no sheet, wind, or gully erosion.[77]

Bennett went at his task with great energy. When an "enemy" of his charged that using public funds on private lands was illegal, Ickes appointed a special committee to investigate SES operations. The committee's report of December, 1934, recommended transfer of the SES to the USDA, "provided that Department will effect a complete consolidation of all . . . agencies working on erosion control on private lands." The report, in effect, commended Bennett's performance.[78] Acting on this report, Roosevelt called Bennett to the White House. Bennett then told Ickes that the President intended to move the SES to the USDA. Ickes was not happy about the transfer, but he did not fight it. On March 25, 1935, under an executive order, Bennett went back to Agriculture. On April 27 Congress passed a bill directing the Secretary of Agriculture to create a Soil Conservation Service as a permanent part of the Department.[79]

Ickes later complained that his false friends Wallace and Tugwell had urged him to rest for a while in the Florida sun, and then, while he was away, had backed a truck up to Interior's rear door, stolen the SES, and renamed it the SCS.[80] Tugwell recalled that he had "stolen" the agency, "but Ickes stole it first." Their original understanding, Tugwell explained, was that there would be an emergency erosion agency in the WPA which neither the USDA nor the USDI would incorporate without first consulting the other Department. When Ickes, who relished every desk and file under his jurisdiction, put the SES in Interior, Tugwell told him he would get it back. When Ickes went to Florida, Tugwell went to the White House and got an executive order.[81] This seemingly frivolous "stealing" of the SES was part of a traditional struggle between Interior and Agriculture to which we shall turn presently. But first we may note that the growth of the SCS continued after Tugwell left Washington at the end of 1936. In 1938 it was given additional duties in order to consolidate in one agency erosion-control and flood-control activities involving actual physical work on individual farms, watersheds, and other areas.[82]

The USDA-USDI conflict ran deeper than a clash of personalities. In fact, Tugwell and Ickes were friends until Ickes died. Tugwell recalled that he had great affection for the Old Curmudgeon, and he believed Ickes liked him too—despite their frequent fights. Ickes seemed to enjoy combat. Tugwell and Hopkins agreed to confine their arguments to the President's office, but Ickes would have no part of any such pact.[83] The USDA-USDI conflict went back many years. It hinged on the jurisdiction of conservation activities. Tugwell was soon aware of the clash. In the latter half of 1933 he encouraged co-operation in solving the dilemma which arose from the AAA's taking land out of production while the USDI's Bureau of Reclamation put more in. Mordecai Ezekiel worked out a practical formula of devoting funds to the two operations on a dollar-for-dollar basis.[84] But interdepartmental co-operation did not last very long. On March 4, 1934, Tugwell wrote to the President, "There is rapidly growing up again the traditional fight between Agriculture and Interior." He suggested Harry Hopkins as mediator.[85]

In June, 1934, Tugwell, Wallace, and Silcox quarreled with Ickes about some provisions of the Taylor Grazing Act.[86] In December, 1934, Tugwell and Ickes discussed at length a reorganization between the two Departments. Ickes wished to group all conservation agencies in the USDI, with Tugwell as Undersecretary in charge.[87] He recorded in his diary, "Tugwell is an able man and if I had him next in line in the Department, it would ease my burdens considerably." [88] Ickes' proposals did not materialize and the fight went on.

Ickes recalled in 1936 how Wallace and Tugwell had agreed to an exchange of agencies, and then Wallace had reneged.[89] In *The Stricken Land* Tugwell stated that before talking to Ickes in 1939 about the position of Director of Territories and Insular Possessions, he had turned down Wallace's offer of Chief Forester several times because "the old quarrel existed between Interior and Agriculture. . . ." Tugwell later learned that Ickes, having finally obtained an Undersecretaryship, could not offer it because it had been promised to Silcox "in a maneuver calculated to bring the Forest Service into Interior." In 1944, Tugwell, now Governor of Puerto Rico, found that Ickes "still resented the President's habit of delaying difficult decisions and of compromising among insistent claimants for power. There had been many such issues in the past, that over control of the Forest Service and other agencies having to do with land having been the hottest and longest-drawn-out of them all." [90]

In conservation, as well as in reorganization, Tugwell combined field trips with desk work. Crossing the plains in the winter of 1933-1934, he reported to Washington that the condition of the land was very discouraging.[91] His misgivings proved all too sound when drought struck in the summer of 1934. He discussed the situation with the President, informing him that USDA experts thought we were about halfway through a fifteen-year cycle.[92] The President gave Tugwell the far from easy assignment of explaining in a national broadcast (CBS, July 31, 1934) the AAA policy of reducing acreage during a drought.

In February, 1935, after the mass firing in the AAA, Tugwell went to the West to check up on drought and rural-relief operations.[93] After May 1, 1935, when he became Resettlement Administrator, he devoted more attention than ever to the drought area (whose southern reaches comprised the "Dust Bowl"). Anticipating a return of dust storms in the winter, accompanied by pressure for federal funds, he appointed a committee of federal and state officials to make a fundamental study of causes and remedies. In December he wrote the President that the committee's report would stress retirement from farming of poor lands. He pointed out that "it costs as much to protect uncovered land for two years as to buy it." Roosevelt expressed his interest in the report, suggesting that Tugwell and Hopkins make recommendations for a program to get under way on July 1, 1936.[94]

Working against time, as he was soon to find out, Tugwell obtained a report on the wind-erosion problem in the "Dust Bowl." He sent it to the President, with preliminary recommendations for a permanent program, on May 4, 1936. Roosevelt promptly replied that every member of Congress should receive a copy.[95] By the summer of 1936 a crash program rather than a carefully planned one was required. The worst drought in American history devastated the plains area. On July 18 Roosevelt appointed a Great Plains Drought Area Committee, naming Morris L. Cooke, Rural Electrification Administrator, as Chairman. Tugwell, Hopkins, John C. Page of the Bureau of Reclamation, Colonel R. C. Moore of the Army Engineers, and F. H. Fowler of the National Resources Committee were the other members.[96] The story of the yeoman service of this committee and the Resettlement Administration during the drought is a long one. The RA was now responsible for all rural relief, and Tugwell "traveled by plane and by car into every center of our vast organization to see that everything possible was done." [97] Tugwell later outlined the story of the calamity of 1936, referring to Roosevelt's meeting with Alfred Landon and other Governors in Des Moines as one of the President's "most elaborate non-political charades," [98] and describing the RA's enormous relief effort.[99] Tugwell also subsequently attributed to the President satisfaction at "this successful succoring effort" and the belief that from the drought would emerge "deeper understanding of what must be done to avoid its happening again in the future." [100]

IV

It has been necessary in the course of this treatment of conservation matters to refer several times to the Resettlement Administration. That agency, however, was not a division of the USDA (see Chapters 21 and 22). It remains here to consider some evaluations of Tugwell's work in the Department of Agriculture.

One of Tugwell's detractors asserted that his chief value to the USDA was as a "court favorite able to keep his pet agencies in funds and protect them from rivals' raids." [101] Ernest K. Lindley looked at Tugwell's protective efforts in another way: "Only the tenacious resistance of Messrs. Wallace, Tugwell, and a few others prevented the wrecking of some of the most valuable and efficiently administered services in the Federal Government. . . ." [102] Lindley also credited Tugwell with pointing out that we must look upon land as "one of the central and controlling elements in our whole national economy" lest we go the way of China. [103] One pair of students of USDA administration concluded that Tugwell's name belonged on the permanent roll of conservationists. [104] Two other students of public administration stressed Tugwell's representation of a new point of view in the USDA, "a concern that no longer emphasizes merely technical and scientific modes of farming but deals with the broader question of the farmer's economic status." [105]

Russell Lord, an informed observer, paid the most glowing tribute to Tugwell as a USDA executive officer. [106] He recalled how Tugwell worked long, mad hours. He praised Tugwell's crossing of the stormy initial approaches to co-ordination (finally achieved "in a measure" in 1938), and his appointment of able young men like Lee Strong of Entomology and Knowles Ryerson of Plant Industry. Indeed, although "There are few questions on which I, and others of conventional college agricultural training, are apt to see eye-to-eye with Tugwell," he applauded Tugwell's contribution to virtually every phase of Agriculture's operations:

A great deal that now goes on in the Department . . . in the way of planning for decent land use, soil conservation, the rehabilitation of tenants, a recognition of the rights of labor, consumer protection, and a valiant clear realism derive directly from Tugwell.

He brought to the Department . . . a new point of view, neither exclusively rural nor urban. He brought a matured economic philosophy, a liberalism beyond that of the Brandeis order. . . .

Because he was not one hundred per cent rural, accustomed to a gradual skinning of farm and range landscapes which seemed to residents to alter little from year to year . . . he saw that what Hugh Bennett said about imperceptible erosion was true. . . . It was due to Tugwell more than to anyone else that Bennett and his new corps of soil rangers . . . could "roll up their sleeves" and go out to "make America over" along the lines of safer farming in a new design.

The stereotyped public picture of Tugwell as an ineffective dreamer is completely discredited by the . . . programs which he initiated. . . . Tugwell had not, of course, "made America over." But I submit that, in the few years given, Tugwell initiated a great deal to make over not only the actual scene of our country, by terraces and strip-field conservation, but greatly to change the governmental attitude and processes with respect to the rural poor.

Tugwell, himself, after his departure from Washington, felt that there was still much to do in soil conservation. In 1941, with Morris L. Cooke and Louis Bromfield, he founded an organization called Friends of the Land.[107] In 1950 he observed that decentralized administration of the SCS to the grass roots enabled local interests to offset serious attempts at regulation, especially "in what will soon again be called the Dust Bowl."[108] Through the 1950's he kept a file of newspaper clippings and pictures which showed the accuracy of his prophecy. But despite his own harsh judgment, or modesty, he must be credited with having done as much as he could, which was a great deal, to conserve the nation's resources.

18. Tugwell as Whipping Boy: The Attack

I

Tugwell's connection with a food and drug bill, introduced in June, 1933, was the most significant single reason for his becoming a prime target for the opposition press. He had been interested in consumer economics at least since his graduate-student days. In his doctoral dissertation, he recalled, he found that in English common law the "salutary doctrine of public interest . . . had always been a protection for consumers. . . ." American judges, with their penchant for confusing business with society, had limited the expansion of this doctrine, misinterpreting it and transforming it into "a protective device for . . . businesses." A "common calling" had come to mean "one which was common to businesses, not to consumers." [1] As a New Dealer, Tugwell continued to assert that the consumer was the key to prosperity and an expanding economy of abundance. Our problem, he stated in a speech in February, 1934, was to discover ways peacefully to "shift from a producer economy to a consumer economy, from habits and institutions which were appropriate to the vast stretches of human scarcity to new institutions and new habits which will be appropriate to the new possibility of plenty for everyone." [2] Inside the administration, he promoted consumerism in more specific terms.

Tugwell had high hopes for the AAA Consumers' Counsel and the NRA Consumers' Advisory Board, but he was compelled to conclude by May, 1934, that they had made "very little progress of an uncertain and feeble sort." [3] He later noted that in the "consequential bargaining going on among the vast powers of industry, it was a small but irritating matter to have a consumers' counsel speaking up against high prices, poor qualities, and insufficient services." Business interests launched vitriolic attacks on the Counsel and the Board, while labor treated the NRA group with contempt. "Both were considered nuisances by the administrators and were reduced to little more than window dressing." [4] Tugwell laid the failure of consumers to enjoy equal representation with producers in the AAA and the NRA to the same difficulty which had always plagued consumerism. Everyone was a consumer, but, before that, he was also something else: a farmer, a worker, an employer, and so forth. Consumers, as such, Tugwell pointed out in May, 1934, did not exert through strong organizations a pressure of interest "for which representation is only an outward manifestation." [5] Thus, consumers, he remarked in August, 1934, were often "parties to the debate who are not present and would be unwelcome to many if they were. . . ." [6]

Tugwell assumed direct responsibility for consumer protection as Assistant Secretary in charge of the old-line bureaus of the USDA. One of them was the Food and Drug Administration. He found that the F&DA had been laboring under several handicaps, including an indifferent public, unenthusiastic Secretaries of Agriculture, and defects in the Pure Food and Drug Act of 1906.[7] After the introduction of new legislation, Tugwell discussed the defects of the Act of 1906 in several articles and speeches. The titles of some of these efforts to reach the public were conventional: "Should Congress Enact a New Food and Drugs Law?," "The Copeland Bill and the Food Industries," "Advertising and the Food Industries." Other titles indicated what was on Tugwell's mind: "Freedom from Fakes" and "The Great American Fraud." [8]

To begin with, Tugwell asserted, the Act of 1906 was outdated. Its authors could not possibly have foreseen the trend of modern advertising, and most of the growth in the cosmetics industry had occurred since 1906. Moreover, a study of the Act disclosed a number of loopholes and omissions. The negative labeling clause indicated only what could *not* appear. The burden of proof that a false label claim was also fraudulent lay with the government, and sometimes a single case required years of legal gymnastics. The "distinctive name" clause enabled the marketing of bogus products. The provision on poisons covered *added* poisons without referring to *naturally occurring* poisons. The regulations on poisonous-spray residue were so complicated that the F&DA had to devote about one-third of its time and funds to this matter. Significant omissions in the Act of 1906, Tugwell noted, were the lack of provisions for regulating package fill, standards designations, and "fiendishly conceived" mechanical devices such as worthless contraptions to treat ruptures. The most serious omission of all was the failure to regulate advertising. A false advertisement in the drugstore window could provide the persuasion which labeling regulations kept off the container. False claims could have harmful effects even when the product was harmless since the consumer might act on them instead of seeing a doctor.

Abuses under the Act of 1906 were shocking. Many medical products and cosmetics contained actually or potentially harmful ingredients.[9] There were even more examples of frauds and misrepresentations in advertising.[10] Tugwell mentioned this fraudulent therapeutic claim for a phony concoction: Glauber's salts, a saline laxative, would cure lumbago, arthritis, neuritis, diabetes, neuralgia, liver and kidney troubles, stomach disorders, rheumatism, and acidosis. He pointed out that it took the government eleven years of legal action to stamp out the sale of "B & M," a mixture of ammonia, turpentine, and eggs which purportedly would cure thirty ailments. "Meanwhile, thousands of credulous souls were taking the concoction in all good faith and getting no better or perhaps even dying from it." The F&DA exploited the overwhelming evidence against the patent-medicine men by setting up an exhibition which reporters called the "Chamber of Horrors." The *pièce de résistance* was a number of testimonials for a diabetes cure accompanied by the death certificates of their writers.[11]

These abuses explain Tugwell's desire to improve consumer protection. In February, 1933, he remarked in his diary that, besides reorganization, the F&DA would be one of the first problems in the USDA. He added this expression of determination: "I'll do the best I can for the consumer regardless of politics; I won't compromise on this." [12] One morning in March he talked to Walter G. Campbell, Chief of the F&DA, about poisonous-spray residue on fruits and vegetables. Then their conversation roamed over the whole field of consumer protection.[13] Tugwell decided to ask at once for the necessary presidential approval of new legislation, and he got it.[14] He later threw some light on one of the important reasons for Roosevelt's favorable response. Tugwell remembered and "used . . . unscrupulously, I am afraid, Mr. Roosevelt's sense of continuity from T.R." He reminded the President that it was the Republican Roosevelt who had sponsored the Act of 1906.[15]

Tugwell's response to Roosevelt's go-ahead signal was, of course, enthusiastic. On March 17 he wrote to the President, expressing his hope for the rapid enactment of a new Food and Drug Act.[16] In his enthusiasm Tugwell decided to do something about the poisonous-spray residue on fruits and vegetables without waiting for new legislation. He issued an administrative order which lowered the maximum allowable residue. Fruit growers and Congressmen of both parties, especially those from apple districts, protested vehemently. This was a portent that the fight over the food and drug bill would be fought on political rather than scientific grounds.[17]

Tugwell arranged to have two law professors, Milton Handler of Columbia and David F. Cavers of Duke, draft a bill.[18] On June 6, 1933, Senator Royal S. Copeland (Dem., N. Y.) introduced S.1944, a bill to "prevent the manufacture, shipment, and sale of adulterated, misbranded food, drugs, and cosmetics, and to regulate traffic therein; to prevent . . . false advertisement. . . ." The regulations on labels required the listing of all active ingredients, the indication of the presence of alcohol, and warning against any habit-forming ingredient. The Secretary of Agriculture could establish standards of identity and quality for all products except fresh fruits and vegetables. The bill provided for a voluntary inspection service, and, if this proved ineffective, operation of factories under federal permit. S.1944 also authorized investigations under the Federal Trade Commission Act and the use of injunctions.[19]

There were objections to all of these provisions, but the clauses on advertising ran into the loudest, stiffest opposition. Manufacturers, distributors, and advertising agencies and media closely scrutinized these words: "An advertisement . . . shall be deemed false if it is misleading in any particular. . . . Any representation concerning any effect of a drug shall be deemed false . . . if such representation is not sustained by demonstrable scientific facts or substantial and reliable medical opinion." Other regulations on advertising assumed the falsity of all claims for drugs of any therapeutic effect in the treatment of Bright's disease, cancer, tuberculosis, poliomyelitis, and venereal diseases; prohibited the advertisement of a palliative as a cure; placed the burden of proof regarding allegedly false statements on the manufacturer, packer, distributor, and seller—not the buyer; and established the "inference and ambiguity" definition of false advertising. None of these provisions applied to advertising "disseminated only to members of the medical or pharmaceutical professions."[20] Thus, S.1944, based on the experience of a quarter of a century, was more comprehensive, more specific, and stricter than the Act of 1906. If Tugwell did not write it, he certainly did not complain that it was too "tough." But, *Time* commented, if it was "much less than Dr. Tugwell and Mrs. Roosevelt had originally planned," it was "much more than . . . Ovaltine et al. cared to accept voluntarily." According to *Time*, S.1944 "frightened even honest advertisers."[21] Formidable opposition to the bill mounted quickly.

Opponents of the bill used both the meat-axe and the rapier. In his articles of 1933 and 1934 Tugwell summarized these sweeping charges which they made against S.1944: (1) it would stop all self-medication; (2) it would enable a single bureaucrat to stifle advertising; (3) by causing the loss of millions of dollars to the important advertising industry it would retard recovery; (4) since the existing Food and Drug Act, Trade Commission Act, and postal laws provided adequate consumer protection, it was unnecessary. The second charge, as explained by Leland J. Gordon, referred to Section 23: "The findings of fact by the Secretary of Agriculture shall be conclusive." It was argued that this section would deprive alleged violators of the right of trial by jury. Opponents of the bill also objected specifically to the establishment of food standards; to the provisions for factory inspection and control, which they called un-American and unconstitutional; and to the proposal to hold corporation officials personally liable in criminal actions.[22]

Tugwell took up the charges, answering the main ones in this fashion: (1) the bill was predicated on the continuation of self-medication, which was older than civilization; (2) an alleged violator could compel the USDA, which had no judicial authority, to prove its charges in court;

(3) the bill would give people confidence in the advertising business, which had slumped and recovered along with business in general and would continue to increase in the future; moreover, with regard to the "recovery" argument, the bill would raise real national income by reducing consumer expenditures on worthless goods; (4) the F&DA was conscientious, but under the Act of 1906 many abuses were beyond its reach. In defending the bill, Tugwell drummed on the theme that it would protect honest dealers against crooked, ruthless competition. The target of legislation for consumer protection, he declared, was a minority—that "contemptible, degraded race of fakers, quacks, and poisonous nostrum makers which is conceived in the slums of public ignorance and nourished by the pain and obsessions of the diseased and ailing."

Some opponents of the bill, whom we may call the inevitability school, shied away from launching a frontal attack. Assuming that new legislation was bound to come, they set out to "soften" it. They maintained that since twenty-seven years of court decisions and the laws of forty-two states were based on the Act of 1906, amendment of the original Act was the best course to follow. They insisted that the Federal Trade Commission rather than the F&DA should regulate advertising; their hope was that a clash between the two agencies would prevent effective regulation.[23] The strengths and weaknesses of the opposition's arguments tended to become lost amid the furor resulting from its principal tactics, which were to suppress news coverage of the bill itself while linking it to Tugwell and discrediting him in the eyes of the public.

II

In the early days of the New Deal the press was generally inclined to give Roosevelt a fair chance to tackle a desperate situation. Most newspapers adopted either a co-operative or a wait-and-see attitude. In time, as the New Deal unfolded, many publishers and editors did not like what they saw, but they hesitated to attack a popular President directly. They attacked his associates. Paul Block, editor of the *Pittsburgh Post Gazette*, expressed his faith in Roosevelt's Americanism but wished the President would get rid of the Socialist and Communist juvenile Brain Trust.[24] P. C. Edwards of the *San Francisco News* asserted that the use of brains and professors in government could be effective, but the Brain Trust, with its half-baked ideas and irresponsible talk, had cast reflections on trained knowledge.[25] Mark Sullivan, commenting in the *New York Herald Tribune* on Tugwell's *The Industrial Discipline*, stated that Roosevelt himself was not a radical—he was under the evil influence of professors. Sullivan quoted a verse by H. I. Phillips of the *New York Sun:*

> School days, school days,
> Good old Golden Rule days,
> Moley and Tugwell and Dr. Berle
> Telling us how to run the worl'! [26]

If the indirect attacks on the President required a whipping boy, here were three likely prospects. They were the original Brain Trusters, and, above all, they were professors. It was a common practice in American life to poke fun at professors involved in practical affairs. Circumstances resulted in the selection of Tugwell. Berle (whose name, despite Phillips' verse, rhymes with "early") did not go to Washington in 1933, and Moley left the government for journalism in the fall of that year. Moley's departure left Tugwell as the most prominent professor in government. And Tugwell's past activities, as well as his present situation, made it easier to make him a whipping boy. In his academic days he had turned out a mass of writings which his attackers could scan for their own purposes. Besides, he continued to write and speak about unfamiliar, unpleasant, and controversial subjects.

Time later remarked that in stating his views Tugwell evoked far more critical comment than the quiet Berle, who was also an unorthodox thinker in economics.[27] There is no doubt that Tugwell's writings and speeches presented a knotty problem in communication. Although he was capable of plain talk, his academic writings were often sophisticated, given to sweeping concepts, and abstruse. Friends of the New Deal searched his works for a rationale. Foes looked for vulnerable points. Both neglected the distinction between the academician and the administrator—another complicating factor in the communication problem.

Not all of the difficulties in reporting Tugwell's remarks arose from the shortcomings or intentions of his interpreters. They had to consider their audience. Journalists who "wrote down" to their readers often knowingly misrepresented Tugwell's ideas. A Washington correspondent explained this practice: "I know that Tugwell is no Communist. I am well aware that he is probably a Social Democrat in the European sense. But how can you convey that impression to your readers? They are ignorant of what a Social Democrat is. They have got to have labels which they understand. They do know what 'radical' means and what 'communist' means." [28] (Even this reporter did not show a clear understanding of Tugwell's "planned capitalism.") Another member of the capital press corps declared, "I'd like to see the Tugwells and Frankfurters try to write up the stories they're making for the big boys and girls who read

Little Orphan Annie. That would be a laugh. . . . I always know I'm doing a better job than they could." [29]

Because Tugwell's "planned capitalism" fell between the doctrinaire extremes of laissez faire and socialism, his words were bound to meet with some disapproval and distortion no matter what he said. The anti-planners wanted to continue to dominate government as they had in the 1920's. The anti-capitalists wanted much more than a New Deal or Tugwell's kind of institutional reform. If it was difficult even for friends to interpret Tugwell's works, his foes combined error with distortion, conscious or unconscious. A typical diatribe from the right, purportedly based on a thorough study of *The Industrial Discipline*, reflected skimming, misunderstanding, or deliberate distortion.[30] The Veblenian conflict between the engineers and the financiers became a dispute between capital and labor. Tugwell's observation that manufacturers were uncoordinated became a charge that they were individually inefficient. And Tugwell's references to the release of labor for alternative pursuits through technological advance became a justification for shirking.

From the left came equally disaparaging estimates of Tugwell. He was a compromiser without courage or sincerity, a "third-rate Voltaire trying to be a second-rate Rousseau," when he should have been a French or English courtier in the infancy of the industrial revolution. He and Wallace, it was alleged, thought they were opening the gates to an abundant life when they were really holding them open for the Trojan horse of reaction. They were judged psychologically immobilized by their middle-class roots, which made the preservation of "human liberties" a prerequisite to change, and they mistook "human liberties" for the "minor privileges and creature comforts" of their middle-class rearing.[31] It is interesting to note that here the rightists' revolutionary was condemned for his emphasis on evolution. The attack from the left reached its logical end result when it included Tugwell, along with the Liberty Leaguers, in a list of Fascists.[32]

In economic terms, a doctrinaire leftist such as Louis C. Fraina judged Tugwell a conservative primarily concerned with assuring markets for the products of capitalism.[33] Another militant reformer was similarly scornful of Tugwell's recommendations for modifying the going system, insisting that any attempt to apply Tugwell's technique of control must "first break the back of monopoly, that is to say, of capitalism itself," if those who now had power were not to continue to hold it and use it for their own ends.[34] This last comment echoed the contention of the rightists that capitalism and planning were incompatible. Thus, given the circumstance of active doctrinaire interests, the content as well as the form of Tugwell's works provoked reactions which did not make for fairness, accuracy, and clarity in communication.

The reaction of idealistic, impatient youth to a speech of Tugwell's in 1933 illustrated the neglect of the distinction between a professor and a public servant. The students at Columbia University were disappointed when he did not elaborate his holistic academic schemes. As an administrator he spoke about meeting the immediate needs of a hungry, cold, and despairing population. The student paper, *Spectator*, criticized him for not getting to the bottom of economic problems and for advising avoidance of commitment to blind doctrine. The paper dismissed his idealistic phrases and his call for experimentation as mere political pragmatism. The students, James Wechsler, who reported this incident, recalled, wanted an all-inclusive "plan." They forgot that "pragmatism is the essence of the American political technique" and that "the minuteness of a blueprint does not establish its validity." [35] On the other hand, advocates of laissez faire, who from another standpoint shared the students' failure to recognize the demands which the emergency imposed on an administrator, feared the same thing the students favored—the implementation of Tugwell's "plan." Again, neither of these unrealistic attitudes was conducive to considered appraisal and communication of Tugwell's ideas.

Thus, Tugwell's status as the most important professor in government and his production of a body of writings, which created problems in communication and provided opportunities for distortion, made him eligible for the role of whipping boy. Once chosen, he was open to attack on additional counts. He was handsome in a way ideal for caricature—something he could not help. Then there was his manner, which, his friends said, was one of gallant confidence. His critics loosed a barrage of adjectives along a different line: disdainful, contemptuous, supercilious, arrogant, pompous, haughty, imperious, conceited. Tugwell was tactless on occasion, and this he could have helped.

Finally, in accounting for Tugwell's becoming a whipping boy, we should note that he volunteered to play the part. In any event, as Russell Lord attested, he obliged the White House by fronting for the food and drug bill in the USDA.[36] He decided that he could serve the President by deflecting attacks against the administration from the Chief Executive to himself. It was not generally known that orders to write the bill came from the White House, which long remained silent on the subject. A letter from Professor Cavers, co-author of the bill, to Tugwell indicated the general unawareness of the ultimate source of the legislation. An opponent of the bill, Cavers wrote, "insists that one man (guess who) is spurning the support of the magazine publishers and their allies to inject a 'personal hobby' into a bill where it does not belong. I resisted with difficulty a temptation to drop a hint or two to the effect that the decision emanated from a point higher up." [37] Not only did the tactic of deflection work, but the amount and virulence of the criticism which it brought down on Tugwell undoubtedly exceeded his and Roosevelt's expectations.

III

The organizer of the attack was one of the noisiest and most determined lobbies of recent times. The vigor of this lobby showed that the drug interests were even more alert to the danger of regulation than they had been in 1906. Its membership included these drug groups: Allied Manufacturers of the Beauty and Barber Industry, Drug Institute, Institute of Medicine Manufacturers, National Association of Retail Druggists, National Drug Trade Conference, National Wholesale Druggists Association, Proprietary Association, United Medicine Manufacturers; and these media organizations: American Newspaper Publishers Association, National Editorial Association (weeklies), National Publishers' Association (slicks). These associations co-ordinated their activities through a Joint Committee for Sound and Democratic Consumer Legislation and the National Advisory Council of Consumers and Producers.[38]

This lobby's motive, according to George Seldes, was its desire to defend the "sacred right of a freeborn American to advertise and sell horse liniment as a remedy for tuberculosis." [39] Its activities, in Stuart Chase's opinion, were the "baldest illustration of the Me First principle I know of." The "Pain and Beauty Boys" did not want to kill people, Chase conceded, but they were "normally in a hurry." [40] James Rorty threw additional light on the medicine men's motives. He listed eight leading lobbyists, linking three to products which had been seized, one to a product which would have been subject to seizure under the proposed law, one to a product on display in the USDA's Chamber of Horrors, and one to a group of religious newspapers which advertised, among other things, rejuvenators. A seventh lobbyist, a food broadcaster and publisher of a vitamin magazine, claimed to speak for Dr. Harvey W. Wiley of 1906 fame, although USDA files contained no correspondence between this gentleman and Wiley. The eighth, head of an advertising agency which handled the Ovaltine account, had written publishers that it would be impossible to sell a "chocolate-flavored dried malt extract containing a small quantity of dried milk and egg" for what it was—at least for a dollar a can.[41]

The basic tactic of the attack was to connect the food and drug bill with Tugwell and discredit him in the eyes of the public. Publishers and advertisers were "up and roaring" against Tugwell from the minute he mentioned food and drug legislation, Russell Lord remarked, and some of the most powerful among them openly threatened to "cut him down." [42] As an economic historian put it, they "ascertained that the bill was sponsored by Rexford Tugwell; Tugwell was a 'brain-truster'; brains were a dangerous ingredient in any government; hence the bill was an-American, revolutionary, bolshevistic, and to be reviled by all good 200% Americans." [43] Thus, if Roosevelt's advisers were targets for violent obloquy and disparagement, the "bullseye of the lot," a capital correspondent commented, was Tugwell.[44] He became a synonym, the *Literary Digest* noted, for everything in the New Deal that the anti-Roosevelt forces disliked.[45]

In the spotlight of publicity, Tugwell could hardly make a move which went unnoticed. For example, *Time,* which resorted to innuendo but did not join the newspaper press in its sanguinary quest for Tugwell's scalp, chose to report a minor incident in May, 1934. *Time* found in the list of USDA judgments for 1933 a fine of fifty dollars on Tugwell and Wiseman of Florida, Inc., for a shipment of citrus juices in cans containing less than the declared volume. The newsmagazine pointed out that Tugwell's father was head of the firm, Tugwell was a stockholder, and Tugwell signed the USDA order.[46] Tugwell later told the rest of the story: "Their account was accurate. I signed the order. That was the going rate under the law for that violation." [47]

Opposing a measure having to do with economics and welfare by resorting to a personal attack was not new to the American scene. Wiley had been the target in 1906. There would be others after Tugwell's time. Professor J. K. Galbraith has explained that "in our tradition of economic debate, a proposition can often be more economically destroyed by association than by evidence. To assail a proposition as un-American, alien, wildeyed, wooly, impractical, or pro-Communist is often effective and invariably more saving of time and energy than the somewhat obsolescent technique of dealing with an issue on its merits." [48]

The chief instrument of the attack was, or course, the press, which aimed to influence Congress by shaping public opinion against the bill. Meanwhile, the lobby did not neglect direct approaches to the politicians. Letters to Roosevelt, Farley, and Hugh Johnson threatened political headache and defeat aside from the merits of the issues.[49] Drug manufacturers, led by the maker of a home remedy supposed to dissolve gallstones, demanded that the administration dismiss for lobbying activities the head of the F&DA, Walter G. Campbell, who had simply testified before a Senate committee at its request.[50] Congressmen were naturally the special objects of the lobbyists' wooing, and this kind of courtship was, as it always is, expensive. There were many avenues of approach to the legislators. For example, J. Bruce Kremer, chief counsel for the Drug Institute, was a former Democratic National Committeeman from Montana and had important friends in the conservative wing of the party.[51]

Tugwell later described him as "one of the most notorious of the fixers who battened on the New Deal." [52]

In seeking the support of the press in carrying on an anti-Tugwell campaign designed for popular consumption, the lobby found the newspapers quite responsive. Stuart Chase told how the drug people obtained the newspapers' co-operation,[53] but there really was no need for persuasion. To Wall Street and the conservative press, Frederick Lewis Allen observed, Tugwell appeared to be practically a Communist, "especially to those newspaper proprietors who feared that his proposal might cut into their revenues." [54] These revenues from patent-medicine advertising were variously estimated between 350 and 400 million dollars annually.[55] The advertising men, moreover, reminded the media of the seriousness of the situation in telling terms. One of their spokesmen warned that Tugwell's aim was not a better food and drug bill but the destruction of advertising.[56] This warning overlooked Tugwell's contention that honesty in advertising would increase revenue in the long run.

That the food and drug bill occasioned the disaffection of a number of newspapers which initially had voluntarily taken a nonpartisan attitude toward the administration's efforts to revive the economy and make it more equitable indicated the importance which the press placed on this matter. A satirist of the Roosevelt administration, in a bit of drama which was in line with the popular notion that this legislation did not have the President's approval, pointed up the predictability of press reaction to any measure affecting advertising:

> (Roosevelt is considering vote-getting measures.)
> Rexford
> I still think a bill to regulate food and drug advertising—
> The Throng
> There he goes! Threatening our press relations again! [57]

In 1934 the Hearst press, which had called for Roosevelt's election in 1932, deserted him, following the lead of Paul Block, who raised the red flag against Tugwell. Frank E. Gannett of Rochester, New York, offered his chain of papers to drug manufacturers and advertising men for the free expression of their opinions.[58] Gannett, a Wilson Democrat, had been favorably disposed toward Roosevelt in 1933. With the growth of central government he became a critic, then a bitter foe of the administration.

The tactics of the attack by the press were both positive and negative. On the positive side, there was the personal attack on Tugwell. The *Chicago Tribune*, he recalled, set the theme, carrying day after day on its front page the "caricature of a college teacher in mortar board and flapping gown offering ridiculous advice to wiser and more experienced men than he. The Hearst papers, very powerful still in those days, and presently the Scripps-Howard chain, joined in the gibing chorus." [59] The "boiler plate" producers in Chicago, suppliers of inside pages to hundreds of small newspapers, also were determined deliberately to discredit the bill by calling it the Tugwell bill and calling him a Red. [60] A variation of the personal attack in the conservative press was to accuse Tugwell of obstructing the enactment of a sound bill by quarreling needlessly with would-be co-operators. [61] (At the same time, the *Nation* charged the administration with insincerity and with backing down repeatedly in the face of opposition from manufacturers, advertisers, and media. [62])

On the negative side, the press, with few exceptions, either omitted coverage of the bill or omitted favorable opinions. The *New York Times* gave the food and drug bill front-page treatment only once in five years. [63] *Collier's*, which had been a leader in the battle of 1906, kept its hands off the story. The *American*, Tugwell learned from a writer, politely ignored an article—"I can't imagine why save for the advertising threat." [64] Tugwell himself soon found opportunities for expressing his views in the press closed to him. In December, 1933, the General Manager of United Features Syndicate wrote him that the hue and cry over the food and drug bill made it very difficult to sell his articles. [65]

When the press did devote space to the bill, it seldom attempted to tell the truth about the fight against fraud. Leo Rosten, in his study of Washington correspondents, found that the press treated the bill with "extraordinary delicacy, and eight separate Washington correspondents stated that they 'wrote around' the story or ignored it" because of their publishers' intense opposition to the measure. Many publishers would not print such unmistakable news as Mrs. Roosevelt's endorsement of the bill. Rosten reported the response of 107 correspondents to this statement: "Most papers printed unfair or distorted stories about the Tugwell Pure Foods Bill": Agreed, 49; Disagreed, 23; Uncertain, 34; No Answer, 1. The percentage in agreement ran far ahead of the percentage accepting statements reflecting on the impartiality of the press with regard to other matters. Rosten concluded that the "famed objectivity of the press . . . is open to serious challenge." [66]

These tactics were the result of intense organizational efforts and enormous pressures. An editor of the *St. Louis Star and Times* informed Tugwell in February, 1934, that the "heat" on the bill was the hottest he had experienced in twenty-five years. [67] Tugwell also learned that David Lawrence was sending publishers confidential letters against the food and drug bill. [68] At the annual meeting of the American Newspaper Publishers Association in New York in May, 1934, General Manager Lincoln B. Palmer aimed some harsh words at Tugwell and reviewed the ANPA's fight against the clauses on advertising in the proposed bill.[69] In July, 1934, the National Publishers' Association issued a statement in which it claimed "due cause to be proud of its operations during the year in the interests of the entire publishing industry. . . . Your committee and executives were finally successful in modifying this legislation." [70]

The press and the GOP stepped up the campaign against Tugwell in the election years of 1934 and 1936. Two incidents in 1934 gave the attack of that year added momentum before the fall elections. In the spring Dr. William A. Wirt, Superintendent of Schools in Gary, Indiana, caused quite a stir with his charge that Tugwell was the leader of a revolutionary group in the government. In May and June a clamor arose over Tugwell's promotion. As the political campaign opened, Republicans hit Tugwell harder than ever. Gaspar Bacon of Massachusetts, in August, 1934, urged a "cracking down on the Tugwells and their many hare-brained experiments." [71] This typified the opposition's line of attack.

As the summer of 1934 began Tugwell started on a proposed speaking tour of the West. He addressed the Iowa Bankers' Association in Des Moines and a farm group in Brookings, South Dakota. Then, in July, he cancelled a speech scheduled for the Commonwealth Club in San Francisco and cut the tour short. Returning to the East, he attacked the foes of the New Deal in a broadcast of late July. In early August he spoke before the Niagara County (N. Y.) Pioneer Association. In early September Tugwell conferred with the President. Later in the month he departed for Europe to attend a meeting in Rome of the International Institute of Agriculture. Before going to Rome, Tugwell observed farming in England and France. In October he was received by Mussolini, delivered an address to the I.I.A., met Ambassador Dodd at Kostanz, Germany, and visited Geneva and Paris. In early November he had a talk with officials of the Ministry of Agriculture of the Irish Free State.[72]

A politician-observer maintained that the farmers' unfavorable reaction to Tugwell's talks and complaints by Congressmen to Farley accounted for the abrupt ending of the speaking tour of the West.[73] One of Tugwell's critics suggested that his absence from the country during the campaign and elections of 1934 was no accident.[74] On the other hand, Tugwell's secretary Paul Appleby, on board ship just before sailing, told reporters that neither the President nor Wallace had pushed the trip to Europe; it was not New Deal stuff but rather the result of Tugwell's interest in scientific agriculture.[75] (There was nothing scientific about this note which Tugwell sent to White House secretary Margaret LeHand: "I have had a week looking at English farming. Tell the President the celebrated English housing scheme is making the whole damn country look like Philadelphia." [76]) We do know that Tugwell was deeply interested in the international aspects of agriculture, and that he was largely responsible for the re-entrance of the United States into the I.I.A. In any event, these developments of 1934 do not appear to have been a direct response to the attack on Tugwell. Suggestions that they were, however, indicate the intensity of the bombardment.

The assault on Tugwell in 1936 was even more formidable. Farley anticipated it, telling Ickes in May that the two points of greatest attack by the GOP in the coming campaign would be the WPA and Tugwell.[77] In fact, the barrage had begun before Farley spoke to Ickes. In January Alfred E. Smith told a gathering of Liberty Leaguers: "Here is the way it happened: the young brain trusters caught the Socialists in swimming and they ran away with their clothes." [78] In March Representative Hamilton Fish, Jr. (Rep., N. Y.), lashed out at Tugwell, and in April the publisher Bernarr MacFadden ridiculed Tugwell's economic thought.[79] The pace of the onslaught quickened as the campaign proper got under way. In September William Randolph Hearst and Paul Block cited Tugwell's "subversive" doctrines, Representative Fish renewed his charges, and George Peek struck at his foe of old; Hearst identified the bulk of Roosevelt's following as "Karl Marx Socialists, the Frankfurter radicals, Communists and anarchists, the Tugwell Bolsheviks and the Richberg revolutionists. . . ." [80] In early October Republican national headquarters protested Roosevelt's retention of Tugwell in the government.[81] In the middle of October the GOP national committee renewed Wirt's charges, declaring that Roosevelt was the Kerensky of the American revolution which, under the leadership of Tugwell, Frankfurter, and Ezekiel, would destroy the capitalistic system.[82] At the end of October Alfred Landon and Alfred E. Smith condemned Tugwell's ideas on economic planning, and Smith repeated his views in early November, just before the election.[83]

Reviewing the Republican tactics of 1936, Farley pointed out a "paradoxical picture which never failed to charm those who drew it." The opposition varied the monotony of campaigning with a unique slogan which, when paraphrased, read, "Turn the Professors Out." The symbol was Tugwell, described as the leader of a cabal of dreamy intellectuals who had taken actual control of policy away from the President. At the same time, GOP literature referred to Farley as the "spoilsman" who had fastened "Farleyism" on the nation to suit the desires of an ambitious President.[84] Had Roosevelt lost control to Tugwell, the dreamer, or was he exercising it through Farley, the Tammany realist?

The defense against the attack on Tugwell and the pure food and drug bill consisted of a comparatively few calm remarks. "Fight the

Tugwell Bill," in the *National Printer Journalist,* January, 1934, was typical of articles in publishing and advertising journals, but *Editor and Publisher* took a fair-minded position. It stated editorially in 1934 that the producers of legitimate products would not suffer from the requirement of honest claims,[85] and in its issue of January 4, 1936, it defended professors in government, carrying an article by Robert S. Mann entitled "Capital Corps No Propaganda Victim." *Advertising and Selling,* in an editorial of November 9, 1933, dismissed fears of catastrophe for 90 per cent of advertising as fanciful, listed undeniable abuses, and urged obstructionists to devote their energy to wise amendment of inevitable legislation.

C. H. McCall, in "That Columbia Crowd," *Credit and Financial Management,* June, 1933, was convinced after trips to various parts of the nation and several visits to Washington that practical businessmen accepted prejudiced generalizations about Moley, Tugwell, and Berle without "a moment's consideration or analysis" of the true facts. The novelist Sherwood Anderson, in a magazine article, "Give Rex Tugwell a Chance," expressed his lack of interest in the clothes Tugwell wore, the kind of cigars he smoked, his age, height, color of hair and eyes. Anderson wanted to know whether Tugwell had, as those who knew him said he did, a dispassionate interest in work and the scientist's attitude.[86]

Editorials in the newspaper press, whose circulation far exceeded that of the trade journals, failed to present Tugwell's side of the story, with very rare exceptions. One of these was a statement by the *Washington Daily News,* December 18, 1933, refuting charges that Tugwell was a socialist, a martyr, and a fanatic. A few reporters and columnists, writing under by-lines, came to Tugwell's defense. Among them, Drew Pearson and Robert S. Allen were particularly outspoken. J. Fred Essary of the *Baltimore Sun* confessed that the professors in government who had been subjected to merciless criticism in the press were "intelligent and decent citizens," and he was "really a little ashamed at some of the derisive matter written about them." *Editor and Publisher,* to its credit, carried Robert Mann's article, just mentioned, which quoted Essary. The implication of Essary's comment was that many journalists who attacked Tugwell did not really believe what they wrote, but there was little consolation in this for the harried whipping boy.

19. Tugwell as Whipping Boy: The Impact of the Attack

I

The public's response to the drug lobby's attack showed that the offense overwhelmed the defense where it counted politically. The popular attitude toward Tugwell, Ernest K. Lindley noted, was marked by near phobia and hysteria. Strong men, presumably in their right minds, saw a sinister threat to the American system if Tugwell merely called for increased security and improvement of the general welfare.[1] Manifestations of an amazing furor over Tugwell appeared throughout the nation. Patriotic societies, village chambers of commerce, and public men of high and low degree expressed their opposition to Tugwell and the food and drug bill.[2] An anti-Tugwell club was formed in Chicago; the *Wichita Beacon* warned parents not to let children see his books; the members of a church in Oregon petitioned the President to dismiss Tugwell because of the way he had spoken about American wines.[3] Foreign studies were generally calmer than most American appraisals of Tugwell,[4] but undoubtedly a distorted picture of him reached other nations. When introduced to him at a social gathering, Takami Miura, a Japanese opera star, said, "Not the man who knows everything in the world?" [5]

The politicians, of course, were quite sensitive to public opinion. Congress dawdled with the food and drug bill for five years. Representative Thomas L. Blanton (Dem., Tex.) made a typical comment when he protested to the House that the food and drug bill would close every country drugstore in the United States.[6] The Democratic leaders decided to keep Tugwell under wraps during the campaign of 1936, much to his chagrin. In the fall of 1936 Farley told Roosevelt that Tugwell and Hopkins should not be used in the campaign. "I agree thoroughly," Roosevelt replied. "I'm going to take steps to eliminate criticism in the future." [7] Tugwell made no speeches, and he was not a member of the speech-writing staff, which included Corcoran and Cohen, Stanley High, Charles Michelson, and Samuel Rosenman.[8] But his silence did not halt the shooting in his direction.

Farley's and Roosevelt's political decisions did not affect their personal attitudes toward Tugwell. Farley, Tugwell recalled, "was pleasant to me, but he was firm to others about my being a detriment. No one ever spoke to me directly, but I knew how I stood." [9] In 1938 Farley wrote: "In view of the real situation, I think the abuse heaped on him was too raw and uncalled for." [10] As for Roosevelt, he was well aware of the "heat" which deflection focused on Tugwell. At the height of the attack he reportedly said to Wallace, "Tell Rex to keep his pajamas on." [11] And he thanked Tugwell a number of times for his services as a whipping boy.[12] In October, 1936, speaking to Ickes of prima donnas, Roosevelt "remarked that no one connected with him or the administration had been subjected to so much criticism as Rex had. Yet Rex has never whimpered or asked for sympathy or run to anyone for help. He has taken it on the chin like a man. The other day the President thanked him for the way he had stood up under fire." [13]

Other men who had personal contact with Tugwell were similarly unaffected by press reports. Their opinions are worth noting, although it should be kept in mind that they did not have many votes. Louis M. Hacker and Harry J. Carman, eminent colleagues at Columbia, retained their respect for Tugwell. Hacker wrote in 1936 that "the Assistant Secretary of Agriculture was made the victim of a good deal of open misrepresentation and covert abuse." [14] Carman and Tugwell, who together had edited some writings in agricultural history and enjoyed in common an upstate New York background, remained good friends. In 1958 Carman paid eloquent tribute to Tugwell, listing five themes of his career: the rejection of doctrinaire attitudes; the taking of inventory; experimentation; courage; and the conviction that a public office is a public trust.[15] (Present at the meeting to which Carman addressed these remarks was the accomplished historian Roy F. Nichols, now of the University of Pennsylvania and formerly a colleague of Tugwell's at Columbia.) And we should not forget Moley, who was much more than a Columbia colleague. He later disagreed with Tugwell's political economics, but he described Tugwell's nearly four years of service in Washington as years of "fame, of bitter and unmerited criticism, and of courageous and intelligent thinking." [16]

In the USDA Henry Wallace and Russell Lord considered the press portrait of Tugwell a caricature. At a press conference Wallace scolded the reporters: "You may not realize it, and some of you apparently do not, but you are insisting on erecting a mythical man. Dr. Tugwell has an excellent scientific and agricultural background. He has worked closely with bureau chiefs." [17] Lord stated in 1942 that "the opposition smacked a red tag on him, and created around that tag an almost completely fictitious character, vain, intellectually arrogant, impractical, dangerous, but—paradoxically—utterly ineffective. That was their story then and they stick to it now and print almost anything which lends credence to this false likeness of their own creation." [18]

Two legislators who had personal contact with Tugwell did not find him the man depicted in the press. Maury Maverick (Dem., Tex.), who spent ten days with Tugwell on a trip through the Southwest in 1935, told the House: "The nation has been washed with a billion barrels of bilge about 'Tugwell philosophy' from critics who know nothing of Tugwell." [19] Senator Robert A. Taft, who in 1941 spoke against the confirmation of Tugwell as Governor of Puerto Rico, later had occasion to discuss Puerto Rican problems with Tugwell. "Mr. Taft," Tugwell recalled, "would be a little embarrassed, I think, when he became acquainted with me later, about this uninformed diatribe. And certainly he *would* turn out to be a useful friend in the exigency of the blockade." [20]

Sumner Welles, who as Undersecretary of State had dealings with Tugwell concerning Puerto Rico, prefaced his review of *The Stricken Land* with these comments: "No member of President Roosevelt's earlier administration was more bitterly derided and more unjustly pilloried as a strange amalgam of a Fascist, a Communist, and a menace to the liberties of the American people than Rexford Guy Tugwell. . . . Those of his fellow citizens—and I fear there are many of them—who, as a result of one of the most vicious and effective campaigns of character assassination in history, have been deluded into believing that Rex Tugwell was a Communist or an authoritarian bent upon depriving them of their rights and liberties, and who are willing to read this book with an open mind, will find conclusive proof to the contrary on every page." [21]

II

The general pattern of Tugwell's own reaction to the attack was sensitiveness at first and growing insensitiveness as time passed. When he arrived in Washington, he was somewhat thin-skinned. Farley found him at a loss as to how to meet the attack.[22] Another report had Tugwell giving up hope that "people who don't know me or anything about me will ever stop talking all-knowingly about me." [23] Surprise at the intensity of the attack contributed to his touchiness. In May, 1933, F. J. Schlink of Consumers' Research warned Tugwell that the facts about the food and drug bill would not reach the public because the press would ignore the story or play it down. Schlink suggested, "If you really want a revision to have a chance, you should spend six months of intensive publicity in educating the public. . . ." [24] The introduction of the bill in June indicates that when Tugwell volunteered to become a whipping boy, he did not fully appreciate what that role would involve.

Disclosures of Tugwell's irritation were largely confined to his private conversation and conduct. If he was bewildered and by no means delighted with being a target, he did not complain in the sense of flinching in his whipping-boy role. Although it was beyond the power of anyone in the administration, including the President, to release him from that role, he could have asked the President to defend him publicly. He did not do this. At the same time, he tried to avoid embarrassing the administration unnecessarily, submitting some of his speeches for White House approval while expressing his willingness to assume full responsibility for his remarks in any case.[25] But, he recalled, "The more pains I took to get out of trouble, the less success I had." [26] As for his private meetings with his foes, contempt rather than co-operation marked Tugwell's attitude. There is a question whether this lack of tact provoked further attack, or whether it resulted from his conclusion that he could not hope for fair treatment even if he sprouted wings and acquired a halo.

Publicly, Tugwell showed sang-froid under fire, which only made his critics more angry. Occasionally he appealed for fair judgment or lashed out at anti-New Dealers without specific reference to himself. Neither of these reactions slowed the attack. In a speech of 1935 on the land program Tugwell urged his audience not to approve because "we mean well or our hearts are in the right place" or to disapprove "on the ground that we are dangerous fellows," but to judge the program by what it accomplished, not by what anyone hoped or feared it would accomplish.[27] Addressing a meeting of newspaper editors in 1934, he referred to distortion and clever selection and remarked, "I may be old-fashioned, but I still think there is much to be said for intellectual honesty." [28] In his hardest-hitting political speech, in 1935, Tugwell asserted that the administration's slight modifications of the system, its checking of the most obvious abuses, and its abridgment of free enterprise and profits only in traditional American ways did not justify the claim that it had committed itself to Communism—"This is an obviously false and vicious statement of the case. . . ." He conceded that part of the press was fair. The attack by that part of it which was an accessory of privileged groups would "cost us only the receivers of unearned income, their hangers-on, and some who confuse laissez faire with the Constitution." [29]

On one occasion Tugwell made a public statement referring specifically to his whipping-boy status. This was in one of his last syndicated columns in early 1934,[30] after his outlets had dropped from fifteen to two when he wrote about the food and drug bill. He used the device of a discussion between himself, Senator Progressive, and Beauregard Boone, a friendly publicist who instructed him in the art of attaining popularity. The dialogue was improbable, and Tugwell was writing mainly for his own amusement.

Boone asked whether Tugwell had ever met a certain columnist who called him a Socialist and a subversive. Tugwell replied, "Once. . . . Of course, a man with his power of divination doesn't need any more than that to go on. He reads people's minds from afar. If he really took the trouble to understand me he would be deprived of a lovely dummy. He gets a great kick out of standing me up and knocking me over." Senator Progressive, seeking further assurance, inquired, "You never were a Socialist, were you?" Boone explained, "He's always been the enemy of any 'ism.' He's what you call an experimentalist, which means, I suppose, that he doesn't think it's possible to read the future in detail; so he won't tolerate any doctrine about it. . . ." Boone then noted the threat in the opposition's harping on dangerous academicians. Tugwell remarked that "the die-hards always have to have a goat," conceding that he was "vulnerable because Americans don't love pedagogues and I seem to be one. Also because I really am the enemy of all these fellows represent. . . . I don't believe the institutions which gave us these years of misery can be altogether sound. I'd like to change them. Why should I hide it?"

When Boone asked Tugwell how he would change things, the reply was a nostalgic reference to Tugwell's boyhood in a small town where no one was either very rich or poor, and Christmas meant "snow on hemlocks, bobsleds and sleighbells, a Christmas tree in the church by the common—all these things. They're really American to me. I can't make this Park Avenue, country-club life seem right, along with slums and bread lines. . . . I'm for decentralization, for simplicity of life, along with a recognition of the complexity of industrial and scientific civilization." Tugwell thought science and technology "ought to make it possible for all of us to approximate that no-riches, no-poverty kind of life in which I grew up. I'd certainly set the sleighbells jingling in thousands of village streets if I could." This discourse suggested what Professor David W. Noble has called "The Paradox of Progressive Thought"—the desire to create out of new elements a new world in which the old ideals would still apply.[31] In any event, it aroused Boone's enthusiasm and led to a discussion of tactics.

"That's the line you ought to develop," Boone commented. "These groups are making you seem like the big, bad wolf. . . . You're always negative these days. You're seeming to object to everything, holding things down, preventing these fellows from getting what they want. Just reverse it. Talk about what you want. People are getting convinced that unless these birds can have their own way, the whole country will go to the dogs pronto." "No, you're wrong," Senator Progressive interjected. He believed that the die-hards were more discredited than ever before. The people really sensed that the administration was sound, and it was neither necessary nor wise to fight fire with fire. The die-hards thought they could run the government if they got rid of Tugwell and a few others. They were wrong. "As for him [Tugwell], personally, it doesn't much matter."

Senator Progressive elaborated his thesis that no one person was as important as the program. He raised the possibility that "someone ought to be sacrificed. Their illusions may be justified. Maybe the whole cause would be served if they did succeed in discrediting him. If we could go on then and seem more respectable for having lost a discreditable colleague, it might quiet down the opposition." "Rats," Boone objected. "That's an old politician's trick." It would work for a short time, he went on to say, but then they would go after others, one by one. They might even be at Senator Progressive next, and someone would then "get the bright idea that you'd better be dropped overboard." "You're right," the Senator replied. "I'll stick." This was the closest Tugwell came to complaining about his position as an undefended target. By 1936 he had no reason to expect the administration to come to his defense, but one can understand why, having taken such a verbal beating, he felt entitled to defend himself. At least he did not enjoy submitting to a silencing which might lend credence to his critics' charges.

To say that Tugwell became insensitive to attack as time passed is to indicate a relative condition, a general trend. He was still capable of resentment. On the other hand, he was learning to live with the attack as a more or less permanent fact of life. This was not an easy adjustment. He recalled how the "constant criticism of Ickes, Frances Perkins, Harry Hopkins, and myself made working very difficult." [32] But he did go through an inuring process, in which "a certain numbness and cynicism about it all . . . would develop in me but . . . in Mr. Roosevelt, with far greater provocation, would gain no foothold. My capacity for indignation would die down, much, I imagine, as does systematic reaction to a drug. I would be educated by experience." [33] In a letter to Arthur Hays Sulzberger, publisher of the *New York Times*, Tugwell revealed his attitude of endurance without complaint. Noting some shortcomings in the corrections of a misleading story on the RA, he concluded, "However, you have gone further to correct an injustice than I had any right to expect, the world being what it is. I appreciate it and I thank you." [34]

Tugwell's reactions also showed that he benefited from a quality which is both a cause and an effect of stability—a sense of humor. An incident in February, 1935, occasioned a lighthearted reaction to the press caricatures which ridiculed his immaculate attire. In connection with a dinner in New York, Moley wrote Tugwell that in order to avoid bookkeeping complications he would pay Tugwell's hotel bill, including valet charges, adding, "I want to contribute to the good reputation of the Brain Trust for marked apparel." Tugwell replied, "I could not think of letting you in on the responsibility for the sartorial effects of the Brain Trust. After all, I must have some distinction." [35] In June, 1936, at Edenton, North Carolina, Tugwell spent half an hour skipping stones, remarking, "If a fellow could do this every day, he could soon forget Frank Kent and Dave Lawrence." [36]

After he left Washington, Tugwell analyzed his detractors' motivation. He used the general term "business" to designate the single most important source of opposition. He saw no economic basis for the attitude of business, which the administration had favored and rehabilitated in order to restore national confidence. The relief program performed for the newly underprivileged what business had a contract with society to do and provided purchasing power to relieve business of its piled-up goods. In fact, under the New Deal profits rose faster than wages or farm income. Yet, Tugwell recalled, businessmen, as soon as they got on their feet, renounced the gratitude they had shown for a moment during the emergency and "arranged to be told daily how badly they were treated." [37] Rejecting an economic explanation of business' behavior, Tugwell turned to psychological causes. To Roosevelt "government was something sacred and business was merely one occupation among others." Thus, the favoring of business was "not done in an atmosphere of adulation, but in one of reproof and coolish tolerance." In view of their dominance in Washington during the 1920's, businessmen interpreted their new status of equality with others outside of government as not only a demotion, but outright persecution. Because they had lost face, they snarled at Roosevelt until he died. And their enmity was far worse, Tugwell observed in completing his psychological analysis, "because he would be recognized secretly as the true, the curative friend." [38]

Within the general category of business the drug interests and advertising agencies and media had the most obvious reasons for seeking to discredit Tugwell. Many advertising men, he noted in 1934, were aware that he had no more to do with the food and drug bill than some others, but they knew an underground, personal attack was more interesting to people and more potent than the public argument.[39] Lobbyists, as well as high-pressure advertisers, were aware of and unconcerned with the merits of the issue. They had to justify their employment. Thus, Tugwell later wrote, they had "a professional as well as an economic reason for making war on newcomers" like himself.[40]

Advertising revenue was not the only, or even the most important, determinant of the publishers' attitudes. They were "compelled to deplore," Tugwell insisted in *The Democratic Roosevelt*, because they "carried the weight of an institution dedicated to the support of policy. They had a policy—the protection of business—because the production of newspapers was a business and because they heard, even to a heightened degree, the prejudices of businessmen. The reporters were their employees and so were far from free to express their opinions." Privately, many of the members of the White House press corps admired Roosevelt's political techniques, giving him "a respect no President had had in the lifetime of any member. Mark Sullivan, David Lawrence, and Frank Kent could have remembered Uncle Ted and made comparisons, but they were hardened old-timers now, turned fearful and reactionary; the comparisons they made were shaped by prejudice. . . . They expressed alarm; they probed their vocabularies for expressive invective; their voices seemed to break with more and more labored satire directed at the New Deal and the New Dealers." At first they refrained from attacking Roosevelt directly, "as is customary in the case of a popular public figure, but they were tuning up for attacks to come as they practiced on lesser figures around him." [41]

Besides the publishers' natural inclination toward the business point of view, the problem of communication made undistorted reporting of events in Washington difficult. Tugwell was aware of this problem. In his address to the American Society of Newspaper Editors in 1934 he commented on the temptation to attach labels to public policies, deploring their indiscriminate use.[42] He also recognized the difficulty in explaining his sophisticated thought simply, recalling that "Adolf Berle and I—I more than he—have, in the course of years, been called some harsh names: Reds, Communists, Socialists, Anarchists, and even on occasion, Fascists. Perhaps the only label which would have been at all accurate would have been Collectivist, although if we were to accept it, we should have to insist on its dictionary definition rather than the one which was intended by those who flung it at us." [43]

Politicians, too, had their stake in their special techniques and in propaganda. In 1940 Tugwell made a comment on this subject which was general but nevertheless applicable to some extent to his own experience as a target. He pointed out that politicians were engaged continuously in a struggle "to attain credit for giving advantages to those who can make private use of them. It is necessary to do this and still maintain a reputation for public service, except when utter cynicism will go unpunished. And it is sometimes, though not often, possible. In this struggle a favorite weapon is the representation of an opponent as the enemy of one after another of these private individuals and groups until the total disaffection is sufficient to discredit him." [44] This reference to the distribution of advantages did not apply to Tugwell's Republican critics who happened to be out of office, but they used some of the techniques he described in seeking to get back in.

In commenting on his whipping-boy role, Tugwell had something to say about his friends as well as his foes. In retrospect he explained the President's position in the matter. If a subordinate got into trouble, "it was your battle and you were expected to fight it. If you ran to the President with your troubles, he was affable and even, sometimes, vaguely encouraging, but he never said a word in public support. If the thing was creditable, he, along with you, profited; but if it was not, the penalties were all your own." The President followed this course because "he was not a person; he was an institution. When he took political chances, he jeopardized not only himself but the whole New Deal. And the New Deal could not afford to be responsible for practitioners who threatened its life—that is, who might lose it votes." And it was the President who decided whether votes were actually involved.[45]

If being sacrificed for the cause made you indignant, "and it practically always did," Tugwell recalled, "there was nothing you could do and, when you thought it over, nothing of any use you could say."[46] This described his own conduct in 1936, although one may doubt whether he then would have made an appraisal of the President's position as objectively as he did when in 1950 he made the one just cited. Still, he carried on, without being directly defended by the President, for nearly three years between the time he rejected Senator Progressive's argument for abandoning individuals subject to heavy attack and his own resignation. And in his resentment he did not question the prerogatives of the President as party leader, but, rather, he doubted the necessity of the action taken—his exclusion from the campaign of 1936 —in his own particular case.

Tugwell was aware that his being a *cause célèbre* also made an impact on his friends in the administration below the level of the President. They did not have the responsibilities of the President, and those who confined their support of Tugwell to private conversations did not win his admiration. In *The Stricken Land* he told how in 1939, desiring to return to the national government as international relations deteriorated into war, he reasoned: "Maybe my friends in the Administration who protested their admiration for my courage but who would just as soon not be seen lunching with me at the Carlton or the Mayflower might have regained their courage or figured I was sufficiently forgot to admit me again to respectable company." Their attitude was quite different from that of President Truman. In 1945 Tugwell offered to resign as Governor of Puerto Rico in order to save the administration from the embarrassment of association with a former Brain Truster. Mr. Truman replied, "Don't worry about your enemies. Everyone who is any good has them. And yours, besides, are all reactionaries."[47]

III

The attack on Tugwell had three main results. First, it ruined his public reputation. This in turn enabled the food and drug interests to delay and weaken legislation—although we cannot be certain as to what would have happened to such a bill if Tugwell had not been involved in it. The discrediting of Tugwell also deprived the Resettlement Administration, created in 1935, of much-needed support, thereby reducing its effectiveness. Perhaps it was unfair to accuse the President of losing interest in the RA because it had become a political liability through misrepresentation growing out of the attack on Tugwell,[48] but it is true that in Tugwell's time in Washington Congress refused to sanction the agency, compelling it to operate under executive order. Certainly criticism of Tugwell for his "presumed general political views was inevitably a factor affecting attitudes concerning the RA, which was also, of course, the subject of attack for its own actions and policies." [49]

It is difficult to exaggerate the success of those who set out to "get" Tugwell. Indeed, the very effectiveness of the attack disheartened some of the men who wanted to "get" Roosevelt. Alva Johnston reported in the *Saturday Evening Post* that Tugwell was an effective shield for the President because people gave credit for the good part of the New Deal to Roosevelt and blamed Tugwell for the bad part. They were not inclined to regard Roosevelt as in any way responsible for Tugwell, "an evil of spontaneous origin, a natural calamity . . . for which no political party can be blamed." [50] Even such a prominent Republican as Frank Knox, who should have been aware of his party's tactics, was taken in by those who concentrated their fire on Tugwell only because they were reluctant to attack the popular Roosevelt. In 1938 Knox frankly admitted that he had once believed Roosevelt to be the victim of his advisers. He no longer believed this because the "mischief" had continued after Corcoran replaced Tugwell as the chief "plotter." [51]

Tugwell himself, in his memoir, described his connection with the food and drug bill as the occasion for "one of my worst defeats." The bill, he recalled, was "a sideline of the New Deal but became a bear by the tail." Its proposals were not drastic to the detached observer, and the fight over it might have remained a tempest in a teapot. Instead, it became "un-American," the pretext for an energetic, expensive, cynical, unscrupulous, and successful attack against him. This assault completely ruined his reputation. It was responsible for the stereotype, used from then on, of "Rex the Red." [52] This stereotype still plagued Tugwell when he was Governor of Puerto Rico, 1941-1946. Because of it, he noted in *The Stricken Land,* it was unlikely that any group of

Congressional investigators "would—or even could—penetrate the layers of falsity and prejudice and reach an impartial judgment. To expect it of them was unreasonable." Thus he was resigned to the prevalence of a public image which

. . . carried over, even after a gap of years, the synthetic personality fastened on me by the embattled advertisers, publicity men, and lobbyists, not to mention the rivals for Presidential favor. The elements of this stereotype were contradictory; that is to say, I was a boondoggling "theorist" and yet so effective as to be "dangerous"; I was extravagant and a waster, yet if I were not watched I should succeed in reorganizing high areas of American life. This kind of jumbled asseveration seemed, however, to frighten certain people because of its very confusion. I was a person to be distrusted, from whom any kind of crazy proposal could be expected together with the insane energy to carry it out. I had always failed in everything I had undertaken; therefore I must be a failure in anything I should undertake in the future. This did not need proof. It was, in fact, impervious to proof of an adverse sort. And if it was not consistent with the fears that I might be effective in an almost revolutionary sense, that inconsistency was a kind of added basis for distrust. If what I wanted to do—which was never exactly explained—was a failure, it proved that I had been wrong; but if it succeeded it was worse because it was anyway "un-American," or "Red" or "Socialistic," and so, "dangerous." [53]

A brief summary of the history of food and drug legislation in the 1930's will indicate how effectively its opponents exploited the public image of Tugwell which they created. He expected opposition, and he hoped to beat it to the draw by getting a bill through Congress before the lobbyists swarmed to Washington.[54] He also hoped to split the opposition by getting the support of "good" firms, newspapers, and broadcasters. He compiled a list of manufacturers, advertisers, consumers' organizations, and Congressmen whom he would try to recruit to his cause, and he had occasion to talk to Father Coughlin about the bill.[55] Unfortunately, Tugwell did not get backing from officials of whom he might have expected it. Henry Wallace, absorbed in the problems of the AAA, showed no interest.[56] The President, Tugwell recalled, undoubtedly concerned with political implications, refrained for some time from translating his interest into public support [57]—although Mrs. Roosevelt, as has been noted, made her position known.

Nor did the opposition split. There was a quarrel between manufacturers and publishers over liability for violations,[58] but this did not significantly weaken the united front. There was, moreover, a historical example of the benefits of unity. Between the introduction of the first food and drug bill in 1889 and the enactment of the Act of 1906, about 140 such bills failed to pass.[59] In the 1930's the opposition did its best to match this record. Between June 12, 1933, and July 25, 1935, the Senate introduced seven bills, starting with S.1944, and the House six.[60] Delay and emasculation were the order of the day. At the hearings representatives of industry outnumbered by far pleaders for the consumers' cause,[61] obtaining one concession after another. With each compromise the opposition demanded another, while advocates of a strong bill became more disgusted.

Senator Copeland bore the brunt of the reformers' criticism. He played an in-between role which is difficult to explain. A physician, he wrote a column of medical hints in the Hearst press and conducted a radio program sponsored by Phillips' Milk of Magnesia, Fleischmann's Yeast, Nujol, and Pluto Water.[62] He assigned the conduct of hearings to Bennett Champ Clark, an avowed opponent of any changes in the Act of 1906.[63] He also accepted amendments freely. On the other hand, he labored to keep food and drug legislation before Congress until it finally passed a bill in 1938. Tugwell's explanation, in retrospect, of Copeland's conduct was that the Senator "was running for reelection in 1936 and saw a chance for an issue. However, he intended to temper the bill's intentions. The President allowed him to sponsor the bill because of the delicate situation in New York." [64] Apparently Copeland attempted the difficult feat of simultaneously doing some good for his clients, his constituents, and himself.

The closest Congress came to passing a bill before 1938 was in 1936. In the spring of 1935 the Senate passed S.5. On June 19, 1936, the House passed an amended version of S.5, but Congress adjourned the next day before a conference committee could meet. At last, in June, 1938, Congress passed a Food, Drug, and Cosmetic Act. Three developments appear to have triggered this action: a number of states introduced bills patterned after the various Copeland proposals; in the fall of 1937 at least seventy-three persons in fifteen states died from taking a drug called Elixir Sulfanilamide; many opponents of legislation decided that continued resistance would damage their public relations. In 1938 Copeland was still working for a bill, even though the advertising of one of his sponsors, Fleischmann, did not meet the tests of the Act of 1938.[65]

Four days after the passage of the Act of 1938 Senator Copeland died. Tugwell was still very much alive, but a year and a half had passed since his resignation on December 31, 1936. It is impossible to say how much he was responsible for the Act of 1938. He would not have been pleased if his responsibility could be proved since he later called the Act a "discredit to everyone concerned in it." [66] It can be argued that Tugwell's sponsorship delayed legislation, or that the commotion he stirred up was a necessary prelude to getting a new law as early as 1938. In any event, it now appears that he and the nation would have been better off if he had kept out of the food and drug fight.

From Tugwell's point of view the Act of 1938 was weak, and it does not seem improbable that Congress would have passed such a law by that year without his urging. If his pleading yielded no greater gain than could have been achieved without it, it resulted in a serious loss. The damage which the drug lobby's smear campaign did to his reputation reduced the effectiveness of the Resettlement Administration in its important attempt to promote the general welfare. Perhaps Tugwell should have known better than to get into the food and drug fight. He anticipated opposition, and, his diary tells us, he considered himself "badly fitted" for guiding a bill through Congress.[67] Yet he must have been somewhat naïve about his battle against evil. His attitude toward the problem of helping sharecroppers showed that this naïveté had disappeared in 1935, but by that time the damage had been done. Finally, we may wonder why the President, with his vast knowledge of politics, lobbies, and the shaping of public opinion, allowed the vulnerable Tugwell to take a public stand on this subject. Both men made a grievous mistake.

It is possible that time will serve to "penetrate the layers of falsity and prejudice." Professor Galbraith has suggested that Tugwell may fare better at the hands of historians than he did among his contemporaries. Referring to the behavior patterns of Roosevelt's subordinates under fire, Galbraith listed four reactions. Some avoided part or most of the assault by keeping themselves a little remote from the President—Hull "did this as a matter of course, while with Jesse Jones it was a matter of elaborate design." Some, including Ickes, Leon Henderson, and Hugh Johnson, matched "criticism with criticism and, if necessary, billingsgate with billingsgate." Some quit. Finally, some adopted the remaining strategy, which was "simply to take it—as long as possible or indefinitely." This was what Mrs. Roosevelt and Miss Perkins did. "And, perhaps better than any other male, so did Rexford G. Tugwell. . . . When his public career was over he went quietly back to teaching. Those who took their medicine in this manner may not fare so badly in the final accounting on F.D.R.—if there ever is one—although those who reversed their field looked a lot better at the time." [68]

20. Promotion: 1934

I

The *New York Times* reported in early January, 1934, that Tugwell might become Undersecretary of Agriculture.[1] On March 26 Congress passed an appropriation act creating the position. The same day Henry Wallace wrote to the President, recommending the appointment of Tugwell under the appropriation act, which was "so worded that the place can be established and filled immediately."[2] On April 24 Roosevelt sent the nomination to the Senate.

Frank Kent, in his column of March 24, asserted that the semiofficial explanations, which referred to "an official promotion, a place of more dignity and prestige, a reward for merit . . . ," concealed a desire to give Tugwell free rein for radical regimentation of the American people. Kent bemoaned the likelihood that Tugwell would have more power than ever to carry out his long-range plans. Regarding New Deal measures, Tugwell, Kent concluded, "knew the talk about these things being temporary was nonsense."[3] In the opinion of *Time* Roosevelt intended a "retort to the clamorous criticism of his Brain Truster by some special mark of public preference for him and his services."[4] An anti-Roosevelt author, James C. Young, later attributed the promotion to the New Deal's "weakness for formalities in titles and long and complex names for its deeds."[5] *Time* probably came closest to the mark, but these commentators overlooked a practical consideration. In going to Washington Tugwell had taken a cut in salary, and he could well use an increase from $7,500 to $10,000.

By the spring of 1934 Tugwell had become a controversial figure. In some quarters, because of his connection with the AAA, the NRA, and a food and drug bill, he personified regimentation. "It was clear," he recalled, "that the appointment to a higher post, just created, would raise a first class storm of protest. . . . I thought and said that my usefulness was too slight to justify the expenditure of any political capital."[6] The President rejected Tugwell's advice, and Tugwell's prediction of opposition proved accurate.

In late April Tugwell made three speeches which were, in effect, pre-confirmation addresses: "The Return to Democracy," American Society of Newspaper Editors, Washington, April 21; "On Life as a Long-Time Enterprise," Dartmouth College, April 26; "Economic Freedom and the Farmer," New York State Bankers Association, Buffalo, April 28.[7] *Newsweek* called the speech to the editors, in which Tugwell declared that the New Deal was in the American tradition and that none of the President's advisers was interested in revolution, the beginning of a counterattack on critics of the administration.[8] Frank Kent commented, "He buttered the editors until they glistened like greased poles in the sunshine." [9] *Time* quoted a passage from the Dartmouth speech in which Tugwell stated, "It is not to be supposed that a generation which made so colossal a failure of social management will succeed much better in reconstruction." He noted that government was "now intrusted to others who always had misgivings concerning the old acquisitive ideas," but "there is everything to be learned about so complicated a business, and . . . new attitudes are not shared by a powerful minority." There would be no "wholly new deal" when the students graduated. "You will confront the same old system with some new changes." These remarks, *Time* commented, "looked like shrewd political opportunism," or else they represented the "natural effort of a man whose ideas have been reviled to win them new esteem." [10]

The gist of the third speech, to the bankers, was that the AAA was an "economic bill of rights" for the farmers, who had made no cries of "regimentation." *Time*, in a general conclusion about the three April addresses, noted that Tugwell's "words and ideas seem to have undergone a marked public change," then conceded that he did not "backtrack from his theories, but he couched them in more conservative terms, gave them a new aspect to refute the charge of radicalism." [11] A Washington correspondent drew a different inference, later stating that in the three speeches Tugwell denied his interest in national planning.[12] After Tugwell's confirmation *Time* observed that he had not begun to picture himself as a conservative until his nomination in April. He appreciated the humor of the situation, *Time* reported, placing on his desk a picture, taken at Dartmouth, of himself standing beside a traffic sign plainly marked: "Safety First—Keep Right." [13]

In early May, at a Department of Commerce exhibition, Roosevelt made an impromptu speech. He said, among other things, "We are going through evolution, not revolution." *Newsweek* related this speech to Tugwell's addresses, as the lead for its story indicated: "Appointment: Critics of Tugwell Balked by Speeches." Now, *Newsweek* concluded, Senators would have "to think up something besides 'radical' and 'revolutionist' to shout into the record." [14] James C. Young, the anti-New Dealer, writing in 1936, interpreted Roosevelt's remarks at the Department of Commerce exhibition as an endorsement of Tugwell's nomination and his ideas on regimentation through national planning.[15] *Newsweek* overestimated the ability of Roosevelt and Tugwell to silence opposition to the appointment with words.

The leader of the opposition, Senator Ellison D. "Cotton Ed" Smith of South Carolina, Chairman of the Senate Committee on Agriculture and Forestry, had weapons in addition to words in his arsenal. Smith used delaying tactics, preventing confirmation by holding up his committee's report on the nomination. He gave two reasons for his stand: (1) Tugwell was not a "dirt farmer"; (2) the position of Undersecretary had been slipped into the agricultural bill without his knowledge when only a few Senators were on the floor.[16] "Cotton Ed," one of the last of the stereotyped old-school Senators, the elderly gentleman of broad accent and string bow tie, fought a hard fight. Henry Wallace, concerned over Smith's tactics, wrote to the President on May 14, passing along the suggestion of Senator James F. Byrnes, also of South Carolina, that a motion in committee by Norris for reporting the nomination favorably would be the best way to get confirmation.[17] In his column of June 5 Frank Kent wrote that there was little sense in Smith's delaying confirmation. Regardless of Senate action or inaction, Tugwell, Kent declared, would continue to remake our civilization. As to the objection that Tugwell was not a "dirt farmer," nothing "could be more ridiculous . . . his home is in the clouds." Kent knew that Roosevelt did not take Smith's opposition so lightly; he noted that in early June the President had asked Smith to let the nomination come out of committee.[18] Meanwhile, some of Smith's colleagues in the Senate were becoming angry with him.

The question of Smith's tactics came up in the Senate on June 8.[19] Senators Huey Long of Louisiana, Joseph Robinson of Arkansas, Burton Wheeler of Montana, and George Norris of Nebraska accused Smith of preventing his committee from taking up the nomination. Senator Carter Glass of Virginia, Chairman of the Appropriations Committee, insisted that the Undersecretaryship had not been "slipped into" the agricultural bill. Members of Smith's committee, Glass explained, had served under Senator Richard Russell of Georgia on a subcommittee of the Glass group, and they sponsored the new position. Senators Harry Byrd of Virginia and Hugo Black of Alabama got off the subject of Smith, offering clashing interpretations of an address, "The Principle of Planning and the Institution of Laissez Faire," which Tugwell had delivered before the American Economic Association in December, 1931. Byrd maintained that Tugwell did not believe in American principles of government. Black saw no basis in the speech for such an inference.

The debate of June 8 did not move Smith, who simply continued to declare that he objected on principle to the creation of an Undersecretaryship, and that, in any event, a "man of the soil" could best fill the position. Finally, Smith agreed to report on the nomination at noon on Tuesday, June 12, and the Senate dropped Joseph Robinson's motion to discharge the nomination from the Committee on Agriculture. But it was not the Senators who caused Smith's change of mind. That was the result of some behind-the-scenes maneuvers. The story around Washington in the spring of 1934 was that Roosevelt threatened Smith with political death over the confirmation.[20] Threats did not frighten "Cotton Ed," who wanted Presidential co-operation, not a scolding. *Time* noted that Smith did not voice his objections to Tugwell as a non-"dirt farmer" until Roosevelt failed to appoint a man of Smith's choice, Reuben Gosnell, as United States Marshal in western South Carolina. At last, as Tugwell's fate hung in the balance, Gosnell's appointment came through to the Capitol.[21] Smith got his appointment, and Roosevelt got his nomination reported.

Ickes described this exchange in his diary under the date May 11. At a Cabinet meeting the President said that he had "traded Rex Tugwell for the favorite murderer of Senator Smith of South Carolina." Ickes explained that Smith had pigeon-holed Roosevelt's nomination of Tugwell and "let word go out to the wide world that he wouldn't report it favorably. It happens that Senator Smith has wanted a certain man appointed United States Marshal. This man is said to have a homicide record, but aside from that seems to have a very good reputation." The outcome, Ickes recorded, was that Roosevelt "sent for Smith and told him he would give him his United States Marshal if he would report Tugwell's name favorably."[22] The date of Ickes' notes, May 11, indicates that Roosevelt did not wait until the last minute to make his offer. *Time's* report that Smith did not relent until Gosnell's appointment came through indicates that "Cotton Ed" would not move until he actually collected on his half of the bargain.

Ickes' diary was not published until 1953, but *Time's* report suggests that Roosevelt's appeasement of Smith through a political appointment was generally known to outsiders as well as Cabinet members. Tugwell, however, writing in 1953, did not have direct knowledge of the details. "Mr. Farley," he recalled, "had been put to work. When it was over, the President said to me, 'You will never know any more about it, I hope, but today I traded you for a couple of murderers.' I do not to this day know precisely what the deal was with which strategic Senator. I could guess, but I have spent much more thought on wondering whether the compromise was worth the price."[23]

Smith's agreement on June 8 to report the nomination on June 12 did not mean that the battle was over. Before a vote was taken on the 14th, there was further debate in the Senate on the 9th, a clamorous hearing on the 11th, and then three additional days of debate. Smith undoubtedly knew that the Senate would confirm Tugwell, but he had committed himself too far to back off his public position. Other opponents of Tugwell, too, intended to have their say. On the 9th

Byrd led the attack. He had written to Tugwell about an article in the press which quoted the Assistant Secretary as saying that proposed amendments to the AA Act "will permit us to continue what we are already doing. If we should get a setback in Court, we would have to stop doing certain things under present circumstances." Tugwell had replied that the quotation was essentially accurate. This showed, Byrd declared, Tugwell's lack of respect for the Constitution, the courts, or the prerogatives of Congress.[24] On the 11th Smith had his day. The battle moved from the floor of the Senate to a committee hearing room, where Tugwell met his foes face to face.

Tugwell's friends took him for a week end in the country in order to prepare him for the hearing by putting him through a mock investigation. They asked him, "Who are you, anyhow?"; "What sort of a guy are you?"; "Are you a Communist?"; "Did you ever spread manure?"[25] Republican Senators also anticipated the hearing. They reportedly gathered quotations from Tugwell's writings and "itched" to get him before them in committee.[26] But at the hearing itself the GOP members kept in the background. Senators Byrd and Smith once again led the attack in a long, loud, colorful, and often irrelevant inquiry.[27] Tugwell brought a statement, "The Amendments to the Agricultural Adjustment Act,"[28] in case Byrd revived that subject—which he did, declaring, "I contend that he has committed acts which he is asking the Congress to ratify. . . . It is inconceivable to me that a man can make a speech in which he says certain things and then say, 'I did not mean what I said.' He has not the sincerity a man should have who holds high public office." Byrd then concentrated on Tugwell's interest in national planning. Tugwell replied that he did not believe in Soviet ideas, that he believed in the kind of national planning which the President proposed. Norris came to Tugwell's defense, dismissing Byrd's opening flag-waving speech as unrelated to confirmation. "The only thing missing," Norris remarked, "was the Marine band."

Smith stuck to his contention that Tugwell failed to qualify because he was not a "dirt farmer" and a graduate of "God's Great University." "Cotton Ed" declared, "He is a handsome, splendidly equipped gentleman. . . . But throw him into the cotton fields and he would starve to death. . . . Before the God that made me I'd do anything for him that did not involve my duty to the farmers." Senator Louis Murphy (Dem., Ia.) sought to turn Smith's tack to Tugwell's advantage. He demanded of Tugwell, "Did you ever follow a plow?"; "Did you ever have mud on your boots?"; "Do you know how hard it is to get a dollar out of the soil?" Tugwell, who had raised a heifer as a boy and had managed his father's orchard farm during summer vacations from college, answered each question with "Yes, sir." Murphy then accused

Smith of attacking the administration. Smith shouted, "By the eternal God, I won't stand for these dirty insinuations. When we took the crown off the head of King George, thank God, we put it. . . ." Murphy shouted back, "When you take the head off President Roosevelt, God only knows where you'll put it."

Tugwell's defenders were as melodramatic as Smith. Senator Black declared, "This man . . . has brains. . . . He has dared to raise his voice in favor of old-age pensions. . . . Treason! Treason! Let him be taken to the stake! Let the inquisition be turned upon him!" Senator Matthew Neely (Dem., W. Va.) refused "to vote for another crucifixion. I refuse to participate in compelling one of the President's most useful friends to drink a bowl of hemlock. I refuse to help bind a Columbus of the New Deal with chains. . . . My act in so doing will be to me in future years—

> A rainbow to the storms of life,
> The evening beam that smiles the clouds away
> And tints tomorrow with prophetic ray."

Tugwell, testifying in his own behalf, referred to several memoranda which he had prepared on the agricultural program and on his general ideas in political economy. The complete statements, in his papers, were entitled "Statistical Information on Agricultural Programs," "Property Rights and the Profit System," and "Constitutionality." He denied that he was a Communist. He told the Senators he was a conservative who desired "to conserve in American life all those things I grew up to respect and love." He expressed his faith in American institutions and his belief that it was not necessary to overstep the Constitution in order to make all necessary reforms. He stated that his "views on the subject of the Constitution of the United States are purely second-hand." He accepted as correct the views of a number of great judges of the Supreme Court. Tugwell quoted Holmes's observations that the Constitution applied to "organic living institutions," did "not enact Spencer's *Social Statics*," and was "not intended to embody a particular economic theory."

Tugwell also quoted Justice Owen J. Roberts: "Neither property rights nor contract rights are absolute"; "Government cannot exist unless it can prevent abuse of these rights." Property rights, Tugwell added, were subject to public regulation in the same way that the citizen's liberty to do as he liked was interfered with, as Holmes pointed out, by school laws and taxes. It was necessary, of course, to make distinctions. The "property of the tiny autocratic minority who, without substantial ownership of shares of stock or bonds, control the property of others" was not the same as "property in houses, farms, or small business enterprises." Confusing these two kinds of property, Tugwell maintained, would lead to the kinds of abuses which government was supposed to prevent. (If Tugwell's differentiation of two types of property sounds similar to views the agrarian John Taylor of Caroline expressed in 1814, it actually reflected the theme of *The Modern Corporation and Private Property,* which his Columbia colleagues Adolf A. Berle, Jr., and Gardiner C. Means published in 1933. Their demonstration of the separation of ownership and management in our corporate industrial economy is vitally relevant to Tugwell's contention that what mattered was not who owned industry but who ran it.) Tugwell concluded that legislation for economic regulation—including price controls—was constitutional so long as it was not, in Roberts' words, "arbitrary, discriminatory, or demonstrably irrelevant to the policy the legislature is free to adopt."

Tugwell affirmed his faith in democracy, which enabled the peaceful accomplishment of the changes that a majority of the voters desired. But the absence of violence did not mean the absence of controversy. Many constitutional measures were controversial. "Some of our most useful laws," Tugwell stated, "evoked the bitterest and most prejudiced opposition when they were proposed. Yet after a short trial they won the approval even of their opponents" (he gave as examples the Hepburn Act, Meat Inspection Act, Food and Drug Act, and Federal Reserve Act). While innovators could start heated arguments, they were not revolutionists. Tugwell called the Old Guard, who opposed "achievable reform while it is possible," the real friends of violent revolution.

Tugwell's answers often had an academic tone. For example, he explained to the Senators that the "anthropomorphic interpretation of events" was very plain. An unfriendly journalist described this tone as "aesthetic exhibitionism" and a flaunting of scorn.[29] The Senators themselves did not appear to resent Tugwell's attitude or ideas at the moment. They were too busy arguing with each other. Partisans in the crowd reinforced the Senators' wrangling by yelling, booing, and applauding while Tugwell sat meekly in his chair, escaping notice a good part of the time.[30] Undoubtedly the conduct of the hearing saved him from any real embarrassment.

The debate in the Senate continued through June 12, 13, and 14.[31] On the 12th Senator W. Warren Barbour (Rep., N. J.) entered in the *Record* a letter from the American Coalition of Patriotic, Civic, and Fraternal Societies which labeled Tugwell a subversive who would destroy the most cherished American institutions. Senator Thomas Schall (Rep., Minn.) made a long speech, the essence of which was that Tugwell's collectivism was strictly a Russian plan. On the 13th Smith and Edward Costigan (Dem., Colo.) quarreled over "Cotton Ed's" insistence on a "dirt farmer." Smith would not go into details, merely repeating his view. Senator Josiah Bailey (Dem., N. C.) conceded that

Tugwell's books did not justify charges of absorption of Russian views, but Bailey thought Tugwell's disavowal of planning to Byrd placed his intellectual honesty in question. He warned that under Tugwell the government would take over the farms of America as in fee-simple with absolute control.

On the 14th the debate dragged on to an end. M. M. Logan (Dem., Ky.), Arthur Robinson (Rep., Ind.), Champ Clark (Dem., Mo.), Henry Hatfield (Rep., W. Va.), Simeon Fess (Rep., O.) and L. J. Dickinson (Rep., Ia.) joined the attack. Phrases such as "the end of laissez faire" and "Russian Communism" filled the air. Tugwell's constitutional thought and intellectual integrity were questioned, and Dickinson quoted his "make America over" poem of 1915. Tugwell's supporters did not take this attack lying down. Norris lauded his knowledge of agriculture, called the hearing an inquisition, and observed that the committee voted 16-2 for reporting favorably. Kenneth McKellar (Dem., Tenn.) asked Dickinson why six of seven Republicans on the committee voted for Tugwell. John Bankhead of Alabama, Joseph Robinson, Wheeler, and Bronson Cutting (Rep., N. M.) defended Tugwell against Byrd on the clarifying amendments to the AA Act. Black repudiated allegations by Byrd and Bailey regarding Tugwell's constitutional and economic views. There was nothing in Tugwell's works, Black asserted, calling for the abolition of private ownership. Toward the end of the debate Neely said Tugwell met with opposition because he was not one hundred per cent reactionary.

The vote was 53-24 in favor of confirmation. Adjusted for absentees with stated positions, the vote would have been 58-28. Tugwell received congratulations in his office, and in the evening his friend Sinclair Lewis gave a party.[32] Roosevelt reacted to the confirmation in his debonair way. He asked Wallace to congratulate Tugwell on his testimony before the committee, adding, "I hope that Rex has enough dirt on him by this time."[33] Attorney-General Cummings had advised Roosevelt in April that Tugwell's taking the oath of office before July 1 would raise accounting questions since the appropriation would not be available until the beginning of the new fiscal year.[34] Tugwell, nevertheless, in a letter to the President, resigned as Assistant Secretary effective at the end of June 18 and accepted the position of Undersecretary effective June 19.[35]

II

In the press criticism of Tugwell's performance at the hearing came from both left and right. A militant reformer asserted in the *Nation* that he "quit under fire" when he told the committee that he was a conservative.[36] The conservative Alva Johnston of the *Saturday Evening Post* noted that Tugwell suddenly "turned 100% American" before the

Senators.[37] According to Mark Sullivan, Tugwell won through sheer skill in words, adroitness of mind, and suave explanation.[38] The *Wall Street Journal* commented, "Had Socrates . . . possessed a tenth of Rexford Guy Tugwell's skill in declining a symbolic role, he would not have had to drink the hemlock." [39] Frank Kent, in his column of June 13, "Tugwell the Tory," made the longest, most sarcastic comment.[40] Tugwell's conservatism, he wrote, was proved by the "enthusiasm with which those famous Conservatives, . . . Norris . . . and Wheeler, clasped him to their reactionary bosoms and defended him against attack by that wild-eyed radical of Virginia, Senator Harry F. Byrd. . . ." It was clear to Kent that Tugwell had fooled the collectivistic, extremely progressive Roosevelt. "The Professor isn't a liberal at all. He does not belong in the administration. With no ideas of his own, he is a meek young Constitutional lamb gleefully gamboling about in the rough skin of a radical wolf."

In a serious vein, Kent believed that Tugwell only superficially came off well at the hearing. The impression of victory for the professor was due to the Senators' ineptitude and their lack of dignity and decorum. Among discriminating people, Kent asserted, Tugwell "did nothing to increase respect for him. . . . Instead of flying his own colors, he ran up another flag." Kent was disappointed at Tugwell's failure to display the independence and firmness of a truly deep thinker. "The Professor side-stepped with the ability of a matador, sought refuge behind the Roosevelt skirts, knowing very well the Senatorial bulls would not pursue him there. . . . Certainly far more clever than the Senators, he seemed to be shrewd, resourceful, alert, with a keen eye for covering up, and with all the sincerity of the well-known china egg."

Tugwell himself did not think he emerged from the hearing unscathed. He later remarked, "Before it was over, I had become even more notorious, having been subjected to Senatorial inquisition and having been publicly castigated by a dozen Democratic Senators." [41] But the question remains whether he had become more notorious among the discriminating people Kent mentioned. An examination of the specific charges against Tugwell shows that it was far easier to make a case against him than for him in the eyes of the general public.

Senator Smith's objection that Tugwell was not a "dirt farmer" may have sounded reasonable to laymen. Certainly the attempt to present Tugwell as a man of the soil did not go over. Paul Porter described Tugwell's boyhood charge as the "most overworked heifer in the history of the United States," but it was hard to imagine Tugwell as a "dirt farmer" as he sat at the hearing in immaculate white, departing "only slightly ruffled, with an air of what seemed to be well-bred amusement." [42] To the public he looked more like a professor than a farmer.

To students of scientific agriculture and public administration, however, being a dirt farmer was not a qualification for the position of Undersecretary. Two serious students of government called Smith's stand amusing.[43] Tugwell himself recalled that the "uncovering of a past for me with vistas of field and stable as well as campus . . . would be phony, just as Mr. Roosevelt's farm experience was, for the tasks he had begun to see ahead. It would contribute exactly nothing to the invention and workmanship to be embodied in the AAA or in Resettlement or in the conservation of soil, forest, and wildlife. Those would be scientific jobs, helped out by strictly acquired craftsmanship in administration, not plowing or seeding." [44]

Byrd's objections to Tugwell's views on proposed amendments to the AA Act were another instance of first-glance plausibility which did not hold up under closer examination. Senator Wheeler pointed out during the debate of June 14 that the courts had upheld the AAA in cases involving marketing agreements, to which the amendments pertained, five to one. Tugwell, rather than ignoring the prerogatives of Congress, was asking for more clarity and specificness in a law which implemented the will of Congress in order to reduce dependence on judicial interpretation of Congressional intent. He did not say, in effect, "We have been flouting the courts' authority." Rather, he said, "If we spell out our intentions in more detail, we stand a better chance of winning judicial approval when cases come up." In citing the courts' power to stop administrative action, Tugwell showed respect for the judiciary and the Constitution. In this light, one can see why Senators Bankhead, Cutting, Robinson (Ark.), and Wheeler rejected Byrd's allegations.

Tugwell's thought on the Constitution was based on the premise that it was a pre-industrial instrument. There were two ways, he believed, of applying the Constitution to modern conditions. Either the courts, putting aside personal social and economic preferences, could permit the legislature to decide what was allowable under the Constitution, as liberals such as Justices Holmes and Stone suggested, or the Constitution could be amended to provide for social and economic regulation. As Tugwell later asserted, amendment "need not present the legislative or executive branches with fundamental powers they did not now possess. It could merely extend the power to regulate into the new areas of technology." [45] Tugwell favored the second solution. There was nothing in this view to justify the charge that he did not believe in constitutional government.

The charge of intellectual dishonesty which Tugwell's alleged disavowal of an interest in national planning evoked was the inevitable result of his serving in government after more than a decade of academic life. When he said he was interested only in the kind of national planning which President Roosevelt wanted, he indicated that he had decided to serve in the emergency, as best he could, the best available leader—not that he had given up his interest in the long-run institutional schemes he had written about. When he told the students at Dartmouth that the New Deal was essentially the old deal patched up, he offered them the same judgment which, as an institutionalist, he would make twenty-five years later. Tugwell was telling the truth—if it is agreed that there is a difference between an academician outside the government and an administrator on the inside. But his foes ridiculed any attempt to make such a distinction.[46] And, having refused to allow a separation of his academic writings from his administrative function, they often distorted the meaning of those writings. Thus, it would not have been possible for Tugwell to follow, either with effect or sincerity, the course recommended by the *Kansas City Star*, which suggested that he should have been sincere by saying his ideas on planning were "a college thesis and you know what that is." [47]

Politics, of course, had more to do with the conduct of the hearing than real intellectual inquiry. Tugwell was in no position to jeopardize the political investment which Roosevelt had made in his promotion, and his opponents were not free to make concessions on intellectual grounds. No doubt, some of the twenty-four men who voted "Nay" sincerely saw intolerable intellectual differences between themselves and Tugwell. Moreover, it is undoubtedly true, as Kent wrote, that some Democratic Senators would have voted "Nay" if it were not for the status of Tugwell's patron, the President.[48] It is also highly probable that some Senators who voted "Nay" did not believe the charges hurled at Tugwell but had to think of their constituents, among whom Tugwell had already acquired a reputation as a radical. As Russell Lord observed in connection with the hearing, "The devices that marshal public opinion, right and left, are as little given to shades of meaning as traffic lights. Red is red." [49]

To political pundit Mark Sullivan red was so red that confirmation of Tugwell also confirmed a turning point in the nation's history—the declaration by one of the major parties of its support of national planning and collectivism.[50] Democrats, *Time* reported, scoffed at Sullivan's conclusion, while Republicans, anticipating the fall elections, "prepared to do their best to scare the country into believing it." [51] The country did not scare, and the Democrats increased their numbers in both Senate and House. On the other hand, Tugwell, now more of a controversial figure than ever, saw his influence wane after 1934. This decline handicapped him as he assumed his duties as Resettlement Administrator in the spring of 1935. His confirmation was a costly victory, his promotion a dubious honor.

21. The Task of the Resettlement Administration

I

The Resettlement Administration was concerned with poor people and poor land. Poor people needed emergency aid. Poor land required long-range conservation measures. The "borderline between the emergency and the basic problem," Tugwell observed in 1936, "is not absolute." To help poor people it was necessary either to help them make their poor land better or to persuade and help them to move to better land. The RA's operations were related to the whole agricultural economy and the national economy. When farm prices rose, farming on poor lands increased, undermining the more efficient farmers' position in the supply-demand situation. When farm prices fell, farmers on submarginal lands, without purchasing power and unable to pay taxes, required constant, sizable expenditures by local and national governments. Thus, Tugwell noted, attempts to cultivate poor land were a drain on the economic well-being of the nation as a whole.[1]

Tugwell advocated the creation of an agency such as the RA because he believed that existing agencies were not doing enough about poor farmers and poor land. He concluded that the AAA was the big staple farmers' agency. It was, he recalled in 1947, "an answer to a lobbyist's dream," bestowing outright benefits without requiring, in return, better conservation practices and a recognition of the national interest in land.[2] It did not, he wrote in 1950, represent the nation or even all farmers. Dominated by the alliance of Extension Service, Land Grant College, and Farm Bureau, the AAA's "grass-roots democracy," like that of the TVA and SCS, served a "very useful purpose for those people who are content with things as they are and for bureaucrats who must come to terms with them."[3] It may be, as Professor Schlesinger has suggested, that Tugwell did not do justice to the county production associations and "the extent to which the vast apparatus of local committees . . . actually did produce both popular education and popular consent."[4] In any event, Tugwell's recollections were consistent with the stand he took in the USDA. In 1933 he said to Wallace, in front of a meeting of state and federal extension officials, "No, I haven't a damn bit of confidence in Extension Directors, Henry."[5]

More important than Tugwell's consistency was the fact that twenty years after the passage of the AA Act four commodities—wheat, corn, dairy products, and cotton and cottonseed oil—comprising 23 per cent of farm marketings and mostly produced by less than half of the nation's farmers, accounted for about nine-tenths of our investment in price supports.[6] These figures described a later stage of the situation which, Russell Lord commented, caused Tugwell to hold that "if one arm of the Department, Triple-A, worked for the advantaged element in the farm population, it was the Department's responsibility equally to advance effective programs to improve the lot of the disadvantaged."[7] But the AAA's "antagonisms and visible exploitations," Tugwell recalled, were not the only reasons why he wanted to establish the RA—there was "the land itself."[8] If the administration was not doing enough about poor people on poor land, what it was doing about poor land it was not doing well. Land-use planning lacked co-ordination, as a mere listing of the various agencies engaged in this work before the creation of the RA will show.

The Public Works Administration created a National Planning Board, which, in turn, organized a Land Planning Committee. An executive order of July 31, 1933, set up a Scientific Advisory Board, which had a Land Use Committee. The AAA's Land Policy Section, the USDI's Division of Subsistence Homesteads, and the Surplus Relief Corporation, using Federal Emergency Relief Administration funds, were concerned with land use. The USDA and the USDI formed a joint committee to reconcile land retirement with reclamation. This committee was to submit its first report to Ickes on August 31, 1933. On April 28, 1934, a Cabinet committee began to study the co-ordination of land-use programs, but it disbanded on June 30, 1934, when the National Resources Board received over-all authority in land-use matters. The NRB was to report to the President on December 1, 1934.[9]

The activities which most directly anticipated the RA got under way with the formation on February 28, 1934, of a Submarginal Land Committee, which comprised representatives of the USDA (including the AAA's Land Policy Section), the USDI (National Park Service and Office of Indian Affairs), the FERA, and the SRC. Meanwhile, in the spring of 1934, the FERA set up state Rural Rehabilitation Corporations. In July, 1934, the FERA's Land Program superseded the Submarginal Land Committee and the SRC in the purchasing of poor land and the resettlement of its occupants. The Land Program was to function through the FERA's Rural Rehabilitation Division in co-operation with the various divisions of the USDA and the USDI. On July 18, 1934, the Special Board for Public Works approved the program outlined by the Director of the Land Program and allotted it $25,000,000.[10]

It was against this background that Tugwell saw the need for co-ordination in a new agency of rehabilitation, resettlement, and land-use programs. He was aware of the confused situation, having taken an interest in these programs since their inception. On December 29, 1933, he had suggested in an address that the government, to start with, purchase and retire from production 50 million acres of submarginal land.[11] On March 2, 1934, he suggested to the President an amendment to the AA Act calling for the retirement of submarginal lands held by local, county, and state governments due to tax delinquencies and by federal land banks as a result of foreclosures.[12] Lewis Douglas, on April 3, 1934, wrote to the President about Tugwell's request for new legislation in support of a long-term land program. Douglas stated that the immense emergency expenditures of 1934 and 1935 would enable a return to "normal maintenance" in 1936.[13]

By the spring of 1934 Tugwell was getting discouraged. The work of the Forest Service and the Soil Erosion Service, the problem of grazing controls for public lands, the revelation of sharecroppers' ills by the AAA, and the Justice Department's difficulties in performing the task of clearing titles all pointed up the need for co-ordination. By 1934, Tugwell's memoir relates, the President agreed on the necessity for co-ordination, "our favorite topic and the one on which we found the most agreement," but nothing happened. And in July, when the Special Board for Public Works granted emergency funds to the FERA's Land Program, Tugwell despaired at the lack of Congressional support for poor farmers (such support would have made it unnecessary to use emergency funds). He was "convinced and ready to quit." Then, in August, the tide turned. Roosevelt, who was not deterred by Douglas' objections to Tugwell's proposals as "indeterminate in scope and cost," asked Wallace where existing land programs stood. Wallace sent Tugwell to the White House to present an answer. In the course of their discussion, the President suggested the possibility of using an executive order to establish a co-ordinating agency operating with emergency funds.[14]

In late August Wallace offered Roosevelt his comments on Tugwell's plan.[15] There was still no probability that Congress would legitimize the new agency, but the developments in August were encouraging. According to his memoir, Tugwell hoped to achieve legitimacy gradually, setting up an independent agency which the USDA would eventually absorb.[16] Meanwhile, discussion and planning continued. In early 1935 Tugwell learned that M. L. Wilson was not happy as head of the Division of Subsistence Homesteads in Interior. More eager than ever to create the RA after Frank's dismissal from the AAA, Tugwell discussed Wilson's dissatisfaction with Wallace, and they reviewed once again the "sprawled and mixed disbursement" through many agencies of rural housing and relief. They decided it was time to consolidate all such work in a new agency under Tugwell.[17] In March and April, 1935, there were rumors that Tugwell would soon take charge of some kind of a land-use, erosion-control, or rural-rehabilitation program.[18] Executive Order 7027 of May 1, 1935, established the RA. Its funds were obtained under the Emergency Relief Act of 1935. Tugwell recalled that the "rehabilitation of poor people and poor land together in one federal agency was my own novel suggestion," which indicates his satisfaction when Roosevelt rejected his recommendation of another Administrator, insisting that this was "his closest interest and he would have no other." [19]

The RA had to join into some kind of a coherent unit an assortment of activities inherited from other government agencies, federal and state. These included the Land Program and the Rural Rehabilitation Division of the FERA, the Division of Subsistence Homesteads of the USDI, the Land Policy Section of the AAA's Program Planning Division, the Farm Debt Adjustment Program of the Farm Credit Administration, and the state Rural Rehabilitation Corporations. The new agency had four main tasks: (1) suburban resettlement; (2) rural rehabilitation; (3) land utilization; (4) rural resettlement. Tugwell was primarily interested in (1) suburban resettlement and (3) land utilization. He was less interested in (2) rural rehabilitation, although he considered it necessary in the emergency, and (4) rural resettlement, particularly when it took the form of subsistence-homesteads communities.

Professor Paul K. Conkin, in *Tomorrow a New World: The New Deal Community Program,* partly based on an exhaustive search of the National Archives, winner of the American Historical Association's 1958 Albert J. Beveridge Memorial Fund Award, and the definitive study of suburban and rural resettlement in the United States, commented that "Tugwell's greatest interest was garden cities or greenbelt cities. For those he followed the well developed ideology of the garden-city movement." Conkin identified these suburban communities as "closest to Tugwell's heart." [20] The biographers of Will W. Alexander, who became Deputy Administrator of the RA, referred to Tugwell's "central conviction . . . that much of the farm problem grew out of a fundamental misuse of land" and stated that Tugwell's "greatest interest remained in reclassification and utilization of land." [21] Alexander's memoir, on which his biographers relied, made this point frequently.[22]

Professor Conkin indicated Tugwell's attitude toward rural rehabilitation, pointing out that in the Resettlement Administrator's view his assignment was "twofold: rehabilitation and permanent reform. . . . But the important task was reform," which meant land utilization.[23] Laurence Hewes of the RA remarked that "Tugwell took no pride in conducting a first-aid program; our real job was to cure the deeper malady." [24] Will Alexander, as one of the nation's leading advocates of rural rehabilitation, was in a good position to give Tugwell's ideas on this subject. Alexander's distinguished career involved four key aspects of life in the

South: religion, race relations, education, and agriculture. He was deeply disappointed when tenants and sharecroppers failed to share in the gains which the AAA brought to the landowners of the South, and in the spring of 1935 he went to Washington to protest that AAA benefits were not getting down to the people who needed them most.[25]

Alexander went to the capital with Edwin Embree, president of the Rosenwald Fund, of which Alexander had been a trustee since 1930. This foundation had sponsored studies of agricultural conditions in the South. These investigations convinced Alexander of the smaller, poorer farmers' need for rehabilitation in the form of loans, credit, equipment, and education. He made his plea to Senator Bronson Cutting, Wallace, Lewis C. Gray, M. L. Wilson, Paul Appleby, and Tugwell (he had met Tugwell once previously, at Columbia University in 1931 through Dr. John Coss, a mutual friend and professor of philosophy). Alexander was aware of Tugwell's primary interest in land utilization, and he was uncertain about the impact of his and Embree's plea. Several weeks later he received a telephone call in his Atlanta office of the Interracial Commission from Tugwell, who wanted Alexander to become Deputy Administrator of the Resettlement Administration.[26]

Thus, Tugwell, despite his lack of interest in rural rehabilitation, had recruited one of its foremost proponents into the RA. In fact, Tugwell maneuvered at the White House in order to obtain an executive order under which the RA replaced Harry Hopkins' FERA as the federal agency co-operating with the state rural rehabilitation corporations.[27] Alexander, in retrospect, concluded that Tugwell decided "he'd better take us into camp if he could and keep all this problem under one tent. I suspect he thought we were a lot of amateurs who would mix things up, and although he didn't think much of what we were doing, he'd come along." [28]

Alexander's biographers characterized Tugwell's attitude toward rural resettlement succinctly: "He did not subscribe to the subsistence homestead idea as preached by M. L. Wilson and the back-to-the-land enthusiasts." [29] Tugwell saw suburban resettlement as the most significant response to coming population movements, stating in 1933 that "we must be prepared to absorb very large numbers of persons from farms into our general industrial and urban life," and that "our subsistence homestead projects . . . will function merely as small eddies of retreat for exceptional persons." [30] In early 1937, just after his resignation, Tugwell re-stated his belief that the subsistence-homesteads projects rested on the invalid theory that industry would move to the workers.[31]

In his later writings Tugwell mentioned his frequent discussions with the President, in the three years preceding the formation of the RA, of resettlement in which subsistence farming was to be supplemented by part-time work in forestry, handicraft and home industries, and near-by small-scale industries. As Governor of New York, Roosevelt had sponsored experimentation in Tompkins County, where submarginal land on the hills around Cornell University was removed from production and returned to grass and trees. Tugwell considered this experiment "a significant intimation of regeneration." He, too, desired to break the vicious circle: "Such lands made people poor, and poor people made such lands so much worse that they became a national problem." But he saw more limitations on the remedial potential of resettlement communities and subsistence farming than Roosevelt did.[32]

Tugwell recalled his emphasis on the necessity of finding economic opportunities for displaced farmers. Roosevelt thought subsistence farming on better land in near-by valleys would take care of them. Tugwell "followed him that far; but when he suggested that this might be done for a lot of idle city folk too, I balked." If they became successful commercial farmers, they would add to existing surpluses. If they engaged in subsistence farming, they would reduce the market for commercial farm products. As for Roosevelt's argument that industries could be induced to move to subsistence-homesteads communities, Tugwell replied that "people had always had to move to industries in the interest of efficiency and that less efficient operations would not attract private enterprise." In retrospect, Tugwell called Roosevelt's "notion that industry could be returned in small units to rural sites with benefit both to industry and the country" one of his "less practical conceptions; . . . it made no sense" to argue for a return to the land during the agricultural depression of the 1920's, and "it would not make much more sense in the depression years to argue that the unemployed could be cared for in this way."[33]

To put it another way, Tugwell told Roosevelt, in effect, that there might be some value in "infiltration" resettlement of individuals on suitable scattered tracts, but that "community" resettlement in self-contained subsistence-homesteads projects was less likely to provide viable havens for submarginal farmers and the urban unemployed. Tugwell's objection to the mixed-economy community was in line with his emphasis on technological efficiency. Professor Conkin has commented that "although he did not exclude a few more subsistence homesteads communities [in addition to those which the RA inherited], Tugwell's main emphasis was to be on all-rural communities for farmers and garden cities for full-time industrial workers, neither depending upon a mixed agricultural and industrial economy."[34] This approach led to some experiments in co-operative farming.

In any case, Roosevelt did not heed Tugwell's advice. Reinforced by

Mrs. Roosevelt and Louis Howe, he authorized the creation in 1933 of the Division of Subsistence Homesteads in the USDI. This Division got under way with an allocation of $25,000,000 under the National Industrial Recovery Act. Moreover, the Division of Subsistence Homesteads became part of the RA in 1935. According to Russell Lord, Tugwell did not want to take over this operation, but the President insisted.[35] According to Harold Ickes' diary, the Secretary of the Interior first tried to trade his reclamation, erosion-control, and subsistence-homesteads programs for the USDA's Bureaus of Roads, Forestry, and Biological Survey, hoping to make Tugwell Undersecretary of the Interior in charge of conservation. Having failed to arrange this exchange and having failed to persuade Hopkins to take over the subsistence homesteads, Ickes talked to Roosevelt in March, 1935, about placing all the community programs in one agency under Oscar Chapman, Assistant Secretary of the Interior. To Ickes' surprise, the President informed him that Tugwell wanted to direct the subsistence-homesteads program.[36] Tugwell himself recalled that the President compelled him to accept this operation.[37]

Lord's and Tugwell's version was probably correct. In speaking to Ickes, Roosevelt may have put words in Tugwell's mouth; or Tugwell may already have acceded to the President's wishes. In brief, Roosevelt told Tugwell that if he wanted a new agency to deal with rural problems, he had to take the whole package. Alexander's biographers noted that it was characteristic of Roosevelt to create a new, independent agency rather than make a determined attempt to change the policies of the USDA.[38] In pushing the subsistence homesteads into the RA, the President adopted the same all-under-one-tent line of reasoning that Tugwell followed in absorbing rural rehabilitation into the new organization.

To sum up, as Tugwell assumed his duties as Resettlement Administrator, he took charge of two programs which he wanted—suburban resettlement and land utilization—and two which he did not really want —rural rehabilitation and rural resettlement (subsistence homesteads). Suburban resettlement and land utilization were both minor aspects of the RA's operations—the former accounting for about $36,000,000 in expenditures, the latter arranging for the retirement of about 9,000,000 of a proposed 50,000,000 or 100,000,000 acres—and both were somewhat controversial. Rural rehabilitation was by far the largest activity of the total program—disbursing about $778,000,000 in loans and about $152,-000,000 in grants—but it was the least controversial. The salient point to bear in mind is that rural resettlement, which Tugwell wanted least, was a relatively minor part of the whole RA operation—costing about $72,000,000—but it was by far the most controversial.

II

The four main tasks of the Resettlement Administration were performed by these Divisions:

Suburban Resettlement
Rural Rehabilitation
Land Utilization
Rural Resettlement

In addition there were twelve co-ordinate Divisions:

Business Management   Management
Construction   Personnel
Finance   Planning
Information   Procedure
Investigation   Special Plans
Labor Relations   Special Skills

Within each Division were Sections, such as the Technical Research Unit of the Suburban Resettlement Division, the Land Planning Section of the Land Utilization Division, and the Economic Development Section and Education and Training Section of the Management Division. Geographically, the RA operated through eleven regional offices and smaller offices in each state and most counties. Decentralization, which followed the pattern of the FERA, was necessary for rural-rehabilitation work. It was least suitable for suburban resettlement, which was controlled from Washington. A combination of regional direction and supervision from Washington was applied to rural resettlement.[39]

The RA acquired 4,200 employees from its inherited agencies, but Tugwell filled most of the higher administrative posts with new appointees. After Tugwell, the two most important executive officers were Will W. Alexander, Deputy Administrator, and Calvin B. Baldwin, one of several Assistant Administrators and erstwhile assistant to Henry Wallace. The Directors of the four main Divisions were: John S. Lansill, a city-planner, Suburban Resettlement; Joseph L. Dailey, a New Mexico lawyer and judge, Rural Rehabilitation; Lewis C. Gray, previously with the Land Policy Section of the AAA, Land Utilization; Carl C. Taylor, formerly of the Division of Subsistence Homesteads of the USDI, Rural Resettlement. Eugene Agger, Tugwell's friend and one-time colleague at Columbia, was Director of the Management Division. The personnel of the RA soon numbered 13,000, and, as Professor Conkin has explained, it definitely was not set up as a temporary agency.[40]

The *Suburban Resettlement Division* acted on Tugwell's expectation that the farm population would continue to decrease, and that some farmers would move to the cities, where, as Professor Conkin pointed out, "a horrible lack of imaginative city planning had created problems in land use even more grave than those in rural areas." This Division was also concerned with resettlement of urban slum dwellers. Suburban Resettlement was largely independent of the other Divisions of the RA. It controlled the greenbelt cities and the uncompleted suburban-type subsistence homesteads. It originally planned twenty-five greenbelt communities, but because of financial and legal obstacles it built only three: Greenbelt, Maryland, near Washington, D. C.; Greenhills, near Cincinnati; Greendale, near Milwaukee. A legal squabble eliminated Greenbrook, which was to be constructed near New Brunswick, New Jersey. Besides designing greenbelt cities or "Tugwell Towns," as the press often called them, Suburban Resettlement modified the plans of two subsistence-homesteads communities—one near Newport News, Virginia, the other near Birmingham, Alabama—changing them to suburban housing projects similar to the greenbelt cities in many ways. Suburban Resettlement also initiated one suburban community, near Ironwood, Michigan, which bore some resemblance to the garden cities. This Division, which had its own Technical Research Unit, relied on the Construction Division for the actual building of its projects.[41] It should be noted that these communities, unlike the subsistence homesteads, were not designed to attract industry, all being located near employment centers.

The greenbelt towns, examples of miniature regional planning, housed 500 to 800 families each. Their officially stated purposes were: (1) to provide useful work for men on unemployment relief; (2) to provide low-rent housing in healthful surroundings for low-income families; (3) to demonstrate the soundness of planning and operating towns according to certain garden-city principles.[42] Tugwell's enthusiasm for these communities, which he communicated to the President in 1935, was exhilarant.[43] In an article of 1936 he referred to the provision of a "more orderly pattern for the inevitable movement from farm to city." [44] In early 1937 he wrote on "The Meaning of the Greenbelt Towns," stating his desire to demonstrate that the peripheral areas of cities offered the "best chance we have ever had in this country for affecting our living and working environment favorably." The towns were designed to assure better living through the prevention of crowding within and encroachment from without. They were surrounded by a "greenbelt" of field and woods. Emphasizing light, air, and space, playgrounds and parks, accessible gardens, and unimpaired foot-traffic ways, they were to be ideal for children. Tugwell predicted that the materials would probably become outmoded, but good design and construction would make the towns attractive for an indefinite time. He believed that the greenbelt projects invited comparison with other suburban projects and the whole current theory of slum clearance.[45]

The *Rural Rehabilitation Division* carried on the bulk of the RA's activities. This work included financial assistance—loans, grants, debt adjustment—and technical, or educational, assistance. There was a precedent for some of the RA's loans in the seed and feed loans which the government had made since 1918 to farmers who were victimized by natural disaster such as flood or drought. The RA responded in addition to the needs resulting from economic disaster, such as the collapse of prices or the foreclosure of mortgages. It made loans to farmers, farm tenants, croppers, farm laborers, and co-operative groups for food, clothing, feed, seed, livestock, equipment, repairs, and land. Financial aid, of course, was not the whole answer. Many farmers, working poor land with poor equipment, also suffered physical, mental, and psychological deficiencies.

During the political campaign of 1936 the Republican National Committee charged that the RA made loans on insufficient security, and Tugwell replied that the rate of repayment to date was 76 per cent.[46] There was some truth in the GOP's charge, but that was because a farmer who could obtain a loan from an established credit agency was ineligible for an RA loan. Statistics, including the years 1937-1943, when the Farm Security Administration (successor to the RA) administered this program, show a small average loan, a large total operation, and an excellent repayment record:

Fiscal years 1936-1943, inclusive

Average original loan	$412
Average supplemental loan	$202
Average interest rate	2.5%
Total amount loaned	$778,000,000
Total amount repaid	$378,000,000
Number of families receiving loans	950,000
Number of families repaying in full	200,000
Amount due, Feb. 28, 1943	$377,000,000
Repayments on amount due, Feb. 28, 1943	$324,000,000
Percentage of repayment on amount due	86% [47]

Besides making these loans, the RA made non-repayable grants of $152,000,000 and conducted a debt-adjustment program to help competent farmers keep their heavily mortgaged farms. The average mortgage debt per farm, Tugwell noted in 1936, had increased in the period 1910-1930 from $1,175 to $3,561; at the same time, interest on old debts ate up profits so that even the farmer on good land could not make ends meet.[48] To ease this burden of mortgage and debt the RA financed meetings of voluntary farm debt-adjustment committees and assisted them with a supervisory staff rather than through direct participation. These committees, appointed by governors and serving without pay, wrote agreements which either reduced indebtedness or extended the time for payment.[49]

There was an urgent, widespread demand for the RA's support of debt adjustment. Life insurance companies, mortgage companies, and other mortgage holders were "little less interested than debtors," Ernest Lindley remarked in 1933, in "giving life to this dead weight of debt." [50] When an administrative complication halted the RA's support of this work on August 1, 1935, several governors protested to the President,[51] who turned the complaints over to Tugwell. The RA, Tugwell explained, had co-operated with the Farm Credit Administration in drawing up a new plan which was to assure the continuance of debt adjustment after August 1, but the plan, submitted on July 8, had neither been approved nor rejected.[52] On August 16, Tugwell finally was able to wire the governors that arrangements were being made to carry on debt-adjustment activities.[53] In the first year after activities were resumed, 31,566 farmers' indebtedness of $102,103,000 was reduced to $76,241,000.[54] In later years agricultural economists disagreed on the impact of the debt-adjustment program.[55]

The RA reinforced financial assistance with technical assistance, setting up more than 200 demonstration projects and providing on-the-farm instruction and supervision. The RA and the FSA gave educational aid to 455,000 farm families in the period 1936-1943. In June, 1936, Roosevelt indicated his interest in this work in a letter to Roger A. Derby of New York: "You are right about the farmers who suffer through their own fault. Some day when you are in Washington I wish you would have a talk with Tugwell about what he is doing to educate this type of farmer to become self-sustaining. During the past year his organization has made 104,000 farm families practically self-sustaining by supervision and education along practical lines. That is a pretty good record!" [56]

The RA's most spectacular effort in the conservation of human and natural resources through relief and rehabilitation was its extensive program of aid to drought-stricken farmers in 1936. It administered this aid under an amendment to Executive Order 7027, obtained by Tugwell in September, 1935, which authorized RA relief in stricken areas.[57] Before his appointment to the Great Plains Drought Committee, Tugwell, in June and early July, 1936, had stepped up relief activities, conferred with the President, traveled through the drought area, and presented a report on relief requirements to the White House.[58] Then he went with the Committee on a 2,000-mile tour, starting in northern Texas on August 17, and meeting the President in Bismarck, North Dakota, in early

September.[59] The Committee reported on the basic problem of conservation, but, Tugwell recalled, "it had to put aside for the moment its
long-range plans and plunge into the emergency job of helping those who
had been demoralized by the implacable hostility of nature." [60]

The RA went into action to aid 400,000 families who had suffered a
loss of $300,000,000 in more than 1,000 counties (of 3,000 in the United
States) which were listed as drought emergency areas.[61] It declared a
one-year moratorium on repayment of rural-rehabilitation loans and
prepared to allot $18,000,000 for crop and forage loans.[62] It also dropped
a number of its projects to permit use of its funds for emergency relief
in the West during the coming winter.[63] Tugwell later noted that two-
thirds to three-quarters of the drought-stricken families received some
kind of assistance: cash grants for supplies, emergency jobs on water-
conservation projects and road and school construction, care for their
livestock. He commented that "it was all done awkwardly and waste-
fully," but in his recollections there was an implication of pride in the
RA's performance: "No one in the short-grass country was happy. The
worst of the region's problems had not been solved. But there was a
general gratefulness that in their extremity no money or effort had
been spared to bring the affected families assistance. There had been a
minimum of red tape; plans for permanent arrangement had not been
much discussed. Help had simply been brought and not too many questions asked. Altogether 1936, although it was a much worse drought
year than 1934, was a far less difficult one for those who were caught
in its burning blast." [64]

The *Land Utilization Division* executed the first half of the retirement-
resettlement sequence. In 1936, describing the RA's program, Tugwell
wrote that when the agency was organized there were 650,000 farm
families on 100,000,000 acres of poor land which even experts could not
have farmed at a profit. He did not suggest acquiring all of this land.
He recommended "adjustment" rather than "simple retirement" as the
best policy. Restoration of the land and education in the right crops and
the right techniques would suffice for some farmers. Others were beyond hope of rehabilitation on the land they occupied. In such cases, retirement was the appropriate action, and the RA, moving cautiously,
initially provided for the retirement of 9,000,000 acres.[65] (As noted
above, this proved to be the final figure.)

The first step in retirement was the RA's purchase, from voluntary
sellers, of worn-out land. The Land Utilization Division, co-operating
with other agencies, then turned the land to nonagricultural uses: wildlife
preserves, recreation facilities, Indian reserves, pasturage, and reforestation. This Division administered over 200 work projects in caring for
retired land and in carrying on certain conservation activities such as
control of soil erosion, seacoast erosion, stream pollution, and flood. The

enabling executive order did not draw a line between the RA's conservation work and that of the Soil Conservation Service. The RA avoided overlapping by confining itself to marginal and submarginal land.[66]

The Land Planning Section of the Land Utilization Division was the RA's main research unit. Co-operating with the USDA's Bureau of Agricultural Economics, it produced valuable studies for Rural Resettlement and Suburban Resettlement as well as for its own Division. The Land Planning Section studied the nation's land problems, located areas for resettlement, and compiled a huge report on resettlement practices. This report recommended "infiltration" (rather than "community") resettlement and encouragement of co-operatives; it counseled against forced co-operation and mixed-economy resettlement communities.[67] Since the RA could not retire land to nonagricultural uses until it had a place for the displaced farmers to go—until, as Tugwell remarked in 1935, there was "effective demand for their employment elsewhere" [68]— it was understandable that a Section of the Land Utilization Division concern itself with resettlement.

The *Rural Resettlement Division* initiated and planned all rural communities. With the assistance of the Special Plans Division, it screened the plans of uncompleted or proposed projects inherited from the Division of Subsistence Homesteads and the Federal Emergency Relief Administration and continued the planning of those communities which were retained. Like the Suburban Resettlement Division, Rural Resettlement depended on the Construction Division for the actual building of its projects. The Management Division assumed responsibility for completed communities: selection of settlers, direction of educational and community activities, organization of government, maintenance of buildings. The Management Division's Economic Development Section dealt with the problem of economic opportunity.[69]

The unspent funds of the Division of Subsistence Homesteads reverted to the Treasury on June 16, 1935. A week later the President allocated $7,000,000 of the emergency-relief appropriation to the RA for the completion of thirty-three communities. The RA was able to spend inherited funds for the completion of the FERA communities. By late 1935 Tugwell assigned 49 millions (of the 375 millions which the RA received under the 4.8 billions Emergency Relief Act of 1935) to rural resettlement.[70] This allocation was subsequently subject to both reductions and increases. It showed, however, that the RA undertaking was much larger than that of the Division of Subsistence Homesteads, which had spent about $8,000,000 in two years.[71]

The Division of Subsistence Homesteads brought to the RA plans for sixty-five communities. The RA (1935-1936) and its successor, the Farm Security Administration (1937-1943), completed thirty-four projects which the Division of Subsistence Homesteads had begun. These communities were classified in several categories:

Industrial	23
Stranded communities	
(Reedsville and Elkins, W. Va.;	
Crossville, Tenn.; Greensburg, Pa.)	4
Farm communities	
(Pender City, N. C.; Jasper City, Ga.;	
Richton, Miss.)	3
Co-operative-industrial	
(Hightstown, N. J.)	1
Resettlement community	
(7 units in 5 counties in Va.)	1
Industrial-small garden city	
(Cahaba, near Birmingham, Ala.)	1
Garden city for Negroes	
(Newport News, Va.)	1

Units: 3,304   Average Unit Cost: $9,114
Total Cost: $30,112,467 [72]

Of the twenty-three industrial communities, eleven (4 in Mississippi, 3 in Texas, 1 each in Alabama, California, Indiana, and Minnesota) were almost finished and were turned over to the Management Division. Seven more (2 in Texas and 1 each in Alabama, Arizona, California, Iowa, and Washington State) were completed by December, 1935. These eighteen communities, Professor Conkin concluded, "gave the Resettlement Administration fewer problems than any other inherited communities, since they were usually located near economic opportunities and usually had excellent settlers." Three other industrial homesteads (2 in Alabama and 1 in Illinois) were completed much later. Duluth Homesteads in Minnesota was drastically modified and became, in effect, an RA community. Dayton Homesteads in Ohio was a special case; it received federal funds, but it was a unique project in that the government never owned the land.[73]

The four stranded communities, Professor Conkin pointed out, "were the real problem children of the Resettlement Administration, even as they had been of the Division of Subsistence Homesteads." [74] Tugwell, as we have seen, did not believe that industry would follow people, and the economies of these projects were in distress. Making the best of a bad situation, Tugwell assigned the stranded communities to the Washington office of the Management Division "in order to spare the regional offices any embarrassment." Management's Economic Development Section attacked the problem of underemployment—of finding outside employment to supplement subsistence farming—in three ways: purchase and addition to the co-operative farms of more land; slowing down of construction to prolong the homesteaders' employment; assistance to various consumer and producer co-operative enterprises—the primary remedy, which Tugwell encouraged. "They became fascinating experiments in co-operation, but never solved the economic problem." [75]

The RA inherited twenty-eight communities from the FERA:

Farm communities
(3 in Ark.; 2 each in N. C., Ga., and
Tex.; 1 each in Ala., N. M., and S. C.)   12
Farm villages
(8 in Neb.; 1 each in S. D. and Tex.)   10
Industrial
(1 in Ariz., 1 in Minn.)   2
Stranded communities
(1 in N. D.; 1 in W. Va.)   2
Farm and rural-industrial
(1 in Fla., 1 in Ga.)   2

Units: 2,426   Average Unit Cost: $8,887
Total Cost: $21,559,325 [76]

Only two were near enough to completion to be turned over to the Management Division. Nearly all of the FERA communities were all-rural and on completion were very similar to the projects of the same type which the RA initiated. The RA frequently added to the acreage of these rural communities in line with its emphasis on an all-farming economy.[77]

The RA itself, through its Rural Resettlement Division, initiated more than 100 rural projects, including thirty-four communities:

Farm communities
(8 in Ark.; 3 each in Miss. and Tex.;
2 each in Ala., La., S. C., and Mo.;
1 each in Ga., Fla., Ky., N. C., Mich.,
and Mont.)   28
Co-operative farms
(1 in Ariz.; 1 in Ark.)   2
Forest homesteads
(1 in Ky.; 1 in Wis.)   2
Co-operative plantation
(Terrebonne Parish, La.)   1
Small garden city
(Ironwood, Mich.)   1

Units: 2,941   Average Unit Cost: $6,878
Total Cost: $20,222,624

The comparable figures for the Suburban Resettlement Division's three greenbelt cities were:

Units: 2,267   Average Unit Cost: $15,968
Total Cost: $36,200,910 [78]

Most of the RA rural projects were all-farming communities, most of them were in the South, and nearly all of them were completed by the FSA. A typical community was either all-white or all-Negro and included about 100 farm units of forty to 100 acres each. Until 1940 tenure was by lease, with rental payments in crops. Each community contained from one to a dozen or more co-operative enterprises. These were run by co-operative associations which the government sponsored and financed. The co-operative farms at Lake Dick, Arkansas, and Casa Grande Valley, Arizona, and the co-operative plantation in Terrebonne Parish, Louisiana, were striking departures from the existing farm pattern, being combined with the village arrangement for residence. All or parts of about a dozen other rural-resettlement projects engaged in co-operative farming, as a number of FERA communities had done, but without the village scheme.[79]

Besides conducting its activities through its sixteen Divisions, with their various Sections, the RA was involved in relations with other government agencies. It took time to get co-operating state agencies to co-ordinate their policies with the RA's. There were complaints, for example, about some of the practices of the State Re-employment Offices, upon which the RA sometimes called for help in procuring qualified personnel. To one protest Tugwell replied that any discriminations in job announcements would be eliminated and were due, in this instance, to the necessity of hiring auditors in a hurry upon taking over the State Rural Rehabilitation Corporations.[80]

In June, 1935, the RA and the Extension Service of the USDA agreed on a Memorandum of Understanding in the planning and supervision of rural communities, but, as Professor Conkin explained, "this never led to a close working relationship, mainly because of conflicting philosophies." The Extension Service was accustomed to dealing mostly with well-to-do, landowning farmers. It abhorred the collectivistic policies which the RA applied to a poverty-stricken clientele.[81] Like Tugwell, who expressed his lack of a "damn bit of confidence" in the Extension Service, Will Alexander pronounced a harsh judgment. He recalled that the Extension Service and the Farm Bureau resented "non-Trade Union members" and deplored their neglect of the poorer farmers.[82]

As Resettlement Administrator, Tugwell had difficulties with the redoubtable Harold Ickes. The RA inherited the FERA's Land Program, but Ickes' National Park Service continued to administer the forty-six recreational areas in that Program. Meanwhile, the RA paid the administrative expenses of half a million dollars a year. The RA, Tugwell informed the President, had the necessary administrative machinery and could save most of the $500,000. It had notified the Park Service of its intention to take over administration, expressing a willingness to retain Park Service personnel necessary to rounding out plans of that agency. Tugwell was stating the RA's intentions "in case there should be some kind of protest from Secretary Ickes. Should such a protest be made, I suggest that he and I be authorized to talk the matter over." [83] There were also jurisdictional conflicts between the RA and Ickes' Bureau of Reclamation over certain land purchases. Tugwell and Ickes were the protagonists, with Dr. Elwood Mead, Commissioner of Reclamation, and the President acting as mediators.[84]

The RA and Harry Hopkins' Works Progress Administration both received their funds under the Emergency Relief Act of 1935, and the RA was required by law to use relief labor under WPA regulations. Thus, there was friction over labor and construction problems and jurisdiction of land-utilization projects, which used WPA labor, as well as continuous competition between Tugwell and Hopkins for executive funds.[85] This scrambling for dollars would not have occurred if the RA had attained legitimacy through the replacement of its enabling executive order by a legislative act. Congress' withholding of such authorization until after Tugwell left Washington at the end of 1936 reflected the criticism which centered on this vast, complex agency and its controversial Administrator.

22. The Performance of the Resettlement Administration under Tugwell: 1935-1936

I

"Rex the Red," the stereotype created by the drug lobby's attack on Tugwell, was also "Rex the Dreamer," and "Rex the Dreamer" was naturally a poor administrator. In terms of a contradictory image, Tugwell was both a dangerous threat to the American way of life and too ineffective to carry out his administrative duties.

In March, 1933, *Business Week* welcomed Tugwell to Washington with the label "pure theorist."[1] In 1934 George M. Verity, Chairman of the Board of the American Rolling Mill Company, unlike most businessmen who disapproved of Tugwell, set down his views at some length. In an article in a trade journal he expressed his concern that a man in a position as important as Tugwell's should show an utter lack of understanding of the actual problems involved in the conduct of business. Verity warned that intellectual development and book knowledge without experience were a dangerous combination when applied to practical things. He did not question Tugwell's sincerity or loyalty, only the soundness of his plans and policies. He conceded that professors might do useful research and scientific work in government, but they should turn over their ideas to an entirely different type of man—the man engaged in the practical application of developed theories. There was one flaw worth noting in Verity's comment. He refuted Tugwell's assertion that industrial experimentation had made men's lives insecure by pointing out the value of experimentation in industry. His frame of reference was technological, whereas Tugwell's was financial—speculative capital investment.[2]

In 1934 James G. Mitchell, a prominent New York City attorney, referred to Tugwell's bureaucratic mentality, which failed, because of a "complete lack of historical and realistic sense," to apprehend that bureaucracy and democracy were mutually exclusive concepts. This bureaucratic mentality also accounted for Tugwell's identifying himself with the larger good. This identification, in turn, resulted in a divorcement from reality which prevented Tugwell from appreciating the implications of his own writings and speeches.[3] In 1933, in *Control from the Top*, Francis Neilson, a staunch advocate of laissez faire, conceded that "Dr. Tugwell is under no sociological delusion as to the social millennium," but Neilson also maintained that Tugwell, having had little contact with laborers and other men who devoted their time to seeking material riches, was not aware that to a London porter another pound a week meant "two more pints, and bet a bob instead of sixpence."[4] Paul Ward, a militant reformer of the *Nation,* considered Tugwell's departure from Columbia University for government unfortunate because fate had cast him for the role of the young professor, found on every campus, who impressed "sophomores with things that neither Marx nor Winchell knew until now." Ward saw Tugwell as a man of ideas who proved a fumbler as a man of action.[5]

The Republicans, of course, contributed their share of references to Tugwell as a dreamer. James C. Young, in his campaign tract of 1936, insisted that Tugwell had come to Washington without any experience in large affairs. Young assumed friction in an administration which was a combination of practical politicians like James A. Farley and ecstatic academic theorists like Tugwell.[6] Among the increasing number of journalists whose support the Republicans enjoyed, Blair Bolles, Alva Johnston, and Frank Kent took particular delight in ridiculing Tugwell's alleged divorcement from reality. In 1936 Bolles called Tugwell a "better poet than administrator."[7] In 1940 Bolles recalled the tragedy of the dismissal of men of affairs as principal advisers to the government and the choice, in their place, of "writers" like Tugwell, whose ideas were the product of compassion and a desire to have all men happy and well fed. The impracticality of these ideas left Tugwell a "frustrated Utopian" who found in business the demon barring the road to heaven.[8] In 1936 Alva Johnston compared Tugwell unfavorably with Colonel House, who understood that a "world-remodeling tête-à-tête man" ought to avoid administrative jobs in order that he might have power without responsibility. Tugwell, Johnston continued, offset any worth which his ideas might have by his self-defeating efforts as an administrator.[9]

Frank Kent deplored the initial allocation of funds to the Resettlement Administration as "quite a lot of money to be spent in a year [by] young and quite advanced . . . thinkers, fitting well into the Tugwell atmosphere and all broken out with theories."[10] Kent's columns were a catalogue of anti-Tugwellisms, flavored with the satirical wit of the slightly veiled or tongue-in-cheek barb. If there were men of more balanced judgment and greater practical experience in public affairs than Professor Tugwell, there were none, Kent asserted, who could see prettier pictures. When it came to long-range vision, Tugwell was "at the top of the class. . . . Through the empurpled haze his keen eyes peer down long, lovely vistas at the end of which lie flowery beds of ease on which everybody leads a happy life. . . . It is not fair, however, to expect the Professor to reveal all his plans . . . and the final promise he holds out . . . is so beautiful that one should not harrow him about details. 'Then,' he quotes, 'shall they sit, each man under his own vine and fig tree and none shall be afraid—a land in order, wisely used, with the hills green and the streams blue.' This will certainly improve the appearance of the Missouri River." But Kent did not want to be too critical of Tugwell's serene confidence, "unshaken and unshakable" in the face of administrative difficulties, that his planned paradise was close at hand. After all, "only the sinister" would suggest that Tugwell's limited experience, cloistered life, and previous lack of success disqualified him from safely guiding 130,000,000 Americans and solving all the problems which had perplexed generations of statesmen.[11]

A recurring theme in the criticism of Tugwell was the one "Cotton Ed" Smith stressed—that he was not a "dirt farmer." Senator Burton K. Wheeler stated that he was favorably disposed toward the AA Act but resented its being promoted by a few professors who sat around the Department of Agriculture and "never saw a bushel of wheat in their lives." [12] Wheeler made this remark after he had soured on the administration, which occurred after he had contracted the presidential virus. *Washington Squirrel Cage,* a scurrilous commentary of 1934 on the New Deal, dismissed Tugwell's study of the farm problem with the observation that he once read a book on the subject and wrote a thesis of such "shallow profundity" that it duly impressed that "sterling dirt farmer from the fish markets of New York, Al Smith." [13] Stanley High remarked in 1937 that Tugwell knew little about agriculture but a great deal about crusades.[14] In 1935, after he had been forced out of the NRA, Hugh Johnson declared, in his inimitable manner, "Rex Tugwell knows as much about agriculture as Haile Selassie knows about Oshkosh, Wisconsin." [15]

After May 1, 1935, criticism of Tugwell was inseparable from criticism of the agency which he headed. Moreover, Tugwell's friends, as well as his foes, were critical of the administration of the RA. Daniel W. Bell, Acting Director of the Bureau of the Budget, wrote to the President in August, 1935, suggesting a reduction in the RA's average salary, which was $3,000, compared to the Veterans Administration's $1,600.[16] In January, 1936, Bell received an anonymous memorandum on waste and extravagances in RA operations. He forwarded it to the White House, describing it as "substantially in accord with some of the rumors about town." He suggested the possibility of a full inquiry by the Bureau of the Budget.[17] In August, 1936, Bell suggested that Admiral Peoples investigate the RA's subsistence-homesteads and suburban-resettlement projects, as he had PWA and WPA construction projects, in order to ascertain the percentage of labor taken from relief rolls, the cost of construction compared with similar work of other government agencies and private enterprise, the probability of the government's being reimbursed, and the desirability of completing specific going projects to full size.[18]

Harold Ickes recorded in his diary in November, 1935, that Tugwell, a man of "real vision and ability," never should have taken the RA job. He did not think that Tugwell was a competent executive. He had received word from various sources that the RA's organization was a "shambles." Ickes noted that Louis Brownlow, a Democrat and a man of social vision, as well as an expert on administration, had recently spoken without prejudice in confirming adverse reports about the RA.[19] The President himself sent Tugwell unfavorable comments on the RA which came to the White House, and he complained in August, 1936, regarding the high unit cost of some resettlement projects, "I do not think we have a leg to stand on." [20]

Consideration of criticism of the RA in some detail discloses disapproval of the agency's eleven-region, sixteen-Division organization. According to Will Alexander, Grace Falke, Tugwell's administrative assistant, was largely responsible for this arrangement.[21] There were objections to this scheme, Professor Conkin noted, "on the grounds that it led to an overlapping of function, to higher administrative expenses, and to difficulties in allotting responsibilities. Many believed that the Resettlement Administration was over-organized." [22] Of the sixteen Divisions in this elaborate system, the two Resettlement Divisions—Rural and Suburban—and their two main co-operating Divisions—Construction and Management—were subject to the most vigorous condemnation. Congressional opposition to the Land Utilization Division's retirement program was comparatively quiet, but it was implacable and decisive in the long run. The activities of other Divisions also provoked unfavorable comment.

The personnel of the Planning Division, unlike the employees of the Land Planning Section of the Land Utilization Division, were mostly of nonrural background. This Division, under Keith Southard, concerned itself with the broad philosophic question of the RA's impact on the course of American development. It recommended suburban decentralization in industrial centers but opposed the subsistence-homesteads idea of combining part-time farming with part-time work in industry, whether attracted from the city or of the handicrafts type. It was less orthodox than the Land Planning Section in emphasizing the possibilities of co-operative enterprises, including experimental co-operative farms and plantations. The Planning Division also advocated, in vain, rehabilitation through grants rather than loans.[23]

Despite its philosophic concerns and its opposition to the subsistence-homesteads idea, the Planning Division hired architects, furniture designers, weavers, and ceramic artisans to help plan the rural communities. Their efforts were akin to some of the work of the Special Skills Division, whose establishment Will Alexander attributed to Grace Falke.[24] Special Skills dealt with the cultural and recreational development of the communities, employing, for example, folk-song collectors. Alexander remembered the Planning Division's personnel as idealistic dreamers.[25] His biographers remarked that the Planning Division "was never a major phase, and yet it revealed in a striking way some of the rarified atmosphere that prevailed in Resettlement and stamped its early image in the public mind." [26] The image outlived the Division, which Tugwell abruptly eliminated in September, 1935—less than five months after the RA got under way.

The Information Division came in for its share of criticism. Marquis Childs, a scholarly columnist, credited the RA's personnel with good intentions and some hard thinking, but they failed to take their case to the American people, whose traditional attitudes ran counter to the "community" idea.[27] Will Alexander concurred, recalling that the Information Division did not tell the public what the RA was actually doing. Instead, the Division concentrated on Tugwell. This was not Tugwell's doing, Alexander pointed out. It was the work of his admirers, who, in typical Washington fashion, sought to enhance the status of their chief.[28]

The general charge against the Personnel Division was that it hired too many people and paid them too much to do too little work. In early 1936 Representative Roy O. Woodruff (Rep., Mich.) stated that the RA expended $13,000 in administration for every $2,500 disbursed to the needy. This allegation, Professor Conkin pointed out, was like "many others that tended to identify the Resettlement Administration's activities only with its communities . . . completely ignoring the vast rehabilitation program which required the largest number of personnel and distributed the largest share of the funds." [29] In late 1935 the *New York Times* had published a widely copied story along these lines. In March, 1936, *Business Week* deplored the RA's high administrative expenses—about twenty cents of every obligated dollar, or $19,000,000 of $98,000,000, including salary payments for 13,045 employees throughout the nation.[30] The official figures, cited by Professor Conkin, revealed that about ten cents of every spent or obligated dollar, or $23,-000,000 of $205,000,000, was chargeable to administrative expenses as of April 30, 1936—"not an enviable record" despite the RA's insistence that unavoidable high costs were involved in starting a new and complicated program.[31]

The Construction Division, in connection with its work for the Rural and Suburban Resettlement Divisions, was also subject to charges of high costs. These claims had a foundation in fact. In September, 1936, the Procurement Division of the Treasury, through which the Construction Division obtained its supplies, investigated RA projects and found costs 33 to 50 per cent higher than those which prevailed under private contracts in open-market conditions.[32] The average unit cost for the greenbelt cities was $15,968. This was not the low-cost housing which, Tugwell maintained, private builders had neglected; at the rents charged, it was heavily subsidized housing.[33]

In early 1937 Tugwell wrote an article in which he summarized the two main arguments of the RA's defense of high construction costs. He conceded that the greenbelt towns were not good examples of low-cost housing. This was true, he stated, because the RA built complete communities, with housing accounting for only about 40 per cent of the total expenditure. The public and community facilities, which were included in the costs, allowed for expansion and would result in lower unit costs for additional housing.[34] This contention was substantiated by drastically lower unit costs for wartime housing at Greenbelt, Maryland.[35] This later experience tended to support Tugwell's claim of 1937 that the limited size of the greenbelt program contributed to higher costs. There would be no low-cost housing, he declared, until there was a housing industry on a factory basis.[36] But, Professor Conkin concluded, "the greenbelt towns indicated that no private corporation could build complete towns, with all their facilities and an expensive greenbelt, and then be able to rent them to low-income families." [37]

The second main line of defense of high costs involved the legal requirement that the RA use relief labor under WPA regulations on all projects. In complying with this order, the RA hired its own subsistence-homesteads clients when possible. It was permissible for the RA to secure the services of certain skilled workers through the United States Employment Service.[38] To charges that high costs were due to poor planning and engineering, the RA replied that the labor regulations under which it operated prevented co-ordination between the planning and construction divisions.[39] Tugwell, in his article of early 1937, held that the use of unskilled relief labor increased total expenditures by about 50 per cent.[40] He had anticipated criticism of high costs due to the employment of WPA workers using shovels instead of bulldozers. Roosevelt, however, wanted to put the maximum number of men to work in the shortest possible time. Tugwell, according to Cleveland Rodgers, infuriated the President by suggesting that the men use spoons instead of shovels.[41] Later the President complained about high unit costs.

Professor Conkin pointed to additional factors contributing to high costs, especially in the first year of "forced haste and expensive experimentation in construction." Seeking new mass-production techniques, the RA experimented with concrete-slab construction, which failed, and rammed-earth construction, which was undertaken successfully at

Mount Olive Homesteads in Alabama. After 1936 the Farm Security Administration conducted valuable experiments in rapid prefabrication of frame-constructed housing. This later resulted in greatly reduced costs of construction. Costs also dropped with the eventual lowering of initially high standards as to toilets, baths, and electric wiring and the adoption of standard house designs. In 1938 the FSA made all the designs and improved techniques available to private builders and the public.[42]

Some critics condemned the subsistence-homesteads projects as financial failures from three standpoints: government expenditures as against government income, sale prices as against client income, and economic viability of the communities. These charges were especially applicable to the four stranded communities inherited from the Division of Subsistence Homesteads of the USDI. Arthurdale (Reedsville, West Virginia) was the subject of a great deal of adverse publicity. Some of its problems were particularly messy. Many of the ready-built houses did not fit their foundations, and others had to be rebuilt.[43] In November, 1933, Louis Howe was negotiating a contract for electricity, and two years later the President requested the "latest news about cheaper electricity for Arthurdale." [44] These examples merely suggest the high government expense incurred. As for sale prices, from across the nation came protests that they were beyond the purchasing power of the people for whom the subsistence homesteads were intended.[45] Regarding economic viability, the Economic Development Section of the Management Division never solved this problem for many communities. In May, 1936, Tugwell himself testified before a subcommittee of the Senate Appropriations Committee that nine projects were "financial failures." [46]

Evaluation of the financial condition of the subsistence-homesteads projects is complicated by their status as social experiments. The administration did not look upon the projects primarily as real-estate investments. They represented an attempt to combat unemployment and economic stagnation in a constructive way which added to the value of rural communities, as did many types of public works constructed with funds the government did not expect fully to recover. On the other hand, according to Lewis Meriam, the projects did not qualify as ordinary public works because the government laid out capital for a specially selected group. Thus, costs were relevant. But, Meriam conceded, selection was "conceivably justifiable" in the conduct of an experiment.[47]

In the selection of clients for subsistence homesteads the Management Division could hardly avoid criticism no matter which way it turned. It had to choose people who indicated that they could make a go of it as subsistence farmers and part-time industrial workers, but they could not be so successful that they did not qualify. As Alva Johnston sarcastically put it, the successful candidate had to demonstrate that he was "below par, but not defective. If you can establish beyond perad-venture that you are not quite all there, you can obtain a Tugwell estate." Johnston also accused the RA of racial discrimination in its selection of clients.[48] James C. Young hurled the charge of social snobbishness.[49] Tugwell maintained that the RA tried to exercise the "utmost care for all the human values immediately concerned."[50] He conceded that there might be some silly descriptions in the thousands of case records of the Family Selection Section.[51]

Charges that the RA was creating federal islands raised the question of the relationship of the communities to state and local governments. The inability of the RA to make payments in lieu of taxes—an incapacity which the objectors to the building of a greenbelt city near New Bruns-wick, New Jersey, stressed—also raised this question. In May, 1936, Representative William B. Bankhead (Dem., Ala.) sponsored a bill, patterned after legislation enacted for the Public Works Administration, which passed a month later. This law placed the RA projects under the political, civil, and criminal jurisdiction of the states and allowed the RA to make payments in lieu of taxes to local governments.[52]

Tugwell had stated in June, 1935, that he did not want to create federal islands, that RA projects "should be geared into the local com-munities as nearly as possible."[53] On the other hand, the RA wished to retain a voice in the future development of its communities. Thus, even with the eventual implementation of the Bankhead law and the integration of the RA projects into state and local political structures, the RA (and its successor, the FSA) kept its hand in community man-agement. In 1937 and 1938 the three greenbelt towns adopted the city-manager form of government under state charters of incorporation, and for many years the freely elected city councils appointed the FSA community managers as town managers. Moreover, the FSA, a non-taxable landowner, while making payments in lieu of taxes to local governments for some services, itself paid for most public services, thereby largely controlling the town budgets. The RA and the FSA sustained their influence in the affairs of the subsistence-homesteads communities, even after their sale, through long-term management con-tracts.[54]

The RA's efforts to retain substantial control of the communities for an indefinite period also involved tenure and ownership—controversial matters which Will Alexander called extremely complex and diffi-cult.[55] On the one hand was the RA's desire to preserve the objectives of the communities, the necessity of providing continuous assistance and supervision for poor, ignorant clients, and concern with the assurance of proper land use from the standpoint of agricultural economics and conservation. On the other hand was the farmers' traditional practice and aspiration of fee simple ownership. The Planning Division recommended long-time or permanent control of real property by the government. The somewhat more conservative Land Planning Section suggested three classifications—permanent leases, trial leases, and forty-year purchase contracts—based on the clients' capabilities. Tugwell felt that the need for a long-time relationship between government and client required some limitations on fee simple ownership.[56] In the short run of about a decade there was a compromise between the RA's position and the agricultural tradition—a compromise heavily weighted toward the RA's viewpoint through long-term lease and purchase agreements. In the long run, at the behest of Congress, the traditional practice triumphed.

The USDI's Division of Subsistence Homesteads had promised ownership to the homesteaders of the industrial communities. The RA inherited this obligation and decided to honor it. In January, 1936, with Roosevelt's approval, Tugwell announced a plan to transfer the completed subsistence-homesteads communities to co-operative associations composed of the homesteaders themselves. Holding title to the land and co-operative property, the associations would issue leases or forty-year purchase contracts, make collections, remit tax and insurance payments, and maintain the communities. The associations would also sign management contracts with the RA, giving that agency or its successors the right to supervise management until final liquidation of the communities. The RA would calculate sale price on the basis of the client's income, appraised value, and original cost to the government. The sale price of an individual homestead would not exceed 25 per cent of the lowest of these three factors.[57]

In 1936 and 1937 the RA and the FSA turned over thirteen industrial communities to homestead associations. Total figures for the first twelve communities so transferred showed sale at 81 per cent of cost. This was a good record, but these communities were the least expensive ones. At about the same time, estimates for twenty-six homesteads projects pointed to a sale price of 43.1 per cent of cost. From 1937 to 1942 the FSA conveyed only one project to a homestead association. In 1942 six associations, the last to be formed, were established, bringing the total to nineteen. In that year, under Congressional pressure, the FSA initiated plans to convey more communities. One stranded community and two industrial projects were placed on sale to individual homesteaders. Several communities which had been retained due to economic problems, the three greenbelt towns, two small garden cities, and one industrial community were being made ready for transfer to special leasing associations.[58]

Regarding the rural communities, Tugwell determined on a temporary leasing policy, leaving the formulation of details of sale for later. Leases involved rental payments in cash and in kind and—the most widely used type—rentals based on a percentage of the crops under a system resembling sharecropping. The FSA did not draw up a single purchase contract for its rural communities until 1940, when, again under Congressional pressure, it started to issue leases and contracts for purchase in most of the nonco-operative rural projects. By 1942 the FSA had sold about 2,500 rural units to individuals, but in all cases the lease or purchase contract was, as Professor Conkin put it, "really a promise of future sale." The farmer received a quitclaim deed when he had paid one-fourth of the purchase price, but he then had to sign a promissory note for the balance (payment in forty years at 3 per cent interest) and execute a mortgage into which the FSA would insert various controls and restrictions. Thus, "few adult men could really look forward to full ownership within their lifetime," and a long relationship between the government and the homesteader was assured.[59]

In 1942 there was a consolidation of all New Deal housing agencies. An executive order of October 1 transferred all FSA housing whose occupants did not receive their main income from agriculture to the Federal Public Housing Authority of the National Housing Agency. The FSA lost twenty-eight subsistence-homesteads communities, the three greenbelt towns, two FERA projects, and one suburban resettlement community. It kept twenty-six FERA and thirty-eight other rural communities. The final disposition of these communities was still a few years away. In 1946, when the Farmers' Home Corporation Act abolished the FSA, Congress instructed the new corporation to liquidate the remaining resettlement projects under its control within eighteen months. The Federal Public Housing Authority finally sold the three greenbelt towns between 1949 and 1954 at a price of $19,559,762 as against a cost of $36,200,910.[60] The desire of the RA and the FSA to maintain a long-time relationship with clients succumbed to the tradition of fee simple ownership sooner than these agencies intended.

Tugwell's foes suspected that he played politics with RA jobs, and their allegations reached his friends. Two editors of the *Portland* (Oregon) *Journal* inquired of the President whether rumors that all subordinate appointments in the RA had to pass political approval were true. They were Democrats, they wrote, but they objected to these practices which hearsay attributed to the RA. Roosevelt replied, undoubtedly using a draft composed in the RA. He explained that the Extension Service nominated the farm and home economics advisers; applicants for nontechnical positions took tests similar to Civil Service examinations; and technical appointees were chosen on merit from lists provided by educational institutions and the other usual sources used by business and industry. In all cases the RA gave preference to eligibles on relief rolls.[61]

Tugwell himself made some general comments on his aversion to mixing politics and relief. In 1934 he asserted that political influence would blight the quality of personnel in relief agencies and subordinate sound policies to political advantage. It would prevent the effective execution of a program of social recovery by organizations which needed competence, courage, continuity, and confidence.[62] In May, 1935, after he became head of the RA, Tugwell said to a meeting of conservationists: "To save the land and the people who depend on it is an aspiration in which all of us can join. It transcends party, creed, and class."[63] In June, 1935, he told some college graduates that national problems calling for national solutions were above considerations of party politics, regional aggrandizement, or power and place for any man.[64] In August, 1935, addressing a meeting of agricultural experts, he referred to the task of establishing a firm foundation for continuous conservation as "the work of a generation." It could not be "approached by slap-dash methods or ballyhoo. . . . This means that, in the deepest sense, this entire program of resettlement and rehabilitation must . . . not be guided by political expediency."[65]

Tugwell's handling of specific situations indicates that he tried to live up to the principles which he laid down publicly. His answers to Congressmen's inquiries—often requests on behalf of constituents for employment—show no disposition to yield to political pressure. On September 16, 1935, he informed Representative H. W. Sumners of Texas that the RA insisted on hiring auditors in that state on merit.[66] A week later he informed Senator Thomas P. Gore of Oklahoma, through the White House, that the appointment of a nonlocal regional attorney in the Texas area was a rare exception to RA practice necessitated by the requirement of experience in government.[67] In a long letter of December 23, 1935, to Representative Edward C. Moran, Jr. (Dem., Me.), Tugwell listed the efforts he had made to satisfy the legislator from Down East regarding RA appointments. There had been some dismissals, but only after careful investigation in every case. Certain considerations, Tugwell continued, outweighed Congressional preferances. He concluded with this professorial lecture: "I should like to impress upon you my desire to be as helpful to you as is consistently possible under the circumstances with which we are faced. I assume from your record in Congress that we have the same general objectives and that the most important consideration, both from a human and political standpoint, is to do our job well."[68]

Ernest K. Lindley observed that there was never any public charge that

Tugwell was amenable to political influence in selecting his administrative and field staffs.[69] Allegations that relief funds went to politicians instead of the unemployed, Lindley noted, were aimed mostly at the WPA.[70] Tugwell was quick to defend Harry Hopkins' administration of the WPA, as well as Ickes' management of the PWA, on this score. In April, 1935, he declared:

> Progress in this program will not be made without opposition of various sorts. Much of it has already appeared. Some is obviously political, coming from those who say, for instance, that the new appropriation bill is merely a huge campaign fund which will be used to buy votes. So long as we have democratic government and political parties, that would be said about any Federal administration which undertook to meet the responsibilities of the present crisis. Certainly the direction given to past expenditures by Mr. Hopkins and Mr. Ickes cannot be fairly criticized in this respect. Both have been actuated by motives which are beyond question. Indeed, they have not been questioned. The partisanship displayed has all been on the other side. The complaints come from those who would like to see the care of the poor and disadvantaged bent toward different purposes.[71]

To say that Tugwell was opposed to playing politics with RA jobs and that he was honest is not to claim, of course, that there were no political maneuvers and corruption in the RA. There was the case, for example, of 1,400 unrequested checks being sent to farmers in Wyoming in December, 1935. Senator Robert D. Carey (Rep., Wyo.) wrote to Tugwell of this "shameful" incident. The official explanation that the RA sent out the checks "in preparation for recommendation for relief prior to investigation" does not appear satisfactory. There was also a charge that the suit by New Jersey residents to enjoin the RA from undertaking a suburban housing project at Greenbrook was withdrawn at one stage of the lengthy litigation when one of the agents of the township was promised a government job for seventy-five dollars a week in return for changing his mind.[72] The disbursal of the checks may have been a gross administrative error, and the charges about the job offer were neither proved nor disproved. In any event, Tugwell could not personally supervise the conduct of all personnel in his far-flung agency. What he could do was fire or prosecute corrupt employees and clients whenever he learned of their activities—and this he did. In March, 1936, for example, the RA brought suit against some allegedly corrupt contractors.[73] In October, 1936, the agency discharged some of its personnel found guilty of malpractices.[74]

In February, 1936, Felix Brunner of the *Washington Post* staff wrote four articles on "Utopia Unlimited," a title consonant with his use of

emotion-laden words in his description of the RA's activities. Nevertheless, this widely reprinted series focused on what was perhaps the most
fundamental criticism of the RA—its exercising of delegated powers
under executive order. The agency, Brunner charged, was not a creation of Congress, its employees were not under civil service regulations,
its programs were not the expressed intent of the people or of Congress,
and its unlimited powers were not subject to outside control.[75] Tugwell
was aware that many RA policies would not have received majority
support in Congress, but, as Professor Conkin remarked, he knew that
America, with respect to its lower third, "needed remaking whether it
wanted it or not." [76]

Tugwell's action in this case raises the question of consistency between
his words and deeds. He "did not expect ideality to be just around the
corner," Professor Conkin noted. "He knew that planning implied a
revolution, with new attitudes, new disciplines, revised legal structures,
unaccustomed limitations on freedom. . . ." [77] In 1939 Tugwell gave
formal expression to these views, presenting a scheme for incorporating
experts' planning into democratic government through an elaborate
procedure of public hearings and legislative ratification—"The Fourth
Power." His conduct as Resettlement Administrator in 1935 and 1936
was not in accord with his previous and subsequent advocacy of evolution and democracy—even though, as Professor Conkin commented,
"Tugwell may have been more nearly right than anyone else. He may
have correctly identified his opposition as the instruments of special
interests." [78]

Tugwell's inconsistency takes on a different aspect if we view democracy in a broad historical context rather than from the standpoint of
the details of political mechanisms. The RA received its funds by executive order under emergency relief acts. Rural poverty in the 1920's
helped to bring about the unusual emergency, which, in turn, called
for unusual action to deal with rural poverty. Moreover, Congressional
deference to the executive was characteristic of a democracy facing a
crisis which was not conducive to patient waiting for evolutionary developments. The emergency banking bill of March, 1933, for example,
received Congressional approval in a matter of hours. This was tanta-
mount to delegation of authority because only a few members of Congress were familiar with the specific provisions of the bill. If we argue
that the majority of Congressmen desired reform of the banking system
but opposed reform of America's rural slums, then we are dealing with
the way in which the executive exercised delegated authority and not
with the act of delegation itself.

The line of reasoning we have just engaged in does not dispose of the
problem of majority preference in a democracy. Congress, if we assume

that it always represents majority opinion, resolved this question in time, reinforcing the emergency banking legislation of March in June, 1933, and again in 1935 but finally dispensing with the Farm Security Administration in 1946. Thus, in retrospect we can see that delegation of power to the executive was a resort of democracy in crisis. With the abatement of the emergency, the legislature regained its confidence and reasserted its prerogatives, selectively confirming or invalidating actions which the executive had taken in meeting its responsibilities, as it understood them, in a time of distress. The development which especially complicated this historical sequence was the executive's attempt to undertake emergency and long-run measures simultaneously. The long-run origins of the crisis and the executive leeway which it produced made this attempt seem in order, even called for by an implied popular mandate, but a number of the long-run measures such as Tugwell's land-use program succumbed to the calmer, sometimes complacent mood which emerged with recovery. The critical thirties was no time to test Tugwell's concept of the "Fourth Power."

II

We cannot judge the performance of the Resettlement Administration under Tugwell without reference to the difficulty of the task the agency faced. Pointing out the herculean nature of an undertaking does not, of course, excuse all shortcomings. It is a negative line of defense but nevertheless an important one. The most obvious handicap under which the RA labored was the very selection of Tugwell as its head. This choice of the administration's principal whipping boy guaranteed hostility toward the RA's program on the part of conservative Congressmen and a large sector of the press. The Information Division did not help matters, nor did Tugwell himself with his display of tactlessness toward Congressmen, journalists, and businessmen. His exhibition of disdain suggests a chicken-or-egg dilemma: was Tugwell's tactlessness a reaction to an antagonistic press, or was the enmity of the press a response to Tugwell's arrogant conduct? A final answer to this quandary would undoubtedly indicate that both of these cause-and-effect sequences were operative. But, in view of the drug lobby's vicious attack on Tugwell beginning in 1933, there is every reason to believe that he and his agency would have received rough treatment at the hands of the press in 1935 and 1936 regardless of his behavior. Nor did his deportment justify character assassination and biased and inaccurate reporting.

Professor Conkin concluded that "the greenbelt cities—like all of Tugwell's ventures—were treated unfairly in a majority of newspapers. . . ." [79] Alexander's biographers noted that "the press had built up a Resettlement Administration stereotype of whimsical impracticality." [80] The main defect in press coverage of the RA was the identification of the agency solely with its project activities. This led to comparisons of personnel figures (and administrative expenses) either with the number of clients on resettlement projects (and the funds expended on them) or with the number of relief laborers employed in the construction of these projects (and the wages they received). The resulting ratios disregarded the tremendous rehabilitation program, which assisted hundreds of thousands of people and, in terms of dollars disbursed, accounted for nine-tenths of the RA's and the FSA's operations (930 of 1,038 millions through fiscal 1943). Thus, Alexander's biographers concluded, "the resettlement idea was publicized out of all proportion to its importance." [81]

A number of inaccurate reports on the RA's program were based on a *New York Times* story of November 17, 1935, by Frank Kluckhorn. This report, which stated that Tugwell employed 12,089 people in order to create 5,012 relief jobs, was copied by papers throughout the nation. The *Times* published corrected figures and, on November 20, Tugwell's letter of protest. Meanwhile, James A. Farley advised Presidential Assistant Marvin McIntyre to look into the matter if the story were true.[82] Tugwell wrote to the President that the "whole affair is calculated to make me more than ever sure that our enemies do not mean to give us a fair shake, but mean to use any tactics which will serve their purpose." He enclosed a report on the news coverage of the *Times* article and an analysis of editorial comment, which, in most cases, used the misleading figures in the original article. Over one hundred papers had not printed the correction.[83] Roosevelt was "outraged by that rotten *New York Times* story . . . a case of deliberate misrepresentation." [84] In his protest Tugwell showed that the misleading charge completely ignored the fact that the largest part of the RA's program had nothing to do with providing jobs. Rural Rehabilitation then cared for 354,000 farm families or 1,500,000 persons (an eventual total of 2,500,000 was expected) without creating any relief jobs. In fact, it took people off relief through loans which would be repaid. Ernest K. Lindley noted that the *Times* story appeared not long after Tugwell had dismissed several thousand employees who had come to the RA with the State Rural Rehabilitation Corporations and other inherited agencies.[85]

The formation of the RA largely through the assumption of functions of other agencies produced some formidable problems. The inherited communities, Professor Conkin noted, "were often considered a burden and a liability pushed upon the Resettlement Administration. . . ." [86] Tugwell called these early New Deal makeshifts "everybody else's headaches." [87] The evaluation and absorption of a conglomeration of inherited projects, of various degrees of feasibility and in various stages of development, was an onerous undertaking. In 1935 Tugwell explained to the White House that in every case RA engineers had to appraise the situation.[88] In 1936 he pointed out that there had been no successful action programs before 1933 in the fields which the RA was entering, and the worth of the 1933 programs had yet to be proved by the time the RA went into operation in 1935. It was very difficult, he asserted, to "revalue and co-ordinate the half-completed efforts of existing agencies." [89]

The integration of the projects which the RA decided to retain was an intricate task. In late June, 1935, when the RA was less than two months old, Tugwell called a conference in order to get various views on the basis of which he could evaluate operations and formulate a program. A report on the conference which Edmund Brunner of Columbia Teachers College made to Professor J. H. Kolb of the FERA on July 5 indicates how difficult it was for the RA to integrate diverse operations while building a unified working organization and staff. "Every agency in America," Brunner noted, "has been bombarding Tugwell with plans . . . and each one of them has literally claimed that complete heaven would come out of its program. . . . Tugwell is very much bothered about the whole matter of achieving the necessary efficient business administration and at the same time the social objectives. . . ." [90]

The RA's origination through inheritance entailed at least two additional problems. Recruitment of employees often ran up against the preference of the best personnel for established agencies.[91] Alexander's biographers remarked that "too few of the employees understood the main objectives of Resettlement, and even fewer were dedicated to the idea of assuring the underdog full opportunity in agriculture." [92] There was also the problem of poor public relations as the result of public forgetfulness. When Senator Harry F. Byrd condemned the Shenandoah Homesteads, it was futile for the RA to point out that it was the purchase by the State of Virginia of land for the Shenandoah National Park which had compelled people to move, and that it was the Division of Subsistence Homesteads which had begun the project. Similarly, Tugwell protested in vain that the stranded communities had been created by someone else on the basis of a theory in which he did not believe.[93]

Some of the RA's most perplexing difficulties arose from the kind of clients it served. Many of them, living on submarginal land, were themselves submarginal from age, ignorance, and poor health. It was hard to help them to a fresh beginning. The RA tried to remove many of these economically displaced people from the relief rolls by starting them in garden farming, which would at least enable them to feed themselves. Much of the RA's rehabilitation work with nearly half a million poverty-stricken farm families was, Tugwell explained in 1936, like relief work.[94] For a time relief was necessary for all of the RA's clients. They were not unemployed in the sense that their need for relief would end with a job. They had work to do, but they needed instruction, guidance, and facilities. Yet, despite their painful experience under traditional practices, they were not satisfied with security of tenure within communal experiments which they did not understand. They wanted economic security immediately and individual ownership ultimately. Thus, Professor Conkin commented, "the community idea, so appealing in the abstract, was much more difficult to achieve than almost anyone believed possible in 1933." [95]

Nor did the large staple farmers and the public at large appreciate the community idea. Accordingly, certain powerful Senators from the South, where most of the communities were located, vigorously opposed the RA's program. An incident in the spring of 1935, when the RA was just getting under way, shows that the administration anticipated this opposition. The Socialist leader Norman Thomas complained to the President that AAA benefits were not reaching the poorer farmers of the South. Chester Davis informed Roosevelt that the AAA was trying to improve enforcement of its acreage-reduction contracts.[96] The legal staff's reinterpretation of these contracts with respect to retention of occupants had resulted in the dismissal of Jerome Frank and his colleagues earlier in 1935. Davis' statement did not satisfy Thomas, and he appealed to Aubrey Williams of the FERA and Tugwell.

Tugwell stressed gradualism and political considerations. He told Thomas that the RA's efforts to improve conditions in the South were only now getting started, and they had very shaky Congressional support. There was no way of changing things overnight. When Thomas gave his opinion to the President that both Williams and Tugwell were afraid of powerful Southern Senators, Roosevelt backed the stand his two subordinates had taken. He expressed sympathy and counseled patience—a new South with new leaders was emerging. In retrospect, Thomas said that Tugwell was the most explicit and honest of the men he talked to in admitting that "that's the way politics has to be in the United States." [97] Professor Schlesinger judged Roosevelt's plea for patience "not insincere." The RA was doing as much as it could, there were limits to federal power, and there were limits to how much he could oppose the conservative Southern leadership in Congress which often determined the nature and fate of his legislative program.[98] The administration's expectations were not amiss. The RA injected change into a static situation in the South, and its ideas of diversification threatened the kingship of cotton.[99] Long-term leases, collective and village forms of agriculture, and efforts to establish industries for homesteaders were departures from tradition which alarmed many Congressmen.[100] The Southerners in the capitol contributed more than their share to a persistent and formidable opposition to the RA.

To sum up, the RA faced imposing obstacles. Its basic task was extremely difficult, calling for vast, scattered, and diverse operations. The press was generally hostile. Most of the agency's clients were poor and ignorant. The community idea encountered a dominating attachment to the traditional on the part of both the clients themselves and the rest of the population, which harbored no deep-felt concern for the plight of the rural poor. Moreover, the RA had to carry out its functions while going through the process of initial organization—a process complicated by the inheritance of projects from other agencies. Stuart Chase compared the RA to the TVA, which exhibited unity, integration, and excellent administration, built around the great dams, in its efforts to re-establish the resource base of the Tennessee Valley. The RA made the same effort in blighted areas scattered from coast to coast. Some were "plain starvation" areas involving all kinds of people in every condition and situated in almost every state. These people were the cumulative wreckage of decades of neglect of resources: the victims of the Dust Bowl, cut-over areas, swamplands, and exhausted mines; the "gray, beaten" army on submarginal lands. Chase urged Tugwell's critics to remember that Americans, in their mad rush to subdue a continent, had stranded and broken these millions of people. It was neither wild extravagance nor radicalism to give them a hand and try to put them on their feet.[101]

In late 1935 Tugwell himself indicated some of the RA's difficulties in getting off the ground when he urged the President to set up no new agencies during the election year of 1936 because "my experience —and Harry's [Hopkins']—has been that it takes almost a year to perfect a country-wide administrative organization and that while it is being done there is political turmoil over the jobs, criticisms of procedure from the field, jealousy on the part of old organizations which fancy their prerogatives are threatened, and other sources of irritation." [102] In March, 1936, Maury Maverick urged his colleagues in the House to consider the gravity and complexity of the problems with which the RA dealt.[103] Even Tugwell's archenemy Alva Johnston conceded, in August, 1936, that the position of Resettlement Administrator was the toughest job of administration in Washington.[104]

Pointing out the difficulty of Tugwell's task is not a direct reply to the charges that he was a dreamer and a deficient administrator. Nor is criticism of his critics an adequate defense—although it is worth noting that it was natural, as Ernest K. Lindley observed, for men who represented special interests, gauged the world by the stock market or profits and losses, and struggled to hold their position in a time of change, to view with hostility academic people possessing a broad social outlook.[105] It seems appropriate at this point to let Tugwell speak in his own behalf and then to consider the comments of his defenders.

Looking back on his experience as a whipping boy, Tugwell noted that the majority of Americans subscribed to the journalistic stereotype of the absent-minded professor. "No one," he wrote, "had taken the trouble to re-examine it for several generations. The fresh-water college Greek professor was the model—as much a stock character as the stage Englishman." [106] Statements which Tugwell made before, during, and after his participation in the New Deal do not indicate the divorcement from reality which the stereotype depicted. For example, in paraphrase and direct quotation:

August 25, 1926 ("Chameleon Words," *New Republic*)

The typical idealist understands neither "a willingness to compromise nor an unwillingness to affiliate." There is nothing wrong with approving of some parts of capitalism and not of others. We can "withhold nothing of energy or loyalty" simply because our ideals have been violated.

1927 (*Industry's Coming of Age*)

"The teaching of economics in school and college went on, as it always had, completely ignoring the study of production and continuing to concentrate largely on the conceptual statements of theory inherited from the contributors to an old tradition."

May 16, 1928 ("Governor or President," *New Republic*)

The economic diseases overcoming both laissez faire and state control are being met with "nostrum hunting."

May 30, 1928 ("Platforms and Candidates," *New Republic*)

Because Wilson's liberal idealism had been unable to meet situations flexibly by finding solutions with direct apprehension, his liberal principles were "wrecked on the reefs of necessity."

December 12, 1928 ("Bankers' Banks," *New Republic*)

The bankers of Wilson's time need not have been so fearful because, as the Federal Reserve Act proved, "Radical talk writes no legislation."

March, 1929 ("Farm Relief and a Permanent Agriculture," *Annals of the American Academy of Political and Social Science*)

"The new agriculture will not develop in any fixed and rigid delineation as may be suggested here, but will create its own forms and social conditions."

August 14, 1930 ("Human Nature and Social Economy," *Journal of Philosophy*)

Some economists hold that is is impossible to experiment with social forces, but their "critic would say that experiments are continually in progress. The world is a laboratory."

January, 1932 (*Mr. Hoover's Economic Policy*)

Hoover's economics is "theological in form and origin . . . a consistent, well-rounded body of principles. They become confused only with contact with unholy reality. For a clergyman or a college professor this is not so important. . . . But a President of the Federal Union in the 1930's is not so lucky. Hobgoblin reality reaches for him from behind every bush." The progress of national disaster has strengthened Hoover's faith, "now magnificent in its repudiation of fact."

1933 ("Trial and Error," syndicated column)

"We have to fall back still, in spite of our developing arts of forecast, . . . on the oldest method of contrivance—trial and error."

December 29, 1933 ("The Place of Government in a National Land Program," address)

"I have indicated only by inference the vast amount of careful investigation and planning which is essential for the establishment of a policy. No one can attempt to say as yet with any exactness how many submarginal acres there are or how rapidly we should attempt to take those acres out of use."

April 28, 1934 ("America Takes Hold of Its Destiny," *Today*)

The administration's experimentalism is in the American tradition—"at least there was a time when Yankee ingenuity was a byword of praise." Action in this tradition will produce "no antiseptic Utopia and no socialistic paradise, but a changing system in which free American human beings can live their changing lives."

May 11, 1934 ("Consumers and the New Deal," address)

Agricultural adjustment is "a colossal job requiring a finesse of judgment and a technique of administration that we are only beginning to master. Mistakes will be made."

May 21, 1934 ("Relief and Reconstruction," address)

"We are faced with the alternatives of making rapid adjustments in our social and economic system which will enlarge its capacity to absorb the young, or of risking the consequences of idleness among millions of them. We have no problem more serious than this and the social service workers of America must help us solve it, without political violence, social demoralization or economic chaos. This is not an issue which can be deferred until some theorist can work out a neat solution. It is terribly urgent."

Winter, 1934 ("The Great American Fraud," *American Scholar,* dealing with the food and drug bill)

"Solon told the Athenians to make, not the best laws that could be written, but the best that could be enforced."

April, 1935 ("The Progressive Tradition," *Atlantic Monthly*)

Americans have always had "a healthy dislike of the doctrinaire. Thus, our faith that objectives can be useful to racial purposes persists and is not discouraged by achievements which turn out to be less than Utopian."

April 22, 1935 ("A Third Economy," address)

All the beating of breasts by the radical and reactionary extremes "is carried on in a vacuum outside reality. The alternatives offered are impossible of achievement. But achievement, of course, is not the purpose."

September, 1936 ("Changing Acres," *Current History,* with reference to retirement of submarginal land)

"We should have a rude awakening if we attempted to do it by a *tour de force.*"

October, 1939 ("The Superpolitical," *Journal of Social Philosophy*)

"Reality is apt to protrude in awkward shapes from the most cherished concepts and to spread embarrassingly across the most elaborate categories."

August 23, 1945 (*The Stricken Land,* quoting Tugwell's diary)

"The President, when I saw him yesterday, was open and cordial. . . .
He went on to say that his administration had to be thought of as no
more than an extension of the Roosevelt regime. . . . I said that
could be true only in a limited and temporary sense, that I had been
a participant in White House activities long enough to recognize that
policies had to be reshaped almost continually."

Winter, 1948 ("The Utility of the Future in the Present," *Public Administration Review*)

"Sir Oliver Franks is no convinced advocate of any ism . . . when
he speaks of what Britain must do, he speaks from the heart and
from experience but not from any theoretical commitment."

More important to Tugwell's defense than his own statements are the
remarks of others who attested to his realism and his administrative
ability. A note which he received from Mordecai Ezekiel indicates
that his co-workers were impressed by his emphasis on practical considerations: "I realize that my discontent with our rate of progress was
due to my not seeing the whole field of campaign as broadly as you saw
it, and not realizing the obstacles in full that you were maneuvering to
overcome. . . . But I appreciate, of course, that we have got to grow
into many of these things, and that public opinion and political support
cannot be forced." [107] John Franklin Carter declared that Tugwell was
neither a socialist, anarchist, nor Utopian; he faced not the conservatives,
but the facts: permanent plenty amid general poverty, mass production
and increasing machine efficiency, and human self-love.[108] James A.
Farley rejected the image of Tugwell as the inveterate dreamer, describing him as "sensible in his approach to particular situations and never
arbitrary." [109]

Tugwell's supporters in Congress included George Foulkes (Dem.,
Mich.) and Fred H. Hildebrandt (Dem., S. D.). Foulkes praised Tugwell as the scientific type, not obstinately tied down to old customs and
institutions.[110] Hildebrandt remarked in 1935 that there were few men
in the nation better equipped to take charge of the land program.[111] Tugwell also enjoyed the respect of a number of agricultural economists.
John D. Black of Harvard University placed him among the men responsible for a "major part of the thinking about effective lines of action
in agriculture." [112] Among journalists, Ernest K. Lindley came forthrightly to Tugwell's defense. He attributed the "Tugwellian menace" not
to theories but to the practical judgment and realism of a man who
was "probably as free from dogma as any official in the administration,
and far less doctrinaire than many of his critics." [113] Lindley attached

some significance to the opening sentence of *The Industrial Discipline:* "The fluidity of change in society has always been the despair of theorists." [114] In 1936 the authors of a biographical sketch claimed that Tugwell was as boldly and brightly active as any of the politicians who opposed him—although these writers misread public opinion when they wrote that "the professor helped to lay for all time the old tradition of the foggy-eyed scholar lost within cloistered walls." [115] Professor Conkin concluded that Tugwell's "famed political ineptitude, if such existed, often indicated only tenacious honesty and high personal integrity." [116]

There were plaudits for the accomplishments of the Resettlement Administration as well as for the realism of its head. After visiting RA projects in the South in 1936, Henry Wallace stated that the agency had done "a marvelous job . . . especially is this true when you consider that all this work was done with emergency funds that made operations other than on a month-to-month basis impossible." [117] Russell Lord credited the RA with having become a strong organization in time.[118] Even *Business Week* conceded that Tugwell had buckled down to his job and appeared to have done it fairly well.[119] Representative Hildebrandt joined in the wide praise for the rehabilitation programs.[120] Senator La Follette declared that history would render a favorable judgment on the RA despite the fun that had been "poked at this program of resettlement by those too stupid or too blind to care about the future." [121]

As the years went by, the greenbelt towns were widely acclaimed. An authority in city planning asserted that these communities planted the seed of future city development and ranked them second only to the TVA as an exception to boondoggling and as a demonstration of future possibilities.[122] Two other students of city planning called the greenbelt towns "outstanding" among New Deal housing projects.[123] Will Alexander later spoke of the "most intelligently planned three communities in this country." [124] Ernest K. Lindley's prediction that "private real estate developers may be compelled to take heed and try to imitate them" [125] was sound. The shift of population to the suburbs, which the greenbelt towns anticipated, got into full swing after World War II. The population of the United States increased from 151.3 millions to 179.3 millions in the years 1950-1960, and two-thirds of the increase of 28 millions took place in the suburbs. Private builders accommodated much of this growth with the mass-production techniques which Tugwell had judged essential to the development of low-cost housing.

Will Alexander also commended Tugwell for his proposals as well as for his accomplishments. Alexander's appraisal of his former chief combined deep affection with critical detachment. He recalled that Tugwell was extremely sensitive to injustice but preferred ideas to action, planning to execution, analysis to remedy. "He is a great economic philosopher," Alexander remarked. "He has a profound understanding of the economic system, and I think he thinks far ahead of everybody else. I think that's one of the reasons he was unpopular. He's usually sound in the long run." Specifically, Alexander thought Tugwell's land-use approach to the farm problem was sound.[126] But the RA retired only about 9 million acres.

Although Alexander contended that his chief preferred ideas to action, Tugwell earned the esteem of a number of colleagues and commentators for his display of administrative ability as Chairman of the New York City Planning Commission (1938-1940) and as Governor of Puerto Rico (1941-1946). Robert Moses, who worked with Tugwell in New York, called him a "first-rate presiding officer." [127] It was Harold Ickes, deplorer of the RA "shambles," who sent Tugwell to Puerto Rico. Louis Brownlow, who reported unfavorably on the RA to Ickes, later said of Tugwell as an administrator, in connection with Tugwell's Puerto Rican performance, "He is one of the finest I have ever known." [128] The liberal writer Oswald Villard, not uncritical of Tugwell, credited him with administrative ability beyond question.[129] In February, 1942, *Time* described Tugwell as a cautious administrator. In June, 1942, *Time* found him "dreamy." But *Time* again changed its view in 1958, stating in an article on Puerto Rico that "Rex Tugwell, named Governor, implanted an efficient civil service and a knack for the kind of economic planning that is flexible enough to improvise when necessary." [130] Actually, Tugwell's chief contribution in Puerto Rico was not planning, which was largely done before his arrival, but administration. He showed the islanders, according to one of the planners of the famous "Operation Bootstrap," how to set up an organization and get things done.[131]

Granting the greater advantages of time and experience which Tugwell brought to bear on his duties in New York and Puerto Rico, we find it difficult to reconcile his alleged ineptitude as Resettlement Administrator with his later proficiency. The difference is probably in large part attributable to the overwhelming obstacles which confronted the RA. Referring solely to that agency, Professor Conkin said of Tugwell's performance, "As a director of a practical program he did compromise, and he was a better, more conservative administrator than his opponents would ever concede." [132]

III

In 1936, Tugwell's last year in Washington, the RA's opponents stepped up their attack. On March 11 Senator W. Warren Barbour (Rep., N. J.) introduced a resolution calling for an investigation of the agency. The Senate tabled this resolution by a vote of 32 to 30 but accepted a resolution directing the RA to make a full report on its work. Tugwell submitted this report to the Senate on May 12. In May the Senate Appropriations Committee amended the RA section of a deficiency appropriation bill, substituting "loans" for "rural rehabilitation" in an attempt to confine the agency's activities. The Senate defeated this amendment, 38-28, but the 1936 deficiency appropriation discontinued the RA's right to purchase land (a right which it continued to exercise under executive order until 1937). On May 18 the residents of Franklin Township in New Jersey obtained an injunction against the construction of Greenbrook. Reacting to this pressure, the RA resorted to a strategic retreat. In September it announced the limitation of its community program to projects already planned (which still left a large number of communities to be completed).[133] The RA also decided not to contest the Greenbrook issue in an election year. Tugwell wrote the President, "This is a formidable attack, and if the Senate lends itself to it you can picture what the publicity would be in a campaign." [134]

In mid-November the President appointed Tugwell and Wallace, among others, to a Presidential Committee on Farm Tenancy. This Committee was to make a 2,000-mile tour of the Southeast, inspecting the RA's work.[135] Earlier in the month Tugwell had recommended the transfer of the RA from independent status to the USDA.[136] This tour, he hoped, would result in favorable action on his recommendation. Some of Wallace's closest advisers told him not to take the RA into Agriculture; Tugwell and Will Alexander challenged the Secretary to see for himself what the RA had accomplished before he made a decision.[137] As the tour began, Tugwell submitted a formal letter of resignation to the President. He confirmed the rumors that he was resigning which had leaked out of Washington, and, in an astonishing manner, told newspapermen that Will Alexander would be the new Resettlement Administrator. "Certainly no one else," Alexander's biographers stated, "would have had the sheer presumption and foresight to announce, without consulting the Secretary of Agriculture or any influential coterie of 'backers,' the man who would be his successor." Moreover, Wallace was convinced that the RA's efforts were still needed. In one stroke, Tugwell designated the leadership of the RA and assured its continuation.[138]

On December 31, 1936, Tugwell's last day as Undersecretary and Resettlement Administrator, Executive Order 7530 transferred the RA to the USDA. In July, 1937, the RA finally received statutory authority under the Bankhead-Jones Farm Tenant Act, which limited the resettlement-community and land-utilization programs to the completion of projects already under way.[139] On September 1, 1937, the RA was renamed the Farm Security Administration. "The fight over the abolition of the Farm Security Administration," wrote Professor Conkin, "was one of the most bitter domestic issues of World War II." [140] He described this battle in detail in a chapter aptly entitled "The Old Society Reasserts Its Claims." The struggle became mortal combat in 1942 when Edward O'Neal of the Farm Bureau and Senators Harry F. Byrd and Kenneth D. McKellar (Dem., Tenn.) opened fire on Calvin B. Baldwin, Farm Security Administrator since 1940, and his agency. The following year a select committee of Congress under Representative Harold D. Cooley (Dem., N. C.) began a full-scale investigation of the FSA.[141]

The report of this select committee in 1944 charged the FSA with distorting the intent of the Bankhead-Jones Act by stretching executive orders and discouraging landownership through the use of ninety-nine-year leases, the retention and initiation of collective farms, and the making of false promises to clients. Carrying out the committee's recommendations, Congress enacted a Farmers' Home Corporation Act in 1946. The Farmers' Home Corporation took over the administration of the forty-year tenant-purchase program and the rehabilitation loans which the Bankhead-Jones Act had authorized. The Corporation, as noted above, was to liquidate the remaining resettlement projects within eighteen months. It could not purchase land, make loans to co-operative associations, or engage in paternalistic supervision of farmers. In April, 1947, only 290 subsistence-homesteads units remained unsold, which moved Representative Everett M. Dirksen to remark, "It appears that in the year ahead there is some likelihood of finally closing out Mr. Tugwell's lovely dream in the field of resettlement." Dirksen overlooked the greenbelt cities and the other projects which the Federal Public Housing Authority still controlled.[142] (In 1948 Tugwell delivered a decennial address at Greendale, Wisconsin, and in 1957 he took up residence at Greenbelt, Maryland, literally living in his dream.)

While Tugwell was responsible for the general orientation of the FSA —its determination to assist the poor, small farmers—he cannot be blamed for the misconduct of that agency under Baldwin. In retrospect, Tugwell wrote in his memoir that the demise of the RA (meaning the FSA) was "a great loss to the nation and I am still bitter about it." He felt that his own notoriety hurt the RA—"In its next reincarnation it will need a more orthodox sponsor"—but he attributed the agency's destruction to the Grange, the Farm Bureau Federation, and the food processors, all of whom had opposed the RA from the beginning. In 1954, in an interview with this writer, Tugwell's first remark about the RA was that the retirement of 9,000,000 acres was "just a demonstration of what could be done"—the land-use approach was still his first love among remedies for the farm problem. In 1958, in an address to a meeting of historians, Tugwell spoke at some length on the opposition to the RA. The *American Historical Review* reported: "This narrative of social organization, political opposition, and eventual defeat was presented for the lessons that it offered posterity, and these were summarized with a wisdom from which bitterness had long since been distilled." [143]

In his 1958 address Tugwell again referred to the prosperous farmers who fought against aid for their poorer neighbors; he mentioned the private builders' opposition to the greenbelt towns; and he rated negative public attitudes toward relief for the destitute as an important obstacle. He recommended caution and political astuteness to the supporters and administrators of a new RA, but he did not regret that he had "annoyed a lot of people who needed to be annoyed." [144] His references to public apathy and the need for political astuteness underlined the inability of the RA's clients to organize for their own good and to defend efforts in their behalf before Congress and the public. In other words, the RA lacked a political constituency—a deficiency which imposed a heavy burden on the sponsors of any attempt to combat rural poverty. Tugwell's reference to a *new* RA indicated, of course, his belief that the need for action in rural slum-clearance was still with us.

Several important studies of the late 1950's and early 1960's confirmed Tugwell's view. In 1959 Columbia University's Conservation of Human Resources Committee published *The Ineffective Soldier*, which showed that rural poverty was one of the three main causes of human failure to meet the minimum requirements for social existence.[145] In November, 1959, the National Conference to Stabilize Migrant Labor discussed the plight of 850,000 migratory farm laborers whose annual average income was $859.[146] In July, 1962, the Committee for Economic Development proposed a "massive adjustment" in agriculture, including reduction of the farm labor force by 2,000,000 workers and the retirement of 20,000,000 acres of cropland to grass for livestock production.[147] It is interesting to note that the CED echoed Tugwell's views of 1929 ("Farm Relief and a Permanent Agriculture"), which stressed land use in conformance with the trend toward a high-protein diet.

If the RA attacked such a persistent fundamental problem, why did it fade from the American scene? The basic dilemma which accounts for its demise was its attempt to undertake short-run and long-run measures simultaneously—the same predicament which confronted the NRA and the AAA. As Tugwell pointed out in *The Democratic Roosevelt*, "the condition had been growing worse for half a century at least; it might well take an equal time to reverse the trend and carry out the relocation of the millions of misplaced families who were doomed to failure. . . ." Meanwhile, the RA "was not ready to tackle on any large scale the rehabilitation of millions of families being starved off their homestead farms. . . ." [148] It was far easier for Congressmen and the public to support or tolerate *on-site* rehabilitation than to understand the need for reform in the allocation of human and natural resources. The laissez faire argument that reform would come anyway as people left the farm of their own accord overlooked the fact that while the trend was working itself out, 1,500,000 farm families required assistance.

Tugwell's policies reflected this basic dilemma and involved him in contradictions. Among agricultural economists, he was a "bulldozer" and not a "spinner." His misgivings about the Committee on Farm Tenancy's traditional "way of life" attitude toward the family farm were in accord with his expectation of invincible technological advance, a decrease in the farm labor force, and growth in the size of productive units. These units, taken together, would constitute, as it were, a national agricultural plant—collectivism in macrocosm. But the RA, in rehabilitating small farmers, restored individual farms and resorted to comparatively small co-operative and collective farms with relatively large labor forces—collectivism in microcosm. Rehabilitation through removal from the land and occupational retraining—as the CED recommended in 1962—was the answer to the dilemma, and it was in accord with Tugwell's basic economic views. He anticipated the movement of population from farm to city, but, as he himself insisted, what profit was there in a farmer's making this move when he was without industrial skills and without job opportunities in cities already burdened with unemployed workers?

Thus, the depression both dramatized rural poverty and prevented its elimination. Tugwell, however, served a worth-while function in annoying "a lot of people who needed to be annoyed." Moreover, with all of his notoriety and despite the fact that he was the wrong man to sponsor a food and drug bill, he was probably one of the few men—if not the only man—in Washington who could have put together an agency to attack rural poverty and misuse of the land. Americans always need to be annoyed, especially in good times when reform is more manageable, about the condition of our poorest citizens, a condition which, in the opinion of some historians, ultimately determines the fate of civilizations.

23. Board Member—Errand Boy—Publicist— Idea Man: 1932-1936

I

The positions of Assistant Secretary (1933-1934) and Undersecretary (1934-1936) of Agriculture and Resettlement Administrator (1935-1936) did not account for all of Tugwell's activities in government. He made additional contributions, official and unofficial. Officially, he often substituted for Henry Wallace at meetings of the Cabinet and on other occasions, and he served on a number of boards and committees. Unofficially, he was an errand boy, a publicist, and an idea man. His functions outside the USDA merit attention, but it should be kept in mind that Roosevelt did not appoint him to the USDA merely as a convenient way of providing a title and a salary for a presidential adviser. Genuinely interested in the farm problem, Tugwell devoted most of his time to his departmental duties. After he became Resettlement Administrator in the spring of 1935, he applied almost all of his energy to that position.

Boards and committees on which Tugwell served were:

> Special Board for Public Works
> Special Industrial Recovery Board
> Committee on Economic Security
> Committee on Farm Tenancy
> Emergency Committee on Housing
> Executive Committee on Commercial Policy
> Great Plains Drought Area Committee

He acted as Wallace's representative on the Executive Committee on Commercial Policy and at nearly all of the meetings of the Special Board for Public Works. The Special Board for Public Works and the Special Industrial Recovery Board grew out of the two titles of the NIR Act. The Public Works Board, headed by the Secretary of the Interior, included members from the Bureau of the Budget and these Departments: Agriculture, Commerce, Justice, Labor, Treasury, and War. To facilitate the expenditure of the 3.3 billions appropriated for public works, the Board created an Allotment Advisory Committee composed of the President, Ickes, Tugwell, Harry Hopkins, and Frank Walker, treasurer of the Democratic National Committee. Tugwell and Hopkins, favoring quick spending for timely stimulation of the economy, met opposition from Ickes and Lewis Douglas. Ickes believed that hasty expenditures by the Public Works Administration would boomerang by giving rise to waste and corruption. Douglas, Tugwell recalled, seemed to be against almost any project that cost money.[1] The Budget Director and the Assistant Secretary had some bitter arguments, especially over funds for research. Tugwell later noted how he concluded that "I couldn't bargain with him and had to defeat him; others did too, and he finally quit." [2]

Ickes proved a more formidable opponent than Douglas. He turned defeat into victory. His policies left millions of people with poor prospects for the winter of 1933-1934, and Hopkins' Civil Works Administration was set up for rapid, large-scale employment. But from Ickes' standpoint this meant that he could continue to administer the kinds of projects he preferred without the risk of being responsible for inefficiency or graft. He was able, besides, effectively to express his strong dislike of non-Presidential direction. The Public Works Board disbanded, a victim of Ickes' desire to work directly under Roosevelt.[3] The Special Industrial Recovery Board suffered a similar fate at the hands of the obstreperous Hugh Johnson. Tugwell and others disagreed with Johnson on NRA price policy in general, and Tugwell also argued with the chairman about the relative rates of advance of agricultural and industrial prices. He thought he represented the President's view, but, he recalled, "I reckoned without political realities." Johnson, taking the businessmen's position, overrode the majority opinion with the President's approval, and by the end of 1933 the Board collapsed.[4] Johnson's days in Washington, however, were numbered, while Ickes was to remain in the capital for years to come.

Tugwell remembered his service on the Public Works Board as being "a good deal more satisfactory" than his efforts on Johnson's Board.[5] His experience on Frances Perkins' Cabinet Committee on Economic Security in the summer of 1934 was the least rewarding of all. He opposed a payroll tax as part of a social security system. He maintained that it was equivalent to a sales tax and would compel those who could least afford it to finance the system.[6] Supported by Harry Hopkins, he also argued against the Brandeis-Frankfurter idea of decentralization to the states. To him this appeared, as he put it in 1950, "so costly an undertaking that it might jeopardize the system. . . ." He and Harry Hopkins "asked the President if it was wrong to go on objecting. The answer was not clear; but it was plain that the objections were not going to win his support. The objectors then withdrew from the committee. . . ." [7]

II

Tugwell later used the term "errand boy" to designate some of the unofficial tasks he performed for Roosevelt.[8] An important activity in this category, especially during the campaign of 1932 and the lame-duck period, was his arranging for various professors to meet with Roosevelt.

After more than a decade at Columbia, Tugwell was aware of which academicians, particularly economists, were pursuing which lines of investigation. He asked a number of them to submit their ideas in writing or in person. These requests, he subsequently explained, did not depend on a scholar's point of view so long as he had no special axe to grind.[9] Among those receiving invitations to Albany, Hyde Park, and New York through Tugwell were Irving Fisher, Professor of Political Economy at Yale; James Harvey Rogers, also of Yale and Tugwell's first choice on monetary matters; E. M. Patterson of the University of Pennsylvania, an authority on trade and tariffs; and H. Parker Willis of Columbia, an expert on banking.[10]

Another errand Tugwell carried out for the President was his acting as a liaison officer linking the White House and Progressive politicians: Senators William E. Borah (Rep., Id.), Edward P. Costigan (Dem., Colo.), Bronson Cutting (Rep., N. Mex.), Hiram W. Johnson (Rep., Calif.), Robert M. La Follette, Jr. (Rep.-Prog., Wis.), George W. Norris (Rep., Nebr.), Gerald P. Nye (Rep., N. D.), Robert F. Wagner (Dem., N. Y.), Burton K. Wheeler (Dem., Mont.); Governors Philip F. La Follette of Wisconsin and Floyd B. Olson of Minnesota; and Fiorello H. La Guardia, Congressman until 1933 and then Mayor of New York City.

Tugwell wrote about this assignment at some length in *The Democratic Roosevelt,* commenting that the President regarded some of these men with "a respect often tinged with affection . . . these were the true breed. If Franklin had not been a Roosevelt I am quite certain he would have liked to be a La Follette." Roosevelt's attitude toward the Progressives involved more than respect and affection. Tugwell made much of something Roosevelt said to him in Albany in 1932: "We'll have eight years in Washington. By that time there may not be a Democratic party, but there will be a Progressive one." Tugwell felt that the word "progressive" was meant to be capitalized. Roosevelt's suggestion to Wendell Willkie twelve years later, in June, 1944, that they discuss the formation of a Progressive party was to Tugwell an indication of the persistence of the President's basic political preference. But, if Roosevelt was a Democrat of convenience, as President he was not in a position to act as the Progressives' leader. Thus, he had asked Tugwell to "keep in touch with these natural allies and had indeed given me the task of holding them together if I could." [11]

The President "was not certain," Tugwell remarked in his memoir, "that I could hold the Progressives together in his name, and he did not count on it; but he didn't select anyone else." Tugwell found his appointive office a handicap in moving among politicians, and he was not able to shape the Progressives, "a scattered but a potential force," into a political movement. He did what he could, and no one else tried.[12] He

was willing to try despite the differences between his own long-run institutional views and the Progressives' ideas. If the Progressives were scattered geographically, they also covered a lot of ground intellectually.
This would be true of Progressives at any given time, and between one
time and another, in American history. In fact, Progressive programs
have sometimes contained regressive elements.

The Progressives Tugwell dealt with rejected the socialists' prescription
for the business system but insisted on making the capitalists behave,
especially through the antitrust laws. The exclusion of the business
system from some enterprises brings to mind, of course, public power
and the name of George Norris. In agriculture the Progressives favored
the farmers as against the processors. They believed in the development of foreign trade. These men, needless to say, advocated the basic
Progressive principle that when necessary the people were to use their
government as a positive instrument to promote the general welfare. In
the depression this meant deficit spending, including appropriations for
relief and public works. All of this, except antitrustism, was acceptable
to Tugwell as an emergency approach. As in the matter of his decision
to work for Roosevelt, he suppressed his long-run policy preferences and
co-operated with men whom he considered the best men available in the
fight against depression. After meeting with La Guardia and some of
his Progressive followers in the House, Tugwell recorded in his diary that
"all but one or two are sincere about solving the nation's problems." [13]

Some of the Progressives had abandoned antitrustism or atomism for
collectivism or holism. Wagner's and Wheeler's interest in the NIR Act
evidenced an appreciation of the collectivists' description of the economy. La Follette was more of a collectivist than the others, which makes
understandable this high tribute afterward paid to him by Tugwell:
"Bob La Follette, of all the progressives of that time, had made the most
complete transition to modernism. He had become a collectivist by
hard thinking and in the course of political experience in a tough school.
He had been his father's secretary for years. Old Bob had been the kind
of fighter who wears himself out in the eternal struggle against evil. Like
George Norris, he was pure in heart and simple in mind. But industrial
technology had created what Tawney called the Great Society under his
eyes without his ever seeing it. Young Bob saw it. He had the mind for
it, but the fighting blood of his father was in his veins too. He was as
tough as they come." For more than two years La Follette had "made
Hoover's nights hideous with stinging criticism." He had also suggested
constructive alternatives to inaction: planning, economic councils, and
massive attacks on unemployment through public works and relief. In
view of his respect for the Senator, it is understandable that Tugwell

vigorously conveyed to the President La Follette's complaints about NRA policies.[14]

Roosevelt's initial rejection of the Progressives' advice on the NRA marked the beginning of their defection. In the middle of 1934, after the Darrow report, Roosevelt finally called for an NRA tailored to the Progressives' taste. This, together with his reversal in 1934 of international currency and trade policies in the direction of the Progressives' preferences, might have been expected to win back their support. But his equivocation in the spring and summer regarding Senator Wagner's proposals for labor legislation deeply offended the Progressives again. And in October the President once more reversed his field on the NRA. These shifts, Tugwell explained in *The Democratic Roosevelt,* were the result of "moving defensively toward the political center." The theme of the President's first address to the new Congress in 1935 was "a very different one from the campaign tactic of keeping to the middle . . . Progressivism had returned to the White House—an orthodox brand, but authentic." Nevertheless, many of the old Progressives were furious.[15]

In retrospect Tugwell could see clearly how hopeless his task was. Difficult at best, it became impossible with the President's political maneuvers. It was not that Roosevelt held the Progressives' attitudes toward him lightly—his "natural affiliation" was with them, whether Republican or Democratic—but his political moves were coldly calculated. He was convinced that the Progressives had no alternative to his policies—"They would not oppose him because they could not." The original bond, however, was destroyed. The Progressives, except for Wagner, protested emphatically over Roosevelt's treatment of labor legislation. After the summer of 1934, except for Norris, they "could not again be counted as certain allies, only ones of convenience. . . ." [16] Thus Tugwell's subsequent efforts were futile. A case in point is the tribute he paid to Bronson Cutting in a speech in the Senator's adopted state of New Mexico in June, 1935.[17] In the summer of 1934 Cutting had bitterly declared that the New Deal was being strangled in the house of its friends, and he and Roosevelt had entered on an estrangement that lasted until Cutting's death in a plane crash. If Cutting were still alive in 1935, it is doubtful that Tugwell could have won him back.

III

Tugwell's efforts as a publicist should be mentioned among his unofficial activities. *Newsweek* commented that his production of articles and speeches made him "the New Deal's No. 1 philosopher." [18] Frank Kent referred to him as the "most prolific and widely interpreted of the New Deal interpreters." [19] The volume of his literary output led some observers to doubt that he wrote his own material. It was alleged, for example, that Paul Porter ghosted his books.[20] The only books Tugwell published while he was in Washington were *The Industrial Discipline,* which he had finished before he left Columbia, and *The Battle for Democracy,* a collection of articles, notes, and speeches. He recalled that he wrote his own material except in rare instances when he got caught short for time. Then Russell Lord or John Fleming would prepare a draft for a speech.[21]

Writing and speaking had been Tugwell's occupational practice for years. Besides, Progressives were in the habit of arguing their case because, as Tugwell pointed out in 1928, "conservatism can afford quiescence; discussion is sure to stir up embarrassment; progressivism is a battle which always must be won by attrition. It cannot proceed by holding its own. It must penetrate the minds of millions, not a few. . . ."[22] Frank Kent, in one of his columns in the *Baltimore Sun* in 1934, ridiculed Tugwell's and Moley's writing and speech-making. He remarked that the two professors reached a height of garrulity rarely attained in public life, concealing their failure as administrators behind a smokescreen of words "beyond computation." Even the most oratorical of the Senators had fallen far behind them in verbal performance. The fame of the two academicians, whose existence was known to only a handful hardly a year before, was achieved, Kent declared, by words rather than deeds: "Theirs is not the field of concrete accomplishment. They dwell on a higher plane, ride upon philosophical clouds, from which they explain, expound, expand, and expose." [23]

Obviously, Presidential disapproval would have prevented Tugwell from pursuing his habitual practice, but, Tugwell's memoir relates, Roosevelt actually encouraged his expository efforts.[24] The President meant "expository" regarding policies and programs which the administration had proposed or adopted. He believed that Tugwell could not present his academic views and expect the public to accept them as such. Thus, Tugwell publicly explained administration policies, some of which he privately opposed. Accordingly, one of his critics charged that as a publicist Tugwell "turned his back on his principles." [25] This allegation overlooked Tugwell's concepts of leadership, loyalty, and service.

Nearly every public administrator, at one time or another, sees his recommendations rejected and must choose between resigning and staying on. Some choose resignation and public criticism of the policies they oppose. Moley, who also composed explanations of policies he disapproved,[26] chose to resign in late 1933, but it was some time before he became an open critic. Tugwell chose to stay on and keep quiet, publicly, because he judged the total program beneficial to the nation and the best available. In late 1936 Tugwell, too, chose to resign, but he still kept quiet. Every man has a right to change his mind, and all of the choices noted here are justifiable. That is why Tugwell was unfair in his unfavorable comments on Moley's resignation.[27] In perspective, one could argue that the only difference in their departures was in timing.

Each man who resigns, of course, has different reasons for deciding that he can no longer stay. Tugwell felt that Moley resigned because his pride had been hurt—insufficient reason for ending one's service to the cause of national welfare. The assumption here was that Moley still considered Roosevelt and his policies contributory to national welfare. Again, every man has a right to change his mind. One can concede, nevertheless, that Moley's turnabout, after two years of working closely with Roosevelt, was difficult for Tugwell to understand. Moley, commenting on Tugwell's *The Democratic Roosevelt*, gave his reasons for resigning and his theory of leadership, which was quite different from Tugwell's, as these titles indicate: "The Leader Above All," *Newsweek*, September 30, 1957, and "A Roosevelt Rhapsody," *The National Review*, November 9, 1957. In *both* cases theory undoubtedly followed fact to some extent and was inseparable from the personality and personal experiences of each man and the psychology of his relationship to the leader.

"To his enemies," a *New York Times* correspondent later noted, Tugwell "was the plausible and sinister apostle of the revolution." [28] In their attacks they called on him to defend his radical views. In reply, Tugwell defined his "liberal" position, as this note he received in February, 1934, from Moley, then editor of *Today*, indicates: "I will advertise your article very extensively in advance and set it forth as a statement of the more liberal view in the administration. . . . In a sense, therefore, you would be answering the current wailings of men like Mark Sullivan." [29] There was some response to Tugwell's stance, and a number of liberals to whom he symbolized modernism considered him their spokesman close to the wheel of the ship of state. On the occasion of some rumors in 1935 that Tugwell was going to resign, the *New Republic* commented editorially, "We are quite sure that if he goes, Mr. Roosevelt's standing among the liberals whose favor he so often courts in his speeches will be even further damaged than it is today." [30]

Nevertheless, from the standpoint of the historian interested in ultimate causation, Tugwell's impact as a publicist was quite limited. In view of the temper of the times, it can be assumed that the major measures of the New Deal would have won acceptance without his expository efforts. As for his long-run institutional ideas, some people looked into them who would not have done so if he had not become nationally known. Many of these inquirers, of course, reacted unfavorably. Moreover, if the institutional changes he recommended were to occur in the year 2100, the historian of say 2300 would conclude that they would have taken place without Tugwell's words. Perhaps the most a publicist can do is to strike a responsive chord. Tugwell's *Mr. Hoover's Economic Policy* did this to a certain extent in the desperate days of early 1932, but in this respect it was by no means in a class with Thomas Paine's *Common Sense* or Mrs. Stowe's *Uncle Tom's Cabin*. In 1942, in a conversation with Abe Fortas, Undersecretary of the Interior, Tugwell got the impression—with reference to his own career in which he had "talked as well as devised"—that "Abe felt the talking, although it may have relieved my feelings, had counted for no real good. He might be right." [31]

IV

After the campaign of 1932 Tugwell continued to fulfill a private educative function as one of Roosevelt's idea men. He tried to be creative in his limited spare time by writing notes on any of his ideas which he thought might interest the President. His private studies, unlike most of his articles and speeches, were exploratory rather than expository. They often approached national problems on an academic level above the turmoil of politics and the exigencies of actual administration. Tugwell used his access to the White House to present some of his views to the President in conversation as well as on paper. Their discussions of rural problems resulted in the creation of the Resettlement Administration, but few of Tugwell's major suggestions elicited such a fruitful response. Perhaps two of them merit special attention: Tugwell's long-run monetary ideas and his suggestion of an undistributed-profits tax.

As an institutionalist Tugwell considered inflation and monetary management inadequate for sustaining a stable, growing economy. He favored reflation and the departure from the gold standard which it required only as emergency measures in the superdeflationary crisis of 1933. Nor did he think that Roosevelt expected to achieve "parity" or "balance" with monetary measures. The President, he recalled, hoped to raise prices, arrest deflation, and save middle-class investments. But, when it came to the gold-buying scheme of Professor George F. Warren of Cornell, Roosevelt succumbed in October, 1933, to the "fascination of all simple solutions for difficult problems. . . ." [32]

In its simplest form, Tugwell noted privately in 1934, Warren's theory held that changes in the price of gold would cause the prices of commodities to vary proportionately. It was expected that the separation of the dollar from a fixed weight of gold, and an increase in the number of dollars which the government would pay for a given weight of gold, would increase the general level of prices. Tugwell, who did not pretend to be an expert on currency matters, based his comments on this theory on the opinions of specialists, and he sent his notes to the President.

First of all, Tugwell pointed out, the theory assumed a relationship between gold and all other media of exchange which did not exist. We did not exchange gold for goods. We used paper money and credit instruments. The price level, moreover, was like the death rate, which could not be controlled by the manipulation of a single factor. Gold was important, especially in international exchange, but its manipulation would not amount to real price management. That would require selective management by commodities and products. In fact, Tugwell noted, the administration as a whole, by going in for the management of some commodities other than gold, showed that it did not accept Warren's theory.[33]

If Tugwell's public support of the gold-buying scheme[34] evoked the criticism that he "turned his back on his principles," in this case Moley was subject to the same accusation. It should be pointed out that Tugwell's note to the President expressed the thought that the scheme might have salutary international effects by preventing foreign manipulation of the dollar,[35] and Moley thought it would do neither good nor harm.[36] Their prediction that the Warren plan would not work proved correct. It produced neither the moderate reflation intended nor the uncontrolled inflation Wall Street predicted. The flow of gold from all over the world into Fort Knox was the principal visible effect. Moley concluded that the devaluation of the dollar in January, 1934, was an acknowledgment of the failure of Warren's scheme. "I was right. It didn't hurt anything except Warren."[37]

In addition to seeing possible salutary international effects in the Warren scheme, Tugwell speculated publicly that it could be a potential first step toward a true commodity dollar. Warren's plan was variously referred to as the quantity theory and the theory of the compensated dollar, the weighted dollar, or the commodity dollar. A genuine commodity dollar, Tugwell commented in a syndicated column in 1933, would treat gold as only one of the commodities useful in backing currency. He suggested a dollar based "perhaps on an index number which expresses the relationship of all commodities to one another." He believed that such a dollar was "feasible with our present statistical resources."[38] It would also meet the requirements of a "sound" or "hard" dollar, which he defined in an address of late 1933 as one having "a substantial equality of purchasing power and debt-paying power from one generation to another."[39]

Tugwell conceded in his ruminations on monetary matters in 1933 and 1934 that a commodity dollar would only theoretically keep purchasing power constant; practically there would be great difficulties.[40] Nor would it be enough to keep purchasing power constant with reference to the medium of exchange.[41] It was "elementary that purchasing power must equal retail prices if activity is to be maintained." [42] In other words, while a change in monetary ideas had a place in the formulation of an effective economic policy, it could not "take the place of honest readjustment through the management of prices." [43] Tugwell's reference to the Warren plan as a first step which "will force us in years to come to look for a really satisfactory medium of exhange" [44] indicates that his remarks on the commodity dollar are best taken as a speculative challenge to unquestioning acceptance of prevailing orthodoxies concerning currency.

V

A. G. Beuhler, a student of the undistributed-profits tax of 1936, writing in 1937, linked it to criticism of corporate saving, "which was popularly held to be an important cause of the depression," and attributed it to the impression which Tugwell and Herman Oliphant, General Counsel of the Treasury on leave from Johns Hopkins University, made on the President with "current oversavings and underconsumption theories." [45] Republican Congressmen, in hearings on the tax before the House Ways and Means Committee, quoted Tugwell's *The Industrial Discipline*, ridiculing Tugwell and Oliphant as "visionaries." [46] A historian of taxation noted that Tugwell, in his book and in his personal advice to the President, suggested the tax as "a means of reducing excessive corporate savings, increasing consumer spending, and stabilizing business. . . . He, Oliphant, and others believed that the tax would give the stockholders more influence in the formulation of corporation dividend and corporation savings policies and would remove certain abuses in corporation finance." [47] Tugwell himself recalled that he was a "chief proponent of the undistributed-profits tax . . . the President was much impressed with the necessity for such a tax." [48]

The pertinent passages in *The Industrial Discipline* appeared in Chapter 8, "Government and Industry," Section 4, "The Allocation of Capital." Referring to the depression, Tugwell asserted that "most of the trouble comes from self-allocation occurring strictly within a single organization." This meant that a company tended to reinvest its surplus in its own operation without having adequate knowledge of its place within an industry, or of the place of that industry in the total economy. Misinvestment led to overproduction of certain goods, eventually producing harmful effects on the whole economy. Tugwell suggested taxation to force surplus (undistributed profits, which we may define as corporation income not paid out to individuals through dividends, salaries, interest, or any other medium) into distribution as dividends. Corporations would then have to seek investment capital through regular channels, and the open investment market would check a firm's plans for expansion, assuring efficient capital investment from a national point of view.

In *The Industrial Discipline* Tugwell also mentioned another means of supervising capital investment—a federal incorporation law under which the revision of original charters would be a prerequisite for obtaining permission to make new capital issues. He worked on such a law with Adolf Berle and Assistant Attorney General Harold M. Stephens.[49] Roosevelt was sympathetic toward these studies, but he and Tugwell agreed in early 1934 that the appropriate time to push a bill had not come.[50] A bank for corporate surplus, as an alternative to an undistributed-profits tax, was another device Tugwell discussed with Roosevelt and others. The idea appealed to the President, but it, too, failed to get beyond the discussion stage.[51]

Roosevelt requested the enactment of an undistributed-profits tax in his Supplemental Budget Message of March 3, 1936.[52] He recommended a measure "which would accomplish an important tax reform, remove two major inequalities in our tax system, and stop 'leaks' in present surtaxes." The reform would be the replacement of the normal corporate-income tax, the capital-stock tax, and the excess-profits tax with a single tax on undistributed corporate profits. The two major inequalities were between small unincorporated firms and large corporations and between small and large stockholders. The leak referred to the large stockholders' practice of avoiding taxes by leaving their dividends with corporations.

Roosevelt did not get the kind of a tax bill he requested. In the Revenue Act of 1936 tax rates on individual incomes, estates, gifts, and excess profits remained virtually the same as the rates in the Revenue Act of 1935. The capital-stock tax was reduced from $1.40 to $1.00 for each $1,000 of declared value of stock. The graduated normal corporate-income tax rates were decreased in the lower brackets; 15 per cent still held for net corporate income of $40,000 or more. The undistributed-profits tax, instead of replacing the normal corporate-income, capital-stock, and excess-profits taxes, was added as a graduated surtax. Rates ran from 7 per cent to 27 per cent, depending on the ratio of undistributed net income to adjusted net income (a.n.i. was net income minus the normal corporate-income tax and interest from government obligations; u.n.i. was a.n.i. minus dividends disbursed and credit allowed prior to May 1, 1936, which restricted dividend payments). The total tax was the sum of the taxes on the various brackets. There was no allowance for losses in previous years.

The President had hardly finished his message when opposition to the undistributed-profits tax arose. A main objection involved the anticipated effect on corporate reserves, which, opponents of the tax stated, were necessary for bad times, payment of debts, maintenance, and expansion. An aspect of the concern about reserves was the question whether the tax would eliminate inequities between small and large corporations. Administration spokesmen asserted that with reduced rates in the lower income brackets, small corporations would now have certain advantages over large ones, especially in the availability for reinvestment of a greater proportion of their earnings. Others concluded that the tax unduly favored large corporations which could obtain capital funds from the sale of securities through the stock exchanges.

Some critics questioned the fiscal soundness of the tax. A group of Republican Congressmen declared that the primary purpose of the bill was "not to raise revenue but to give effect to the Tugwellian philosophy of forcing the distribution of corporate earnings. . . ."[53] Businessmen complained about the novelty of the tax, holding that departures from fixed principles of corporate taxation would create administrative difficulties. Besides objecting to the immediate impact of the tax on reserves, revenue, and administration, some of its opponents stressed its long-run implications of what they considered undue intrusion by government into the field of economic control.

The administration based its defense of the undistributed-profits tax mainly on two arguments. One was the thesis that Roosevelt had presented in his acceptance address of July 2, 1932—that misuse of corporate surplus in the 1920's was a cause of the depression. The other was the denial that the tax, either in intent or effect, would undermine corporate reserves. This defense caused a controversy among economists as to the anticipated impact of the undistributed-profits tax on the business cycle. This discussion, in turn, led them back to the causes of the depression, which they debated vigorously.

Several scholars attempted to evaluate the undistributed-profits tax after it had been in operation.[54] This was a difficult undertaking. As one analyst, M. S. Kendrick, concluded, the tax "created a series of new differentials . . . throughout the whole range of individual and income situations."[55] Moreover, the tax they studied was not the single tax on corporate profits which the President proposed. Finally, the tax was short-lived. It continued in effect in the same form in the Revenue Act of 1937, was emasculated beyond resemblance to its original form in the Revenue Act of 1938, and was dropped after 1939. We cannot be sure about either its short-run impact or what its long-run effects would have been if it had remained in operation for some time. Certainly it did not test Tugwell's ideas on "external" scrutinization of investment. Another student of the tax, G. E. Lent, doubted whether outside funds replaced those taken by the tax.[56] Figures for later years showed that American corporations obtained only about 6 per cent of their funds for capital expansion from net new stocks.[57] This last figure may have been greater if there had been forced distribution of profits, but it indicates that raising capital funds through the sale of securities is perhaps more easily said than done, and it tends to confirm Lent's doubt.

It is quite possible that the administration did not want to establish "external" control of investment through the undistributed-profits tax. Tugwell's influence in this matter may not have been as great as some observers, including Tugwell himself, thought. The undistributed-profits tax was enacted during the Second New Deal, and the transition from the First New Deal to the Second involved the rise of the trustbusters' and the decline of the collectivists' influence at the White House. An important trustbuster was Herman Oliphant, who shared credit for the undistributed-profits tax with Tugwell in the opinion of a number of observers. Moley considered Oliphant more influential than Tugwell in "selling" the undistributed-profits tax to Roosevelt.[58] And the Commissioner of Internal Revenue and the Director of Research and Statistics of the Treasury, Oliphant's Department, presented the administration's case at Congressional hearings.

It was not unusual during the New Deal for members of different schools of economic thought to support the same measure, each seeing in a complicated proposal a means of advance toward his own objectives. Oliphant and Tugwell were diametrically opposed in their economic thought. Oliphant, according to Moley, was an "evangelical trustbuster" who believed that the tax would prevent the growth of monopoly.[59] Tugwell, writing about the tax in *The Industrial Discipline*, stated that the regulation of capital investment "would need to be developed side by side" with integration.[60] This difference helps us to see how Oliphant might desire forced distribution of profits to promote democracy among stockholders, while Tugwell might desire it as a means of injecting a scrutinizing factor—investors and bankers—into investment decision-making. This difference would be between atomizing the locus of decision-making among amateurs and allowing it to concentrate while subjecting it to a check by "external" professionals.

It is impossible, of course, to give exact weights to the influences which worked in Roosevelt's mind. This writer has concluded in a detailed study of the undistributed-profits tax [61] that the trustbusters were more influential in bringing about its proposal and had more to say about its content than Tugwell. John M. Blum, in his study based on the diary of Secretary of the Treasury Morgenthau, confirmed this conclusion, noting that the advocates of the tax, except Tugwell, were interested in its antitrust possibilities.[62] It appears that contemporary estimates of Tugwell's influence with reference to the undistributed-profits tax should be revised downward. But some good came from the attention Roosevelt's proposals drew to Tugwell's writings—even though the writings did not prompt the proposals. The discussion of the causes of the depression was worth while. Those who denied Tugwell's prognosis of the 1920's and the ability of stockholders, bankers, and investors to do better in investment than corporate managers assumed the burden of proof. Since the depression corporations have stressed improved market analysis and careful planning of capital investment. This emphasis amounts to a tacit admission of careless, abusive practices in the past.

VI

Frank Kent, in his column for November 2, 1935, remarked that Tugwell "seems to combine the function of administration soothsayer and seer with that of practical man of affairs and national planner par excellence." [63] Two students of public administration commented that Tugwell's dual function as an executive officer in the USDA and as a nonpolitical general-staff assistant to the President made his position "anomalous." [64] But the two roles were not of equal significance. Tugwell was only one "educator" among many at the White House. Tugwell himself recalled that his errand-boy role ended with his USDA field trip in the fall of 1933.[65] As for his activities as a publicist, he made only one-third as many public addresses in 1935 as in 1934 and none in 1936. And the treatment here of two of the suggestions he made as an idea man is an academic matter rather than administrative history. His greatest contribution as an idea man was the intellectual curiosity he helped to arouse in the Democratic candidate in 1932.

24. Resignation: 1936

I

In November, 1935, Harold Ickes recorded in his diary that there seemed to be a "pretty general feeling that Rex Tugwell will soon be out of the government. He has been under terrific attack lately on account of a speech he made in Los Angeles. . . . I have no doubt, however, that one of these days I will find myself the subject of sharp attacks because of some statement taken out of the context of a speech and distorted by Hearstian editorial writers." Ickes also noted a conversation he had had with Harry Hopkins, who remarked that Tugwell had a lifetime job at Columbia at $9,000 a year and would have to decide soon whether he was going back to teaching. "I will be sorry," Ickes concluded, "to see Tugwell go because I think he is a man of real vision and ability." [1] In Washington discussions about the possibility of the resignation of a high official do not remain private very long. Tugwell's case was no exception. In early 1936 the *New York Times* reported the typical sequence of premature rumors and denials.[2] Later in the year Tugwell's silence during the campaign was the occasion for rumors which had a basis in fact. Tugwell's muteness was not voluntary. James A. Farley decided that keeping Tugwell quiet would be a way of avoiding criticism, and Roosevelt agreed. A number of observers took this strategy as an indication that Tugwell's departure was imminent.[3] They were correct in a way. Roosevelt did not intend to fire Tugwell, but this strategy, which did not work anyway, was strongly resented by the Undersecretary.

Meanwhile, foes of the New Deal disregarded Tugwell's silence. Joseph B. Ely of Massachusetts warned that Roosevelt's re-election would be immediately construed as the "mandate which Mr. Tugwell has asked . . . in order to create what they speak of as a 'planned economy.' . . ."[4] Frank Kent made this prediction: "If the More Abundant Life is sustained by the voters next November, this silly stuff about economy, the Constitution, the courts and individual liberty can be tossed out of the window and Dr. Tugwell will be able to transplant people by a mere wave of the hand. And if the transplanted are not happy it will be their own fault."[5] Kent did not have to wait long to see his prophecy disproved. In mid-November, flying with Tugwell to Memphis to begin the tour of the South which was to convince Wallace of the RA's value, Felix Belair of the *New York Times* "scooped" the resignation story. After breakfast the next day Tugwell surrendered to the other news-

men: "O.K., boys, I guess I may as well give in. The report is true."
Then he basked in a friendliness of a sort he had missed during recent
years and joked with the reporters.[6] On November 18 the White House
announced the text of the letters exchanged by Tugwell and the President:

November 17, 1936

My dear Mr. President:

For reasons which have been discussed between us more than once,
I should like to be permitted to resign from the Government and return to private life within the next few months. I have served the
better part of your first term as President with growing confidence in
your policies and in you. I do not need to say that if you ever have
real need for me again, I shall be on call.

Respectfully yours,
R. G. Tugwell

Dear Rex:

I fully understand the reasons that make you feel you should, for a
while at least, return to private life within the next few months. You
have given generously and efficiently of your services to the Government for these past four years, and I want you to know that later on
I fully expect you to come back to render additional service.

Later on when I have returned from my trip to South America, we can
talk over the actual date on which you will want your resignation to be
effective.

With my warm regards,
As ever yours,
Franklin D. Roosevelt [7]

Tugwell's resignation was effective as of the close of business on December 31, 1936. He immediately assumed the position of traveling consultant and Executive Vice-President in the American Molasses Company under his friend Charles Taussig, a presidential adviser on Caribbean affairs. His acceptance of this position had been announced along
with his resignation. At that time, when reporters questioned him
about the RA, Tugwell replied, "But don't ask me about cotton. I'm a
molasses man." To some Washingtonians it was amusing that the aus-
tere, immaculate Tugwell should go into the molasses business. He told
his friends with glee, "Our leading brand is 'Grandma,' and the slogan
on the label, so help me, is 'Look for Grandma on the Can.'" [8] There
was another aspect of Tugwell's going into the molasses business which
was not humorous, although the President, Tugwell recalled, treated it

lightly in a conversation of November, 1936. Roosevelt said he would be looking for a new job in 1941. "We laughed and speculated about what it might be. I told him he too ought to go to work for Charles Taussig— no other businessman would have either of us. 'Yes,' he said, 'and we can't either of us be professors after our unorthodox behavior.' " [9] Roosevelt's remark was too true. Tugwell later observed, "I couldn't go back to Columbia. I wasn't reputable. I was a 'crackpot.' My resignation was written out. My greatest humiliation was that the propaganda about me had even 'gotten' the faculty at Columbia." [10]

The press suggested several reasons for Tugwell's resignation.[11] He needed more money to support his family. His leave of absence from Columbia was going to expire in 1937. His official position had grown uncomfortable. He anticipated difficulty in getting appropriations from Congress for the RA. The farm tenancy committee's tour left Wallace unimpressed with the RA's work and unwilling to take the agency into the USDA. Tugwell's influence at the White House had faded. He was no longer in a position within the administration to get much accomplished. To this contemporaneous list a Washington correspondent of the *New York Times* later added the "explosive force" with which Tugwell's effort to "sell" the RA, an "incredibly gaudy and expensive" brochure issued in 1936, backfired.[12] Except for the references to Tugwell's leave of absence from Columbia and Wallace's attitude toward the RA, there was something to all of these suggestions. As for the reactions to Tugwell's departure, some conservatives were relieved at the stepping down and out of the "leftist left-winger of the New Deal," [13] but many of them were satisfied to leave well enough alone. Ickes was surprised at the number of conservatives present at a farewell dinner for Tugwell, which was "all in a light vein." [14] Perhaps they knew that many of the things which they had said about Tugwell were not true. This was indicated in *Newsweek*, which had lost its original New Deal orientation but entitled its story: "New Deal's Leading 'Red' Gets Job on Wall Street," using punctuation which indicated that "Red" was to be taken with several grains of salt.[15] *Time* used only slight sarcasm, heading its story: "Molasses Man." [16] John T. Flynn, it is true, later stated that Tugwell "hid his scorn under a bushel while he crawled onto the payroll of one of those great enemies of the Common Man—a big Puerto Rican sugar corporation." [17] But the most acid comments came from the militant left. Paul W. Ward, Washington correspondent of the *Nation*, called Tugwell a weakling who withdrew at the prospect of a fight to keep the RA intact and deserted the progressive cause for money and security.[18] Editorially, the *Nation*, which had hoped Tugwell would lead progressive forces, stated that his acceptance of a "lucrative post as a business executive puts an end to such hopes. Molasses is a sticky substance, and any prospect of Mr. Tugwell's being able to detach himself from it to become a leader of the progressive forces seems very distant." [19] But molasses did not prove to be so sticky after all. In February, 1938, Tugwell became Chairman of the New York City Planning Commission.

Tugwell's co-workers and friends expressed regret at his resignation. Henry Wallace declared: "You know, Rex has been one of the most vigorous fighters for the capitalistic system I know of. Men of Tugwell's courage and insight are rare. We shall all regret he is no longer in Government." [20] Will Alexander said: "Dr. Tugwell is the sanest, clearest-thinking man in the Government." [21] Skeptics could write off these remarks as accolades for public consumption. This could not be done with Ickes' privately recorded comment: "I am sorry to see Rex go. I think that he has been terribly misrepresented by the public press and enemies of the Administration. . . ." [22] Other private comments were made by employees of the RA. Perhaps only the regretful ones wrote Tugwell. On the other hand, they had nothing to gain from him, and their remarks were unsolicited. D. P. Trent, Regional Director in Dallas, expressed "admiration for the manner in which you have stood for your convictions . . . and for the constructive contributions which you have made to the underlying purposes of the RA." [23] R. A. Pearson wrote: "You have helped enormously to put on their feet a great many people who otherwise would be a burden to society. Things you have been doing will stand to your credit after critics are gone and forgotten." [24]

Examining the reasons for Tugwell's decision more closely, we find that by 1936 his personal influence at the White House had dwindled, and that he was no longer in a position to get as much done as before —as the press suggested. At the same time, his decline compelled him to consider some developments in which his interest was at least partly impersonal. He thought about the work of the RA, and he pondered the eclipse of the kind of progressivism which he thought best for the promotion of the general welfare in the long run. An uproar had arisen in Congress over the RA, and there was no doubt that it was going to be difficult—as the press suggested—to get appropriations adequate for the continuation of the agency's program. [25] It would undoubtedly be easier to get funds if Tugwell resigned. It is not true, as reported in the press, that Wallace was unimpressed by his tour of RA operations. The tour virtually clinched the transfer of the RA to the USDA, and that absorption did take place on December 31, 1936—Tugwell's last day on the job. Undoubtedly his departure facilitated this union. Thus, it can be argued that, rather than running from a fight, he sacrificed his personal position for the good of the RA and its work. Two students of public administration commented: "The administrative ramifications of the RA multiplied the possible points of attack. Tugwell's withdrawal seemed tactical." [26]

At the White House the rise of Corcoran and Cohen signaled the triumph of atomism over collectivism. Corcoran revealed the personal animosity of the victors toward Tugwell when he told Moley, on November 13, 1936, that "we'll take care of him. Not that he doesn't serve a useful function. He is sort of a catfish to keep the herrings from getting sluggish when the fishermen take them back in tanks to port. But the Skipper shouldn't get the idea that he is an edible fish." "That," Moley concluded, "seemed to dispose of Rex." [27] Tugwell's own recollection of his recognition of the atomists' victory is informative:

I had another reason for going when the campaign was over. The Brandeis-Frankfurter-Corcoran influence had prevailed. Franklin did not doubt my loyalty any more than he ever had, I am sure, but he had been half persuaded—and Eleanor even more than he—that I had totalitarian leanings. I had spoken too highly of planning and had not succeeded in persuading those who heard me that it was, as I believed it to be, an essential device for democratic government.

My ideas concerning the necessity for coordination and conjunction were interpreted over and over as similar to those which underlay the corporate state. Franklin never argued this with me. He must have understood that this was a misinterpretation; but he was a politician. He could support only so much disapproval of an intimate; when the tolerance was exceeded, friendship must not be put before expediency. [28]

Will Alexander, years later, said that he still did not know why Tugwell resigned. He guessed that the anticipation of difficulty in legitimizing the RA because of Tugwell's unpopularity with Congress was a factor. He thought the main reason for Tugwell's decision involved a personal matter. Tugwell and Grace Falke, his administrative assistant, were deeply in love, and Tugwell, according to Alexander, did not think that Washington was the place to be while he obtained a divorce. [29] (Tugwell was divorced, after twenty-three years of marriage, in early 1938 and married Grace Falke in late 1938. His second marriage is in its twenty-third year as this is written, and he has two sons in college.)

Tugwell himself indicated that the specific development which, more than any other, moved him to act on his general uncomfortableness was the politicians' decision that he remain offstage during the campaign of 1936. "I was through unconditionally," he later wrote, "when Roosevelt agreed with Farley to keep me quiet and hidden during the 1936 campaign. I had worked hard and felt I was entitled to speak." [30]

He decided to wait until after the election before resigning, he recalled, because he did not want to appear to be quitting under fire. He was especially resentful because he felt that Roosevelt would win with ease.[31] In fact, he regretted that Roosevelt did not ask for a mandate for further social legislation. But, as he pointed out in *The Art of Politics*, politicians tend to play it safe, to give too much for what they gain in the way of approval; and "as submission to decision—electoral, legislative, or merely in public opinion—approaches, there tends to be a panic conviction that more must be done." [32] In the light of Roosevelt's overwhelming victory in 1936, we can now safely say that he would have won whether or not he asked for a mandate and whether or not Tugwell participated in the campaign.

If the question whether Roosevelt had enough political capital to afford the liability of Tugwell now seems academic, it did not appear this way to the President and others in 1936. Ickes, for example, referring to Tugwell late in that year, noted that "undoubtedly he has been a good deal of a political load for the President to carry." [33] Tugwell himself considered Roosevelt's decision to silence him a political one. He resented it as being incorrect or unnecessary, not because it grew out of politics, in which "friendship must not be put before expediency." In *The Democratic Roosevelt* Tugwell asserted that Roosevelt early in his life, in family matters, seized and protected "an essential independence. It might have to be got by dissimulation and a continual tactical management, which meant sacrifice and exclusion even for those who were dear enough to him. . . ." [34] This applied even more to Roosevelt's profession. As Tugwell remarked in *The Art of Politics*, "friendship is a difficult—almost an impossible—luxury for a leader. Sooner or later he sacrifices loyalty to a friend for some other value— usually his own ambition in combination with a conviction that it also involves a people's interest." [35]

Tugwell's relations with Roosevelt after November, 1936, show that his later comments on politics and friendship were not just afterthoughts. A few days after he resigned, Tugwell took the President to see the RA's Greenbelt town near Washington,[36] and their relations remained cordial until Roosevelt died. In fact, the President's reference in his letter of November 17 to Tugwell's return to government proved to be more than a mere formality. In 1938 Ickes stated in his diary: "I think that this administration owes it to Tugwell to get him back again. He suffered more cruel treatment than anyone from the beginning of the administration, and he is an able and resourceful man." [37] It was under Ickes' sponsorship that Tugwell became Governor of Puerto Rico in 1941.

The reasons for Tugwell's resignation add up not to a nervous breakdown but, nevertheless, to a serious personal crisis, emotional and intellectual. This outcome was probably inherent in his attempt to act as a Presidential adviser, an administrator, and an academic observer. Trying to keep practical and intellectual approaches to national problems separate was bound to produce a strain. This tension was compounded by Tugwell's belief that Roosevelt was at heart a collectivist who would move in that direction in time. But when? In *The Democratic Roosevelt* Tugwell stated that the President let the collectivistic Progressives know that "they ought to be more willing than they were to believe that Franklin's intentions were the same as their own and that his tactics and his timing ought to be accepted as essential to the common end. To me, to Harry [Hopkins], and to Bob [La Follette] it meant more than that. It was as if he said, 'I am the progressive way; only through me can the common intention be realized.' That was not necessary to say to me; I had long ago granted him leadership without reserve. When I could not sustain that loyalty I would not stay in his service." [38]

Can we say that Tugwell was simply impatient? Roosevelt, after all, was still talking about forming a Progressive party in 1944—twelve years after he admitted Tugwell to his circle. But to call Tugwell impatient is to rely too much on hindsight. Twelve years, or even four, is a long time to a man in the thick of things in Washington. Moreover, it was difficult for him to interpret the rise of the trustbusters and the request for his own silence as aspects of a merely temporary maneuver. Was it that he could no longer see the collectivistic forest for the atomistic trees? Or was it another kind of forest? In retrospect Tugwell wrote that he finally found himself "in such confusion about what I had always believed and about the possibilities which had always seemed inherent in American life, that my longing for simple withdrawal would become unbearable. I might hope to find some certainty again if I could escape from the center of the struggle." [39]

II

Thus, "simple withdrawal" became the dominating impulse of this complex man in an unbearably complex situation. One aspect of Tugwell's complexity arises from the clash between anti-determinism and cultural lag. His anti-determinism is essentially optimistic, representing his faith that man can control the course of history, subject to certain limitations. The principal force circumscribing man's influence in the area of political economy is invincible technological advance. Man cannot hold back this development, but he can accommodate it and benefit from it through the conscious creation of appropriate institutions (rather than through the unconscious, determined reactions of the Marxist historical prognosis). Cultural lag, on the other hand, represents man's inability to adjust his thinking, and thereby his institutions, as rapidly as conditions change. Certain momentous events caused Tugwell to conclude that as a result of cultural lag man would make the wrong choices or refrain from making any choice, becoming the slave of machines. Since the solution was not for man to exchange regimentation by machines for regimentation by some men of others, democracies had more to lose than dictatorships through failure to cope with technology. Not only did democratic societies have more to lose than totalitarian ones, but they were in great danger of losing it if their reliance on evolution through popular education and persuasion precluded the use of expert planning. Burdened by such thoughts, the advocate of democratic evolution became impatient, the exponent of optimistic anti-determinism became pessimistic.

World War I deeply shook Tugwell's faith that man would progress while avoiding senseless self-destruction on a massive scale, but in 1920 he returned to the problem of human control of human creations as he participated in the designing of Columbia University's famous course, Contemporary Civilization. In the years 1929-1932, the Hoover administration's fatalistic reaction to the depression led Tugwell to doubt that anyone could or would do anything about the disintegrating situation. But indignation accompanied this doubt, producing a vigorous protest in *Mr. Hoover's Economic Policy*. Roosevelt's accession to the presidency raised Tugwell's enthusiasm and expectations in the field of institutional reconstruction. He soon learned that there would be no quick change from an individualistic to a more collectivized society, that the New Deal would comprise measures which, from his standpoint, were essentially superficial. Yet, he was determined to go on with a kind of personal, as distinguished from historical, fatalism. Thus, the ideologist became a pragmatist. He was already that insofar as his ideology itself emphasized experimentation. Now, in addition, he made the pragmatic decision to suppress his personal policy preferences. The contrast between Tugwell's recognition of earthbound obstacles to reform and the soaring imagery of his descriptions of human potentialities made him a realistic romantic, what Russell Lord called a "Tough Poet."

The end of the First New Deal, signified by the launching of the Second New Deal in 1935 and the silencing of Tugwell in 1936, finally brought him to bewilderment, to an inability to span the gap between his basic ideas about planning and the actual New Deal program. As Professor Richard Hofstadter remarked, "Genuine planners like Rexford Guy Tugwell found themselves floundering amid the cross-currents of the New Deal, and ended in disillusionment." [40] In his later writings Tugwell recovered from this disillusionment, concluding, as a political scientist rather than as an economist, that Roosevelt had accomplished about as much as could be expected under the circumstances. Finally, the dropping of the atomic bomb on Hiroshima drove Tugwell to despair at the prospects for survival not only of democracy but of the human race. He expressed his dismay in *A Chronicle of Jeopardy: 1945-55.* He wrote about "the general conviction that all of us had at last been delivered over to Fate or Chance, that implacable and inscrutable fashioner of events which under so many names has always terrorized mankind." The coming of the atomic age meant that "we had . . . a choice between untold luxury for everyone and the total destruction of everything. And damned if I didn't half-believe that we would choose destruction." [41] Tugwell further examined his philosophical doubt in *The Light of Other Days,* attempting to determine through his own life's story why his generation had been responsible for dropping the bomb. Again, his mood was not one of unmitigated hopelessness as indignation and inquiry accompanied his despair.

This picture of the impatient evolutionary, the pessimistic optimist, the pragmatic ideologist, the realistic romantic, the indignant despairer is complicated by additional juxtapositions of opposites: the standoffish democrat, the pro-business antagonist of the titans of business, the flippant foe and the warm friend—the tactless gentleman. Sumner Welles believed that the compelling motive throughout Tugwell's life was his sympathy for the underprivileged and his passionate desire to serve their interests.[42] *Time* put it another way: "He loves the people to beat hell." [43] Tugwell himself said, "Gambling with human lives was to be closed to speculation." [44] But this middle-class champion of the common man was disinclined to rub shoulders with the masses. Similarly, if Tugwell was pro-business in that his institutional thought pointed to business as the instrument of recovery and reconstruction, he was imperious toward the individual practitioners of business, or their sycophants, as he called them, in Congress and the press. Yet, if he was a supercilious antagonist, he was a devoted friend.

Blair Bolles maintained that Tugwell conducted himself in a curt, contemptuous manner which showed the dormitory esthete's scorn for homely ideas, plain people, and politicians. This arrogance arose from a consciousness of intellectual superiority and a romantic imagination. It produced a tactlessness which Tugwell practiced with deliberate finesse, making an avocation of being unpleasant to Congressmen, businessmen, politicians, and petitioning citizens. He flaunted his idealistic scorn before anyone who doubted his romantic nostrums.[45] The *Chicago Tribune* described Tugwell as living in a "perpetual state of astonishment . . . at his own intellect and his own beauty." [46] John T. Flynn asserted that Tugwell, having looked at the world in his college years and having found it strictly third-class, perfected himself in the fine art of being contemptuous, especially toward legislators.[47] Paul Ward of the *Nation* remarked that Tugwell was essentially an academician, aloof and cold almost to the point of snobbishness.[48]

Reports of specific incidents tend to verify this portrayal of Tugwell as the haughty court favorite, with smug confidence in his own theories, whose conduct gave his foes an abundance of ammunition. One story told of an editor who asked him to explain certain features of the AA Act. Tugwell asked the editor whether he had read the bill. The editor had—three times. Tugwell replied, "Then what more can I say?" [49] Another incident, reported by an eyewitness, described a press conference in the USDA on March 7, 1933. Tugwell, in his best classroom manner, told the newsmen that everything was simple and all would be straightened out by the end of the summer. Then he left without answering any questions.[50] Even Tugwell's friends commented on his lack of tact. Henry Wallace once said, "The trouble with Rex as a public man is that he *exhibits* disdain." [51] Sumner Welles conceded that Tugwell was "intellectually arrogant, perhaps, and frequently tactless with those whose purposes he combatted, or whose views he held in contempt." [52] Russell Lord admitted that it was true, as an eminent Senator said somewhat wistfully, that Tugwell, in displaying disdain, broke the first rule of politics.[53] Frances Perkins recalled that Tugwell was "too professoryish." [54] Congressman Byron Harlan of Ohio, who wished to protect the RA against adverse criticism, complained to the White House that he had tried for four days to get an appointment with Tugwell. He might just as well have tried, Harlan grumbled, to get an appointment with the Mikado.[55]

For all his bumptiousness under the circumstances we have indicated, Tugwell enjoyed cordial relations with his colleagues. To them he was charming and engaging, and friendships developed which he valued highly. A letter which Charles G. Proffitt, manager of the Columbia University Press, wrote in 1933 suggests the informality which characterized relations between Tugwell and his acquaintances. Referring to Tugwell's official designation as "The Honorable," Proffitt remarked, "I expressed surprise at the above handle, but my secretary tells me that it is correct." [56] Russell Lord described Tugwell as a man who usually did not unbend in public, but who was friendly and considerate to co-workers.[57] "He hates a heel and a hack," Lord wrote, "but he is a companionable and gallant man with whom to work." [58] Lord reported an incident which showed the good fellowship Tugwell and his co-workers enjoyed. When the lady readers of a Hearst paper in Washington chose Tugwell as the most handsome New Dealer, his associates tried to pull his leg at lunch the next day. He "responded with words which showed that while in the strictest sense of the term he may be no farmer, he at least grew up in a small country town with comfortable access to the livery stable." [59]

Tugwell and Harry Hopkins did not become close friends, but this note which Tugwell wrote to the President on March 3, 1934, evinces sensitivity: "I had a long talk yesterday with Harry. I am sure you do not know how serious his financial situation is. He really has not enough money to get on. He is trying to devise ways and means, but he ought not to have to think of such things now. Perhaps I shouldn't worry you with this but I know he would never tell you, and I thought you ought to know." [60] Will Alexander, who became a devoted friend and admirer of Tugwell, recalled that Tugwell was more at ease with intellectual Congressmen such as La Follette and treated others with disdain. But, Alexander observed, Tugwell was no egoist either in the sense of intellectual snobbishness or certitude, or desire to further his own career.[61]

It can be said in Tugwell's defense that there were certain circumstances which meant that his conduct was bound to be criticized anyway. It was inevitable, as Frank Kent pointed out, that the New Deal appointees should arouse Congressional resentment. Old political rules and images did not cover their activities. Soon after the newcomers arrived in Washington, Vice-President Garner warned them at a Sulgrave Club party to settle down and mind their political manners. Garner said it was a new experience to him to hand the top cards to "boys who had never worked a precinct," but the politicians would go along with the President for the time being if that is what he wanted.[62] Having granted broad powers to the executive branch, and being quick to interpret an action by an appointed administrator as tactless, the politicians turned to their friends among the veterans of the Washington press corps when they wanted to circulate tales which put Tugwell in an unfavorable light. Many of the capital correspondents, of course, needed neither tips nor encouragement to attack Tugwell, particularly after the introduction of the food and drug bill, and some reports of his tactlessness represented distortions. One such incident involved Frank Kent. The story in the press told how Alice Longworth invited Tugwell to a dinner, offering to introduce him to her friend and guest of honor, Frank Kent. Tugwell asked, "Kent? Kent? Who is Mr. Kent, anyway?" From that time on, the press version continued, Kent sought revenge through his column.[63] Actually, Kent had been attacking Tugwell for some time, and the Assistant Secretary asked his question as a joke—which, he recalled, brought the house down.[64] Perhaps this gag was not in the best of taste, but it amused rather than offended those present.

Besides distortions, misunderstandings inevitably cropped up. For example, when Tugwell was aboard ship, about to depart for Europe, in September, 1934, he locked himself in his stateroom and let Paul Appleby explain that the Undersecretary was not snooty but had a lot of last-minute work to do. Reporters attributed Tugwell's behavior to arrogance and tactlessness. The President explained to the press that process-servers, looking for Tugwell in connection with a suit filed against the USDA, accounted for his furtive departure.[65] Occasionally, what seemed to be a misunderstanding was really a case of hyper-criticism. Commenting on the farm program, Tugwell once said, "One move compels another, as in a game of chess." Reporters treated this remark with derision. They may have misunderstood it as evidence of Tugwell's snobbishness, but probably they were just being captious. Russell Lord thought it nothing more or less than an accurate description of the situation. "It would have sounded homlier, more country-like," Lord noted, "if he had said 'checkers.'" [66]

Reminiscing about his tactlessness, Tugwell traced it back to the 1920's, when, in vain, he and many other dissenters had pointed out flaws in the economy and warned against disastrous potentialities. When the collapse came, he had little patience with men whom he considered representative of the ideas and forces which had been responsible for the depression. They had run this country, and they had run it aground. Now it was "their turn to step aside and let someone else take a crack at it" [67]—take responsibility, that is, for the nation's economic stability. Professor Schlesinger called this attitude a "chilly refusal to accept busi-nessmen at their own evaluation." [68] But Tugwell did not exonerate himself, despite the circumstances of previous frustration and the un-justifiably hostile press and politicians, from responsibility for inappro-priate and unnecessary tactlessness. He remarked in retrospect that "When I first went to Washington I expected to stay only a few months. My situation was an impossible one, and I knew it. It grew worse as time went on, which made me careless, or more so than I might other-wise have been. There was no virtue and a certain unreality about my conduct . . . I was a nuisance at times, especially to Henry Wallace. My intention to leave was frustrated again and again." [69]

Considering Tugwell's career in all its aspects, we cannot attain a full understanding of why he acted as he did. Despite this limitation, and notwithstanding the caution with which we must evaluate a man's comments on his own conduct, we may find it enlightening to examine Tugwell's statements—two in particular—on the subject of motivation. Visiting England in 1927, he wrote for his own instruction and private circulation "Meditation in Stinsford Churchyard," a commentary on Thomas Hardy, his favorite author. This treatise, which Jacques Barzun praised, included these revealing remarks:

A certain deep loneliness resides in man which has awakened deep pity many times. It may be largely out of pity that poets have turned again and again to comforting those who find, at intervals, the victories a little dull, or feeble, or impertinent. Never mind, they say, there will be flower and fruit and childhood always. Your thought, your hands, even the dissolution of your body is part of a cycle. . . . And whatever you do, even if you only are, you have a contribution to make without which the race would be, by a significant measure, much the poorer.

Hardy had not this kind of pity. Fate had the power to anger him. It was pure anger, however; there was no whine in it; and no particular softness for the weakening of others. There are bleak winds that blow from eternity. But for all his large defeatist principles, he lived as though he were important, as though it always mattered what he did.[70]

In various other writings Tugwell rejected Hardy's determinism and lack of pity while sharing his anger and sense of personal worth and duty. But to Tugwell, according to views he expressed in an address at Dartmouth College in 1934, the performance of his duty, although important to society and *to* himself, was not important *for* himself in the sense of achieving, in addition to personal satisfaction, rewards and acclaim. He told the Dartmouth student body that the desire to avoid suffering in this world or punishment in the next, and the desire to survive in the race's memory and records, were inadequate incentives for making a contribution to the advancement of civilization:

To the inclination toward these attitudes I would object merely that, in your judgment, when you are old and living largely on a diet of recollection, these will not seem sufficient. You will then say that you could have lived differently and better. You will have become mellow, benevolent, and unafraid, rather than active, self-regardful, and cautious. You will say that you have not done what you should have done; that the world is not better for your having been in it; that in living for selfish certainties and an assured supply of things, you sacrificed the chance that the race to which you belong might once for all come into the promise which was set in its mind from its first appearance on this earth.

No, there is no legitimate threat that I know of. But there is the tremendous challenge of opportunity which, once it has been seen by man, has never yet failed to stir the blood. There is something deep within us which responds to the growing challenge of the tyranny of things and calls out efforts which no other reward could possibly evoke.

The incentive, I suppose, which has changed the world most, is exactly this.

To have lived—in the definition you will sometime formulate for yourselves—you must have participated livingly in the decisions of your time which matter. You must have done even more than that—you must have set your race forward in some positive way by a contribution which only you could possibly have made.[71]

There is evidence that Tugwell did not express idealistic concern for the general interest merely for public consumption. In September, 1940, he wrote to the President, requesting that at least one campaign speech rise above politics and include a statement of what America wanted in the world:

Total disarmament.
A kind of money which keeps production up and gets the goods to people.
Security against the risks of age, illness, disaster, and unemployment.
The chance to train ourselves and after that the grateful discipline of work.
Freedom of thought and speech.
A union of peoples through trade, common access to education and opinion, and free travel.

Tugwell thought Roosevelt would win the election easily, "but I know that what lies in your heart now is not that. It is where we shall be when the great showdown comes." He thought that the President "might rally unexpected forces to us, so that our might will have a great moral ally when it is next needed." [72]

There is also evidence that in his actions, as well as his words, Tugwell placed the public interest above his own. James A. Farley recalled that Tugwell never took advantage of his closeness to the President, stayed in his own backyard, and kept his hands off politics—"an example that could have been followed with profit by some of his successors." Farley found Tugwell reasonable, honest, and sincerely interested in improving economic conditions.[73] John Franklin Carter noted that Tugwell was ready to resign whenever he became an embarrassment to the administration.[74] One of the reasons Tugwell resigned in 1936 was his conclusion that his presence hurt the RA. Concerning Tugwell's service on the New York City Planning Commission, 1938-1940, Cleveland Rodgers, knowledgeable about the affairs of Gotham, concluded that Tugwell was devoted to the public interest and opposed to special interests of any kind.[75]

Of his resignation in 1946 from the governorship of Puerto Rico, Tugwell later remarked: "Realizing that my ineffectiveness in Washington [under President Truman] would be a progressive weakness Puerto Rico could ill afford, I resolved not to delay my going beyond summer."[76] He recalled his thoughts as he left Puerto Rico for the University of Chicago: "I might be forgiven, I thought, if I regarded my work in Puerto Rico, as in New York with the Planning Commission, and in Washington with the RA, as oriented against destruction. It had always been overwhelmed by those who represented a temporarily successful laissez faire. But it had been true enough. And, Chicago, I hoped, was to be its extension."[77] He also recalled that Roosevelt had preferred advice from business people and, by proxy, from Justice Brandeis to his own, "But that was his responsibility. I had done what I could. . . ."[78] "I had always given him what I had to give and had not asked anything except—and this I did not ask—to be of service."[79]

Part V
An American's Challenge to America

━━━━◆◆━━━━

25. Tugwell the "Subversive"

Tugwell's critics saw no selflessness in his motivation. In their view he strove mightily and successfully for personal power, which he used to implement his unorthodox ideas—and unorthodoxy was *ipso facto* un-American. The presentation and rebuttal of these allegations in the first three chapters of this concluding section may seem to some readers as if we are setting up a straw man. Yet, if the orthodox thinkers do not enjoy exclusive possession of patriotism, their pretension to this monopoly and the resultant charges, whether valid or not, are important historical facts.

I

Tugwell's critics traced his driving personal ambition back to 1915, when he expressed in blank verse his determination to "make America over." As a New Dealer, Tugwell often heard this somewhat theatrical composition of his college days. In 1934 Senator L. J. Dickinson (Rep., Ia.) read the poem to his colleagues.[1] H. L. Mencken paraphrased it in his column of August 17, 1936.[2] These citations implied that Tugwell saw in his association with Roosevelt an opportunity to make his youthful dreams come true. Frank Kent contrasted Tugwell's frustration during years of studying and writing and of imagining a world organized and managed according to his theories with his exhilaration as he found his ideas adopted by the President, accepted by the nation, and he, himself, in a position to play a key role in their execution—"What a transformation for this young man from his cloistered college circle to the center of power in the world! . . . What a thrill he must be having now."[3] Blair Bolles conceded that Tugwell was not enthusiastic about going to Washington in 1933 and did not enjoy his official position at first, but, Bolles explained, the delights of office-holding grew on him. Here was his chance, after years of soulful writing, to "curb, lead, regiment, and dominate" 130,000,000 people.[4] Alva Johnston asserted that "we" in Tugwell's speeches first meant Roosevelt and Tugwell, then Tugwell alone.[5]

It is difficult to tell how seriously accomplished journalists like Bolles, Kent, and Johnston, with their flair for exaggeration, took the threat of Tugwell as a potential dictator. Inevitably, some of their readers accepted their warnings at face value. On the other hand, some observers made the same charge in a satirical manner:

> The Tugwell and the Frankfurter
>   Had matters nicely planned;
> "We're what this country needs!" they said.
>   "It would be simply grand
> If Franklin D. put you and me
>   Completely in command."
>
> "If we could only work without
>   These constitutional checks,
> We might make every citizen
>   Obey our nods and becks,
> And be a little Frankfurter
>   Or else a little Rex." [6]

This ditty inadvertently indicated that the United States was still a democracy in which writers could use nicknames for high officials.

In fact, Tugwell was far from eager to go to Washington in early 1933. Entries in his diary from December, 1932, into February, 1933, show his real uncertainty as he weighed the pros and cons of following Roosevelt to the capital. He wanted to "put off the decision about government service as long as possible" (Dec. 30, 1932). In the middle of January he did not know "whether I'll be in the new government" (Jan. 13, 1933). At the end of January he recorded Moley's intention of asking for jobs for both of them—"I said, 'Not for me.' I will help in the emergency" (Jan. 31, 1933). In February, Tugwell noted that "I can be Assistant Secretary of Commerce, Tariff Commissioner, or Federal Trade Commissioner. I'll think it over a while; from professor to the government is a great transformation" (Feb. 10, 1933). "If I am in the administration," he told himself two days later, "I'll have to make endless compromises—a far different position from that of critical observer" (Feb. 12, 1933). In the middle of February Nicholas Murray Butler advised Tugwell not to make a formal connection with the government, but on the same day Tugwell wrote, "I seem to have capitulated on going to Washington" (Feb. 15, 1933).

There is also evidence that before he went to Washington, and after he got there, Tugwell did not expect to stay very long. On March 17, 1933, after the farm bill went to Congress, Tugwell wrote the President, "Now if we can do as much for consumers with a new Food and Drug act I can return happily to academic life!" [7] In requesting a leave of absence for the fall semester of 1933, he wrote Dean H. E. Hawkes of Columbia College that he was not sure when his work in Washington would be finished.[8] In December, 1933, he informed the owners of his New York apartment that he hesitated to remove his furniture because he did not know when he would return to Columbia.[9] At about the same time he requested leave of absence for the spring semester, adding, "further into the future I can not see very clearly." [10]

The months and the years slipped by, leaving Tugwell enmeshed in his governmental activities. It was especially difficult for him to disentangle himself after the spring of 1935, when he became Resettlement Administrator, responsible for setting up a new agency and getting it on its feet. Nor would he withdraw against Roosevelt's wishes, as he indicated in a letter to Butler in January, 1936: "It is my desire to return to the University. My hesitation involves no lack of loyalty; merely a feeling that the situation has become more complex than can be resolved by a simple decision flowing from my own wishes." [11] In February, replying to an inquiry from Butler, Roosevelt expressed his attitude, thanking Butler for the use of Tugwell's services and explaining that "because of our Constitution (in which I still believe) no one can tell who will be responsible for the Resettlement Administration after January 20, 1937. To lose Tugwell before that time, however, would really seriously affect government work. . . ." [12] At the end of February Columbia granted Tugwell a third leave of absence.[13]

As for the contention that Tugwell found his work in Washington a sheer delight, there is counter evidence that he was by no means ecstatic as he performed his official duties. His diary shows that as early as April 2, 1933, he was having a rough time of it and expecting more of the same: "Regulatory acts always cause friction. I have been criticized in the House already. . . . I will be unpopular in the Department when the reorganization bill comes up. This and the necessity for economy will make my position difficult, even useless. I shall be a soldier and do what seems best." On April 14 he recorded this attitude: "While I am in this, I suppose I may as well see it through as best I can." If, in Blair Bolles's opinion, this initial uneasiness gradually gave way to delight, James A. Farley, who conferred with Tugwell a number of times, found him apparently unhappy in public life.[14] Tugwell himself, reviewing a book in 1948, remarked, "His book came out of a Washington experience which evidently was not a happy one—as whose, for that matter, ever is?" [15]

In any event, Tugwell's foes held that he assiduously strove for power and that his quest for dominance was successful. In 1934 David Lawrence asserted that the Brain Trust controlled the making of laws.[16] In 1935 Frank Kent stated that "officially" Tugwell came to the capital as Assistant Secretary of Agriculture, but unofficially he began as and remained a first-rank Presidential adviser.[17] In the election year of 1936 claims of Brain Trust influence focused almost exclusively on Tugwell, increasing in scope and frequency. Blair Bolles commented: "Soon Rexford in the government was by way of becoming the Government." [18] James C. Young called Tugwell the man of the hour.[19] In Alva Johnston's opinion the favorable verdict, "Well, Roosevelt has been trying to do something," was "based largely on Tugwell-inspired measures of the New Deal." [20] Lawrence proclaimed Tugwell "the true author of most of the New Deal principles of the last three years" and more dominant than ever.[21] After the election Walker S. Buel of the *Cleveland Plain Dealer* predicted that Tugwell, whose "star blazes as brightly as ever," would continue to be the "ace of the braintrusters." [22]

Commentators often treated Tugwell's statements as expressions of Roosevelt's views. There was a striking example of this even before Tugwell went to Washington. On January 26, 1933, he was interviewed by Forrest Davis of the *New York World Telegram*. In what Tugwell thought was an off-the-record conversation, Davis sought advance information on the incoming administration's policies. Tugwell outlined a seven-point program. Very quickly headlines in newspapers across the nation announced this program. *Time's* reaction was typical. The newsmagazine accepted Tugwell's views, "though he spoke only for himself," as an "authoritative reflection of the Roosevelt mind." [23] The interview, *Business Week* noted, gave Wall Street a severe attack of "jitters." [24] When *The Industrial Discipline* appeared in the spring of 1933, some of Tugwell's critics recommended it as a guide to New Deal legislation. When he expressed his personal long-run views on international trade in a speech at Rome in October, 1934, the press assumed that the address indicated Roosevelt's views. When he referred briefly to fiscal matters in his controversial Los Angeles speech of October, 1935, newspapers played up his comments on the budget as if they were the President's.

Concerning his interview of January 26, 1933, Tugwell recalled how he "incautiously confided to Mr. Forrest Davis of Scripps-Howard, and to my confusion and chagrin it was plastered over front pages everywhere. It was not my first lesson in the irresponsibilities in public life; but it was the most embarrassing one. I was still merely an academic

Roosevelt attaché without writ or title. Ray Moley went to Warm Springs and 'fixed' it with our principal. But to this day I blush when I think of my naivety and brashness." [25] As for the claim that *The Industrial Discipline,* published a few months after the Davis interview, was a guide to New Deal legislation, C. H. McCall observed in *Credit and Financial Management,* "This is merely another example of the puerile reasoning applied to anything and everything Tugwell may do." [26]

Tugwell's articles and speeches, it is true, were sometimes subjected to advance scrutiny at the White House.[27] But usually only digests were submitted, and checks could not always be made. This incomplete kind of review left ample room for divergence from White House views or from preferences for silence on certain subjects. Thus, the President would have been just as happy if Tugwell had not made his Rome speech of October, 1934. Tugwell's Los Angeles speech of October, 1935, proved particularly thorny. On November 1, in a long letter to Roosevelt, Tugwell said that he was "terribly disturbed" that his fiscal references embarrassed the President. He went on to explain: "I still don't understand why it should have happened in view of what I actually said, its context, etc. Of course, the news reports must have perverted its meaning. What I actually said was only an incidental part of a speech in which I made the strongest plea I could for progressive unity under your leadership. . . . Anyway, I am embarrassed beyond telling that it should have been thought any kind of a prediction or official estimate. I guess the mistake was to use any figures. . . . Good intentions are no excuse I know. But anyway I claim them." Tugwell covered his letter with a note to Margaret LeHand: "Dear Missy, Will you give the enclosed to the President. . . . I'm scared to come home in view of what the newspapers have done to me again. But really everything is not so bad. Thanks, Rex." [28]

Louis Hacker concluded that conservative critics gave the "sometimes unguarded and often airily delivered" statements of New Dealers much greater significance than they merited. Hacker specifically mentioned Hugh Johnson and Tugwell.[29] In 1937 Tugwell himself, in a letter to the President, remarked, "There was a time, now happily past, when everything I said was immediately attributed to you. That cramped my style more than you know; and it caused you, I am sure, a lot more embarrassment than you let on." [30] On the other hand, Roosevelt, apparently amused at declarations in the press that Tugwell was the real power in the New Deal, once told Tugwell to keep his sense of reality and to remember the source.[31]

Many critical commentators, and some friendly ones, concluded that Tugwell often acted as well as spoke for the President. Not only was he the uncontrolled creator and designer of the AAA, the NRA, the CCC, the "Tugwell bill" for food and drugs, and the RA, but his dominance extended into many other fields. Ernest K. Lindley credited Tugwell with preparing a plan for stabilizing the dollar.[32] Ruth Finney, a Scripps-Howard staff writer, reported that he drafted the administration's power program.[33] There were reports that he determined railroad policies, and *Time* listed him as an important delegate to the London Economic Conference.[34] It was not always easy to tell just how much Tugwell had to do with the formulation of some policies because he was often, as he recalled, "in and around" many important discussions.[35] His only connection with monetary matters was his arranging for certain professors to give their views to Roosevelt. As for power policy, Tugwell remembered that the President invited him to sit in as an observer at a conference in Warm Springs of the Federal Power Commissioners. Roosevelt, with Tugwell seated beside him, then answered reporters' questions, ending each remark with "Isn't that right, Rex?" Tugwell's affirmations were his contribution to power policy.[36] Similarly, his contribution to railroad policy was his mere presence at a conference of the Interstate Commerce Commissioners at Roosevelt's New York City residence in January, 1933.[37] He did not attend the London Economic Conference. He did participate in the preliminary preparations, it is true, but primarily as Moley's assistant—and Moley did not determine United States policy at London.

Walker S. Buel inadvertently illustrated these overestimations when he wrote that Tugwell's "star blazes as brightly as ever" more than two years after it had begun to fade and less than two weeks before Tugwell resigned. Nevertheless, the net effect of exaggerations of Tugwell's influence, whether or not they resulted from honest mistakes, was the widely held belief that he was the dominating figure in the New Deal. A letter to the editor of the *New York Times* in early 1936 expressed this belief forthrightly: "The newspaper report that Professor Tugwell has been lent to the United States by Columbia University for another year came as a shock to me. I had been under the impression that the United States had been lent to Columbia University for experiments by Professor Tugwell." [38]

There were some denials, both contemporary and later, that Tugwell dominated the New Deal. *Business Week* commented in March, 1933, that the President's "classroom cabinet" commanded his "ear but not his decisions," providing him with "facts and broad conclusions which he accepts or rejects." [39] In 1935 the *New Republic* asserted that the degree to which Roosevelt's policies departed from Tugwell's ideas was "patent to every observer not blinded by Tory high blood pressure." [40] In 1938 Frank Knox referred to "all the so-called conspirators," judging their advice subordinate to the desires, aims, and purposes of only one man—the President.[41] In 1940 Joseph Alsop and Robert Kintner mentioned Hull's defeat of Moley, Tugwell, and Peek on the question of trade policy.[42] In 1941 *Current Biography* remarked that Tugwell opposed internationalism, argued for very rapid expenditure of public works appropriations, fought for consumer protection, and was "defeated on all scores." [43] These disavowals, however, did not receive the wide circulation that the opposing claims in the newspapers enjoyed, and the image of Tugwell as a powerful personage persisted through the years following his resignation. In 1943, according to Oswald Villard, many reactionaries in Congress regarded Tugwell as the real author of the New Deal.[44]

The specific key to Tugwell's power, in the opinion of those who assigned him a dominating role in the New Deal, was his intellectual domination of the President. His article, "The Ideas behind the New Deal," in the *New York Times Magazine* of July 16, 1933, convinced Frank Kent that Tugwell had laid down the New Deal program of which Roosevelt "had no idea" on March 4, 1933.[45] Alva Johnston attributed Tugwell's influence, which had produced "profound" changes in Roosevelt, to a hypnotic persuasiveness in tête-à-têtes.[46] Peter Crosby, in his campaign diatribe of 1936, *Three Cheers for the Red, Red, and Red,* asserted that Tugwell did Roosevelt's thinking for him.[47]

Blair Bolles diluted Tugwell's intellectual influence somewhat by listing him, Frankfurter, Wallace, Frank, Herman Oliphant, and Thurman Arnold as the intellectual writers who defined New Deal democracy—spending, expertise, and centralization. They were "philosophers who prompted Franklin Roosevelt to climb a political peak in Darien and drove him to exploration far into the new world they showed him." [48] Bolles neglected to point out that Tugwell and the trustbusters—Frankfurter, Oliphant, and Arnold—could not have described this new world in similar terms. Joseph B. Ely, a conservative Massachusetts Democrat, likewise had Tugwell sharing intellectual domination of the New Deal with others, especially Wallace and Ickes.[49] Kent was inconsistent with his conclusion of 1933 when he wrote, in early 1935, that changes in Roosevelt's ideas and policies were due to the influence of several Progressive Republicans in the Senate and the Cabinet, Keynes, and Tugwell. He ascribed these changes to "the combination of all these elements rather than to one." Two months later Kent noted that Keynes, La Follette, Norris, and Tugwell changed the President into a spender.[50] In addition to diluting Tugwell's influence, Kent and Bolles became entangled in other self-contradictions. In May, 1935, Kent called wholesale attacks on the administration off the target because the New Dealers and Brain Trusters "were all subordinates." [51] Bolles observed that Tugwell was as "charmed" by Roosevelt's experimental approach as Roosevelt was by his economic thought.[52]

Two assumptions underlying allegations of Tugwell's intellectual domination of Roosevelt were that the President was intellectually shallow, and that the professors in his inner circle had exclusive access to his ear. In the 1930's and afterward it became commonplace among anti-New Dealers to hold that Roosevelt knew little about economics and took his cue in this area from his advisers. Professor Daniel Fusfeld, in *The Economic Thought of Franklin D. Roosevelt and the Origins of the New Deal*,[53] showed that Roosevelt had good academic training in economics. He continued to read and study in the field after graduation. Before he became Governor, he displayed some familiarity with economic concepts that became important in the New Deal: deficit spending, regional planning, the "yardstick" approach to controlling private profits, and a "concert of interests" among economic groups. His governorship foreshadowed significant phases of the New Deal. He advocated social security, extensive public relief, public power projects, and labor's right to organize and bargain collectively.

Perhaps it was just as well that Roosevelt's training in economics at Harvard, which included courses in currency legislation and the economics of transportation, banking, and corporations, was not more thorough —insofar as additional training might have imbued him with classical convictions. The classical economists had little to offer in 1933. Roosevelt recalled, "I took economics courses in college for four years, and everything I was taught was wrong." [54] It should be said, however, that there was little likelihood of his becoming a doctrinaire adherent of classical economics since his intellect was not given to full acceptance of any system of thought. Roosevelt discovered the inadequacy of classical economics long before he met the Brain Trusters. "Tugwell's perception of one of the main causes of the depression in the failure of the capitalistic system to distribute the surplus piled up by the astonishing growth of industrial efficiency in the nineteen-twenties harmonized," Ernest K. Lindley pointed out, "with Mr. Roosevelt's own observations." [55] Roosevelt, John Franklin Carter noted, saw the causes of the depression as human and psychological rather than natural or physical before Moley ever brought Tugwell to Hyde Park.[56]

As for Roosevelt's general philosophy of political economy, Lindley maintained that it antedated both the political opportunities of the depression and the summoning of the professors to Hyde Park and Albany in 1932. Roosevelt, Lindley wrote, "though some were slow to believe it . . . had developed his fundamental attitude toward the American experiment long before he met the first member of the group which came to be known as the brains trust." [57] Elsewhere Lindley commented that the Governor "did not recruit his professional advisers to provide him with a point of view; he drew them to him because their point of view was akin to his own." [58] In *After Seven Years* Moley "agrees with Lindley" that long before the depression Roosevelt had adopted a point of view which the professors "had to match." [59] In an article of 1953 Tugwell traced Roosevelt's basic philosophy back to childhood. Later experiences, including the struggle for recovery from infantile paralysis, simply reinforced this philosophy, for the "inner convictions which made Franklin Roosevelt the instrument of his nation's return to health were his own. They were so sturdy and fully fed, so ardently and with such artfulness fought for, that they can only have been the extension of his own nature, at last come to full ripeness through suffering, contemplation, and conviction, but not created by those experiences." [60]

In referring to Roosevelt's customary practice of obtaining the advice of a great many types of individuals,[61] Lindley refuted the second assumption underlying allegations of Tugwell's intellectual domination of the President—the supposition that the President consulted only the professors. Tugwell himself recalled that the Brain Trust grew, adding to its ranks a number of "orthodox, business-minded people." [62] Indeed, in the end these late-comers defeated the professors because Roosevelt determined that they should. But to hold that the professors did not dominate the President or determine New Deal policies in the manner popularly ascribed to them is not to deny that they had a lot of work to do. Their task, Lindley remarked, was to learn the main trends of Roosevelt's thought and discover the kind of information he wanted in order that he might enlarge and co-ordinate his knowledge of economics. They had to help him apply his philosophy to the specific conditions of 1932 and 1933. They worked hard in giving force and direction to Roosevelt's general interpretations. As a result of these efforts, Tugwell became, in Lindley's words, "the philosopher, the sociologist, and the prophet of the Roosevelt Revolution, as well as one of its boldest practitioners. He had provided the movement with much of its rationale (to use one of his favorite words)." [63]

But Tugwell, and Moley, knew who was boss. Moley recalled wondering in early 1933 whether a possible reason for Roosevelt's stand on the Stimson Doctrine was a desire to prove independence of any one kind of advice or any adviser at all. Moley, "God knew, required no such proof. . . ." In *After Seven Years* Moley also briefly described Roosevelt's manner of mental activity, indicating that the professors' function was an educative one, with Roosevelt making the final decisions. The President, Moley noted, showed an astonishing energy and vitality and an amazing interest in things as he skipped and bounced through seemingly intricate subjects. He got most of his information from talking to people, storing away the "net" of each conversation. This approach to many subjects at various levels through the Socratic method seemed "to give Tugwell some worries because he wants people to show familiarity with pretty elementary ideas," but Moley considered Roosevelt's lack of dogmatism, compared to Hoover's imprisonment by his own knowledge, a virtue in 1932 and 1933.[64]

Tugwell did not write about this educative process until the late 1940's. He did declare in 1935 that the New Deal was no "academic brainstorm . . . no group of pallid professors enacted its main features." [65] In his later writings he went into more detail about the intellectual relationship between the President and the professors. In an article, "The Progressive Orthodoxy of Franklin D. Roosevelt," Tugwell stated that the phraseology of Roosevelt's 1932 campaign speeches indicated the results of the professors' educative efforts. That is, Roosevelt "sometimes spoke with the voice of a learning we made available" when he summarized information with which the professors provided him in phrases which they suggested. This did not mean that the Brain Trusters transformed his basic general views. Tugwell took no pride in the candidate's use of his data and words: "The creation was not ours. We were merely the middlemen of modernism. . . ." [66] In "The Two Great Roosevelts" Tugwell compared Franklin's talents with words unfavorably with Uncle Ted's, but to refer to the Democratic Roosevelt's use of literary people in the preparation of speeches was "not to say that the policies they expressed were anyone else's, for they were not . . . the future President was his own man." [67]

In "The Preparation of a President" Tugwell systematically analyzed the professors' experience as educators from March to November, 1932, when he, Moley, and the others spent the "most gruelling six months of our lives having part of that candidate's education dug out of our entrails." Gradually the Brain Trusters "learned . . . the trick of moving with his mind and supplying its needs." This meant learning how to desystematize. Pieces of theory which the professors threw out or relations which they suggested sometimes attracted Roosevelt's notice, "but the tapestry of the policy he was weaving was guided by a conception which was not made known to us." There was "no question in anyone's mind of sharing Mr. Roosevelt's generalship." [68] No one knew this better than Tugwell himself. In May, 1933, he received a copy of a letter in which the President assured Senator F. R. Duffy (Dem., Wis.) that professors did not run the government.[69] And he was aware, he recalled, that the more attention he got in the press, the less influence he actually had.[70]

II

In the eyes of his critics, who ignored evidence to the contrary, the Tugwell phenomenon, as we have seen, was simple: his main motivation was his desire for power, this desire was fulfilled by his acquisition of power, and this acquisition was effected through his intellectual domination of the President. This clear-cut image raises the obvious question of what Tugwell planned to achieve through the exercising of his prodigious power. His critics, naturally, did not neglect this question. They often charged that he was a serious threat to the American way of life, a dangerous advocate of revolution and political and economic dictatorship. A statement of Alva Johnston's in the *Saturday Evening Post* in 1936 amounted to a concise summary of these charges. According to Johnston, Tugwell, in his speeches, rolled up his sleeves, dismissed the Constitution and existing institutions, abolished property and profit, organized all activities into government monopolies, and planned every man's life and forcibly made him comfortable and happy.[71]

Johnston's ability to read clearly the revolutionary import of Tugwell's speeches was not unique. It was obvious, an industrialist stated in 1934, that the young intellectuals in Washington, led by Tugwell, thought they could make the world over in a day; they did not understand that we progress through evolution, not revolution.[72] Blair Bolles remarked in September, 1936, that Tugwell had been disgusted with democracy since 1932.[73] A corporation executive of Wilmington, Delaware, did not have to read Tugwell's words; he could identify a subversive just by looking at him. An acquaintance of Jerome Frank's from the latter's days as a corporation lawyer, this gentleman returned to Wilmington after a visit to Washington and sent a telegram to Frank: BEWARE COMMA JEROME BEWARE STOP THIS MORNING AT YOUR BREAKFAST TABLE I SAW THE FACE OF ROBESPIERRE STOP THAT MAN WOULD WILLINGLY GO TO THE GUILLOTINE FOR AN IDEAL AND TAKE HIS FRIENDS WITH HIM STOP BEWARE. One evening as they were driving home, Frank read the telegram. Tugwell, usually a careful driver, swung a corner without signaling and grazed a curb. He said it was a hell of a life when idiots came in to look at you and then just said what they read in the papers. "In any event," Frank replied, "you drive like Robespierre."[74]

Tugwell's fighting address, couched in military terms, to the Democratic State Central Committee at Los Angeles in October, 1935, evoked more flat accusations that he was an advocate of class warfare and violent revolution than any other of his public statements. Fred R. Marvin, author of a campaign bromide in 1936, considered this address a clear indication of the Communist connections of the New Deal.[75] Elizabeth

Dilling, in *The Roosevelt Red Record and Its Background,* which she published herself in 1936, labeled this speech a "Call to the Barricades." [76] Alva Johnston treated the revolutionary implications of this talk by Tugwell with irony: "No bloodshed . . . Not even a chairman of the board is to be slain in his bed. Tugwell is a great peace lover, like Benvolio, who used to enter a tavern swishing a sword and slapping it on the table, with the exclamation, 'God send me no need of thee!' " [77] Raoul Desvernine, a spokesman for the Liberty League, commented on Tugwell's Los Angeles address in a campaign piece of 1936, *Democratic Despotism* —his version of Tugwell's "democratic discipline." The speech suggested to Desvernine the mood of Mussolini just before the March on Rome, of the Bolsheviki in 1917, and of Hitler in the late 1920's. It was the "most startling and challenging" discourse by a New Dealer to date, coming from the "boldest, the most outspoken" of Roosevelt's prophets, the "psychoanalyst" of the New Deal. And, Desvernine noted, Tugwell had not been repudiated by the President. [78]

Obviously, Tugwell's foes considered the Los Angeles talk clear evidence of his revolutionary intentions. Thus, according to the theory of the functioning of a free press in a democracy, there was little to fear from Tugwell. Being a known revolutionary, he could be watched closely. As Alva Johnston put it, Tugwell, like the American Communist leader William Z. Foster, was a man whose books prematurely gave away his schemes and whose big talk interfered with big acts. [79] But a number of his critics still professed to fear Tugwell as the leader of a subtle, silent, secret revolution.

Time, in March, 1936, itself called Tugwell a "Parlor Pink" but quoted Representative Hamilton Fish, Jr. (Rep., N. Y.), who contended that the open attacks by Communists against American institutions were far less dangerous than the subtle and insidious attacks by New Deal spokesmen such as Tugwell. [80] Percy L. Crosby, in his *Three Cheers for the Red, Red, and Red,* maintained that Roosevelt was not a socialist but an "agitator of the worst sort." He pointed to Tugwell as the real mastermind of the New Deal, warning the people not to permit "Roosevelt (Tugwell)" to think for them. Crosby concluded his chapter on "The Constitution and Tugwell" with this prediction, italicized: "*A vote for Roosevelt in 1936 is a vote for bloodshed in 1937.*" [81] Crosby, too, feared Tugwell as the power behind the throne. Mark Sullivan, columnist and confidant of Herbert Hoover, was the most persistent proponent of the "secret revolution" thesis. In a series of columns in the *New York Herald Tribune* in December, 1933, he repeatedly declared that Tugwell was the leader of a group of young intellectuals who were "gradually" and "quietly" transforming the familiar American type of social organization into one which the word "Russian" described best. Tugwell and his followers, Sullivan alleged, were able to bring about a silent revolution because they had gotten hold of the "key places in government." Sullivan demanded publicity about the revolution in order that the public might be able to see the struggle and choose sides. When the activities of the twenty or thirty young radicals, typified and led by Tugwell, were made known, there could then be a roll call in Congress for or against Tugwell's "Workers' World." [82]

Tugwell the revolutionary—open or secret or both—could logically be expected to destroy the Constitution. Again, Tugwell's subversive intentions were both apparent and hidden. In Desvernine's opinion, careful consideration of Tugwell's statements made it obvious that constitutional limitations gave the crusading doctor no great concern.[83] Senator L. J. Dickinson (Rep., Ia.) saw in Tugwell's writings an eagerness to get at the Constitution first in a *tour de force* aimed at overthrowing precedents and changing the government once and for all.[84] David Lawrence cited Tugwell's remarks on the confusion of ends with means, and on the emotional attachment to the instruments of social life which resulted in some Americans' "unreasoning, almost hysterical" attachment to the Constitution, as proof of the professor's dangerous disregard for precedents.[85] Blair Bolles, on the other hand, thought that the key to Tugwell's success was his outward obeisance to the Constitution, his public pretensions of respect for democracy. Tugwell's theology was orthodox, but his practice was irregular, "like a Renaissance cardinal with children." [86]

Tugwell's commencement address at the University of New Mexico in June, 1935, "Your Future and Your Nation," included some references to judicial review and the regulation of industry amid changing conditions. In this address, according to Desvernine, Tugwell showed defiance and contempt for law in expressing his impatience with judicial restraints which prevented the acceptance of his views.[87] Frank Kent commented that Tugwell's "disturbing" New Mexico speech was the kind of statement which would make it impossible for Democratic allegiance to the Constitution and respect for the Supreme Court to go unquestioned during the campaign of 1936.[88] Blair Bolles summarily dismissed Tugwell's contention that the absence of any reference in the Constitution to industry and the subsequent formulation of public policy by the courts were plain evidence of the flexibility of the Constitution. This meant, Bolles inferred, that anything which was not protected by a specific constitutional reference was subject to extermination—for example, cockroaches.[89]

The implication of Bolles's comment was that Tugwell intended to use the absence of constitutional reference to industry as the basis for economic revolution, not regulation. Desvernine drew the same conclusion regarding Tugwell's address to the Rochester, New York, Teachers Association in April, 1935: "A Third Economy." Tugwell spoke of the economic sphere which belonged neither to free enterprise nor to state socialism. What he proposed, in essence, was a permanent public-works program to absorb surplus labor into activities which were essential to the community, including business, but which would be unprofitable to private enterprise. In Desvernine's view, Tugwell's constitutional ideas would enable the arbitrary classification of enterprises as being affected with a public interest and so subject to governmental control, and the "Third Economy" would inevitably become the total economy. We would then have an entirely new social and economic order with a definite fascist orientation, for there was a striking similarity between the ideas of Mussolini—who spoke of "liberalism," "socialism," and "corporationism," the latter being "above" the first two—and Tugwell—who mentioned "socialism, individualism, and the Third Economy," the latter to "reconcile" the first two.[90]

Thus, Tugwell the revolutionary, having subverted the Constitution, would impose on the nation total economic planning akin to foreign totalitarian systems. This prognosis arose from the proposition that any planning inevitably leads to total planning. In other words, planning, as European history shows, is national socialism in its first stage. In 1935 David Lawrence, in his *Stumbling into Socialism*, pointed out that European Socialists, after believing for decades in the necessity of revolution, finally concluded that acquisition of political power rather than economic collapse was the way to victory and would enable them to prevent during the transitional period the disintegration which leads to dictatorship. New Deal philosophers entertained "somewhat the same hope," but veteran Socialists knew better. Mussolini and Kerensky had been Socialists, and Hitler had initially drawn his support from the Socialist party.[91] In the same year Herbert Agar expressed views similar to Lawrence's. He asserted that it was hypocritical of Tugwell to mention in the same book his desire to save the native American system and his idea of a planned economy, because a planned economy was synonymous with a tyrant state.[92] John T. Flynn later wrote that Tugwell's mind, "keen, busy, and widely enriched with economic and social history," had gradually infected the far less able Wallace with the idea of state planning for the welfare of all. Unfortunately, Wallace failed to recognize the basic affinity between state planning, fascism, and communism; he did not understand that "they all belong to one great generic philosophy."[93]

The assumption of an automatic planning-socialism-dictatorship sequence relieved Tugwell's foes of the task of studying his ideas in detail, and it enabled them to call him a socialist, communist, or fascist in a haphazard manner. Nevertheless, they most often attributed his thought to a Russian influence which stemmed specifically from his tour of the Soviet Union in 1927. In a speech in 1934 Tugwell said, "Seven years ago I visited Russia for two months. That visit has often been considered sufficient proof of my adherence to communism, as though communism could be caught by contagion like mumps or measles." [94] He did not exaggerate. Conservative members of Congress seemed horrified at his having been to Russia. At the time of his promotion in June, 1934, Senator Thomas D. Schall (Rep., Minn.) devoted a long speech to a description of Tugwell's collectivism as strictly a Russian plan.[95] Senator Henry D. Hatfield (Rep., W. Va.) declared that Tugwell and his kind had all but Russianized the nation.[96] Senator Arthur R. Robinson (Rep., Ind.) called Tugwell's thought "Russian communism." [97] In 1935, in the House, William H. Wilson (Rep., Pa.) referred to Tugwell's visit to Russia, labeling him an advocate of revolutionary socialism.[98] Blair Bolles called the tour of 1927 the "supreme experience" of Tugwell's personal education. "Tugwell Rex, as the New Deal's master romanticist and collectivist, was forged in Russia." Bolles conceded that it was not apparent at the time how much the trip had affected Tugwell, who "proved that he still had a good deal of the sophomore in him" by having "fun playing the bad boy away from home." Tugwell's chapter on Russian agriculture, in the book written by members of the visiting group, contained no propaganda about democratic discipline and industrial regimentation, but such propaganda, Bolles explained, appeared in his later writings "when the Russian idea had more thoroughly filtered through his romantic brain. . . ." [99]

In the early 1930's a number of anti-New Dealers saw a Russian influence, which they attributed to Tugwell, in the AA Act. Representative Wilson, in a speech just quoted, called him "Assistant Commissar of Agriculture." [100] Charges that Tugwell aped the Russians also included specific references to his remarks on industrial planning. This did not surprise Tugwell, who, in 1932, had quoted a statement by President Hoover in 1931 as typical of many politicians' penchant for dismissing any suggestion of planning as a dangerous infection from Russia.[101] David Lawrence and James C. Young were shocked at Tugwell's suggestion in a textbook (*American Economic Life and the Means of Its Improvement*, 3rd ed., 1930, 711-12) that the challenge to America of developments in Russia lay neither in comparative standards of living, alleged or actual merits of the Russian scheme, nor in agreement or disagreement with Russia's philosophy; it lay, rather, in the idea of planning—the demonstration of man's ability intelligently to control economic forces for the achievement of desired ends, as a substitute for an outdated laissez faire philosophy.[102]

The particular part of Tugwell's Los Angeles speech of October, 1935, which evoked charges that he imitated the Russians was his call for resistance to the Republicans' attempt to separate the two great groups which had benefited most from New Deal policies. He told the Democratic leaders of California to forge a "farmer-worker alliance in this country which will carry all before it." [103] This statement, in Frank Kent's opinion, expressed the viewpoint of the school of New Deal politicians who saw the way to victory in 1936 in a bold summons to the farmers and the workers to rally against the bourgeoisie and support Tugwell's "new order"—a dictatorship with total planning.[104] According to Raoul Desvernine, Tugwell had picked up in Russia the communistic concept of a combination of farmers and workers bringing about a new social and economic order.[105] Garet Garrett of the *Saturday Evening Post* noted the similarity between Tugwell's remarks in Los Angeles and some statements in early March, 1936, by Earl Browder and the *Daily Worker*. Garrett also pointed out that in order to assure the triumph of Communism, Lenin had grafted onto Marxism the policy of "Smychka" —the Russian word denoting the theoretical community of interests of workers and peasants. "Smychka," of course, required the re-education of the peasants.[106]

In two cases charges against Tugwell of subversion received especially intensive and wide publicity. These instances involved Dr. William A. Wirt, Superintendent of Schools in Gary, Indiana, in 1934, and George Peek, whose book, *Why Quit Our Own*, written in collaboration with Samuel Crowther, appeared in 1936 after pre-publication release in May and June in the form of six articles, entitled "In and Out," in the *Saturday Evening Post*. Wirt's charges became public in April, 1934, when he put them in a letter and sent it to various persons, adding that he had not written his accusations for publication but that recipients were free to make use of his letter in any way they saw fit. James H. Rand, Jr., Chairman of the Committee for the Nation, offered Wirt's letter to a Congressional committee as evidence of a conspiracy in government, thereby touching off a storm of controversy. There are numerous accounts of this incident, including an objective summary of the charges and denials in the *New York Times*.[107] Here we shall follow James C. Young's anti-administration account in his *Roosevelt Revealed* in order to present Wirt's case in its most forceful form.[108]

Wirt's charges consisted of revelations made to him by certain youthful satellites of the Brain Trust about the secret aims of that group. Wirt's informants regarded Roosevelt as the Kerensky of the New Deal and expected a Stalin to replace him. To hasten the coming of a dictatorship, the Brain Trust intended to postpone recovery, convincing the people that government ownership was the only solution to economic problems. Then a Stalin would take over. The New Dealers' reactions to these charges, Young commented, were marked by a significant self-consciousness. Even the occasionally hysterical Washington of the early 1930's had experienced nothing like the excitement stirred up by Wirt's accusations. Young implied that the New Dealers would have appeared in a better light if they had reacted calmly to Wirt's attack. Instead, being egoists, they showed no ability to laugh at themselves. Led by Mrs. Roosevelt, they issued denials, and with "longest faces and a pompous manner" they named a special committee to investigate the charges. They also launched a pre-hearing campaign to discredit Wirt. Representative Alfred L. Bulwinkle (Dem., N. C.), Chairman of the special committee of three Democrats and two Republicans, told the House that Wirt had served time in prison during World War I for pro-German activities. Bulwinkle had to retract this statement.

At the hearing, with Wirt occasionally nodding his approval, Bulwinkle read the charges into the record. They were by no means complimentary to the President, who apparently had been duped into believing that he was making decisions for himself. The key question was, "Who was the Lenin?" Everyone saw the person of Dr. Tugwell "looming in the shadows," and Wallace came to his defense. Meanwhile, the two Republicans on the committee complained of the unfair treatment of Wirt. The New Dealers, possessing "too sure a knowledge of public psychology," arranged two hurried meetings of the committee, which then adjourned over the protest of its Republican members. Wirt fired his parting shot: "I regard Professor Tugwell as the motivating force behind the plan to overthrow our established American liberties. He is the real brains of the brain trust. The others are satellites."

During the remainder of Tugwell's stay in Washington, his foes repeated Wirt's charges that he was the Stalin or the Lenin—Lenin was historically accurate—of the New Deal. With his promotion coming up for hearing and debate, it was to be expected that the opposition would keep the kettle boiling on the issue of a Red conspiracy. Senator Hatfield entered in the *Congressional Record* an editorial from the *Washington Herald* of May 15, 1934, on Tugwellism, which the *Herald* said was so obviously revolutionary, subversive, and communistic that Wirt's accusations were unnecessary.[109] In August, 1936, Alva Johnston noted that although Wirt had failed to sustain his charges, Peek's book and other observations made it appear "highly probable that there was some sort of intrigue" in 1934.[110] As late as 1953 Fulton Lewis, Jr., stated that the subsequent uncovering of the fact that there were Communists in Washington in 1933 vindicated Wirt.[111]

George Peek, in commenting on the basic division of opinion in the AAA, identified Tugwell as the leader of the "collectivists" who were responsible for the policies which he, Peek, opposed. Peek recalled that the collectivistic group comprised a number of intense young men in the Legal and Consumers' Divisions who were determined to destroy the profit system, although they were not sure what they would do after they had accomplished this destruction. Peek deplored the status among the collectivists of Lee Pressman, noting that Tugwell took Pressman into the Resettlement Administration. Peek's only other reference to Tugwell in connection with implied allegations of subversion in *Why Quit Our Own* was a summary of a report from a friend who had attended several parties of Tugwell's and Frank's. Peek's friend, like Wirt, heard some amazing talk of a social revolution, which would begin in agriculture because in other nations farmers had been the staunchest foes of socialism.[112]

Peek's authoritative biographer, Gilbert C. Fite, stated that among the fifty-five lawyers in the AAA there were some whose economic thought was collectivistic. Disillusioned by the depression, they had "permanent" ideas about remedies for America's social and economic ailments. They were idealistic, impractical, and inexperienced. Peek, according to Fite, soon saw that the urban leftwing lawyers were attempting to employ the AAA's powers, especially its authority to license processors, for "purposes not originally contemplated." They were not just aiming for farm recovery; they sought permanent socialization of the processing and distributing business. Peek balked at incorporating their principles in AAA codes and marketing agreements, rejecting their talk and ideas as nonsense. He did not know of any actual card-carrying Communist employees in the AAA, but, Fite concluded, Peek was one of the first to notice that the reformers in Washington included men "who would solve the nation's problems in some authoritative fashion outside of the American tradition." [113]

In the 1950's investigations established that some of the Communists of the Ware cell were employees of the AAA. The Internal Security Subcommittee of the Senate Judiciary Committee listed as being among the first organized Communists in Washington these men: Harold Ware, Alger Hiss, Nathan Witt, Charles Kramer, Victor Perlo, John Abt, Henry Collins, Nathaniel Weyl, Nathan Silvermaster, William Ullmann, and Lee Pressman, the latter three having been employed at one time or another by the Resettlement Administration.[114] In July, 1936, *Time* linked Tugwell to Pressman, reporting that John L. Lewis and Tugwell had dinner together shortly before Pressman, General Counsel of the RA, began to serve the Steel Organizing Committee in the same capacity. Meanwhile, Lewis' United Mine Workers had recently raised bail for some sharecroppers arrested in Memphis, and sharecroppers, *Time* noted, were one of Tugwell's gravest concerns.[115] In 1937 Harold Ickes recorded in his diary a statement by Thomas Corcoran, who hoped Pressman "won't ruin Lewis as he . . . had almost ruined Rex Tugwell and Hopkins." [116]

We should mention an additional association of Tugwell's which occasioned comments linking him to Communism.[117] This was his support, for a time, of Henry Wallace's candidacy for the presidency in 1948 under the banner of the Progressive party. It later became generally known that there was a potent Communist influence in that organization.[118]

III

If the proposition of Tugwell's critics—that he sought and acquired immense power and exercised it with the intention of destroying the Constitution and imposing a Russian system on the nation—were valid, we would be living in the United Soviet States of America. Since we do not, we can raise at least two obvious questions about the proposition: Did Tugwell really wield stupendous power? Did he really intend to Sovietize America? A negative answer to the first question has recurred throughout this book. Perhaps we can most meaningfully summarize and underline this denial of Tugwell's power by briefly considering his evaluation of the New Deal in terms of his institutional thought with its emphasis on "social management."

In this light, Roosevelt did barely save the capitalistic system and democracy, but he "spent a lot of time . . . planting protective shrubbery on the slopes of a volcano." In *The Stricken Land* Tugwell judged the effects of his own educative efforts in this way: "I had given him the explanation he needed of the crisis of 1928-32; and naturally, since he accepted the explanation, I expected him to accept the logical resolution. The cure lay in the cause. But that was not his way, whatever had been his intention." [119] Tugwell did not oppose the Progressives' reforms as such. Except for trustbusting, they were all to the good as far as they went, but they were not genuinely vital, he stated in *The Art of Politics,* because they, and the whole New Deal, never got at the real source of difficulty—the problems arising from machine production.[120] In an article of 1941 Tugwell called trustbusting literally reactionary—an attempt to turn back the clock to a previous stage of technological development.[121] Nor were Progressive reforms and improvement in business ethics adequate for sustaining the long-run growth of the economy. Thus, the New Deal, Tugwell remarked in 1949, was never able successfully to abandon its inflationary supports.[122]

In general retrospective comments Tugwell referred to the Progressives' equipment as of 1933 as the strategies of the New Freedom and nothing more.[123] Or, as he put it elsewhere, the New Deal was just catching up with La Follette thirty years later.[124] Accordingly, it was a series of expediencies, one after another as issues arose, designed to make the old economy a going concern again. This was mild medicine considering the seriousness of the patient's sickness. It was patching the walls and roof of the national house without strengthening the foundation, because patching, Tugwell asserted, was "all the New Dealers knew how to do or all their enemies would let them do." [125] He thought this Progressive nature of the New Deal became apparent in retrospect when one could see that the differences between Democrats and Republicans were basically not so great as conflicts in campaigns seemed to indicate.[126] Against this general evaluation of the New Deal, however, Tugwell did place the prevalent acceptance of the concept of a public interest in business. At least business was public enough to be regulated negatively, if not enough to be directed positively. But even this was a far remove from 1928.[127]

Tugwell's judgment that the New Deal will go down in history as an old-fashioned Progressive patch-up of the traditonal economic system is, of course, unacceptable to those who consider the New Deal radical and Tugwell even more so. If any of these critics would give ground on part of their proposition and concede that Tugwell was not powerful, they might still maintain that one of the reasons the New Deal was not even more radical was Tugwell's inability to carry out his revolutionary plans. Thus, it remains for us to consider Tugwell's intentions in terms of his attitudes and actions with respect to Communism on the one hand and the American tradition on the other.

26. Tugwell and Communism

I

The image of Tugwell which emerges from the various charges against him is that of a revolutionary who aimed to destroy the Constitution and, following the Russian model, impose total economic planning and totalitarianism on the American people. Tugwell's intentions, moreover, were reinforced by the automaticity of the planning-socialism-dictatorship sequence. William Wirt and George Peek contributed broad strokes to this portrait, and there were some detailed lines: Communists in the AAA and the RA, particularly Lee Pressman, and the pinkish, sometimes Red, Progressive party of 1948. Turning to counter evidence which paints a quite different picture, we find in this case, as in nearly all others of its kind, that it takes longer to rebut a charge of subversion than it does to make it. Brief reference to two general points—the planning-socialism-dictatorship sequence and the climate of accusation—is a necessary preface to a rebuttal in specific terms.

Those who assumed that any economic planning automatically led to total planning and dictatorship drew analogies between the histories of certain European nations and made the further assumption that the patterns they saw in European history were universal axioms, that they would apply to all countries, including the United States. David Lawrence drew parallels between the histories of Italy, Germany, and Russia, which was perhaps justifiable at a superficial level—fascism is gangsterized capitalism and communism is gangsterized socialism. There was also some substance to John T. Flynn's contention that the totalitarian systems all sprang from "one great generic philosophy." They did have at least two traits in common: they placed the state above the individual, and they claimed to be riding the "wave of the future," to be in tune with an inexorably unfolding pattern of history. But, as Professor William Ebenstein has pointed out, there are more sophisticated distinctions between the various isms which may be made "through the *way of life* concept rather than through one particular aspect such as government or economics." [1]

Ebenstein's *way of life* approach suggests that Lawrence and Flynn were dealing with effects rather than causes. It was not that totalitarianism inevitably resulted from planning. It was, rather, that the whole planning-socialism-dictatorship sequence resulted from a particular nation's unique nature and historical experience. To deny this was, as Walter Lippmann asserted in 1935, to take for granted "something ex-

tremely improbable, namely that nations which have had different histories will henceforth have the same future." To accept Lawrence's and
Flynn's sequence, Lippmann went on to say, would be to deprive
democracy of its flexibility, leaving it helpless in a crisis. Those who took
this rigid view renounced their "title to govern a modern democratic
state." [2] In short, Lippmann rejected as invalid the attempts by Lawrence, Flynn, Hoover, and others to draw analogies between European
and American history. He also agreed, in effect, with Tugwell's anti-
deterministic contention that no one could blueprint the future.

What we have referred to as the climate of accusation was a product
of the depression. When the American economy broke down, it was not
unusual for people in all walks of life to criticize the traditional economic
system. A very small minority of the critics became Communists, and
a very small minority of the Communists became subversives. The subversives created a difficult problem in a democracy which wished to remain a democracy while defending itself against an internal and international conspiracy. This problem was aggravated by reformers who
carelessly pooh-poohed any references to Communists in government,
and by die-hard conservatives who were inclined to lump almost any
advocate of reform together with the Communists, engaging in a kind
of verbal vigilantism without waiting for official proof of their direct and
indirect charges. It was unrealistic to maintain that there were no subversives, and it was not in the democratic tradition to label everyone
who had ever worn a red necktie a subversive. The challenge to a
democracy was to identify the right, or wrong, people in the right way
by means of established public agencies and Congressional committees
using fair procedures. Unfortunately, irresponsibility was the order of
the day. Loose accusations unnecessarily created fear and divisiveness
in American society at a time when it could use all the stability it could
muster in facing its trying problems.

Congressional committees were as irresponsible as various commentators and the public at large. In 1938 the Dies Committee to Investigate
Un-American Activities allowed unscreened witnesses to denounce their
enemies as Red sympathizers, and the press gave elaborate coverage
to even the most fantastic portions of this testimony.[3] Governor Frank
Murphy of Michigan was an example of an unimpeachable target for
lurid charges. In the 1950's, amid the frustrations and bewilderment of
the Cold War, Senator Joseph R. McCarthy used the shot-gun accusation of subversion with devastating effects on national morale and unity.
His supporters contended that he drew attention to a serious problem,
but the burden was on them to show that this could not have been done
in a responsible way. We are getting ahead of our time, but the fact to
note here is the hysteria which has been both a cause and an effect of

attempts in America to deal with subversion—in the 1920's (the Red Scare), the 1930's, and the 1950's. It should also be pointed out that the prevalence of the loose accusation in the 1950's, when Communists of the 1930's were identified, resulted in its retroactive application—to Tugwell's detriment. Thus, Fulton Lewis, Jr., could say that the revelations of the 1950's confirmed Wirt, even though the Republicans had won the White House and Tugwell, the Lenin of the New Deal, having failed to bring off the revolution and eliminate the opposition, was teaching at the University of Chicago.

One can readily understand that in the kind of reaction to real and imagined subversion which America has periodically experienced, the lunatic fringe, as well as fishers in muddy waters like McCarthy and die-hards like Mark Sullivan, will be active. Percy Crosby and Elizabeth Dilling qualify for this category, along with Gerald Winrod, author of *Communism and the Roosevelt Brain Trust*.[4] Winrod has been grouped with the likes of Fritz Kuhn and William Dudley Pelley as a breeder of hate and poison among his fellow men.[5] It is not surprising to find Winrod quoting Elizabeth Dilling's descriptions of Stuart Chase as a "long-time subversive" and Donald Richberg as a "leading red light."[6] Unfortunately, we also find Representative William Wilson, who called Tugwell "Assistant Commissar of Agriculture," quoting the Dilling book of biographical sketches in his anti-Tugwell speech to the House.[7] But few of Tugwell's critics were in the lunatic fringe, and, in any event, *argumentum ad hominem* is an indirect and inadequate defense. There are direct answers to the charges against Tugwell.

II

Tugwell's observations on "Russian Agriculture" were published in 1928,[8] a year after the Russian tour which his critics often pointed to as the source of his collectivistic ideas. One of the obvious aspects of Tugwell's critique—a chapter in *Soviet Russia in the Second Decade*—is that he was writing as a social scientist in whose view any social phenomenon was a proper subject for scholarly examination. Qualifications characteristic of the academic approach occurred throughout his report. At the beginning he stipulated that the tests of success of Russia's rural economic policies would "have to be kept pretty much on the objective levels susceptible of investigation to the outsider." He remarked that because his time in Russia had been short, there would be gaps and misinterpretations. He continually injected a note of caution with regard to various details. He stated, for example, with respect to the collective farm system, "it must be admitted that reports differ." Another passage showed his awareness of investigatory problems: "Apparently the gathering of prices in central localities and the construction of indexes from them would lead to the conclusion that the Russian peasants are much better off than they are actually. Suspicion of such general figures is justifiable. No real notion of the situation can be got without the use of indexes constructed from figures actually taken on the ground." Tugwell also recognized that since he had had no previous experience with Russian life, he could not tell what had been lost. He concluded his study on a typically academic note. A series of trifles taken together, he observed, amounted to a stirring of new life hardly yet come to birth, but held close within the strong peasant culture. "What will be its maturity no one knows."

Another conspicuous theme in Tugwell's chapter was his emphasis on the differences between conditions and problems in the U.S.S.R. and those in the U.S.A. He found the rural standard of living in Russia depressed beyond Americans' comprehension. The disadvantageous price position of the peasants, he wrote, involved "less ability to buy furniture, soap, textiles, and other amenities of civilization upon which our own rural population has come to depend. But if one thinks himself back about fifty years in America, he will realize that most of these were then produced locally here. And this is the present situation in Russia." In the 1930's the picture in Tugwell's mind was one of a Russian agricultural problem—underproduction—exactly the reverse of the American.

Tugwell's chapter also showed that his call for farmer-labor unity in his Los Angeles speech of 1935 had nothing to do with what he had seen in Russia in 1927. This was not the first time he made such a plea—in July, 1934, he had accused the "Tories" of "trying to array labor against the farmers, with the sole if unconfessed object of perpetuating the speculative conditions" which "Tories" exploited.[9] Nor was he the first to make it. There had been farmer-labor political movements in the United States since some time before the Russian revolution. They had not, it is true, attained national significance. In 1933, in the 73rd Congress, there was only one Farmer-Labor Senator, Henrik Shipstead of Minnesota, and only five Farmer-Labor Representatives, all from Minnesota. The point to note here is that Tugwell made his plea on behalf of an administration which, as he indicated in his Los Angeles address, had helped both farmers and workers in an undoctrinaire way. In Russia the situation in 1927 was quite different. Marx had not provided the leaders of the revolution with any doctrinal guidance on policy for rural Russia, but this policy was, nevertheless, indirectly shaped by doctrine—the Marxist concern with the urban worker. Thus, Tugwell noted in his essay of 1928, the peasant "has a serious economic handicap in any economic struggle which may come. . . . The government of Russia is a dictatorship of the proletariat; and all the recent talk about united 'workers and peasants' cannot alter the fundamental fact of institutions managed, so far as is expedient, for the enhancement of the proletarian power."

Tugwell explained in some detail the "serious discriminations" which the peasant suffered in credit, tax, and price policies. He conceded that there had been some encouragement of agriculture since the period of military communism, when the Soviet government had looked upon rural districts as colonies to be exploited, but a vigorous dissenting group, including Trotsky, disputed the wisdom of this change. At any rate, "the greatest benefits have undoubtedly gone to city workers so far." Nor could it be "disguised that heavy burdens are borne in the service of the socialistic ideal. It would seem, also, in the face of it, that they are borne most heavily by the peasants." Thus, the peasants had supported the revolution only to find themselves in what Tugwell called an anomalous position in a socialistic state.

When the Soviet government abolished peasant home industry in 1928, Tugwell called this action, which came at a time when difficulties in grain collection were most acute, an astonishing, contradictory, and ruthless suppression of the one factor which made the goods famine endurable to the peasant.[10] In responding to such measures, the peasant proved a formidable fighter. This did not surprise Tugwell, who had stated in his account of his observations of 1927 that the peasant employed "the tactic of a fighter who opposes his adversary's skill with a steady resistance to punishment, and who, when fatigue has become his ally, wins without recourse to strategy. This describes, precisely, rural Russia." The peasant was still winning in 1961 when Tugwell judged the Russian system a failure in agriculture. Communization of farming, he wrote, created problems of overmanning, incentives, and delegation of authority which the Russians had not been able to solve. While we had our difficult surplus problem, we were successful in terms of national productivity. The American solution was not perfect, but it did "have the advantage of flexibility; it allows technical considerations to determine the size of units and the amounts of capital to be applied. Furthermore, it provides for delegation of authority in a way that bureaucracies have not been able to match." [11]

Internal analysis of Tugwell's report of his trip to Russia in 1927 does not indicate in any way that he had lost faith in the American creed of freedom or was sympathetic with revolutionary tactics. Russell Lord wrote that Tugwell was sympathetic to the march away from family-line Czarism but critical of the regimentation of the Russian system.[12] John Franklin Carter stressed Tugwell's academic function and attitude as an "interested observer" of the Soviet experiment.[13] Senator Josiah Bailey (Dem., N. C.), in accusing Tugwell of seeking to regiment American farming, conceded that Tugwell's comments on Russian agriculture did not justify any suspicion that he had absorbed the Russian leaders' views.[14] *Newsweek* noted that Tugwell produced a "critical and realistic" assay of Russian agriculture.[15] Drew Pearson and Robert S. Allen maintained that Tugwell, who "wrote an appraisal of the Russian system with . . . calm deliberation," was "cussed out by both Right and Left" mainly because he was a scientist.[16] Apparently many of Tugwell's critics did not read his report on Russia. According to Blair Bolles, that would not have made any difference, since the impact of the Russian tour on Tugwell was delayed several years.

Continuing to rebut the charges against Tugwell, let us take up the cases of Wirt and Peek. James C. Young thought the New Dealers' reactions to Wirt's charge were suspiciously serious. But when Roosevelt responded with tongue in cheek to the observation, in connection with Wirt's charge, that no leader had ever retained power through the three phases of a revolution, Young considered the President's attitude smart alecky. Roosevelt's reply was, "Well, Cromwell did," and Young's comment was that that was "what may come from knowing a bit of history." Although a New Dealer of the inner circle saw a little joke in the Wirt affair, saying that "some of the boys in good spirits kidded the old duffer," Young thought this comment came "too late." Young held that if someone had laughed at the right time, the public would have laughed too.[17] Yet neither he nor a good part of the press would accept a joke as sufficiently funny or timely if a New Dealer told it.

Some observers did consider the Wirt matter the result of a hoax. Even Alva Johnston believed Wirt's charge was based on the "loose conversation of some Tugwell worshipers." [18] Oswald Villard could not understand why, if the Tugwell idolizers were going to reveal their hands so completely, they selected the mere superintendent of the Gary schools as their confidant.[19] And there were other weaknesses in Wirt's reasoning. The Brain Trust theory, in the sense of a group of plotters controlling the administration, was without foundation in fact. The investigation by a select committee of the House, which Professor Schlesinger reported in some detail, showed that what had indeed happened was that some of the boys and girls, none of whom was prominent in the New Deal, had kidded the old duffer.[20] Tugwell, who was far from indifferent in 1934 to the appeal Wirt's charge might have, later remarked that "those present seem to have had a lot of fun with the scary old gentleman. . . . The publicity this trivial farce commanded can hardly be imagined at a distance in time. What is hard to credit is the prevalence of fear in the minds of most of the nation's pundits and former decision-makers. It was upon this hysteria that such silly allegations as Wirt's fed." [21]

Finally, we should note something about the Wirt incident which was not brought out at the time. The Committee for the Nation, which first released Wirt's charge, would, as Tugwell recalled, "have relied altogether on currency manipulation" for achieving recovery.[22] Its chairman, James H. Rand, Jr., had a speculator's interest in inflation. Wirt, to complete the circle, had been a publicist for the Committee for the Nation—in April, 1933, Tugwell mentioned in his diary a pamphlet by Wirt with a foreword by Rand.[23] In this light the Wirt charge can be understood as an attempt to present conspiracy as the cause of the administration's neglect of monetary panaceas.

George N. Peek's personal references to Tugwell in *Why Quit Our Own* contradicted his implications elsewhere in that book that Tugwell was a conspirator and a revolutionary. Peek wrote, "I never personally had any serious differences with Dr. Tugwell—which simply means that he never clearly got in my way." Tugwell, Peek continued, was bright but not profound, never let himself get too far out on a limb, loved words and speeches, and failed to appreciate the gap between words and action. While Tugwell's speeches expounded some "deep and fine" social theory and his writings showed "a deep familiarity with 'revolutionary technique,'" he "starts and stops with words. It does not occur to him perhaps that there is a world where actions must eventually take the place of words." Peek completed his personal comments on Tugwell with the remark that "neither Dr. Tugwell nor Mr. Frank is the kind of man to get into a dispute. They both seem to believe that he who fights and runs away will live to fight another day." [24]

In drawing his contradictory sketch of a dangerous-harmless Tugwell, Peek resorted to loose name-calling. According to Gilbert Fite this was Peek's usual practice. Fite found no evidence in Peek's personal files indicating that he had information about actual Communist party members in the AAA. Some of his closest friends did not recall his having made such a charge in 1933. Peek, Fite explained, was inclined to group all leftwingers in the subversive category: "'Communist' was a term which he frequently used to stigmatize extreme liberals with whom he disagreed." *Why Quit Our Own*, moreover, reflected the sensationalist techniques of Samuel Crowther, who assisted in its writing. Crowther warned Peek that people would not read an objective book. He insisted on stressing personalities and radicalism in the New Deal. He inserted phrases which made the account more dramatic than Peek really intended. Only in some instances, Fite noted, did Peek make Crowther tone down his exaggerations.[25] It is pertinent to note that Roger Burlingame found Crowther an unreliable amanuensis of Henry Ford.[26] Tugwell himself commented in *The Stricken Land* that Peek did not worry about the "economy." This was a "generalization beyond his range." He worried about the farmer. As for sharecroppers, tenants, and hired hands, they were "help" who had to look to the farmer for aid. Thus, "it was a short leap, for a mind as simple as Mr. Peek's, from the suggestion that government might assist the underprivileged farm folk along with the well-to-do proprietors, all the way to Communism with a capital 'C' . . . many of Peek's followers would say this, but they did not believe it." [27]

We may dispose of Tugwell's relations with Lee Pressman and with the Progressive party briefly and together. Tugwell apparently allowed Henry Wallace to persuade him to support the Progressive party. In April, 1948, Tugwell made two speeches in Wallace's cause. In August he appeared at the party's convention in Philadelphia. On the surest test issue of the day, foreign policy, he found that the party, led by Lee Pressman, acted like a Communist cell. When Tugwell tried in the Resolutions Committee to win approval of the Marshall Plan, he was summarily voted down.[28] He expressed his fear that the "wrong people" might get control of the Progressive party. When asked to identify the "wrong people," he replied, "I certainly don't know whether they are Communists, but they certainly act like them." [29] Then he fell silent, taking no active part in the campaign. Undoubtedly, as Will Alexander asserted, some of the RA's experiments reflected Pressman's influence,[30] but Tugwell was not taken in by Pressman when the latter's actions ran counter to American interests.

III

Tugwell's critics who attributed any ideas about economic planning to European sources would not concede that he could have arrived at his views on the basis of his observation of the American scene. Ernest K. Lindley, on the other hand, stated that if Tugwell was convinced of the need to overhaul the American economy, he was also convinced that the new model was not to be found in foreign creeds.[31] John Franklin Carter noted Tugwell's "staunch and Whitmanesque" Americanism and his belief in the necessity of our working out our own destiny by applying our own ideas and methods.[32] In this Tugwell followed the lead of his teacher Simon Nelson Patten, who, he recalled, "took no stock in European doctrines; rather he set out to create one out of American stuffs—and he succeeded." [33]

In 1927 Tugwell made a statement which shows that his criticism of the American economy arose from a desire to improve it, not replace it with a foreign system: "We are conscious of the great good luck it is to be Americans just now. We should probably not have bathrooms if we lived anywhere else. We should not have telephone service, an automobile, or a radio; we should not have electric cleaners and washers; we should not in fact carry on with anything like our present efficiency and comfort if we happen to have been a French, German, or Russian family. But we are conscious, too, that many Americans are not so lucky, and this is disturbing." [34] In poorer times, in 1935, Tugwell continued to reject foreign doctrines: "Rather than feverishly scan all horizons—England whose fiscal recovery so enamors our bankers, Russia whose collectivism is so enchanting to our radicals, Italy and Germany upon whose system some of our industrialists cast so wistful a gaze—it would pay them to study the American spirit . . . in a disciplined effort to find and cling to the social ethic which must give direction to our national policy as it always finally has done." [35]

In his speech at Dartmouth in 1934 Tugwell told the students to use some of their free time to "explore the American character, the development of our traditions, our background of thinking" so that they could test public policies in terms of their contribution to "those aims which Americans hold in common." [36] A month later he captured the American spirit for a group of social workers in these words: " 'Oh, Susannah, don't you cry for me!' was the marching song of a generation of Americans who set out to conquer the West. Americans want no pity, no one crying for them. They want opportunity to use their energy and talents." He also told the social workers that their task was "helping people to help themselves—to take advantage, for the reconstruction of American life, of those springs of individual initiative which are so native to the American culture." [37] In the early 1930's, in another statement which merits quotation, Tugwell tried to explain why the literary economists were "tormented by the unrepentant originality of events," and why the New Deal had not failed even though "it is not this or that." It was, he said,

an indigenous development; the confusion arises because our literary folk know everything except American history. The clue they are looking for exists in their own rural past. Let me suggest, therefore, that they try to visualize the homestead and the village of a generation or two ago right here in the Eastern States. And let me give them a word to embroider and elaborate to see whether more can not be made of it than of Communism, Fascism, Capitalism or any other of the terms which are being so overworked. The word is neighborliness.[38]

Of course, one could call these statements lip service to the American tradition if there were no specific examples of Tugwell's rejection of foreign isms. His dealings with two individuals, one a radical and the other an anti-radical, illustrate his loyalty to American values. Donald Henderson was a young teacher at Columbia who was supposed to be working on his Ph.D. in economics. He did nothing on it for two years, then begged Tugwell for another year of employment. In his third year he became an agitator, a Socialist, and finally a Communist—mostly, Tugwell thought, for reasons of injured pride. He neglected his work, and Tugwell received complaints. The problem was complicated by Henderson's radicalism since the young radicals on campus wanted to make an issue on the grounds of academic freedom. Finally Tugwell fired Henderson, issuing a public statement to the effect that Henderson refused to others the tolerance they gave to him and furthered his philosophy with methods of force. While Henderson neglected his duties, the real issue, Tugwell said, was "freedom from compulsion and loyalty to the traditions of scholarship." [39] Thus, Tugwell rejected the Communist tactic of overriding other viewpoints through force as well as argumentation. Henderson became a hero to the Communists as the result of this "affront" to his academic freedom.[40] Tugwell, for his part, learned a lesson, as he recalled, from the Henderson affair. He decided that in the future he would avoid working with Communists if he possibly could.[41] That is why the young Communists in the AAA and the RA had to conceal their affiliation.

Pare Lorentz's case was the opposite of Henderson's. Lorentz produced a motion picture, "The Plow That Broke the Plains," for the USDA. In making this film about the Dust Bowl, he suffered a personal financial loss. He was irritated, moreover, by some of his colleagues, who wanted "The Plow" to be "all about human greed and how lousy our social system was." Lorentz objected violently to being called a "leftist" or any other cultist, artistic or political. He could not see the connection between comment on the social system and dust storms. Discouraged, he went into Tugwell's office to voice his complaints and announce his departure. Tugwell refused to accept Lorentz's resignation and increased his per diem allowance.[42] This was one more instance justifying C. H. McCall's earlier observation in *Credit and Financial Management* that Tugwell's supposed desire to Sovietize America was an "absolute myth." [43] Moley later condemned Tugwell's collectivism but insisted that it had nothing to do with the kind of Communism Lenin brought to the world.[44] Hugh Johnson called Tugwell "about as Red as a blue hen." [45]

As for the New Deal in general, the claims that it promoted the cause of Communism ran along contradictory lines. There was Wirt's contention that the New Deal conspirators hoped to prolong the depression, creating chaos and setting the stage for a revolution. On the other hand, Earl Browder, as quoted by Alva Johnston, said in Moscow that the American Communist party did not oppose the New Deal because it was helping the movement toward revolutionary objectives.[46] Thus, the New Deal was bringing the revolution closer both by inaction and action. Nevertheless, James Burnham, in his *The Web of Subversion* (1954), maintained that for the Communists in the economic agencies of the

1930's "the aim of influencing policy on the whole was more important than espionage." But Burnham's evidence, Professor Schlesinger replied, simply failed to establish this fact.[47] If the subversives obtained a living from their government jobs while gaining an entrance which enabled eventual espionage, no one has demonstrated how they affected the depression-combatting measures of Tugwell's time in a way advantageous to international Communism. Indeed, given the mood of the American people in early 1933, one can make a strong case for the New Deal reforms as preventive of the rise of Communism in the United States.

IV

On the subject of Communism as an international movement and an external threat to the United States, Tugwell was alert and consistent through the years. His academic interest in the Soviet experiment did not blind him to the harshness of Stalin's methods. In his essay on Russian agriculture he remarked how factory managers were dismissed "with characteristic Communist ruthlessness."[48] In 1928 he wrote an article, "Communist Theory and Russian Fact," in which he commented on the unrealistic observations of recent visitors to the Soviet Union. He also noted that some people had thought Trotsky's exile was a prelude to conservatism, "yet, it now begins to look as though Stalin had stolen some of Trotsky's thunder and the quarrel was mainly . . . over who should make the noise."[49] Tugwell saw the Stalin regime as an expansive as well as a ruthless one. In his argument to Roosevelt against the Stimson Doctrine in early 1933, he referred to Japanese power in Asia as an obstacle to Russian imperialism.[50]

Tugwell came into direct contact with Communists when he served as Governor of Puerto Rico from 1941 to 1946. Both the Communists and the Falangistas, he wrote in *The Stricken Land*, could not admit that they were anti-American, but they "took oaths which no American could take. . . ." The Communists were,

> for the moment, because it was party policy, in favor of the war and so somewhat cautious about the use of the strike. But in typical communist fashion they worked night and day, admitted no scruple in making decisions, and conducted themselves in ways which indicated their contempt for such bourgeois concepts as promises and contracts. Because they were allied with the *independentistas* Munoz granted them too much. So he came to extend a dangerous tolerance to the communistas, forgetting that they had no directed interest in Puerto Rico but were only using independence as a means of causing trouble for another "capitalist" nation.

Elsewhere in *The Stricken Land* Tugwell stated that "it was obvious that the Communists were getting ready for the day when the party line of international communism would diverge from policies of the United States." [51]

In October, 1941, referring to systems—Communism, Democracy, Capitalism, Fascism, and National Socialism—Tugwell asserted: "To the extent which each pretends to world domination in the same subject-matter, no two can exist in tolerance, though there may be temporary defensive alliances. . . ." [52] A month later we were in the war and allies of Russia. Soon after the end of the war the Grand Alliance fell apart, and we were aligned against Russia in a Cold War which would last, unless it became a hot war, so long as Russia pretended to world domination. In the light of these events Tugwell's remark of October, 1941, seems prescient. In any event, the Cold War imposed on the United States great new responsibilities. Tugwell recognized these in 1947 as the Cold War came out into the open. He pointed out how the Soviet Union had exploited Britain's weakness and our own faltering and demobilization. At the eastern end of the Mediterranean "we were exposed to the consequences of any incident which the brutish Russians might make too hard for them [the British] to accept." [53] Our responsibility was to assume burdens Britain could no longer bear and to provide the free world with strength and leadership.

Tugwell wrote at some length on the Cold War in 1958 in *The Art of Politics*. He suggested that if Roosevelt had lived, he would have found ways to reduce antagonisms.[54] He thought it was "arguable, at least, that Roosevelt might have averted both of these catastrophes"—the loss of Eastern Europe and China—because he "saw the Russian fear of Western aggression" and understood Stalin as a politician.[55] Samuel Lubell, in a review of *The Art of Politics*, commented: "To Tugwell Russia appears just as a misunderstood juvenile delinquent." [56] The book itself provides refutations of Lubell's observation. Tugwell explicitly stated that his line of reasoning was "conjecture." [57] He stressed the differences between the Communist way of life and ours, stating that the governments of the United States and the U.S.S.R. "stood in complete contrast theoretically, and almost as complete contrast actually." [58] He pointed out that to Communists "the party was everything . . . and individuals nothing," and he noted the superiority of the state to the individual in Russia.[59] Tugwell also described the Russians as tough tacticians who found it "all too easy to play on the very human sentiment of envy among those who were less well off." [60] Tugwell may have overestimated Roosevelt, but he did not underestimate the Russians. In 1961, in a long letter to the editor of the *Washington Post* about the origins of the Monroe Doctrine, Tugwell remarked that the Russians were "then interested in extending and protecting the holy alliance . . . now they are interested in extending and protecting another kind of system [to Cuba]. But its headquarters would be in Moscow and its policy makers Russian." [61]

If irresponsible anti-Communists found Tugwell "guilty by association," they neglected a connection which made him "innocent by association." That was his relationship with Adolf A. Berle, Jr., often a co-recipient with Tugwell of the Red label. It was Assistant Secretary of State Berle to whom Whittaker Chambers, in a now well-known incident of August 23, 1939, gave information about Communists in government. Berle circulated to high officials a confidential memorandum summarizing Chambers' disclosures.[62] It was Berle who, on July 10, 1941, warned J. Edgar Hoover against Russian espionage in the United States.[63] And it was Berle who, in the fall of 1944, wrote a memorandum on the danger of Soviet postwar domination of Central and Eastern Europe.[64] Tugwell shared Berle's attitude, expressing in *The Stricken Land* his lack of toleration of Americans who became Communists in these words: "Those who honor truth and whose integrity is uncompromising are in no way excused from going on. Nor are they forgiven for becoming—as some did—communists or any other kind of un-American pledgee. This is even worse for the soul than becoming a compromiser. Because the way is strait the believer is not excused from going down it." [65]

27. Tugwell and the American Tradition: Evolution—Democracy—the Constitution

In 1933 in *The Industrial Discipline* Tugwell made this distinction: "The essential contrast between the liberal and the radical view of the tasks which lie before us is that liberalism requires this experimenting and that radicalism rejects it for immediate entry on the revolutionary tactic. Liberals would like to rebuild the station while the trains are running; radicals prefer to blow up the station and forego service until the new structure is built." [1] A critic contended that Tugwell, in making this distinction, failed to put himself in either camp. [2] This contention did not take into account other passages in *The Industrial Discipline*, and in other works, in which Tugwell definitely placed himself in the camp of the evolutionary liberals.

The two foundation stones of Tugwell's evolutionary position were his rejection of force and his elevation of reason. He accepted a rule from his teacher Simon Nelson Patten, who said to him during World War I, "Force, my boy, force never settles anything." [3] In *The Industrial Discipline* Tugwell wrote, "I have never found myself greatly in sympathy with the revolutionary tactic. 'Force never settles anything' has always seemed to me a sufficient axiom. It is my reading of history that reconstruction is about as difficult after a revolutionary debacle as it would have been in a process of gradual substitution." [4] In 1935 Tugwell stated that the Civil War "should have taught us . . . that force is, of itself, incapable of altering the basic habits and institutions of mankind and that unless they are assessed realistically no corrective policy can be formed. Changes of this sort come slowly in spite of heat or strife. They never yield to unreason or violent action. The use of force would have no better results today if it is really reconstruction we want rather than a bloody overturn and the replacement of one government by another." [5]

Preceding the title page of *The Industrial Discipline* appeared this quotation from Francis Amasa Walker: "Happy is that people, and proud may they be, who can enlarge their franchises and perfect their political forms without bloodshed or threat of violence, the long debate of reason resulting in the glad consent of all." The last sentence of the book read: "There is a kind of duty among civilized beings now not to desert reason but to press its claims insistently." During his career in the capital Tugwell reiterated this enshrinement of reason. In 1934 he re-

marked that in the history of America some of our departures from tradition had done great harm because they were not discussed and thoroughly
understood beforehand.[6] In 1936 he insisted that research and analysis
must precede action.[7] In 1949, after serving governments in Washington,
New York, and San Juan, and with specific reference to planning, Tugwell pointed out how much we had to learn about the evolution of
human societies (the "transfer of directive authority from the cell to the
multicellular organism—from the individual to society—and, indeed, the
whole relation of parts to wholes in human association") before we could
develop any effective conjunctural apparatus.[8]

Tugwell dealt at some length with evolutionary reform in America
in an article about "The Progressive Tradition," published in 1935.[9] He
outlined the battle for democracy since Cleveland's time, listing occasional advances interspersed among truces and retreats. After the lesser
advances in the time of Cleveland and Bryan, the greater ones under the
Republican Roosevelt and Wilson, the sidetracking of reform during the
war, and the tense truce of the 1920's, came the advances under the
Democratic Roosevelt. Tugwell attributed the continual attack on economic discriminations and privileges, and its occasional successes, to the
"stream of American purpose, a steady underground river beneath an
artificially ordered and documented landscape." This stream flowed continuously, but only now and then did it come to the surface. Then it
carried all before it. The statesman's function was to moderate and
direct—he could not oppose. (In this article of 1935 Tugwell implied
a grandfather-father-son relationship between Populism, Progressivism,
and the New Deal which historians have since disproved, although his
references elsewhere to trustbusting as being literally reactionary are in
accord with the recent differentiation by Richard Hofstadter, Arthur
Mann, George E. Mowry, and others between the three main phases of
the reform tradition.)

Tugwell took great pains to explain that Americans regarded natural
forces and man-made privileges as obstacles to be overcome for "some
deeper purpose." "Clever dodges of the privileged" could deflect this
deeper purpose, but they could not stop it. It was the American faith,
something difficult to describe, although a study of our history helped
one to feel and understand it. It lay in the realm of morals and religion,
having to do with the good life. The law of Western religions taught
that the good life was the purpose of life, that life was barren without
living and achieving and human dignity. The highest values of the good
life were above the material: "Those who accuse us of always living
for material things fail to penetrate the surface of our life. The ingenuity
which produces goods for use has a source outside the things themselves
. . . that life is good which seems good to the men and women who live

it. With us, with our free traditions . . . it is conditioned on free institutions and comprehensive if unavowed desires. It reflects our belief that human dignity is more important than numbers or wealth."

The American people showed during the depression that their highest values were nonmaterial: "Economic hardships have never greatly mattered to our people, so long as elemental virtues were possible." The tremendous protest after the collapse arose because our institutions had affronted human dignity. Fortunately, if our institutions "fail us, we can change them; but if this purpose departs then we are lost indeed." The people demanded that their leaders find a system which would make the good life possible, and conformity to their demands was imperative: "We shall see some amazingly disturbed and unhappy years if our present social and industrial leaders prove themselves unable to conform to the American faith." (Tugwell's emphasis in this article on above-the-material values conflicts with Richard Hofstadter's conclusion—in the frequently quoted final chapter of *The Age of Reform*—that the Brain Trusters were morally relativistic, opportunistic improvisers, manipulators, organizers, and technicians whose concern was means rather than ends.)

Thus, the stage was set for a New Deal, an attempt by society to adapt itself to the undefined ethic "through the materials put at its disposal by the recent technological revolution in industry and agriculture." Technology introduced no new factor into our political life; it simply intensified our determination to resolve economic problems. The New Deal, the "first chance we have had to do this coherently," was a great opportunity. It belonged to all the people and their tradition, and it could be reshaped every day. It would determine whether the political forces of democracy were "wise and strong enough to rearrange the economic and social environment on terms satisfactory to the general ethical and moral sense." Its success would amount to the "most merciful of recorded human revolutions."

This summary of "The Progressive Tradition" suggests several pertinent conclusions. Tugwell appreciated the American tradition of evolution, based on a faith which raised men by "slow, but certain stages." That faith gave first place to values diametrically opposed to the values of the economic determinism and dialectical materialism espoused by revolutionary Communists. Intolerable violations of that faith resulted in the people's irresistible demands for rectification—irresistible because they lived in a democracy. The very difficulty of defining that faith showed that the essence of democracy was process—a way of meeting problems flexibly and of reconciling differences peacefully through compromise. And democracy both promoted and benefited from a striving for the attainable. Tugwell used the term American "faith" rather than "dream," he noted, because "dream" connoted the unattainable.

When we come to Tugwell's emphasis on the opportunities attendant on the New Deal, and his subsequent disappointment at its achievements, we face some facts which require further elaboration of his concept of evolution. The difficulty with reform in spurts or in crises was that the people and their leaders, through lack of education, were unprepared to adopt new social devices adequate to the new age which had come into being since the last spasm of reform. Tugwell referred to this difficulty, recalling that he, like Ickes, had known Progressive struggles too,

> but my generation had redefined the issues and used other terms. They were, for all that, perhaps the same. We had more of an agreed positive program in contrast to their negative one; but we were not such good fighters and we probably had less public support because our concepts were, necessarily, more difficult. Denouncing the "interests" and "busting trusts" had been more conducive to adrenalin flow than advocating more effective administrative arrangements for specific social functions.[10]

In retrospect Tugwell observed that the people were reluctant to go beyond rudimentary patchwork in institutional matters. They knew a bridge was "something which cannot be built with elementary arithmetic; yet it is expected that the more complicated social processes may be provided for without the use of devices for measurement, of institutions for co-ordination, or reference to the relevant body of social science." [11] The pent-up desire for reform was rapidly expended, and soon "every reform had to be fought for inch by inch, and the fight grew harder as recovery proceeded." [12] The "national house was in ruins, but we were not yet ready for a new one." [13] Consequently the New Deal only began the vital task of changing habits and bringing policy within the influence of modern thought.[14] And the back-to-freedom urge after World War II "made it impossible, when victory had come, to plan or act in the public interest except as it might accidentally emerge from the conflicts among extremely complex interests." [15] Tugwell's comment on the postwar period was a key to his thought on evolution. He wanted continuous concern—in prosperity and peace as well as in depression and war—with the development of new social devices to meet new needs. Perhaps this was too much to expect of the general public. Social scientists, however, could pursue these problems with more zeal and realism than they had in the 1920's and publicize their findings more widely and effectively, disturbing public complacency to some extent. None of this meant a rejection of the American evolutionary tradition; it was, rather, a call for its perfection.

Before, during, and after his term in the USDA, Tugwell described the development of planning as a gradual process. In 1928 he suggested that the insertion of public regulation "gently and gradually," as the official theory of competition disappeared, would enable us to face the evolution of industrial technique with more equanimity.[16] In the same year, in his report to Alfred E. Smith, he stressed popular acceptance as a prerequisite for planning, stating with regard to price controls: "I am convinced that in time we shall see that this is the only road to an ordered national economic life, but perhaps that time has not yet come."[17] A decade later he noted that "the instruments of wholeness are not ones which can be perfected overnight. They require long preparation and maturation,"[18] and only their effective functioning could justify their existence.[19] Two decades later he did not expect planners to accomplish much in the way of procedural or theoretical advances until they had finished telling each other, as they were still doing, how wonderful planning was.[20] Still, there was a need for planning which caused us "tentatively but persistently" to feel our way toward an acceptable agency of conjuncture.[21]

In the 1940's Tugwell also commented on the history of actual planning agencies, including the National Resources Planning Board, its successor under the Unemployment Act of 1946, and the New York City Planning Commission. He concluded that the development of such agencies, strong enough to promote the general welfare in the face of opposition from private interests, would be a sequence of birth, death, and reincarnation.[22] In 1950 Tugwell referred to a directive mechanism enabling expansion, along with fair exchange between groups, as "something to be worked out over considerable time."[23] In March, 1953, he tried to explain, in an article in the *Revue Economique*, "L'Attitude Reticente des Etats Unis a L'Egard de la Planification." Tugwell's belief that planning could be gradually grafted onto capitalism attested his belief that that system itself was changing. Static interpretations of the word "capitalism," he wrote in 1926, were invalid descriptions of an evolving economy.[24] An aspect of this evolution was changes in public law, subject to judicial interpretation. Disagreeing with a court decision in 1928, Tugwell commented that the only hope for a desirable judicial opinion lay in time and a change in the court.[25]

In 1929, in his article, "Farm Relief and a Permanent Agriculture," Tugwell stated, "We shall not in our generation be witness to great changes. The forces which affect agriculture do not come in revolutionary ways."[26] With the depression changes in agriculture did come faster, however, than Tugwell expected in 1929, but, as an official of the administration sponsoring new public policies, he was assigned to what one observer, familiar with USDA operations, called "eminently conservative" tasks.[27] He did not turn out to be the dangerous radical whom the rightists feared, and he failed to satisfy the leftists, who disapproved because he did not always act consistently with his views on the rational planning of economic life.[28] Beginning with Jefferson, public officials in our democracy have seldom proved as "bad" as their detractors thought they would be or as "good" as their admirers expected them to be—especially regarding the matter of change. Policy is both impelled and limited, in both formulation and execution, by going concerns and accepted ways of doing things which no single official can disregard or oppose with impunity. Besides, Tugwell's task was literally conservative. The USDA and the RA, although their methods, it is true, were sometimes novel and dramatic, acted to conserve human and natural resources. Tugwell remarked in 1935 that the RA's activities seemed dramatic only because it applied the principles of sound agriculture, such as drainage, fencing, and crop rotation, on a regional and national scale.[29]

To this task of conservation Tugwell brought a moderation in philosophy and method consistent with his pre-Washington attitude. In late 1933 General Westervelt of the AAA reported to Peek that Tugwell had expressed an interest in getting codes and agreements through as rapidly as possible; that under no circumstances did he wish to be placed in the position of delaying action; and that while he favored complete government access to company books, he was willing to settle on some satisfactory middle ground.[30] In 1934 Tugwell described the mediating function of the Secretary of Agriculture in this way: "Among the special pleas which are offered, a public servant must always pick and choose, modify and correct, granting what can be given, rejecting that which cannot." [31] In 1935 Tugwell wrote: "A sound agricultural program, a sound program for the use of our natural resources, and a sound program of industrial development cannot be established in a day after a period of misdirected efforts ending in a great national disaster." [32] In 1936 Tugwell explained how the RA, through its appraising program, proceeded with caution in its land-purchase and resettlement program. There were no forced removals. Careful planning and checking of soil quality, types of buildings, and families' prospects for success preceded the development of a project.[33] Thus, as an administrator in a crisis Tugwell was, in a sense, evolutionary with regard to specifics in a brief time span in a manner consistent with his views on long-term general evolution.

II

Tugwell's elevation of reason, one of the foundation stones of his ideas on evolution, was related to his thought on democracy. The use of reason to advantage required investigation and education. Action would necessarily be evolutionary if it were to proceed from time-consuming education, and education would necessarily be precisely that—rather than indoctrination—if it were both to reflect and foster democracy in which agreement on ends and means rests on voluntarism and consent.

Tugwell stated in 1928 that the ease of enforcing a program of production controls in agriculture would depend on popular support.[34] As a New Dealer, in 1934, he stressed the importance of consent in several of his articles and speeches. We could have nothing new in government, he wrote, which did not "correspond to a new need on the part of our people and of their economic institutions." [35] He told a Consumers' League meeting, "Government can do no more than is wanted of it." [36] Commenting on the NRA codes, he stated that no one could foresee the final structure of industry which might result from the "essentially voluntary and democratic process now going on." [37] In an address at Clemson College on the farm problem Tugwell would not "do more than state the problem at this time—the solution must, of necessity, come from you." [38] Twenty years later, in 1953, he referred to "one of society's most serious problems: the securing of change within a desired pattern without serious departure from voluntarism." [39]

Underlying this insistence on consent was a certain concept of equality as a central aspect of democracy. Foreigners, Tugwell noted in 1938, often found it difficult to grasp the American attitude toward democracy.[40] In America, he later wrote, "Democracy is a word which is capable of touching off . . . emotions of various sorts, but all of them mixed with a genuine reverence. Our peculiar history makes equality more real to us than to people in some other lands." [41] This, to Tugwell, did not mean that all men were equal in every respect. If it was self-evident that all men were created equal, it was also obvious that they did not end up that way. As Tugwell pointed out in *The Art of Politics*, "There has been a rags-to-riches myth in America, a kind of leveler tradition, part, probably, of the whole equality misconception. The extreme form of this notion is that all men are interchangeable; that is anyone can do any job as well as anyone else. After Jackson's day and down to Lincoln's—and even beyond—this was a quite prevalent view, one that was acknowledged by most politicians; it tended to die out as the age of large-scale enterprise with corollary specialization advanced and as higher education became widely available." [42]

Thus, equality meant to Tugwell the opportunity to develop to the limits of one's capacity and to participate according to one's ability to contribute. It also meant equality before the law and equal consideration of all men when measures for the promotion of the general welfare were being formulated. The burden of his article of 1928, "Bankers'

Banks," was that we needed a financial mechanism to protect "all of us," not just bankers,[43] for the tradition of democracy, he wrote in a commentary of the same year on Alfred E. Smith's candidacy, was the protection of all vital social interests, not just those of one class.[44] Finally, equality meant that the general public would have an ultimate check on the formulations of the "unequal" experts.

The discussion in Chapter 9 of the reconciliation of the esoteric and exoteric, of expertise and public opinion, concentrated on mechanism —the "Fourth Power." Tugwell also referred in general terms to the nature of this problem in a democracy. In his address at Dartmouth College in 1934 he pointed out how we never worried about our failure to understand the principles behind many things we used every day, such as radios and motor cars. These principles were "utterly mysterious to all but the highly trained expert," and we did not take a vote on the use of the vacuum tube or the internal combustion engine. "Yet these things affect the common life as widely and as deeply as any legislative change could possibly do." Nevertheless, there was resistance to "numerous suggestions that the fields of government and economics ought to be likewise specialized." [45]

Tugwell accepted the general opinion that "abdication" in the less exact social sciences was dangerous, that the "basic decisions ought not to be by other than general consent. This, I think, is sound." But there still was a problem with respect to social decisions in a democracy. There was a "need for definition of the fields within which expertness may be trusted and of those within which a more democratic procedure is necessary. We have developed rather carelessly, in our generation, a policy of autocratic decision about matters with momentous social effects; and perhaps we have kept democratic some decisions in which a degree of expertness would be desirable." Tugwell held up this task of definition to the undergraduates as a challenge to their generation. In the past "our autocratic theory in one field and our democratic theory in the other" had prevented adjustments to great technical and industrial changes, which thus had "effects for which society was totally unprepared." The New Deal, Tugwell pointed out, had to make decisions on the use of expertness. It tipped the scales in favor of democracy because its administrators were prejudiced in that direction. They believed that democratic methods, which won co-operation, were best in the long run.[46]

In 1930 Tugwell had written, regarding the use of experts, "There should be no aristocracy of deciders and proletariat of consenters." [47] If this were to hold, the answer lay in education—which made it fitting that he should speak of this matter to the students at Dartmouth. Democracy could develop leadership and the consent necessary to leadership in a democracy, he stated in 1933, once people knew where they were going and why they were going there.[48] This did not mean suppression of dissent. Criticism, he remarked in 1940, was essential to the educative process and inseparable from democracy. There could be no suppression of a free press, for example, because the "battle, if kept up and won, could not be one of those instances, in which, in order to save democracy, what was best in democracy had been sacrificed." [49] But education among free men was no magic formula for *quick* obtainment of consent. Roosevelt's greatest efforts, Tugwell recalled, were in educating toward a national policy. His successes in that direction were few, limited, and temporary. "Congress, and most other people as well, would not have advanced far enough in this kind of learning even to follow willingly." [50]

With his basic belief in a "concert of interests," Tugwell saw two other gaps to span, or reconciliations to make, in a democracy. These were the clashes between special and general interests and between local and national interests, the second being a particular form of the first. In his arguments the balance of weight fell on the side of the general and the national. Government in a democracy, he noted in 1935, could not suppress any pressure. It had to identify and consider all views. In the past government had responded to the strongest pressures. The New Deal, Tugwell asserted, showed an unashamed preference for pressures exerted on behalf of human rights. Then it attempted to make specific interests coincide with an acceptable concept of national interest. In order to do this, it needed the courage to oppose wrong methods and the energy and imagination to take steps toward sound objectives. In the short run the government determined the steps, but in the long run the voters made the choices. Neither voters nor administrators were wholly objective. Still, the administrator had to assay all pressures in the light of his own concept of the national interest. "Once this is understood . . . government ceases to be a citadel to be stormed, but instead becomes a living organism, combining some of the best and some of the poorest features of mankind." [51]

In defining these ideals, Tugwell, in effect, exaggerated the accomplishments of the New Deal in reconciling conflicts between special interests and between them and the general interest. What he described in early 1934 as the "essentially voluntary and democratic process now going on" in the NRA turned out to be self-government by only one of the several interested parties. This showed, Tugwell asserted in 1935, that business feared real democracy.[52] Regarding the reconciliation of local and national interests, Tugwell later accepted Philip Selznick's views on this question. In a book review-article of 1953, "Grass Roots Democracy—Myth or Reality?," he found appearances deceiving.

He agreed with Selznick that promotion of the national interest by the TVA, the AAA, and the Soil Conservation Service had been hampered by "co-optation," the process whereby these agencies, in order to avert threats to their stability or existence, shared policy determination with "grass-tops" local interests which stood for the status quo.[53]

Tugwell saw the whole problem of operating in the national interest on the local level as exceedingly complex. There was a difference, he explained, between participation and simple involvement. It was a sham to call the latter, in which an unorganized citizenry became a "reliable instrument for achieving administrative goals," democracy. This was not in accord with the views which David Lilienthal expressed in his book, *TVA: Democracy on the March*. Tugwell maintained that as a result of "co-optation" the TVA's decisions "ran not only against the interest but also the express wishes of the American people. It is therefore an expression of the weakness of our ways of making democracy effective." He concluded that the "wider the issue, the wider must be the public that decides it; but to the extent that an issue is local, authority to deal with it must be decentralized so that local opinion may be brought to bear on it. This is surely a most delicate and intricate operation in administration, but it is in this way that real and responsible publics will be brought into existence." [54]

While accomplishment fell short of ideals, Tugwell showed that he had done some hard thinking about democracy and its problems. Out of this reflection, Sumner Welles observed, emerged a belief in a "positive, progressive, and dynamic" form of democracy.[55] Tugwell's statements in the 1930's of his faith in democracy appear to be more than outward obeisance for political purposes when we note their similarity to this expression in 1962 of his current belief:

> I am seldom heard to say that the good old days were really better than later ones, but in this matter of deciding I have no doubt that what we reached for and got was of the utmost importance. It is, after all, the individuals of this world who are its irreducible units. Everything that is sought or done is for them. If it is done by them or with their express consent, it will have the authentic title it must acquire to be accepted and permanent. Otherwise it will always be in jeopardy, subject to upheaval and revolt. This is the argument for democracy. It seems to me incontrovertible. People acquiring their own information, making their own decisions—even to delegate—and establishing their own institutions seem to me to have reached the ultimate relationship with each other. The problem of future generations will be to preserve this relationship in the difficult circumstances of an increasingly crowded and complex civilization.[56]

III

In several articles published in 1939, 1941, and the early 1950's Tugwell surveyed constitutional history down to 1933.[57] He considered the events at Philadelphia in 1787, finding that they paved the way for the triumph of laissez faire in the nineteenth century in two ways, one having to do with the times, the other with the fifty-five men meeting in Convention Hall. The times, or the stage of economic development in America, resulted in a vague and carelessly drawn commerce clause. "Commerce" then meant shipping—the commerce clause was an outgrowth of the Alexandria Conference of 1785, which dealt with traffic near the capes of the Potomac and on that river. In the Constitution "the word 'industry' does not occur anywhere; there is no smell of smoke, noise of factories, suggestion of men working together in planned fashion. Fifty years later it must have been a different document."

The men of 1787 could not foresee new conditions in which Americans, depending on unified social organization, would seek to protect themselves *with*, rather than *from*, government. The delegates at Philadelphia performed their task on the verge of the industrial revolution: "There was a moment in history when inventions should have been suppressed or social management should have been greatly extended. It was of great consequence that the American Constitution should have been formulated almost at that moment"—"almost," but not quite. Thus, the men of 1787, in controlling "a commerce among the states which was even then getting out of hand," thought they had settled a controversy, when, in fact, they had launched one. They had drafted a commerce clause which, in succeeding years, was responsible for arguments but not really relevant to those arguments. They were not aware, of course, that they had set the stage for an inevitable, continuing conflict: "It is not possible to make a convincing argument that the nationalists intended the commerce clause to cover the intimate conduct of industrial life, but neither did they intend that its conduct should be beyond the reach of interference. To them it had perhaps been unimportant, a matter already settled and not a matter of controversy. Its future significance, however, had been underestimated."

The other advantages which the nineteenth-century advocates of laissez faire inherited from 1787 derived from the compromises which settled the conflict between the two main groups at the Convention— the eighteenth-century mercantilist-nationalists and the enterprisers, typified by Roger Sherman of Connecticut. It should be noted that Tugwell, in referring to these groups, did not accept Charles A. Beard's economic interpretation of the Constitution: "Our Constitution had been written not by simple men but by worldly ones with complex intelligences and mixed motives." They had opposed the control of Parliament, but they did not oppose control as such. Adam Smith's ideas had not yet become part of their thinking. The eighteenth-century "gentlemen" among them reached farther back for their ideology to mercantilism and nationalism. The Constitution, "so far as it reflected economic ideas at all (which was amazingly little)," reflected old rather than current ones.

Although the Constitution "had not been written altogether by and for . . . enterprisers, they had had an important part in shaping it, and were able, during the next century to adapt it to their needs," transforming a mercantilist document into one of laissez faire. They came off best in their clash with the mercantilists. Their victory did not affect the wording of clauses relating to economics. They triumphed in another way, in matters of structure and distribution of power. They were able to win because the eighteenth-century gentlemen did not quite understand the conflict, while they, the enterprisers—not theorizers but representatives of businessmen—knew what they were after.

The eighteenth-century gentlemen—Washington, Hamilton, and Madison—intended to eliminate the states if they could. Hamilton, in particular, had no local loyalties, and he hoped to deflate the inflated pretensions of state politicians. He took a pro-union stand because America's international position was humiliating to him. His mind was not on commerce and business. Meanwhile, the enterprisers, who did have their minds on commerce and business, acquired supporters. A "curious alliance of literary folk and speculative merchants" fought for the balance-of-power concept. The literary folk saw in it assurance of "deliberation, dignity, and a circumscribed sphere of action." The enterprisers knew it would "insure a minimum of interference with business." The nationalists gave in because "the necessity for compromise seemed to them, as it often has to others, controlling." They ended up fighting during the ratification struggle for compromises they had originally opposed. The enterprisers emerged with dual sovereignty, national and state, and a Senate which was to harass even the strong Presidents and dominate the weak ones, standing for Smithian economics while serving as a barrier between the executive and the rights of business.

Laissez faire entered in full force with Jefferson, and Adam Smith's influence became pervasive after the generation of 1787 had passed on. Laissez faire seemed to win the first round of the constitutional conflict through the default of its potential critics. In the nineteenth century no one caught a glimpse of the economic essence of American constitutional progress "because it had been not only a hidden but also an unwanted evolution," usually unacknowledged and often deliberately camouflaged. Few Americans noticed the dominance of speculation, exploitation, competition, and money-making over planning, conservation, co-operation, and service. The majority adhered to the orthodoxy of free enterprise. Economists generally echoed Smith and his successors —Ricardo, Mill, and Marshall. Some intellectuals dissented when they saw in Spencer's *Social Statics* where laissez faire led, but they were few in number. Men of affairs and statesmen left constitutional interpretation alone—"they operated on the going theory." Judges were among the few who considered constitutional questions, but they "had to risk either their reputation as scholars or their duty to American business."

The judges, it is true, had an exceedingly difficult task in applying a vague commerce clause to a modern industrial society. Responding to pressure from the Senate, they allowed pro-business constitutional lawyers to define the place of industry, once it became interstate, in society. The lawyers' principal weapons were the legal status of corporations as individuals and the Fifth and Fourteenth Amendments. Noting that the corporation was a Roman concept which English common law had recognized before the rise of industry, Tugwell maintained that the legal status of the corporation in the United States in the 1800's was a concept possessing unique and priceless attributes for industry. The law gave the corporation "a fictional individuality" so that "it could perform many acts with which few individuals would care to be associated directly." Corporations also benefited when the granting of charters fell among the residual powers of the competing states.

As for the Fifth and Fourteenth Amendments, history showed that they guaranteed liberties which antedated the modern corporation and inhered in human beings: "It would have surprised the drafters . . . to know that the Bill of Rights [Fifth Amendment] would prove to be as important a protection for corporate as for individual interests; that in the years to come, the personal 'liberty,' which English colonists thought ought to be inviolate even against the state, would serve to elevate corporations beyond the reach of the government." The Fourteenth Amendment, of course, protected the liberties of Negroes against the states as well as the federal government. When the corporations seized upon the "due process" clauses in order to establish their rights, they began a controversy "too long and too bitterly fought to have been settled satisfactorily to anyone who lived through it." Lawyers cited the Fifth Amendment to protect business from the federal government and the Fourteenth when the states threatened. They found the commerce clause harder to handle, but they made a brave try.

Tugwell outlined the interpretation of the commerce clause, and the related question of jurisdiction as between the federal government and the states, from the time of Chief Justice John Marshall, 1801-1835, to the time of Chief Justice William Taft, 1921-1930. Marshall, in Gibbon vs. Ogden, prevented the states from regulating interstate trade. This did not mean a spate of federal regulations. He was less concerned that commerce be regulated than that the states should regulate it. Marshall also defined commerce as something more than "traffic," creating more implied powers. Chief Justice Roger B. Taney, 1836-1864, had a states'-right bias. He allowed the states to regulate in instances in which the federal government failed to act. Unlike Marshall's position, Taney's tended to hold back commercial expansion. Business benefited when the Wabash Case of 1886 reversed Taney, making federal jurisdiction over interstate commerce exclusive by preventing the states from acting even when Congress did not. Congress acted in 1887, but the Interstate Commerce Act, Tugwell asserted, "merely settled where an old power was to lie in a single instance of control."

The struggles of an expanding industrial society followed as the people fought for legislative fulfillment of their demand for control over business. There was still the problem of where the due-process and commerce clauses applied, and in "every case there had been the matter of jurisdiction"—state and federal. Down to Taft's time the courts persistently refused "to give up for the states all that Taney had kept for them." But the states lost effective control of business anyway. They fell victim to the commerce clause where business was interstate and to the due-process clauses where business was local. The result was renewed popular demands for federal legislation, and the Sherman Antitrust Act of 1890 gave the federal government power to control business. "But when even the lobbies had failed big business, the courts had stood firm." Chief Justice Melville W. Fuller's opinion in the Sugar Trust Case of 1895 emasculated the Sherman Act. It was, Tugwell declared, a "deliberate misinterpretation of legislative intent."

Meanwhile, business thrived. The once boiling controversy over government's power in economic matters simmered. The government seemed at first to be reopening the debate when it assumed war powers in 1917, but the court made exception in a "controlling emergency," evading the basic issue. The controversy apparently ended after the war. The courts reduced the states' powers to practically nothing, and Chief Justice Taft delivered a "ringing declaration of business immunities." Then the depression and the "policeman" government's failure to meet the exigencies of the crisis reopened the whole controversy. The people elected a new administration, which determined that only national action could salvage something from the wreckage of the national economy. But what powers might the federal government have? There was no answer. Laissez faire was firmly entrenched with the American people, who did not see that much of it was inconsistent with the Constitution. Accepting the "policeman" concept of government, they had only superficially considered the problem of regulation in a national economic state. There was, moreover, Taft's dictum. Thus, "about the control of business we were still in the dark in 1933, and still at the Senate's mercy." In 1926 Taft had said in the Tyson case that business could not be controlled, and "that in 1933 was the last word."

Roosevelt knew quite well that there was a slim chance of getting the Justices to reverse Taft's opinion. At the same time, amending the Constitution would be hopelessly slow. The only available course was to obtain Senate co-operation in the emergency and seek, despite the Court's inclinations, an extension of federal power through reinterpretation of the commerce clause. During the depression a widespread demand had already arisen for a search backward to find the beginning of the "stretching"—the transfer of the tradition of individual liberty to the corporation. This had been a prelude to the demand for a reinterpretation of the Constitution. This approach, of course, once again imposed a difficult burden on the Court, which, along with the framers of legislation, had to "torture meanings into a document which was broad and elastic on nearly every question it touched, but could hardly be so on one which had not been thought of at the time it was written." This was a problem which "perhaps it would be unfair to force the Court to face," but the "need for governmental powers to meet the challenge of defiant business was imperative, even though the attempts to create them might be fumbling and awkward." Defiant business, it should be noted, was not so obstinate during the crisis as it had been in the happier days of the 1920's. It was frightened enough to accept aid from the RFC, "but its lawyers would never lose sight of the permanent questions involved even in this." When the Liberty League was formed by businessmen who had got over their fright, its most numerous and ardent members were corporation lawyers who would not "admit even to themselves that they had all along supported what was merely expedient and even, perhaps, wrong."

Perhaps one could largely discount Tugwell's retrospective writings about his and the New Deal's broad-constructionist constitutional position if a study of his career did not show his earlier expression of opinions consistent with the views of his later writings and his concern as a New Dealer with the constitutionality of specific measures. In 1928, in an article entitled "That Living Constitution," he called for judicial interpretations which took a pragmatic view of human necessity, enabling the Constitution to grow as a "living instrument." [58] In his agricultural memorandum to Alfred E. Smith of 1928 he reasoned that the Court probably would have declared the McNary-Haugen proposals unconstitutional. He suggested that "this difficulty may as well be avoided in future proposals, and price relief sought by a means to which all assent." Of his own advance-ratio-price plan he said, "From the constitutional point of view, there are two difficulties": Would it abridge the right of contract unreasonably? Would it fall within the prohibitions of the Fifth Amendment? [59]

Correspondence between M. L. Wilson and Tugwell in the fall of 1932 shows their concern with constitutionality as they worked on the domestic-allotment plan. They studied the opinions of Judge Hulbert of the Farm Board's legal staff, Stanley Reed, Solicitor of the Farm Board, and others.[60] This study resulted in a shift from the sale of allotment certificates to a processing tax (which still did not satisfy the Court). During the lame-duck period proposals for legislation poured into Tugwell's office. Professor J. S. Long of Lehigh University suggested a plan requiring a percentage of alcohol in commercial gasoline. Tugwell replied: "The plan . . . is very interesting. . . . You must realize, however, that this is a state matter rather than a national one, and while some experimental work might be carried on by the Federal Government, there is little else that can be done." [61]

At the end of June, 1933, after the sweeping legislation of the Hundred Days, Tugwell addressed a group of lawyers on constitutional questions, mainly with reference to the AA Act and the NIR Act. He pointed out that opponents of these measures based their arguments on economic as well as constitutional grounds. They considered laissez faire and democracy "two aspects of one and the same value." "Certainly," Tugwell declared, "the Constitution was never designed to impose upon one era the absolute economic dogma which have been glorified under it in an earlier one." He then inquired whether the President and the Congress had violated the republican form of government explicit in the Constitution, or had infringed on the philosophy of checks and balances. These questions, he averred, "command respect, for they concern our faith in the organization and functioning of our national government." Answering his own questions, he conceded that the emergency had called for quick enactment of legislation which required "little policing, but, instead, much co-ordinated administration and negotiation." But the new laws were still the laws of Congress, which could amend or repeal them, and their content, in the light of the events of 1787 and subsequent economic developments, represented an attempt "to rediscover the Constitution, to revitalize the powers it was intended to create, many of which had been obscured in the interest of economic aims and purposes which have now become oppressingly obsolescent." [62]

In his first year on the job in the capital Tugwell was more directly concerned, with respect to constitutional considerations, with the food and drug bill than the NIR and AA Acts. David Cavers, co-author of the bill, wrote Tugwell in the spring of 1933: "We must fall back . . . on the sort of statute which can withstand judicial interference—and worse. This calls in some cases for extreme specification, in others for language as loose as the Constitution will permit." [63] Tugwell publicly defended the bill against charges of violation of the Constitution, stating in 1934 that the Food and Drug Administration could not violate the separation-of-powers doctrine because it had no judicial authority.[64] This contention was borne out in 1934 in an analogous case (Morgan vs. U. S., 298 US 468), which established that the Secretary of Agriculture's authority was not above the courts' jurisdiction.[65]

In an article of April, 1934, Tugwell called government sacred, but it had to change to remain so. Otherwise, it would become "atrophied and obsolete," ignored or brushed aside. Timely change required a broad construction of the Constitution. Institutions, after all, did not spring full-grown from legislative acts. Nor did our government emerge complete from the Constitutional Convention: "We had to learn about democratic government in practice; we had to grow into it by trying various devices. . . . We express determination to move forward in a general direction and within an agreed framework of rules. . . ." [66] Two months later, in June, 1934, Tugwell stated his views on the Constitution at the hearing on his promotion. He stressed the lack of any reference to industry in the Constitution, and his general position—"a Constitution is not intended to embody a particular economic theory"—was in line with Holmes's famous dictum.

In June, 1935, in his commencement address at the University of New Mexico, Tugwell made some remarks which obviously referred to the Supreme Court's action of two weeks before, the invalidation of the NIR Act. This was the speech which provoked Frank Kent and others to deplore Tugwell's defiance of the Court. Tugwell was simply asking the Court to adopt a broad constructionist view by way of allowing a new generation to meet its new problems. This was a common plea at the time. Moley made it in an article, "A Living Constitution"—a title, Kent noted, similar to one Tugwell used in 1928.[67] In 1936 another critic of the Court accused it of "veto-mindedness" and failure to fulfill its responsibility of clarifying the Constitution with regard to freedom and the general welfare. In vetoing methods as well as powers, the Court, this critic held, usurped legislative functions. It applied an eighteenth-century Constitution to twentieth-century problems in terms of nineteenth-century economic theories.[68]

But criticism was not defiance. After the Court invalidated the AA Act in January, 1936, Tugwell remarked in July that the new agricultural act did not influence economic balance as directly as the old one did, "and no certain way seems open to do that under the dictum of the Court." [69] Nor did he support Roosevelt's court-packing scheme. In mid-1937 he wrote to the President: "I still think the unwillingness of the Senate to submit to the popular will is your real problem and that the Court issue is secondary." He recommended no Pride's Purge such as Roosevelt attempted in 1938; he suggested a study of the legislative branch on the same high level as the Report on Management, a survey of the executive branch.[70] Tugwell's identification of the Senate as obstructive raised a serious question for political scientists (as did the same charge when it was revived, now against the House, in the 1960's). Meanwhile, he favored seeking the Constitutional amendment, ensuring the federal regulatory power, for which there had been no time in 1933. "The progressives," he recalled, "generally felt more or less deeply this way. Of these I may say I was one. But my protests, like those of others, were ineffective." [71]

In retrospect, Tugwell saw definite gains, despite the Court and the Senate, for the nationalists. The period 1880-1933 had "no parallel in all history for sheer disorder, confusion, and paradox." Nevertheless, in those years there had been a discernible double trend—a reduction in state power and an increase in federal power. The New Deal's interstate commerce cases provoked a "long overdue Constitutional debate in which, however the victory might appear to run, the power of the national government in economic matters would be immensely increased, if not established beyond argument." [72] Roosevelt had been "enough of a lawyer—and, if he was not, Attorney General Cummings was—to know that he walked here in a no man's land of doubtful legality; and he must rely on recognition, even in judges' minds, of contemporary reality." [73] At the same time, the judges learned, as they had in the past, that the right of judicial review which John Marshall had established in a no man's land, "depended very considerably on discretion. The Court must not allow itself to be maneuvered into untenable positions. . . . The justices, in the larger strategic sense, must be politicians. They were vulnerable. And the continuance of their prerogatives depended upon their holding the substantial confidence of the country." [74]

Looking to the future, Tugwell wrote, in 1949, that central economic planning involved "matters which have constitutional implications and need exploration in terms appropriate to their legality." He was aware that "constitutionally . . . the difficulties of recognizing the American economy as an articulate whole are considerable but not absolute." He did not expect the Court to adopt holistic economic views when there was so little recognition elsewhere of "essential economic and social unity." If proposed changes were sufficiently important and sound, they could be argued for—"otherwise not." Constitutional change had to follow a change of public feeling in fundamental matters. The courts would grant full recognition of new social concepts and devices "if they should be generally demanded . . . the courts cannot go faster than is demanded." [75]

In 1956 Merlo J. Pusey, the eminent student of the Supreme Court, stated that "some of the early New Deal statutes were passed under the pressure of emergency without the slightest regard for constitutional limitations." [76] There is something to this statement—as far as it goes. It needs to be checked against the attitudes of particular individuals working on particular bills. Documentary evidence shows that Tugwell and others were concerned with the constitutionality of legislation they helped to formulate. One cannot say that the New Dealers did not care one jot about the Constitution. Nor can one say that they strove to conform scrupulously to prevailing strict-constructionist views. When in doubt, during the period of formulation, they tipped the scales in favor of action, seeing some justification in broad constructionism. But being by no means sure of the Court's approval, they had no intention of defying the Court's disapproval in some illegal manner. Even the court-packing scheme rested on the Constitutional authority of Congress to ordain and establish courts (Article III, Section 1) and of the President to appoint judges of the Supreme Court (Article II, Section 2, Paragraph 2). Nevertheless, as Tugwell recalled, he told Roosevelt the scheme would "constitute a successful aggression against one co-ordinate branch of government by the other two branches." [77] In Sumner Welles's opinion, Tugwell "sought consistently, according to the best lights available to him, to rectify the social injustices of our modern civilization in the truly liberal and democratic tradition of the principles of the Constitution." [78]

IV

Any attempt to find a place for Tugwell in the political spectrum in terms of his attitudes toward the American tradition requires a definition of terms. It is commonly held that the terms "liberal" and "conservative" have become meaningless in American society because it is essentially an undifferentiated, middle-class, Lockean mass. It is true that "liberal" and "conservative" do not lend themselves to precise definition solely in terms of policy proposals, at a given time or at one time as compared to another. For example, one wing of the Democratic party is now more Hamiltonian than Jeffersonian, while the reverse is true of one wing of the Republican party. But some attempt at definition is in order if the application of these terms to Tugwell is not to become mere verbal gymnastics.

Perhaps it is useful to formulate definitions in terms of attitudes toward change. The conservatives do not dismiss the need to adjust to and accommodate new conditions, but they tend to emphasize the importance of those things which have proved valuable in the past. The liberals do not dismiss the importance of those things which have proved valuable in the past, but they tend to emphasize the need to adjust to and accommodate new conditions. The reactionary opposes change in a doctrinaire way, while the radical favors change in a doctrinaire way. Both conservatives and liberals believe that policies based on their respective attitudes toward change will best promote the dignity and the free, full development of the individual. Conservatives consider collectivistic (public or governmental) action a threat to these values. Liberals (M. Morton Auerbach and William J. Newman, for example) attribute to conservatives a Quixotic yearning for an uncomplicated past and a simplistic view of the world in which these values are to be realized.[79] Liberals see an ever-new world in which new means, some of them collectivistic, are appropriate to the preservation of the values relating to the individual and to the retention of as much of the past in general as is possible under the circumstances. Thus, a liberal like Tugwell will sometimes claim to be conservative in the sense of conservational and in the limitive sense of calling for no more action than the situation demands. Conservatives' estimates of what circumstances require will, of course, differ from liberals' assessments of the needs of the times. (Even definition in terms of attitudes toward change requires a supplementary note. The Populists' and Progressives' desire for change places them in the liberal or reform tradition, yet the change they desired—their policy—was in large part the restoration of conditions which they thought had existed in the past.)

When Tugwell declared himself a conservative, Frank Kent made a joke of it. On the other hand, Professors Arthur W. Macmahon and John D. Millett of Columbia, writing in 1939, called Tugwell "inherently conservative" although "daring in the conception of remedies."[80] In a special context Louis Hacker did not think it humorous of Tugwell to refer to himself as a conservative, "which economically speaking," Hacker noted, "he really was."[81] The conservative aspect of Tugwell's thought from the standpoint of economics was his emphasis on efficiency. This he shared with the classical economists, but, as he saw it, the means of achieving efficiency were quite different in the technologically advanced economy of the twentieth century from what they had been in terms of the classical model of many, small, equal, com-

peting enterprises. The attainment of efficiency now involved the creation of larger economic units. In recognizing the trend toward larger,
interrelated units, Tugwell, according to John Franklin Carter, was a
collectivist only in the sense that J. P. Morgan was.[82]

Seven years after Carter made this remark, in 1941, Burnham expressed
his fear that through *The Managerial Revolution* Morgan's "socialism"
would lead to totalitarian technocracy. In 1942 Joseph Schumpeter asserted that Morgan's "socialism" would eventually give way to classical
socialism. Tugwell and Berle, the latter in *Property without Power* (1959),
denied that our corporate economy must inevitably develop in either of
these directions. It was necessary to live with bigness, Tugwell insisted
in 1939, because it was invincible: "What orthodoxy disapproves, what
educators resist, what our moral leaders want to reverse—and what industrialists all-unknowingly are precipitating—is a vast-scale modernism
which no resistance can stop." [83] Interchangeable parts, scientific management, and machine costing, he commented in 1941, had, in an instant,
removed the rule-of-thumb factory manager to the dinosaur class.[84]

This technological advance, Tugwell asserted in 1939, made "articulation of the whole the emergent need of society." [85] Thus, he advocated
co-ordination through planning, only to see business condemn him as a
radical. In 1935 Stuart Chase advised business that if it were to continue to hold its position in the future, it should stop damning Tugwell,
a "safe and sane intellectual," as a symbol for socialistic penetration and
concentrate on the march of events. Business, Chase continued, had to
come to terms not with a few personalities like Tugwell, but with a
maelstrom of impersonal historical forces.[86] Tugwell was saying the
same thing as Chase. He was insisting that invincible economic trends
compelled adjustment for survival. Of course, mere recovery from the
depression would not constitute adequate adjustment. Survival required thinking in long-run terms and with a sense of urgency as great
as that which applied to immediate measures. Tugwell was aware of
the great resistance to planning, but he saw it as his duty to point out
probable threats to survival and the means of their avoidance: "The
planner," he wrote in 1949, "like other social scientists, may not have great
hope of modification of these attitudes and the attainment of freedom
in time to avert calamity; but he must be forgiven for insisting that
materials are being played with which are likely to destroy the world
if they are not made to conform to civilized disciplines." [87] He could
not have stated the problem in graver terms.

There was no telling, Tugwell warned in 1939, what the details of
our decline would be if we neglected adjustment. Opposing forces
could delay the adaptive process of articulation to the point where the
American state would be reduced to ineffectiveness, and "the whole

system would either be subjected to a foreign executive or submerged in chaos out of which anything might emerge—anything that is except institutions with fundamental provision for the participation of every citizen after his sort, which is, after all, the democratic *sine qua non*." [88] One possible result was autarchy, which could come about by some industrial *tour de force*—"it even seems more likely to come about that way, so great is the moral objection to the enlargement or the revision of governmental powers." [89] In the face of such dire consequences Tugwell's recommendations for adjustment seem conservative both in the sense of conservational and of a minimum of change under the circumstances.

Tugwell was concerned with efficiency as an economic objective (Taylor), planning as a means of achieving that objective (Patten and Veblen), and experimentation as the technique of planning (Dewey). This technique neither rejected capitalism nor accepted socialism. It was not dictatorial but evolutionary. For example, Tugwell agreed with the classical contention that tariffs were a hindrance to efficiency, but he would not support immediate adoption of a free-trade policy or any other program which did not take into account maintenance of the American workers' standard of living in the going world as it was. [90] Evolution in formulation was to be accompanied by consent in adoption. Given the fact that technology would overcome all obstacles in any case, it was incumbent upon us, Tugwell declared in 1935, to reject the violent course of other nations which had eliminated the evolutionary and democratic process and at the same time produce leadership and administration capable of creating institutions "suited to the world in which they are expected to operate." [91] Tugwell had asserted in 1934 that no one "with the slightest sense of history" would attempt to fit the American people into a regimented scheme, for "law, government, and social organization for such a people must be instruments through which their characteristic actions, resistances, and imaginations could find appropriate expression. Law, government, and social organization will inevitably fail if they are not this. In this respect I unhesitatingly avow myself a thorough conservative." [92]

The implication of Tugwell's insistence on the invincibility of technological advance and the necessity of adjusting to it in an evolutionary way was that he did not favor collectivism for its own sake. Advocacy of planning, co-ordination, and regulation was his response to the failures of haphazard and unrestrained profit-making. The principal failure of our system had arisen out of the problem of distributing the enormous product of Taylorized industry. This failure had been one of the basic causes of the depression. It had been the failure of "private" collectivists, who, John Franklin Carter pointed out, cried out the loudest against

New Deal "collectivism." [93] They had interfered, Tugwell stated in 1935, with the "natural—as distinguished from the financial—laws of supply and demand." [94] Neither competition nor antitrustism had made them operate in the general interest, or even in their own—for only wide distribution would enable capitalism to survive.

Tugwell preferred action by business itself—co-operation on policies of low prices, high wages, planned use of capacity, and the foregoing of speculative profits and deficits—to government intervention as the means of assuring continuity. No one would know, he wrote in 1934, "to what lengths the government will have to go until it is seen whether industry is capable . . . of arranging itself so that the full resources of our productive capacities can be used." If industry did not provide its own government, there would be serious government intervention. This would involve the "less efficient policy of rigorous regulation, extreme taxation, and of widespread provision of free social goods." A lot of expensive and otherwise unnecessary machinery would be needed. [95] These remarks fitted in with Tugwell's institutionalist thought which gave first place to business as the instrument of recovery.

The original Brain Trusters were to the right of their successors, Corcoran and Cohen, because, as Professor Schlesinger has commented, they believed in collaboration with the business community. Their long-run economic views required the "transformation of business rather than its isolation and terrorization." [96] John Franklin Carter concluded that Tugwell was a "genuine conservative" who desired to save the profit system and private property by adjusting them to the technical conditions of the power age. If the New Deal succeeded in this objective, Tugwell would go down in history as one of the men who saved capitalism. If it failed, he would be written off as a "poor, deluded, right-wing liberal" who was foolish enough to hope that the great forces of the industrial revolution could find expression in an orderly way within the channels of democratic institutions. [97]

The New Deal did save the profit system and private property, barely, although it did not take as much conservational action as Tugwell would have liked. It was caught in the dilemma of combining immediate and long-run measures. As Ernest K. Lindley put it, the New Deal was engaged in shoring up useful portions of the old structure while remodeling. [98] It is difficult to overestimate the urgency of immediate measures. Tugwell's involvement in them caused a resident of Detroit to ask his Senator in 1934 to try to get rid of the notorious professor. Senator James Couzens, a renegade Republican, replied, "I am unwilling to sit by and see millions of our people in distress because they are unable to secure work, and if that is what Professor Tugwell is driving at, then I am for it." [99] Yet, some historians have underestimated the depth of the crisis of 1933. Professor Edward C. Kirkland, for example, has suggested that Hoover's policies should not be judged only by short-term considerations, that "over a longer period than the 1930's and 1940's they may have contained deeper insights than we realize." [100]

Kirkland was certainly correct if he meant that the New Deal had changed the relationship between government and society, and he had every right to prefer that relationship as of 1885-1932 to its New Deal form. He may eventually prove correct if he meant to imply that the planning-socialism-dictatorship sequence will run its course in America —although we have not been a civilization like those which have made this sequence seem automatic. Nor was he alone if he meant to deplore continuing deficit financing, although in this connection one must consider, besides the New Deal, wars both hot and cold. But we must judge Hoover's policies by short-term considerations because there could be no survival in the long run without survival in the short run. The first question is not whether we *should* have continued Hoover's policies. It is, rather, whether we *could* have.

Edgar Eugene Robinson contended in *The Roosevelt Leadership* that the New Deal made Americans "less able to perform the function of a self-supporting people." William Miller, replying to Robinson, maintained that Americans "either as individuals or a nation have not been a 'self-supporting people' for generations. Fortunately, in politics in the 'thirties they continued to act as if they were. In an unprecedented crisis in which their self-appointed leaders had thrown up their hands in fear and panic, it is to be wondered what the neo-Hooverites might deem the 'function of a self-supporting people' if not to vote in by orderly and constitutional means new leaders of their own choosing." [101] Professor Frank Freidel has remarked that critics of the New Deal "succeeded in creating the impression in the prosperous years since 1945 that the depression really did not amount to much. How bad it was is worth remembering since this is a means of gauging the enormous pressure for change." [102] Those who underestimated the crisis accused the New Deal of taking away from the American people something which they certainly did not have in 1933. Those who contended, nevertheless, that Hoover's policies would not have harmed the American people as the New Deal did were contradicted by other Hooverites who called their man the "real father of the New Deal." Some claimants of Hoover's paternity based their case on excerpts from Walter Lippmann's *The New Imperative* (1935). Lippmann remarked that Hoover and Roosevelt, reacting to the same new economic forces, sponsored governmental intervention in a number of the same sectors of the economy: fiscal policy, public works, relief, farm "disparity," industrial co-operation, monetary management. Thus, the real break with the past took place not in 1933 but in 1929. Supporters of Hoover's progenitorship overlooked Lippmann's references to significant differences between Hoover and Roosevelt in implementation. Dixon Wecter and Broadus Mitchell also concluded, in effect, that differences in degree were substantial.[103]

Miller made a case for the New Deal as an effort on the part of the "politically self-supporting people" to save their constitutional system, restore their national morale, and strengthen their political morality "by confronting it at long last with the facts of life." [104] No one knew better than Tugwell the shortcomings of this emergency effort, which he publicly admitted in 1934.[105] But the real source of these mistakes, he later asserted, was the neglect of adjustment in the past.[106] Thus, in 1933 we faced a crisis requiring tremendous efforts in relief and reconstruction. If there had been adjustment in the past, Hoover's kind of individualism would have faded without the New Deal. Its flourishing amid neglect of adjustment to technological advance suggests that history, which finally sprang the trap on the neglectors, not the New Deal, changed the relationship between government and society. In this view, the superiority of Hoover's kind of individualism is an academic matter. Our problem now is to combine co-operation with individualism in a new kind of world. If we fail, we can not attribute our failure to the New Deal. It alleviated some problems and created others in struggling to respond to historical forces. The new problems were left to succeeding generations, who would enjoy no shortage of challenges.

David Lawrence and James C. Young were shocked at Tugwell's suggestion in a textbook that the challenge to America of developments in Russia lay in the idea of planning. Their shock implied that Tugwell's comment reflected a pro-Soviet attitude. What he meant was that both the United States and the Soviet Union were dealing with technological forces which Marx never heard of and which would exist in the United States even if there were no Soviet Union. This did not mean that the other aspects of the two civilizations which were facing these forces had anything in common. This, in turn, meant that we could meet the Soviet challenge, as C. H. Carr suggested in *The Soviet Impact on the Western World*, through a "successful search for new forms of economic and social action in which what is valid in individualist and democratic tradition can be applied to the problems of mass civilization." [107] Carr wrote in 1947 when it was impossible to shrug one's shoulders at the Soviet challenge which Tugwell had pointed to in 1928, before the U.S.S.R. became a superpower. In the 1950's references to the Soviet challenge did not evoke charges of pro-Sovietism, and they comprised a growing shelf of literature which included *The Communist Challenge to American Business*, the work of an outstanding industrialist like Clarence B. Randall.[108]

The Soviet challenge was another fact we had to face in a new world. Tugwell's feelings about this new world as he expressed them in *The Stricken Land* showed that he did not preach institutional adjustment for its own sake:

My parents do not know what changed their world—and neither do I for that matter. The one we now have seems to have evolved mysteriously out of that simpler, perhaps more satisfying and certainly more secure one into which I was born. I am at least privileged to feel that my experience spans the transition from one kind of civilization to another. Like others of my age I cannot tell whether I like the old or the new. My parents have no such doubts—perhaps because they have outlived insecurity. They like the new. They do not like everything. But they consider wars, heavy taxes, governmental regulation of people's lives and so on to be errors which will be corrected. They like automobiles and good roads, airplanes, radios, improved bathrooms, and all appurtenances of modernity which I am inclined to regard as too high a price for wars, governmental interests, and all the rest of it.[109]

These are the words of a man who criticized the capitalistic system not because he wished to destroy it, as all of its critics desire to do according to Ludwig von Mises, but because he wished to improve it. His proposals were in the pragmatic-idealistic tradition of frontally attacking injustice and oppression—the American tradition.

28. Tugwell's Thought and America Today

I

Historians have raised the question whether the New Deal was evolutionary or revolutionary.[1] Mario Einaudi has written about *The Roosevelt Revolution,* and Carl N. Degler has called the New Deal "The Third American Revolution." [2] Each historian makes his judgment in a particular frame of reference. Tugwell stressed evolution, concluding that in terms of his institutional thought the New Deal did not basically change the capitalistic game but provided some new rules and, through social security, sought to give everyone a chance to play. Since welfare statism, concentration-and-control, and Progressive antitrustism and reform all go back many years in the history of American thought, intellectual historians have tended to label the New Deal evolutionary. At the same time, in many instances the *actual adoption* of certain measures was new. In this sense, the New Deal was revolutionary in practice, at least in its novelty. Besides the matters of conception and adoption, there is, of course, the question of impact. Whether the New Deal was evolutionary or revolutionary, we live in a society quite different from the America of 1933.

The prevailing opinion is that our complex technological economy will not run well the way Topsy grew. This abandonment of automaticity, Professor J. K. Galbraith has stated, "requires that nearly everyone be socially responsible in some degree at some time. No business decision is any longer quite private. Economic depression has been an unhappy experience with us. No one can lightly risk the charge that he is contributing to such a disaster." [3] Thus, as Berle, David Lilienthal, Peter F. Drucker, and others have pointed out, corporations have become more socially conscious than they were in the 1920's. The private sector of the economy displays more wisdom and foresight, exercising greater care in making investment decisions and recognizing the necessity of widespread, adequate purchasing power.

There have been developments in the distribution of control and of income which would surprise Theodore Roosevelt and Woodrow Wilson, and which Karl Marx would not believe. Berle has described the concentration of great economic power in about 500 corporations. But this does not mean, as Marx assumed, concentration of economic power in 500 families. Control has become separated from ownership ("management control"), and ownership and benefits through stockholding have become so widespread that it is difficult to describe our system in traditional terms. It has been called "people's capitalism," a "paraproprietal society" (a society beyond property), and "company socialism" (a collective system administered by business rather than by the state).[4]

There have been equally striking changes in the distribution of income. In 1935 the median income was $2,048; in 1959 it was $4,400—in constant dollars.[5] The labor unions and progressive taxation have contributed to this redistribution. The unions, in raising real wages about 3 per cent annually for the past thirty years, have had an impact which the Marxist analysis did not allow them. Similarly, progressive taxation is a governmental measure which Marx ruled out—in his system the government was the tool of the bourgeoisie. Indeed, the whole list of the New Deal's measures affecting the economy, in enactment and effect, represents a rejection of the fatalism of Marx, who said that capitalism is automatically self-destroying, and the classical economists, who said that capitalism is automatically self-preserving. Capitalism in the United States adjusted for survival. It acquired "built-in stabilizers," which, despite their defects, give us confidence that we shall not see another 1929. Tugwell commented in 1958, "The bulwarks built by Roosevelt were not altogether proof against conservative sabotage, but it was unlikely that after his work was done such a calamity as 1929 would happen again." [6]

Confirmation of this new society is seen in its acceptance by the Republican party. Berle noted in 1958 that the Republicans, whose alliance with ultraconservative Democrats gave them control of legislation most of the time, had not in six years "cared or dared to change any essential part of the institutional structure they inherited." They were as proud as anyone, Berle continued, of the American "economic record and achievements under the rules set up by Franklin Roosevelt and maintained by Harry Truman." During the recession of 1957-1958 they boasted that "thanks to (New Deal) social legislation," the economy had built-in stabilizers to prevent another crash like that of 1929.[7] Berle's parenthetical insertion of "New Deal" suggests a phenomenon on which Professor Galbraith has commented. Those who argue for automaticity because "the American economy is very different from what it was in 1929" are usually those who are least inclined to give the New Deal credit for therapeutic qualities.[8]

Leading Republicans, however, have made specific statements indicating acceptance of the New Deal or, at least, a lack of intention of undoing it. In 1956, Dr. Raymond J. Saulnier, Chairman of the President's Council of Economic Advisers, declared, "We take the view that the Federal Government has a heavy responsibility to moderate economic fluctuations." [9] At about the same time Gerard B. Lambert, of the

Listerine fortune, published his autobiography in which he recalled his increasing liberalism over the years and his changed attitude toward unions: "Now I am glad that they have enforced their demands. It has brought a more stable economy by shifting our wealth from a few to the masses, strangely enough aiding industry while doing so." [10] In 1957 Cabell Phillips of the *New York Times* described the program outlined in President Dwight D. Eisenhower's State of the Union Message as "quite a progressive one when measured by Republican standards of only ten years ago . . . and even moderately progressive when measured by the standards of the New and Fair Deals." [11] In 1959, speaking at a banquet for Mr. Khrushchev, Henry Cabot Lodge, Jr., said, "We live in a welfare state which seeks to put a floor below which no one sinks but builds no ceiling to prevent men from rising." These words, Arthur Krock commented, could have been those of Franklin D. Roosevelt.[12] This change in the views of the GOP, or one wing of the party, fits in with Walter Lippmann's conclusion that the historical function of the Democratic party has been innovation, of the Republican consolidation.[13] This change gives people confidence that regardless of which political party is in power, "whatever action may be required to prevent anything resembling the debacle of 1929 will be taken." [14]

Nevertheless, the performance of our economy leaves much to be desired. We do have "built-in stabilizers"—measures for the maintenance of financial liquidity in a business downturn, supports for purchasing power, and a better understanding of compensatory fiscal effects—but a number of analysts, differing in their definitions of "built-in stabilizers," agree that they are not in themselves adequate preventives of severe decline.[15] Despite the recent rise in median income, 25.8 per cent or 14,044,000 of the nation's families earn less than $2,500 a year net according to a report by *Sales Management Magazine* in July, 1962. Our economy certainly lacks the "continuity" which Tugwell stressed, as this sequence indicates:

> Recession 1948-1949
> Recovery 45 months
> Recession 1953-1954
> Recovery 35 months
> Recession 1957-1958
> Recovery 25 months
> Recession 1960-1961
> Recovery ? [16]

In late September, 1962, Richard Rutter of the *New York Times* reported that "the recovery from the 1960-1961 recession had obviously failed to meet expectations and . . . signs of a real fall pick-up were still missing." [17] Rutter's report confirmed the findings of the Cleveland Trust Company in July, 1962, which showed these percentages of increase in industrial production in the sixteen-month period following the low point of each of the last four recessions: 30.7, 17.2, 18.9, 15.4 (February, 1961-June, 1962).[18] Moreover, with each recovery unemployment has remained high:

> 1953 peak 2.9 per cent
> 1957 peak 4.3 per cent
> 1959 peak 5.0 per cent
> 1961 peak 6.0 per cent (estimated) [19]

In late September, 1962, a presidential committee of economists reported these unemployment rates for the industrial nations of the free world:

Canada	7.0 per cent
United States	5.6 per cent
Italy	4.3 per cent
Britain	2.4 per cent
France	1.9 per cent
Sweden	1.5 per cent
Japan	1.1 per cent
West Germany	1.0 per cent [20]

Discussions of the causes of recession invariably involve references to overexpansion of capital plant (the kind of overinvestment which Tugwell described in the 1920's) in relation to declining demand and reductions in government expenditures (the kind of "withdrawal" which Tugwell saw as preceding the recession of 1937-1938).[21] Discussions of recovery from recessions inevitably refer to increased government expenditures—the policy which Tugwell recommended in 1938 and again in 1958.

Was Tugwell a victim of what Carey McWilliams, in an article entitled "Taps for the 1930's," called the acute nostalgia for the days of the depression and the New Deal which many liberals suffered? [22] Hardly. He still looked upon monetary and fiscal policies as crude devices for maintaining economic stability. Spending in an emergency, when the trickle-down theory held little promise, was one thing. Spending on a continuous basis to sustain prosperity was another. It characterized an economy to which the classical rules did not apply: in the recession of August, 1957-April, 1958, a decline in production and employment (5%) was accompanied by a *slight* decline (1%) in personal income and consumer spending and a slight *increase* (2-3%) in wage rates and prices.[23] Nor is there agreement among economists on the causes—government spending, "administered" prices, or wage increases in excess of productivity gains—or the effects—fundamental danger or necessary growth stimulant—of the inflationary tendencies which persisted through the recession. Moreover, many economists, confirming Tugwell's views, consider both monetary and fiscal policies ineffective, unreliable contracyclical instruments.[24]

On page 118 of *The Art of Politics* Tugwell stated his collectivistic position, his belief in the need for planning and co-ordination, without socialism, if the economy were to achieve growth with balance and continuity. This statement was essentially like others he made thirty years before. Berle, too, wrote about an increased growth rate and more planning.[25] Neither of these men was nostalgic because the kinds of reforms they had in mind had the newness of never having been tried. That Tugwell's scheme was never tried involved the fundamental question of change in a democratic society, which was the question underlying his study of Roosevelt's career.

There was no apparatus available in the 1930's for executing a collectivistic scheme in the general interest. Tugwell knew this, as evidenced in his early criticism of the NRA. On the other hand, he believed that Roosevelt underestimated his freedom of action in refraining from pushing the NRA in the "right" direction. Still, there was the problem of personnel. Tugwell showed his awareness of this problem as Governor of Puerto Rico, in which position he stressed the thorough training of civil servants to carry out a long-maturing development program (unlike Castro, Munoz-Marin had some place to go in an evolutionary manner when he attained power). The recent troubles in the federal regulatory agencies, moreover, underline the probability of difficulty in executing Tugwell's kind of program. He commented on these troubles in 1958, noting the historic pattern of the regulated taking over the agency that is supposed to be regulating them.[26] Finally, and foremost, there is the matter of public opinion. The American people will tolerate a great deal of difficulty and hardship before they will forego clinging to familiar ways, even myths, and respond to the argument for efficiency.

Thus, the adoption and effective execution of a collectivistic policy like Tugwell's would require a deeply and widely felt need on the part of the people; long and careful pre-planning; and thorough training, oriented toward the public interest, of highly competent personnel. Adoption, in particular, would require political astuteness to gain Congressional support, and execution would require judicious administration to retain that support. Tugwell's experience in the RA convinced him of the importance of these last two requirements.

If Roosevelt appears vulnerable to the charge that he had "followers"

rather than "disciples" because his appeal was personal rather than ideological, Professor Walter Johnson has taken an opposing position. We
cannot be certain, Johnson asserted, that " 'long-range' plans would have
been more successful than what was tried" by the New Deal.[27] Professor
Schlesinger seconded this judgment with reference to Tugwell's proposals.
Tugwell's contribution was his reinforcement of Roosevelt's conclusion
that the old explanations were invalid. In seeking new solutions, Roosevelt
did not accept Tugwell's institutionalism as the only remedy. In fact, the
President was more of an experimentalist than Tugwell. As Professor
Schlesinger has so shrewdly pointed out, Tugwell and others "were ready
to experiment *within* their systems. But Roosevelt transcended systems for
the sake of a more complex vision of America, which included elements of
co-ordination and of decentralization, of nationalism and of internationalism, and thus also included means of preventing any system from being
pushed to logical—and probably—destructive extremes." [28] But since the
performance of our economy leaves much to be desired, we still cannot
evade the question which Tugwell's career and commentary raised so
magnificently—can we get the most out of our modern industrial plant
without planning and co-ordination?

II

In the early summer of 1958 Houghton Mifflin published *The Affluent Society* by J. K. Galbraith, who rejected the "conventional wisdom"
which assumed that all profit-yielding enterprises produced wealth and
that government expenditures were wasteful. This was a stifling double
standard, Galbraith maintained as he called for the allocation of a
greater portion of national income to the public sector: health, education,
welfare, urban renewal, housing, transportation, recreation, conservation. *The Affluent Society* sold about 100,000 copies—an amazing total
for a work by an academic economist. Its ideas provoked what Edwin
L. Dale, Jr., reporting from Washington in the *New York Times* of
February 7, 1960, called the "Great Debate in Capital: Is U. S. Misusing
Its Wealth?" In the *Times* of March 13, 1960, Dale analyzed the "Big
Debate: Public versus Private Spending." The discussions which Dale
described did not satisfy his colleague James Reston, who, also in the
Times of March 13, 1960, called upon the leaders of both major political
parties to discuss the basic philosophical, economic, political, and moral
issues involved in the question of allocation of resources. Similarly,
Barbara Ward, in the *New York Times Magazine* of May 8, 1960, complained about "The Great Silence in the Great Debate," deploring
widespread apathy toward the question of private versus public spending which she considered the issue of transcendent importance facing
the free world.

Despite these misgivings, discussion of Galbraith's ideas produced a ream of literature in each of several areas besides the debate concerning the *inner consistency and empirical validity of Galbraith's thesis* itself.[29] In his column of March 9, 1960, Walter Lippmann contended that we could meet the challenge of public needs with only a slight increase in the share of national income spent by the government—if we could bring the annual *growth rate of the economy* up to 4.7 per cent. Thus, the question of allocation of resources tied in with the problem of economic growth. In June, 1960, W. Allen Wallis, Special Assistant to President Eisenhower, held that those who argued that growth would provide more funds for federal spending also pointed to federal spending as the way to growth. Thus, the question of growth tied in doubly with the issue of *collectivism*—collective public, or governmental, action —the subject of a debate whose manifestations in print would fill a long library shelf. Suffice it to say for the moment that works by Arthur M. Schlesinger, Jr., and Senator Barry Goldwater appeared simultaneously on the best-seller lists in 1960 and that in late 1961 Henry Regnery, the conservative publishing house, advertised, "If you've read Galbraith and Schlesinger—you owe it to yourself to read *Prosperity through Freedom* by Lawrence Fertig." Finally, the question of allocation of resources raised issues which transcended the realm of economic and political means. In the last analysis the relative amounts of steel which we allocated to schools, tail fins, and missiles had to do with ends and philosophical values, with the kind of a society we wanted to be. Thus, the question of allocation of resources tied in with the searching, endless discussion of the *national purpose*, which, in turn, brought us back to the question of collectivism—if we decided that a collective sense of purpose were desirable, could we attain our goals with noncollective means?

Some people, John K. Jessup noted, believe that only individuals, not nations, are capable of high purposes.[30] Henry Hazlitt declared that the "'national purpose' is no different from the purposes of the individuals who compose the nation." [31] Others, such as Charles Darlington, held that "it is not enough to do right as individuals. The nation has also a moral life which we must fill by public effort imbued with spiritual purpose." [32] Michael Polyani maintained that a free society can sustain itself only by dedicating itself to a distinctive set of beliefs.[33] Some economists—Milton Friedman, Henry Hazlitt, Henry C. Wallich, John Chamberlain, Friedrich Hayek, Ludwig von Mises—rejected collectivism of purpose and held up free enterprise as an end in itself.[34] In this vein, Raymond J. Saulnier remarked, "As I understand our economy, its ultimate purpose is to produce more consumer goods." [35] *Nation's Business* observed editorially, "Barring a dedicated few in religion, education, science or medicine, a sense of purpose which attracts men toward new frontiers is another name for profits." [36]

Walter Lippmann replied to Saulnier that "the object of our economy is . . . to use the wealth and power which our economy can produce to support the national purposes which we so frequently proclaim." [37] Charles Darlington insisted that in charting our future as a nation we should not allow the "virtue" of free enterprise to become a "vice." [38] Father R. L. Bruckberger, commenting on Henry Charles Carey, the American economist whose chief works appeared between 1837 and 1859, called Carey's contention that wealth should be put to man's service in the pursuit of ends which transcend the realm of the material "in the best American tradition" and "characteristically American." [39] Adolf A. Berle, Jr., also took the view that an economy is an instrument for the attainment of a larger purpose. He insisted that our economy must grow faster not to keep ahead of Russian production, not just to make up a lag in certain armaments, but primarily to make America the kind of a country we want it to be.[40]

Tugwell, like Galbraith, raised the question of allocation of resources. Tugwell's immediate concern was quantitative—efficiency, or the effect of allocation of resources on economic stability. Galbraith's emphasis was qualitative—the public sector had to do with the quality of life in America rather than the bread-and-butter issues which had concerned the New Dealers. But the contrast was not so clear-cut. Tugwell believed that Americans' highest purposes transcended the realm of the material. Thus, from economic efficiency would emerge a life of higher general quality. In a broad sense, both Tugwell and Galbraith raised the issue denoted in William James's famous phrase, "A Moral Equivalent for War." Of course, this concern with ends is inseparable from the question of means, and it would not be accurate to imply a parallel between Tugwell and Galbraith in this respect. Tugwell's "planned capitalism" was *direct* collectivism, while Galbraith's ideas on the expenditure of some of the funds which capitalism produced were *indirect* collectivism —in the sense that all public or governmental action is collectivistic. Collective decisions had always determined allocations to the public sector. Galbraith was essentially asking for a change in value judgments regarding the relative importance of public needs. He asserted that his proposals were not "merely a renewal of the ancient argument over socialism." [41]

Nevertheless, Henry Hazlitt, referring to Galbraith's ideas, stated that since socialization of production "is in disrepute in the Western world, a new brand of socialism is now on sale. It does not insist on the socialization of production but on the socialization of consumption." [42] W. Allen Wallis, Special Assistant to President Eisenhower, declared that "the public squalor argument is, in fact, simply this decade's battlecry of socialism. . . ." [43] Some objections to Galbraith's proposals rested on the proposition that in the first place there was no need for larger allocations to the public sector. In an article entitled "Affluent Government," Hazlitt, citing figures on government income and government expenditures as percentages of gross national product, called claims of poverty in the public sector absurd. [44] *Fortune* referred editorially to "That 'Starved' Public Sector." [45] Francis M. Bator arrived at a different conclusion. He found that while total government purchases of goods and services had increased fourfold between 1929 and 1957, nondefense public spending had only doubled. On a per capita basis, Bator found, there had been no increase in nondefense spending since 1939. [46]

This debate over collectivism is merely the most recent phase of a controversy which public action and proposals for public action have long stimulated in American history—whether positive government will give the American people national security, personal freedom, and economic abundance or lead them to regimentation and misery. It is unfortunate that as this is written the "New Conservatives" look to Senator Barry Goldwater as their spokesman in this controversy. [47] Goldwater's relative emphasis on the past is so great that he has been called a "Restorationist" by Clinton Rossiter, [48] whose own presentation of the conservative position is on a far higher intellectual level than Goldwater's. [49] Goldwater's reasoning is marked by oversimplification. He is given to such either-or statements as "I do not undertake to promote welfare, for I propose to extend freedom." [50] (This reminds us of Russell Kirk's remark that he would "rather lose with Socrates, let us say, than win with Lenin." [51]) The Senator frequently refers to the unchanging quality of man's nature, especially his spiritual nature, in the midst of a changing environment. The man in the Roman chariot and the man in the jet airplane are the same man. Institutionalists would not accept this separation of human nature from the environment, which, they hold, encourages or discourages the expression of the various facets of man's comparatively unchanging nature. Nor would theologians accept Goldwater's total division of man's spiritual nature and his environment. At least at a certain level theologians see a relationship between the two. Otherwise, we could account neither for Reinhold Niebuhr's writings in history and international affairs nor papal encyclicals such as Leo XIII's *Rerum Novarum: The Condition of the Working Classes* and John XXIII's *Mater Magistra: Christianity and Social Progress.*

When Senator Goldwater refers to "what has always worked to provide the most in a material way for the people, namely, our free enterprise system," [52] he employs a vague, unqualified generalization which suggests three favorite conservative contentions: (1) laissez faire is the best system of political economy because the economic growth rate was highest in the nineteenth century when that system prevailed; (2) the depression of 1929-1941 really was not very serious; (3) the New Deal never got us out of the depression.

Regarding (1), eminent historians such as Allan Nevins, Thomas C. Cochran, and Edward C. Kirkland (who are not advocates of laissez faire in the twentieth century) have revised the "robber baron" estimate of the captains of industry, defending their motives and praising their ability and contribution to American development.[53] Good motives, sincerely held, could nevertheless lead to some bad results such as those mentioned by Sidney Hook, who, replying to (1), attributed to the welfare state "the absence today of the degree of poverty and deprivation which existed among large sections of the population even during the golden age of free enterprise . . . child labor, sweated factory and mine labor, and especially the evils of unemployment. . . ."[54] That the "robber barons" were also creative organizers does not conflict with the contention that they must be considered in the context of a particular stage of economic development, at a particular time, in a particular nation—a combination of the personal and impersonal. Walt W. Rostow has pointed out that different kinds of societies have gone through similar sequences of stages of economic growth.[55] Henry C. Wallich, a staunch advocate of free enterprise, has conceded that our economy is still essentially one of free enterprise whose maintenance requires some sacrifice of economic growth.[56] In expressing his willingness to make this sacrifice in order to avoid government action, Wallich, in effect, admitted that laissez faire would not produce the results in the twentieth century which it had yielded in the nineteenth. As Wallich indicated in his treatment of details, aside from his general propositions, we were in a new stage of development which went unrecognized by most twentieth-century advocates of nineteenth-century laissez faire.

Regarding (2), Goldwater's statement that free enterprise "always worked" did not even grant that there had been a depression. We need only repeat that it is difficult to exaggerate the despair which gripped the nation in the early 1930's. Regarding (3), contentions that the New Deal did not get us out of the depression emphasized unemployment as a criterion and translated partial failure into total failure—just as some admirers of Roosevelt translated partial success into total success. Moreover, the persistence of chronic unemployment in prosperous times calls for a re-evaluation of the New Deal as an agent of recovery on the part of those who stress unemployment as grounds for a blanket condemnation.

Indeed, many historians and economists attributed the New Deal's failure to achieve full employment to its neglect of full-fledged

Keynesian spending.[57] Either contemporaneously or in retrospect, this policy would not have met with the conservatives' approval. Nor would Tugwell favor massive public spending as a *continuous* policy, although he did advocate it in the crisis of the 1930's. Certainly World War II saw a demonstration of how massive government spending can quickly raise Gross National Product (70 per cent, 1939-1945) and eliminate unemployment. As Robert L. Heilbroner remarked regarding World War II, "In the end, it was not theory that settled the history of compensatory government spending, but history that settled the theory." [58] Nevertheless, from Tugwell's institutionalist standpoint, massive government spending as a permanent policy was reacting after the fact—rectifying imbalances instead of operating efficiently to begin with. His "Third Economy" of public works was not compensatory in the Keynesian sense, but, rather, it would compensate in good times as well as bad for our habitual neglect of needed public facilities. Moreover, many economists considered the heavy taxation which accompanied continuous deficit spending, and the effects of which Tugwell had warned against, a drag on our economic growth in the 1960's.[59]

The unemployment problem of the 1960's provoked suggestions for retraining workers [60] and re-examination of income-price relationships [61]—matters Tugwell had discussed three decades earlier. There was controversy over the means to stimulate economic growth in order to maintain full employment. James Tobin called for a shift in allocation of national output from private consumption to the public sector and private investment.[62] Oscar Gass and Leon Keyserling were not so concerned with private investment when many basic industries were operating below capacity. Gass asserted that meaningful growth must be sustained from an initial position of full employment.[63] Keyserling emphasized lagging demand and called for building up the purchasing power of the poorer portion of the population.[64] Gunnar Myrdal prescribed a sweeping program of public works, an agreement by industry to invest accompanied by tax cuts, tax cuts in the lower- and middle-income brackets to build up purchasing power, and a pause in wage increases.[65]

Myrdal criticized the failure of Americans "to do what we do in every European country—make an analytical forecast of what a greater growth rate for five or ten years implies." [66] Meanwhile, Dr. Walter W. Heller, Chairman of the President's Council of Economic Advisers, and other American economists were studying the economies of Europe, where socialism was dwindling but many interesting applications of guided capitalism were under way.[67] An approximation of Tugwell's "few but momentous steps" in over-all co-ordination appeared in France, which enjoyed full employment and vigorous economic growth. The French method depended upon defining and planning for the achievement of national goals by a highly trained civil service and its counterpart in business and banking. The government, like ours, also exerted considerable leverage on the economy, but, unlike ours, used its influence to promote widely agreed-upon goals. The French government employed a dual system of budgeting (administrative and capital-investment budgets, similar to practices Tugwell initiated as Chairman of the New York City Planning Commission), control of interest rates, monetary policy, loans, and capital formation in nationalized industries to promote pursuit of the established goals. (Planning in France, we must recognize with misgivings, has also been easier because of inflation and restrictions on imports, and the French economy will undoubtedly grow more slowly when it reaches "maturity.") [68]

Belgium, Britain, and Italy studied the French program, and the Morgan Guaranty Trust Company of New York prepared an analysis of the French plan. Did this mean that the economic institutions of one nation could work effectively in other nations, each with its unique civilization? With reference to the United States there was a prior question—could French practices gain acceptance? The answer for the present is no. The French scheme depends upon the persuasion of private industrialists to play a part in full co-operation with the government. American business and the people in general instinctively oppose the rigidity of centralized co-ordination and favor the American historical idea of a freely functioning market economy in which the consumer is the final judge.[69] Indeed, the United States is the only capitalistic country in which Keynes's thesis that the market economy, left to itself, tends to equilibrate below the optimum level of full employment is not widely taken for granted. Thus, talk of adaptation before adoption occurs is necessarily academic. But we should note Marquis Childs's report that developments in France are divorced from politics.[70] This suggests Tugwell's contention that planning is politically neutral, that it can be used in different ways by different, unique societies, that it need not automatically lead to totalitarianism. This contention represents a noneconomic interpretation of history. It assumes not that a nation's economy will determine everything else about that nation's society, but that everything else about a nation's society will determine the way that nation handles its economic problems.

III

If the New Conservatives' analyses of the past—the rise of industry, the depression, the New Deal—were inadequate, their view of the present and future was myopic, oversimplified, unrealistic. Change was the order of the day. As C. P. Snow put it, "The danger is that most of us in the prosperous West are becoming existential societies living in the same world with future-directed societies. We don't know how to change, but change is just what we must do." [71] And the trend toward collectivism was an undeniable aspect of invincible change. Friedrich Hayek, relating free enterprise to freedom in general in *The Road to Serfdom*, did not think so. He asserted that welfare measures could lead to the destruction of the "bases of an economy based on the market and gradually smother the creative powers of a free civilization. . . ." [72] William R. Allen also urged the preservation of the market mechanism. [73]

Robert L. Heilbroner, on the other hand, observed that the mechanism of the competitive market, the "traditional means of control over business as well as labor," was being eroded by the waning of economic necessity. Who, for example, would want to do society's necessary menial tasks as affluence increased and spread? Another taskmaster, Heilbroner held, would have to be found. Thus, the "road to abundance leads subtly but surely into the society of control" and into the "socialization of life." The increasing penetration of science and technology—as in automation, mechanization of home tasks, refinement of the arts of communication— weakened the private person's "solitary capacity to cope with life." [74] Heilbroner believed that we had to adjust to the collectivistic trend involved in the emergence of abundance. Machines would master men "as long as the control of technology rests primarily on economic calculation." Therefore, social planning and control were required. But Heilbroner was not a determinist. Despite powerful trends, we could, he concluded, exercise historic control in important areas. Our choice was between "subservience" to powerful trends and "perilous freedom"—an attempt to control them. [75]

The debate over determinism in connection with the industrial revolution went back at least to the controversy between the Conservative Social Darwinists such as Herbert Spencer and William Graham Sumner and the Liberal Social Darwinists such as Lester Frank Ward and William James. The Conservatives based their case on the comparative immutability of the human organism and the environment. The Liberals believed that man could alter the environment and in the process altered himself. "To let things alone was to deny human intelligence; to deny man's intelligence was to deny man's humanity. The debate hinged on the power of man to mold his own destiny." [76] Tugwell stood with the anti-determinists. Goldwater would call him one of "those gentler collectivists who ask our permission to play God with the human race." [77] Tugwell did not think that man was God, but he believed that God had given man a brain with which to attack complex social problems. Thus, the anti-determinist enshrined reason.

This enshrinement raises the whole subject of the "gadfly" role of the intellectual, the significance of which Professor Charles Frankel has sharply defined.[78] The gadfly has run into obstacles in the United States in what Professor Merle Curti has called "The Conflict of Thought and Action." [79] But we must reduce those obstacles, for we cannot afford to ignore our intellectuals. They may be inevitably "in advance" in politics, as Richard Crossman has written,[80] but, as Berle has declared, while proposals for present action must be "framed within the limit of what is politically possible in America," we must "lay out facts, analyze situations, state conditions, and propose ideas that will bring today's impossible into tomorrow's field of political feasibility." [81] Robert L. Heilbroner called the "respectable" Victorian economists' attitude toward their unorthodox colleagues an "intellectual tragedy of the first order" which allowed the cataclysm of the twentieth century to "burst on a world utterly unprepared for social change. It teaches us, in retrospect, that ideas —however heretical—cannot be safely ignored. One need not adopt the prescriptions of the discontents, the unfashionables, and the dissenters to profit by their insight." [82] The neglect of the dissenters of the 1920's like Tugwell provided a similar lesson. The nation could not afford the shabby treatment which this man, whose intellect a veteran capital commentator called "one of the most profound and prolific that has operated in this country in the last quarter-century," [83] received at the hands of the press.

Fortunately, in the early 1960's the public response to the employment of professors in government was far more favorable than it was in the 1930's. Berle attributed this change to the professors' effective performance.[84] Perhaps the public recognized in calm retrospect, while heaving a retroactive sigh of relief, that Roosevelt's academic advisers were not the irresponsible screwballs depicted in the newspapers. Perhaps this change was due to a rise in the educational level of the population. Perhaps it was the result of a pendulum-like reaction rather than an evolutionary development. That is, Americans may have been reacting to what Tugwell, in 1961, called a previous "flight from intellect." [85] Academicians as well as the public at large favored the involvement of professors in public affairs (there were some exceptions [86]). Compare Nicholas Murray Butler's advice to Tugwell with these words of President Nathan Pusey of Harvard: "This natural process [of turnover in personnel] has perhaps recently had a bit more assistance from Washington than we might selfishly like. But at the same time we can only admire the taste which our colleague, the President-elect, has shown in his choice of our officers. Actually we are both pleased and proud if Harvard's losses can make easier for Mr. Kennedy the incredibly difficult task to which he has been called." [87] Students, too, displayed a desire for involvement in public affairs in contrast to the 1950's, when a university dean said, "They seem to think that God will automatically provide for them." [88] Their involvement was as much of the liberal as it was of the more publicized conservative variety, although it was limited and practical.[89]

Yet, the nation still showed little inclination to adopt the collectivistic means adequate to its widely professed collective ends.[90] We had not found a "moral equivalent for war" even though we were in a war—"cold" but mortal combat. Our reaction to this conflict was collective agreement on one national purpose—survival. In supporting this purpose Americans gave decisive weight to the necessity, aside from the desirability, of collectivistic means. But we approached survival on a minimal basis. Indeed, as Robert L. Heilbroner asserted, military spending amounted to "covert" or "disguised" planning because, by injecting large amounts of public funds into the economy without encroaching on the traditional areas of private enterprise, it sustained our growth and enabled us to enjoy the advantages of planning "without actually confronting the problems of a true 'mixed' economy." Disarmament, Heilbroner maintained, would demonstrate that we are subject to the trend toward planning of all industrial nations, and that this trend "cannot be considered a scheme being foisted on us by 'socialistic' thinkers" or alien ideologies. The socialistic ideal has practically disappeared in the United States. Planning here would have a conservative, not a radical, objective. It would be our "defensive . . . response to the changed environment of history," including the requirements of technology, public morale, and international competition. We must assure growth in the event of a breakdown of private investment, and we must maintain the prestige and power of capitalism in the face of the Soviet challenge.[91]

Even with the stimulation of defense spending, we suffered economic stagnation, which, in Gunnar Myrdal's opinion, posed a danger to the entire non-Communist world.[92] In Marriner S. Eccles' view, we were only tinkering with an economic situation which was out of control and getting worse.[93] We had to consider the health of our economy for its own sake aside from the Cold War. In the end, of course, a healthy economy was a key factor in the Cold War. There is a historical truism, which the New Conservatives denied, that domestic and foreign affairs are inseparable. The force of our example is as important as the force of our arms. What we are counts as much as what we say or how hard we can hit.

We can preserve the values of Western civilization only by thinking and acting *together* as never before. Three hundred years ago, Professor Frankel wrote, reason began a revolution in the West, now worldwide, and "the hopes with which the modern world began are still the hopes by which we may steer our course." [94] Tugwell would agree, although he would not hold that reason is an infallible instrument. He is no longer on the firing line. He tends his garden, writes, lectures, and visits old Washington friends, or resides in Rio Piedras, where he serves as Special Assistant to the Chancellor of the University of Puerto Rico. He would be the last to claim that his generation left us without problems. "Our troubles," he wrote in 1957, "are not over; they will never be over." [95] But his legacy is a challenge. Can we adopt the collectivistic means adequate to our collective ends, using our brains to go forward in a changing, shrinking, perilous, challenging world, and still preserve our democracy? This is a challenge for every American, for Tugwell, the anti-determinist, did not accept that distortion of Freud, who really illuminated the search for rational control of irrational sources of behavior, which relieves men of responsibility for their conduct. In our democracy we shall get the kind of economy, government, and civilization we ask for. As Gunnar Myrdal stated, we must make our demands in the "daredevil spirit for which America has been noted." He said this spirit was best expressed by the motto that Newton D. Baker, Secretary of War in World War I, had on his office wall: "It can't be done, but here it is." [96]

In *The Light of Other Days* Tugwell looked back six decades to his boyhood at the turn of the century:

> Going to school day after day, playing games, going summers to Bemus Point, I gradually absorbed the idea that in getting on in the world I should also be making myself a good citizen. The Union that had been fought for so short a while ago, the nation that Washington had almost singlehandedly, it seemed, brought into existence—helped, of course, by John Jay, Ben Franklin and others—was part of me and I was part of it. When I sang its songs in school or on social occasions, when I read of its heroes, when I heard of all its distant wonders—the mountains, prairies, rivers, and bordering seas—the swelling pride in my heart was sometimes almost too much to conceal. [97]

This was the nation to which Tugwell made his challenge, the nation to which he gave his best—his faith as well as his reason—the nation which can no longer rely on the policy of crossing its bridges when it comes to them, the nation which must possess in peace or in cold war the sense of purpose it displayed at Chateau-Thierry, Guadalcanal, and Normandy, the nation which embodies no static "system," the nation which must be a thinking, dynamic, daring, noble America.

The Works and Papers of
Rexford Guy Tugwell

Books

Author

The Economic Basis of Public Interest, Menasha, Wisconsin: George Banta
Publishing Company, 1922.

Industry's Coming of Age, New York: Harcourt, Brace, 1927.

Mr. Hoover's Economic Policy, New York: John Day, 1932.

The Industrial Discipline and the Governmental Arts, New York: Columbia
University Press, 1933.

The Battle for Democracy, New York: Columbia University Press, 1935.

*Changing the Colonial Climate: the Story, from His Official Messages, of
Governor Rexford Guy Tugwell's Efforts to Bring Democracy to an Island
Possession Which Serves the United Nations as a Warbase*, selection and
explanatory comments by J. Lear, San Juan: Bureau of Supplies, Printing,
and Transportation, 1942.

Puerto Rican Public Papers of R. G. Tugwell, Governor, San Juan: Service
Office of the Government of Puerto Rico, Printing Division, 1945.

Forty-Fifth Annual Report of the Governor, 1945, San Juan: Government of
Puerto Rico, 1945.

The Stricken Land: The Story of Puerto Rico, Garden City, New York:
Doubleday, 1947.

The Place of Planning in Society: Seven Lectures, San Juan: Office of the
Government Planning Board, 1954.

A Chronicle of Jeopardy, 1945-1955, Chicago: University of Chicago Press,
1955.

The Democratic Roosevelt: A Biography of Franklin D. Roosevelt, Garden
City, New York: Doubleday, 1957.

*The Art of Politics, As Practiced by Three Great Americans: Franklin Delano
Roosevelt, Luis Munoz Marin, and Fiorello H. LaGuardia*, Garden City,
New York: Doubleday, 1958.

The Enlargement of the Presidency, Garden City, New York: Doubleday,
1960.

The Light of Other Days, Garden City, New York: Doubleday, 1962.

Co-Author

and Howard C. Hill, *Our Economic Society and Its Problems*, New York:
Harcourt, Brace, 1934.

and Joseph Dorfman, *Early American Policy: Six Columbia Contributors*,
New York: Columbia University Press, 1960, including five articles previously published in the *Columbia University Quarterly*, listed below, and
a new article on John Jay.

Joint Author

and Thomas Munro, and Roy E. Stryker, *American Economic Life and the Means of Its Improvement*, 2d ed., New York: Harcourt, Brace, 1925.

Editor

Simon N. Patten, *Essays in Economic Theory*, New York: Knopf, 1924.
The American Year Book and Directory of the American-Russian Chamber of Commerce, 1928-29 (published in Russia, in the Russian language).

Co-Editor

Eliot Jared, *Essays upon Field Husbandry in New England, and Other Papers, 1748-1762*, ed. by Harry J. Carman and Rexford G. Tugwell, Columbia University Studies in the History of American Agriculture, No. 1, New York: Columbia University Press, 1934.

Editor and Contributor

The Trend of Economics, ed. by R. G. Tugwell; "Experimental Economics," by R. G. Tugwell, New York: Knopf, 1924.

Co-Editor and Contributor

Redirecting Education, ed. by Leon Keyserling and R. G. Tugwell, 2 volumes; "Social Objectives in Education," Vol. I, by R. G. Tugwell, New York: Columbia University Press, 1934-35.

Joint Editor and Contributor

Soviet Russia in the Second Decade, ed. by Stuart Chase, Robert Dunn, and R. G. Tugwell; "Russian Agriculture," by R. G. Tugwell, New York: John Day, 1928.

Contributor

"Resettlement Administration," in *The Democratic National Convention, 1936.*
Review, *This Ugly Civilization*, by Ralph Borsodi, in *Designed for Reading: Anthology from the Saturday Review of Literature, 1924-1934*, New York: Macmillan, 1936.
"Economics," in *Roads to Knowledge*, ed. by W. A. Neilson, New York: Halcyon House, 1937.
"Caribbean Obligations," in *The Caribbean*, ed. by A. C. Wilgus, Gainesville: University of Florida Press, 1952.
"New York," in *Great Cities of the World*, ed. by William A. Robson, London: Allen and Unwin, 1954.

Articles

and Charles Reitel, "Meaning and Making of Farm Strikes," *Pennsylvania Farmer*, September 22, 1917.
"The Marketing of Farm Products," *Pennsylvania Farmer*, December 22, 1917.

"The Casual of the Woods," *The Survey*, July 3, 1920.

"The Outlaw," *The Survey*, August 16, 1920.

"The Philosophy of Despair: Outlawing the I.W.W.," *New York Call*, magazine section, October 17, 1920.

"The Gipsey Strain," *The Pacific Review*, September, 1921.

"The Economic Basis for Business Regulation," *American Economic Review*, December, 1921.

Review, *Guild Socialism and the Industrial Future*, by G. D. H. Cole, in *The International Journal of Ethics*, April, 1922.

"Human Nature in Economic Theory," *Journal of Political Economy*, June, 1922.

"Country Life for America," *The Pacific Review*, March, 1922; to have been continued in June, but *The Pacific Review* failed.

"Some Formative Influences on the Life of Simon Nelson Patten," *American Economic Review, Supplement*, March, 1923.

"Economic Theory and Practice," *American Economic Review, Supplement*, March, 1923.

"Notes on the Life and Work of Simon Nelson Patten," *Journal of Political Economy*, April, 1923.

"Bibliography of the Works of Simon Nelson Patten," *The Annals of the American Academy of Political and Social Science*, May, 1923.

"Distortion of Economic Incentive," *International Journal of Ethics*, April, 1924.

"Economics and Ethics," *Journal of Philosophy*, December 4, 1924.

"The Problem of Agriculture," *Political Science Quarterly*, December, 1924.

"The Woman in the Sunbonnet," *Nation*, January 21, 1925.

"Hired Man," *Nation*, August 5, 1925.

"An Economist Reads Dark Laughter," *New Republic*, December 9, 1925.

"Henry Ford in This World," *Saturday Review of Literature*, August 7, 1926.

"Chameleon Words," *New Republic*, August 25, 1926.

"The End of Laissez Faire," *New Republic*, October 13, 1926.

"America's Wartime Socialism," *Nation*, April 6, 1927.

"What Will Become of the Farmer?," *Nation*, June 15, 1927.

"Economics as the Science of Experience," *Journal of Philosophy*, January 19, 1928.

"High Wages and Prosperity: Discussion," *Bulletin of the Taylor Society*, February, 1928.

"Paradox of Peace," *New Republic*, April 18, 1928.

"Hunger, Cold, and Candidates," *New Republic*, May 2, 1928.

"Governor or President?," *New Republic*, May 16, 1928.

"Communist Theory vs. Russian Fact," *New Republic*, May 16, 1928.

"Contemporary Economics," *New Republic*, May 16, 1928.

"Platforms and Candidates," *New Republic*, May 30, 1928.

"What Is a Scientific Tariff?," *New Republic*, June 13, 1928.

"That Living Constitution," *New Republic*, June 20, 1928.

"Experimental Control in Russian Industry," *Political Science Quarterly*, June, 1928.

"A Plank for Agriculture," *New Republic*, July 4, 1928 (unsigned).

"Wage Pressure and Efficiency," *New Republic*, July 11, 1928.

"Governor Smith's Dilemma," *New Republic*, August 1, 1928.

"The Liberal Choice," *New Republic*, September 5, 1928.

"Bankers' Banks," *New Republic*, December 12, 1928.

"Reflections on Farm Relief," *Political Science Quarterly*, December, 1928.

"Farm Relief and a Permanent Agriculture," *The Annals of the American Academy of Political and Social Science*, March, 1929.

"Agricultural Policy of France," *Political Science Quarterly*, June-December, 1930.

"Human Nature and Social Economy," *Journal of Philosophy*, August 14 and 28, 1930.

"Elements of a World Culture: Economics," *World Unity*, November-December, 1930.

"Occupational Obsolescence," *Journal of Adult Education*, January, 1931.

"Theory of Occupational Obsolescence," *Political Science Quarterly*, June, 1931.

and Joseph Dorfman, "The Reverend John McVickar: Christian Teacher and Economist," *Columbia University Quarterly*, December, 1931.

and A. T. Cutler, and G. S. Mitchell, "Flaws in the Hoover Economic Plan," *Current History*, January, 1932.

"What the World Economic Conference Can Do," *New York Herald Tribune*, April 12, 1933.

"The Role of the State in American Economic Life," *L'Esprit International*, April, 1933.

"Government in a Changing World," *Review of Reviews*, August, 1933.

"Advertising and the New Food and Drugs Bill," *Editor and Publisher*, September 16, 1933.

"The Copeland Bill and the Food Industries," *Grocery Trade News*, October 24, 1933; also *USDA Press Release*.

"New Monetary Policy Regarded Logical Step," *Washington Star*, November 5, 1933.

"One Aim of the *Consumer's Guide* of the Agricultural Adjustment Administration," *Consumer's Guide*, November 14, 1933.

"Freedom from Fakes," *Today*, November 17, 1933.

"The Farm Price Level," *Fortune*, November, 1933.

"Are the Increasing Powers of the President Improving the American Government?," *Congressional Digest*, November, 1933.

" 'Grasping' Congressmen Feel Constituents' Need," *Washington Star*, December 10, 1933.

and Joseph Dorfman, "Henry Vethake: A Chapter in the Development of Higher Learning in the United States," *Columbia University Quarterly*, December, 1933.

"How Shall We Pay for All This?," *American Magazine*, December, 1933.

"Planned Use of the Land," *Today*, January 20, 1934.

"The Price Also Rises," *Fortune*, January, 1934.

"The Road to Economic Recovery," *Extension Service Review*, March, 1934.

"Should Congress Enact a New Pure Food and Drugs Law?," *Congressional Digest*, March, 1934.

"Tariff Revision Certain to Come," *British Industries*, March, 1934.

"New Deal as Brain Trust Sees It," *United States News and World Report*, April 23, 1934.

"America Takes Hold of Its Destiny," *Today*, April 28, 1934.

"The Great American Fraud," *American Scholar*, Winter, 1934.

"Agriculture and the Consumer," Washington, USDA, 1934.

"A Fireside Symposium," *Columbia University Quarterly*, March, 1935.

"The Progressive Tradition," *Atlantic Monthly*, April, 1935.

"No More Frontiers," *Today*, June 22 and 29, 1935.

and Joseph Dorfman, "William Beach Lawrence: Apostle of Ricardo," *Columbia University Quarterly*, September, 1935.

"National Significance of Recent Trends in Farm Population," *Social Forces*, October, 1935.

"Spain as a Colonizer," *Bulletin of the Pan American Union*, October, 1935.

"New Deal Objective," *United States News and World Report*, November 18, 1935.

"Our New National Domain," *Scribner's Magazine*, March, 1936.

"New Frontier: The Story of Resettlement," *Chicago Sun-Times*, April 19, 1936.

"Should the Administration's Housing Policy Be Continued?," *Congressional Digest*, April, 1936.

"Why Resettlement?," *Labor Information Bulletin*, May, 1936.

"Down to Earth," *Current History*, July, 1936.

"Changing Acres," *Current History*, September, 1936.

"Grass Did Not Grow," *Fortune*, October, 1936.

"The Future of National Planning," *New Republic*, December 9, 1936.

"The Meaning of the Greenbelt Towns," *New Republic*, February 17, 1937.

"Will Government Aid for Small Farm Purchasers Solve the Tenancy Problem?," *Congressional Digest*, February, 1937.

"Co-operation and Resettlement," *Current History*, February, 1937.

"Is a Farmer-Labor Alliance Possible?," *Harper's Magazine*, May, 1937.

"On the Troublesome 'X,'" *Philosophy of Science*, October, 1937.

"Wesley Mitchell: An Evaluation," *New Republic*, October 6, 1937.

and Joseph Dorfman, "Alexander Hamilton: Nation Maker," *Columbia University Quarterly*, December, 1937, and March, 1938.

"Land of Plenty," *Current History*, February, 1938.

and Joseph Dorfman, "Francis Lieber: German Scholar in America," *Columbia University Quarterly*, September and December, 1938.

Annual Report of the City Planning Commission of the Department of City Planning, The City of New York, 1938.

"Veblen and 'Business Enterprise,'" *New Republic*, March 29, 1939.

"Notes on the Uses of Exactitude in Politics," *Political Science Quarterly*, March, 1939.

"It's Tough," *Radio Digest*, May, 1939.

"Frightened Liberals," *New Republic*, April 26, 1939.

"The Fourth Power," *Planning and Civic Comment*, Part II, April-June, 1939.

"After the New Deal: 'We Have Bought Ourselves Time to Think,'" *New Republic*, July 26, 1939.

"When the Usha Buys Land," *New Republic*, October 25, 1939.

"The Superpolitical," *Journal of Social Philosophy*, October, 1939-July, 1940.

"The City Planning Commission," *New York Advancing*, 1939.

Annual Report of the City Planning Commission of the Department of City Planning, The City of New York, 1939.

"Does Roosevelt Want a Third Term?," *Look Magazine*, January 16, 1940.

"What Should America Do for the Joads?," *Town Meeting Bulletin*, March 11, 1940.

"Planning in New York City," *Planner's Journal*, April, 1940.

"The Sloping Walls of Casa Grande," *Atlantic Monthly*, April, 1940.

"Parts of a New Civilization," *Saturday Review of Literature*, April 13, 1940.

"Must We Draft Roosevelt?," *New Republic*, May 13, 1940.

"Forester's Heart," *New Republic*, May 13, 1940.

"Roosevelt Will Not Run for a Third Term," *Look Magazine*, June 18, 1940.

"Planning for Living," *Child Study*, Summer, 1940.

"Must We Socialize Business to Restore Prosperity?," *American Economic Foundation Bulletin*, November 18, 1940.

"Implementing the General Interest," *Public Administration Review*, Autumn, 1940.

"Crisis of Freedom," *Common Sense*, October, 1941.

"The Directive," *Journal of Social Philosophy and Jurisprudence*, October, 1941.

"Investigation into the Administrative Responsibilities under the 500 Acre Limitation on Land Holdings," *Report*, Department of the Interior, 1941.

"Puerto Rico Also Serves," *New Republic*, July 13, 1942.

"Puerto Rico and Its Housing Problem," *American City*, July, 1942.

"The Real Estate Dilemma," *Public Administration Review*, Winter, 1942.

"In Defense of Puerto Rico," *New Republic*, April 15, 1946.

and Grace F. Tugwell, "Puerto Rico's Bootstraps," *Harper's Magazine*, February, 1947.

Review, *Welfare and Planning in the West Indies*, by T. S. Simey, in *Journal of Political Economy*, October, 1947.

"Notes on Some Implications of Oneness in the World," *Common Cause*, November, 1947.

Review, *The United States and the Caribbean*, by Dexter Perkins, in *Saturday Review of Literature*, December 27, 1947.

Review, *Henry Wallace*, by Dwight MacDonald, in *Chicago Sun-Times*, February 23, 1948.

and others, "Preliminary Draft of a World Constitution," *Common Cause*, March, 1948.

"The Preparation of a President," *Western Political Quarterly*, June, 1948.

"An Open Reply to Mr. Borgese," *Common Cause*, October, 1948.

"The New Deal in Retrospect," *Western Political Quarterly*, December, 1948.

"The Utility of the Future in the Present," *Public Administration Review*, Winter, 1948.

and E. C. Banfield, "Can the United Nations Become a World Government?," *Common Cause*, February, 1949.

"A Planner's View of Agriculture's Future," *Journal of Farm Economics*, February, 1949.

Review, *Property, Wealth, Land: Allocation, Planning and Development*, by M. S. McDougal and D. Haber, in *Yale Law Journal*, April, 1949.

"Progressives and the Presidency," *The Progressive*, April, 1949.

"Beyond Malthus: Numbers and Resources," *Common Cause*, May, 1949.

"Variation on a Theme by Cooley," *Ethics*, July, 1949.

and E. C. Banfield, "Great Rehearsal or Great Compromise?," *Common Cause*, July, 1949.

" 'Looking Outward' of the Americans," *Antioch Review*, September, 1949.

"The New Deal: The Available Instruments of Governmental Power," *Western Political Quarterly*, December, 1949.

"Earthbound: The Problem of Planning and Survival," *Antioch Review*, December, 1949.

"Letters from Latter-Day Britain," 15 articles, *Common Cause*, March, 1950-June, 1951.

"To Succor the Weak," *Common Cause*, April, 1950.

"Welfare State," *Common Cause*, July, 1950.

"The Experimental Roosevelt," *Political Quarterly*, July, 1950.

"Wonders May Not Cease," *British Agricultural Economics Society, Transactions*, Summer, 1950.

"The New Deal: The Progressive Tradition," *Western Political Quarterly*, September, 1950.

and E. C. Banfield, "Grass Roots Democracy—Myth or Reality?," *Public Administration Review*, Winter, 1950.

"One World—One Wealth," *Ethics*, April, 1951.

"The Consequences of Korea," *Bulletin of the Atomic Scientists*, May, 1951.

and E. C. Banfield, "Governmental Planning at Mid-Century," *Journal of Politics*, May, 1951.

"The New Deal: The Decline of Government," Parts I and II, *Western Political Quarterly*, June and September, 1951.

"Beyond Nationalism," *Political Quarterly*, October, 1951.

Foreword, *Government Project*, by E. C. Banfield, 1951.

"The Two Great Roosevelts," *Western Political Quarterly*, March, 1952.

"The New Deal: The Rise of Business," Parts I and II, *Western Political Quarterly*, June and September, 1952.

Review, *Roosevelt and Daniels*, by Carroll Kilpatrick, in *Western Political Quarterly*, December, 1952.

"What Next for Puerto Rico?," *The Annals of the American Academy of Political and Social Science*, January, 1953.

"L'Attitude Reticente des Etas Unis a l'Egard de la Planification," *Revue Economique*, March, 1953.

"The Compromising Roosevelt," *Western Political Quarterly*, June, 1953.

"The Progressive Orthodoxy of Franklin D. Roosevelt," *Ethics*, October, 1953.

"The Protagonists: Roosevelt and Hoover," *Antioch Review*, December, 1953.

"The Sources of New Deal Reformism," *Ethics*, July, 1954.

"Roosevelt and Howe," *Antioch Review*, September, 1954.

Review, *Transformation: The Story of Modern Puerto Rico*, by Earl P. Hanson, in *Saturday Review*, February 12, 1955.

"Fuel of Magnificence: The Case of Puerto Rico," *Confluence*, October, 1955.

"The Fallow Years of Franklin D. Roosevelt," *Ethics*, January, 1956.

"Franklin D. Roosevelt on the Verge of the Presidency," *Antioch Review*, March, 1956.

"F. D. R.: Living Memorials," *Nation*, April 7, 1956.

Review, *Roosevelt: The Lion and the Fox*, by James M. Burns, in *Chicago Sun-Times*, August 12, 1956.

Review, *The Crisis of the Old Order*, by Arthur M. Schlesinger, Jr., in *Chicago Sun-Times*, March 3, 1957.

Review, *Franklin D. Roosevelt and Conservation, 1911-1945*, 2 vols., comp. and ed. by Edgar B. Nixon, in *American Historical Review*, April, 1958.

"A Memorable Christmas," *The Evening Star*, Washington, D. C., December 9, 1958.

Review, *La Guardia: A Fighter against His Time, 1882-1933*, by Arthur Mann, in *New York Times Book Review*, November 15, 1959.

Foreword, *Puerto Rican Politics and the New Deal*, by Thomas G. Mathews, 1960.

"The View from Puerto Rico," *Nation*, June 10, 1961.

"The Farmer and the Commissar," *Nation*, July 29, 1961.

In *New York Times*

"Ideas behind the New Deal," July 16, 1933 (Magazine).

"Resettling America," January 14, 1934, VIII.

"Resettling America: A Fourfold Plan," July 28, 1935 (Magazine).

"Where the New Deal Succeeds," April 22, 1934.

"Problems—and Goal—of Rural Relief," December 15, 1935 (Magazine).

"Behind the Farm Problem: Rural Poverty," June 10, 1937 (Magazine).

"The New Deal Interpreted," May 28, 1933, VIII; brief statements on basic policy by Raymond Moley, Harold Ickes, Rexford Tugwell, et al.

Syndicated Columns: 1933-1934

In *The Battle for Democracy*

The Senior Partner

An Experiment in Reconstruction

Our Weight in Gold

Banking for the People

Trial and Error

Freedom and Business

Prices and Dollars

Later Moral Equivalents

Senator Progressive
Senator Progressive Again
The Senator and Beauregard Boone
International Economic Policy
Wind, Water, and Soil

In *Tugwell Papers*

Purchasing Power
Reduce the Spread
Religious Reformation in Economics
Diversified Attack
The President's Monetary Policy
Nationalism and Internationalism
A More Abundant Life
Henry Wallace

Published Notes

In *The Battle for Democracy*

When Corporations Save; notes made in February, 1934.

Letters to the Editor

New York Times

November 20, 1935.
December 15, 1935.

New Republic

December 25, 1935.
March 18, 1936.

Washington Post

April 27, 1961.

Published Addresses

"The Principle of Planning and the Institution of Laissez Faire," American
   Economic Association, December, 1931; in *American Economic Review,
   Supplement,* March, 1932.
"Responsibility and Economic Distress," National Advisory Council on Edu-
   cation, Economic Series, Lecture Number 14, National Broadcasting Com-
   pany, January 30, 1932; Chicago: University of Chicago Press, 1932.
"Jobs in the Woods," Columbia Broadcasting System, March 18, 1933; *USDA
   Press Release* (in National Archives).
"Design for Government," Eighth Annual Meeting of the Federation of Bar
   Associations of Western New York, June 24, 1933; in *The Battle for Democ-
   racy.*

"Sound Money," Adult Education Association, Chicago, October 29, 1933; *USDA Press Release* (in National Archives).

"The Prospect for the Future," Chicago Forum, October 29, 1933; in *The Battle for Democracy*.

"The Economics of the Recovery Program," Institute of Arts and Sciences, Columbia University, November 16, 1933; in *The Battle for Democracy*.

"New Strength from the Soil," Swarthmore College, November 26, 1933; in *The Battle for Democracy*.

"The Place of Government in a National Land Program," Joint Meeting, American Economic Association, American Statistical Association, Farm Economic Association, Philadelphia, December 29, 1933; *USDA Press Release;* also in *Journal of Farm Economics,* January, 1934.

"Wine, Women, and the New Deal," Women's Democratic Club, Washington, D. C., February 5, 1934; in *The Battle for Democracy*.

"A New Deal for the Consumer," Columbia Alumni Luncheon, New York, February 12, 1934; in *The Battle for Democracy;* also *USDA Press Release*.

"The Return to Democracy," American Society of Newspaper Editors, April 21, 1934; in *The Battle for Democracy*.

"On Life as a Long-Time Enterprise," Dartmouth College, April 26, 1934; in *The Battle for Democracy;* also *USDA Press Release*.

"Economic Freedom and the Farmer," New York State Bankers Association, Buffalo, April 28, 1934; in *The Battle for Democracy*.

"The Social Responsibilities of Technical Workers," Organizations of Government Employees, Washington, D. C., May 1, 1934; in *The Battle for Democracy*.

"Consumers and the New Deal," Consumers' League of Ohio, Cleveland, May 11, 1934; in *The Battle for Democracy*.

"Bread or Cake," Oberlin College, May 12, 1934; in *The Battle for Democracy*.

"Relief and Reconstruction," National Conference of Social Workers, Kansas City, May 21, 1934; in *The Battle for Democracy;* also in Conference *Proceedings*.

Farm Policy, Columbia Broadcasting System, July 31, 1934; *USDA Press Release* (in National Archives).

New Deal Policies, Niagara County Pioneer Association, Olcott Beach, New York, August 8, 1934; *USDA Press Release* (in National Archives).

AAA Policies, Clemson College, South Carolina, August 15, 1934; *USDA Press Release* (in National Archives).

"The New Course of International Trade," International Institute of Agriculture, Rome, Italy, October, 1934; in *International Problems of Agriculture, 12th Meeting, General Assembly, International Institute of Agriculture,* Rome: 1935.

"Needed Social and Political Adjustments," in *Vital Speeches,* November 19, 1934.

"A Third Economy," Rochester Teachers Association, Rochester, New York, April 9, 1935; *USDA Press Release;* also in *Vital Speeches,* April 22, 1935.

"Conservation Redefined," Fiftieth Anniversary of the Founding of New York's

Forest Preserve, Albany, May 15, 1935; *USDA Press Release* (in National Archives).

"Your Future and Your Nation," Commencement Address, University of New Mexico, Albuquerque, June 10, 1935; *USDA Press Release;* also in *New Mexico Quarterly,* August, 1935.

Regional Directors of the Land Program, June 18, 1935 (in National Archives).

Land-Use, Tompkins County Development Meeting, Ithaca, New York, August 7, 1935; *USDA Press Release* (in National Archives).

"The Progressive Task Today and Tomorrow," Democratic State Central Committee, Los Angeles, October 28, 1935; *RA Press Release* (in *Tugwell Papers*); also in *Vital Speeches,* November 16, 1935.

"The Reason for Resettlement," National Broadcasting Company, December 2, 1935; *Tugwell Papers.*

Regional Directors of the Resettlement Administration, January 28, 1936 (in National Archives).

"For a Third Term," New York Herald Tribune Forum, October 25, 1938; *Report of the Eighth Annual New York Herald Tribune Forum,* 1938.

"The Study of Planning as a Scientific Endeavor," The Michigan Academy of Science, Arts, and Letters, 1948; in *Fiftieth Annual Report of the Michigan Academy of Science, Arts, and Letters, 1948.*

"The Spread of Industry into Rural Areas," opening address, Seventh Conference of the International Agricultural Economics Society, 1949; in Conference *Proceedings.*

"The Resettlement Idea," joint meeting, Agricultural History Society and American Historical Association, Washington, D. C., December 30, 1958; in *Agricultural History,* October, 1959.

Published Interviews

"An Interview between Mrs. Isabella Greenway, Congresswoman-elect from Arizona, and Dr. R. G. Tugwell, Assistant Secretary of Agriculture," Columbia Broadcasting System, October 30, 1933; *Agricultural Adjustment Administration Press Release* (in National Archives).

"Memoirs of the New Deal," interview with Dean Zelman Cowen, University of Melbourne Law School, Tape No. 15, Center for the Study of Democratic Institutions, Santa Barbara, California.

Unpublished Addresses

"Discourse in Depression," Columbia Teachers College, 1932.

"Taking Stock," University of Cincinnati, February 5, 1934.

"The Responsibilities of Partnership," Iowa Bankers Association, June 27, 1934.

Farm policy, Brookings, South Dakota, July, 1934.

Cancelled address, Commonwealth Club, San Francisco; cancellation reported in *New York Times,* July 15, 1934.

"Fateful Choice," George Washington University, June 7, 1940.

Introductory address, Henry Osborne Lectures, University of Chicago, October 9, 1947.

Progressive Citizens of America, DuSable High School, Chicago, October 29, 1947.
"The Elements of a Progressive Foreign Policy," New York, January 23, 1948.
Henry Wallace Rally, Chicago Stadium, April 10, 1948.
Henry Wallace Dinner, Hotel Commodore, New York, April 19, 1948.
Greendale Decennial Celebration, Milwaukee, June 5, 1948.
Homecoming Dinner, University of Chicago, October 1, 1948.
"Washington without Roosevelt," Phi Alpha Theta, Honorary History Fraternity, University of Maryland, January 9, 1958.

Unpublished Lectures

"The President and the Congress," Lecture in the American Presidency Series, University College, University of Chicago, October 19, 1948.
"The President and His Cabinet," Lecture in the American Presidency Series, University College, University of Chicago, October 22, 1948.
"The Practice of Democracy," Sidney Hillman Lectures, Howard University, December 8, 9, 10, 1959.

Unpublished Memoir

"A New Deal Memoir: Early Days, 1932-1933," *Tugwell Papers*.

Unpublished Diary

"Notes from a New Deal Diary," *Tugwell Papers*. (Portions covering the periods December, 1932-February 27, 1933, and March 31, 1933-May 31, 1933, are available at the Franklin D. Roosevelt Library, Hyde Park, N. Y.)
"Addendum to the Diary for the 100 Days," *Tugwell Papers*.

Unpublished Interview

Oral History Research Office, Columbia University.

Tugwell Papers

Files, including correspondence (and carbon copies of outgoing items), relating to the Department of Agriculture.
Personal correspondence.
Scrapbooks, including magazine and newspaper clippings.
Memorandum on farm problem prepared for Alfred E. Smith.
Miscellaneous notes and statements.
"Meditation in Stinsford Churchyard," 1927; on Thomas Hardy; privately circulated.
Tugwell's Preliminary Draft of a World Constitution, Document No. 100, October 17, 1946, Committee to Frame a World Constitution.
Mordecai Ezekiel, "Notes on the 100 Days."

Addendum

"When the Constitution Is Silent, Bold Voices Speak," *Columbia University Forum*, Spring, 1963.
(*Unpublished items, except Columbia interview, in Mr. Tugwell's possession*)

Notes

The preceding section, "The Works and Papers of Rexford Guy Tugwell," lists the complete titles and gives the locations of the materials in this category, including those designated in the notes as: Tugwell, *Diary;* Tugwell, *Memoir;* and *Tugwell Papers.* The items in the preceding section whose location in the National Archives is indicated are deposited in Records of the Office of Secretary of Agriculture, RG 16, with two exceptions; Tugwell's address to the Regional Directors of the Land Program, June 18, 1935, and his address to the Regional Directors of the Resettlement Administration, January 28, 1936, are in Records of the Farmers Home Administration, RG 96. The citation in the notes, Tugwell, *interview with writer,* refers to a series of interviews at the University of Chicago over a two-week period in April, 1954.

The collection of interviews of the Oral History Research Office at Columbia University contains a wealth of material on the agricultural aspect of the New Deal, including details of the strife within the Agricultural Adjustment Administration in the years 1933-1935. In addition to the interviews of Will W. Alexander and Norman Thomas, which are cited here, the writer has examined these interviews at the Oral History Research Office: Louis H. Bean, Samuel B. Bledsoe, William W. Cumberland, Rudolph M. Evans, John P. Frey, Arthur Krock, Harry L. Mitchell, Cleveland Rodgers, Lindsey Rogers, Oscar C. Stine, and, of course, Rexford Guy Tugwell.

The abbreviations used in the notes in references to the *Roosevelt Papers* designate these files in the Franklin D. Roosevelt Library at Hyde Park:

OF 1, 466c, 1568, 2700: Official File 1, etc.
PPF 180, 564, 758: President's Personal File 180, etc.
PSF-T: President's Secretary's File-Tugwell
PSF-GC: President's Secretary's File-General Correspondence

The following abbreviations appear in the text:

AAA	Agricultural Adjustment Administration
AA Act	Agricultural Adjustment Act
AF of L	American Federation of Labor
ANPA	American Newspaper Publishers Association
CBS	Columbia Broadcasting System
CCC	Civilian Conservation Corps
CED	Committee for Economic Development
FCA	Farm Credit Administration
F&DA	Food and Drug Administration
FERA	Federal Emergency Relief Administration
FHA	Federal Housing Authority

FSA	Farm Security Administration
GOP	Grand Old (Republican) Party
HOLC	Home Owners' Loan Corporation
IIA	International Institute of Agriculture
NCC	National Credit Corporation
NIR Act	National Industrial Recovery Act
NRA	National Recovery Administration
PWA	Public Works Administration
RA	Resettlement Administration
RFC	Reconstruction Finance Corporation
SCS	Soil Conservation Service
SEC	Securities and Exchange Commission
SES	Soil Erosion Service
SRC	Surplus Relief Corporation
TVA	Tennessee Valley Authority
USDA	United States Department of Agriculture
USDI	United States Department of the Interior
VDAP	Voluntary Domestic Allotment Plan

With respect to notes, each chapter is a unit. A source is presented in complete form upon its first appearance in a given chapter; in subsequent references to a source, in the same chapter, short titles are used. The numerous references to Tugwell's works made it impossible to use *op. cit.* and *loc. cit.*

The notes, of course, do not include references to all of the materials and works consulted. A number of recent publications have been examined for evidence calling for substantive change but have not been cited. These include the following books which should be mentioned:

Christiana McFayden Campbell, *The Farm Bureau and the New Deal: A Study of the Making of National Farm Policy, 1933-40,* Urbana: University of Illinois Press, 1962, analyzes the opposition of the Farm Bureau and the Extension Service to the Resettlement Administration and is pertinent to Chapters 21 and 22. Mrs. Campbell also refers to the Bureau's desire to enjoy parity without government subsidies or controls, a position which Tugwell and M. L. Wilson anticipated in 1932 (Chapter 15).

Felix Frankfurter, *Felix Frankfurter Reminisces,* Recorded in Talks with Harlan B. Phillips, New York: Reynal, 1960, is pertinent to Chapter 10 and should be consulted for Frankfurter's disavowal of his own influence in the New Deal.

Laurin L. Henry, *Presidential Transitions,* Washington: Brookings Institution, 1960, is relevant to Chapter 6.

Louis Koenig, *The Invisible Presidency,* New York: Holt, Rinehart and Winston, 1960, deals with a key figure in Chapter 11 in a section, "Tommy the Cork."

Thomas Mathews, *Puerto Rican Politics and the New Deal,* Gainesville: University of Florida Press, 1960, treats briefly but in some detail Tugwell's concern with Puerto Rico and his visit there in 1934, a matter mentioned in Chapter 17.

James W. Prothro, *Dollar Decade: Business Ideas in the 1920's,* Baton Rouge: Louisiana State University Press, 1954, especially 209-21, supports Tugwell's judgment (Chapter 3) that during the depression businessmen were "poor sports." At least in Prothro's view businessmen were "poor sports" in effect if not in intent. He does not question the "honesty and depth of feeling with which [their] assumptions were held." He concludes, however, that "its concern for the immediate and narrow interests of the economic elite was so overweening that business leadership was blind to the most urgent needs of the public at large. Alarmed for its prestige and profits, the business community—after assuming full credit for prosperity—could generate no meaningful sense of public responsibility in the face of the depression."

Karl M. Schmidt, *Henry A. Wallace: Quixotic Crusade, 1948,* Syracuse: Syracuse University Press, 1960, relates to portions of Chapter 26.

Harris G. Warren, *Herbert Hoover and the Great Depression,* Toronto: Oxford University Press, 1959, makes a judgment of Hoover's policies quite different from that presented in Chapters 3, 5, 6, and 7; this writer agrees with Edward C. Kirkland (*American Historical Review,* July, 1959, 976-77) that Harris' attempt to defend Hoover is unsuccessful.

This article is pertinent:

Arthur H. Carhart, "Shelterbelts: A 'Failure' That Didn't Happen," *Harper's,* October, 1960, corrects some popular misconceptions about this project and is relevant to Chapter 17.

Hardly a month passes without the publication of materials pertinent to one or another aspect of this book. Several books and articles which appeared too late for incorporation here of their relevant points should also be mentioned. Alfred B. Rollins, Jr., *Roosevelt and Howe,* New York: Knopf, 1962, shows that the relationship between Howe and the Brain Trusters changed somewhat after the election of November, 1932. Gilbert C. Fite, "Farmer Opinion and the Agricultural Adjustment Act, 1933," *Mississippi Valley Historical Review,* March, 1962, is relevant to Chapter 15 and demonstrates that in 1933 "farmer" opinion was "farm-leader" opinion so far as the Roosevelt administration was concerned. Lewis S. Feuer, "American Travelers to the Soviet Union 1917-32: The Formation of a Component of New Deal Ideology," *American Quarterly,* Summer, 1962, in a brief quotation of Tugwell on page 124, and Raymond Moley, *The Republican Opportunity,* New York: Duell, Sloan and Pearce, 1962, in a chapter entitled "The Cult of Planning," attribute to Tugwell's trip to Russia in 1927 a greater impact on his thinking than this writer does in view of the basic themes in both what Tugwell wrote before 1927 and what he wrote and did after 1927. Gabriel Kolko, *Wealth and Power in America: An Analysis of Social Class and Income Distribution,* New York: Praeger, 1962, and Herman P. Miller, "Is the Income Gap Closed? No!," *New York Times Magazine,* November 11, 1962, show that the shift toward greater income equality in America, mentioned in Chapter 28, came to an end more than a decade ago. Michael Harrington, *The Other America,* New York: Macmillan,

1962, supports the reference made in Chapter 28 to those Americans who do not share in our general affluence. In his study of J. A. Schumpeter, J. K. Galbraith, A. H. Hansen, and J. M. Clark, *Revolution, Evolution, and the Economic Order*, Englewood Cliffs, N. J.: Prentice-Hall, 1962, Allan M. Sievers finds that the consensus of both conservative and liberal is that we have not yet fully solved the serious difficulties of the 1930's, and that our economy is not as sound as postwar prosperity seems to indicate—a point made in Chapter 28. As this is written, an announcement of an address relevant to Chapters 18 and 19 is in hand: J. Harvey Young, "The 1938 Food, Drug, and Cosmetic Act," Annual Meeting, American Historical Association, Chicago, December, 1962.

1. A Biographical Sketch: 1891-1931

1. Russell Lord, *The Wallaces of Iowa* (Boston: Houghton Mifflin, 1947), 348, incorporating material from a "Profile" by Lord in the *New Yorker*, March 23 and 30, 1935; Tugwell, *The Light of Other Days* (Garden City, N. Y.: Doubleday, 1962), 21, 138, 146, 161.
2. Russell Lord, *The Wallaces of Iowa*, 349.
3. Mrs. Allen Hinchliffe, Wilson, N. Y., *interview with writer*.
4. Blair Bolles, "The Sweetheart of the Regimenters," *American Mercury*, September, 1936, 79.
5. Mrs. Allen Hinchliffe, *interview with writer*.
6. *Ibid.*
7. Blair Bolles, "The Sweetheart of the Regimenters," 79.
8. Tugwell, "Conservation Redefined," address, Fiftieth Anniversary of the Founding of New York's Forest Preserve, Albany, May 15, 1935, *USDA Press Release*, 8.
9. Tugwell, address, Clemson College, S. C., August 15, 1934, *USDA Press Release*, 1-2.
10. Tugwell, address, Niagara County Pioneer Association, Olcott Beach, N. Y., August 8, 1934, *USDA Press Release*, 1-2.
11. Mrs. Allen Hinchliffe, *interview with writer*.
12. Tugwell, *The Stricken Land* (Garden City, N. Y.: Doubleday, 1947), 663.
13. Russell Lord, *The Wallaces of Iowa*, 349.
14. Blair Bolles, "The Sweetheart of the Regimenters," 80.
15. Quoted in "Tugwell's Dream," *Newsweek*, July 1, 1946, 28; Blair Bolles, "Prose and Politics: Writers in the New Deal," *Saturday Review*, March 30, 1940, 4.
16. Lightner Witmer, *The Nearing Case* (New York: B. W. Huebsch, 1915) is a detailed account.
17. Russell Lord, *The Wallaces of Iowa*, 350.
18. *Ibid.*, 349.
19. Blair Bolles, "The Sweetheart of the Regimenters," 80.
20. Tugwell, ed., *The Trend of Economics* (New York: Knopf, 1924), 493.
21. Quoted in Allan C. Gruchy, *Modern Economic Thought: The American Contribution* (New York: Prentice-Hall, 1947), 406, 406n.

22. Quoted in *ibid.*, 406n., 407.
23. Russell Lord, *The Wallaces of Iowa,* 350.
24. Blair Bolles, "The Sweetheart of the Regimenters," 80.
25. Tugwell, ed., *The Trend of Economics*, notes on contributors.
26. Tugwell, *letter to writer,* June 18, 1953.
27. Letter, N. M. Butler to Roosevelt, February 13, 1936, *PPF 564 Roosevelt Papers.*
28. Tugwell, "The Fourth Power," *Planning and Civic Comment,* Part II, April-June, 1939, 3.
29. Blair Bolles, "Prose and Politics," 4.
30. "Territories: Rumbles in Puerto Rico," *Time,* June 15, 1942, 12.
31. Paul W. Ward, "The End of Tugwell," *Nation,* November 28, 1936, 623.
32. Tugwell, *Industry's Coming of Age* (New York: Harcourt, Brace, 1927), 211.
33. Tugwell, *The Stricken Land,* 441, 443.
34. Cleveland Rodgers, *Robert Moses* (New York: Henry Holt, 1952), 129.
35. A. Gillis and R. Ketcham, *Our America* (Boston: Little, Brown, 1936), 362-63.
36. Samuel Pettengill, *Smoke-Screen* (New York: Southern Publishers, 1940), 22.
37. Tugwell, unpublished statement, *Tugwell Papers.*

2. *Tugwell's Institutionalism and the Coming of the Depression*

1. Tugwell, "After the New Deal: 'We Have Bought Ourselves Time to Think,'" *New Republic,* July 26, 1939, 325.
2. Tugwell, *Industry's Coming of Age* (New York: Harcourt, Brace, 1927), 212.
3. Tugwell, "After the New Deal," 325.
4. Tugwell, "A Fireside Symposium," *Columbia University Quarterly,* March, 1935, 31.
5. C. H. McCall, "That Columbia Crowd," *Credit and Financial Management,* June, 1933, 17.
6. Tugwell, "Human Nature and Social Economy," Part I, *Journal of Philosophy,* August 14, 1930, 242.
7. Tugwell, "Implementing the General Interest," *Public Administration Review,* Autumn, 1940, 34.
8. Tugwell, "After the New Deal," 325.
9. Tugwell, "Notes on the Uses of Exactitude in Politics," *Political Science Quarterly,* March, 1939, 15.
10. Tugwell, "The Fourth Power," *Planning and Civic Comment,* April-June, 1939, Part II, 30.
11. Tugwell, "The New Deal: The Rise of Business," Part II, *Western Political Quarterly,* September, 1952, 484-85.
12. *Ibid.,* 484.
13. Tugwell, address, Democratic State Central Committee, Los Angeles, October 28, 1935, *Resettlement Administration Press Release,* 9.

14. Tugwell, "The Superpolitical," *Journal of Social Philosophy*, October, 1939-July, 1940, 107.
15. Tugwell, "Design for Government," address, Eighth Annual Meeting of the Federation of Bar Associations of Western New York, June 24, 1933, in Tugwell, *The Battle for Democracy* (New York: Columbia University Press, 1935), 14.
16. Tugwell, "The New Deal: The Rise of Business," Part II, 486.
17. Tugwell, "The Directive," *Journal of Social Philosophy and Jurisprudence*, October, 1941, 9.
18. Tugwell, "Design for Government," 3-4.
19. Allan G. Gruchy, *Modern Economic Thought: The American Contribution* (New York: Prentice-Hall, 1947), 412-16.
20. Blair Bolles, "Prose and Politics: Writers in the New Deal," *Saturday Review*, March 30, 1940, 4.
21. Tugwell, "The Preparation of a President," *Western Political Quarterly*, July, 1948, 150.
22. Ernest K. Lindley, "War on the Brains Trust," *Scribner's Magazine*, November, 1933, 264.
23. Tugwell, "The Preparation of a President," 150.
24. Ernest K. Lindley, "War on the Brains Trust," 264.
25. Tugwell, "The Directive," 10.
26. Tugwell, "The Progressive Tradition," *Atlantic Monthly*, April, 1935, 413.
27. *Ibid.*
28. Blair Bolles, "The Sweetheart of the Regimenters," *American Mercury*, September, 1936, 79.
29. Joseph B. Ely, *The American Dream* (Boston: B. Humphries, 1944), 225.
30. Tugwell, address, Niagara County Pioneer Association, Olcott Beach, N. Y., August 8, 1934, *USDA Press Release*, 7.
31. Tugwell, address, Columbia Broadcasting System, July 31, 1934, *USDA Press Release*, 3-4.
32. Tugwell, "Earthbound: The Problem of Planning and Survival," *Antioch Review*, Winter, 1949-50, 482.
33. Tugwell, "The Fourth Power," 30.
34. Tugwell, "The Directive," 10.
35. Tugwell, "Earthbound," 477-81.
36. Tugwell, "Variation on a Theme by Cooley," *Ethics*, July, 1949, 242.
37. *Time*, May 2, 1949, 36.
38. Tugwell, "Human Nature and Social Economy," Part II, *Journal of Philosophy*, August 28, 1930, passim.
39. *Ibid.*, 490.
40. Tugwell, "The Directive," 22-24.
41. Tugwell, "The New Deal: The Rise of Business," Part I, *Western Political Quarterly*, June, 1952, 275.
42. Ernest K. Lindley, "War on the Brains Trust," 286.
43. Tugwell, *The Stricken Land* (Garden City, N. Y.: Doubleday, 1947), 441.
44. Tugwell, "The Superpolitical," 112.
45. Tugwell, *The Stricken Land*, 441.

46. Tugwell, *The Economic Basis of Public Interest* (Menasha, Wis.: George Banta, 1922), doctoral dissertation; also see Tugwell, "The Economic Basis for Business Regulation," *American Economic Review,* December, 1921.

47. Tugwell, "America Takes Hold of Its Destiny," *Today,* April 28, 1934, in Tugwell, *The Battle for Democracy,* 258.

48. Tugwell, "The New Deal: The Decline of Government," Part II, *Western Political Quarterly,* September, 1951, 471.

49. Tugwell, "The New Deal: The Rise of Business," Part II, 496.

50. *Ibid.*

51. Tugwell, "The Future of National Planning," *New Republic,* December 9, 1936, 162.

52. Tugwell, "The New Deal: The Rise of Business," Part I, 276.

53. Tugwell, "The Fourth Power," 8.

54. Tugwell, *The Democratic Roosevelt* (Garden City, N. Y.: Doubleday, 1957), 229-30.

55. Tugwell, "The Superpolitical," 109.

56. Tugwell, *The Democratic Roosevelt,* 230.

57. Quoted in Tugwell, *Mr. Hoover's Economic Policy* (New York: John Day, 1932), 12.

58. Ernest K. Lindley, *The Roosevelt Revolution: First Phase* (New York: Viking, 1933), 7-12.

59. G. Burck and C. E. Silberman, "What Caused the Great Depression," *Fortune,* February, 1955, 96-97.

60. Tugwell, "The New Deal: The Rise of Business," Part I, 275.

61. Tugwell, address, Democratic State Central Committee, 3.

62. Tugwell, "America's Wartime Socialism," *Nation,* April 6, 1927; "Paradox of Peace," *New Republic,* April 18, 1928; "Later Moral Equivalents," in Tugwell, *The Battle for Democracy.*

63. Tugwell, "The Fourth Power," 23.

64. Tugwell, "A Third Economy," address, Rochester (N. Y.) Teachers Association, April 9, 1935, *USDA Press Release,* 16.

65. Tugwell, "The Theory of Occupational Obsolescence," *Political Science Quarterly,* June, 1931, passim.

66. Tugwell, "The New Deal: The Rise of Business," Part II, 501.

67. Tugwell, A. T. Cutler and G. S. Mitchell, "Flaws in the Hoover Economic Plan," *Current History,* January, 1932, 527.

68. Tugwell, "Wage Pressure and Efficiency," *New Republic,* November 11, 1928, passim.

69. Tugwell, "The New Deal: The Rise of Business," Part I, 284-85.

70. Tugwell, "Flaws in the Hoover Economic Plan," 525-26.

71. Tugwell, "Hunger, Cold, and Candidates," *New Republic,* May 2, 1928, 323-24.

72. Tugwell, "The Progressive Orthodoxy of Franklin D. Roosevelt," *Ethics,* October, 1953, 11-12.

73. Tugwell, "Hunger, Cold, and Candidates," 323.

74. Tugwell, address, Niagara County Pioneer Association, 7.

75. "Scowl at Billboards," *Business Week,* July 8, 1939, 30.

76. Tugwell, "Freedom from Fakes," *Today*, November 17, 1933, in Tugwell, *The Battle for Democracy*, 103.
77. W. Groom, "Tugwell's Mischievous Ideas about Advertising," *Printer's Ink*, March 1, 1934, 33.
78. *New York Times*, October 23, 1934, reported the meeting.
79. Tugwell, *interview with writer*.
80. Tugwell, "The Progressive Orthodoxy of Franklin D. Roosevelt," 6.
81. Francis Neilson, *Control from the Top* (New York: G. P. Putnam's, 1933), 34-35.
82. Tugwell, "Chameleon Words," *New Republic*, August 25, 1926; "The End of Laissez Faire," *New Republic*, October 13, 1926; "Hunger, Cold, and Candidates," 323-24; "The Liberal Choice," *New Republic*, September 5, 1928, 75.
83. Quoted in *Editor and Publisher*, February 2, 1934, 5.

3. Mr. Hoover's Economic Policy: 1928-1932

1. Tugwell, "Platforms and Candidates," *New Republic*, May 30, 1928, 44.
2. Tugwell, "Hunger, Cold, and Candidates," *New Republic*, May 2, 1928, 325.
3. Tugwell, "The Liberal Choice," *New Republic*, September 5, 1928, 74.
4. Tugwell, "The Progressive Orthodoxy of Franklin D. Roosevelt," *Ethics*, October, 1953, 7.
5. Tugwell, note, *Tugwell Papers*.
6. Tugwell, "The New Deal: The Rise of Business," Part II, *Western Political Quarterly*, September, 1952, 494.
7. Tugwell, *The Democratic Roosevelt* (Garden City, N. Y.: Doubleday, 1957), 198.
8. Tugwell, "The Liberal Choice," 74.
9. *Ibid.*
10. Tugwell, *The Democratic Roosevelt*, 449.
11. Tugwell, "The Progressive Orthodoxy of Franklin D. Roosevelt," 7-8.
12. Louis B. Wehle, *Hidden Threads of History: Wilson through Roosevelt* (New York: Macmillan, 1953), 87.
13. Quoted in Kenneth E. Tromblyn, *The Life and Times of a Happy Liberal: A Biography of Morris Llewellyn Cooke* (New York: Harper, 1954), 95.
14. Tugwell, *Mr. Hoover's Economic Policy* (New York: John Day, 1932), 23.
15. *Ibid.*, 13-14.
16. *Ibid.*, 5-6.
17. *Ibid.*, 7-10.
18. Tugwell, "Hunger, Cold, and Candidates," 323.
19. Tugwell, *Mr. Hoover's Economic Policy*, 11.
20. Tugwell, *The Democratic Roosevelt*, 198.
21. Herbert Hoover, *American Individualism* (Garden City, N. Y.: Doubleday, Doran, 1928), 53-54.
22. Tugwell, *The Democratic Roosevelt*, 322.

23. Tugwell, "The Protagonists: Roosevelt and Hoover," *Antioch Review,* Winter, 1953-54, 419.
24. Basil Rauch, *The History of the New Deal, 1933-1938* (New York: Creative Age Press, 1944), 15.
25. Tugwell, "The Directive," *Journal of Social Philosophy and Jurisprudence,* October, 1941, 21.
26. Tugwell, *interview with writer.*
27. Tugwell, address, Democratic State Central Committee, Los Angeles, October 28, 1935, *Resettlement Administration Press Release,* 14; Tugwell, "Discourse in Depression," address, *Tugwell Papers.*
28. Tugwell, "Prices and Dollars," in Tugwell, *The Battle for Democracy* (New York: Columbia University Press, 1935), 48.
29. Tugwell, "A Fireside Symposium," *Columbia University Quarterly,* March, 1935, 25.
30. Tugwell, "Bankers' Banks," *New Republic,* December 12, 1928, 95-96.
31. Tugwell, "Banking for the People," in Tugwell, *The Battle for Democracy,* 30.
32. Tugwell, *Mr. Hoover's Economic Policy,* 15.
33. Tugwell, "Discourse in Depression," address, *Tugwell Papers.*
34. Tugwell, "The Progressive Orthodoxy of Franklin D. Roosevelt," 9.
35. Tugwell, *Mr. Hoover's Economic Policy,* 15.
36. Basil Rauch, *The History of the New Deal, 1933-1938,* 18.
37. Tugwell, A. T. Cutler and G. S. Mitchell, "Flaws in the Hoover Economic Plan," *Current History,* January, 1932, 525.
38. Basil Rauch, *The History of the New Deal, 1933-1938,* 21.
39. Tugwell, *Mr. Hoover's Economic Policy,* 11.
40. Tugwell, *The Democratic Roosevelt,* 250.
41. *Ibid.,* 132.
42. *Ibid.,* 201.
43. *Ibid.,* 198.
44. Tugwell, *Mr. Hoover's Economic Policy,* 20.
45. Tugwell, "Relief and Reconstruction," address, National Conference of Social Workers, Kansas City, Mo., May 21, 1934, in Tugwell, *The Battle for Democracy,* 309.
46. Tugwell et al., "Flaws in the Hoover Economic Plan," 529.
47. Tugwell, *Mr. Hoover's Economic Policy,* 24.
48. Tugwell et al., "Flaws in the Hoover Economic Plan," 528, 530.
49. *Ibid.,* 529.
50. Tugwell, *Mr. Hoover's Economic Policy,* 24.
51. Tugwell et al., "Flaws in the Hoover Economic Plan," 531.
52. Tugwell, *Mr. Hoover's Economic Policy,* 17-22.
53. Tugwell, "A Third Economy," address, Rochester (N. Y.) Teachers Association, April 9, 1935, *USDA Press Release,* 5.
54. Tugwell, *Mr. Hoover's Economic Policy,* 16.
55. Tugwell et al., "Flaws in the Hoover Economic Plan, 530.
56. Tugwell, "Discourse in Depression," address, *Tugwell Papers.*
57. Tugwell et al., "Flaws in the Hoover Economic Plan," 529.

58. Tugwell, *The Democratic Roosevelt*, 203.
59. *Ibid.*, 251.
60. Tugwell, "The Protagonists: Roosevelt and Hoover," 429.
61. Tugwell et al., "Flaws in the Hoover Economic Plan," 529-31.
62. *Ibid.*, 529.
63. *Ibid.*, 531.
64. Tugwell, "Discourse in Depression," address, *Tugwell Papers.*
65. Basil Rauch, *The History of the New Deal, 1933-1938,* 17, 20.
66. Dixon Wecter, *The Age of the Great Depression, 1929-1941* (New York: Macmillan, 1948), 44-45.
67. Basil Rauch, *The History of the New Deal, 1933-1938,* 17-18.
68. Marriner S. Eccles, *Beckoning Frontiers* (New York: Knopf, 1951), 101-02.
69. Dixon Wecter, *The Age of the Great Depression, 1929-1941,* 50.
70. Tugwell, *Mr. Hoover's Economic Policy,* 12-13.
71. Tugwell, "Discourse in Depression," address, *Tugwell Papers.*
72. Tugwell, *The Democratic Roosevelt,* 198.
73. Basil Rauch, *The History of the New Deal, 1933-1938,* 10, 21.
74. Quoted in *Boston Globe,* June 29, 1958.
75. Tugwell, *The Democratic Roosevelt,* 198.

4. Brain Trust—Campaign—Election: 1932

1. Raymond Moley, *After Seven Years* (New York: Harper, 1939), 5-23; Samuel Rosenman, *Working with Roosevelt* (New York: Harper, 1952), 59, 64.
2. Tugwell, *interview with writer.*
3. Lela Stiles, *The Man behind the President: The Story of Louis McHenry Howe* (New York: World, 1954), 275.
4. Tugwell, *The Democratic Roosevelt* (Garden City, N. Y.: Doubleday, 1957), 219n.
5. Tugwell, "Discourse in Depression," address, 1932, *Tugwell Papers.*
6. Tugwell, *letter to writer,* May 18, 1955.
7. Tugwell, note, *Tugwell Papers.*
8. Tugwell, *The Democratic Roosevelt,* 212-15.
9. Ernest K. Lindley, "War on the Brains Trust," *Scribner's Magazine,* November, 1933, 259.
10. Tugwell, *The Democratic Roosevelt,* 351.
11. *Ibid.*, 218.
12. *Ibid.*, 218-20, 219n.
13. Raymond Moley, *After Seven Years,* 27, 30.
14. Tugwell, *interview with writer.*
15. Raymond Moley, *After Seven Years,* 31.
16. Tugwell, "The Preparation of a President," *Western Political Quarterly,* June, 1948, 143.
17. Tugwell, *The Democratic Roosevelt,* 233-34, 233n.
18. *Ibid.*, 234-35.
19. *Ibid.*, 235.

20. John Gunther, *Roosevelt in Retrospect* (New York: Harper, 1950), 269.
21. Raymond Moley, *After Seven Years*, 29.
22. *Ibid.*, 29, 36-37.
23. Lela Stiles, *The Man behind the President*, 276.
24. Mrs. Louis M. Howe, *interview with writer*, Fall River, Mass.
25. Lela Stiles, *The Man behind the President*, 254.
26. Tugwell, "The Progressive Orthodoxy of Franklin D. Roosevelt," *Ethics*, October, 1953, 21.
27. Tugwell, *interview with writer*.
28. Raymond Moley, *After Seven Years*, 37-39, 45-46.
29. Tugwell, "The Progressive Orthodoxy of Franklin D. Roosevelt," 21.
30. Tugwell, *The Democratic Roosevelt*, 217.
31. *Ibid.*, 217-18.
32. *Ibid.*, 216.
33. *Ibid.*
34. Ernest K. Lindley, "War on the Brains Trust," 264.
35. Samuel Rosenman, *Working with Roosevelt*, 80.
36. Tugwell, "The Preparation of a President," 143.
37. Tugwell, "The Progressive Orthodoxy of Franklin D. Roosevelt," 21.
38. Quoted in Ernest K. Lindley, "War on the Brains Trust," 264.
39. Raymond Moley, *After Seven Years*, 41.
40. Gilbert C. Fite, *George N. Peek and the Fight for Farm Parity* (Norman: University of Oklahoma Press, 1954), 239.
41. Raymond Moley, *After Seven Years*, 41-44.
42. Letter, M. L. Wilson to Tugwell, September 28, 1932, *Tugwell Papers*.
43. Tugwell, *The Democratic Roosevelt*, 246.
44. *Ibid.*
45. Tugwell, "Design for Government," address, Eighth Annual Meeting of the Federation of Bar Associations of Western New York, June 24, 1933, in Tugwell, *The Battle for Democracy* (New York: Columbia University Press, 1935), 7.
46. Raymond Moley, *After Seven Years*, 62.
47. Frank Freidel, *Franklin D. Roosevelt: The Triumph* (Boston: Little, Brown, 1956), 357.
48. *Ibid.*, 361-63, 362n.
49. Raymond Moley, *After Seven Years*, 62.
50. *Ibid.*, 63.
51. Tugwell, *The Democratic Roosevelt*, 215, 216-17.
52. *Ibid.*, 214-15.
53. *Ibid.*, 220-21.
54. *Ibid.*, 220-21, 224.
55. Tugwell, "The Progressive Orthodoxy of Franklin D. Roosevelt," 10-17.
56. Tugwell, *The Democratic Roosevelt*, 219.
57. *Ibid.*, 218.
58. Tugwell, "The Progressive Orthodoxy of Franklin D. Roosevelt," 20-21.
59. Tugwell, *The Democratic Roosevelt*, 242.
60. *Ibid.*, 241.

61. *Ibid.*, 247.
62. Tugwell, "The Progressive Orthodoxy of Franklin D. Roosevelt," 20.
63. Tugwell, *The Democratic Roosevelt*, 247.
64. Tugwell, "The Progressive Orthodoxy of Franklin D. Roosevelt," 20.
65. Tugwell, *The Democratic Roosevelt*, 216.
66. Tugwell, "The Progressive Orthodoxy of Franklin D. Roosevelt," 21.

5. Nationalism versus Internationalism

1. Raymond Moley, *After Seven Years* (New York: Harper, 1939), 23-24.
2. Letter, Gardiner C. Means to Tugwell, October 1, 1934, *Tugwell Papers.*
3. Raymond Moley, *After Seven Years*, 108.
4. Harold B. Hinton, *Cordell Hull* (London: Hurst and Blackett, 1941), 158.
5. Tugwell, note, *Tugwell Papers.*
6. Raymond Moley, *After Seven Years*, 48.
7. Tugwell, *The Democratic Roosevelt* (Garden City, N. Y.: Doubleday, 1957), 231.
8. *Ibid.*, 254.
9. Ernest K. Lindley, *The Roosevelt Revolution: First Phase* (New York: Viking, 1933), 185.
10. Tugwell, *The Democratic Roosevelt*, 291.
11. Raymond Moley, *After Seven Years*, 48, 368.
12. Tugwell, "Must We Draft Roosevelt?," *New Republic*, May 13, 1940, 630.
13. Tugwell, "International Economic Policy," in Tugwell, *The Battle for Democracy* (New York: Columbia University Press, 1935), 166.
14. *Ibid.*, 164.
15. Tugwell, "The Preparation of a President," *Western Political Quarterly*, June, 1948, 149.
16. Tugwell, "The Place of Government in a National Land Program," address, Joint Meeting, American Economic Association, American Statistical Association, Farm Economic Association, Philadelphia, December 29, 1933, *USDA Press Release*, 9.
17. Tugwell, "International Economic Policy," 167.
18. Tugwell, "The Preparation of a President," 149.
19. Raymond Moley, *After Seven Years*, 86-99.
20. Tugwell, A. T. Cutler and G. S. Mitchell, "Flaws in the Hoover Economic Plan," *Current History*, January, 1932, 28.
21. Tugwell, *The Democratic Roosevelt*, 255.
22. Tugwell, "The Progressive Orthodoxy of Franklin D. Roosevelt," *Ethics*, October, 1953, 8.
23. Quoted in Edward Angly, ed., *Oh Yeah?* (New York: Viking, 1932), 47.
24. Quoted in Tugwell et al., "Flaws in the Hoover Economic Plan," 28.
25. *Ibid.*, 29.
26. Raymond Moley, *After Seven Years*, 76-77.
27. Theodore G. Joslin, *Hoover off the Record* (Garden City, N. Y.: Doubleday, Doran, 1934), 342.
28. *Ibid.*, 254-56, 315.

29. *Ibid.*, 256, 260.
30. Tugwell, "The Preparation of a President," 148.
31. Raymond Moley, *After Seven Years*, 70, 78-79, 87-88.
32. William Miller, *A History of the United States* (New York: Dell, 1958), 407.
33. Morit J. Bonn, *Prosperity: Myth and Reality in American Life* (London: M. Hopkinson, 1931), 7-10.
34. Tugwell, "The Progressive Orthodoxy of Franklin D. Roosevelt," 8.

6. Roosevelt versus Hoover: The Lame-Duck Interlude

1. Tugwell, "The Protagonists: Roosevelt and Hoover," *Antioch Review*, Winter, 1953-54, 419.
2. *Ibid.*, 423.
3. Ernest K. Lindley, *The Roosevelt Revolution: First Phase* (New York: Viking, 1934), 18-19.
4. *Ibid.*, 19.
5. Quoted in *Time*, February 6, 1933, 14.
6. Memorandum, Tugwell to Roosevelt, September 8, 1934, *PPF 180 Roosevelt Papers*.
7. Tugwell, *interview with writer*.
8. Tugwell, syndicated column, *Tugwell Papers*.
9. F. D. Roosevelt, address, Oglethorpe University, cited in Tugwell, "The Progressive Orthodoxy of Franklin D. Roosevelt," *Ethics*, October, 1953, 13.
10. Tugwell, "The New Deal: The Decline of Government," Part II, *Western Political Quarterly*, September, 1951, 483.
11. G. Burck and C. E. Silberman, "Why the Depression Lasted So Long," *Fortune*, March, 1955, 194.
12. Basil Rauch, *The History of the New Deal, 1933-1938* (New York: Creative Age Press, 1944), 106.
13. Raymond Moley, *After Seven Years* (New York: Harper, 1939), 162; Tugwell, *interview with writer*.
14. Tugwell, "The Preparation of a President," *Western Political Quarterly*, June, 1948, 144; unpublished statement on balanced exchangeability, no date, *Tugwell Papers*.
15. Tugwell, "The New Deal: The Rise of Business," Part II, *Western Political Quarterly*, September, 1952, 497-501.
16. Raymond Moley, *After Seven Years*, 157-61.
17. Tugwell, "The Compromising Roosevelt," *Western Political Quarterly*, June, 1953, 334.
18. Tugwell, "The New Deal: The Decline of Government," Part II, 483.
19. Raymond Moley, *After Seven Years*, 72-77.
20. Tugwell, A. T. Cutler and G. S. Mitchell, "Flaws in the Hoover Economic Plan," *Current History*, January, 1932, 529.
21. Basil Rauch, *The History of the New Deal, 1933-1938*, 48-49.
22. Raymond Moley, *After Seven Years*, 76.

23. *Ibid.*, 49.
24. Tugwell, *The Democratic Roosevelt* (Garden City, N. Y.: Doubleday, 1957), 314-17, 315n.
25. Raymond Moley, *After Seven Years*, 141.
26. Tugwell, *The Democratic Roosevelt*, 260.
27. Theodore G. Joslin, *Hoover off the Record* (New York: Doubleday, Doran, 1934), 363, 365.
28. J. F. T. O'Connor, *The Banking Crisis and Recovery under the Roosevelt Administration* (Chicago: Callaghan, 1938), 9, 12.
29. Raymond Moley, *After Seven Years*, 143-46.
30. *Ibid.*, 145-46.
31. Theodore G. Joslin, *Hoover off the Record*, 333.
32. Raymond Moley, *After Seven Years*, 142.
33. Tugwell, "The Protagonists: Roosevelt and Hoover," 424.
34. Theodore G. Joslin, *Hoover off the Record*, 341, 346-47, 355-57.
35. *Ibid.*, 332, 351-53.
36. *Ibid.*, 350-53.
37. *Ibid.*, 330, 351-53.
38. William S. Myers and Walter H. Newton, *The Hoover Administration: A Documented Narrative* (New York: Scribner, 1936).
39. Basil Rauch, *The History of the New Deal, 1933-1938*, 48.
40. H. Hoover, *The Memoirs of Herbert Hoover: The Great Depression, 1929-1941* (New York: Macmillan, 1952), 269.
41. J. F. T. O'Connor, *The Banking Crisis and Recovery*, 9.
42. Theodore G. Joslin, *Hoover off the Record*, 354, 359.
43. Basil Rauch, *The History of the New Deal, 1933-1938*, 52.
44. Quoted in Theodore G. Joslin, *Hoover off the Record*, 357.
45. Quoted in Tugwell, "The Protagonists: Roosevelt and Hoover," 420.
46. Lawrence Sullivan, *Prelude to Panic: The Story of the Bank Holiday* (Washington: Statesman Press, 1936), for example.
47. Dixon Wecter, *The Age of the Great Depression, 1929-1941* (New York: Macmillan, 1948), 51.
48. Basil Rauch, *The History of the New Deal, 1933-1938*, 51-52.
49. Ernest K. Lindley, *The Roosevelt Revolution: First Phase*, 44, 46, 75.
50. Basil Rauch, *The History of the New Deal, 1933-1938*, 50, 53; Raymond Moley, *After Seven Years*, 143.
51. Raymond Moley, *After Seven Years*, 105, 141-42, 144, 144n.
52. Tugwell, *The Democratic Roosevelt*, 272.
53. Tugwell, "The Protagonists: Roosevelt and Hoover," 420.
54. E. E. Agger, "Money and Gold," forwarded to Roosevelt by Tugwell, May 28, 1936, *PPF 180 Roosevelt Papers*.
55. Tugwell, "Our Weight in Gold," in Tugwell, *The Battle for Democracy* (New York: Columbia University Press, 1935), 26.
56. *Ibid.*, 27.
57. Tugwell, unpublished statement, *Tugwell Papers;* "Prices and Dollars," in Tugwell, *The Battle for Democracy*, 49.

58. Basil Rauch, *The History of the New Deal, 1933-1938,* 64.
59. Raymond Moley, *After Seven Years,* 155.
60. Tugwell, *The Democratic Roosevelt,* 273.

7. Tugwell versus Hoover: The Twenty-Five-Year Debate

1. Quoted in William S. Myers and Walter H. Newton, *The Hoover Administration: A Documented Narrative* (New York: Scribner, 1936), 356.
2. John T. Flynn, *The Roosevelt Myth* (New York: Devin-Adair, 1948), 24.
3. Lawrence Sullivan, *Prelude to Panic: The Story of the Bank Holiday* (Washington: Statesman Press, 1936), 99.
4. Quoted in William S. Myers and Walter H. Newton, *The Hoover Administration,* 341.
5. Lawrence Sullivan, *Prelude to Panic,* 99.
6. Marriner S. Eccles, *Beckoning Frontiers* (New York: Knopf, 1951), 114-15.
7. Tugwell, *The Democratic Roosevelt* (Garden City, N. Y.: Doubleday, 1957), 262.
8. Tugwell, *interview with writer.*
9. Letters, James H. Rand, Jr., to Tugwell, March 14, 1933, and November 15, 1933, *Tugwell Papers.*
10. Herbert Hoover, *The Memoirs of Herbert Hoover: The Great Depression, 1929-1941* (New York: Macmillan, 1952), 214.
11. *Ibid.,* 471.
12. Tugwell, "The Protagonists: Roosevelt and Hoover," *Antioch Review,* Winter, 1953-54, 427-28.
13. Tugwell, *The Democratic Roosevelt,* 240.
14. Tugwell, "A Planner's View of Agriculture's Future," *Journal of Farm Economics,* February, 1949, 36.
15. Tugwell, *The Democratic Roosevelt,* 240.
16. Tugwell, "The Protagonists: Roosevelt and Hoover," 428.
17. *Ibid.,* 438-39.
18. *Ibid.,* 430.
19. Tugwell, "A Planner's View of Agriculture's Future," 37.
20. G. Burck and C. E. Silberman, "Why the Depression Lasted So Long," *Fortune,* March, 1955, 200.
21. Tugwell, *The Democratic Roosevelt,* 442-43.
22. Walt W. Rostow, *The Stages of Economic Growth: A Non-Communist Manifesto* (Cambridge: At the University Press, 1960), 78.
23. Tugwell, "The Protagonists: Roosevelt and Hoover," 421-22, 424-27.
24. *Ibid.,* 421.
25. *New York Times,* February 28, 1958.
26. Tugwell, *The Democratic Roosevelt,* 263.
27. Tugwell, "The Protagonists: Roosevelt and Hoover," 427.
28. *Ibid.,* 428.
29. *Ibid.,* 422.
30. David Lawrence, "1933 Bank Holiday Was Unnecessary," *Rochester (N. Y.) Democrat and Chronicle,* March 5, 1958.

31. David Lawrence, *United States News and World Report*, February 21, 1958, 120.
32. Tugwell, "The Protagonists: Roosevelt and Hoover," 439.
33. Tugwell, "The New Deal: The Decline of Government," Part II, *Western Political Quarterly*, September, 1951, 485.
34. Ernest K. Lindley, "War on the Brains Trust," *Scribner's Magazine*, November, 1933, 264.
35. George M. Verity, "Appraises Prof. Tugwell," *Iron Age*, July 26, 1934, 34.
36. Tugwell, "The Preparation of a President," *Western Political Quarterly*, June, 1948, 151.
37. Tugwell, "The Compromising Roosevelt," *Western Political Quarterly*, June, 1953, 330.
38. Tugwell, "The New Deal: The Rise of Business," Part II, *Western Political Quarterly*, September, 1952, 491.
39. Tugwell, "The Protagonists: Roosevelt and Hoover," 437-39.
40. *Ibid.*, 428-31, 442.
41. *Ibid.*, 429-32.
42. *Ibid.*, 431, 442.
43. Tugwell, "The New Deal: The Progressive Tradition," *Western Political Quarterly*, September, 1950, 426-27.
44. William E. Leuchtenburg, *The Perils of Prosperity, 1914-32* (Chicago: University of Chicago Press, 1958), 264.
45. Tugwell, "The Protagonists: Roosevelt and Hoover," 437.
46. Tugwell, *The Stricken Land* (Garden City, N. Y.: Doubleday, 1947), 441, 681.
47. Mario Einaudi, *The Roosevelt Revolution* (New York: Harcourt, Brace, 1959), 67.
48. Tugwell, *The Stricken Land*, 441-42.
49. Tugwell, "The Protagonists: Roosevelt and Hoover," 427.
50. *Ibid.*, 423.
51. *Ibid.*, 422.
52. *Ibid.*, 419-20, 436-37.
53. Arthur S. Link, *American Epoch* (New York: Knopf, 1955), 708; John D. Hicks, *Republican Ascendancy: 1921-1933* (New York: Harper, 1960), 284.
54. Paul Seabury, review, *The Kaiser*, by J. von Keurenberg, in *Saturday Review*, August 20, 1955, 14.
55. John T. Flynn, *The Roosevelt Myth*, 182.
56. Raymond Moley, *After Seven Years* (New York: Harper, 1939), 376.
57. Tugwell, *The Art of Politics* (Garden City, N. Y.: Doubleday, 1958), 86, 197.
58. Tugwell, *The Stricken Land*, 681.
59. Tugwell, *The Art of Politics*, 184-88.
60. David Reisman and Michael Maccoby, "The American Crisis," in James Roosevelt, ed., *The Liberal Papers* (Garden City, N. Y.: Doubleday, An Anchor Book, 1962), 13.
61. *New York Times*, December 29, 1937; January 15, 1938.

62. Tugwell, "The New Deal: The Rise of Business," Part I, *Western Political Quarterly*, June, 1952, 282.
63. Tugwell, "The Compromising Roosevelt," 322.
64. James M. Burns, *Roosevelt: The Lion and the Fox* (New York: Harcourt, Brace, 1956), 368-69.
65. Dexter Perkins, *The New Age of Franklin Roosevelt, 1932-45* (Chicago: University of Chicago Press, 1957), 80.
66. Arthur Krock, *New York Times*, March 21, 1958.
67. Robert L. Heilbroner, *The Worldly Philosophers* (New York: Simon and Schuster, 1953), 267.
68. G. Burck and C. E. Silberman, "Why the Depression Lasted So Long," 199.
69. Alvin H. Hansen, letter to the editor, *New York Times*, May 21, 1961.
70. Tugwell, "The Protagonists: Roosevelt and Hoover," 427-28.
71. Basil Rauch, "Roosevelt and the Historians," *Yale Review*, Summer, 1958, 620.

8. *Officialdom and the End of the Brain Trust*

1. Cabel Phillips, "The New Dealers—Where Are They Now?," *New York Times Magazine*, September 29, 1946, 52.
2. George N. Peek with Samuel Crowther, *Why Quit Our Own* (New York: D. Van Nostrand, 1936), 22.
3. Raymond Moley, *27 Masters of Politics* (New York: Funk and Wagnalls, 1949), 80.
4. Raymond Moley, *After Seven Years* (New York: Harper, 1939), 123n.
5. Raymond Moley, *27 Masters of Politics*, 80.
6. Tugwell, *interview with writer*.
7. Paul W. Ward, "Henry Morgenthau and His Friends," *Nation*, August 14, 1935, 83.
8. Raymond Moley, *After Seven Years*, 124.
9. Harold L. Ickes, *The Secret Diary of Harold L. Ickes, Part One* (New York: Simon and Schuster, 1953), 239-40.
10. Tugwell, "The Utility of the Future in the Present," *Public Administration Review*, Winter, 1948, 49.
11. George N. Peek, *Why Quit Our Own*, 73.
12. Russell Lord, *The Wallaces of Iowa* (Boston: Houghton Mifflin, 1947), 323-24.
13. Raymond Moley, *After Seven Years*, 124n.
14. Russell Lord, *The Wallaces of Iowa*, 324.
15. Frank Kent, *Without Grease* (New York: William Morrow, 1936), 82.
16. Blair Bolles, "The Sweetheart of the Regimenters," *American Mercury*, September, 1936, 83.
17. Quoted in Raymond Moley, *27 Masters of Politics*, 81.
18. Letter, Henry A. Wallace to Roosevelt, February 22, 1933, *Tugwell Papers*.
19. Arthur W. Macmahon and John D. Millett, *Federal Administrators* (New York: Columbia University Press, 1939), 215.

20. Russell Lord, *The Wallaces of Iowa*, 323.
21. Tugwell, *The Stricken Land* (Garden City, N. Y.: Doubleday, 1947), 24-25.
22. Raymond Moley, *After Seven Years*, 124n.
23. David Lawrence, *Beyond the New Deal* (New York: Whittlesey House, 1934), 205.
24. David Lawrence, *Stumbling into Socialism* (New York: Appleton-Century, 1935), 16.
25. David Lawrence, *Beyond the New Deal*, 206.
26. Leo C. Rosten, *The Washington Correspondents* (New York: Harcourt, Brace, 1936), 268.
27. Ernest K. Lindley, "War on the Brains Trust," *Scribner's Magazine*, November, 1933, 260.
28. Max Lerner, *It Is Later than You Think* (New York: Viking, 1939), 156-58.
29. George Soule, *The Coming American Revolution* (New York: Macmillan, 1934), 207-08.
30. *Ibid.*, 208.
31. Ernest K. Lindley, "War on the Brains Trust," 258.
32. Samuel Rosenman, *Working with Roosevelt* (New York: Harper, 1952), 81, 87-88.
33. Raymond Moley, *After Seven Years*, 65-66.
34. Tugwell, note on "Discourse in Depression," *Tugwell Papers*.
35. Raymond Moley, *After Seven Years*, 83.
36. Samuel Rosenman, *Working with Roosevelt*, 88.
37. Telegram, Tugwell to D. Geddes, June 19, 1933, *Tugwell Papers*.

9. *Tugwell's Institutionalism and Economic Planning*

1. Cited in Stuart Chase, *The Economy of Abundance* (New York: Macmillan, 1934), 202.
2. Tugwell, "Ideas behind the New Deal," *New York Times Magazine*, July 16, 1933, 2.
3. Tugwell, "Design for Government," address, Eighth Annual Meeting of the Federation of Bar Associations of Western New York, June 24, 1933, in Tugwell, *The Battle for Democracy* (New York: Columbia University Press, 1935), 6.
4. *Ibid.*, 6-7.
5. Tugwell, "The New Deal: The Decline of Government," Part II, *Western Political Quarterly*, September, 1951, 478.
6. Tugwell, "The Utility of the Future in the Present," *Public Administration Review*, Winter, 1948, 57-58.
7. Tugwell, *Mr. Hoover's Economic Policy* (New York: John Day, 1932), 10.
8. *Ibid.*, 9-10.
9. Tugwell, *The Industrial Discipline and the Governmental Arts* (New York: Columbia University Press, 1933), 19.
10. Tugwell, "Chameleon Words," *New Republic*, August 25, 1926, 163.

11. Quoted in Blair Bolles, "The Sweetheart of the Regimenters," *American Mercury*, September, 1936, 79.
12. Tugwell, "The Superpolitical," *Journal of Social Philosophy*, October, 1939-July, 1940, 98.
13. Allan G. Gruchy, *Modern Economic Thought: The American Contribution* (New York: Prentice-Hall, 1947), 450.
14. Tugwell, "Hunger, Cold, and Candidates," *New Republic*, May 2, 1928, 323-24.
15. Tugwell, "The New Deal: The Decline of Government," Part II, 470-71.
16. Tugwell, "The New Deal: The Decline of Government," Part I, *Western Political Quarterly*, June, 1951, 308.
17. Allan G. Gruchy, *Modern Economic Thought*, 446.
18. Tugwell, "Implementing the General Interest," *Public Administration Review*, Autumn, 1940, 34.
19. Tugwell, "The Fourth Power," *Planning and Civic Comment*, April-June, 1939, Part II, 27.
20. Tugwell, "Implementing the General Interest," 34.
21. Tugwell, "Variation on a Theme by Cooley," *Ethics*, July, 1949, 236-37.
22. Tugwell, "Implementing the General Interest," 34.
23. Tugwell, "The Superpolitical," 113.
24. Tugwell, "Chameleon Words," 163.
25. Tugwell, "The Superpolitical," 113.
26. Tugwell, "Land of Plenty," *Current History*, February, 1938, 483.
27. Tugwell, "The Principle of Planning and the Institution of Laissez Faire," *American Economic Review, Supplement*, March, 1932, 89.
28. Quoted in letter, M. L. Wilson to Tugwell, July 25, 1932, *Tugwell Papers*.
29. 73 Congress, 2 Session, *Congressional Record*, June 14, 1934, 11349.
30. Tugwell, unpublished statement, December, 1933, *Tugwell Papers*.
31. Tugwell, "A Third Economy," address, Rochester (N. Y.) Teachers Association, April 9, 1935, *USDA Press Release*, 9.
32. Tugwell, *The Stricken Land* (Garden City, N. Y.: Doubleday, 1947), 56-57.
33. Letter, Tugwell to Harold L. Ickes, 1941; cited in Russell Lord, "Governor Rex of Puerto Rico," *Common Sense*, July, 1942, 28.
34. Tugwell, "The Directive," *Journal of Social Philosophy and Jurisprudence*, October, 1941, 34.
35. Tugwell, "The Superpolitical," 103-04.
36. James G. Mitchell, "The Precocious Juvenility of the 'Brain Trust,'" *Annalist*, June 1, 1934, 849.
37. Tugwell, "The Superpolitical," 102.
38. *Ibid.*, 104-05.
39. James G. Mitchell, "The Precocious Juvenility of the 'Brain Trust,'" 849.
40. Tugwell, "Chameleon Words," 162-63.
41. Tugwell, "A Fireside Symposium," *Columbia University Quarterly*, March, 1935, 28.
42. Tugwell, "A Third Economy," 10.
43. Tugwell, "The New Deal: The Decline of Government," Part II, 478.

44. Tugwell, "The Superpolitical," *Journal of Social Philosophy*, October, 1939-July, 1940.

45. Tugwell, "Earthbound: The Problem of Planning and Survival," *Antioch Review*, Winter, 1949-50, 492.

46. Tugwell, "The Directive," 25-26.

47. Tugwell, "The Fourth Power," *Planning and Civic Comment*, April-June, 1939, Part II.

48. Tugwell, "The Superpolitical," 97-101, 111-12.

49. Francis Neilson, *Control from the Top* (New York: G. P. Putnam's, 1933), 39.

50. Tugwell, "The Fourth Power," 30.

51. Allan G. Gruchy, *Modern Economic Thought*, 448.

52. Tugwell, "The Utility of the Future in the Present," 52.

53. Tugwell, "The Protagonists: Roosevelt and Hoover," *Antioch Review*, Winter, 1953-54, 431n.

54. Tugwell, "The Superpolitical," 111-12.

55. Tugwell, "The Directive," 11.

56. Tugwell, "A Planner's View of Agriculture's Future," *Journal of Farm Economics*, February, 1949, 31.

57. Tugwell, "The Fourth Power," 6.

58. Tugwell, "Variation on a Theme by Cooley," 241.

59. Tugwell, "The Directive," 11.

60. Tugwell, "The Future of National Planning," *New Republic*, December 9, 1936, 162.

61. Tugwell, "Variation on a Theme by Cooley," 238-41.

62. Tugwell, "The Fourth Power," 2.

63. Ernest K. Lindley, *Halfway with Roosevelt* (New York: Viking, 1937), 32-34.

64. Tugwell, "Chameleon Words," 9.

65. Paul W. Ward, "Wallace the Great Hesitator," *Nation*, February 20, 1935, 535.

66. Tugwell, "The Superpolitical," 103.

67. Tugwell, "The Fourth Power," 3.

68. Tugwell, "A Planner's View of Agriculture's Future," 31.

69. Tugwell, "Variation on a Theme by Cooley," 243.

70. Tugwell, "The Fourth Power," 2.

71. *Ibid.*, 24.

72. Tugwell, "The Superpolitical," 113.

73. Tugwell, *The Democratic Roosevelt* (Garden City, N. Y.: Doubleday, 1957), 454.

74. Frank R. Kent, *Without Gloves* (New York: William Morrow, 1934), 273, 289.

75. *Time*, August 13, 1934, 11-12.

76. Tugwell, "A Planner's View of Agriculture's Future," 46.

77. Tugwell, column, United Features Syndicate, January 28, 1934.

78. Ernest K. Lindley, *Halfway with Roosevelt*, 130.

79. Cable, S. Early to Tugwell, October 12, 1934; memorandum, M. McIntyre to Roosevelt, October 20, 1934; memorandum, S. Early to H. A. Wallace, October 23, 1934, *OF 1 Roosevelt Papers.*
80. *Time,* November 5, 1934, 16.
81. Tugwell, address, Democratic State Central Committee, Los Angeles, October 28, 1935, *Resettlement Administration Press Release,* 2.
82. Alva Johnston, "Tugwell, the President's Idea Man," *Saturday Evening Post,* August 1, 1936, 9.
83. Harold L. Ickes, *The Secret Diary of Harold L. Ickes, Part One* (New York: Simon and Schuster, 1953), 473.
84. Tugwell, "America Takes Hold of Its Destiny," *Today,* April 28, 1934, in Tugwell, *The Battle for Democracy,* 264.
85. Tugwell, "The Fourth Power," 12.
86. *Ibid.,* 4.

10. The Ideological Split in the New Deal

1. Tugwell, *The Democratic Roosevelt* (Garden City, N. Y.: Doubleday, 1957), 375.
2. Tugwell, "The New Deal: The Decline of Government," Part I, *Western Political Quarterly,* June, 1951, 308.
3. Dexter Perkins, *The New Age of Franklin Roosevelt, 1932-45* (Chicago: University of Chicago Press, 1957), 70-74.
4. Leon Keyserling, " 'Liberal' Government Is Not Enough," *Reporter,* May 31, 1956, 18.
5. Tugwell, "The Fourth Power," *Planning and Civic Comment,* April-June, 1939, Part II, 13.
6. Tugwell, "The New Deal: The Rise of Business," Part II, *Western Political Quarterly,* September, 1952, 495.
7. Tugwell, "The Progressive Orthodoxy of Franklin D. Roosevelt," *Ethics,* October, 1953, 16.
8. Tugwell, "The New Deal: The Rise of Business," Part I, *Western Political Quarterly,* June, 1952, 281.
9. Tugwell, "The New Deal: The Decline of Government," Part II, *Western Political Quarterly,* September, 1951, 485.
10. Tugwell, "The Progressive Orthodoxy of Franklin D. Roosevelt," 19.
11. James M. Burns, *Roosevelt: The Lion and the Fox* (New York: Harcourt, Brace, 1956), 334.
12. Raymond Moley, *After Seven Years* (New York: Harper, 1939), 13-14.
13. Tugwell, "The New Deal: The Decline of Government," Part I, 312.
14. Tugwell, *The Stricken Land* (Garden City, N. Y.: Doubleday, 1947), 563.
15. Tugwell, "After the New Deal: 'We Have Bought Ourselves Time to Think,' " *New Republic,* July 26, 1939, 324.
16. Tugwell, "The Preparation of a President," *Western Political Quarterly,* June, 1948, 139.
17. Dixon Wecter, *The Age of the Great Depression, 1929-1941* (New York: Macmillan, 1948), 59.

18. Tugwell, "The New Deal: The Rise of Business," Part I, 281.
19. Tugwell, "The New Deal: The Rise of Business," Part II, 503.
20. Tugwell, "The Preparation of a President," 142.
21. *Ibid.*, 152.
22. Tugwell, "The New Deal: The Rise of Business," Part I, 279.
23. Quoted in Tugwell, "The Two Great Roosevelts," *Western Political Quarterly*, March, 1952, 189n.
24. Tugwell, *The Art of Politics* (Garden City, N. Y.: Doubleday, 1958), 33.
25. *Ibid.*, 263.
26. Tugwell, "The Two Great Roosevelts," 89.
27. Tugwell, *The Democratic Roosevelt*, 369.
28. Tugwell, "The New Deal: The Rise of Business," Part II, 503.
29. Tugwell, "The Preparation of a President," 138.
30. Cited in 73 Congress, 2 Session, *Congressional Record*, May 8, 1934, 8267-68.
31. Raymond Moley, 27 *Masters of Politics* (New York: Funk and Wagnalls, 1949), 157.
32. Letter, Frankfurter to Tugwell, December 12, 1933, *Tugwell Papers.*
33. Memorandum, Roosevelt to Tugwell, May 28, 1934, *Tugwell Papers.*
34. Tugwell, "The New Deal: The Decline of Government," Part II, 482.
35. Tugwell, "The New Deal: The Rise of Business," Part I, 275n.
36. Tugwell, *The Art of Politics*, 247.
37. Tugwell, *The Democratic Roosevelt*, 326.
38. *Ibid.*, 247-48.
39. Tugwell, "The Compromising Roosevelt," *Western Political Quarterly*, June, 1953, 329.
40. Tugwell, "Must We Draft Roosevelt?," *New Republic*, May 13, 1940, 630.
41. Tugwell, *The Democratic Roosevelt*, 239; Tugwell, *interview with writer.*
42. Margaret Coit, *Mr. Baruch* (Boston: Houghton Mifflin, 1957), 450.
43. Tugwell, *The Democratic Roosevelt*, 327.
44. Margaret Coit, *Mr. Baruch*, 409.
45. *Ibid.*, 440.
46. *Ibid.*, 441.
47. *Ibid.*, 439, 440.
48. Tugwell, "The New Deal: The Decline of Government," Part II, 486.
49. Tugwell, *The Democratic Roosevelt*, 307.
50. Tugwell, "The Compromising Roosevelt," 320-21, 322n.
51. Tugwell, "The Progressive Tradition," *Atlantic Monthly*, April, 1935, passim.
52. Tugwell, "The Compromising Roosevelt," 325.
53. Basil Rauch, *The History of the New Deal: 1933-1938* (New York: Creative Age Press, 1944), 138, 159.
54. James M. Burns, *Roosevelt: The Lion and the Fox*, 224-25.
55. Tugwell, *The Democratic Roosevelt*, 327.
56. *Ibid.*, 349-50.
57. *Ibid.*, 350, 429.
58. *Ibid.*, 298, 430.

59. *Ibid.*, 348, 429-30.
60. *Ibid.*, 348.
61. *Ibid.*, 328.
62. *Ibid.*, 326.
63. Tugwell, *The Art of Politics*, 248.
64. Tugwell, *The Democratic Roosevelt*, 415.
65. Tugwell, *The Art of Politics*, 121.
66. *Ibid.*, 20-23.
67. Tugwell, *The Democratic Roosevelt*, 328.
68. *Ibid.*, 415-16.
69. Tugwell, *The Art of Politics*, 119.
70. Tugwell, *The Democratic Roosevelt*, 416.
71. Samuel Lubell, *The Future of American Politics* (New York: Doubleday, An Anchor Book, 1956), 46-53.
72. Elmo Roper, *You and Your Leaders: Their Actions and Your Reactions, 1936-1956* (New York: William Morrow, 1957), 28, 28-29n.
73. James M. Burns, *Roosevelt: The Lion and the Fox*, 487n; "Two-Party Stalemate: The Crisis in Our Politics," *Atlantic*, February, 1960, 205.
74. Tugwell, "After the New Deal," 322.
75. Tugwell, "The Superpolitical," *Journal of Social Philosophy*, October, 1939-July, 1940, 99.
76. Tugwell, *The Democratic Roosevelt*, 370.
77. Richard Hofstadter, "Franklin D. Roosevelt: The Patrician as Opportunist," in Hofstadter, *The American Political Tradition and the Men Who Made It* (New York: Knopf, 1948), 311-47.
78. Tugwell, *The Art of Politics*, 47, 85.
79. Quoted in David Hawke, "Interview: Richard Hofstadter," *History 3* (New York: Meridian Books, 1960), 139.
80. Tugwell, *The Art of Politics*, 240-41.
81. Tugwell, *The Democratic Roosevelt*, 329.

11. The Two New Deals: 1933-1938

1. James M. Burns, *Roosevelt: The Lion and the Fox* (New York: Harcourt, Brace, 1956), 226.
2. Eugene O. Golub, *The "Isms": A History and Evaluation* (New York: Harper, 1954), 141-42.
3. Eric F. Goldman, *Rendezvous with Destiny* (New York: Vintage Books, 1956), 287.
4. Daniel R. Fusfeld, "The New Deal in Retrospect," *Challenge*, June, 1959, 65-66.
5. Tugwell, *The Democratic Roosevelt* (Garden City, N. Y.: Doubleday, 1957), 465.
6. Tugwell, *The Art of Politics* (Garden City, N. Y.: Doubleday, 1958), 184-85.
7. *Ibid.*, 186; Tugwell, *The Democratic Roosevelt*, 342.

8. Alfred Kazin, "The Historian as Reporter: Edmund Wilson and the 1930's," *Reporter*, March 20, 1958, 43-44.
9. Tugwell, *The Democratic Roosevelt*, 342.
10. Tugwell, *The Art of Politics*, 47, 85.
11. Tugwell, review, *Roosevelt: The Lion and the Fox*, by James M. Burns, in *Chicago Sun-Times*, August 12, 1956.
12. Tugwell, *The Democratic Roosevelt*, 308.
13. Tugwell, *The Art of Politics*, 186.
14. Granville Hicks, "Father Bruckberger's America," *Saturday Review*, July 11, 1959, 33.
15. Tugwell, "Bankers' Banks," *New Republic*, December 12, 1928.
16. Tugwell, "Discourse in Depression," address, *Tugwell Papers*.
17. Tugwell, "Banking for the People," syndicated column, in Tugwell, *The Battle for Democracy* (New York: Columbia University Press, 1935), 30-32.
18. Tugwell, *Diary*, April 21, 1933.
19. Tugwell, "The Preparation of a President," *Western Political Quarterly*, June, 1948, 147.
20. Tugwell, "The Compromising Roosevelt," *Western Political Quarterly*, June, 1953, 333-34.
21. Tugwell, *The Democratic Roosevelt*, 263-64.
22. Tugwell, "The Preparation of a President," 147.
23. Tugwell, "The Compromising Roosevelt," 334.
24. Tugwell, "The Preparation of a President," 145.
25. Tugwell and E. C. Banfield, "Grass Roots Democracy—Myth or Reality," *Public Administration Review*, Winter, 1950, 50.
26. Tugwell, "The Progressive Orthodoxy of Franklin D. Roosevelt," *Ethics*, October, 1953, 16.
27. Tugwell, "A Planner's View of Agriculture's Future," *Journal of Farm Economics*, February, 1959, passim.
28. Tugwell, "The Compromising Roosevelt," 334-35.
29. Tugwell, *The Democratic Roosevelt*, 326.
30. *Ibid.*, 324-25, 325n.
31. *Ibid.*, 339-40.
32. *Ibid.*, 375-76, 378-83.
33. *Ibid.*, 383.
34. *Ibid.*, 326-27.
35. Franklin D. Roosevelt, *The Public Papers and Addresses of Franklin D. Roosevelt*, S. Rosenman, arr. (New York: Random House, 1938), IV, 15-25.
36. Basil Rauch, *The History of the New Deal, 1933-1938* (New York: Creative Age Press, 1944), 157.
37. *Ibid.*, 158, 163-64.
38. Tugwell, *The Democratic Roosevelt*, 343-44n.
39. *Ibid.*, 375.
40. *Ibid.*, 328.
41. *Ibid.*, 344.

42. *Ibid.*, 376.
43. *Ibid.*, 376-77.
44. *Ibid.*, 377-78.
45. *Ibid.*, 420-21, 563.
46. *Ibid.*, 449.
47. Tugwell, "The New Deal: The Rise of Business," Part I, *Western Political Quarterly*, June, 1952, 282, 282n.
48. Tugwell, "The Compromising Roosevelt," 329, 340.
49. Tugwell, *The Stricken Land* (Garden City, N. Y.: Doubleday, 1947), 436.
50. *Ibid.*, 442, 541-42.
51. *Ibid.*, 69.
52. Tugwell, *The Art of Politics*, 248.
53. Frank R. Kent, *Without Grease* (New York: William Morrow, 1936), 398.
54. Tugwell, address, Niagara County Pioneer Association, Olcott Beach, N. Y., August 8, 1934, *USDA Press Release*, 4.
55. Quoted in Harold L. Ickes, *The Secret Diary of Harold L. Ickes, Part One* (New York: Simon and Schuster, 1953), 302.
56. Marriner S. Eccles, *Beckoning Frontiers* (New York: Knopf, 1951), 118.
57. Tugwell, *The Democratic Roosevelt*, 443.
58. Tugwell, "The Compromising Roosevelt," 334.
59. *Ibid.*, 334-35.
60. Tugwell, *The Democratic Roosevelt*, 443.
61. Tugwell, "The Protagonists: Roosevelt and Hoover," *Antioch Review*, Winter, 1953-54, 429-30.
62. Tugwell, *The Democratic Roosevelt*, 449.
63. Tugwell, "The Compromising Roosevelt," 334.
64. Tugwell, "The Protagonists: Roosevelt and Hoover," 430.
65. Tugwell, *The Democratic Roosevelt*, 444.
66. Tugwell, "The Protagonists: Roosevelt and Hoover," 430.
67. Memorandum, D. W. Bell to Roosevelt, June 16, 1935, *OF 1568 Roosevelt Papers*.
68. Memorandum, Tugwell to Roosevelt, July 15, 1935, *OF 1568 Roosevelt Papers*.
69. Tugwell, *The Democratic Roosevelt*, 240, 261.
70. Tugwell, "The Protagonists: Roosevelt and Hoover," 430.
71. Tugwell, *The Democratic Roosevelt*, 265, 319.
72. Harold L. Ickes, *Back to Work: The Story of WPA* (New York: Macmillan, 1935), 25-27; Marriner S. Eccles, *Beckoning Frontiers*, 118.
73. Tugwell, "After the New Deal: 'We Have Bought Ourselves Time to Think,'" *New Republic*, July 26, 1939, 325.
74. Raymond Moley, *After Seven Years* (New York: Harper, 1939), 172-74, 367.
75. Tugwell, *The Democratic Roosevelt*, 274-75.
76. Tugwell, "After the New Deal," 325.
77. Tugwell, *The Democratic Roosevelt*, 280.
78. *Ibid.*, 448.

79. Marriner S. Eccles, *Beckoning Frontiers*, 98-99.
80. Tugwell, *The Democratic Roosevelt*, 445, 447-49.
81. *Ibid.*, 375.
82. *Ibid.*, 374.
83. Tugwell, *Mr. Hoover's Economic Policy* (New York: John Day, 1932), 11, 14, 16, 21, 25.
84. Tugwell, A. T. Cutler and G. S. Mitchell, "Flaws in the Hoover Economic Plan," *Current History*, January, 1932, 329.
85. Tugwell, *The Democratic Roosevelt*, 240, 262.
86. Marriner S. Eccles, *Beckoning Frontiers*, 85-87, 114.
87. Tugwell, *Diary*, April 2, 3, and 14, 1933.
88. Tugwell, "The Budget," unpublished statement, *Tugwell Papers*.
89. Tugwell, "The New Deal: The Decline of Government," Part II, *Western Political Quarterly*, September, 1951, 481.
90. Harold L. Ickes, *Back to Work: The Story of WPA*, 28-30.
91. Tugwell, "Relief and Reconstruction," address, National Conference of Social Workers, Kansas City, Mo., May 21, 1934, in Tugwell, *The Battle for Democracy*, 311.
92. Tugwell, "Your Future and Your Nation," Commencement Address, University of New Mexico, June 10, 1935, *USDA Press Release*, 8.
93. Tugwell, *The Stricken Land*, 57.
94. *Ibid.*, 82.
95. Tugwell, address, Democratic State Central Committee, Los Angeles, October 28, 1935, *Resettlement Administration Press Release*, 8.
96. Tugwell, *interview with writer*.
97. Frank R. Kent, *Without Grease*, 276-77.
98. Tugwell, *The Stricken Land*, 39.
99. Tugwell, "A Fireside Symposium," *Columbia University Quarterly*, March, 1935, 30; Tugwell, "A Third Economy," address, Rochester (N. Y.) Teachers Association, April 9, 1935, *USDA Press Release*, 5.
100. Tugwell, *The Democratic Roosevelt*, 240.
101. Tugwell, "The Compromising Roosevelt," 334.
102. *New York Times*, December 29, 1937; January 15, 1938.
103. John T. Flynn, *The Roosevelt Myth* (New York: Devin-Adair, 1948), 182.
104. Basil Rauch, *The History of the New Deal, 1933-1938*, 157-59; William Miller, *A History of the United States* (New York: Dell, 1958), 417-18.
105. Arthur M. Schlesinger, Jr., *The Coming of the New Deal* (Boston: Houghton Mifflin, 1959), 183-84.
106. Tugwell, *The Democratic Roosevelt*, 348, 415.
107. *Ibid.*, 376.
108. Tugwell, *Memoir*.
109. John Kenneth Galbraith, *Economics and the Art of Controversy* (New York: Vintage Books, 1959), passim.
110. Marcus Cunliffe, *The Nation Takes Shape, 1789-1837* (Chicago: University of Chicago Press, 1959), 8.
111. Tugwell, *The Art of Politics*, 61.

12. Intellectual Approaches to Crisis

1. Tugwell, *Mr. Hoover's Economic Policy* (New York: John Day, 1932), 15.
2. *Ibid.*, 15-16.
3. Tugwell, note on "Discourse in Depression," *Tugwell Papers.*
4. Tugwell, "The Preparation of a President," *Western Political Quarterly,* June, 1948, 135.
5. Tugwell, "The Progressive Orthodoxy of Franklin D. Roosevelt," *Ethics,* October, 1953, 20.
6. Tugwell, "The New Deal: The Rise of Business," Part II, *Western Political Quarterly,* September, 1952, 502-03.
7. Tugwell, "The Progressive Tradition," *Atlantic Monthly,* April, 1935, 411, 413-14.
8. Tugwell, *The Stricken Land* (Garden City, N. Y.: Doubleday, 1947), 444.
9. Tugwell, "The Compromising Roosevelt," *Western Political Quarterly,* June, 1953, 334.
10. 73 Congress, 2 Session, *Congressional Record,* June 14, 1934, 11440-41.
11. Tugwell, *The Stricken Land,* 39, 180.
12. Tugwell, "Discourse in Depression," address, 1932, *Tugwell Papers.*
13. Tugwell, *The Industrial Discipline and the Governmental Arts* (New York: Columbia University Press, 1933), 229.
14. Tugwell, "America Takes Hold of Its Destiny," *Today,* April 28, 1934, in Tugwell, *The Battle for Democracy* (New York: Columbia University Press, 1935), 257.
15. Tugwell, "Relief and Reconstruction," address, National Conference of Social Workers, Kansas City, Mo., May 21, 1934, in Tugwell, *The Battle for Democracy,* 316.
16. Tugwell, Statement Prepared for Hearing, *Tugwell Papers.*
17. Tugwell, "A Third Economy," address, Rochester (N. Y.) Teachers Association, April 9, 1935, *USDA Press Release,* 14.
18. Tugwell, address, Democratic State Central Committee, Los Angeles, October 28, 1935, *Resettlement Administration Press Release,* 2.
19. Tugwell, "The Fourth Power," *Planning and Civic Comment,* April-June, 1939, Part II, 22.
20. Tugwell, "Earthbound: The Problem of Planning and Survival," *Antioch Review,* Winter, 1949-50, 492-94.
21. Tugwell, "Governor or President?," *New Republic,* May 16, 1928, 381.
22. Tugwell, "On Life as a Long-Time Enterprise," address, Dartmouth College, April 26, 1934, *USDA Press Release,* 4.
23. Tugwell, "Relief and Reconstruction," 307.
24. Tugwell, address, Clemson College, S.C., August 15, 1934, *USDA Press Release,* 14.
25. Tugwell, "Your Future and Your Nation," Commencement Address, University of New Mexico, June 10, 1935, *USDA Press Release,* 15-16.
26. Tugwell, "The Superpolitical," *Journal of Social Philosophy,* October, 1939-July, 1940, 106.
27. Tugwell, "The Fourth Power," 5-6.

28. Tugwell, "Implementing the General Interest," *Public Administration Review*, Autumn, 1940, 34.

29. Tugwell, "The Sources of New Deal Reformism," *Ethics*, July, 1954, 250-51, 273-74.

30. Raymond Moley, *After Seven Years* (New York: Harper, 1939), 124n., 130-31.

31. Tugwell, "Chameleon Words," *New Republic*, August 25, 1926, 6.

32. Letter, Tugwell to Basil O'Connor, August 9, 1932, *Tugwell Papers*.

33. Tugwell, "Relief and Reconstruction," 311.

34. Tugwell, "National Significance of Recent Trends in Farm Population," *Social Forces*, October, 1935, 4.

35. Tugwell, *The Democratic Roosevelt* (Garden City, N. Y.: Doubleday, 1957), 59-60.

36. Tugwell, "The Fourth Power," 23.

37. Tugwell, "Implementing the General Interest," 43.

38. Tugwell, "Relief and Reconstruction," 317.

39. *Ibid.*, 302-04, 320.

40. *Ibid.*, 305, 313.

41. Tugwell, "The Directive," *Journal of Social Philosophy and Jurisprudence*, October, 1941, 11.

42. Tugwell, "The Fourth Power," 29-30.

43. Tugwell, "The Progressive Orthodoxy of Franklin D. Roosevelt," 10.

44. Tugwell, "Relief and Reconstruction," 305.

45. Tugwell, "The New Deal: The Decline of Government," Part I, *Western Political Quarterly*, June, 1951, 306.

46. Tugwell, "The Progressive Tradition," 415.

47. Tugwell, "America Takes Hold of Its Destiny," 256.

48. Tugwell, "Relief and Reconstruction," 305.

49. Tugwell, "The New Deal Reinterpreted," *New York Times*, May 28, 1933.

50. Tugwell, *The Democratic Roosevelt*, 218.

51. Tugwell, "The Preparation of a President," 135.

52. Tugwell, syndicated column, United Features Syndicate, November 26, 1933, *Tugwell Papers*.

53. Tugwell, address, Democratic State Central Committee, 7.

54. Tugwell, "The Place of Government in a National Land Program," address, Joint Meeting, American Economic Association, Farm Economic Association, and American Statistical Association, Philadelphia, December 29, 1933, *USDA Press Release*, 12.

55. Tugwell, "The Preparation of a President," 141-42.

56. Tugwell, "A Planner's View of Agriculture's Future," *Journal of Farm Economics*, February, 1949, 35-42, is the source of the references in the remainder of this chapter.

13. The National Industrial Recovery Act and the NRA: 1933-1935

1. Tugwell, *The Democratic Roosevelt* (Garden City, N. Y.: Doubleday, 1957), 308-09.

2. *Ibid.*, 309.
3. Tugwell, *The Industrial Discipline and the Governmental Arts* (New York: Columbia University Press, 1933), 211-16.
4. Tugwell, *The Democratic Roosevelt*, 309.
5. *Ibid.*, 283.
6. Marshall E. Dimock, *Business and Government* (New York: Henry Holt, 1949), 186.
7. Tugwell, *The Democratic Roosevelt*, 283, 283-84n.
8. *Ibid.*, 284.
9. *Ibid.*, 282-83.
10. *Ibid.*, 91-92, 142-43.
11. *Ibid.*, 142-43, 281.
12. *Ibid.*, 230.
13. Quoted in Tugwell, "The Progressive Orthodoxy of Franklin D. Roosevelt," *Ethics*, October, 1953, 17.
14. Tugwell, *Diary*, April 21 and May 30, 1933.
15. Arthur M. Schlesinger, Jr., *The Coming of the New Deal* (Boston: Houghton Mifflin, 1959), 96-97.
16. Raymond Moley, *After Seven Years* (New York: Harper, 1939), 185-88.
17. Ernest K. Lindley, *The Roosevelt Revolution: First Phase* (New York: Viking, 1933), 156.
18. Arthur M. Schlesinger, Jr., "The First Hundred Days of the New Deal," in Isabel Leighton, ed., *The Aspirin Age, 1919-1941* (New York: Simon and Schuster, 1949), 289.
19. Frances Perkins, *The Roosevelt I Knew* (New York: Viking, 1947), 198.
20. Raymond Moley, *After Seven Years*, 189.
21. Tugwell, *Diary*, May 30, 1933.
22. Arthur M. Schlesinger, Jr., *The Coming of the New Deal*, 108-10.
23. Hugh Johnson, *The Blue Eagle from Egg to Earth* (New York: Doubleday, Doran, 1935), 204.
24. Donald Richberg, *The Rainbow* (Garden City, N. Y.: Doubleday, 1936), 107.
25. Frank R. Kent, *Without Gloves* (New York: William Morrow, 1934), 43-44.
26. Blair Bolles, "The Sweetheart of the Regimenters," *American Mercury*, September, 1936, 83.
27. Tugwell, *The Democratic Roosevelt*, 285.
28. *Ibid.*, 230, 285-86, 309.
29. *Ibid.*, 230, 284-85.
30. *Ibid.*, 283, 285, 286.
31. *Ibid.*, 309.
32. *Ibid.*, 310-11.
33. Marshall E. Dimock, *Business and Government*, 182.
34. *Special Industrial Recovery Board, Proceedings,* July 18 and 19, 1933; cited in Arthur M. Schlesinger, Jr., *The Coming of the New Deal*, 113.
35. Tugwell, *The Democratic Roosevelt*, 311-12.
36. Arthur M. Schlesinger, Jr., *The Coming of the New Deal*, 111, 116.

37. Arthur M. Schlesinger, Jr., "The First Hundred Days of the New Deal," 294.
38. Raymond Moley, *After Seven Years*, 190.
39. Arthur M. Schlesinger, Jr., *The Coming of the New Deal*, 124.
40. Marshall E. Dimock, *Business and Government*, 183.
41. *Ibid.*
42. Tugwell, *The Democratic Roosevelt*, 326.
43. *Ibid.*, 231, 292, 308, 313, 324, 326.
44. *Special Industrial Recovery Board, Proceedings,* November 15 and 27, December 12, 1933; cited in Arthur M. Schlesinger, Jr., *The Coming of the New Deal,* 123.
45. Letter, Tugwell to Johnson, June 29, 1933, *Bureau of the Budget Papers;* cited in Arthur M. Schlesinger, Jr., *The Coming of the New Deal,* 123-24.
46. Tugwell, *Diary,* May 30, 1933.
47. Tugwell, *The Democratic Roosevelt*, 330.
48. Letters, Tugwell to Roosevelt, September 5 and 7, 1934, *Roosevelt Papers;* cited in Arthur M. Schlesinger, Jr., *The Coming of the New Deal,* 156.
49. Hugh Johnson, *The Blue Eagle from Egg to Earth,* 291.
50. Tugwell, *Diary,* April 2 and 3, 1933.
51. Frances Perkins, *The Roosevelt I Knew,* 271.
52. Raymond Moley, *After Seven Years,* 172-73.
53. *Ibid.,* 173-74.
54. *Ibid.,* 190.
55. Hugh Johnson, *The Blue Eagle from Egg to Earth,* 367.
56. Tugwell, "America Takes Hold of Its Destiny," *Today,* April 28, 1934, in Tugwell, *The Battle for Democracy* (New York: Columbia University Press, 1935), 260.
57. Maurice Parmelee, *Farewell to Poverty* (New York: John Wiley, 1935), 284.
58. Raoul Desvernine, *Democratic Despotism* (New York: Dodd, Mead, 1936), 98.
59. J. Franklin Carter, *The New Dealers* (New York: Simon and Schuster, 1934), 90.
60. Lewis Corey (Fraina), *The Decline of American Capitalism* (New York: Covici-Friede, 1934), 195.
61. Tugwell, address, Democratic State Central Committee, Los Angeles, October 28, 1935, *Resettlement Administration Press Release,* 6.
62. Tugwell, *The Stricken Land* (Garden City, N. Y.: Doubleday, 1947), 435.
63. *Ibid.*
64. Tugwell, "The Directive," *Journal of Social Philosophy and Jurisprudence,* October, 1941, 9.
65. *Ibid.,* 10.
66. Tugwell, "The New Deal: The Rise of Business," Part I, *Western Political Quarterly,* June, 1952, 279-80.
67. Tugwell, newspaper clipping, *Tugwell Papers.*
68. Tugwell, "After the New Deal: 'We Have Bought Ourselves Time to Think,'" *New Republic,* July 26, 1939, 323.

69. Tugwell, "The New Deal: The Decline of Government," Part I, *Western Political Quarterly*, June, 1951, 307.
70. *Ibid.*, 303.
71. Tugwell, *The Democratic Roosevelt*, 143, 230, 285, 310-14, 329-31, 413, 416.
72. Tugwell, "Must We Draft Roosevelt?," *New Republic*, May 13, 1940, 632.
73. Tugwell, newspaper clipping, *Tugwell Papers*.
74. Arthur M. Schlesinger, Jr., *The Coming of the New Deal*, 169-75.
75. *Ibid.*, 172.
76. Memorandum, Tugwell to Roosevelt, September 8, 1934, *PPF 180 Roosevelt Papers*.
77. Arthur M. Schlesinger, Jr., *The Coming of the New Deal*, 172.
78. *Ibid.*, 176.
79. Tugwell, *The Democratic Roosevelt*, 416.
80. Arthur M. Schlesinger, Jr., *The Crisis of the Old Order* (Boston: Houghton Mifflin, 1957), 160.
81. Tugwell, "The Economic Basis for Business Regulation," *American Economic Review*, December, 1921, passim.
82. Tugwell, *The Democratic Roosevelt*, 231.

14. Proposals for Farm Relief: 1922-1933

1. Tugwell, *The Democratic Roosevelt* (Garden City, N. Y.: Doubleday, 1957), 158-59.
2. Tugwell, "Hunger, Cold, and Candidates," *New Republic*, May 2, 1928, 323-24.
3. Basil Rauch, *The History of the New Deal, 1933-1938* (New York: Creative Age Press, 1944), 8.
4. Tugwell, "Consumers and the New Deal," address, Consumers' League of Ohio, Cleveland, May 11, 1934, in Tugwell, *The Battle for Democracy* (New York: Columbia University Press, 1935), 274.
5. Tugwell, "The Place of Government in a National Land Program," address, Joint Meeting, American Economic Association, American Statistical Association, Farm Economic Association, Philadelphia, December 29, 1933, *USDA Press Release*, 4-5.
6. Tugwell, "A Planner's View of Agriculture's Future," *Journal of Farm Economics*, February, 1949, 33n.
7. Tugwell, "The Place of Government in a National Land Program," 5.
8. Tugwell, "The New Deal: The Rise of Business," Part II, *Western Political Quarterly*, September, 1952, 489, 500.
9. Tugwell, *The Democratic Roosevelt*, 159.
10. Wesley McCune, *The Farm Bloc* (Garden City, N. Y.: Doubleday, Doran, 1943), 16.
11. Tugwell, *The Democratic Roosevelt*, 159.
12. Gilbert C. Fite, *George N. Peek and the Fight for Farm Parity* (Norman: University of Oklahoma Press, 1954), 222, 232.
13. Tugwell, *The Democratic Roosevelt*, 260.

14. Murray R. Benedict, *Farm Policies of the United States, 1790-1950* (New York: Twentieth Century Fund, 1953), 268.
15. Quoted in Wesley McCune, *The Farm Bloc*, 17.
16. Quoted in Tugwell, *The Battle for Democracy*, 228.
17. Mordecai Ezekiel, "Notes on the Hundred Days," *Tugwell Papers*.
18. Tugwell, "A Planner's View of Agriculture's Future," 33n.
19. Gilbert C. Fite, *George N. Peek*, 230.
20. *Ibid.*, 230-31.
21. Henry A. Wallace, "Stabilization of Farm Prices and the McNary-Haugen Act," *Annals of the American Academy of Political and Social Science*, March, 1929, 402-05.
22. George Creel, *Rebel at Large* (New York: G. P. Putnam's, 1947), 273.
23. William E. Dodd, *Ambassador Dodd's Diary, 1933-38*, ed. by W. E. Dodd, Jr., and Martha Dodd (New York: Harcourt, 1941), 212.
24. Tugwell, *Memoir*.
25. Tugwell, Memorandum Prepared for Alfred E. Smith, *Tugwell Papers*.
26. Tugwell, *Memoir*.
27. Tugwell, *interview with writer*.
28. Gilbert C. Fite, *George N. Peek*, 232.
29. Quoted in *ibid.*, 227.
30. *Ibid.*, 224.
31. Quoted in *ibid.*, 247, 249-50.
32. *Ibid.*, 235-36.
33. Tugwell, "Farm Relief and a Permanent Agriculture," *Annals of the American Academy of Political and Social Science*, March, 1929, 279-81.
34. Tugwell, *The Democratic Roosevelt*, 232.
35. *Ibid.*, 160, 275-76.
36. Gilbert C. Fite, *George N. Peek*, 245-46.
37. *Ibid.*, 234-35.
38. Tugwell, *The Democratic Roosevelt*, 159.
39. Tugwell, "International Economics," syndicated column, in Tugwell, *The Battle for Democracy*, 169.
40. Gilbert C. Fite, *George N. Peek*, 234.
41. Tugwell, *The Democratic Roosevelt*, 232.
42. Gilbert C. Fite, *George N. Peek*, 234.
43. Wesley McCune, *The Farm Bloc*, 17-18.
44. Quoted in Gilbert C. Fite, *George N. Peek*, 237-40.
45. Murray R. Benedict, *Farm Policies of the United States*, 267.
46. Quoted in Gilbert C. Fite, *George N. Peek*, 231.

15. The Agricultural Adjustment Act: 1932-1933

1. Russell Lord, *The Wallaces of Iowa* (Boston: Houghton Mifflin, 1947), 310-11.
2. Tugwell, *Diary*, December 31, 1932.
3. Gilbert C. Fite, *George N. Peek and the Fight for Farm Parity* (Norman: University of Oklahoma Press, 1954), 233.

4. Russell Lord, *The Wallaces of Iowa,* 311.
5. *Ibid.,* 322; Ernest K. Lindley, "War on the Brains Trust," *Scribner's Magazine,* November, 1933, 264.
6. Tugwell, "The Preparation of a President," *Western Political Quarterly,* June, 1948, 132.
7. Tugwell, *Diary,* December 31, 1932.
8. Tugwell, *The Democratic Roosevelt* (Garden City, N. Y.: Doubleday, 1957), 233.
9. Tugwell, *Diary,* December 31, 1932.
10. Letter, M. L. Wilson to Tugwell, July 25, 1932, *Tugwell Papers.*
11. Letter, M. L. Wilson to Tugwell, August 7, 1932, *Tugwell Papers.*
12. Ernest K. Lindley, "War on the Brains Trust," 264.
13. Letter, M. L. Wilson to Tugwell, September 28, 1932, *Tugwell Papers.*
14. Gilbert C. Fite, *George N. Peek,* 240.
15. Letter, M. L. Wilson to Tugwell, October 8, 1932, *Tugwell Papers.*
16. Letter, M. L. Wilson to Tugwell, October 24, 1932, *Tugwell Papers.*
17. Letters, Tugwell to M. L. Wilson, November 3, 1932, and M. L. Wilson to Tugwell, November 28, 1932, *Tugwell Papers.*
18. Tugwell, *Diary,* December 31, 1932.
19. Joseph S. Davis, *Wheat and the AAA* (Washington: Brookings Institution, 1935), 34n.
20. Tugwell, *Diary,* December 27, 1932; January 5, 6, 1933.
21. *Ibid.,* January 7, 12, 17, 1933.
22. *Ibid.,* January 7, 14, 17, 24, 1933.
23. Ernest K. Lindley, "War on the Brains Trust," 264.
24. Tugwell, *The Democratic Roosevelt,* 266.
25. Tugwell, *Diary,* February 27, 1933.
26. *Ibid.,* January 12, 13, 1933.
27. Tugwell, *The Democratic Roosevelt,* 158, 160-61, 175.
28. Tugwell, *Diary,* January 21, 1933.
29. *Ibid.*
30. *Ibid.,* no date; the sequence indicates late March, 1933.
31. Arthur M. Schlesinger, Jr., *The Coming of the New Deal* (Boston: Houghton Mifflin, 1959), 27-28.
32. Tugwell, *Diary,* no date; the sequence indicates late March, 1933.
33. *Ibid.*
34. *Ibid.*
35. Gilbert C. Fite, *George N. Peek,* 227-49; George N. Peek with Samuel Crowther, *Why Quit Our Own* (New York: D. Van Nostrand, 1936), 64-66, 80-85, 89-93, 98-100.
36. Memorandum, Henry A. Wallace to Roosevelt, April 22, 1933, *OF 1 Roosevelt Papers.*
37. Tugwell, "A Planner's View of Agriculture's Future," *Journal of Farm Economics,* February, 1949, 35.
38. Arthur M. Schlesinger, Jr., *The Coming of the New Deal,* 39.
39. Ernest K. Lindley, *The Roosevelt Revolution: First Phase* (New York: Viking, 1933), 51, 97.

40. Tugwell, *The Democratic Roosevelt*, 103, 233-34.
41. Gilbert C. Fite, *George N. Peek*, 252.
42. George N. Peek, *Why Quit Our Own*, 71.
43. *Ibid.*, 73, 75, 82, 93.
44. Richard Barry, *Theme Song—1936* (Indianapolis: Bobbs-Merrill, 1936), 81-82.
45. Gilbert C. Fite, *George N. Peek*, 223.
46. *Ibid.*, 222.
47. *Ibid.*, 226.
48. Charles A. Beard and George E. Smith, *The New Deal and the Old* (New York: Macmillan, 1940), 190.
49. Henry A. Wallace, *New Frontiers* (New York: Reynal and Hitchcock, 1934), 164.
50. George N. Peek, *Why Quit Our Own*, 93.
51. *Ibid.*, 75.
52. Gilbert C. Fite, *George N. Peek*, 249.
53. Russell Lord, *The Wallaces of Iowa*, 312.
54. Tugwell, *The Democratic Roosevelt*, 265.
55. Ernest K. Lindley, *The Roosevelt Revolution: First Phase*, 99.
56. Basil Rauch, *The History of the New Deal, 1933-1938* (New York: Creative Age Press, 1944), 68.
57. Henry A. Wallace, *New Frontiers*, 164.
58. Stuart Chase, *Democracy under Pressure* (New York: Twentieth Century Fund, 1945), 99.
59. Gilbert C. Fite, *George N. Peek*, 223.
60. Basil Rauch, *The History of the New Deal, 1933-1938*, 67-68.
61. Edwin G. Nourse, *Marketing Agreements under the AAA* (Washington: Brookings Institution, 1935), 3-5, 9-13.
62. Tugwell, "A Planner's View of Agriculture's Future," 35.

16. Tugwell versus Peek and the Purge in the AAA: 1933-1935

1. Tugwell, *Diary*, April 3, 1933.
2. *Ibid.* and editorial note.
3. *Ibid.*, December 31, 1932, and January 6, 1933.
4. Tugwell, *The Stricken Land* (Garden City, N. Y.: Doubleday, 1947), 23.
5. J. Franklin Carter, *The New Dealers* (New York: Simon and Schuster, 1934), 147, 149.
6. Tugwell, *The Stricken Land*, 23.
7. Tugwell, *The Democratic Roosevelt* (Garden City, N. Y.: Doubleday, 1957), 371.
8. Tugwell, *Diary*, February 17, 1933.
9. Tugwell, "Consumers and the New Deal," address, Consumers' League of Ohio, Cleveland, May 11, 1934, in Tugwell, *The Battle for Democracy* (New York: Columbia University Press, 1935), 275.
10. Tugwell, "Reduce the Spread," syndicated column, October 22, 1933, *Tugwell Papers*.

11. Tugwell, "Consumers and the New Deal," 280.
12. Tugwell, *Memoir*.
13. Edwin G. Nourse, *Marketing Agreements under the AAA* (Washington: Brookings Institution, 1935), 43.
14. *Ibid.*
15. Tugwell, *The Democratic Roosevelt*, 230.
16. Tugwell, "Consumers and the New Deal," 281.
17. Quoted in Edwin G. Nourse, *Marketing Agreements under the AAA*, 38.
18. *Ibid.*, 41.
19. Gilbert C. Fite, *George N. Peek and the Fight for Farm Parity* (Norman: University of Oklahoma Press, 1954), 257.
20. Edwin G. Nourse, *Marketing Agreements under the AAA*, 21.
21. Tugwell, *Memoir*.
22. Tugwell, unpublished statement, *Tugwell Papers*.
23. George N. Peek with Samuel Crowther, *Why Quit Our Own* (New York: D. Van Nostrand, 1936), 132.
24. *Ibid.*, 146.
25. Edwin G. Nourse, *Marketing Agreements under the AAA*, 40-41.
26. Russell Lord, *The Wallaces of Iowa* (Boston: Houghton Mifflin, 1947), 395.
27. Quoted in Wesley McCune, *The Farm Bloc* (Garden City, N. Y.: Doubleday, Doran, 1943), 9-10, 268-69.
28. Quoted in *ibid.*, 272.
29. Tugwell, *The Democratic Roosevelt*, 371.
30. Memorandum, March, 1935, *Tugwell Papers*.
31. Edwin G. Nourse, *Marketing Agreements under the AAA*, 44.
32. *Ibid.*, 32-36.
33. Margaret Coit, *Mr. Baruch* (Boston: Houghton Mifflin, 1957), 443.
34. Arthur M. Schlesinger, Jr., *The Coming of the New Deal* (Boston: Houghton Mifflin, 1959), 51.
35. Tugwell, *Diary*, April 21, 1933; "Addendum to the Diary for the 100 Days."
36. Russell Lord, *The Wallaces of Iowa*, 340.
37. *Ibid.*, 395.
38. George N. Peek, *Why Quit Our Own*, 113.
39. J. Franklin Carter, *The New Dealers*, 146.
40. Russell Lord, *The Wallaces of Iowa*, 400.
41. Tugwell, *Diary*, April 13, 1933.
42. Gilbert C. Fite, *George N. Peek*, 256.
43. Letter, Henry A. Wallace to Roosevelt, May 15, 1933, *OF 1 Roosevelt Papers*.
44. Quoted in Gilbert C. Fite, *George N. Peek*, 255.
45. George N. Peek, *Why Quit Our Own*, 132.
46. Arthur M. Schlesinger, Jr., *The Coming of the New Deal*, 56.
47. Gilbert C. Fite, *George N. Peek*, 259-60.
48. George N. Peek, *Why Quit Our Own*, 149-50.
49. J. Franklin Carter, *The New Dealers*, 99.

50. George N. Peek, *Why Quit Our Own*, 131, 151-54.
51. Gilbert C. Fite, *George N. Peek*, 263.
52. Tugwell, *interview with writer*.
53. George N. Peek, *Why Quit Our Own*, 154.
54. Tugwell, *Memoir*.
55. *Time*, December 18, 1933, 9.
56. J. Franklin Carter, *The New Dealers*, 84.
57. Edwin G. Nourse, *Marketing Agreements under the AAA*, 45, 278, 358.
58. *Time*, December 18, 1933, 9.
59. Gilbert C. Fite, *George N. Peek*, 265.
60. George N. Peek, *Why Quit Our Own*, 155.
61. *Time*, December 18, 1933, 9; Gilbert C. Fite, *George N. Peek*, 266.
62. Gilbert C. Fite, *George N. Peek*, 265.
63. Tugwell, *The Art of Politics* (Garden City, N. Y.: Doubleday, 1958), 122-23.
64. Tugwell, *The Democratic Roosevelt*, 313, 371.
65. Quoted in "Mr. Sullivan Bores from Without," editorial, *Nation*, January 17, 1934, 61.
66. *Time*, December 18, 1933, 9.
67. *Des Moines Register*, quoted in Gilbert C. Fite, *George N. Peek*, 293.
68. Gilbert C. Fite, *George N. Peek*, 261-62.
69. Jerome Frank, *Save America First* (New York: Harper, 1938).
70. Raymond Moley, *After Seven Years* (New York: Harper, 1939), 128-29.
71. Quoted in *Time*, November 11, 1935, 11.
72. J. Franklin Carter, *The New Dealers*, 145, 148.
73. Gilbert C. Fite, *George N. Peek*, 302.
74. Edwin G. Nourse, *Marketing Agreements under the AAA*, 43.
75. Quoted in Gilbert C. Fite, *George N. Peek*, 266.
76. Russell Lord, *The Wallaces of Iowa*, 400-02.
77. Tugwell, "The Responsibilities of Partnership," address, Iowa Bankers Association, June 27, 1934, *Tugwell Papers*.
78. Edwin G. Nourse, *Marketing Agreements under the AAA*, 48.
79. Russell Lord, *The Wallaces of Iowa*, 404-05.
80. Quoted in *ibid.*, 406-09.
81. Raymond Gram Swing, "The Purge at the AAA," *Nation*, February 20, 1935, 216.
82. *Time*, February 18, 1935, 14.
83. Harold L. Ickes, *The Secret Diary of Harold L. Ickes, Part One* (New York: Simon and Schuster, 1953), 250, 292, 302-03.
84. *Time*, February 18, 1935, 14.
85. Raymond Gram Swing, "The Purge at the AAA," 216.
86. Harold L. Ickes, *The Secret Diary of Harold L. Ickes, Part One*, 302.
87. Tugwell, *Memoir*.
88. Tugwell, *The Stricken Land*, 24.
89. Tugwell, *The Art of Politics*, 201.
90. *Time*, February 18, 1935, 14.

91. Raymond Gram Swing, "The Purge at the AAA," 216.
92. Arthur M. Schlesinger, Jr., *The Coming of the New Deal,* 53-54.
93. Murray Kempton, *Part of Our Time* (New York: Simon and Schuster, 1955), 56.
94. Raymond Gram Swing, "The Purge at the AAA," 216.
95. Quoted in Arthur M. Schlesinger, Jr., *The Coming of the New Deal,* 77.
96. Quoted in *Time,* February 18, 1935, 14.
97. Arthur W. Macmahon and John D. Millett, *Federal Administrators* (New York: Columbia University Press, 1939), 211.
98. Tugwell, *The Democratic Roosevelt,* 267, 360.
99. Tugwell, review, *Henry Wallace: The Man and the Myth,* by Dwight MacDonald, in *Chicago Sun-Times,* February 23, 1948.
100. Tugwell, *The Stricken Land,* 24.
101. Quoted in Russell Lord, *The Wallaces of Iowa,* 402.

17. The Department of Agriculture—Conservation: 1933-1936

1. John T. Flynn, *The Roosevelt Myth* (New York: Devin-Adair, 1948), 224.
2. Raymond Moley, *27 Masters of Politics* (New York: Funk and Wagnalls, 1949), 80.
3. John Chamberlain, *The American Stakes* (New York: Carrick and Evans, 1940), 117.
4. Russell Lord, *The Wallaces of Iowa* (Boston: Houghton Mifflin, 1947), 335, 345-46.
5. Arthur W. Macmahon and John D. Millett, *Federal Administrators* (New York: Columbia University Press, 1939), 211.
6. *Ibid.*
7. Tugwell, *Diary,* April 3, 1933.
8. Tugwell, *The Stricken Land* (Garden City, N. Y.: Doubleday, 1947), 543.
9. Harold L. Ickes, *The Secret Diary of Harold L. Ickes, Part One* (New York: Simon and Schuster, 1953), 241.
10. *Ibid.,* 194.
11. Russell Lord, *The Wallaces of Iowa,* 343.
12. Arthur M. Schlesinger, Jr., *The Coming of the New Deal* (Boston: Houghton Mifflin), 1959, 354-55.
13. Tugwell, *Diary,* February 18, 1933.
14. Russell Lord, *The Wallaces of Iowa,* 323, 381.
15. Tugwell, "Addendum to the Diary for the 100 Days."
16. Tugwell, *Diary,* March 18, April 3, 1933; Tugwell, *Memoir.*
17. Tugwell, "Addendum to the Diary for the 100 Days."
18. Tugwell, *Diary,* December 26, 1932; January 5 and 7, 1933.
19. Log of Trip, *Tugwell Papers;* Tugwell, *Memoir.*
20. Tugwell, *The Democratic Roosevelt* (Garden City, N. Y.: Doubleday, 1957), 267n.
21. Frank R. Kent, *Without Gloves* (New York: William Morrow, 1934), 273.
22. Tugwell, *The Stricken Land,* 32-34.

23. Harold L. Ickes, *The Secret Diary of Harold L. Ickes, Part Three* (New York: Simon and Schuster, 1954), 269.

24. Letter, Roosevelt to Hopkins, June 24, 1934, *OF 1 Roosevelt Papers.*

25. Tugwell, *The Stricken Land,* 33.

26. Memorandum, Tugwell to Roosevelt, March 3, 1934, *OF 1 Roosevelt Papers.*

27. *New York Times,* March 13, June 21, 22, and 30, 1934.

28. Tugwell, *The Stricken Land,* 34-35.

29. *Ibid.,* 24.

30. Letter, O. Butler to Tugwell, March 17, 1933, *Tugwell Papers.*

31. Tugwell, "Conservation Redefined," address, Fiftieth Anniversary of the Founding of New York's Forest Preserve, Albany, May 15, 1935, *USDA Press Release,* 3, 5.

32. Tugwell, "Your Future and Your Nation," Commencement Address, University of New Mexico, June 10, 1935, *USDA Press Release,* 10.

33. Tugwell, "A Third Economy," address, Rochester (N. Y.) Teachers Association, April 9, 1935, *USDA Press Release,* 6.

34. Tugwell, "Planned Use of the Land," *Today,* January 20, 1934, 6.

35. Tugwell, address, Tompkins County Development Meeting, Ithaca, N. Y., August 7, 1935, *USDA Press Release,* 5, 8.

36. Tugwell, "The Progressive Tradition," *Atlantic Monthly,* April, 1935, 413.

37. Tugwell, "A Third Economy," 6.

38. Tugwell, "Conservation Redefined," 1.

39. Tugwell, *The Democratic Roosevelt,* 45, 81.

40. *Ibid.,* 44.

41. Tugwell, "Conservation Redefined," 2-4.

42. Tugwell, address, Tompkins County Development Meeting, 5.

43. Tugwell, "The Protagonists: Roosevelt and Hoover," *Antioch Review,* Winter, 1953-54, 433.

44. Tugwell, "The Preparation of a President," *Western Political Quarterly,* June, 1948, 133.

45. *Time,* December 3, 1934, 13.

46. Edgar B. Nixon, compiler and ed., *Franklin D. Roosevelt and Conservation, 1911-1945,* 2 vols. (Hyde Park: Franklin D. Roosevelt Library, 1957), I, 340-41.

47. Note, Tugwell to Roosevelt, May 20, 1934, *OF 1 Roosevelt Papers.*

48. Blair Bolles, "The Sweetheart of the Regimenters," *American Mercury,* September, 1936, 83.

49. Lela Stiles, *The Man behind Roosevelt: The Story of Louis McHenry Howe* (Cleveland: World, 1954), 266-67.

50. Tugwell, "The Preparation of a President," 132.

51. Tugwell, *The Democratic Roosevelt,* 278.

52. Letters, Stuart to Tugwell, December 6, 7, and 14, 1932, *Tugwell Papers.*

53. Tugwell, *Diary,* March 17, 1933.

54. Tugwell, *The Democratic Roosevelt,* 279.

55. Tugwell, "Jobs in the Woods," address, CBS Radio, March 18, 1933, *USDA Press Release,* 4.

56. Tugwell, *Diary*, March 17, 1933.
57. Letter, O. Butler to Tugwell, March 17, 1933, *Tugwell Papers.*
58. Letter, P. A. Herbert to Tugwell, no date, *Tugwell Papers.*
59. Tugwell, *interview with writer.*
60. Tugwell, "Relief and Reconstruction," address, National Conference of Social Workers, Kansas City, Mo., May 21, 1934, in Tugwell, *The Battle for Democracy* (New York: Columbia University Press, 1935), 316.
61. Lewis Meriam, *Relief and Social Security* (Washington: Brookings Institution, 1946), 434-35.
62. Tugwell, *The Democratic Roosevelt*, 82n.
63. Tugwell, "F.D.R.: Living Memorials," *Nation*, April 7, 1956, 276.
64. Tugwell and E. C. Banfield, "Grass Roots Democracy—Myth or Reality?," *Public Administration Review*, Winter, 1950, 47.
65. *Ibid.*, 47-50.
66. Edgar B. Nixon, *Franklin D. Roosevelt and Conservation, 1911-1945,* I, 218.
67. *Ibid.*, 218-19.
68. Harold L. Ickes, *The Secret Diary of Harold L. Ickes, Part Two* (New York: Simon and Schuster, 1954), 41-42.
69. Tugwell, *The Stricken Land,* 57.
70. Tugwell, "Forester's Heart," *New Republic*, March 4, 1940.
71. Edgar B. Nixon, *Franklin D. Roosevelt and Conservation, 1911-1945,* I, 326.
72. *Ibid.*, 207-08.
73. *Ibid.*, 419.
74. *Ibid.*, 212-16, 224, 276-77, 291-92.
75. Arthur W. Macmahon and John D. Millett, *Federal Administrators,* 326-27.
76. Quoted in Wellington Brink, *Big Hugh: Father of Soil Conservation* (New York: Macmillan, 1951), 83-84.
77. *Yearbook of Agriculture, 1936* (Washington: USDA), 61.
78. Wellington Brink, *Big Hugh: Father of Soil Conservation*, 99-100.
79. *Ibid.*, 100-01.
80. Russell Lord, *The Wallaces of Iowa,* 373; *Time*, April 8, 1935, 17.
81. Tugwell, *interview with writer.*
82. Arthur W. Macmahon and John D. Millett, *Federal Administrators,* 70, 326.
83. Tugwell, *interview with writer.*
84. Tugwell, *Memoir.*
85. Letter, Tugwell to Roosevelt, March 4, 1934, *OF 1 Roosevelt Papers.*
86. Harold L. Ickes, *The Secret Diary of Harold L. Ickes, Part One,* 169-70.
87. *Ibid.*, 250.
88. *Ibid.*, 241.
89. *Ibid.*, 534.
90. Tugwell, *The Stricken Land,* 62-63, 657.
91. Arthur M. Schlesinger, Jr., *The Coming of the New Deal,* 69.
92. Harold L. Ickes, *The Secret Diary of Harold L. Ickes, Part One,* 165-66.

93. Russell Lord, *The Wallaces of Iowa*, 409.
94. Edgar B. Nixon, *Franklin D. Roosevelt and Conservation, 1911-1945*, I, 456-57.
95. *Ibid.*, 519-20.
96. *Ibid.*, 541-42.
97. Tugwell, *The Art of Politics* (Garden City, N. Y.: Doubleday, 1958), 10.
98. *Ibid.*, 10-14.
99. Tugwell, *The Democratic Roosevelt*, 421-25.
100. *Ibid.*, 424.
101. Paul W. Ward, "The End of Tugwell," *Nation*, November 28, 1936, 623.
102. Ernest K. Lindley, *Halfway with Roosevelt* (New York: Viking, 1937), 268.
103. *Ibid.*, 130-31.
104. John R. Gaus and Leon C. Wolcott, *Public Administration and the United States Department of Agriculture* (Chicago: Public Administration Service, 1940), 143.
105. Arthur W. Macmahon and John D. Millett, *Federal Administrators*, 211.
106. Russell Lord, *The Wallaces of Iowa*, 345-47, 459; "Governor Rex of Puerto Rico," *Common Sense*, July, 1942, 224.
107. Kenneth Trombley, *The Life and Times of a Happy Liberal: A Biography of Morris Llewellyn Cooke* (New York: Harper, 1954), 225.
108. Tugwell and E. C. Banfield, "Grass Roots Democracy—Myth or Reality?," 52.

18. Tugwell as Whipping Boy: The Attack

1. Tugwell, "The New Deal: The Decline of Government," Part I, *Western Political Quarterly*, June, 1951, 303.
2. Tugwell, "A New Deal for the Consumer," address, Columbia Alumni Luncheon, February 12, 1934, *USDA Press Release*, 1.
3. Tugwell, "Consumers and the New Deal," address, Consumers' League of Ohio, Cleveland, May 11, 1934, in Tugwell, *The Battle for Democracy* (New York: Columbia University Press, 1935), 268.
4. Tugwell, *The Democratic Roosevelt* (Garden City, N. Y.: Doubleday, 1957), 335n.
5. Tugwell, "Consumers and the New Deal," 268.
6. Tugwell, address, Niagara County Pioneer Association, Olcott Beach, N. Y., August 8, 1934, *USDA Press Release*, 17.
7. Tugwell, "Addendum to the Diary for the 100 Days," *Tugwell Papers*.
8. Tugwell, "Freedom from Fakes," *Today*, November 17, 1933, in Tugwell, *The Battle for Democracy*, 97-104, and "The Great American Fraud," *American Scholar*, Winter, 1934, 85-95, are the sources of all references to Tugwell in this chapter not attributed to other sources.
9. George Seldes, *You Can't Do That* (New York: Modern Age Books, 1938), 95.
10. *New York Times*, December 11, 1933.

11. A. Gillis and R. Ketchum, *Our America* (Boston: Little, Brown, 1936), 368.
12. Tugwell, *Diary*, February 26, 1933.
13. Ruth Lamb, *American Chamber of Horrors* (New York: Farrar and Rinehart, 1936), 279.
14. Tugwell, *Diary*, April 21, 1933.
15. Tugwell, "The Preparation of a President," *Western Political Quarterly*, June, 1948, 134.
16. Letter, Tugwell to Roosevelt, March 17, 1933, *PPF 564 Roosevelt Papers*.
17. Arthur M. Schlesinger, Jr., *The Coming of the New Deal* (Boston: Houghton Mifflin, 1959), 356.
18. Tugwell, *Diary*, April 21, 1933.
19. Leland J. Gordon, *Economics for Consumers*, 2d ed. (New York: American Book Company, 1950), 608, 611, 614.
20. Quoted in *ibid.*, 611.
21. *Time*, June 25, 1934, 11; April 1, 1935, 68.
22. Leland J. Gordon, *Economics for Consumers*, 609 and Chapter 25.
23. *Ibid.*, 610.
24. Quoted in George M. Verity, "Appraises Prof. Tugwell," Part II, *Iron Age*, July 26, 1934, 33.
25. Quoted in Peter H. Odegard and E. A. Helms, *American Politics* (New York: Harper, 1938), 557.
26. Quoted in Earle Looker, *The American Way: Franklin D. Roosevelt in Action* (New York: John Day, 1933), 71.
27. "Taxes: Mr. Tugwell's Ideas," *Time*, November 25, 1940, 86.
28. Quoted in Leo C. Rosten, *The Washington Correspondents* (New York: Harcourt, Brace, 1937), 268.
29. Quoted in *ibid.*, 95.
30. Francis Neilson, *Control from the Top* (New York: G. P. Putnam's, 1935), 31-34, 44, 49, 69-70.
31. Paul W. Ward, "The End of Tugwell," *Nation*, November 28, 1936, 623; "Wallace the Great Hesitator," *Nation*, May 8, 1935, 535.
32. Ernest K. Lindley, *Halfway with Roosevelt* (New York: Viking, 1937), 6.
33. Lewis Corey (Fraina), *The Decline of American Capitalism* (New York: Covici-Friede, 1934), 95.
34. Mauritz Hallgren, *Seeds of Revolt* (New York: Knopf, 1933), 343.
35. James A. Wechsler, *The Age of Suspicion* (New York: Random House, 1953), 44.
36. Russell Lord, *The Wallaces of Iowa* (Boston: Houghton Mifflin, 1947), 345-46.
37. Letter, David F. Cavers to Tugwell, January 18, 1934, *Tugwell Papers*.
38. Stuart Chase, *Democracy under Pressure* (New York: Twentieth Century Fund, 1945), 41-42; James Rorty, "Who's Who in the Drug Lobby," *Nation*, February 21, 1934, 213.
39. George Seldes, *You Can't Do That*, 95.
40. Stuart Chase, *Democracy under Pressure*, 41-42.
41. James Rorty, "Who's Who in the Drug Lobby," 213-15.
42. Russell Lord, *The Wallaces of Iowa*, 346.

43. Fred A. Shannon, *America's Economic Growth,* 3d ed. (New York: Macmillan, 1951), 799.
44. Cabell Phillips, "The New Dealers—Where Are They Now?," *New York Times Magazine,* September 29, 1946, 52.
45. "Exit Brain Trust," *Literary Digest,* November 28, 1936, 6.
46. *Time,* May 7, 1934, 14.
47. Tugwell, *interview with writer.*
48. John Kenneth Galbraith, *Economics and the Art of Controversy* (New York: Vintage Books, 1959), 55-56.
49. James Rorty, "Who's Who in the Drug Lobby," 213.
50. Fred A. Shannon, *America's Economic Growth,* 799-800.
51. Editorial, "Poison versus Honesty," *Nation,* January 1, 1934, 6.
52. Tugwell, *The Democratic Roosevelt,* 402n.
53. Stuart Chase, *Democracy under Pressure,* 42.
54. Frederick L. Allen, *Since Yesterday* (New York: Harper, 1940), 173.
55. Harold J. Laski, *The American Democracy* (New York: Viking, 1948), 639, 673; Leo C. Rosten, *The Washington Correspondents* (New York: Harcourt, Brace, 1937), 287.
56. William S. Groom, "Tugwell's Mischievous Ideas about Advertising," *Printer's Ink,* March 1, 1934, 36.
57. Howard Wolf, *Greener Pastures: A New Deal Fable* (Caldwell, Idaho: Caxton, 1936), 72.
58. George Seldes, *Lords of the Press* (New York: Julian Messner, 1938), 212.
59. Tugwell, *The Democratic Roosevelt,* 354.
60. Tugwell, *Memoir.*
61. Alva Johnston, "Tugwell, the President's Idea Man," *Saturday Evening Post,* August 1, 1936, 8.
62. Editorial, "Advertising as Usual," *Nation,* July 4, 1934, 5.
63. Arthur M. Schlesinger, Jr., *The Coming of the New Deal* (Boston: Houghton Mifflin, 1959), 359.
64. Letter, December 16, 1933, *Tugwell Papers.*
65. Letter, December 11, 1933, *Tugwell Papers.*
66. Leo C. Rosten, *The Washington Correspondents,* 217-18, 229, 287.
67. Letter, February 12, 1934, *Tugwell Papers.*
68. Tugwell, *Memoir.*
69. *Time,* May 7, 1934, 50.
70. Quoted in George Seldes, *One Thousand Years* (New York: Boni and Gaer, 1947), 62-63; Jerome Davis, *Capitalism and Its Culture* (New York: Farrar and Rinehart, 1935), 303.
71. Gaspar Bacon, address, Lincoln Club of Cumberland County, Maine, in Bacon, *Individual Rights and Public Welfare* (Boston: privately printed, 1935), 263.
72. *New York Times,* June 24 and 28, July 15, August 1, September 1, October 23, 25, and 30, November 7, 1934; *Time,* September 24, 1934, 55; William E. Dodd, *Ambassador Dodd's Diary, 1933-1938,* ed. by W. E. Dodd, Jr. and Martha Dodd (New York: Harcourt, 1941), 181.
73. George Michael, *Handout* (New York: G. P. Putnam's, 1935), 171.

74. Alva Johnston, "Tugwell, the President's Idea Man," 8-9.
75. *Time,* September 24, 1935, 55.
76. Letter, Tugwell to Margaret LeHand, September 25, 1934, *OF 1 Roosevelt Papers.*
77. Harold L. Ickes, *The Secret Diary of Harold L. Ickes, Part One* (New York: Simon and Schuster, 1953), 580.
78. Quoted in Oscar Handlin, *Al Smith and His America* (Boston: Little, Brown, 1958), 180.
79. *New York Times,* March 7, April 9, 1936.
80. *Ibid.,* September 8, 21, 24, and 29, 1936; William Randolph Hearst, *New York American,* September 20, 1936; quoted in W. A. Swanberg, *Citizen Hearst* (New York: Scribner's, 1961), 478.
81. *New York Times,* October 8, 1936.
82. Charles M. Smith, Jr., *Public Opinion in a Democracy* (New York: Prentice-Hall, 1939), 182.
83. *New York Times,* October 25 and 27, November 1, 1936.
84. James A. Farley, *Behind the Ballots* (New York: Harcourt, Brace, 1938), 219.
85. Quoted in "Poison versus Honesty," 6.
86. Magazine clipping, *Tugwell Papers.*

19. Tugwell as Whipping Boy: The Impact of the Attack

1. Ernest K. Lindley, *Halfway with Roosevelt* (New York: Viking, 1937), 359.
2. Fred A. Shannon, *America's Economic Growth,* 3d ed. (New York: Macmillan, 1951), 800.
3. Russell Lord, *The Wallaces of Iowa* (Boston: Houghton Mifflin, 1947), 42-43.
4. A. Chalufour and S. Desternes, "Deux Theoricians de la Crise Americaine: Rexford Tugwell et A. Berle," *Revue des Sciences Politiques,* April, 1934, 221-25.
5. Quoted in Helen Lombard, *Washington Waltz* (New York: Knopf, 1941), 186.
6. 73 Congress, 2 Session, *Congressional Record,* April 23, 1934, 7166.
7. Quoted in James A. Farley, *Jim Farley's Story* (New York: Whittlesey, 1948), 57.
8. Harold F. Gosnell, *Champion Campaigner: Franklin D. Roosevelt* (New York: Macmillan, 1952), 160.
9. Tugwell, *The Democratic Roosevelt* (Garden City, N. Y.: Doubleday, 1957), 414.
10. James A. Farley, *Behind the Ballots* (New York: Harcourt, Brace, 1938), 219.
11. Quoted in Drew Pearson and Robert S. Allen, "Valentino of the Revolution," magazine clipping, *Tugwell Papers.*
12. Tugwell, *Memoir.*

13. Harold L. Ickes, *The Secret Diary of Harold L. Ickes: Part One* (New York: Simon and Schuster, 1953), 692.

14. Louis M. Hacker, *A Short History of the New Deal* (New York: F. S. Crofts, 1936), 108.

15. Harry J. Carman, introductory remarks, Joint Meeting, American Historical Association and Agricultural History Society, Washington, D. C., December 30, 1958.

16. Raymond Moley, *After Seven Years* (New York: Harper, 1939), 124n.

17. Quoted in Russell Lord, *The Wallaces of Iowa*, 406.

18. Russell Lord, "Governor Rex of Puerto Rico," *Common Sense*, July, 1942, 224.

19. 74 Congress, 2 Session, *Congressional Record*, March 19, 1935, 4068.

20. Tugwell, *The Stricken Land* (Garden City, N. Y.: Doubleday, 1947), 142-43.

21. Sumner Welles, review, *The Stricken Land*, by Tugwell, in *Saturday Review*, December 28, 1946, 9.

22. James A. Farley, *Behind the Ballots*, 219.

23. Quoted in M. Block, ed., *Current Biography, 1941* (New York: H. W. Wilson, 1941), 875.

24. Letter, F. J. Schlink to Tugwell, May 26, 1933, *Tugwell Papers*.

25. Letter, Tugwell to S. Early, May 16, 1934, *Tugwell Papers*.

26. Tugwell, *The Stricken Land*, 347.

27. Tugwell, address, Tompkins County Development Meeting, Ithaca, N. Y., August 7, 1935, *USDA Press Release*, 7.

28. Tugwell, "The Return to Democracy," address, American Society of Newspaper Editors, April 21, 1934, in Tugwell, *The Battle for Democracy* (New York: Columbia University Press, 1935), 199.

29. Tugwell, address, Democratic State Central Committee, Los Angeles, October 28, 1935, *Resettlement Administration Press Release*, 1-2, 5.

30. Tugwell, "The Senator and Beauregard Boone," syndicated column, 1934, in Tugwell, *The Battle for Democracy*, 137-42.

31. David W. Noble, *The Paradox of Progressive Thought* (Minneapolis: University of Minnesota Press, 1958), passim.

32. Tugwell, *The Democratic Roosevelt*, 327.

33. Tugwell, "The Preparation of a President," *Western Political Quarterly*, June, 1948, 152.

34. Letter, Tugwell to A. H. Sulzberger, November 27, 1935, *PSF-T Roosevelt Papers*.

35. Letters, Moley to Tugwell, Tugwell to Moley, February, 1935, *Tugwell Papers*.

36. Quoted in *Time*, June 22, 1936, 38.

37. Tugwell, "The New Deal: The Decline of Government," Part I, *Western Political Quarterly*, June, 1951, 302; "After the New Deal: 'We Have Bought Ourselves Time to Think,'" *New Republic*, July 26, 1939, 323.

38. Tugwell, "The New Deal: The Decline of Government," Part I, 301-02; "The Preparation of a President," 151.

39. Tugwell, "A New Deal for the Consumer," address, Columbia Alumni Luncheon, New York, February 12, 1934, *USDA Press Release*, 5.

40. Tugwell, *The Stricken Land*, 22.
41. Tugwell, *The Democratic Roosevelt*, 304-05.
42. Tugwell, "The Return to Democracy," 199.
43. Tugwell, "The Progressive Orthodoxy of Franklin D. Roosevelt," *Ethics*, October, 1953, 3.
44. Tugwell, "Implementing the General Interest," *Public Administration Review*, Autumn, 1940, 48.
45. Tugwell and E. C. Banfield, "Grass Roots Democracy—Myth or Reality?," *Public Administration Review*, Winter, 1950, 47.
46. *Ibid.*
47. Tugwell, *The Stricken Land*, xviii, 62.
48. Editorial, "Tugwell to the Wolves?," *New Republic*, December 25, 1935, 187.
49. John M. Gaus and Leon C. Wolcott, *Public Administration and the United States Department of Agriculture* (Chicago: Public Administration Service, 1940), 241-42n.
50. Alva Johnston, "Tugwell, the President's Idea Man," *Saturday Evening Post*, August 1, 1936, 74.
51. Frank Knox, *We Planned It That Way* (New York: Longmans, Green, 1938), vi-vii.
52. Tugwell, *Memoir*.
53. Tugwell, *The Stricken Land*, 456.
54. Tugwell, *Diary*, March 17, 1933.
55. *Ibid.*, April 21, 1933.
56. *Ibid.*
57. Tugwell, "The Preparation of a President," 134.
58. George Seldes, *Lords of the Press* (New York: Julius Messner, 1938), 12.
59. Leland J. Gordon, *Economics for Consumers*, 2d ed. (New York: American Book Company, 1950), 601.
60. Ruth Lamb, *American Chamber of Horrors* (New York: Farrar and Rinehart, 1936), 329.
61. Paul Y. Anderson, "Washington Side Show," *Nation*, March 21, 1934, 331.
62. Oswald G. Villard, "Let Us Abate Senator Copeland," *Nation*, April 18, 1934, 433.
63. Leland J. Gordon, *Economics for Consumers*, 613.
64. Tugwell, *letter to writer*, May 11, 1955.
65. Leland J. Gordon, *Economics for Consumers*, 608, 614-17.
66. Tugwell, *The Democratic Roosevelt*, 464.
67. Tugwell, *Diary*, April 21, 1933.
68. John Kenneth Galbraith, "The 'Landlord of the Public Estate,'" review, *The Democratic Roosevelt*, by Tugwell, in *Reporter*, October 31, 1957, 45.

20. Promotion: 1934

1. *New York Times*, January 3, 1934.
2. Memorandum, Henry A. Wallace to Roosevelt, March 26, 1934, *OF 1 Roosevelt Papers*.
3. Frank R. Kent, *Without Gloves* (New York: William Morrow, 1934), 217.

4. *Time*, May 7, 1934, 14.

5. James C. Young, *Roosevelt Revealed* (New York: Farrar and Rinehart, 1936), 149.

6. Tugwell, "The Compromising Roosevelt," *Western Political Quarterly*, June, 1953, 339.

7. These speeches appear in Tugwell, *The Battle for Democracy* (New York: Columbia University Press, 1935); the Dartmouth speech was issued as a *USDA Press Release*.

8. *Newsweek*, May 5, 1934, 9.

9. Quoted in *Time*, May 7, 1934, 14.

10. *Ibid.*, 14-15.

11. *Ibid.*, 15.

12. Blair Bolles, "The Sweetheart of the Regimenters," *American Mercury*, September, 1936, 86.

13. *Time*, June 25, 1934, 10.

14. *Newsweek*, May 5, 1934, 10.

15. James C. Young, *Roosevelt Revealed*, 149.

16. *Time*, May 7, 1934, 14.

17. Letter, Henry A. Wallace to Roosevelt, May 14, 1934, *OF 1 Roosevelt Papers*.

18. Frank R. Kent, *Without Gloves*, 272-73.

19. 73 Congress, 2 Session, *Congressional Record*, June 8, 1934, 10816-36.

20. George Michael, *Handout* (New York: G. P. Putnam's, 1936), 6.

21. *Time*, June 25, 1934, 10.

22. Harold L. Ickes, *The Secret Diary of Harold L. Ickes, Part One* (New York: Simon and Schuster, 1953), 164.

23. Tugwell, "The Compromising Roosevelt," 339.

24. 73 Congress, 2 Session, *Congressional Record*, June 9, 1934, 10913.

25. *Time*, June 25, 1934, 10.

26. *Ibid.*, May 7, 1934, 14.

27. 73 Congress, 2 Session, Senate Committee on Agriculture and Forestry, *Hearings, June 11, 1934, on the Confirmation of Rexford Guy Tugwell for the Position of Undersecretary of Agriculture*, Superintendent of Documents, 1934, is the complete record; *Time*, June 18 and 25, 1934, quotes several of the more colorful statements.

28. Tugwell, statement on S. 3326, *Tugwell Papers*.

29. Blair Bolles, "The Sweetheart of the Regimenters," 78.

30. *Time*, June 18, 1934, 12.

31. 73 Congress, 2 Session, *Congressional Record*, June 12, 1934, 11156-60, 11170; June 13, 1934, 11340-41; June 14, 1934, 11427-62.

32. *Time*, June 25, 1934, 10.

33. Quoted in Russell Lord, *The Wallaces of Iowa* (Boston: Houghton Mifflin, 1947), 348.

34. Letter, Homer Cummings to Roosevelt, April 23, 1934, *OF 1 Roosevelt Papers*.

35. Letter, Tugwell to Roosevelt, no date, *PSF-T Roosevelt Papers*.

36. Paul W. Ward, "The End of Tugwell," *Nation*, November 28, 1936, 623.

37. Alva Johnston, "Tugwell, the President's Idea Man," *Saturday Evening Post*, August 1, 1936, 74.
38. Quoted in George M. Verity, "Appraises Prof. Tugwell," *Iron Age*, July 26, 1934, 33.
39. Quoted in *ibid.*, 33.
40. Frank R. Kent, *Without Gloves*, 288-89.
41. Tugwell, "The Compromising Roosevelt," 339.
42. Russell Lord, *The Wallaces of Iowa*, 347-48.
43. Arthur W. Macmahon and John D. Millett, *Federal Administrators* (New York: Columbia University Press, 1939), 211n.
44. Tugwell, "The Preparation of a President," *Western Political Quarterly*, June, 1948, 140.
45. Tugwell, *The Democratic Roosevelt* (Garden City, N. Y.: Doubleday, 1957), 389-90.
46. See George M. Verity, "Appraises Prof. Tugwell," 33.
47. "A Hint to Prof. Tugwell," editorial, *Kansas City Star*, June 12, 1934, entered in *Congressional Record*, June 15, 1934, 11682, by Senator Bennett Champ Clark (Dem., Mo.).
48. Quoted in *Time*, June 25, 1934, 10.
49. Russell Lord, *The Wallaces of Iowa*, 348.
50. Quoted in "Action on Elevation of Tugwell Watched as Indicative of Political Trend," *New York Herald Tribune*, June 6, 1934, entered in *Congressional Record*, June 8, 1934, 10831, by Senator Warren R. Austin (Rep., Vt.).
51. *Time*, June 25, 1934, 11.

21. The Task of the Resettlement Administration

1. Tugwell, "Down to Earth," *Current History*, July, 1936, passim; "Changing Acres," *Current History*, September, 1936, 59.
2. Tugwell, *The Stricken Land* (Garden City, N. Y.: Doubleday, 1947), 24.
3. Tugwell and E. C. Banfield, "Grass Roots Democracy—Myth or Reality?," *Public Administration Review*, Winter, 1950, 55.
4. Arthur M. Schlesinger, Jr., *The Coming of the New Deal* (Boston: Houghton Mifflin, 1959), 73.
5. Quoted in Russell Lord, *The Wallaces of Iowa* (Boston: Houghton Mifflin, 1947), 381.
6. Ezra T. Benson, "A Workable Farm Policy," *Atlantic Monthly*, July, 1954, 54.
7. Russell Lord, *The Wallaces of Iowa*, 459.
8. Tugwell, *The Stricken Land*, 25.
9. Tugwell, *Memoir*.
10. *Ibid.*
11. Tugwell, "The Place of Government in a National Land Program," address, Joint Meeting, American Economic Association, Farm Economic Association, American Statistical Association, Philadelphia, December 29, 1933, *USDA Press Release*, 14-19.

12. Edgar B. Nixon, compiler and ed., *Franklin D. Roosevelt and Conservation, 1911-1945,* 2 vols. (Hyde Park: Franklin D. Roosevelt Library, 1957), I, 262-63.
13. *Ibid.,* 268-71.
14. *Ibid.*
15. Letter, Henry A. Wallace to Roosevelt, August 25, 1934, *OF 1 Roosevelt Papers.*
16. Tugwell, *Memoir.*
17. Russell Lord, *The Wallaces of Iowa,* 248.
18. *New York Times,* March 26 and 28, April 25, 1933.
19. Tugwell, *Memoir.*
20. Paul K. Conkin, *Tomorrow a New World: The New Deal Community Program* (Ithaca, N. Y.: Cornell University Press for the American Historical Association, 1959), 160, 166.
21. Wilma Dykeman and James Stokley, *Seeds of Southern Change: The Life of Will Alexander* (Chicago: University of Chicago Press, 1962), 216, 218.
22. Will W. Alexander, *Interview, Oral History Research Office,* Columbia University, 384-87, 395.
23. Paul K. Conkin, *Tomorrow a New World,* 153.
24. Quoted in Wilma Dykeman and James Stokely, *Seeds of Southern Change,* 219.
25. *Ibid.,* 207-08, 211-12.
26. *Ibid.,* 175, 185, 211, 213, 216.
27. Will W. Alexander, *Interview, Oral History Research Office,* Columbia University, 397-400.
28. Quoted in Wilma Dykeman and James Stokely, *Seeds of Southern Change,* 212-13.
29. *Ibid.,* 212.
30. Tugwell, "The Place of Government in a National Land Program," 14.
31. Tugwell, "Co-operation and Resettlement," *Current History,* February, 1937, 74.
32. Tugwell, "The Preparation of a President," *Western Political Quarterly,* June, 1948, 132; *The Democratic Roosevelt* (Garden City, N. Y.: Doubleday, 1957), 423.
33. Tugwell, "The Preparation of a President," 132-33; Tugwell, *The Democratic Roosevelt,* 157, 159.
34. Paul K. Conkin, *Tomorrow a New World,* 159.
35. Russell Lord, *The Wallaces of Iowa,* 429.
36. Paul K. Conkin, *Tomorrow a New World,* 142-43.
37. Tugwell, *interview with writer.*
38. Wilma Dykeman and James Stokely, *Seeds of Southern Change,* 212.
39. Paul K. Conkin, *Tomorrow a New World,* 155-56; Will W. Alexander, *Interview, Oral History Research Office,* Columbia University, 404-05, 465-66.
40. Paul K. Conkin, *Tomorrow a New World,* 155-56.
41. *Ibid.,* 153-54, 156, 166, 167.

42. Clarence S. Stein, *Toward New Towns for America* (The University Press of Liverpool, 1951), 101.
43. Letter, Tugwell to Roosevelt, December 12, 1935, *PSF-T Roosevelt Papers.*
44. Tugwell, "Down to Earth," 38.
45. Tugwell, "The Meaning of the Greenbelt Towns," *New Republic,* February 17, 1937, 42-43.
46. *New York Times,* October 26 and 29, November 4, 1936.
47. Lewis Meriam, *Relief and Social Security* (Washington: Brookings Institution, 1946), 295, 299-300.
48. Tugwell, "Changing Acres," 59.
49. *Ibid.*
50. Ernest K. Lindley, *The Roosevelt Revolution: First Phase* (New York: Viking, 1933), 108-09.
51. Telegrams, August, 1935, *OF 1568 Roosevelt Papers.*
52. Letter, Tugwell to M. H. McIntyre, August 5, 1935, *OF 1568 Roosevelt Papers.*
53. Letter, Tugwell to M. H. McIntyre, August 16, 1935, *OF 1568 Roosevelt Papers.*
54. Tugwell, "Changing Acres," 59.
55. H. C. M. Case, "Farm Debt Adjustment during the Early 1930's," *Agricultural History,* October, 1960; Ernest Feder, "Farm Debt Adjustment during the Depression—the Other Face of the Coin," *Agricultural History,* April, 1961.
56. Letter, Roosevelt to R. A. Derby, June 23, 1936, *PPF 758 Roosevelt Papers.*
57. Memoranda, Tugwell to D. Bell, Acting Budget Director, September 23, 1935; Bell to Attorney General, September 24, 1935; Roosevelt to Tugwell, September 30, 1935, *OF 1568 Roosevelt Papers.*
58. *New York Times,* June 23, July 7, 11, 14, 19, 22, 1936.
59. *Ibid.,* August 18, 1936; *Time,* September 7, 1936, 7.
60. Tugwell, *The Democratic Roosevelt,* 424.
61. *Time,* July 20, 1936, 22.
62. *Ibid.,* August 31, 1936, 15.
63. *New York Times,* September 2 and 29, 1936.
64. Tugwell, *The Democratic Roosevelt,* 423-24.
65. Tugwell, "Down to Earth," "Changing Acres," passim.
66. Note, *Tugwell Papers.*
67. Paul K. Conkin, *Tomorrow a New World,* 156-58.
68. Tugwell, "National Significance of Recent Trends in Farm Population," *Social Forces,* October, 1935, 7.
69. Paul K. Conkin, *Tomorrow a New World,* 156, 161-62, 165.
70. *Ibid.,* 161.
71. *Ibid.*
72. Based on tables in *ibid.,* 332-37.
73. *Ibid.,* 108, 162.
74. *Ibid.,* 164.
75. *Ibid.,* 165.
76. Based on tables in *ibid.,* 332-37.

77. *Ibid.*, 166.
78. Based on tables in *ibid.*, 332-37.
79. *Ibid.*, 167-69.
80. Letters, Congressman H. W. Sumners (Dem., Tex.) to Roosevelt, August 28, 1935; M. H. McIntyre to H. W. Sumners (prepared by Tugwell), September 20, 1935, *OF 1568 Roosevelt Papers*.
81. Paul K. Conkin, *Tomorrow a New World*, 160.
82. Will W. Alexander, *Interview*, 425-27.
83. Letter, Tugwell to Roosevelt, June 24, 1936, *OF 1568 Roosevelt Papers*.
84. Letters, Tugwell to Mead, Mead to Tugwell, Ickes to Mead, Ickes to Roosevelt, Roosevelt to Tugwell, Tugwell to Roosevelt, July, 1935, *OF 1568 Roosevelt Papers*.
85. *Time*, April 8, 1935, 17; May 25, 1936, 13-14; Paul K. Conkin, *Tomorrow a New World*, 161.

22. *The Performance of the Resettlement Administration under Tugwell: 1935-1936*

1. "The Brain Trust," *Business Week*, March 22, 1933, 16.
2. George M. Verity, "Appraises Prof. Tugwell," Parts I and II, *Iron Age*, July 5, 1934, 34-35, 42B; July 26, 1934, 33-34.
3. James G. Mitchell, "The Precocious Juvenility of the 'Brain Trust,'" *Annalist*, June 1, 1934.
4. Francis Neilson, *Control from the Top* (New York: G. P. Putnam's, 1933), 20-21.
5. Paul W. Ward, "The End of Tugwell," *Nation*, November 28, 1936, 623.
6. James C. Young, *Roosevelt Revealed* (New York: Farrar and Rinehart, 1936), 114, 149.
7. Blair Bolles, "The Sweetheart of the Regimenters," *American Mercury*, September, 1936, 85.
8. Blair Bolles, "Prose and Politics: Writers in the New Deal," *Saturday Review*, March 30, 1940, 4, 17.
9. Alva Johnston, "Tugwell, the President's Idea Man," *Saturday Evening Post*, August 1, 1936, 8-9.
10. Frank R. Kent, *Without Grease* (New York: William Morrow, 1936), 231-32.
11. Frank R. Kent, *Without Gloves* (New York: William Morrow, 1934), 147-50, 172, 227.
12. Quoted in James C. Young, *Roosevelt Revealed*, 41.
13. Morris Bealle, *Washington Squirrel Cage* (Washington: The Author, 1934), 31.
14. Stanley High, *Roosevelt—and Then?* (New York: Harper, 1937), 160.
15. Quoted in *Time*, November 11, 1935, 11.
16. Letter, D. W. Bell to Roosevelt, August 8, 1935, *OF 1568 Roosevelt Papers*.
17. Memorandum, D. W. Bell to Roosevelt, January 8, 1936, *OF 1568 Roosevelt Papers*.

18. Letter, D. W. Bell to Roosevelt, August 15, 1936, *OF 1568 Roosevelt Papers*.
19. Harold L. Ickes, *The Secret Diary of Harold L. Ickes, Part One* (New York: Simon and Schuster, 1953), 473.
20. Memorandum, Roosevelt to W. W. Alexander, August 28, 1936, *OF 1568 Roosevelt Papers*.
21. Will W. Alexander, *Interview, Oral History Research Office*, Columbia University, 395.
22. Paul K. Conkin, *Tomorrow a New World: The New Deal Community Program* (Ithaca, N. Y.: Cornell University Press for the American Historical Association, 1959), 156.
23. *Ibid.*, 158-59.
24. Will W. Alexander, *Interview*, 395, 465-66.
25. *Ibid.*, 403.
26. Wilma Dykeman and James Stokely, *Seeds of Southern Change: The Life of Will Alexander* (Chicago: University of Chicago Press, 1962), 219.
27. Marquis Childs, *I Write from Washington* (New York: Harper, 1942), 10-14.
28. Will W. Alexander, *Interview*, 548-49.
29. Paul K. Conkin, *Tomorrow a New World*, 178.
30. "What's Tugwell Doing?," *Business Week*, March 21, 1936, 30.
31. Paul K. Conkin, *Tomorrow a New World*, 178.
32. *Ibid.*, 172.
33. *Ibid.*, 320.
34. Tugwell, "The Meaning of the Greenbelt Towns," *New Republic*, February 17, 1937, 42.
35. Paul K. Conkin, *Tomorrow a New World*, 320.
36. Tugwell, "The Meaning of the Greenbelt Towns," 42.
37. Paul K. Conkin, *Tomorrow a New World*, 320.
38. *Ibid.*, 170.
39. *Ibid.*, 173.
40. Tugwell, "The Meaning of the Greenbelt Towns," 43.
41. Cleveland Rodgers, *Robert Moses* (New York: Henry Holt, 1952), 131.
42. Paul K. Conkin, *Tomorrow a New World*, 170-72.
43. Tugwell, *interview with writer*; Russell Moore, *Roosevelt Riddles* (Garden City, N. Y.: Doubleday, Doran, 1936), 7-8.
44. Telegram, Howe to Col. Greer, Preston Light and Power Co., November 27, 1933; memorandum, Roosevelt to Tugwell, May 19, 1935, *OF 2700, OF 1568 Roosevelt Papers*.
45. Letter, C. D. Beebe, Kalamazoo, Mich., to Roosevelt, October 16, 1936, *OF 466c Roosevelt Papers*.
46. *New York Times*, May 28, 1936.
47. Lewis Meriam, *Relief and Social Security* (Washington: Brookings Institution, 1946), 312-13.
48. Alva Johnston, "Tugwell, the President's Idea Man," 9.
49. James C. Young, *Roosevelt Revealed*, 269-70.

50. Tugwell, "National Significance of Recent Trends in Farm Population," *Social Forces,* October, 1935, 4.
51. Tugwell, letter to the editor, *Nation,* December 25, 1935, 742.
52. Paul K. Conkin, *Tomorrow a New World,* 175.
53. Quoted in letter, Edmund Brunner, Columbia Teachers College, to J. H. Kolb, FERA, July 5, 1935, *Tugwell Papers.*
54. Paul K. Conkin, *Tomorrow a New World,* 215, 318-19.
55. Will W. Alexander, *Interview,* 414-17.
56. Paul K. Conkin, *Tomorrow a New World,* 158-60, 170, 214.
57. *Ibid.,* 162-63, 214-15.
58. *Ibid.,* 215-17.
59. *Ibid.,* 218-19.
60. *Ibid.,* 217-18, 322-25.
61. Letter, B. F. Irvine and M. N. Dana to Roosevelt, July 12, 1935; reply, no date, *OF 1568 Roosevelt Papers.*
62. Tugwell, "Relief and Reconstruction," address, National Conference of Social Workers, Kansas City, Mo., May 21, 1934, in Tugwell, *The Battle for Democracy* (New York: Columbia University Press, 1935), 310.
63. Tugwell, "Conservation Redefined," address, Fiftieth Anniversary of the Founding of New York's Forest Preserve, Albany, May 15, 1935, *USDA Press Release,* 10.
64. Tugwell, "Your Future and Your Nation," Commencement Address, University of New Mexico, June 10, 1935, *USDA Press Release,* 2.
65. Tugwell, address, Tompkins County Development Meeting, Ithaca, N. Y., August 7, 1935, *USDA Press Release,* 8.
66. Draft of reply, Tugwell to M. McIntyre, September 16, 1935, *OF 1568 Roosevelt Papers.*
67. Letter, Roosevelt to Gore, September 24, 1935, *OF 1568 Roosevelt Papers.*
68. Letter, Tugwell to E. C. Moran, Jr., December 23, 1935, *OF 1568 Roosevelt Papers.*
69. Ernest K. Lindley, *Halfway with Roosevelt* (New York: Viking, 1937), 210.
70. *Ibid.,* 21.
71. Tugwell, "A Third Economy," address, Rochester (N. Y.) Teachers Association, April 22, 1935, *USDA Press Release,* 15.
72. Alva Johnston, "Tugwell, the President's Idea Man," 73-74.
73. *New York Times,* March 22, 1936.
74. *Ibid.,* October 10 and 16, 1936.
75. Felix Brunner, "Utopia Unlimited," *Washington Post,* February 10, 11, 12, 13, 1936; quoted in Paul K. Conkin, *Tomorrow a New World,* 176.
76. Paul K. Conkin, *Tomorrow a New World,* 176.
77. *Ibid.,* 151.
78. *Ibid.,* 177.
79. *Ibid.,* 319.
80. Wilma Dykeman and James Stokely, *Seeds of Southern Change,* 221.
81. *Ibid.,* 220.

82. Letter, J. A. Farley to M. McIntyre, November 19, 1935, *OF 1568 Roosevelt Papers.*

83. Letter, Tugwell to Roosevelt, November 26, 1935, *PSF-T Roosevelt Papers.*

84. Letter, Roosevelt to Tugwell, November 25, 1935, *OF 1568 Roosevelt Papers.*

85. Ernest K. Lindley, *Halfway with Roosevelt*, 210.

86. Paul K. Conkin, *Tomorrow a New World*, 166.

87. Quoted in Russell Lord, *The Wallaces of Iowa* (Boston: Houghton Mifflin, 1947), 429.

88. Letter, Tugwell to M. McIntyre, August 31, 1935, *OF 1568 Roosevelt Papers.*

89. Tugwell, "Changing Acres," *Current History*, September, 1936, 59, 62.

90. Letter, Edmund Brunner, Columbia Teachers College, to J. H. Kolb, FERA, July 5, 1935, *Tugwell Papers.*

91. Lewis Meriam, *Relief and Social Security*, 296.

92. Wilma Dykeman and James Stokely, *Seeds of Southern Change*, 221.

93. Paul K. Conkin, *Tomorrow a New World*, 163-65.

94. Tugwell, letter to the editor, *Nation*, March 18, 1936, 362.

95. Paul K. Conkin, *Tomorrow a New World*, 329.

96. Arthur M. Schlesinger, Jr., *The Coming of the New Deal* (Boston: Houghton Mifflin, 1959), 378.

97. Norman Thomas, *Interview, Oral History Research Office*, Columbia University, 98.

98. Arthur M. Schlesinger, Jr., *The Coming of the New Deal*, 378-79.

99. Wilma Dykeman and James Stokely, *Seeds of Southern Change*, 220-21.

100. Paul K. Conkin, *Tomorrow a New World*, 170, 177.

101. Stuart Chase, *Rich Land, Poor Land* (New York: Whittlesey House, 1936), 362.

102. Letter, Tugwell to Roosevelt, December 21, 1935, *OF 1568 Roosevelt Papers.*

103. 74 Congress, 2 Session, *Congressional Record*, March 19, 1936, 4069-70.

104. Alva Johnston, "Tugwell, the President's Idea Man," 9.

105. Ernest K. Lindley, "War on the Brains Trust," *Scribner's Magazine*, November, 1933, 286.

106. Tugwell, "The Progressive Orthodoxy of Franklin D. Roosevelt," *Ethics*, October, 1953, 4.

107. Note, Ezekiel to Tugwell, no date, *Tugwell Papers.*

108. J. Franklin Carter, *The New Dealers* (New York: Simon and Schuster, 1934), 86.

109. James A. Farley, *Behind the Ballots* (New York: Harcourt, 1938), 219.

110. 73 Congress, 2 Session, *Congressional Record*, June 11, 1934, 11088-89.

111. 74 Congress, 1 Session, *Congressional Record*, March 27, 1935, 4535.

112. Quoted in John M. Gaus and Leon C. Wolcott, *Public Administration and the United States Department of Agriculture* (Chicago: Public Administration Service, 1940), 66.

113. Ernest K. Lindley, *Halfway with Roosevelt*, 43.

114. Ernest K. Lindley, "War on the Brains Trust," 259.
115. A. Gillis and R. Ketcham, *Our America* (Boston: Little, Brown, 1936), 367.
116. Paul K. Conkin, *Tomorrow a New World*, 328.
117. Quoted in *New York Times*, November 26, 1936.
118. Russell Lord, "Governor Rex of Puerto Rico," *Common Sense*, July, 1942, 224.
119. "What's Tugwell Doing?," 29.
120. Paul K. Conkin, *Tomorrow a New World*, 179.
121. Quoted in *ibid.*
122. Clarence S. Stein, *Toward New Towns for America* (The University Press of Liverpool, 1951), 101.
123. C. Tunnard and H. H. Reed, *American Skyline: The Growth and Form of Our Cities and Towns* (New York: New American Library, 1956), 180.
124. Will W. Alexander, *Interview*, 410.
125. Ernest K. Lindley, *Halfway with Roosevelt*, 186.
126. Will W. Alexander, *Interview*, 470-71, 633.
127. Quoted in Paul W. Ward, "Wallace the Great Hesitator," *Nation*, May 8, 1935, 533.
128. Louis A. Brownlow, *A Passion for Anonymity: The Autobiography of Louis Brownlow, Second Half* (Chicago: University of Chicago Press, 1958), 459.
129. Oswald G. Villard, "That Man Tugwell," *Christian Century*, April 5, 1944, 430.
130. *Time*, February 2, 1942, 19; June 15, 1942, 12; June 23, 1958, 32.
131. Earl P. Hanson, *Transformation: The Story of Modern Puerto Rico* (New York: Simon and Schuster, 1945), chapter entitled "Tugwell."
132. Paul K. Conkin, *Tomorrow a New World*, 328-29.
133. *Ibid.*, 174, 178-80.
134. Memorandum, Tugwell to Roosevelt, September 3, 1936, *OF 1568 Roosevelt Papers.*
135. Russell Lord, *The Wallaces of Iowa*, 460.
136. *New York Times*, November 11, 1936.
137. Russell Lord, *The Wallaces of Iowa*, 429, 460.
138. Wilma Dykeman and James Stokely, *Seeds of Southern Change*, 222.
139. Paul K. Conkin, *Tomorrow a New World*, 184.
140. *Ibid.*, 220.
141. *Ibid.*, 224-25.
142. *Ibid.*, 227, 230-31.
143. *American Historical Review*, April, 1959, 795.
144. Tugwell, "The Resettlement Idea," address, Joint Meeting, American Historical Association and Agricultural History Society, Washington, D. C., December 30, 1958.
145. Robert V. Smuts, "Causes of Human Failure," *Challenge*, October, 1959, 18-22.
146. *New York Times*, November 1, 1959.

147. *Ibid.*, July 17, 1962.
148. Tugwell, *The Democratic Roosevelt* (Garden City, N. Y.: Doubleday, 1957), 424.

23. *Board Member—Errand Boy—Publicist—Idea Man: 1932-1933*

1. Tugwell, *interview with writer.*
2. Tugwell, *Memoir.*
3. *Ibid.*
4. *Ibid.*
5. *Ibid.*
6. Arthur M. Schlesinger, Jr., *The Coming of the New Deal* (Boston: Houghton Mifflin, 1959), 308.
7. Tugwell and E. C. Banfield, "Grass Roots Democracy—Myth or Reality?," *Public Administration Review*, Winter, 1950, 50.
8. Tugwell, *interview with writer.*
9. *Ibid.*
10. Tugwell, *Memoir;* Tugwell, *Diary*, January 14, 23, 1933.
11. Tugwell, *The Democratic Roosevelt* (Garden City, N. Y.: Doubleday, 1957), 298, 329, 409-15, 658-59.
12. Tugwell, *Memoir.*
13. Tugwell, *Diary*, January 7, 1933.
14. Tugwell, *The Democratic Roosevelt*, 219-20, 329.
15. *Ibid.*, 326, 330-31, 339-41.
16. *Ibid.*, 328, 340, 360.
17. Tugwell, "Your Future and Your Nation," Commencement Address, University of New Mexico, June 10, 1935, *USDA Press Release*, 13-14.
18. *Newsweek*, July 1, 1946, 28.
19. Frank R. Kent, *Without Grease* (New York: William Morrow, 1936), 231.
20. George Michael, *Handout* (New York: G. P. Putnam's, 1935), 82.
21. Tugwell, *letter to writer*, May 11, 1955.
22. Tugwell, "The Liberal Choice," *New Republic*, September 5, 1928, 74.
23. Frank R. Kent, *Without Gloves* (New York: William Morrow, 1934), 227.
24. Tugwell, *Memoir.*
25. Blair Bolles, "The Sweetheart of the Regimenters," *American Mercury*, September, 1936, 85.
26. Raymond Moley, *After Seven Years* (New York: Harper, 1939), 281-82.
27. Tugwell, *The Democratic Roosevelt*, 238.
28. Cabell Phillips, "The New Dealers—Where Are They Now?," *New York Times Magazine*, September 29, 1946, 52.
29. Letter, Raymond Moley to Tugwell, February 19, 1934, *Tugwell Papers.*
30. Editorial, "Tugwell to the Wolves?," *New Republic*, December 25, 1935, 186.
31. Tugwell, *The Stricken Land* (Garden City, N. Y.: Doubleday, 1947), 349.
32. Tugwell, "The Preparation of a President," *Western Political Quarterly*, June, 1948, 144.

33. Tugwell, "Managing Money," unpublished notes, 1934, *Tugwell Papers.*
34. Tugwell, "New Monetary Policy Regarded Logical Step," *Washington Star,* November 5, 1933.
35. Tugwell, "Managing Money."
36. Raymond Moley, *After Seven Years,* 282.
37. *Ibid.,* 269, 281.
38. Tugwell, "Prices and Dollars," syndicated column, in Tugwell, *The Battle for Democracy* (New York: Columbia University Press, 1935), 48-49.
39. Tugwell, "Sound Money," address, Adult Education Association, Chicago, October 29, 1933, *USDA Press Release,* 1.
40. Tugwell, "Prices and Dollars," 50.
41. Tugwell, "Managing Money."
42. Tugwell, "Sound Money," 3.
43. *Ibid.*
44. Tugwell, "Our Weight in Gold," syndicated column, in Tugwell, *The Battle for Democracy,* 27.
45. A. G. Beuhler, *The Undistributed Profits Tax* (New York: McGraw-Hill, 1937), 14, 153.
46. 74 Congress, 2 Session, *Hearings before the House Committee on Ways and Means on the Revenue Act of 1936,* 38.
47. Sidney Ratner, *American Taxation* (New York: W. W. Norton, 1942), 474.
48. Tugwell, *letter to writer,* May 18, 1955.
49. Letter, Louis Brownlow to Tugwell, November 29, 1933, *Tugwell Papers.*
50. Letters, Tugwell to Roosevelt, February 24, 1934; Roosevelt to Tugwell, February 28, 1934, *PSF-T Roosevelt Papers.*
51. Tugwell, "Addendum to the Diary for the 100 Days," *Tugwell Papers.*
52. F. D. Roosevelt, *The Public Papers and Addresses of Franklin D. Roosevelt,* S. Rosenman, arr. (New York: Random House, 1938), V, 102-06.
53. R. G. Blakey and G. C. Blakey, *The Federal Income Tax* (New York: McGraw-Hill, 1937), 422.
54. A. G. Beuhler, *The Undistributed Profits Tax;* M. S. Kendrick, *The Undistributed Profits Tax* (Washington: Brookings Institution, 1937); G. E. Lent, *The Impact of the Undistributed Profits Tax, 1936-37* (New York: Columbia University Press, 1948).
55. M. S. Kendrick, *The Undistributed Profits Tax,* 83.
56. G. E. Lent, *The Impact of the Undistributed Profits Tax, 1936-37,* 188.
57. *Economic Affairs,* June 30, 1959, 2.
58. Raymond Moley, *After Seven Years,* 309.
59. *Ibid.*
60. Tugwell, *The Industrial Discipline and the Governmental Arts* (New York: Columbia University Press, 1933, 205.
61. B. Sternsher, "The Undistributed Profits Tax of 1936," Seminar Paper, Harvard University, 1951.
62. John Morton Blum, *From the Morgenthau Diaries: Years of Crisis, 1928-1938* (Boston: Houghton Mifflin, 1959), 305-19.
63. Frank R. Kent, *Without Gloves,* 231.

64. John M. Gaus and Leon C. Wolcott, *Public Administration and the United States Department of Agriculture* (Chicago: Public Administration Service, 1940), 241n.
65. Tugwell, *Memoir*.

24. Resignation: 1936

1. Harold L. Ickes, *The Secret Diary of Harold L. Ickes, Part One* (New York: Simon and Schuster, 1953), 473-75.
2. *New York Times*, January 2, 1936.
3. Charles W. Smith, Jr., *Public Opinion in a Democracy* (New York: Prentice-Hall, 1939), 182.
4. Joseph B. Ely, *The American Dream* (Boston: B. Humphries, 1944), 179.
5. Frank R. Kent, *Without Gloves* (New York: William Morrow, 1934), 297-98.
6. "Tugwell: New Deal's Leading 'Red' Gets Job on Wall Street," *Newsweek*, November 28, 1936, 16.
7. Letters, Tugwell to Roosevelt, November 17, 1936, and Roosevelt to Tugwell, November 18, 1936, *PPF 564 Roosevelt Papers*.
8. Quoted in Russell Lord, *The Wallaces of Iowa* (Boston: Houghton Mifflin, 1947), 458.
9. Tugwell, *The Art of Politics* (Garden City, N. Y.: Doubleday, 1958), 194.
10. Tugwell, *Memoir*.
11. "Tugwell: New Deal's Leading 'Red' Gets Job on Wall Street," 16; "Molasses Man," *Time*, November 30, 1936, 13; editorial, *Nation*, November 28, 1936, 618; Paul W. Ward, "The End of Tugwell," *Nation*, November 28, 1936, 623.
12. Cabell Phillips, "The New Dealers—Where Are They Now?," *New York Times Magazine*, September 29, 1946, 52.
13. *Review of Reviews*, December, 1936, 52.
14. Harold L. Ickes, *The Secret Diary of Harold L. Ickes: Part Two* (New York: Simon and Schuster, 1954), 48.
15. "Tugwell: New Deal's Leading 'Red' Gets Job on Wall Street," 16.
16. "Molasses Man," 13.
17. John T. Flynn, *The Roosevelt Myth* (New York: Devin-Adair, 1948), 150.
18. Paul W. Ward, "The End of Tugwell," 623.
19. Editorial, *Nation*, November 28, 1936, 618.
20. Quoted in "Molasses Man," 13.
21. Quoted in *ibid*.
22. Harold L. Ickes, *The Secret Diary of Harold L. Ickes, Part Two*, 9.
23. Letter, D. P. Trent to Tugwell, January 20, 1937, *Tugwell Papers*.
24. Letter, R. A. Pearson to Tugwell, December 30, 1936, *Tugwell Papers*.
25. Russell Lord, *The Wallaces of Iowa*, 429.
26. Arthur W. Macmahon and John D. Millett, *Federal Administrators* (New York: Columbia University Press, 1939), 212.
27. Raymond Moley, *After Seven Years* (New York: Harper, 1939), 355.

28. Tugwell, *The Democratic Roosevelt* (Garden City, N. Y.: Doubleday, 1957), 414.

29. Will W. Alexander, *Interview, Oral History Research Office,* Columbia University, 633-34.

30. Tugwell, *Memoir.*

31. Tugwell, "The Compromising Roosevelt," *Western Political Quarterly,* June, 1953, 324.

32. Tugwell, *The Art of Politics,* 61, 74.

33. Harold L. Ickes, *The Secret Diary of Harold L. Ickes, Part Two,* 9.

34. Tugwell, *The Democratic Roosevelt,* 58.

35. Tugwell, *The Art of Politics,* 222.

36. "Molasses Man," 13.

37. Harold L. Ickes, *The Secret Diary of Harold L. Ickes, Part Three* (New York: Simon and Schuster, 1954), 6.

38. Tugwell, *The Democratic Roosevelt,* 414.

39. Tugwell, "The Preparation of a President," *Western Political Quarterly,* June, 1948, 153.

40. Richard Hofstadter, *The Age of Reform: From Bryan to F.D.R.* (New York: Knopf, 1955), 305.

41. Tugwell, *A Chronicle of Jeopardy: 1945-1955* (Chicago: University of Chicago Press, 1955), 13, 24.

42. Sumner Welles, review, *The Stricken Land,* by Tugwell, in *Saturday Review,* December 28, 1946, 9.

43. "Rex in Puerto Rico," *Time,* February 2, 1942, 19.

44. Quoted in newspaper clipping, *Tugwell Papers.*

45. Blair Bolles, "The Sweetheart of the Regimenters," *American Mercury,* September, 1936, 77-78.

46. Quoted in Elizabeth Dilling, *The Roosevelt Red Record and Its Background* (Chicago: the author, 1936), 351.

47. John T. Flynn, *The Roosevelt Myth,* 149.

48. Paul W. Ward, "Wallace the Great Hesitator," *Nation,* May 8, 1935, 536.

49. Quoted in James G. Mitchell, "The Precocious Juvenility of the 'Brain Trust,'" *Annalist,* June 1, 1934, 848.

50. George Michael, *Handout* (New York: G. P. Putnam's, 1935), 128-29.

51. Quoted in Russell Lord, *The Wallaces of Iowa,* 346.

52. Sumner Welles, review, *The Stricken Land,* by Tugwell, 9.

53. Russell Lord, "Governor Rex of Puerto Rico," *Common Sense,* July, 1942, 224.

54. Frances Perkins, *interview with writer,* University of Rochester, 1958.

55. Letter, B. Harlan to M. H. McIntyre, August, 1935, *OF 1568 Roosevelt Papers.*

56. Letter, C. G. Proffitt to Tugwell, November 27, 1933, *Tugwell Papers.*

57. Russell Lord, *The Wallaces of Iowa,* 348.

58. Russell Lord, "Governor Rex of Puerto Rico," 224.

59. Russell Lord, *The Wallaces of Iowa,* 348.

60. Letter, Tugwell to Roosevelt, March 3, 1934, *OF 1 Roosevelt Papers.*

61. Will W. Alexander, *Interview, Oral History Research Office,* Columbia University, 472, 598.
62. Frank R. Kent, *Baltimore Sun,* July 21, 1933; quoted in Russell Lord, *The Wallaces of Iowa,* 353-55.
63. *Time,* June 25, 1934, 11.
64. Tugwell, *interview with writer.*
65. *Time,* September 24, 1934, 55.
66. Russell Lord, note, in Russell Lord and Kate Lord, eds., *Forever the Land* (New York: Harper, 1950), 51.
67. Tugwell, *interview with writer.*
68. Arthur M. Schlesinger, Jr., *The Coming of the New Deal* (Boston: Houghton Mifflin, 1959), 360.
69. Tugwell, *Memoir.*
70. Tugwell, "Meditation in Stinsford Churchyard," *Tugwell Papers.*
71. Tugwell, "On Life as a Long-Time Enterprise," address, Dartmouth College, April 26, 1934, *USDA Press Release,* 9-10.
72. Letter, Tugwell to Roosevelt, September 16, 1940, *PSF-GC Roosevelt Papers.*
73. James A. Farley, *Behind the Ballots* (New York: Harcourt, Brace, 1938), 219-20.
74. J. Franklin Carter, *The New Dealers* (New York: Simon and Schuster, 1934), 91.
75. Cleveland Rodgers, *Robert Moses* (New York: Henry Holt, 1952), 129.
76. Tugwell, *The Stricken Land* (Garden City, N. Y.: Doubleday, 1947), xxi.
77. *Ibid.,* xxxi.
78. Tugwell, "The Progressive Orthodoxy of Franklin D. Roosevelt," *Ethics,* October, 1953, 21-22.
79. Tugwell, *The Stricken Land,* 681.

25. Tugwell the "Subversive"

1. 73 Congress, 2 Session, *Congressional Record,* June 14, 1934, 11445.
2. H. L. Mencken, *H. L. Mencken on Politics: A Carnival of Buncombe,* ed. by Malcolm Moos (New York: Vintage Books, 1960), 323.
3. Frank R. Kent, *Without Gloves* (New York: William Morrow, 1934), 45.
4. Blair Bolles, "The Sweetheart of the Regimenters," *American Mercury,* September, 1936, 12, 83, 86.
5. Alva Johnston, "Tugwell, the President's Idea Man," *Saturday Evening Post,* August 1, 1936, 9.
6. Berton Braley, *New Deal Ditties* (New York: Greenberg, 1936), 20.
7. Letter, Tugwell to Roosevelt, March 17, 1933, *PPF 564 Roosevelt Papers.*
8. Letter, Tugwell to H. E. Hawkes, no date, *Tugwell Papers.*
9. Letter, December 22, 1933, *Tugwell Papers.*
10. Letter, Tugwell to John J. Coss, December 27, 1933, *Tugwell Papers.*
11. Letter, Tugwell to N. M. Butler, January, 1936, *PPF 564 Roosevelt Papers.*

12. Letter, Roosevelt to N. M. Butler, February 10, 1936, *PPF 564 Roosevelt Papers.*
13. *New York Times,* February 25, 1936.
14. James A. Farley, *Behind the Ballots* (New York: Harcourt, 1938), 219.
15. Tugwell, "The Utility of the Future in the Present," *Public Administration Review,* Winter, 1948, 56.
16. David Lawrence, *Beyond the New Deal* (New York: Whittlesey House, 1934), 205.
17. Frank R. Kent, *Without Grease* (New York: William Morrow, 1936), 231.
18. Blair Bolles, "The Sweetheart of the Regimenters," 83.
19. James C. Young, *Roosevelt Revealed* (New York: Farrar and Rinehart, 1936), 419.
20. Alva Johnston, "Tugwell, the President's Idea Man," 9.
21. David Lawrence, column in *New York Sun,* May 11, 1936, cited by Senator J. G. Townsend, Jr. (Rep., Del.) in 74 Congress, 2 Session, *Congressional Record,* June 16, 1936, 9530-31.
22. Quoted in "Molasses Man," *Time,* November 30, 1936, 12.
23. *Time,* February 6, 1933, 14.
24. "The Brain Trust," *Business Week,* March 22, 1933, 17.
25. Tugwell, note, *Tugwell Papers.*
26. C. H. McCall, "That Columbia Crowd," *Credit and Financial Management,* June, 1933, 17.
27. Memoranda, Early to Tugwell, no date, indicating the President's approval of a speech to a social workers' conference, May, 1934, and an article in *Fortune,* October, 1936, *OF 1 Roosevelt Papers.*
28. Note, Tugwell to Margaret LeHand, November 1, 1935, *PPF 564 Roosevelt Papers.*
29. Louis M. Hacker, *A Short History of the New Deal* (New York: F. S. Crofts, 1936), 108.
30. Letter, Tugwell to Roosevelt, August 26, 1937, *PPF 564 Roosevelt Papers.*
31. Tugwell, *Memoir.*
32. Ernest K. Lindley, "War on the Brains Trust," *Scribner's Magazine,* November, 1933, 264.
33. Newspaper clipping, April 12, 1936, *Tugwell Papers.*
34. *Time,* June 19, 1933, 25.
35. Tugwell, *interview with writer.*
36. *Ibid.*
37. Claude M. Fuess, *Joseph B. Eastman* (New York: Columbia University Press, 1952), 192.
38. *New York Times,* March 22, 1936.
39. "The Brain Trust," 16.
40. Editorial, "Tugwell to the Wolves?," *New Republic,* December 25, 1935, 186.
41. Frank Knox, *We Planned It That Way* (New York: Longmans, Green, 1938), vii.

42. Joseph Alsop and Robert Kintner, *American White Paper: The Story of American Diplomacy in the Second World War* (New York: Simon and Schuster, 1940), 83.
43. *Current Biography* (New York: H. W. Wilson, 1944), 875.
44. Oswald G. Villard, "Tugwell, Puerto Rico, and Washington," *Christian Century*, January 27, 1943, 107.
45. Frank R. Kent, *Without Gloves*, 44-45.
46. Alva Johnston, "Tugwell, the President's Idea Man," 8.
47. Peter Crosby, *Three Cheers for the Red, Red, and Red* (McLean, Va.: Freedom Press, 1936), 458.
48. Blair Bolles, "Prose and Politics: Writers in the New Deal," *Saturday Review*, March 3, 1940, 3.
49. Joseph B. Ely, *The American Dream* (Boston: B. Humphries, 1944), 172-77.
50. Frank R. Kent, *Without Grease*, 54-55, 121.
51. *Ibid.*, 142.
52. Blair Bolles, "The Sweetheart of the Regimenters," 86.
53. Daniel Fusfeld, *The Economic Thought of Franklin D. Roosevelt and the Origins of the New Deal* (New York: Columbia University Press, 1956).
54. Quoted in James M. Burns, *Roosevelt: The Lion and the Fox* (New York: Harcourt, Brace, 1956), 157.
55. Ernest K. Lindley, "War on the Brains Trust," 258.
56. J. Franklin Carter, *The New Dealers* (New York: Simon and Schuster, 1934), 87.
57. Ernest K. Lindley, "War on the Brains Trust," 258.
58. Ernest K. Lindley, *The Roosevelt Revolution: First Phase* (New York: Viking, 1933), 7.
59. Raymond Moley, *After Seven Years* (New York: Harper, 1939), 13.
60. Tugwell, "The Protagonists: Roosevelt and Hoover," *Antioch Review*, Winter, 1953-54, 432-33.
61. Ernest K. Lindley, "War on the Brains Trust," 258.
62. Tugwell, "The Progressive Orthodoxy of Franklin D. Roosevelt," *Ethics*, October, 1953, 21-22.
63. Ernest K. Lindley, "War on the Brains Trust," 259-63.
64. Raymond Moley, *After Seven Years*, 11, 95.
65. Tugwell, "The Progressive Tradition," *Atlantic Monthly*, April, 1935, 409.
66. Tugwell, "The Progressive Orthodoxy of Franklin D. Roosevelt," 4.
67. Tugwell, "The Two Great Roosevelts," *Western Political Quarterly*, March, 1952, 87.
68. Tugwell, "The Preparation of a President," *Western Political Quarterly*, June, 1948, 131, 135, 142.
69. Tugwell, *Diary*, May 21, 1933.
70. Tugwell, *Memoir*.
71. Alva Johnston, "Tugwell, the President's Idea Man," 9.
72. George M. Verity, "Appraises Prof. Tugwell," *Iron Age*, July 5, 1934, 42B.
73. Blair Bolles, "The Sweetheart of the Regimenters," 80.

74. Quoted in Russell Lord, *The Wallaces of Iowa* (Boston: Houghton Mifflin, 1947), 347.

75. Fred R. Marvin, *Fool's Gold* (New York: Madison and Marshall, 1936), 19.

76. Elizabeth Dilling, *The Roosevelt Red Record and Its Background* (Chicago: the author, 1936), 352.

77. Alva Johnston, "Tugwell, the President's Idea Man," 9.

78. Raoul Desvernine, *Democratic Despotism* (New York: Dodd, Mead, 1936), 101-02.

79. Alva Johnston, "Tugwell, the President's Idea Man," 74.

80. *Time*, March 16, 1936, 20.

81. Percy L. Crosby, *Three Cheers for the Red, Red, and Red*, 458, 460, 485.

82. Mark Sullivan, *New York Herald Tribune*, December 12, 13, 17, 18, 20, 22, 24, 28, 1933.

83. Raoul Desvernine, *Democratic Despotism*, 106.

84. *Time*, May 7, 1934, 14.

85. David Lawrence, *Stumbling into Socialism* (New York: D. Appleton-Century, 1935), 24.

86. Blair Bolles, "The Sweetheart of the Regimenters," 83.

87. Raoul Desvernine, *Democratic Despotism*, 180.

88. Frank R. Kent, *Without Grease*, 165.

89. Blair Bolles, "The Sweetheart of the Regimenters," 84.

90. Raoul Desvernine, *Democratic Despotism*, 100-01, 107.

91. David Lawrence, *Stumbling into Socialism*, 27.

92. Herbert Agar, *Land of the Free* (Boston: Houghton Mifflin, 1935), 126.

93. John T. Flynn, *The Roosevelt Myth* (New York: Devin-Adair, 1948), 224.

94. Tugwell, "The Return to Democracy," address, American Society of Newspaper Editors, April 21, 1934, in Tugwell, *The Battle for Democracy* (New York: Columbia University Press, 1935), 200.

95. 73 Congress, 2 Session, *Congressional Record*, June 12, 1934, 11156-60.

96. *Ibid.*, June 14, 1934, 11460.

97. *Ibid.*, 11453.

98. 74 Congress, 1 Session, *Congressional Record*, June 27, 1935, 10332.

99. Blair Bolles, "The Sweetheart of the Regimenters," 80-81.

100. 74 Congress, 1 Session, *Congressional Record*, June 27, 1935, 10333.

101. Tugwell, *Mr. Hoover's Economic Policy* (New York: John Day, 1932), 20.

102. David Lawrence, *Stumbling into Socialism*, 16; James C. Young, *Roosevelt Revealed*, 125.

103. Tugwell, address, Democratic State Central Committee, Los Angeles, October 28, 1935, *Resettlement Administration Press Release*, 5-6.

104. Frank R. Kent, *Without Grease*, 284.

105. Raoul Desvernine, *Democratic Despotism*, 105.

106. Garet Garrett, "National Hill Notes," *Saturday Evening Post*, May 16, 1936, 13.

107. *New York Times*, April 11, 1934.

108. James C. Young, *Roosevelt Revealed*, 145-49.

109. 73 Congress, 2 Session, *Congressional Record*, May 25, 1934, 9585-86.
110. Alva Johnston, "Tugwell, the President's Idea Man," 9.
111. Fulton Lewis, Jr., *Boston Daily Record*, August 8, 1953.
112. George N. Peek with Samuel Crowther, *Why Quit Our Own* (New York: D. Van Nostrand, 1936), 1, 107, 114, 140.
113. Gilbert C. Fite, *George N. Peek and the Fight for Farm Parity* (Norman: University of Oklahoma Press, 1954), 261-62.
114. Internal Security Subcommittee of Senate Judiciary Committee, *Report*, August 24, 1953; "The Story of Spies in Government," *United States News and World Report*, November 27, 1953, 21-22.
115. *Time*, July 6, 1936, 17.
116. Harold L. Ickes, *The Secret Diary of Harold L. Ickes: Part Two* (New York: Simon and Schuster, 1954), 34-35.
117. Frank Hughes, *Prejudice and the Press* (New York: Devin-Adair, 1950), 169-70, 426, 528.
118. Jacob Spolanski, *The Communist Trail in America* (New York: Macmillan, 1951), 187-97.
119. Tugwell, *The Stricken Land* (Garden City, N. Y.: Doubleday, 1947), 681-82.
120. Tugwell, *The Art of Politics* (Garden City, N. Y.: Doubleday, 1958), 271-73.
121. Tugwell, "The Directive," *Journal of Social Philosophy and Jurisprudence*, October, 1941, 27.
122. Tugwell, "A Planner's View of Agriculture's Future," *Journal of Farm Economics*, February, 1949, 136-37.
123. Tugwell, "The New Deal: The Decline of Government," Part II, *Western Political Quarterly*, September, 1951, 480.
124. Tugwell, "After the New Deal: 'We Have Bought Ourselves Time to Think,'" *New Republic*, July 26, 1939, 320-22.
125. Tugwell, *The Stricken Land*, 22.
126. Tugwell, "The Protagonists: Roosevelt and Hoover," passim.
127. Tugwell, "The Fourth Power," *Planning and Civic Comment*, April-June, 1939, Part II, 13n.

26. Tugwell and Communism

1. William Ebenstein, *Today's Isms* (Englewood Cliffs, N. J.: Prentice-Hall, 1958), vii.
2. Walter Lippmann, *The New Imperative* (New York: Macmillan, 1935), 4-7.
3. Peter H. Odegard, *Prologue to November, 1940* (New York: Harper, 1940), 26.
4. Gerald Winrod, *Communism and the Roosevelt Brain Trust* (Wichita, Kans.: Defender Press, 1933).
5. Drew Pearson, "Merry-Go-Round," *Boston Traveler*, March 3, 1954.
6. Gerald Winrod, *Communism and the Roosevelt Brain Trust*, 351.
7. 74 Congress, 1 Session, *Congressional Record*, June 27, 1935, 10332-33.

8. Tugwell, S. Chase and R. Dunn, eds., *Soviet Russia in the Second Decade* (New York: John Day, 1928), Chapter III.

9. Tugwell, address, Columbia Broadcasting System, July 31, 1934, *USDA Press Release*, 4.

10. Tugwell, "Communist Theory vs. Russian Fact," *New Republic*, May 16, 1928, 367.

11. Tugwell, "The Farmer and the Commissar," *Nation*, July 29, 1961, 59.

12. Russell Lord, *The Wallaces of Iowa* (Boston: Houghton Mifflin, 1947), 350-51.

13. J. Franklin Carter, *The New Dealers* (New York: Simon and Schuster, 1934), 88.

14. 73 Congress, 2 Session, *Congressional Record*, June 13, 1934, 11337.

15. "Tugwell: He Blazed a New Path in 'Dismal Science,'" *Newsweek*, April 8, 1933, 16.

16. Drew Pearson and Robert S. Allen, "Valentino of the Revolution," magazine clipping, *Tugwell Papers*.

17. James C. Young, *Roosevelt Revealed* (New York: Farrar and Rinehart, 1936), 46, 48.

18. Alva Johnston, "Tugwell, the President's Idea Man," *Saturday Evening Post*, August 1, 1936, 74.

19. Oswald G. Villard, "Issues and Men: The Communistic Brain Trust," *Nation*, April 4, 1934, 377.

20. Arthur M. Schlesinger, Jr., *The Coming of the New Deal* (Boston: Houghton Mifflin, 1958), 457-59.

21. Tugwell, *The Democratic Roosevelt* (Garden City, N. Y.: Doubleday, 1957), 323.

22. *Ibid.*, 322.

23. Tugwell, *Diary*, April 21, 1933.

24. George N. Peek with Samuel Crowther, *Why Quit Our Own* (New York: D. Van Nostrand, 1936), 108-09, 117.

25. Gilbert C. Fite, *George N. Peek and the Fight for Farm Parity* (Norman: University of Oklahoma Press, 1954), 262, 289.

26. Roger Burlingame, *Henry Ford* (New York: New American Library, 1954), 132.

27. Tugwell, *The Stricken Land* (Garden City, N. Y.: Doubleday, 1947), 23.

28. Eric F. Goldman, *Rendezvous with Destiny* (New York: Knopf, 1952); cited in C. Canby and N. Gross, eds., *The World of History* (New York: New American Library, 1954), 175.

29. Quoted in *New York Times*, August 11, 1948.

30. Will W. Alexander, *Interview, Oral History Research Office*, Columbia University, 417.

31. Ernest K. Lindley, "War on the Brains Trust," *Scribner's Magazine*, November, 1933, 264.

32. J. Franklin Carter, *The New Dealers*, 91.

33. Tugwell, "The New Deal: The Progressive Tradition," *Western Political Quarterly*, September, 1950, 405.

34. Tugwell, *Industry's Coming of Age* (New York: Harcourt, Brace, 1927), 252-53.
35. Tugwell, "The Progressive Tradition," *Atlantic Monthly*, April, 1935, 412.
36. Tugwell, "On Life as a Long-Time Enterprise," address, Dartmouth College, April 26, 1934, *USDA Press Release*, 14.
37. Tugwell, "Relief and Reconstruction," address, National Conference of Social Workers, Kansas City, Mo., May 21, 1934, in Tugwell, *The Battle for Democracy* (New York: Columbia University Press, 1935), 309, 320.
38. Tugwell, newspaper clipping, *Tugwell Papers*.
39. Tugwell, *Diary*, April 5, 1933.
40. Benjamin Stolberg, *Story of the C.I.O.* (New York: Viking, 1938), 242.
41. Tugwell, *interview with writer;* Tugwell, *Memoir*.
42. W. L. White, "Pare Lorentz," *Scribner's Magazine*, January, 1939, 9-10.
43. C. H. McCall, "That Columbia Crowd," *Credit and Financial Management*, June, 1933, 17.
44. Raymond Moley, "A Roosevelt Rhapsody," *National Review*, November 9, 1957, 427.
45. Quoted in Arthur M. Schlesinger, Jr., *The Coming of the New Deal*, 360.
46. Alva Johnston, "Tugwell, the President's Idea Man," 74.
47. Arthur M. Schlesinger, Jr., review, *The Web of Subversion*, by James Burnham, in *Saturday Review*, March 20, 1954, 16-17.
48. Tugwell, in Tugwell, S. Chase and R. Dunn, eds., *Soviet Russia in the Second Decade*, 95.
49. Tugwell, "Communist Theory vs. Russian Fact," 367.
50. Tugwell, *interview with writer;* Tugwell, *Diary*, Introduction; B. Sternsher, "The Stimson Doctrine: FDR versus Moley and Tugwell," *Pacific Historical Review*, August, 1962, 284.
51. Tugwell, *The Stricken Land*, 80, 568.
52. Tugwell, "The Directive," *Journal of Social Philosophy and Jurisprudence*, October, 1941, 35-36.
53. Tugwell, *The Stricken Land*, x-xi.
54. Tugwell, *The Art of Politics* (Garden City, N. Y.: Doubleday, 1958), 154.
55. *Ibid.*, 207, 212, 266-67.
56. Samuel Lubell, review, *The Art of Politics*, by Tugwell, in *Saturday Review*, January 3, 1959, 16.
57. Tugwell, *The Art of Politics*, 154.
58. *Ibid.*, 157.
59. *Ibid.*, 83, 267.
60. *Ibid.*, 65.
61. Tugwell, letter to the editor, *Washington Post*, April 27, 1961.
62. "The Story of Spies in Government," *United States News and World Report*, November 27, 1953, 24.
63. *United States News and World Report*, July 4, 1958, 73.
64. Hanson W. Baldwin, "Churchill Was Right," *Atlantic Monthly*, July, 1954, 26.
65. Tugwell, *The Stricken Land*, 442.

27. Tugwell and the American Tradition:
Evolution—Democracy—the Constitution

1. Tugwell, *The Industrial Discipline and the Governmental Arts* (New York: Columbia University Press, 1933), 229.
2. James G. Mitchell, "The Precocious Juvenility of the 'Brain Trust,'" *Annalist*, June 1, 1934, 849.
3. Quoted in Tugwell, "Frightened Liberals," *New Republic*, April 26, 1939, 328.
4. Tugwell, *The Industrial Discipline and the Governmental Arts*, 228.
5. Tugwell, "A Third Economy," address, Rochester (N. Y.) Teachers Association, April 9, 1935, *USDA Press Release*, 2.
6. Tugwell, "On Life as a Long-Time Enterprise," address, Dartmouth College, April 26, 1934, *USDA Press Release*, 12.
7. Tugwell, "The Future of National Planning," *New Republic*, December 9, 1936, 162.
8. Tugwell, "Variation on a Theme by Cooley," *Ethics*, July, 1949, 239-40.
9. Tugwell, "The Progressive Tradition," *Atlantic Monthly*, April, 1935.
10. Tugwell, *The Stricken Land* (Garden City, N. Y.: Doubleday, 1947), 348.
11. Tugwell, "The Progressive Orthodoxy of Franklin D. Roosevelt," *Ethics*, October, 1953, 2.
12. Tugwell, "The Compromising Roosevelt," *Western Political Quarterly*, June, 1953, 329.
13. Tugwell, *The Stricken Land*, 22.
14. Tugwell, "After the New Deal: 'We Have Bought Ourselves Time to Think,'" *New Republic*, July 26, 1939, 325.
15. Tugwell, "A Planner's View of Agriculture's Future," *Journal of Farm Economics*, February, 1949, 39.
16. Tugwell, "That Living Constitution," *New Republic*, June 20, 1928, 120.
17. Tugwell, Memorandum Prepared for Alfred E. Smith, *Tugwell Papers*.
18. Tugwell, "The Fourth Power," *Planning and Civic Comment*, Part II, April-June, 1939, 17.
19. Tugwell, "After the New Deal," 325.
20. Tugwell, "The Utility of the Future in the Present," *Public Administration Review*, Winter, 1948, 49.
21. *Ibid.*, 58.
22. Tugwell, *The Stricken Land*, 437; "The Utility of the Future in the Present," 57; "Implementing the General Interest," *Public Administration Review*, Autumn, 1940, 48-49.
23. Tugwell, "Relief and Reconstruction," address, National Conference of Social Workers, Kansas City, Mo., May 21, 1934, in Tugwell, *The Battle for Democracy* (New York: Columbia University Press, 1935), 315.
24. Tugwell, "Chameleon Words," *New Republic*, August 25, 1926, 16.
25. Tugwell, "That Living Constitution," 122.
26. Tugwell, "Farm Relief and a Permanent Agriculture," *Annals of the American Academy of Political and Social Science*, March, 1929, 277.

27. J. Franklin Carter, *Our Lords and Masters* (New York: Simon and Schuster, 1935), 286.

28. Editorial, *Nation*, November 28, 1936, 618.

29. Tugwell, address, Tompkins County Development Meeting, Ithaca, N. Y., August 7, 1935, *USDA Press Release*, 5-6.

30. George N. Peek with Samuel Crowther, *Why Quit Our Own* (New York: D. Van Nostrand, 1936), 151.

31. Tugwell, address, Niagara County Pioneer Association, Olcott Beach, N. Y., August 8, 1934, *USDA Press Release*, 6.

32. Tugwell, "National Significance of Recent Trends in Farm Population," *Social Forces*, October, 1935, 6-7.

33. Tugwell, "Changing Acres," *Current History*, September, 1936, 61-62.

34. Tugwell, Memorandum Prepared for Alfred E. Smith, *Tugwell Papers*.

35. Tugwell, "America Takes Hold of Its Destiny," *Today*, April 28, 1934, in Tugwell, *The Battle for Democracy*, 266.

36. Tugwell, "Consumers and the New Deal," address, Consumers' League of Ohio, Cleveland, May 11, 1934; in Tugwell, *The Battle for Democracy*, 273.

37. Tugwell, "America Takes Hold of Its Destiny," 261.

38. Tugwell, address, Clemson College, S. C., August 15, 1934, *USDA Press Release*, 9, 13.

39. Tugwell, "Earthbound: The Problem of Planning and Survival," *Antioch Review*, Winter, 1949-50, 486.

40. Tugwell and Joseph Dorfman, "Francis Leiber: German Scholar in America," *Columbia University Quarterly*, September and December, 1938, passim.

41. Tugwell, "The New Deal: The Rise of Business," Part I, *Western Political Quarterly*, June, 1952, 280.

42. Tugwell, *The Art of Politics* (Garden City, N. Y.: Doubleday, 1958), 139.

43. Tugwell, "Bankers' Banks," *New Republic*, December 12, 1928, 96.

44. Tugwell, "Governor or President?," *New Republic*, May 16, 1928, 382.

45. Tugwell, "On Life as a Long-Time Enterprise," 11.

46. *Ibid.*, 12-13.

47. Tugwell, "Human Nature and Social Economy," Part II, *Journal of Philosophy*, August 28, 1930, 489.

48. Tugwell, "The Place of Government in a National Land Program," address, Joint Meeting, American Economic Association, American Statistical Association, Farm Economic Association, Philadelphia, December 29, 1933, *USDA Press Release*, 17.

49. Tugwell, "Must We Draft Roosevelt?," *New Republic*, May 13, 1940, 630.

50. Tugwell, "The Preparation of a President," *Western Political Quarterly*, June, 1948, 141.

51. Tugwell, "A Fireside Symposium," *Columbia University Quarterly*, March, 1935, 34-36.

52. Tugwell, address, Democratic State Central Committee, Los Angeles, October 28, 1935, *Resettlement Administration Press Release*, 2.

53. Tugwell and E. C. Banfield, "Grass Roots Democracy—Myth or Reality?," *Public Administration Review*, Winter, 1950, 50-55.
54. *Ibid.*, 51.
55. Sumner Welles, review, *The Stricken Land*, by Tugwell, in *Saturday Review*, December 28, 1946, 9.
56. Tugwell, *The Light of Other Days* (Garden City, N. Y.: Doubleday, 1962), 83.
57. Tugwell, "The Fourth Power," 7, 19-20, 23, 27; "The Decline of Government," *Western Political Quarterly*, Part I, June, 1951, 295-300, and Part II, September, 1951, 470-79; "The New Deal: The Rise of Business," Part II, *Western Political Quarterly*, September, 1952, 484-86, 491-93; "The Directive," *Journal of Social Philosophy and Jurisprudence*, October, 1941, 24, are the sources of all references not attributed to other sources in this summary of Tugwell's constitutional ideas.
58. Tugwell, "That Living Constitution," 121.
59. Tugwell, Memorandum Prepared for Alfred E. Smith, *Tugwell Papers*.
60. Letters, M. L. Wilson to Tugwell, September 28 and October 24, 1932, *Tugwell Papers*.
61. Letter, J. S. Long to Tugwell, January 23, 1933, *Tugwell Papers*.
62. Tugwell, "Design for Government," address, Eighth Annual Meeting of the Federation of Bar Associations of Western New York, June 24, 1933, in Tugwell, *The Battle for Democracy*, 5-13.
63. Letter, D. Cavers to Tugwell, May 13, 1933, *Tugwell Papers*.
64. Tugwell, "The Great American Fraud," *American Scholar*, Winter, 1934, 92.
65. Merlo J. Pusey, *Charles Evans Hughes*, 2 vols. (New York: Macmillan, 1951), II, 707-08.
66. Tugwell, "America Takes Hold of Its Destiny," 258-60.
67. Frank R. Kent, *Without Grease* (New York: William Morrow, 1936), 165.
68. Francis P. Miller, *The Blessings of Liberty* (Chapel Hill: University of North Carolina Press, 1936), 79-81.
69. Tugwell, "Down to Earth," *Current History*, July, 1936, 37.
70. Letter, Tugwell to Roosevelt, August 26, 1937, *PPF 564 Roosevelt Papers*.
71. Tugwell, *The Democratic Roosevelt* (Garden City, N. Y.: Doubleday, 1957), 391, 414-15.
72. Tugwell, "The New Deal: The Decline of Government," Part II, 474, 479.
73. Tugwell, *The Democratic Roosevelt*, 290.
74. *Ibid.*, 395.
75. Tugwell, "A Planner's View of Agriculture's Future," 39-42.
76. Merlo J. Pusey, review, *Harlan Fiske Stone*, by A. T. Mason, in *New York Times Book Review*, November 11, 1956, 1.
77. Tugwell, *The Democratic Roosevelt*, 414.
78. Sumner Welles, review, *The Stricken Land*, by Tugwell, 9.
79. M. Morton Auerbach, *The Conservative Illusion* (New York: Columbia University Press, 1959); William Newman, *The Futilitarian Society* (New York: George Braziller, 1961).

80. Arthur W. Macmahon and John D. Millett, *Federal Administrators* (New York: Columbia University Press, 1939), 212.
81. Louis M. Hacker, *A Short History of the New Deal* (New York: F. S. Crofts, 1936), 108.
82. J. Franklin Carter, *The New Dealers*, 87-88.
83. Tugwell, "After the New Deal," 325.
84. Tugwell, "The Directive," 27-28.
85. Tugwell, "The Fourth Power," 11.
86. Stuart Chase, *Government in Business* (New York: Macmillan, 1935), 6.
87. Tugwell, "A Planner's View of Agriculture's Future," 47.
88. Tugwell, "The Fourth Power," 1-2.
89. *Ibid.*, 12.
90. Tugwell, unpublished statement, *Tugwell Papers*.
91. Tugwell, address, Democratic State Central Committee, 3.
92. Tugwell, "The Return to Democracy," address, American Society of Newspaper Editors, April 21, 1934, in Tugwell, *The Battle for Democracy*, 194.
93. J. Franklin Carter, *The New Dealers*, 87.
94. Tugwell, "A Third Economy," 8.
95. Tugwell, "America Takes Hold of Its Destiny," 265-66.
96. Arthur M. Schlesinger, Jr., "The First Hundred Days of the New Deal," in Isabel Leighton, ed., *The Aspirin Age, 1919-1941* (New York: Simon and Schuster, 1949), 286.
97. J. Franklin Carter, *The New Dealers*, 86.
98. Ernest K. Lindley, *The Roosevelt Revolution: First Phase* (New York: Viking, 1933), 327.
99. Quoted in Harry Barnard, *Independent Man: The Life of Senator James Couzens* (New York: Scribner's, 1958), 291.
100. Edward C. Kirkland, review, *Herbert Hoover and the Great Depression*, by Warren G. Harris, in *American Historical Review*, July, 1959, 977.
101. William Miller, *A History of the United States* (New York: Dell, 1958), 410.
102. Frank Freidel, *The New Deal in Historical Perspective* (Washington, D. C.: Service Center for Teachers of History, 1959), 1.
103. Walter Lippmann, *The New Imperative* (New York: Macmillan, 1935), 1-26; Dixon Wecter, *The Age of the Great Depression, 1929-1941* (New York: Macmillan, 1948), 55-56; Broadus Mitchell, *Depression Decade: From New Era to New Deal, 1929-1941* (New York: Rinehart, 1947), 404.
104. William Miller, *A History of the United States*, 411.
105. Tugwell, address, Niagara County Pioneer Association, 4.
106. Tugwell, "The New Deal: The Decline of Government," Part I, 23.
107. Quoted in Clyde Kluckhorn, *Mirror for Man* (New York: Fawcett, 1957), 197.
108. Clarence B. Randall, *The Communist Challenge to American Business* (Boston: Little, Brown, 1959).
109. Tugwell, *The Stricken Land*, 663.

28. Tugwell's Thought and America Today

1. Edwin C. Rozwenc, ed., *The New Deal: Revolution or Evolution?*," rev. ed. (Boston: D. C. Heath, 1960).
2. Mario Einaudi, *The Roosevelt Revolution* (New York: Harcourt, Brace, 1959); Carl N. Degler, *Out of Our Past* (New York: Harper, 1959), 379-416.
3. John Kenneth Galbraith, *Economics and the Art of Controversy* (New York: Vintage Books, 1959), 46.
4. Adolf A. Berle, Jr., *Power without Property* (New York: Harcourt, Brace, 1959), passim; "Marx Was Wrong and So Is Khrushchev," *New York Times Magazine*, November 1, 1959, 9, 95; "Whose Socialism?," *Reporter*, October 30, 1958, 13.
5. *Economic Affairs*, February 14, 1959, 3.
6. Tugwell, *The Art of Politics* (Garden City, N. Y.: Doubleday, 1958), 88.
7. Adolf A. Berle, Jr., "Whose Socialism?," 12.
8. John Kenneth Galbraith, *Economics and the Art of Controversy*, 54.
9. Quoted in *New York Times*, November 25, 1956.
10. Quoted in Cleveland Amory, review, in *New York Times Book Review*, November 18, 1956, 38.
11. Cabell Phillips, *New York Times*, January 13, 1957.
12. Arthur Krock, *New York Times*, September 20, 1959.
13. Walter Lippmann, column, *Rochester* (N. Y.) *Democrat and Chronicle*, October 5, 1956.
14. Joseph Spigelman, "If We Were Faced with Depression," *New York Times Magazine*, August 5, 1956, 56.
15. Edwin L. Dale, Jr., "Lessons of the 1957-58 Recession," *New York Times Magazine*, October 5, 1958, 7, 70, 72-73; Ernest Bloch, N. Y. Federal Reserve Bank, quoted in *Economic Affairs*, October 15, 1959, 4; Paul A. Baran, "The Coming Depression," *Nation*, December 21, 1957, 467-70.
16. *Newsweek*, January 9, 1961, 57.
17. Richard Rutter, *New York Times*, September 30, 1962.
18. *New York Times*, July 25, 1962.
19. Newsweek, April 17, 1961, 91.
20. *Newark* (N. J.) *Star Ledger*, September 30, 1962.
21. Leonard Silk, "What Caused the Recession?," *Challenge*, May, 1958, 10-12; Federal Reserve Bank of N. Y., *Perspective on 1960* (New York: 1961), 1-6; *Time*, March 3, 1961, 21-22.
22. Carey McWilliams, "Taps for the 1930's," *Nation*, April 7, 1956, 269.
23. Arthur F. Burns, "Some Lessons of the Recession," *Reporter*, December 11, 1958, 16-17.
24. *Time*, March 3, 1961, 21; Paul W. McCracken, W. Allen Wallis, Elmer C. Bratt, quoted in *United States News and World Report*, February 13, 1961, 60-63; Stephen W. Rousseas, "What Politicians Want—and Cannot Do," *Challenge*, October, 1960, 6-7; Federal Reserve Bank of N. Y., *Perspective on 1960*, 5; Edwin L. Dale, Jr., "Lessons of the 1957-58 Recession," 72; Paul A. Baran, "The Coming Depression," 470.

25. Adolf A. Berle, Jr., *Power without Property,* passim.

26. Tugwell, *The Art of Politics,* 239-40.

27. Walter Johnson, review, *Roosevelt: The Lion and the Fox,* by James M. Burns, in *New York Times Book Review,* August 12, 1956, 1.

28. Arthur M. Schlesinger, Jr., *The Coming of the New Deal* (Boston: Houghton Mifflin, 1959), 193-94.

29. Ernest Van Den Haag, "Galbraith, Affluence, and Democrats," *Commentary,* September, 1960, 206-14; Lewis A. Coser and Ben B. Seligman versus Ernest Van Den Haag, "Affluence," *Commentary,* January, 1961, 70-75; Leon Keyserling, "Eggheads and Politics," *New Republic,* October 27, 1958; "Galbraith and Schlesinger Reply to Leon Keyserling," *New Republic,* November 10, 1958; "Leon Keyserling on Economic Expansion," *New Republic,* November 17, 1958; Leon Keyserling, "Less for Private Spending?," *New Republic,* May 23, 1960; Leon Keyserling, "Public Weal —and Private, Too," *New York Times Magazine,* August 21, 1960; Leon Keyserling, "Investment and Consumption," *New Republic,* October 10, 1960; Henry Hazlitt, columns, *Newsweek,* February 22, 1960, June 27, 1960, July 18, 1960, November 7 and 14, 1960, October 9, 1961; "That 'Starved' Public Sector," editorial, *Fortune,* August, 1960; Francis M. Bator, *The Question of Government Spending* (New York: Harper, 1960); Henry C. Wallich, "'Private versus Public': Could Kenneth Galbraith Be Wrong?," *Harper's Magazine,* October, 1961.

30. John K. Jessup, "A Noble Framework for a Great Debate," in Oscar Handlin, ed., *The National Purpose* (New York: Holt, Rinehart and Winston, 1960), 2-3, 18-19.

31. Henry Hazlitt, "The New Collectivism," *Newsweek,* July 18, 1960, 75.

32. Charles Darlington, "Not the Goal, Only the Means," *New York Times Magazine,* July 3, 1960, 25.

33. Michael Polyani, *The Logic of Liberty* (Chicago: University of Chicago Press, 1951), passim.

34. Milton Friedman, *Capitalism and Freedom* (Chicago: University of Chicago Press, 1962); Henry Hazlitt, "The New Collectivism"; Henry C. Wallich, *The Cost of Freedom: A New Look at Capitalism* (New York: Harper, 1960); John Chamberlain, *The Roots of Capitalism* (Princeton, N. J.: D. Van Nostrand, 1959); Friedrich Hayek, *The Road to Serfdom* (Chicago: University of Chicago Press, 1944); Ludwig von Mises, *The Anti-Capitalist Mentality* (Princeton, N. J.: D. Van Nostrand, 1956).

35. Quoted in Walter Lippmann, "President's Messages Betray Dangerous Complacency," *Rochester* (N. Y.) *Democrat and Chronicle,* January 22, 1960.

36. "How to Be Bold and Imaginative," editorial, *Nation's Business,* February, 1961, 98.

37. Walter Lippmann, "President's Messages Betray Dangerous Complacency"; "Consumer Spending Not Highest U. S. Goal," *Rochester* (N. Y.) *Democrat and Chronicle,* January 18, 1961.

38. Charles Darlington, "Not the Goal, Only the Means," 5.

39. R. L. Bruckberger, *Image of America* (New York: Viking, 1959), 156-58.

40. Adolf A. Berle, Jr., "Why Our Economy Must Grow Faster," *New York Times Magazine*, February 7, 1960, 18, 72-74.
41. John Kenneth Galbraith, letter to the editor, *New York Times*, August 3, 1960.
42. Henry Hazlitt, "The New Collectivism," 75.
43. W. Allen Wallis, "Economic Growth: What, Why, How," *White House Press Release*, June 8, 1960, 7.
44. Henry Hazlitt, "Affluent Government," *Newsweek*, June 27, 1960, 89.
45. "That 'Starved' Public Sector," 87-88, 90.
46. Francis M. Bator, *The Question of Government Spending*, passim.
47. Barry Goldwater, "A Conservative Sets Out His Credo," *New York Times Magazine*, July 31, 1960, 16, 18, 20-21; "How to Win in '60: No Molly-coddling," *Newsweek*, August 1, 1960, 19; *The Conscience of a Conservative* (New York: Hillman Books, 1960).
48. Clinton Rossiter, letter to the editor, *Time*, March 31, 1961, 2.
49. Clinton Rossiter, "Toward an American Conservatism," *Yale Review*, March, 1955, 353-72.
50. Barry Goldwater, *The Conscience of a Conservative*, 23.
51. Russell Kirk, "Conservative versus Liberal: A Debate," *New York Times Magazine*, March 4, 1956, 64.
52. Barry Goldwater and Eugene McCarthy, "Does Big Federal Government Threaten Our Freedom?," Face the Nation, CBS Television, *transcript*, 12.
53. Edward C. Kirkland, "The Robber Barons Revisited," *American Historical Review*, October, 1960, 68-73.
54. Sidney Hook, letter to the editor, *New York Times Magazine*, December 11, 1960, 4.
55. Walt W. Rostow, *The Stages of Economic Growth: A Non-Communist Manifesto* (Cambridge: At the University Press, 1960), passim.
56. Henry C. Wallich, *The Cost of Freedom*, passim.
57. James M. Burns, *Roosevelt: The Lion and the Fox* (New York: Harcourt, Brace, 1956), 335-36; Arthur Smithies, "What Government Can and Cannot Do," *Challenge*, March, 1961, 35.
58. Robert L. Heilbroner, *The Making of Economic Society* (Englewood Cliffs, N. J.: Prentice-Hall, 1962), 167.
59. Graham Hutton, "Does Maturity Bring Stagnation," *Challenge*, October, 1962, 6-9.
60. Editorials, *Rochester* (N. Y.) *Democrat and Chronicle*, February 12 and 28, 1961.
61. Robert Theobald, letter to the editor, *New York Times*, April 17, 1961.
62. James Tobin, "Growth through Taxation," *New Republic*, July 25, 1960, 15-18.
63. Oscar Gass, "Growth! Growth! Growth!," *New Republic*, November 7, 1960, 21-23.
64. Leon Keyserling, "Less for Private Spending?," "Public Weal—and Private, Too," "Investment and Consumption."
65. *New York Times*, July 22, 1962.
66. Quoted in *ibid*.

67. *New York Times,* June 5, June 22, July 14, 1962.
68. Sam Dawson, column, *Newark* (N. J.) *Evening News,* June 15, 1962; Doris Fleeson, column, *ibid.,* July 17, 1962; Marquis Childs, columns, *ibid.,* October 1 and 2, 1962; Thomas Wilson, "National Planning in a Free Economy," *Challenge,* July, 1962, 31; Graham Hutton, "Does Maturity Mean Stagnation?," *Challenge,* October, 1962, 6-7.
69. Sam Dawson, column, June 15, 1962.
70. Marquis Childs, column, October 2, 1962.
71. Quoted in *Life,* April 7, 1961, 134.
72. Friedrich Hayek, *The Road to Serfdom,* x.
73. William R. Allen, "Thoughts on Economic Growth: The Full and Efficient Use of Resources," *New Republic,* June 6, 1960, 13-16.
74. Robert L. Heilbroner, "The Future in America: II. Dilemma of Abundance," *Reporter,* January 21, 1960, 29-31.
75. *Ibid.,* 32.
76. Bert J. Loewenberg, *Darwinism: Reaction or Reform?* (New York: Rinehart, 1957), 5.
77. Barry Goldwater, *The Conscience of a Conservative,* 13.
78. Charles Frankel, "Definition of a True Egghead," *New York Times Magazine,* October 21, 1956, 58, 60.
79. Merle Curti, *American Paradox: The Conflict between Thought and Action* (New Brunswick, N. J.: Rutgers University Press, 1956).
80. Richard Crossman, Introduction, *The God That Failed* (New York: Bantam Books, 1952), 3.
81. Adolf A. Berle, Jr., "The Problems Overlap," *Reporter,* May 31, 1956, 15.
82. Robert L. Heilbroner, *The Worldly Philosophers* (New York: Simon and Schuster, 1953), 198.
83. Cabell Phillips, review, *A Chronicle of Jeopardy, 1945-55,* by Tugwell, in *New York Times Book Review,* August 14, 1955, 3.
84. Adolf A. Berle, Jr., "Case for the Professor in Washington," *New York Times Magazine,* February 5, 1961, 17, 84, 86-87.
85. Quoted in Gerald W. Johnson, "Return Flight," *New Republic,* January 30, 1961, 10.
86. Loren Baritz, "The Lonely Intellectual," *Nation,* January 21, 1961, 50-52.
87. Harvard University, *The President's Report, 1959-60,* 4.
88. Quoted in *Look,* January 5, 1960, 5.
89. John P. Sisk, "Conservatism on Campus," *Commonweal,* January 27, 1961, 451-54; Peter Schrag, "Stirrings on Campus," *New Republic,* April 17, 1961, 9-11.
90. Stephen Rousseas, "What Politicians Want—and Cannot Do," passim.
91. Robert L. Heilbroner, "The Future in America: I. The Price of Growth," *Reporter,* January 7, 1960, 29-33; *The Future as History* (New York: Grove Press, 1962), 143, 145, 148, 168, 177, 188.
92. *New York Times,* July 22, 1962.
93. Quoted in Doris Fleeson, column, *Newark* (N. J.) *Evening News,* August 21, 1962.

94. Charles Frankel, *The Case for Modern Man* (Boston: Beacon Press, 1959), 2.
95. Tugwell, *The Democratic Roosevelt* (Garden City, N. Y.: Doubleday, 1957), 11.
96. Quoted in *New York Times,* July 22, 1962.
97. Tugwell, *The Light of Other Days* (Garden City, N. Y.: Doubleday, 1962), 94.

Index

Abbreviations of New Deal Alphabetical Agencies, 425
Abt, John, 354
Acheson, Dean, 6
Adams, Henry, *The Degradation of the Democratic Dogma*, 102
Advance Ratio Price Plan, R. G. Tugwell, 176, 181-82, 385
Advertising, R. G. Tugwell, 24, 115, 249; Pure Food and Drug Act, 224, 244
Affluent Society, The, John K. Galbraith, 401
After Seven Years, R. G. Tugwell, 42, 345
Agar, Herbert, 350
Age of Reform, The, Richard Hofstadter, 372
Agricultural Adjustment Administration (AAA) trade, 52; George E. Peek, 86, 194-95; reactionaries, 115; McNary-Haugen Bill, 172; Domestic Allotment Plan, 183; Democratic Party, 183; R. G. Tugwell, 183 ff., 193 ff.; Communism, 205, 363; national economy, 378; Supreme Court, 386
Agricultural Advisory Committee, Henry Morgenthau, Jr., 86; R. G. Tugwell, 144
Agricultural Marketing Act, 188
Agricultural Reform in the United States, John D. Black, 174
Agriculture, R. G. Tugwell, 5, 9, 23, 39, 46, 87, 107, 146, 208 ff., 281; Herbert Hoover, 19, 35-36; F. D. Roosevelt, 41, 43, 86, 183, 209, 213, 220, 258, 260, 267; "Topeka Address," 46; trade, 53, 180; Thomas Amendment, 62; price controls, 97; relief, 149; national economy, 152; National Recovery Administration, 163; tariff, 170, 175, 182; Domestic Allotment Plan, 170, 178; Advance Ratio Price Plan, 177, 181; Agricultural Adjustment Act, 183; M. L. Wilson, 184; New Deal, 193; controversy in, 199; Conservation, 212, 260, 264; Resettlement Administration, 266, 296; migrant workers, 305; Soviet Union, 360-61; depression, 374
Agriculture, Department of, Henry Wallace, 87 ff.; R. G. Tugwell, 88, 91, 251; inefficiency of, 87 ff.
Alexander, Will W., Resettlement Administration, 265, 269, 277, 294, 303; Rosenwald Fund, 266; press, 292-93; greenbelt towns, 301-02; R. G. Tugwell, 324-25, 331
Alexandria Conference, 380
Allen, Frederick L., 233
Allen, Robert S., R. G. Tugwell, 237, 362
Allen, William R., 408
Allotment Plan. *See* Domestic-Allotment Plan
Alsop, John, 343
American Economic Association, R. G. Tugwell, 10
American Economic Life and the Means of Its Improvement, R. G. Tugwell, 351
American Federation of Labor, 19

American Forestry Association, 212

American Historical Review, The, Resettlement Administration, 304

American Individualism, Herbert Hoover, 30

American Molasses Company, R. G. Tugwell, 322-23

American Scholar, 299

American University Union in Paris, R. G. Tugwell, 6

Anderson, Sherwood, 237

Annals of the American Academy of Political and Social Service, R. G. Tugwell, 10, 174-75, 179, 298

Anti-trustbusting, R. G. Tugwell, 93, 105, 196-97; taxation, 115; big business, 140, 154, 166, 310, 392; Sherman Anti-trust Law, 383

Anti-trust laws, big business, 18-19; Herbert Hoover, 29; R. G. Tugwell, 93; Sherman Anti-trust Law, 383

Appleby, Paul, agriculture, 198, 266; R. G. Tugwell, 235, 332

Arnold, Thurman, trustbusting, 132, New Deal, 343

Art of Politics, The, R. G. Tugwell, 84, 123, 326, 355, 376, 400

Atlantic Monthly, 299

Atomic bomb, 329

Atomism, James M. Burns, 111; Louis D. Brandeis, 151; progressivism, 310; Thomas Cocoran, 325; R. G. Tugwell, 325. *See also* anti-trustbusting.

Auerbach, M. Morton, 389

Bacon, Gasper, 235

Bailey, Josiah, R. G. Tugwell, 257, 361

Baker, Newton D., 411

Balancing the Farm Output, W. J. Spillman, 173

Baldwin, Calvin B., Agriculture, 198; Farm Security Administration, 269, 304

Baltimore Sun, 312

Bankhead-Jones Farm Tenant Act, land utilization, 303-04

Bankhead, John, 258

Bankhead, William B., Bankhead-Jones Farm Tenant Act, 303-04

Banking, public welfare, 23-24, 124-25, 377; depression, 31, 252; Herbert Hoover, 33-34, 62, 65; loans, 36; Export-Import Banks, 54; gold standard, 55; collapse of, 56, 64, 73; debts, 57; reflation, 60; Bernard Baruch, 61; Detroit Clearing House, 64; David Lawrence, 89; government, 97, 130, 138; progressivism, 109; R. G. Tugwell, 136, 314-15; farmers, 271, 292, 304; Resettlement Administration, 283; Congress, 291; H. Parker Willis, 309; international currency, 311; Civil Service, 407. *See also* Monetary Affairs

Banking Act, New Deal, 129; R. G. Tugwell, 133

Barbour, Warren W., R. G. Tugwell, 259, 302

Barry, Richard, 192

Bartlett, F. B., 210

Baruch, Bernard, Campaign of 1932, 42; Hugh Johnson, 45, 156; "sound money," 61; F. D. Roosevelt, 114, 117, 121, 124; Margaret Coit, 116; Alfred E. Smith, 116; Supreme Court of Industry, 116; Agricultural Adjustment Administration, 163; War Industries Board, 172; Farm Recovery program, 189, 194; George Peek, 198

Barzun, Jacques, R. G. Tugwell, 7, 332

Bator, Francis M., 404

Battle for Democracy, The, R. G. Tugwell, 312

Bean, Louis, R. G. Tugwell, 148, 198

Beard, Charles A., 380

Belair, Felix, 321

Bell, Daniel W., 134, 281

Bennett, Hugh H., 217-18

Berle, Adolf A., Jr., Brain Trust, 10, 48, 156, 228; R. G. Tugwell, 41, 138, 228, 257, 317, 369; Hugh Johnson, 45; agriculture, 46, 269; F. D. Roosevelt, 47, 124; New Deal, 124; press, 237, 245; Columbia University, 257; *Property Without Power,* 390; socialism, 390; national economy, 396, 400, 403; Republican Party, 397; government, 409

Beuhler, A. G., 316

Beveridge, Albert J., 265

Big Business, government, 17, 27, 69, 85, 90, 93, 95, 374; anti-trustbusting, 18, 140, 154, 166, 310, 392; "confidence," 28, 123; capitalism, 165; Constitution, 380

Bill of Rights, 382

Biology, 104

Black, Hugo, capitalism, 99; R. G. Tugwell, 253, 256, 258

Black, John D., thirty hour week, 160; Domestic-Allotment Plan, 173-74; *Agricultural Reform in the United States,* 174; tariff, 182; agricultural economist, 300

Blanton, Thomas L., 238

Block, Paul, F. D. Roosevelt, 227; R. G. Tugwell, 233, 236

Blum, John M., 319

Blue Eagle, Re-employment Agreement, 161; failure of, 167. *See also* National Industrial Recovery Act

Bolles, Blair, Henry Wallace, 88; press, 280, 338; R. G. Tugwell, 329, 337, 339-40, 347, 349, 351, 362

Books by R. G. Tugwell. *See* page 413 ff.

Boone, Beauregard, 241

Borah, William E., 309

Brand, Charles, Agricultural Adjustment Administration, 192; George Peek, 198, 201

Brandeis, Louis, progressivism, 114-15, 121; Brain Trust, 125; F. D. Roosevelt, 128-29, 325, 335; Atomism, 151; decentralization, 308

Brain Trust, history of, 10, 39, 41, 43, 48, 372; Adolph A. Berle, Jr., 10, 48, 156, 228; R. G. Tugwell, 27, 38 ff., 86 ff., 143, 243; Hugh Johnson, 45; monetary policies of, 90, 124-25, 138; Second New Deal, 128; "concert of interest," 157; NIRA, 159; agriculture, 184; F. D. Roosevelt, 39, 48, 227, 345, 409; David Lawrence, 340; New Deal, 343

Bromfield, Louis, 222

Browder, Earl, *Daily Worker,* 352; Communism, 366

Brownlow, Louis, New Deal, 148; Resettlement Administration, 282, 302

Bruckberger, R. L., 403

Brunner, Edmund, 294

Brunner, Felix, 290-91

Bryan, William Jennings, progressivisim, 131, 371; democracy, 371

Buffalo Courier, R. G. Tugwell, 4

Buel, Walker S., 340-42

Bulwinkle, Alfred L., 353

Burlingame, Roger, 363

Burnham, James, *The Web of Subversion,* 366; *The Managerial Revolution,* 390

Burns, James M., depression, 84; atomism, 111; conservatism, 117; R. G. Tugwell, 119-20; F. D. Roosevelt, 121

Business Week, R. G. Tugwell, 279; Resettlement Administration, 283, 301

Butler, Nicholas Murray, R. G. Tugwell, 7, 328, 338, 409; F. D. Roosevelt, 121

Butler, Ovid, American Forestry Association, 212; employment, 214

Byrd, Harry F., national economy, 134; laissez faire, 253; agriculture, 258, 304; radicalism, 259, 260; Resettlement Administration, 294

Byrnes, James F., Brain Trust, 44; F. D. Roosevelt, 46; farm organizations, 186, 210; R. G. Tugwell, 253

Cabinet, F. D. Roosevelt, 128, 342; R. G. Tugwell, 190, 307; Harold Ickes, 254

Campaign of 1928, R. G. Tugwell, 8; Herbert Hoover, 8, 26; Alfred E. Smith, 8, 26, 116, 174

Campaign of 1932, Bernard Baruch, 42; F. D. Roosevelt, 59 ff.; R. G. Tugwell, 314, 320

Campaign of 1936, Republican Party, 271; F. D. Roosevelt, 321, 348, 352; R. G. Tugwell, 349

Campbell, Walter G., pesticides, 225; Food and Drug Administration, 232

Capitalism, Herbert Hoover, 30; R. G. Tugwell, 91-92, 143, 147, 229, 297, 324; Hugo Black, 99; democracy, 102, 105, 397; progressivism, 109; big business, 165; static interpretation of, 374; Europe, 406

Cardozo, Benjamin, 111

Carey, Henry C., 403

Carey, Robert D., 290

Carman, Harry J., 239

Carr, C. H., *Soviet Impact on the Western World,* 394

Carter, John F., equalization, 202; R. G. Tugwell, 300, 334, 344, 361, 364; depression, 344; collectivism, 391-92

Castro, Fidel, 400

Cavers, David F., Food and Drug Bill, 225, 230; legislation, 386

Chamberlain, Edward, 22

Chamberlain, John, R. G. Tugwell, 208; free enterprise, 402

Chambers, Whittaker, 369

Chapman, Oscar, 268

Chase, Stuart, Soviet Union, 9; M. S. Eccles, 133; New Deal, 193; Food and Drug Bill, 231; Resettlement Administration, 296; subversion, 359; industrial revolution, 390

Cheap money, 61

Chicago Convention of 1932, 42

Chicago, University of, R. G. Tugwell, 6, 117, 335, 359

Childs, Marquis, Resettlement Administration, 283; politics, 407; France, 409

Chronicle of Jeopardy, A, R. G. Tugwell, 329

Civil liberties, Fifth Amendment, 382, 385; Fourteenth Amendment, 382

Civil Liberties Union, 9

Civil Service, R. G. Tugwell, 209, 400; Resettlement Administration, 288, 291; Banking, 407; France, 409

Civil Works Administration, 308

Civilian Conservation Corps, F. D. Roosevelt, 214; Congress, 215, 245

Clark, Bennett Champ, 249, 258

Clark, John, 17

Classical economists, 23

Clemson College, R. G. Tugwell, 376

Cleveland, Grover, 371

Cobb, Cully, *Kiplinger Farm Letter*, 87

Cochran, Thomas C., 405

Cohen, Benjamin, progressivism, 114; Second New Deal, 128; F. D. Roosevelt, 238; atomism, 325; Brain Trust, 392

Coit, Margaret, 116

Cold War, F. D. Roosevelt, 368; Soviet Union, 368, 370; national economy, 410-11

Collective bargaining, 156

Collectivism, New Deal, 109-10, 127, 130; F. D. Roosevelt, 111, 117, 327; George Peek, 116; R. G. Tugwell, 139, 245, 257, 351, 353, 366, 389, 390, 400; Adolph Berle, 151; Soviet Union, 257; progressivism, 310; John F. Carter, 391; government, 404. *See also* holism

Collier's Magazine, 234

Collins, Henry, 354

Columbia University, R. G. Tugwell, 6, 7, 230, 266, 280, 309, 321, 323; Brain Trust, 39; Adolph A. Berle, Jr., 257; Donald Henderson, 365

Commerce, Department of, 28

Commerce Clause, 380

Committee for the Nation, R. G. Tugwell, 60; James H. Rand, Jr., 76; William Wirt, 362

"Common Man," R. G. Tugwell, 323

Common Sense, 314

Communications Act, 127

Communism, Agricultural Adjustment Administration, 205-06, 363; R. G. Tugwell, 228, 236, 241, 347, 355 ff.; Soviet Union, 258; New Deal, 347, 366-67; John Abt, 354; American society, 358-59; Earl Browder, 366; Puerto Rico, 367; dialectical materialism, 372

Communism and the Roosevelt Brain Trust, Clarence B. Randall, 394

Communist Challenge to American Business, The, Clarence B. Randall, 394

"Concert of Interests," F. D. Roosevelt, 108, 151, 157; R. G. Tugwell, 378

Confidence, Herbert Hoover, 28; big business, 28, 123

Congress, inflation, 62, 291; Lame Duck session, 88, 190; R. G. Tugwell, 117, 349, 378; New Deal, 132; chaos in, 144; National Industrial Recovery Act, 158; McNary-Haugen Bill, 172; Civilian Conservation Corps, 215, 245; investigations, 288; Resettlement Administration, 325; legislation, 385

Congressional Committees, 358

Congressional Record, 353

Conkin, Paul K., *Tomorrow a New World*, 265; subsistence homesteads, 267, 275; Resettlement Administration, 269, 282-83, 291 ff.; greenbelt towns, 270, 284, 288; R. G. Tugwell, 301-02.

Conservation, R. G. Tugwell, 10, 88, 175, 205, 208 ff., 260, 375; F. D. Roosevelt, 113, 213, 220, 267; agriculture, 212, 260, 264; Soil Conservation Service, 217; Resettlement Administration, 262, 268, 287; Soil Erosion Service, 264

Conservatism, American Society, 358, 408; Morton N. Auerbach, 389; explanation of, 389

Constitution, R. G. Tugwell, 260, 347 ff., 357, 395; F. D. Roosevelt, 339; big business, 380-81; laissez faire, 384; legislation, 384, 386; Supreme Court, 388

Constitutional Convention, 380, 386

Consumers' Advisory Board, 160

Control From the Top, Francis Neilson, 279

Cooke, Morris L., Rural Electrification Administration, 28; New Deal, 148; Great Plains Drought Area Committee, 220; Friends of the Land, 222

Cooley, Harold, 304

Coolidge, Calvin, tariff, 26; administration, 32-33; debts, 55; R. G. Tugwell, 145; farm problems, 192

Copeland, Royal S., 225, 249

Corcoran, Thomas, progressivism, 114; New Deal, 116, 128, 247; atomism, 325; R. G. Tugwell, 354; Brain Trust, 392

Corey, Lewis, 165

Coss, John, R. G. Tugwell, 7, 266

Costigan, Edward, public works, 164; R. G. Tugwell, 257; progressivism, 309

Coughlin, Charles, demagogue, 118; R. G. Tugwell, 248

Couzens, James, 392

Credit and Financial Management, C. H. McCall, 341, 366

Credit systems, 23-24

Croly, Herbert, 8

Cromwell, Oliver, 362

Crosby, Percy L., subversives, 348; *Three Cheers for the Red, Red and Red*, 359

Crossman, Richard, 409

Crowther, Samuel, *Why Quit Our Own*, 352, 363

Cuba, R. G. Tugwell, 211; Soviet Union, 369

Cummings, Homer, banking, 64; Hugh Johnson, 164; agriculture, 190; F. D. Roosevelt, 258; legislature, 387

Current Biography, R. G. Tugwell, 342

Current History, R. G. Tugwell, 26; submarginal land, 299

Curti, Merle, 409

Cutler, A. T., 26

Cutting, Bronson, Agricultural Adjustment Administration, 258; Will Alexander, 266; progressivism, 309; New Deal, 311

Dailey, Joseph L., 269

Daily Worker, 352

Dale, Edwin L., Jr., 401

Darlington, Charles, 402

Darrow, Clarence, 127, 161, 167, 311

Dartmouth College, R. G. Tugwell, 147, 251, 333, 365; New Deal, 261; democracy, 377

David, Charles, Agricultural Adjustment Administration, 192; production controls, 201

Davis, Chester C., New Deal, 148; foreign trade, 181; R. G. Tugwell, 189; George Peek, 198, 203, 205; Jerome Frank, 206

Davis, Forrest, 340

Debt Commission, Raymond Moley, 58; gold standard, 62

Debts, Coolidge administration, 55; inflation, 59; gold standard, 62; farmers, 185, 271

Deflation, lame-duck interregnum, 59; gold standard, 70, 314; National Industrial Recovery Act, 168

Degler, Carl N., 396

Degradation of the Democratic Dogma, The, Henry Adams, 102

Delano, Frederick, 148

Delta Upsilon Fraternity, R. G. Tugwell, 5

Derby, Roger A., 272

Democratic Despotism, Raoul Desvernine, 105, 348

Democracy, capitalism, 102, 105, 397; R. G. Tugwell, 329, 338, 370 ff.; totalitarianism, 358; Thomas Jefferson, 375; education, 376-77; laissez faire, 385

Democratic Party, R. G. Tugwell, 8, 89, 288, 347; inflation, 68; Agricultural Adjustment Administration, 183; F. D. Roosevelt, 309; farmers, 352; Republicans, 356

Democratic Roosevelt, The, R. G. Tugwell, 27, 30, 37, 40, 44, 46, 48, 55, 57, 63, 73, 75, 123, 126, 135, 138, 148, 154, 156, 162, 165-66, 169, 172, 193, 195, 244, 247, 305, 309, 311, 313, 326-27, 371

Depression, R. G. Tugwell, 10 ff.; *Fortune* Magazine, 20; F. D. Roosevelt, 20, 43, 51, 72; monetary policy, 31, 252; Herbert Hoover, 32, 68, 72, 76, 143, 328; Adolph A. Berle, Jr., 51, 396; internationalism, 53; World War I, 55; theory of, 48, 82, 373, 396; lame-duck interregnum, 59; James M. Burns, 84; public works, 137; rural poverty, 306; taxes, 316; John F. Carter, 344; agriculture, 374; New Deal, 405

Desvernine, Raoul, *Democratic Despotism*, 105, 348; R. G. Tugwell, 349, 352

Determinism, Communism, 372; religion, 408

Detroit Clearing House, The, 64

Dewey, John, social experiences, 6; education, 8; pragmatism, 15; optimism, 16; techniques of planning, 391

Dialectical materialism, 372. *See also* Soviet Union

Dickinson, John, Department of Commerce, 157; Wagner-Dickinson Act, 158

Dickinson, Lester J., R. G. Tugwell, 258, 337; Constitution, 349

Dictatorships, totalitarianism, 357; Soviet Union, 360

Dilling, Elizabeth, 347-48, 359

Dirksen, Everett M., 304

Disarmament, R. G. Tugwell, 334; national economy, 410

"Discourses in Depression," R. G. Tugwell, 31, 36-37, 40

Doctrinaire socialism, R. G. Tugwell, 9, 100, 105, 229

Dodd, William E., agriculture, 174; R. G. Tugwell, 235

Domestic-Allotment Plan, M. L. Wilson, 46, 87, 184; agriculture, 170, 178, 183; McNary-Haugen Bill, 181; George Peek, 188, 193; constitutionality of, 385

Dorfman, Joseph, R. G. Tugwell, 7

Douglas, Lewis, Director of Budget, 134, 158; Hugh Johnson, 164; agriculture, 190, 210; land program, 264; Public Works Administration, 307-08

Douglas, Paul, 9

Drucker, Peter F., 396

Duffy, Francis R., 346

Dunn, Robert, 9

Dust Bowl, Resettlement Administration, 296; Pare Lorentz, 366

Ebenstein, William, 357

Eccles, Marriner S., banking, 75; recession, 97; public works, 133 ff.; national economy, 410

Economic Conference, 56-57

Economic Planning, R. G. Tugwell, 91 ff., 357, 364; Soviet Russia, 359-60; F. D. Roosevelt, 400; national economy, 410

Economic Security Committee, R. G. Tugwell, 307; Frances Perkins, 308

Economic Thought of Franklin D. Roosevelt and the Origin of the New Deal, Daniel Fusfeld, 344

Economy Act, F. D. Roosevelt, 124-25, Public works, 134

Education, R. G. Tugwell, 4 ff., 143, 230, 250, 260, 279, 301, 320, 328, 330, 337-38; John Dewey, 8; Alfred E. Smith, 8; Resettlement Administration, 266; F. D. Roosevelt, 344, 378; reform, 373; democracy, 376, 401, 411

Edwards, P. C., 227

Einaudi, Mario, F. D. Roosevelt, 82; *The Roosevelt Revolution,* 396

Eisenhower, Dwight D., 398

Ely, Joseph B., R. G. Tugwell, 321, 343

Embree, Edwin, 266

Emergency Banking Act, 62, 124-25

Emergency Relief Act, Resettlement Administration, 265, 274; Works Program Administration, 278. *See also* Relief

Employment, Civil Works Administration, 308; New Deal, 405; Public works, 406. *See also* Unemployment
England. *See* Great Britain
Equality for Agriculture, George Peek, 172
Essary, J. Fred, R. G. Tugwell, 237
Europe, relief, 34; economy, 75; recession, 77; socialism, 407; monetary policies, 408
Experimentalism, Scott Nearing, 5; R. G. Tugwell, 242, 401; F. D. Roosevelt, 401
Ezekiel, Mordecai, New Deal, 148; Federal Farm Bureau, 173; agriculture, 184, 186; Farm programs, 188-89; Agricultural Adjustment Administration Act, 192, 198, 219; capitalism, 236; R. G. Tugwell, 300

Fair Labor Standards Act, R. G. Tugwell, 131; National Industrial Recovery Act, 156
Fair Deal, 398
Falke, Grace, Resettlement Administration, 282; wife of R. G. Tugwell, 325
Farley, James A., F. D. Roosevelt, 43, 236, 238; agriculture, 190; Jerome Frank, 198; politician, 232, 280; R. G. Tugwell, 235, 240, 254, 293, 300, 325, 334, 339
Farm Bureau Federation, Edward O'Neal, 198, 264; Resettlement Administration, 304
Farm Credit Administration, Henry Morgenthau, Jr., 87; Resettlement Administration, 265, 271-72
Farm Management, Office of, R. G. Tugwell, 171
Farm Marketing Act, M. L. Wilson, 185
Farm problems, R. G. Tugwell, 107, 170 ff., 281, 302; McNary-Haugen Act, 172; Advance Ratio Price Plan, 178; tariff, 181-82; Dust Bowl, 220; Migrant workers, 305; Resettlement Administration, 375; Clemson College, 376; Stanley Reed, 385
Farm Program, F. D. Roosevelt, 41, 267; Thomas Bill, 62; George E. Peek, 86, 202; Wages, 97, 170; R. G. Tugwell, 146, 208 ff., 332, 339; Agricultural Adjustment Administration, 183, 192, 206, 262; Domestic Allotment Plan, 184; M. L. Wilson, 188, 209; Soviet Russia, 360-61. *See also* Agriculture
Farm Security Administration, banking, 271, 292; subsistence homesteads, 274, 285, 303; Calvin D. Baldwin, 304
Farm Tenancy Committee, R. G. Tugwell, 307
Farmer's Home Corporation Act, 288, 304
Farmer's Union Act, 184
Fechner, Robert, 214
Federal Emergency Relief, 263
Federal Farm Board, 173, 179
Federal Public Housing Authority, 304
Federal Reserve Act, politicians, 31; R. G. Tugwell, 257, 297
Federal Reserve Board, 64
Federal Reserve System, Herbert Hoover, 33; R. G. Tugwell, 124, 133

Federal Trade Commission, National Industrial Recovery Act, 156; Meat
    Packers Union, 196; Pure Food and Drug Act, 226-27
Federalism, Founding Fathers, 383; Supreme Court, 387
Fertig, Lawrence, *Prosperity Through Freedom*, 402
Fess, Simon, 258
Fifth Amendment, 382, 385
Finney, Ruth, 342
Fish, Hamilton, Jr., R. G. Tugwell, 236, 348
Fisher, Irving, 309
Fite, Gilbert, George Peek, 179, 363; Domestic Allotment Plan, 184; "Farm
    Board Interlude," 188; Agricultural Adjustment Administration, 192, 200;
    collectivism, 354
"Flaws in the Hoover Economic Plan," R. G. Tugwell, 33, 35-36
Fleming, John, 312
Flynn, John T., Glass Bill, 65; banking, 73-74; depression, 83, 138; World
    War II, 83; R. G. Tugwell, 208, 323, 329, 350; totalitarianism, 357
Food and Drug Act. *See* Pure Food and Drug Act
Food Industries Advisory Board, 197
Ford, Henry, 363
Foreign Markets, R. G. Tugwell, 180, 311; progressivism, 310. *See also* Trade
Foreign Policy, Frank Freidel, 47, 393; R. G. Tugwell, 364
Forest Service, conservation, 217, 253; Resettlement Administration, 264, 268
"Forgotten Man" speech, Raymond Moley, 42; F. D. Roosevelt, 49
Fortune Magazine, 20, 77, 404
Foster, William Z., 348
Fourteenth Amendment, 382
"Fourth Power," R. G. Tugwell, 102-03, 377
Foulkes, George, 300
Fowler, F. H., 220
Fraina, Louis C., 165, 229
France, monetary policy, 57, 62, 407; agriculture, 235; unemployment, 399
Frank, Jerome, New Deal, 148, 343; National Industrial Recovery Act, 157;
    agriculture, 189, 198, 199, 200, 264, 295; Marxism, 202; Peek-Tugwell
    controversy, 203-04; Surplus Relief Corporation, 208, 210; R. G. Tugwell,
    347, 354, 363
Frankel, Charles, education, 409; democracy, 410
Franklin, Benjamin, 411
Frankfurter, Felix, R. G. Tugwell, 114, 198, 338; F. D. Roosevelt, 117, 125;
    decentralization, 308, 343
Franks, Oliver, 300
Free Enterprise, government, 93, 334, 382, 391, 408; R. G. Tugwell, 350;
    Charles Darlington, 403; Barry Goldwater, 405
Freedom of speech, R. G. Tugwell, 334
French Revolution, 12
Freidel, Frank, 47, 393
Friedman, Milton, 402
Friends of the Land, R. G. Tugwell, 222

Fuller, Melville W., 383
Fusfeld, Daniel, New Deal, 122-23; *Economic Thought of Franklin Delano Roosevelt and the Origin of the New Deal,* 344

Galbraith, John K., national economy, 140; R. G. Tugwell, 232, 250; social conscience, 386, 403; New Deal, 397; *The Affluent Society,* 401; socialism, 404
Gannett, Frank E., 233
Garner, John N., banking, 66; recovery, 76; politicians, 331
Garrett, Garet, R. G. Tugwell, 352
Gass, Oscar, 406
Gaston, Herbert E., 46
Geddes, Donald, 90
Giannini Foundation of Agricultural Economics, 46
Glass, Carter, R. G. Tugwell, 253
Glass Bill, 65
Gold buying, R. G. Tugwell, 125-26
Gold Clause Act, 129
Gold Reserve Act, 127
Gold standard, R. G. Tugwell, 31, 147, 314; Herbert Hoover, 55, 57; Great Britain, 55, 71; trade, 56; F. D. Roosevelt, 57, 61, 70, 89, 167; George W. Warren, 61, 89; Emergency Banking Act, 62; hoarding of, 67; James H. Rand, Jr., 76; New Deal, 123
Goldwater, Barry, national economy, 402; The New Conservatives, 404; free enterprise, 405; determinism, 408
Goldwin, Eric F., 122
Golub, Eugene C., economic security, 122; New Deal, 123
Gordon, Leland, J., 226
Gore, Thomas P., 289
Gosnell, Reuben, 254
Government, big business, 17, 27, 69, 85, 90, 93, 95, 374; public works, 25, 122; Hugh Johnson, 45; banking, 96; spending, 123, 406; F. D. Roosevelt, 244, 393, 396; Constitution, 260, 349; socialism, 298; intervention, 376, 386, 391
Governmental Arts, The, R. G. Tugwell, 96
Governor's Tri-State Milk Commission, R. G. Tugwell, 5
Grange, 304
Gray, Lewis C., 266, 269
Great Britain, monetary policies, 55, 57, 71, 365, 407; unemployment, 76, 399; democracy, 105; R. G. Tugwell, 235, 300, 332; Soviet Union, 368
Great Plains Drought Committee, Resettlement Administration, 272; R. G. Tugwell, 307
Greenbelt towns, R. G. Tugwell, 204; Resettlement Administration, 210, 270, 277, 301; high cost of, 284

Hacker, Louis M., R. G. Tugwell, 239, 389; New Deal, 341
Hamilton, Alexander, 381

Handler, Milton, 225

Hansen, Alvin H., 85

Harding, Warren G., government, 32, 145; National Agricultural Conference, 173

Hardy, Thomas, 332

Harlan, Byron, 330

Harriman, Henry I., capitalism, 99, 155; Boston Chamber of Commerce, 174; R. G. Tugwell, 184; agriculture, 186

Harvard University, 344

Hatfield, Henry D., 351, 353

Haugen, Gilbert N. *See* McNary-Haugen Bill

Hawkes, H. E., 339

Hayek, Friedrich, free enterprise, 402; *The Road to Serfdom*, 408

Hazlitt, Henry, individualism, 402; socialism, 403

Hearst, William R., trade, 181; agriculture, 188; R. G. Tugwell, 233, 236, 321, 330

Heilbroner, Robert L., government, 85, World War II, 406; labor, 408; press, 409; free enterprise, 410

Heller, Walter W., 406

Henderson, Donald, 365

Henderson, Leon, 250

Herbert, P. A., 214

Hewes, Lawrence, 265

Hicks, Granville, 124

Hicks, John D., 83

High, Stanley, F. D. Roosevelt, 238; R. G. Tugwell, 281

Hildebrandt, Fred H., land program, 300; rural rehabilitation, 301

Hiss, Alger, Agricultural Adjustment Administration, 204; subversives, 354

History, R. G. Tugwell, 327, 365, 391; Constitution, 380; national economy, 410

Hitler, Adolph, demagogue, 348; socialism, 350

Hobson, John A., 139

Hofstadter, Richard, F. D. Roosevelt, 121; New Deal, 328; *The Age of Reform*, 371-72

Holism, R. G. Tugwell, 138 ff., 171; progressivism, 310; Supreme Court, 387

Holman, Charles, 197

Holmes, Oliver W., Jr., Louis Brandeis, 115; Constitution, 256, 260

Home Economics, Bureau of, 51

Home Loan Banks, 36

Homesteads. *See* Subsistence Homesteads

Hook, Sidney, 405

Hoover, Calvin B., 204

Hoover, Herbert, campaign of 1928, 8, 26; American Federation of Labor, 19; "confidence" theme, 28, 85; relief, 29, 34, 85, 393; *American Individualism*, 30; economic planning, 30, 105, 151; National Credit Corporation, 31; depression, 32, 55, 145, 298, 328; Home Loan Banks, 36; Wagner-Garner Relief Bill, 36; lame duck interregnum, 51, 59 ff., 72 ff.; F. D.

Roosevelt, 51, 59 ff., 73 ff., 346; trade, 54, 154; monetary policy, 55, 57, 62, 65, 73, 83, 135; *Memoirs,* 79; individualism, 135, 166, 394; agriculture, 183, 188, 191; Jones Bill, 186; Mark Sullivan, 348; Soviet Union, 351; Europe, 358

Hoover, J. Edgar, 369

Hopkins, Harry, Chicago Convention of 1932, 32; public works, 87; F. D. Roosevelt, 117, 133; Works Progress Administration, 128, 278, 290; New Deal, 148; R. G. Tugwell, 201, 218 ff., 243, 296, 321, 327, 331; Federal Emergency Relief Administration, 266; Subsistence homesteads, 268; Allotment Advisory Committee, 307; Civil Works Administration, 308

House, Edward M., 280

Housing, 128

Howard, Roy, 130

Howe, Frederic C., Brain Trust, 39; Chicago Convention of 1932, 42; Raymond Moley, 43, 87; agriculture, 86; New Deal, 148; R. G. Tugwell, 198; progressivism, 202

Howe, Louis, F. D. Roosevelt, 214; Subsistence homesteads, 268, 285

Hughes, Charles Evans, 114

Hulbert, Judge, 385

Hull, Cordell, F. D. Roosevelt, 48, 250; trade, 52, 343; nationalism, 54; recovery, 77

Humanitarianism, F. D. Roosevelt, 124; R. G. Tugwell, 137, 139, 150, 328; New Deal, 378

"Hundred Days," F. D. Roosevelt, 137, 146, 385

Hunt, Henry, labor, 114; New Deal, 148

Hyde, Arthur M., 173

Ickes, Harold L., Henry Morgenthau, Jr., 87; R. G. Tugwell, 107, 133, 205, 209, 211, 219, 236, 243, 323, 326, 373; F. D. Roosevelt, 117, 135, 164; Works Progress Administration, 137, 239; New Deal, 134, 148, 343; conservation, 217; Securities and Exchange Commission, 218; *Diary,* 254, 321, 354; Resettlement Administration, 263, 282, 302; National Park Service, 277; politicians, 290

Individualism, concept of, 13, 92, 94, 99, 107, 389; government, 166; agriculture, 172; Herbert Hoover, 394

Industrial Discipline and the Governmental Arts, The, R. G. Tugwell, 10, 96, 145, 155, 227, 229, 301, 312, 316, 319, 340, 370

Industrial Revolution, R. G. Tugwell, 17, 390; agriculture, 171; Constitution, 349, 380; Bill of Rights, 382; government, 382

Industry's Coming of Age, R. G. Tugwell, 10, 20, 297

Ineffective Soldier, The, 305

Inflation, government, 27, 138; national economy, 59, 189; cheap money, 61, 184; Congress, 62; Committee for the Nation, 76

Intercollegiate Magazine, R. G. Tugwell, 5

Interior, Department of, land agencies, 171; Forest Service, 219, 268; M. L. Wilson, 264

Internal Revenue Service, 319
International Institute of Agriculture, R. G. Tugwell, 210
Internationalism, nationalism, 51 ff.; Debt Commission, 58; inflation, 77; R. G.
    Tugwell, 343. *See also* Foreign Trade and Foreign Policy
Institutionalism, R. G. Tugwell, 9, 11, 91 ff., 138, 147, 261, 314, 328, 392,
    395, 401, 406
Isolation, 62

Jackson, Andrew, 376
Jackson, Gardiner, 204
James, William, "Moral Equivalent for War," 21, 403; Liberal Social Darwin-
    ists, 408
Janeway, Eliot, 84
Jay, John, 410
Jefferson, Thomas, democracy, 375; laissez faire, 381
Jessup, John K., 402
Johnson, Alva, R. G. Tugwell, 247, 280, 338, 340, 343, 348; Saturday Eve-
    ning Post, 258, 285, 347; Resettlement Administration, 285, 296; William
    Wirt, 353, 362; New Deal, 366
Johnson, Hiram W., 309
Johnson, Hugh, Brain Trust, 45; agriculture, 46, 201; F. D. Roosevelt, 47, 128,
    250; progressivism, 114; Bernard Baruch, 116; Labor, 157; National In-
    dustrial Recovery Act, 159, 162; Blue Eagle, 161; R. G. Tugwell, 164,
    281, 366; *Equality for Agriculture*, 172; Pure Food and Drug Bill, 232;
    Special Industrial Recovery Board, 308; New Deal, 341
Johnson, Tom, 114
Johnson, Walter, 401
Johnson Bill, 158
Jones, Jesse, 250
Jones, Marvin, 185
Jones Bill, F. D. Roosevelt, 185; Herbert Hoover, 186; George Peek, 189
Joslin, Theodore, 64, 66, 73
Journal of Philosophy, R. G. Tugwell, 298
Journal of Social Philosophy, R. G. Tugwell, 299
Jump, William, 210

Kansas City Star, R. G. Tugwell, 261
Kazan, Alfred, 123
Kendrick, M. S., 318
Kennedy, John F., 409
Kent, Frank, Henry Wallace, 88; New Deal, 106, 331, 352; Public works,
    137; National Recovery Act, 158; R. G. Tugwell, 211, 244, 251, 259,
    281, 311, 320, 337, 340, 349, 386, 389; F. D. Roosevelt, 132, 245, 253,
    321, 343; Resettlement Administration, 280
Kerensky, Alexander, Soviet Union, 236, 352; socialism, 350

Keynes, John M. (Keynesian), R. G. Tugwell, 24, 135 ff., New Deal, 77, 135; F. D. Roosevelt, 84, 111, 129, 131, 133, 136, 343; employment, 406; national economy, 407

Keyserling, Leon H., New Deal, 110; National Recovery Act, 157; monetary policies, 406

Kieran, James M., Brain Trust, 39; F. D. Roosevelt, 42

King, Clyde, 5

Kintner, Robert, 343

Kirk, Russell, 404

Kirkland, Edward C., individualism, 99; Herbert Hoover, 393; national economy, 405

Kolb, J. H., 294

Kluckhorn, Frank, 293

Knox, Frank, R. G. Tugwell, 247; F. D. Roosevelt, 342

Kondratieff, Russian economist, 9

Kramer, Charles, 354

Kremer, J. Bruce, 232

Krock, Arthur, unemployment, 85; welfare state, 398

Khrushchev, Nikita, 398

Kyhn, Fritz, 359

Labor, wages, 97, 334; progressivism, 114; Labor Disputes Act, 127; National Labor Relations Act, 129; national economy, 142, 154, 398; Works Progress Administration, 278; National Conference to Stabilize Migrant Labor, 305; F. D. Roosevelt, 344

La Follette, Philip F., 309

La Follette, Robert M., Jr., public works, 34, 77, 134-36, 164; F. D. Roosevelt, 42, 49, 343; collectivism, 110, 130; progressivism, 114, 131, 135, 309, 327; Resettlement Administration, 301; R. G. Tugwell, 331; New Deal, 356

La Guardia, Fiorello H., 185, 309

Laissez faire, Herbert Hoover, 8, 26, 81, 376; R. G. Tugwell, 12, 229, 279, 380; national economy, 18, 80, 95, 147; big business, 22, 99, 150, 383; F. D. Roosevelt, 48; Cordell Hull, 52; democracy, 103; progressivism, 109, 139; agriculture, 176, 181, 306

Lambert, Gerard B., 397

Lame Duck Interregnum, depression, 51; national economy, 59; Roosevelt versus Hoover, 59 ff., 72 ff.; banking, 67; agriculture, 88, 173, 184, 210, 385; R. G. Tugwell, 308

Land Banks, Herbert Hoover, 33; Agricultural Adjustment Administration, 264

Land Economics, Division of, 171, 300

Land use programs, agriculture, 26, 183, 268, 282; Resettlement Administration, 262, 269, 273, 302, 375; Bankhead-Jones Farm Tenant Act, 303

Land Utilization, 183

Landon, Alfred, F. D. Roosevelt, 220; economic planning, 236

Laura Spelman Rockefeller Fund, 46

Lawrence, David, banking, 79; Brain Trust, 89, 340; Pure Food and Drug Bill, 234; R. G. Tugwell, 244, 249, 351, 394; F. D. Roosevelt, 245; New Deal, 340; *Stumbling Into Socialism*, 350; dictatorships, 357; democracy, 358

Le Hand, Margaret, 341

League for Industrial Democracy, 9

Lee, Frederick P., 185, 187, 189, 192, 199

Lemke, William, 118

Lenin, Nicolai, Marxism, 352; communism, 366; Russell Kirk, 404

Lent, G. E., 318

Lerner, Max, 89

Leuchtenburg, William E., 8

Lewis, Fulton, Jr., 353, 359

Lewis, John L., 354

Lewis, Sinclair, 358

Liberalism, Benjamin Cardoza, 111; progressivism, 115; R. G. Tugwell, 370; social conscience, 388

Liberty League, Alfred E. Smith, 236; Raoul Desvernine, 348

Light of Other Days, The, R. G. Tugwell, 329, 411

Life Magazine, 84

Lilienthal, David, Tennessee Valley Authority, 215; *TVA: Democracy on the March*, 379; social conscience, 396

Lincoln, Abraham, 376

Lindley, Ernest K., Brain Trust, 41, 89; R. G. Tugwell, 45, 220, 289, 300, 364; New Deal, 59, 392; inflation, 60; Lame Duck interregnum, 69, 186; democracy, 105; agriculture, 190, 193; Pure Food and Drug Bill, 238; Resettlement Administration, 272, 293; Works Progress Administration, 290; Wall Street, 297; greenbelt towns, 301; monetary policies, 342; F. D. Roosevelt, 344

Link, Arthur A., 83

Lippmann, Walter, *The Public Philosophy*, 102; economic planning, 357; *The New Imperative*, 393; Herbert Hoover, 394; political parties, 398; national economy, 402

Literary Digest, 232

Lodge, Henry Cabot, Jr., 398

London Economic Conference, nationalism, 54; gold standard, 62; R. G. Tugwell, 342

Long, Huey, demagogue, 118; F. D. Roosevelt, 186; agriculture, 253

Long, J. S., 385

Longworth, Alice, 331

Lord, Russell, Henry Wallace, 88, 308; Unfair Trade Practice, 197; Agricultural Adjustment Administration, 199, 263; Chester Davis, 203; R. G. Tugwell, 221, 261, 312, 328, 361; Pure Food and Drug Bill, 230; Subsistence Homesteads, 268; politicians, 330; press, 332, 339

Lorentz, Pare, 366

Lowden, Frank, 174

Lubell, Samuel, social legislation, 120; R. G. Tugwell, 368

Lubin, David, 210
Lubin, Simon J., 210

MacFadden, Bernarr, 236
MacMahon, Arthur W., R. G. Tugwell, 389
Madison, James, 381
Managerial Revolution, The, James Burnham, 390
Mann, Arthur, 371
Mann, Robert S., 237
Marshall, John, industrial revolution, 17; free enterprise, 382; commerce clause, 383; judicial review, 387
Marshall Plan, R. G. Tugwell, 364
Marvin, Fred R., 347
Marx, Karl (Marxism), dogmas of, 15, 394; totalitarianism, 98; doctrinaire socialism, 100, 236, 396; R. G. Tugwell, 105, 147, 280; Granville Hicks, 124; Jerome Frank, 202; rural Russia, 360; technological revolution, 394
Mater Magistra: Christianity and Social Progress, 404
Maverick, Maury, R. G. Tugwell, 239; Resettlement Administration, 296
McCall, C. H., *Credit and Financial Management,* 237, 341, 366
McCarthy, Joseph R., subversives, 358; demagogue, 359
McCune, Wesley, 197
McIntyre, Marvin, 293
McKellar, Kenneth, 258
McNary, Charles L. *See* McNary-Haugen Bill
McNary-Haugen Bill, Domestic Allotment Plan, 170 ff., 203; Alfred E. Smith, 174, 384; agriculture, 175, 188; Advance Ratio Price Plan, 177; Supreme Court, 178; laissez faire, 180; George Peek, 191, 198
McReynolds, James C., 115
McWilliams, Carey, 399
Mead, Elwood, 278
Means, Gardiner C., R. G. Tugwell, 51, 168; *The Modern Corporation and Private Property,* 257
Mercantilism, 381
Mellon, Andrew, 27
Memoirs of Herbert Hoover, banking, 65; New Deal, 73, 79
Meriam, Lewis, Civilian Conservation Corps, 215; public works, 285
Meyer, Eugene, 28
Michelson, Charles, 238
Michigan State Bankers Association, 64
Migrant workers, 305
Mill, John Stuart, industrial revolution, 17; laissez faire, 382
Miller, William, trade, 58; R. G. Tugwell, 138; individualism, 393; New Deal, 394
Millett, John D., 359
Mills, Frederic, 61
Mills, Ogden, Herbert Hoover, 49; gold standard, 62
Mises, Ludwig von, R. G. Tugwell, 395; free enterprise, 402

Mitchell, Broadus, 394

Mitchell, G. S., 26

Mitchell, Wesley C., 6

Moley, Raymond, Brain Trust, 10, 39, 90, 126, 144, 148; R. G. Tugwell, 40, 243, 313, 338; speeches of, 42, 46, 312; Louis Howe, 43; Hugh Johnson, 45; State Department, 45; depression, 51, 83; free trade, 52; nationalism, 54; monetary policies, 58, 61, 315, 319; Lame Duck interregnum, 59; agriculture, 86, 184, 187, 190, 202; F. D. Roosevelt, 111, 344 ff.; National Recovery Act, 114, 134, 154, 157, 162; big business, 138; press, 237; London Economic Conference, 342; collectivism, 366; Supreme Court, 386

Monetary policies, R. G. Tugwell, 107, 138, 155, 279, 314, 342; national banking system, 124; gold buying, 125; Resettlement Administration, 269, 271, 283; Congress, 291; James H. Rogers, 309; economic planning, 377, 407; government, 393, 399. *See also* Banking

Monopolies, R. G. Tugwell, 106; government, 347, 383

Monroe Doctrine, 368

Moore, R. C., 220

Moran, Edward C., Jr., 289

Morgan, Arthur E., 215

Morgan, Harcourt A., 215

Morgan, J. P., 390

Morgenthau, Henry, Jr., Agricultural Advisory Committee, 41; agriculture, 46, 86, 184, 186 ff.; recovery, 77; gold buying, 125; Cabinet, 128; recession, 135; New Deal, 148; Hugh Johnson, 164; Brain Trust, 183; taxation, 319

Moscowitz, Belle, 175

Mowry, George E., 371

Mr. Hoover's Economic Policy, R. G. Tugwell, 26, 29, 31, 34, 93, 298, 314, 328

Munoz-Marin, Luis, Puerto Rico, 367; civil servants, 400

Murphy, Frank, 358

Murphy, Louis, 255

Mussolini, Benito, press, 24; fascism, 159, 350; R. G. Tugwell, 235; demagogue, 348

Myers, William I., monetary policies, 73; New Deal, 148; agriculture, 186

Myrdal, Gunnar, public works, 406; national economy, 410; individualism, 411

Nation, The, R. G. Tugwell, 8, 10, 174, 258, 280, 323, 330; Brain Trust, 205; Pure Food and Drug Bill, 234

National Agricultural Conference, Warren G. Harding, 173; R. G. Tugwell, 174

National Agricultural Research Center, 210

National Business Survey Conference, 55

National Co-operative Milk Producers Federation, 197

National Credit Corporation, Herbert Hoover, 31, 33, 55; banking, 57

National Industrial Recovery Act, trade, 52; price fixing, 60, 154 ff.; Supreme Court, 115, 156, 386; New Deal, 138; public works, 154; Congress, 158; institutionalism, 168; Jerome Frank, 198; Resettlement Administration, 268; Robert La Follette, 311; F. D. Roosevelt, 400. *See also* Blue Eagle

National Labor Relations Act, New Deal, 129; collective bargaining, 156

National Park Service, 277
National Resources Planning Board, R. G. Tugwell, 374
National Review, The, 313
National Socialism, 350
Nationalism, versus internationalism, 51 ff.; European nations, 54; New Deal, 54, 113, 372; monetary affairs, 57; Constitution, 381; Supreme Court, 387
Nation's Business, 402
Nearing, Scott, R. G. Tugwell, 5
Neely, Matthew, 256
Negroes, 382
Neilson, Francis, *Control From the Top,* 279
Nevins, Allan, 99, 405
New Conservatives, Barry Goldwater, 404; national economy, 407, 410
New Deal, *Intercollegiate Magazine,* 5; competition, 22; Brain Trust, 39, 198; trade, 52, 387; nationalism, 54, 113, 372; production, 59; Hoover *Memoirs,* 73; recovery, 73, 82, 152, 392, 397; unemployment, 85, 405; economic planning, 91 ff.; socialism, 99; collectivism, 109, 122; philosophy of, 109 ff., 140; reactionaries, 115; progressivism, 122, 139, 355, 371; Second New Deal, 122 ff.; National Industrial Recovery Act, 139; agriculture, 193; Civilian Conservation Corps, 215; F. D. Roosevelt, 227; R. G. Tugwell, 232, 313, 337, 341, 396; Dartmouth College, 261; taxation, 319; *Time* Magazine, 323; communism, 347, 366; social conscience, 365, 378; Supreme Court, 388; individualism, 394
New Freedom, New Deal, 122; progressivism, 355
New Imperative, The, Walter Lippmann, 393
New Mexico, University of, R. G. Tugwell, 349, 386
New Nationalism, 122
New Republic, R. G. Tugwell, 7, 25, 175, 297, 313, 343; F. D. Roosevelt, 342
New York City Planning Commission, R. G. Tugwell, 102, 302, 324, 334, 374, 407
New York Stock Exchange, 30
New York *Times,* R. G. Tugwell, 283, 293, 323, 401
Newman, William, 389
Newspaper Editors, American Society of, R. G. Tugwell, 250
Newspapers. *See* Press
Newsweek, R. G. Tugwell, 174, 240, 251, 311, 313, 323, 362
Newton, Walter A., 73
Nichols, Roy F., 239
Niebuhr, Reinhold, 404
Noble, David W., 242
Norbeck, Peter, 174
Norris, George W., R. G. Tugwell, 253, 255, 258; progressivism, 309, 311; public power, 310; F. D. Roosevelt, 343
Nye, Gerald P., 309

O'Connor, Basil, F. D. Roosevelt, 39; R. G. Tugwell, 40, 144
Ogburn, William F., R. G. Tugwell, 6

Oliphant, Herman, monetary policies, 316; trustbusting, 319; New Deal, 343
O'Neal, Edward, agriculture, 186, 304; George Peek, 198
Olson, Floyd, 309
Other People's Money, Louis D. Brandeis, 115

Page, John C., 220
Palmer, Lincoln B., 234
Parker, Carleton H., R. G. Tugwell, 6
Patten, Simon Nelson, institutionalism, 5, 16; R. G. Tugwell, 5, 8, 15, 106, 364, 370; economic planning, 13, 391
Pearson, Drew, R. G. Tugwell, 237, 362
Pearson, R. A., 324
Peek, George E., Agriculture Adjustment Administration, 86, 163, 188, 353, 357, 375; R. G. Tugwell, 87, 187, 236, 362 ff.; collectivism, 116; F. D. Roosevelt, 128; New Deal, 148; Hugh Johnson, 164; *Equality for Agriculture*, 172; McNary-Haugen Bill, 178; Production controls, 179 ff.; Domestic Allotment Plan, 184, 188, 193; Jones Bill, 189; Department of Agriculture, 190, 198
Pelley, William D., 359
Pennsylvania, University of, R. G. Tugwell, 4; E. M. Patterson, 309
Pennsylvania Rural Progress Association, R. G. Tugwell, 5
Perkins, Dexter, "capital strike" theory, 84; F. D. Roosevelt, 110
Perkins, Frances, unemployment, 30, 157; F. D. Roosevelt, 117, 250; public works, 137; agriculture, 148, 190; Department of Labor, 214; R. G. Tugwell, 243, 308, 330
Perlo, Victor, 354
Pesticides, 225
Phillips, Gabell, 398
Phillips, H. I., 228
Pinchot, Gifford, 5
Pittman, Key, Brain Trust, 44; F. D. Roosevelt, 47
Plow, The, Dust Bowl, 365
Political Science Quarterly, R. G. Tugwell, 10, 298
Political Treatise, Baruch Spinoza, 14
Politicians, versus academicians, 44; Herbert Hoover, 81; R. G. Tugwell, 93, 102, 238, 245, 296, 301, 331; F. D. Roosevelt, 118, 121, 152, 246, 309, 325; Democratic Party, 288; Harold L. Ickes, 290; Josef Stalin, 368
Politics of Upheaval, The, Arthur M. Schlesinger, Jr., 126
Porter, Paul, R. G. Tugwell, 259, 312
Polyani, Michael, 402
Populism, 371, 389
Pragmatism, public works, 139; R. G. Tugwell, 230, 328, 395
Presidential Campaigns. *See* Campaigns of
President's Emergency Unemployment Relief Committee, 35
Press, freedom of, 24; Hearst papers, 233, 321; R. G. Tugwell, 233, 241, 245, 248, 292, 323, 338, 340, 409; Resettlement Administration, 296; editors, 330; Dies Committee, 358

Pressman, Lee, 354, 357, 364

Price fixing, R. G. Tugwell, 60, 155; government, 96, 166, 392; National Industrial Recovery Act, 155, 161; agriculture, 177

Proffett, Charles G., 330

Progressivism, economic planning, 105; New Deal, 109, 113, 148, 356, 371; public works, 115, 310; monetary policy, 126; Second New Deal, 139; Federal Trade Commission, 156; National Industrial Recovery Act, 162; R. G. Tugwell, 185, 324, 373, 384; Frederic C. Howe, 202; Robert La Follette, 309; F. D. Roosevelt, 309, 327, 346; Republican Party, 343; Henry Wallace, 355, 364; Populists, 371, 389

Property Without Power, Adolf A. Berle, Jr., 390

Proskauer, Joseph M., 175

Prosperity Through Freedom, Lawrence Fertig, 402

Protagonists, The: Roosevelt and Hoover, R. G. Tugwell, 73

Proxmire, William, 85

Public Administration Review, R. G. Tugwell, 300

Public Philosophy, The, Walter Lippmann, 102

Public Works, national economy, 21, 77; government, 25, 87, 139, 393, 406; Marriner S. Eccles, 36; F. D. Roosevelt, 66, 118, 128, 134, 344; R. G. Tugwell, 108, 307, 350; progressivism, 115, 310; National Industrial Recovery Act, 152, 163; high cost of, 285

Public Works, Special Board for, R. G. Tugwell, 210, 307; Resettlement Administration, 263

Public Works Administration, conservation, 217; Resettlement Administration, 263; Harold L. Ickes, 290, 308

Puerto Rico, R. G. Tugwell, 211, 219, 240, 246, 323, 326; Communism, 367

Pure Food and Drug Bill, F. D. Roosevelt, 113; R. G. Tugwell, 124, 224, 231, 247, 257, 331, 339, 342; press, 331; David Cavers, 386

Pusey, Merlo J., 388

Pusey, Nathan, 409

Radicalism, R. G. Tugwell, 349, 370; Agricultural Adjustment Administration, 363; individualism, 389

Railroads, Herbert Hoover, 33; Taylorism, 115; R. G. Tugwell, 136, 342; Donald Richberg, 157

Rand, James H., Jr., R. G. Tugwell, 73, 75; Committee for the Nation, 352, 363

Randall, Clarence B., *The Communist Challenge to American Business*, 394

Rauch, Basil, Wall Street, 10; Herbert Hoover, 32, 37; Campaign of 1932, 36; Lame Duck Interregnum, 68; banking, 71; unemployment, 85; F. D. Roosevelt, 117, 126; R. G. Tugwell, 119, 138; New Deal, 122; agriculture, 193

Reactionaries, Oswald Villard, 343; national economy, 389

Recession, national economy, 398; New Deal, 405

Reciprocity Trade Agreements Act, nationalism, 54; progressivisim, 127

Reclamation, Bureau of, Agricultural Adjustment Administration, 219; Resettlement Administration, 278

Reconstruction Finance Corporation, Herbert Hoover, 55; John N. Garner, 66; banking, 67; Jerome Frank, 206; created, 281

Recovery, big business, 138, 398; agriculture, 149; National Recovery Administration, 167; R. G. Tugwell, 329, 392

Red Cross, 34

Reed, David, 74

Re-employment Agreement, 161

Reflation, 60

Reform, progressivism, 109, 373, 389; Congress, 291, agriculture, 306; R. G. Tugwell, 400

Regenery, Henry, 402

Relief, New Deal, 129, 152; agriculture, 149, 263, 293; Surplus Relief Corporation, 210; Farm Credit Administration, 272; politicians, 289, 393; Resettlement Administration, 294, 303; progressivism, 310; F. D. Roosevelt, 344

Religion, American Way of Life, 371; Papal encyclicals, 404

Reno, Milo, 118

Republican Party, R. G. Tugwell, 8, 235, 245, 255; rural reform, 80, 388, 397; Frank Knox, 247; farmers, 252; Resettlement Administration, 271; Democratic Party, 356

Rerum Novarum: The Condition of the Working Classes, Papal encyclical, 404

Resettlement Administration, R. G. Tugwell, 91, 122, 197, 205 ff., 247, 261, 279 ff.; relief, 129; agriculture, 206; drought, 220; Pure Food and Drug Law, 250; Submarginal Land Committee, 263; Subsistence Homesteads, 263; greenbelt towns, 270, 277; Dust Bowl, 296

Reston, James, 401

Revenue Act, 130, 317

Revue Economique, R. G. Tugwell, 374

Rexford, Dessie, mother of R. G. Tugwell, 3

Ricardo, David, industrial revolution, 17; laissez faire, 382

Richberg, Donald, National Industrial Recovery Act, 158; communism, 359

Ringland, Arthur C., 217

Road to Serfdom, The, Friedrich Hayek, 408

"Roaring Twenties," 11, 17, 19, 332, 344

Roberts, Owen, 256

Robespierre, Maximilien, 347

Robey, Ralph, 61

Robinson, Arthur, R. G. Tugwell, 258, 260, 351

Robinson, Edgar E., *The Roosevelt Leadership,* 393

Robinson, Joseph, R. G. Tugwell, 253, 258

Rogers, Cleveland, R. G. Tugwell, 284, 334

Rogers, James H., 89, 309, 389

Rogers, Lindsay, 10

Roosevelt, Eleanor, social programs, 148; F. D. Roosevelt, 250; Subsistence Homesteads, 268; R. G. Tugwell, 325; New Deal, 353

Roosevelt, Franklin D., Rexford G. Tugwell, 8, 10, 27, 40, 119, 128, 151, 200, 232, 238, 243, 250, 252, 254, 258, 300, 307, 322, 326, 337, 340,

344, 352; humanitarianism, 14, 124, 398; presidency, 20, 42, 59 ff., 318, 321, 348, 352; depression, 20, 43, 51, 72, 77, 135, 144, 397; Brain Trust, 39, 48, 227, 346, 409; Robert M. La Follette, Jr., 42, 49, 343; agriculture, 43, 86, 183, 213, 220, 260, 264, 267, 272, 303; James Farley, 43, 236, 238; personal magnetism, 46, 50, 246, 344; Adolph Berle, Jr., 47, 124; Hugh Johnson, 47, 128, 250; Herbert Hoover, 51, 59 ff., 69, 73 ff., 346; Lame Duck Interregnum, 51, 59 ff., 72 ff., 309; gold standard, 57, 61, 70, 89, 167; public works, 66, 118, 128, 134, 164, 308; banking, 74, 134, 342; Keynesian, 84, 111, 129, 131, 133, 136, 343; trust busting, 109, 343; progressivism, 110, 112, 117, 127, 131, 309, 346, 371; as politician, 110, 118, 121, 152, 246, 254, 288, 321, 325; Raymond Moley, 111, 344 ff.; collectivism, 111, 117, 327; conservation, 113, 213, 220, 267; Theodore Roosevelt, 113, 346; Bernard Baruch, 114, 117, 121, 124; Felix Frankfurter, 117, 125; Frances Perkins, 117, 250; Harry Hopkins, 117, 133; Harold L. Ickes, 117, 135, 164; Basil Rauch, 117, 126; New Deal, 126, 227, 343, 355, 362, 394, 405; Louis D. Brandeis, 128, 325, 335; social security, 128, 130, 344, 400; Frank Kent, 132, 245, 253, 321, 343; Supreme Court, 129, 384, 387; "hundred days," 137, 146, 385; National Recovery Administration, 158, 160, 166, 169, 311; government, 244, 393, 396; Resettlement Administration, 247, 268, 288, 293, 295, 314, 339; Stimson Doctrine, 345, 367; education, 378. *See also*, 52, 54, 60, 62, 75, 108, 118, 156, 184, 186, 344, 368, 401

Roosevelt, Theodore, F. D. Roosevelt, 112 ff., 346; "Square Deal," 112; progressivism, 113, 131; reform, 114, 371; national economy, 386; government, 396

Roosevelt Leadership, The, Edgar E. Robinson, 393
Roosevelt Red Record and Its Background, The, Elizabeth Dilling, 347
Roosevelt Revealed, James C. Young, 352
Roosevelt Revolution, The, First Phase, 69; Mario Einaudi, 396
Roper, Daniel, 164
Roper, Elmo, 120
Rorty, James, 231
Rosenman, Samuel, Brain Trust, 39, 90; R. G. Tugwell, 40, 144; F. D. Roosevelt, 44, 238
Rosenwald Fund, 266
Rossiter, Clinton, 404
Rosten, Leo, 234
Rostow, Walter W., employment, 78; national economy, 405
Rotnem, Victor, 204
Ruml, Beardsley, Domestic-Allotment Plan, 47, 173; farm organization, 183
Rural Electrification Administration, Morris L. Cooke, 28; New Deal, 129
Rural Rehabilitation Division, Resettlement Administration, 263, 265, 271, 293; relief, 303
Russell, Richard, 253
Russia. *See* Soviet Union
Rutter, Richard, 398
Ryerson, Knowles, 221

Sargent, John G., 178

Saturday Evening Post, Alva Johnson, 247, 347; Garet Garrett, 352

Saulnier, Raymond J., President's Council of Economic Advisers, 397; free enterprise, 402

Save America First, Jerome Frank, 202

Say's Law, 23

Schall, Thomas, R. G. Tugwell, 257, 351

Schlesinger, Arthur M., Jr., *The Politics of Upheaval,* 126; national economy, 138, 332, 392, 402; National Recovery Administration, 162, 168, 262; Agricultural Adjustment Administration, 205; R. G. Tugwell, 209, 362, 401; F. D. Roosevelt, 295; subversives, 367; Brain Trust, 392

Schick, Sir William, 213

Schlink, F. J., 240

Scientific Advisory Board, 263

Scripps-Howard Newspapers, R. G. Tugwell, 234

Securities and Exchange Commission, 113

Securities Exchange Act, 127

Selassie, Haile, 281

Seldes, George, 231

Selznick, Philip, 378

Shea, Francis, 204

Sherman, Roger, 380

Sherman Anti-Trust Act, 383

Shipstead, Henrik, 360

Silcox, Ferdinand, Forest Service, 216; Taylor Grazing Act, 219

Silvermaster, Nathan, 354

Simpson, John, 184

Smith, Adam, Ethics, 14; capitalism, 30; laissez faire, 381

Smith, Alfred E., campaign of 1928, 8, 26, 116, 174; R. G. Tugwell, 10, 174, 181, 209, 236, 281, 373, 384; Bernard Baruch, 42, 116; monetary policies, 61, 377; progressivism, 114; McNary-Haugen Bill, 172, 174

Smith, Earl, 186, 188

Smith, Ellison S., farm program, 186, 253; R. G. Tugwell, 252 ff., 281; F. D. Roosevelt, 254

Smith, Gerald L. K., 118

Smoot-Hawley Tariff Act, 55

Snow, C. P., 407

Social conscience, development of, 4, 120, 122, 229, 408; F. D. Roosevelt, 289; R. G. Tugwell, 333, 365; big business, 396

Social management, national economy, 7, 109, 138, 148; political campaigns, 49; Resettlement Administration, 285; Soviet Union, 348, 360; history, 380

Social security, progressivism, 109; Huey Long, 118; F. D. Roosevelt, 128, 130, 344; New Deal, 129, 397; R. G. Tugwell, 334

Social Statics, Herbert Spencer, 256, 382

Socialism, free enterprise, 99, 350; taxation, 165; young liberals, 199; government, 298; agriculture, 354; R. G. Tugwell, 400; Europe, 406

Socrates, 404

Soil Conservation Service, R. G. Tugwell, 217, 379; land utilization, 274
Soil Erosion Service, 264
Soule, George, Brain Trust, 89; monetary policies, 90
"Sound money," deflation, 61; F. D. Roosevelt, 70; Alfred E. Smith, 377
Southard, Keith, 282
Soviet Impact on the Western World, C. H. Carr, 394
Soviet Russia in the Second Decade, R. G. Tugwell, 9, 351, 359
Soviet Union, R. G. Tugwell, 9, 174, 348, 351, 359; doctrinaire socialism, 100; collectivism, 257, 365; agriculture, 367; economic planning, 394, 403; cold war, 410
Special Industrial Recovery Board, National Industrial Recovery Act, 161; Hugh Johnson, 308; economic planning, 357
Specie payment, 70
Spencer, Herbert, *Social Statics*, 256, 382; Conservative Social Darwinist, 408
Spencer, William, 8
Spillman, W. J., 171-73
Spinoza, Baruch, 14
Sprague, O. M. W., 61
Stalin, Josef, New Deal, 352; communism, 367; politicians, 368
Statism, F. D. Roosevelt, 112; Department of Agriculture, 218; R. G. Tugwell, 374, 411
Stephens, Harold M., 317
Stimson, Henry L., 345, 367
Stimson Doctrine, 345, 367
Stock Market, 31
Stone, Alf, 190
Straus, Jesse, 42
Stricken Land, The, R. G. Tugwell, 4, 132, 195, 205, 211, 219, 246, 300, 355, 363, 367-69, 395
Strong, Lee, 210, 221
Stuart, Robert J., 214, 216
Stumbling Into Socialism, David Lawrence, 350
Submarginal Land Committee, 263
Subsistence Homesteads, 263, 268, 270, 275, 285
Suburban Resettlement Division, R. G. Tugwell, 269
Sullivan, Lawrence, 73
Sullivan, Mark, Peek-Tugwell controversy, 202; Brain Trust, 227; R. G. Tugwell, 261, 313, 349; F. D. Roosevelt, 345; Herbert Hoover, 348
Sulzberger, Arthur Hays, 243
Sumner, William Graham, 408
Sumners, H. S., 289
Supreme Court, National Industrial Recovery Act, 115, 156, 159, 386; R. G. Tugwell, 129, 256, 349, 374, 386; collectivism, 139; agriculture, 178; commerce clause, 383; F. D. Roosevelt, 384, 387; Merle J. Pusey, 388
Surplus Relief Corporation, Jerome Frank, 208; R. G. Tugwell, 210; Resettlement Administration, 263
"Sweetheart of the Regimenters, The," R. G. Tugwell, 15

Swing, Raymond Gram, R. G. Tugwell, 204
Swope, Gerard, 155

Taber, John, 134
Taft, Robert A., R. G. Tugwell, 240
Taft, William H., big business, 97, 383; Supreme Court, 384
Taney, Roger B., 383
Tariff, Herbert Hoover, 26, 29; F. D. Roosevelt, 41, 62, 66, 184; Cordell Hull,
    52; Smoot-Hawley Tariff Act, 55-56; R. G. Tugwell, 147, 175; agricul-
    ture, 170, 184, 187; Domestic Allotment Plan, 182; E. M. Patterson, 309
Taussig, Charles, trade, 52; American Molasses Company, 322-23
Taxation, depression, 55, 152, 316; expenditures, 107, 137-38, 286; anti-trust-
    busting, 115; national economy, 115; socialism, 165, 397; agriculture,
    175, 262; inflation, 406
Taylor, Carl C., Resettlement Administration, 269; national economy, 391
Taylor, Frederick W., 115
Taylor, John, 257
Taylorism, R. G. Tugwell, 20, 25; industry, 22, 391; railroads, 115
Technological revolution, R. G. Tugwell, 21, 390-91
Tennessee Valley Authority, conservation, 215; Resettlement Administration,
    296, 379
TVA: Democracy on the March, David Lilienthal, 379, 384
"Third Economy," R. G. Tugwell, 350, 406
Thomas, Norman, 295
Thomas Amendment, 62
Three Cheers for the Red, Red and Red, Peter Crosby, 343
Time Magazine, R. G. Tugwell, 8, 232, 251-52, 323, 329, Brain Trust, 205;
    Pure Food and Drug Act, 226, 232; F. D. Roosevelt, 54; Puerto Rico,
    302; New Deal, 323
Tobin, James, 406
Today, R. G. Tugwell, 298; Raymond Moley, 313
Tomorrow a New World; The New Deal Community Program, Paul K.
    Conkin, 265
Totalitarianism, R. G. Tugwell, 15, 325, 350, 407; economic planning, 357
Townsend, Francis, 118
Trade, nationalism, 51, 54; economic collapse, 56, 162; gold standard, 62;
    R. G. Tugwell, 107; World War I, 181; Domestic Allotment Plan, 182;
    E. M. Patterson, 309; progressivism, 310
Trade, socialism, 100; National Recovery Administration, 156-57; price fixing,
    168
Trade Association Movement, Herbert Hoover, 81; F. D. Roosevelt, 156-57
Trade Union, Soviet Union, 9; R. G. Tugwell, 154
Trading with the Enemy Act, gold exports, 56; banking, 64-65
Trend of Economics, The, R. G. Tugwell, 8
Trent, D. P., 324
Trotsky, Leon, communism, 361; Josef Stalin, 367
Truman, Harry S., R. G. Tugwell, 246, 335; social legislation, 397

Trust Busters, progressivism, 109, 355, 371; F. D. Roosevelt, 109, 343; Thurmond Arnold, 132. *See also* Anti-trustbusting

Tugwell, Charles Henry, father of R. G. Tugwell, 3

Tugwell, Dessie Rexford, mother of R. G. Tugwell, 3

Tugwell, Rexford Guy (analytical index only, arranged alphabetically for convenient reference. For individuals see specific names in general index). Advance Ratio Price Plan, 176-77, 181, 385; advertising, 24, 115, 249; Agricultural Adjustment Administration, 23, 183 ff., 192 ff.; Agricultural Advisory Committee, 144; agriculture, 5, 9-10, 23, 39, 46, 87, 107, 146-47, 152, 175-76, 208 ff., 210, 212, 239, 253; Agriculture, Department of, 45, 86, 88, 91, 208, 212, 251, 255-56, 258, 307, 340; American Economic Association, 10; American Molasses Company, 322-23; American University Union in Paris, 6; Ancestry and birth, 3; anti-trustbusting, 93, 105, 156, 196-97, 325; banking, 23, 124-25, 136, 233, 314-15; books and articles by, see bibliography on page 413 and specific titles in general index; Brain Trust, 10, 27, 38 ff., 48, 86 ff., 143, 243; Buffalo Courier, 4; *Business Week*, 279; Cabinet, 190, 307; capitalism, 91, 143, 147, 229, 297, 324; Chicago, University of, 6, 117, 335, 359; Civil Liberties Union, 9; Civil Service, 209, 400; Civilian Conservation Corps, 214; Clemson College, 376; collectivism, 139, 245, 257, 351 ff., 366, 389-90, 400; Columbia University, 6-8, 86, 88, 205, 230, 266, 280, 309, 321, 323; Committee for the Nation, 60; communism, 228, 236, 241, 247, 258, 355 ff.; Congress, 117, 349, 378; conservation, 10, 88, 174-75, 208 ff., 260-61, 264, 375; Constitution, 260, 347 ff., 357, 395; Cuba, 211; Dartmouth College, 147, 333, 351, 365; democracy, 329, 338, 370 ff.; Democratic Party, 8, 145, 288-89, 347; depression, 10, 51, 79; doctrinaire socialism, 9, 100, 105, 229; Domestic Allotment Plan, 172, 184; economic planning, 91 ff., 357, 364; education, 4 ff., 143, 230, 250, 260, 279, 301, 320, 328, 330, 337-38; experimentalism, 242, 401; farm problems, 107, 146, 153, 170 ff., 188, 208 ff., 281, 302, 332, 339; Federal Reserve System, 124, 133, 297; foreign affairs, 52, 190, 311, 364; "Fourth Power," 102-03, 292, 377; free enterprise, 334, 350; Friends of the Land, 222, 296; gold policies, 31, 61-62, 71, 125-26, 147, 314-15; Great Britain, 235, 300, 332; Great Plains Drought Committee, 307; greenbelt towns, 204, 270, 287, 303; health of, 6, 46, 204; holism, 138 ff., 171, 230; humanitarianism, 137, 139, 150, 328-29; industrial revolution, 17, 390; laissez faire, 12, 229, 258, 279, 306, 351, 380; lame duck interregnum, 59, 210, 308; London Economic Conference, 342; marriage to Grace Falke, 325; monetary policies, 55, 58, 107, 138, 155, 279, 314, 342; National Recovery Administration, 154, 268; National Resources Planning Board, 374; New Deal, 22, 73, 143, 232, 247, 261, 313, 337, 341-42, 396; *New Republic*, 7, 25, 175, 297, 313, 343; New York City Planning Commission, 102, 302, 324, 334, 374, 407; politicians, 44, 93, 102, 117, 238, 245, 288-89, 296, 301, 326, 331; pragmatism, 230, 328, 395; presidential campaigns, 8, 38, 42, 50, 320, 340, 349; press, 233, 241, 244, 248, 292, 312, 323, 329, 338, 340, 409; progressivism, 85, 242, 324, 373, 384; public works, 108, 210, 307, 350; Puerto Rico, 211, 219, 246-47, 267, 302, 323, 326;

Pure Food and Drug Bill, 122, 124, 224, 231, 234, 247-48, 257, 331, 339, 342; radicalism, 349, 370; relief, 34, 149, 303, 307; Republican Party, 8, 235, 245, 255; Resettlement Administration, 122, 197, 205 ff., 219-20, 247, 250, 261, 279 ff., 292, 301, 307, 314, 354; rural rehabilitation, 266, 269, 303; Second New Deal, 122, 133; social conscience, 333, 365; socialism, 9, 202, 229, 241, 247-48, 350-51, 400; Soil Conservation Service, 217, 379; Soviet Union, 9, 174, 348, 351, 359; statism, 374, 411; Suburban Resettlement Division, 269; Supreme Court, 129, 165, 256, 349, 374, 386; tariff, 147, 175; Taylorism, 20, 25; technological revolution, 21, 390-91; "Third Economy," 350, 406; totalitarianism, 5, 325, 350, 407; trade, 9, 107, 154; unemployment, 21, 31, 85, 174, 392, 399; White House, 309, 314; Works Progress Administration, 133

Tugwell, Rexford Guy

Advance Ratio Price Plan, 176-77, 181, 385

Advertising, 24, 115, 249

After Seven Years, 42, 345

Agricultural Adjustment Administration, 23, 183 ff., 192 ff.

Agricultural Advisory Committee, 144

Agriculture, 5, 9-10, 23, 39, 46, 87, 146-47, 107, 175-76, 152, 210, 212, 239, 208 ff., 253

Agriculture, Department of, 45, 86, 88, 91, 208, 212, 251, 255-56, 258, 307, 340

Alexander, Will W., 324-25, 331

Allen, Robert S., 237, 362

American Economic Association, 10

American Economic Life and the Means of its Improvement, 351

American Molasses Company, 322-23

American University Union in Paris, 6

Ancestry and Birth, 3

Annals of the American Academy of Political and Social Service, 10, 174-75, 179, 298

Anti-trustbusting, 93, 105, 156, 196-97, 325

Appleby, Paul, 235, 332

Art of Politics, The, 84, 123, 326, 355, 376, 400

Bailey, Josiah, 257, 361

Banking, 23, 124-25, 136, 233, 314-15. *See also* Monetary Policies

Barbour, Warren W., 259, 302

Barzun, Jacques, 7, 332

Baruch, Bernard, 42

Battle for Democracy, The, 312

Bean, Louis, 148, 198

Berle, Adolf A., Jr., 41, 138, 228, 257, 317, 369

Black, Hugo, 253, 256, 258

Block, Paul, 233, 236

Bolles, Blair, 329, 337, 339-40, 347, 349, 351, 362

Books. *See* bibliography on page 413

Tugwell, Rexford Guy (cont.)
  Brain Trust, 10, 27, 38 ff., 48, 86 ff., 143, 243
  Buffalo Courier, 4
  Burns, James M., 119-20
  Business Week, 279
  Butler, Nicholas Murray, 7, 328, 338
  Byrnes, James, 253

  Cabinet, 190, 307
  Capitalism, 91, 143, 147, 229, 297, 324
  Carter, John F., 300, 334, 344, 361, 364
  Chamberlain, John, 208
  Chase, Stuart, 9
  Chicago, University of, 6, 117, 335, 359
  Chronicle of Jeopardy, A, 329
  Civil Liberties Union, 9
  Civil Service, 209, 400
  Civilian Conservation Corps, 214
  Clemson College, 376
  Collectivism, 139, 245, 257, 351 ff., 366, 389-40, 400. *See also* Holism
  Columbia University, 6-8, 86, 88, 205, 230, 266, 280, 309, 321, 323
  Committee for the Nation, 60
  "Common Man," 323
  Communism, 228, 236, 241, 247, 258, 355 ff.
  "Concert of Interests," 378
  Congress, 117, 349, 378
  Conkin, Paul K., 301-02
  Conservation, 10, 88, 174-75, 208 ff., 260-61, 264, 375
  Constitution, 260, 347 ff., 357, 395
  Coolidge, Calvin, 145
  Corcoran, Thomas, 354
  Coss, John, 7, 266
  Costigan, Edward, 257
  Coughlin, Charles, 248
  Cuba, 211
  Current Biography, 342
  Current History, 26

  Dartmouth College, 147, 351, 333, 365
  Davis, Chester C., 189
  Delta Upsilon Fraternity, 5
  Democracy, 329, 338, 370 ff.
  Democratic Party, 8, 145, 288-89, 347
  Democratic Roosevelt, The, 27, 30, 37, 40, 44, 48, 55, 57, 63, 73, 75, 123, 126, 135, 138, 148, 154, 162, 166, 169, 172, 193, 195, 244, 247, 305, 309, 311, 313, 326-27, 371
  Depression, 10 ff., 51, 79
  Deservnine, Raoul, 349, 352

Tugwell, Rexford Guy (cont.)
  Dewey, John, 8
  Dickinson, Lester J., 258, 337, 349
  Disarmament, 334
  "Discourses in Depression," 31, 36-7, 40
  Doctrinaire socialism, 9, 100, 105, 229
  Dodd, William E., 235
  Domestic Allotment Plan, 172, 184
  Dorfman, Joseph, 7
  Douglas, Paul, 9
  Dunn, Robert, 9

  Ely, Joseph B., 321, 343
  Essary, J. Fred, 237
  Economic planning, 91 ff., 357, 364
  Economic Security Committee, 307
  Education, 4 ff., 143, 230, 250, 260, 279, 301, 320, 328, 330, 337-38
  Ethics, 14, 328
  Experimentalism, 242, 401
  Ezekiel, Mordecai, 300

  Fair Labor Standards Act, 131
  Falke, Grace, 282, 325
  Farley, James A., 235, 240, 254, 293, 300, 325, 334, 339
  Farm Management, Office of, 171
  Farm Problems, 107, 170 ff., 281, 302
  Farm Program, 146, 153, 188, 208 ff., 332, 339
  Farm Tenancy Committee, 307
  Federal Reserve Act, 297
  Federal Reserve System, 124, 133
  Fish, Hamilton, Jr., 236, 348
  "Flaws in the Hoover Economic Plan," 33, 35-36
  Flynn, John T., 208, 323, 329, 350
  Foreign markets, 52, 190, 311. See also Trade
  Foreign Policy, 364
  "Fourth Power, The," 102-03, 292, 377
  Frank, Jerome, 203-04, 347, 354, 363
  Frankfurter, Felix, 114, 198, 338
  Free enterprise, 350
  Freedom of speech, 334
  Friends of the Land, 222, 296

  Galbraith, John K., 232, 250
  Garrett, Garet, 352
  Glass, Carter, 253
  Gold policies, 31, 61-2, 71, 125-26, 147, 314-15
  Governmental Arts, The, 96
  Governor's Tri-State Milk Commission, 5

Tugwell, Rexford Guy (cont.)
    Great Britain, 235, 300, 332
    Great Plains Drought Committee, 307
    Greenbelt towns, 204, 270, 287, 303

Hacker, Louis M., 239, 389
Harriman, Henry I., 184
Health of, 6, 46, 204
Hearst, William R., 233, 236, 321, 330
High, Stanley, 281
History, 327, 365, 391
Holism, 138 ff., 143, 171, 230. *See also* Collectivism
Hoover, Herbert, 8, 26 ff., 54, 73, 143
Hopkins, Harry, 42, 201, 218 ff., 243, 296, 321, 327, 331
Howe, Frederic C., 198
Howe, Louis, 42
Humanitarianism, 137, 139, 150, 328-29

Ickes, Harold L., 107, 133, 205, 209, 211, 219, 236, 243, 323, 326, 373
Industrial Discipline and the Governmental Arts, The, 10, 96, 145, 155, 227, 229, 301, 312, 316, 340, 370
Industrial revolution, 17, 390
Industry's Coming of Age, 10, 20, 297
Intercollegiate Magazine, 5
International Institute of Agriculture, 210
Internationalism, 343. *See also* Foreign Trade and Foreign Policy

Johnson, Alva, 247, 280, 338, 340, 343, 348
Johnson, Hugh, 164, 281, 366
Jones Bill, 186
Journal of Philosophy, 298
Journal of Social Philosophy, 299

Kansas City *Star*, 261
Kent, Frank, 244, 251, 259, 281, 311, 320, 337, 340, 349, 386, 389
Keynes, James M., 24, 135 ff.
Knox, Frank, 247
Kondratieff, 253

La Follette, Robert M., Jr., 331
Laissez faire, 12, 13, 229, 258, 279, 306, 351, 380
Lame Duck Interregnum, 59, 210, 308
Lawrence, David, 244, 249, 351, 394
League for Industrial Democracy, 9
Liberalism, 370
Light of Other Days, The, 329, 411
Lindley, Ernest K., 45, 220, 289, 300
London Economic Conference, 342
Lord, Russell, 221, 261, 312, 328, 361
Lubell, Samuel, 368

Tugwell, Rexford Guy (cont.)
MacMahon, Arthur W., 389
Marriage to Grace Falke, 325
Marshall Plan, 364
Marx, Karl, 105, 147, 280, 326, 360
Maverick, Maury, 239
Means, Gardiner C., 51, 168
Miller, William, 138
Mitchell, Wesley C., 6
Moley, Raymond, 10, 40, 52, 90, 154, 243, 313, 325, 338
Monetary policies, 55, 58, 107, 138, 155, 279, 314, 342. *See also* Banking
Monopolies, 106
Mr. Hoover's Economic Policy, 26, 29, 31, 34, 93, 298, 314, 328
Mussolini, Benito, 24, 235, 345, 350

Nation, The, 8, 10, 174, 258, 280, 323, 330
National Agricultural Conference, 174
National Industrial Recovery Administration, 154, 268
National Resources Planning Board, 374
Nationalism, 51, 54
Nearing, Scott, 5
New Deal, 22, 73, 143, 232, 247, 261, 313, 337, 341-42, 396
New Mexico, University of, 349, 386
New Republic, 7, 25, 26, 175, 297, 313, 343
New York City Planning Commission, 102, 302, 324, 334, 374, 407
New York *Times*, 283, 293, 323, 401
Newspaper Editors, American Society of, 250
Newsweek, 174, 251, 311, 313, 323, 362
Niagara Preserving Corporation, 6
Norris, George W., 253, 255, 258

O'Connor, Basil, 40, 144
Ogburn, William F., 6

Parker, Carleton H., 6
Patten, Simon Nelson, 5, 8, 15, 106, 364, 370
Pearson, Drew, 237, 362
Peek, George E., 87, 128, 187, 190, 200, 202 ff., 236, 362 ff.
Pennsylvania, University of, 5
Pennsylvania Rural Progress Association, 5
Perkins, Frances, 243, 308, 330
Political Science Quarterly, 10, 298
Politicians, 44, 93, 102, 117, 238, 245, 288-89, 296, 301, 326, 331
Porter, Paul, 259, 312
Pragmatism, 230, 328, 395
Presidential campaigns, 8, 38, 42, 50, 320, 340, 349
Press, 233, 241, 244, 248, 292, 312, 321, 323, 329, 338, 340, 409
Price fixing, 60, 155

Tugwell, Rexford Guy (cont.)
  Progressivism, 85, 242, 324, 373, 384
  Protagonists, The: Roosevelt and Hoover, 73
  Public Administrator Review, 300
  Public Works, 108, 210, 307, 350
  Puerto Rico, 211, 219, 240, 246-47, 267, 302, 323, 326
  Pure Food and Drug Bill, 122, 124, 224, 231, 234, 247-48, 257, 331, 339, 342

Radicalism, 349, 370
Railroads, 136, 342
Rand, James H., Jr., 73, 75
Rauch, Basil, 119, 138
Reconstructions Finance Corporation, 28
Recovery, 329, 392
Reflation, 61
Reform, 400
Relief, 34, 149, 303, 307
Republican Party, 8, 235, 245, 255
Resettlement Administration, 122, 197, 205 ff., 219-20, 247, 250, 261, 279 ff., 292, 301, 307, 314, 354
Revue Economique, 374
Rexford, Dessie, 3
Robespierre, Maximilien, 347
Robinson, Arthur, 258, 260, 351
Robinson, Joseph, 253, 258
Rogers, Cleveland, 284, 334
Rogers, Lindsey, 10
Roosevelt, Eleanor, 325
Roosevelt, Franklin D., 8, 10, 27, 40, 119, 128, 151, 200, 232, 238, 243, 250, 252, 254, 258, 300, 307, 322, 326, 337, 340, 341, 344, 352
Rosenman, Samuel, 40, 144
Rural Rehabilitation, 266, 269, 303

Schall, Thomas, 257, 351
Schlesinger, Arthur M., Jr., 209, 362, 401
Scripps-Howard Newspapers, 234
Second New Deal, 122, 133
Smith, Alfred E., 8, 10, 26, 174 ff., 181, 209, 236, 281, 373, 382, 384
Smith, Ellison S., 252 ff., 281
Social Conscience, 333, 365
Social Security, 334
Socialism, 9, 202, 229, 241, 247-48, 350-51, 400
Soil Conservation Service, 217, 379
Soviet Russia in the Second Decade, 9, 351, 359
Soviet Union, 9, 174, 348, 351, 359
Statism, 374, 411

Tugwell, Rexford Guy (cont.)
  Stricken Land, The, 4, 132, 195, 205, 211, 219, 246, 300, 355, 363, 367, 369, 395
  Suburban Resettlement Division, 269
  Sullivan, Mark, 202, 261, 313, 349
  Supreme Court, 129, 165, 256, 349, 374, 386
  Surplus Relief Corporation, 210
  "Sweetheart of the Regimenters, The," 15
  Swing, Raymond Gram, 204

Taft, Robert A., 240
Tariff, 147, 175
Taylorism, 20, 25
Technological revolution, 21, 390-91
"Third Economy," 350, 406
Time Magazine, 8, 201, 232, 251-52, 329
Today, 298
Totalitarianism, 5, 325, 350, 407
Trade, 9, 107, 154
Trend of Economics, The, 8
Truman, Harry S., 246, 335

Unemployment, 21, 31, 85, 174

Veblen, Thorstein B., 16, 18
Villard, Oswald, 302, 362
Von Mises, Ludwig, 395

Wages, 392, 399
Wall Street Journal, 258
Wallace, Henry A., 86, 88, 163, 208, 218, 221, 238, 250, 258, 262, 307, 324, 330, 332, 353
Ward, Paul W., 280, 323, 330
Washington, University of, 6
Welles, Sumner, 240, 329
Western Political Quarterly, 79
Wharton School of Finance and Commerce, 4
Wheeler, Burton K., 144, 253, 258
White House, 309, 314
Wilson, Woodrow, 297
Wirt, William A., 235, 357
Works Progress Administration, 133
World Wars, 328, 370

Young, James C., 280

Ullman, William, 354
Uncle Tom's Cabin, Harriet B. Stowe, 314
Un-American Activities, 358

Unemployment, public works, 21, 84, 278; Herbert Hoover, 29, 36; Great Britain, 76; New Deal, 85, 123, 405; F. D. Roosevelt, 128; national economy, 152, 166, 277, 399, 406; progressivism, 310
Unemployment Act of 1946, R. G. Tugwell, 374
United Features Syndicate, 234
United Mine Workers, 354
United States Chamber of Commerce, 68

Van Devanter, Willis, 115
Van Hise, Charles R., 95, 154
Veblen, Thorstein B., pessimism, 16; R. G. Tugwell, 18; economic planning, 391
Villard, Oswald, R. G. Tugwell, 302, 362; reactionaries, 343
Viner, Jacob, recovery, 77; recession, 135
Voluntary Domestic Allotment Plan, 46. *See also* Domestic Allotment Plan
Von Mises, Ludwig, capitalism, 395; free enterprise, 402

Wages, economic stability, 21; Herbert Hoover, 30, 36; free trade, 53; Government, 97, 334; New Deal, 122, 244; labor, 131, 154, 293, 397; price fixing, 156; National Industrial Recovery Act, 168; R. G. Tugwell, 392, 399
Wagner-Connery Act, 129
Wagner-Dickinson Bill, 158
Wagner-Garner Relief Bill, 36
Wagner, Robert F., unemployment, 34, 157; F. D. Roosevelt, 42, 158; public works, 77, 134, 310; recession, 135; collectivism, 159; progressivism, 309; labor, 311
Walker, Francis A., 370
Walker, Frank, 307
Wall Street, Herbert Hoover, 30; 1929 collapse, 113; national economy, 296; gold standard, 315
Wall Street Journal, R. G. Tugwell, 258
Wallace, Henry A., agriculture, 46, 186, 189; R. G. Tugwell, 86, 88, 163, 208, 218, 221, 238, 250, 258, 262, 307, 324, 330, 332, 353; Department of Agriculture, 87; F. D. Roosevelt, 135, 138, 158, 239; New Deal, 148, 343; H. Johnson, 164; Domestic Allotment Plan, 174, 184; Agricultural Adjustment Administration, 183, 192, 248; cabinet, 190; Peek-Tugwell controversy, 194, 200, 204; Ellison D. Smith, 253; land program, 264; C. B. Baldwin, 269; Resettlement Administration, 301, 321; farm tenancy, 303, 323; social history, 350; state planning, 350; progressivism, 355, 364
Wallich, Henry C., 402, 405
Wallis, W. Allen, 402
Walsh, Thomas, 64
War Finance Corporation, 33
War Industries Board, 116, 156, 172
Ward, Barbara, 401
Ward, Lester F., 408
Ward, Paul W., R. G. Tugwell, 280, 323, 330

Ware, Harold, 354

Warren, George F., gold buying, 61, 89, 125, 167, 314-16; agriculture, 86, 186; Henry Morgenthau, Jr., 87

Washington *Post*, 290

Washington Squirrel Cage, 281

Washington, University of, R. G. Tugwell, 6

Web of Subversion, The, James Burnham, 366

Wechsler, James, 230

Wector, Dixon, Herbert Hoover, 36; New Deal, 112; monetary policies, 394

Welfare State, 398

Wehle, Louis B., 28

Welles, Sumner, R. G. Tugwell, 240, 329; democracy, 379; Constitution, 388

Westervelt, William I., 375

Western Political Quarterly, R. G. Tugwell, 79

Weyl, Nathaniel, 354

Wharton School of Finance and Commerce, R. G. Tugwell, 4

Wheeler, Burton K., R. G. Tugwell, 144, 253, 258; farm program, 187, 260, 281; National Industrial Recovery Act, 310

White House, R. G. Tugwell, 309, 314

White, Leonard, 148

Whitlock, Brand, 114

"Why the Depression Lasted So Long," *Fortune* Magazine, 77

Why Quit Our Own, George Peek and Samuel Crowther, 191, 352, 354, 363

Wickens, D. L., 186

Wiley, Harvey W., 231

Williams, Aubrey, 295

Willis, H. Parker, 65, 309

Willkie, Wendell, 119, 309

Wilson, Milburn L., voluntary domestic allotment plan, 46; Domestic Allotment, 87, 174, 184, 190, 385; tariff, 182; *Land Utilization*, 183; Agricultural Adjustment Administration, 183, 192; farm program, 188, 209; Division of Subsistence Homesteads, 264, 266

Wilson, William, 359

Wilson, Woodrow, progressivism, 113; reform, 114, 371; R. G. Tugwell, 297; national economy, 396

Winrod, Gerald, *Communism and the Roosevelt Brain Trust*, 359

Winship, Blanton, 211

Wirt, William A., James H. Rand, Jr., 76; R. G. Tugwell, 235, 357; subversives, 352; New Deal, 353, 362, 366; Committee for the Nation, 363

Witt, Nathan, 354

Woodin, William, Emergency Banking Act, 62, 71; banking, 71, 74; agriculture, 190

Woodruff, Roy O., 283

Works Progress Administration, F. D. Roosevelt, 128; R. G. Tugwell, 133; H. L. Ickes, 236, 278

World War I, Herbert Hoover, 55; War Industries Board, 156; foreign markets, 181; R. G. Tugwell, 328, 370

World War II, F. D. Roosevelt, 84; Farm Security Administration, 303; depression, 373; unemployment, 406

"Year of Decision," Samuel Lubell, 120
Young, James C., New Deal, 251; R. G. Tugwell, 280; Resettlement Administration, 286; *Roosevelt Revealed,* 352